# REAL ESTATE TRANSACTIONS

## Examples and Explanations

# REAL ESTATE TRANSACTIONS

## Examples and Explanations

## D. Barlow Burke, Jr.

*Professor of Law*
*American University*

**LITTLE, BROWN AND COMPANY**
Boston   New York   Toronto   London

Library of Congress Catalog Card No. 93-77379

ISBN 0-316-11773-0

Third Printing

EB

Published simultaneously in Canada
by Little, Brown & Company (Canada) Limited

Printed in the United States of America

# Contents

Preface                                                                vii
Acknowledgments                                                         ix


**PART ONE:  LAW OF CONVEYANCING**                                       1

   1.  Introduction to American Conveyancing                             3
   2.  Professional Responsibility in Real Property Transactions         9
   3.  Real Estate Brokers                                              19
   4.  Contract Risk of Loss                                            43
   5.  The Statute of Frauds in Real Property Transactions              55
   6.  Contract of Sale Conditions                                      63
   7.  Remedies for Breach of a Contract of Sale                        89
   8.  Remedies for Breach of a Contract of Sale (continued)           107
   9.  Closings:  Deeds and Escrows                                     115
  10.  Escrows and Escrow Instructions                                  127
  11.  Deed Descriptions                                                135
  12.  Implied Warranties for Housing                                   145
  13.  Slander of Title                                                 159
  14.  Recording Acts                                                   163
  15.  Title Searches, Abstracts, and Title Insurance                   181
  16.  Model Marketable Title Act and Curative Statutes                 195
  17.  The Torrens System                                               205


**PART TWO:  LAW OF MORTGAGES**                                         209

  18.  Mortgage Lenders and Markets                                     211
  19.  Mortgages                                                        215
  20.  Junior Liens                                                     243
  21.  Transfers of the Mortgage                                        249
  22.  Foreclosures                                                     279
  23.  Real Estate in Trouble                                           317
  24.  Installment Land Sale Contracts                                  337

**PART THREE:   INVESTING IN REAL ESTATE**                          351

  25.   Real Property Owners and the Internal Revenue Code        353
  26.   Real Estate Planning:  Investment Strategy                359
  27.   Tax Events:  *Tufts* and *Lyon*                            373
  28.   General and Limited Partnerships                           393
  29.   Real Property Transfer Taxes                               419
  30.   Construction Agreements and Finance                       425
  31.   Shopping Center Covenants                                  455
  32.   Commercial Leases                                         463

     *Index*                                                487

# Preface

This book is intended as a supplement to law school elective courses in real estate conveyancing and transactions, mortgages and real estate finance, and business planning and investment for real estate. Its triad of objectives is to provide basic information needed in these three types of courses, to deal with the basic questions that course casebooks are likely to ask, and to cover some of the same leading cases used in the casebooks. Its first part covers transactions, the second finance, and the third — and last — covers business planning. Students in courses that cover all these subjects will read from cover to cover with profit, using the book as a supplement to the casebook at the end of the term and in preparation for the exam.

Some first-year students will also find the book useful. Those students whose professors have stressed conveyancing, in the latter stages of a required first-year course on real property, will find large portions of the first part of the book useful because there is more detail here than the usual real property student books provide.

The topics in this book are arranged in two ways: first, in such a way that the book starts out discussing simple residential transactions and then proceeds to treat more complex commercial ones. Second, the topics are so arranged that the basic residential transaction is presented chronologically, introducing the actors involved in it in the same sequence as they will appear in real life. This reflects, by and large, the organization of the casebooks in the area.

I once heard of a teacher in a course on real estate transactions announce, to student cheers, that his course was *not* a continuation of the first-year property course. This announcement is both good and bad news. The good news is that any transactions course, almost by definition, has a nuts-and-bolts approach for which some law students crave after completing the first year. The bad news is that any transactions course assumes a knowledge of not just property law, but of contracts and torts as well — and of corporations, tax, and agency law — on and on. This book, like its casebook counterparts, provides some background in all these subjects but, inevitably, assumes some as well.

On the advice of many students who have read this book in manuscript, I have provided my explanations immediately following the example, which sets out a problem or issue. This sequence is for convenience only: After reading the problem and before reading its explanation, pause and think. You will profit from the pause and will have the fun of arguing with me as you read what I think. That mental engagement is the real value of a book like this one.

Preparation of this book began in the heyday of the real estate boom of the 1980s but was substantially affected by the bust that followed, so that its present virtue is that it is a book for both good times and bad in real estate markets. I have used the examples and explanations that I and my students have found entertaining, useful, and instructive in classes over many years. Some wag said that a teacher is someone who is incapable of ever just saying something once. For some students, this is a blessing: No example is as instructive as the ability to hear, once more, what the professor said in class. This book aims at providing one professor's version, not only of what deserves emphasis but also of what's worth repeating. My hope is that students will find the book a useful review of this area, long a mainstay of the general practice of law.

*Barlow Burke*

March 1993

# Acknowledgments

I have benefited from the comments and questions raised by many students over the past four years while this manuscript was in preparation. Too many to name all of them, I thank them all. They pushed me to expand on one topic, compress my treatment of another, and in general kept me sensible to my obligations as a teacher.

My research assistants over the last several years deserve a special mention for editing and spading the manuscript in its several stages of development. To the last four of them — Keith Allen, Darby Jones, Esten Goldsmith, and Patricia Hammes — I owe a large debt.

At Little, Brown and Company, Rick Heuser and, later, Carol McGeehan provided steady encouragement, Betsy Kenny tactfully blind reviews, and Lisa Wehrle a close and cheerful edit of the final submission.

# REAL ESTATE TRANSACTIONS

**Examples and Explanations**

# PART ONE

*Law of Conveyancing*

# 1

## *Introduction to American Conveyancing*

First, some history. (But if you are not inclined to use history as an explanation for current problems, then proceed on to the next chapter and return to this one as you feel the need.) American appellate cases show only the slightest use of the oldest of common law conveyances — enfeoffment by livery of seisin — in which the grantor and grantee go onto the property and the grantor, in the presence of witnesses, hands the grantee some symbol of ownership (a bit of soil or a twig, for instance). The near-total neglect of this method of transfer is evident in every colony and in the early case reports of the states down to the mid-nineteenth century. Early in U.S. history, most of the states instead adopted statutes authorizing transfer of title by simple forms of deeds, and all of the states used the recording acts from our formative era forward. R. Patton, 1 Titles §4 (2d ed. 1938). Recording the contract of sale or the deed for real property was a public act that enrolled the document on the public records. These records became a substitute for older common law methods of transfer.

Early opinions do show the courts extolling the virtues of the recording acts, obviously to educate the bar in their use. See, e.g., Norcross v. Widgery, 2 Mass. 506 (1807) (Parsons, C.J.). Moreover, the earliest recording acts embodied a rule of first to record, first in right (known as a race type act). The draconian effects of a late recording meant that the bar and the public needed little encouragement to record. The beauty of the recording system is that it is self-executing, relying as it does on the incentive that every purchaser has to record. In addition, some of the early recording acts made recording a substitute for enfeoffment. Mass. Col. & Prov. L. 303 (1697).

3

But, of course, the purchaser has to record a contract of sale or a deed, so American conveyancing was documentary from the beginning. The presence of public records had another effect on our conveyancing. It meant that early on Americans abandoned the English system of abstracts of title; these abstracts were compilations of deeds, passed from vendor to purchaser and growing thicker with each transfer, that showed the chain of title devolving on the latest purchaser of the property. In the United States, proof of title came instead from searching the public records at each transfer to establish the abstract anew. Thus Americans needed contracts of sale to activate this search process and define the state of the title that would be acceptable to the purchaser. When the purchaser executed such a contract, the closing on it was usually "subject to proof of title." When the contract was silent as to the standard for that title, the standard implied by law was "marketable title."

## The English Background: Two Statutes

The mechanism for interjecting a contract of sale into the conveyancing process had started more than two centuries prior to the United States when England passed its Statute of Uses in 1535.[1]

This statute was received at the inception of the United States as part of our law. It provided that a person who transferred real property to another "to the use of" himself, his family, or a third person, without giving any real power to use it to another, was "seised" of the property — that is, given the legal rights of one with seisin to the property and thus made the holder of both the equitable and the legal title. The statute said that:

> where any person or persons stand or are seised of any honors,
> etc., land, tenements, etc. to the use, confidence, or trust of
> any other person or persons, by reason of any bargain, sale,

---

1. The Statute of Uses was enacted to deal with a revenue problem encountered by Henry VIII. The Tudors, of which royal English house Henry VIII was the most ambitious, gained control of the English throne by being the victors in the civil war known as the War of the Roses (1455-1485). Before going off to this war, the English nobility on both the contending sides put the legal title to their property into the hands of trustees. The only trustee neutral in this war was the church, so generally a church institution, such as a monastery, would become the trustee. By the terms of the trust, however, the trustee could only hold the title; it did not manage the property, control any rents and income generated from it, or take possession of it. Management, rents and income, and possession all stayed where they had been, in the hands of the nobleman's family. Thus after the war, the victors, the Tudors, could not get at the property of the losers. And because church property was not subject to royal taxation, the "use" (the early name for this type of trust) became a tax shelter as well.

feoffment, etc., such person that have such use shall be deemed
and adjudged in lawful seisin, estate, and possession thereof,
to all intents and purposes, of or in such like estates as they have
in the use . . . after such quality, manner etc. as they had
before, in, or to the use.

27 Hen. VIII, ch. 10 (1535).[2]

The modern contract of sale is the present-day equivalent of the old use
executed by the statute. The holder of an equitable interest in property, such
as a purchaser holding a contract of sale, could be made the legal title holder
by removing all conditions to the closing in the title. When these conditions
are removed, the vendor holds the title "to the use of" the purchaser. The
Statute of Uses then "executes the use" — in other words, it adds the legal
interest to the purchaser's equitable interest, thereby transferring the whole
title to the purchaser. French v. French, 3 N.H. 234 (1825), reviews this
history in more detail than presented here.

Looking at this matter another way may help. The Statute of Uses came
to be interpreted generally as authority for the creation of those common
law estates known as executory interests. This interpretation of the statute is
consistent with the modern-day contract of sale, in which the vendor conveys
his interest in real property "to myself for 90 days or the (executory) period
specified in this contract, but if during that time the title proves marketable,
then to P (the purchaser)." The interest P has at the moment of this conveyance
is one that will cut short the previous estate and vest the title in himself.[3]
This description does not take account of the modern contract of sale, filled
as it is with conditions, contingencies, and "subject to" clauses, but in this
quotation one easily detects the beginnings of the doctrine of equitable conversion, which you studied in first-year property.

While the Statute of Uses provided a legal mechanism for the effectiveness
of a contract of sale, another English statute had sounded the death knell of
enfeoffment in England. The Statute of Frauds required that after 1677, the
effective date of the statute, deeds of transfer for real property be in writing.
In large part the rationale for passing the Statute of Frauds was conveyancing

---

2. This statute had two immediate effects: First, it eliminated the use as a tax shelter
by giving the seisin to the taxpayer. Second, it gave what had been work for equity
lawyers (licensed to litigate chancery court matters) to common law lawyers (and
courts); thus it was a widening of jurisdiction in the latter courts and was supported
in Parliament by — guess which block? The common law lawyers. Henry's deal with
them gave the statute the votes it needed to pass.

3. As the *French* opinion states: "On this statute the conveyance, which has been
called a bargain and sale, is founded. The bargainer contracts to sell the land, and
receives the purchase money; after this, he is, in equity, considered as seised of the
land to the use of the bargainee; and this statute unites the possession to the use, so
that the very instant the use is raised, the possession is joined to it, and the bargainee
becomes seised of the land." French v. French, 3 N.H. 234 (1825).

reform. Some in Parliament at the time advocated a system of public records for title deeds but settled for getting them in writing.[4]

With the Statute of Uses providing a legal mechanism for executing contract of sale, and the Statute of Frauds requiring written contracts and deeds, Americans added another new element to their conveyances — the public record, from which vendors could show title to their purchasers.

# American Conveyancing Reforms: The First Generation

The earliest purchasers were interested in only one interest or estate in real property — the full fee simple absolute. Anything less felt reminiscent of the feudal tenure relationships that Americans had left the Old World to escape.

Thus early American legislatures enacted legal reforms to make the fee more freely alienable with regard to feudal interests: They abolished primogeniture, abolished the common law presumption for the joint tenancy with a right of survivorship in favor of the tenancy in common, and limited the common law marital estates of dower and curtesy to land seised at death. Thus far did they go to make real property free of familial interests. Yet, at the same time and in line with the view of land as a commercial commodity, state legislatures also created restraints on the fee for commercial interests (such as mechanics' liens, permission to tack junior and senior mortgages, and new forms of mortgage foreclosure) — interests unknown in Great Britain. Thus, at one and the same time, conveyancing was made both simpler and more complex.

While the public records reflected the state of the title, it yielded its answers as to what a particular grantor has to transfer with some difficulty. With the passage of time, as the records came to reflect a greater number of transfers, this difficulty became extreme. In theory, the records had to be searched on each and every transfer back to the sovereign — the proprietor of the colony, the king, or the state or federal land office patent. Eventually, on the mistaken notion that the Statute of Limitations on every conceivable common law writ had run after 60 years, that length of time came to be the period of search for real property titles. See, e.g., Morris's Lessee v. Vanderen, 1 Pa. 67 (1782). However, in states where land was obtained out of the public domain of the federal government (not subject, after all, to state statutes of limitations), title is often still searched "back to the sovereign."

Attorneys early acquired the skills necessary to search titles, and the law

---

4. What made all of these written documents possible, of course, were advances in the technology of papermaking, and what made the pursuit of this technology practical was the availability of linen, the raw material for paper at that time. Linen was used in underwear at the time. So in a sense, what made the Statute of Frauds possible was underwear!

of conveyancing and title search became considered their domain. Of course, attorneys were not available everywhere. A regrettable situation (in this case!) because deeds drafted by laypersons became confused. If a deed of bargain and sale (or, in New York, a deed of lease and release) was not used, the lay conveyancer and often the attorney threw in every legal verb coming to mind. Thus the vendor would "give, enfeoff, grant, convey, bargain and sell, lease and release, covenant to stand seised, assign and transfer" whatever property it was that was changing hands. This potpourri of legal verbs eventually came to mean "what I (vendor) have, I transfer it to you (purchaser)." Thus the quitclaim deed was recognized. This type of deed is another American conveyancing invention intended to make a title more freely transferable.

A title search is necessary because in all states a purchaser wants to know not only that the vendor is transferring the title, but that the title is "marketable" — that is, is transferred in such a state that it in turn can be transferred to another future purchaser. Even in a quitclaim deed, therefore, the law read a standard of marketable title as an implied term. The attorney's job is not just to determine that the vendor will transfer the title, but is also to determine that the title is marketable. Thus the title searching attorney determines the state of the title, as well as thereafter evaluates its marketability.

As attorneys did more and more title searches, they accumulated stacks of abstracts as their work product; these abstracts had value if and when they handled a later transfer of the same property. Some firms hired nonattorney employees as title searchers. Thus began the practice of having a lay abstractor search the title and an attorney review the resulting abstract and issue an opinion on the state of the title.

The next question was what to do about abstractor negligence. The possibility of an expensive and time-consuming lawsuit always loomed. Title insurance was devised in response to this threat. The earliest policies were designed to provide a remedy for abstracting mistakes, as well as to protect against interests that the abstractor could not discover by searching the public records. Thus title insurance policies protected against both record and non-record defects. This double coverage became their great selling point. By the beginning of the twentieth century, title insurers were established as abstractors, reviewers, and insurers of titles in many large urban areas. In rural communities, attorneys and abstractors continued to do the business of conveyancing as before. Now, however, the conveyancing industry evidenced three patterns for attorney participation. Attorneys functioned as title searchers, title reviewers, or employees of title insurance companies.

This pattern of participation means, moreover, that attorney involvement comes usually after the contract of sale is executed and the executory period under way, at a time when real estate brokers, lender mortgagees, appraisers, property inspectors, and title insurers — and in some regions of the West, escrow agents — are also involved. Some attorneys bemoan this lateness, arguing that the provisions of the contract of sale determine what will happen during the executory period and that, consequently, vendors and purchasers need legal advice while they are still able to affect the provisions of the contract. What do you think of this argument? You will confront the question again as you deal with the materials in Chapters 6-8.

# The Second Generation of Reforms

In the twentieth century, the reform of American conveyancing patterns has been statutory. One spate of statutes took, the other didn't.

First, the failed effort. From the 1890s to the 1930s, more than 20 state legislatures enacted Torrens, or title registration, statutes. Under them, a title search was performed, and a certificate of title was issued; thereafter, a transfer of the certificate was a transfer of the title. The states enacting such laws acted with many jurisdictions around the world to implement some versions of a title registry (as opposed to a public records office), but in this country, this reform did not take. For many reasons, the Torrens statutes were repealed or fell into disuse during the 1930s, and a conveyancing reform that proved suitable for many countries around the world was here discarded. We will deal with this type of reform in Chapter 17. A title registry is still available in a few states as an alternative form of conveyancing.

However, the problem of title searches becoming increasingly longer and ever more mired in paper did not go away. After the Second World War, the process of searching title, no matter how conducted, needed further definition, and another series of statutes, less comprehensive in their reforms than the Torrens acts, followed. The problem was this: As time passed, title searches covered a longer and longer period of time and involved ever more diverse types of interests. The need to shorten and simplify them was addressed by two types of state legislation. First, Marketable Record Title Acts shortened the period for the search to less than the period of the 60-year, common law search to periods of 30 to 40 years. Second, statutes of various types enacted shorter statutes of limitations for encumbrances on the fee simple (particularly for the enforcement of old mortgage liens) and for curing defects appearing on the face of documents on the public records for a certain length of time. Over the years, attorneys have sought enactment of these two types of legislation at the state level.

These second generation statutes are still with us. We will deal with such reforms in Chapter 16.

# 2

## Professional Responsibility in Real Property Transactions

## The Attorney's Role

Typically the attorney first becomes involved in a real property transaction as, or shortly after, the contract of sale is drafted by the parties. For many attorneys, involvement after the execution of the contract comes too late — too late, that is, to advise either the vendor or the purchaser in framing the provisions of the contract in their best interest. For this reason, for example, the standard form contract of sale drafted jointly by the New Jersey Bar Association and Board of Realtors contains an attorney review clause, permitting either party to have the contract reviewed by an attorney of his or her choice within three business days of its execution. See, e.g., Kargen v. Kerr, 248 N.J. Super. 91, 590 A.2d 255 (Ch. Div. 1991). Attorneys in other regions of the country, though, might find this incredible because they are so seldom involved in transactions at this stage.

Often the first issues that an attorney considers in a real estate transaction are ethical, and it is to those that this chapter turns. Like it or not, real estate transactions generate a substantial volume of all the malpractice claims against attorneys. See Gates, The Newest Data on Lawyer's Malpractice Claims, 70 Am. Bar Assn. J. 78 (Apr. 1984) (reporting that 24.9 percent of 1981-1983 claims involved real estate and that 5 percent involved the issuance of title opinions by attorneys).

An attorney involved in real property transactions (and generally) has to keep two documents of the American Bar Association (ABA) in mind: its Model Rules of Professional Conduct (1983) and its Code of Professional

Responsibility (1979). The latter contains the Canons of Ethics, along with their ancillary disciplinary rules (the DRs — mandatory in nature) and ethical considerations (the ECs — "aspirational" in nature). See Ethical Canon 5b, from which DR 5-105(A)-(D) and EC-14 to -16 are derived. Canon 5b states: "A lawyer should exercise independent professional judgment on behalf of a client." This canon embodies a prohibition on (1) attorneys representing clients in transactions in which they themselves are interested, and (2) dual representation, meaning that attorneys should not represent clients with adverse interests either in the same transaction or generally.

However, the prohibition against dual representation is subject to exceptions. The exceptions are applicable when the dual representation has been fully disclosed to the parties, and an informed consent to such representation has been given. See ABA Model Rules of Professional Conduct Rule 1.7(a)(2) (1983) (hereafter ABA Model Rule). The ABA intends these rules to supplant its Code of Professional Responsibility. These rules have been adopted by state bar associations in 29 states; most of the other states have adopted a modified version of the code or, like New York, some combination of the rules and the code.

As a preliminary matter, consider whether we shouldn't just prohibit dual representation outright. For decisions advocating exactly that, see In re Dolan, 76 N.J. 1, 384 A.2d 1076 (1978); In re Lanza, 65 N.J. 347, 322 A.2d 445 (1974) (Pashman, J., concurring in both cases). Wouldn't that be a neater solution than having a rule that, in order to be applied, requires a definition of what constitutes full disclosure, informed consent, and so forth? Those issues present sticky questions of facts. For one thing, a prohibition on dual representation would require independently employed counsel for each party to a transaction. Each attorney must be paid. In the corporate takeover setting, the economics of the transaction generally justify independent counsel, with the attendant multiple payments. Yet this justification is not so clear in the small residential real estate transaction in which the attorney provides documents, some of which are dictated by a third party such as a mortgage lender. Moreover, the competition often sets itself up as representing both parties: Escrow agents handle many aspects of real estate transactions as stakeholders for the parties in the West and Southwestern parts of the country; they are not really the parties' agents but act as their intermediaries in implementing the contract of sale.

ABA Model Rule 1.7 provides:

> (a) A lawyer shall not represent a client if the representation of that client will be directly adverse to another client, unless:
> (1) the lawyer reasonably believes the representation will not adversely affect the relationship with the other client; and
> (2) each client consents after consultation.
> (b) A lawyer shall not represent a client if the representation of that client may be materially limited by the lawyer's

responsibilities to another client or to a third person, or by the lawyer's own interests, unless:

(1) the lawyer reasonably believes the representation will not be adversely affected; and

(2) the client consents after consultation. When representation of multiple clients in a single matter is undertaken, the consultation shall include explanation of the implications of the common representation and the advantages and risks involved.

Compare Model Rule 1.7 with DR 5-105(A), which provides as follows:

A lawyer shall decline proffered employment if the exercise of his independent professional judgment in behalf of a client will be or is likely to be adversely affected by the acceptance of the proffered employment, or if it would be likely to involve him in representing differing interests, except to the extent permitted under DR 5-105(C).

DR 5-105(A) certainly sounds much more restrictive than Model Rule 1.7, but consider also DR 5-105(B) and (C):

(B) A lawyer shall not continue multiple employment if the exercise of his independent professional judgment in behalf of a client will be or is likely to be adversely affected by his representation of another client, or if it would be likely to involve him in representing differing interests . . . .

(C) A lawyer may represent multiple clients if it is obvious that he can adequately represent the interest of each and if each consents to the representation after full disclosure of the possible effect of such representation on the exercise of his professional judgment on behalf of each.

Do the model rule and the DR quoted here amount to the same thing?

In the normal case, the parties to a transaction may approach the attorney thinking that he or she will without pause clothe the transaction with documents. In such a situation, the attorney has a duty to test the waters for potential conflicts. If a conflict is reasonably foreseeable, then the attorney must decline to serve one party or the other. This foreseeability is that of a reasonably prudent attorney, not just that of a layperson. The attorney must give a monologue on the typical pitfalls and problems that beset the type of transaction that the parties propose. The monologue must be of some length and quite specific; it must probe the troublesome areas of potential disagreement between the parties. If the parties are not at each other's throats after this session, then the attorney can conclude that no conflicts are foreseeable and proceed to outline whatever dual representation he or she proposes. In this way, the exceptions to the prohibition on dual representation kick in only after the attorney has made an independent inquiry into the possibility of conflicts of interest between the parties.

When an actual conflict develops, at whatever stage of the transaction, the attorney has an obligation to withdraw. DR 5-105(B); and see In re Disciplinary Proceedings against Flynn, 122 Wis. 2d 649, 363 N.W.2d 440 (1985); see generally, Annot., Attorney and client: conflict of interest in real estate closing situations, 68 A.L.R.3d 967 (1976).

New Jersey case law provides two good opinions in this area: In re Kamp, 40 N.J. 588, 194 A.2d 236 (1963) (representation of purchaser under contract with vendor previously employing the attorney requires more than attorney reliance on contract provision informing the purchaser that all parties "agree to have attorney handle the closing"; attorney must disclose prior employment and obtain purchaser's personal consent), and In re Lanza, 65 N.J. 347, 322 A.2d 445 (1974) (imposing a reprimand on an attorney who sought consent to dual representation with a bare statement that he did not foresee any conflict of interest). *Kamp* proscribes representation when the attorney's prior work for another client is adverse to an interest that he or she is later asked to represent, and *Lanza* proscribes switching sides in midtransaction unless disclosure is made and consent is obtained. But see Richards v. Wright, 45 N.M. 540, 119 P.2d 102 (1941) (finding no improper conduct when vendor requires purchaser to employ vendor's attorney).

Opinions addressing the issue of dual representation are also found in Oregon reports. See In re Conduct of Robertson, 290 Or. 639, 624 P.2d 603 (1981) (attorney representing both vendor and purchaser did not inform purchaser that the vendor's takeback mortgage was subordinate to another mortgage of which the vendor was unaware); In re Baer, 298 Or. 29, 688 P.2d 1324 (1984) (attorney represented his spouse as purchaser and vendor in the sale of a home). Both of these opinions resulted in a one- or two-month suspension from practice of the attorney involved.

Model Rule 1.7 and DR 5-105 quoted previously require that an attorney exercise "independent professional judgment." This standard is required of professionals as they gain knowledge of the client's needs and evolves as a transaction proceeds to its conclusion.

Test your understanding of the bounds of dual representation and conflicts of interest in the following situations.

# EXAMPLES AND EXPLANATIONS

1.  V and P — vendor and purchaser — agree on the terms of a contract of sale for the sale of V's real property Blackacre. They both ask you to draft the contract for them. Will you?

**Explanation:**   You could. See DR 5-105(A). If the parties have reached a complete agreement on the terms of the sale, then an attorney is not "representing" them but is acting as their scrivener — not drafting the terms of their agreement but writing down the predetermined terms that prior negotiations have produced. This situation is the so-called scrivener's exception to the prohibition on dual presentation. How would the attorney's conduct in determining the foreseeability of conflicts and whether full disclosure of the dual representation was made differ in this situation? It probably wouldn't. The attorney would still have to provide the monologue and test both the breadth of the parties' areas of agreement as well as any areas left out of their agreement. DR 5-105(C). If that agreement is incomplete in any area required for a mutually binding contract of sale (for example), the attorney should send them back to the negotiating table before becoming their scrivener. When contract negotiations are ongoing, dual representation is clearly unethical. See N.J. Advisory Comm. on Professional Ethics, Op. 243, 95 N.J.L.J. 1145 (1972); see also Blevin v. Mayfield, 189 Cal. App. 2d 649, 11 Cal. Rptr. 882 (1961).

Once the attorney has acted as a scrivener for the contract of sale, who better to implement its terms and carry the transaction to a closing? However, authority to draft the contract does not provide the attorney with a consent to proceed further. See, e.g., ABA Comm. on Ethics and Professional Responsibility, Informal Op. 923 (1966) (when the vendor and purchaser present final instructions for an escrow closing, it is not improper for an attorney to represent both, but only if both consent). In this regard, moreover, a decision to leave to an attorney the judgment about when to discontinue dual representation may be taken as authority to continue that representation until a conflict actually develops. But the authority is one implied from the rules, not one that is expressly stated there. Furthermore, if an escrow agent or title company employee can close the instructions or carry out the terms of a contract, why can't an attorney (better trained, etc.) do the same work? However, a decision to use an escrow agent to close the transaction is a decision by the parties to leave the implementation of their contract of sale to third parties. Their decision leaves the attorney to carry out the parties' prior instructions. If the parties wanted to attend the closing and review the closing documents, the attorney dual representation would be on less firm footing.

2a. Assuming that you proceed with the drafting of the contract requested by V and P, what course of conduct will you follow if and when the previously agreed-to contingency for mortgage financing proves unacceptable to P?

**Explanation:** Assuming that what is involved is not an all-cash deal, then the lack of agreement over the financing contingency goes to the legal heart of the contract of sale — the consideration — and the attorney should withdraw at this point.

2b. Should you represent either party beyond this point? Should you continue to represent one of them?

**Explanation:**  No. The parties' lack of agreement over this term has brought them back to square one, and so a new disclosure of multiple representation should be given them and their renewed consent should be obtained. Cf. DR 5-105(D).

3a. What if, under the same facts as in the foregoing two problems, V is a real estate developer for whom you had performed, at cost, a title search for the subdivision as a whole. Is it now proper for you to search the title to P's lot in that subdivision and to represent P at his closing on one lot in the subdivision? How would this affect your answers to the previous questions?

**Explanation:**  This new fact standing alone may not affect your prior answers, but the appearance of impropriety in the prior employment is heightened, and so might judicial scrutiny be. See DR 5-105(A). In addition, consider that V here is in an analogous position to the "ambulance chaser" for the personal injury attorney: He serves as a runner and touter for the attorney. In such a situation, the attorney may be tempted to do her legal work for the developer at cost and recoup the profit margin from unsuspecting lot purchasers.

In the pre-model rules era, the ABA Committee on Ethics and Professional Responsibility held, in Informal Opinion 886 (1965), that it was unprofessional for an attorney representing a developer-vendor of residential real property to continue her representation of the vendor while accepting employment from a purchaser of one of the vendor's residences to close a contract of sale on the property, even with full disclosure of the possible conflict and with consent. So there is some authority strongly suggesting that this relationship is improper.

3b. If your prior employment as an attorney had been in the context of legal work done for a lender, would your answer to this third problem change? See In re Chase, 68 N.J. 392, 346 A.2d 89 (1975) (held that dual representation in a lending transaction is prohibited. Read this holding carefully before reading the next paragraph.)

**Explanation:**  Maybe. What is known as a closing often involves two separate transactions: (1) the closing of the title, and (2) the closing of the mortgage loan. Should an attorney represent the purchaser in the first and the lender in the second? Are these transactions sufficiently different that the attorney's actions in one won't affect her judgment in the other? That's the issue. See Note, One for All Is Worth Two in the Bush: Mixing Metaphors Creates Lawyer Conflict of Interest Problems in Residential Real Estate Transactions, 56 Cinn. L. Rev. 639 (1987).

# Attorney Advertisements

Here it might be well to add a word on professional advertising. After Bates v. State Bar of Arizona, 433 U.S. 350 (1977), it is no longer unprofessional to send out a letter offering legal services to large numbers of homeowners who represent potential vendors of property and clients as long as the letter is not misleading. Direct solicitation of clients, while regulated, is also possible. Koffler v. Joint Bar Assn., 51 N.Y.2d 140, 432 N.Y.S.2d 872, 412 N.E.2d 927 (1980), cert. denied sub nom., Joint Bar Assn. v. Koffler, 450 U.S. 1026 (1981). However, a letter extending the same services at the same rates but sent to brokers to pass along to homeowners has been found to constitute an unprofessional practice. This is reverse competition — competing not for the business of consumers, but of providers of services. In re Greene, 54 N.Y.2d 118, 444 N.Y.S.2d 883, 429 N.E.2d 390 (1981), cert. denied sub nom., Greene v. Grievance Comm., 455 U.S. 1035 (1982); contra Kentucky Bar Assn. v. Stuart, 568 S.W.2d 933 (Ky. 1978). Brokers in this instance would be performing an intermediary function for the attorney similar to that performed by developers and lenders in the preceding Example 3 (on page 14).

# EXAMPLES AND EXPLANATIONS

4. Assume that you had previously performed a title search for V, the residential subdivision developer of Example 3, and discovered that each lot in the subdivision was subject to a drainage easement. How would this affect your answer to Example 3a?

**Explanation:** Here the attorney knows something that the purchaser would want to know before closing the deal. If the purchaser retains the attorney, the attorney's knowledge as the purchaser's agent may be imputed to the principal, the purchaser, who thereafter will be taken to have known of the easement. Representation of the purchaser would be improper. See Farr v. Newman, 14 N.Y.2d 183, 250 N.Y.S.2d 272, 199 N.E.2d 369, 4 A.L.R.3d 215 (1964), noted at 9 Utah L.Rev. 493 (1964).

5. P procures independent counsel who then calls you up and requests that you send her your abstract compiled in the prior title search on Blackacre. Will you send it to her?

**Explanation:** Absent a provision in the contract of sale about this, an attorney is under no obligation to comply with such a request. The abstract is the attorney's work product. This suggests, however, that the well-drafted contract of sale should make provision for the intervention of other counsel.

Does this give you another practical reason why dual representation is permitted in some situations? In some locales, the attorney by custom would provide the abstract to the new attorney. In the Washington, D.C., suburbs of northern Virginia, an abstract provided in this situation is known as a back-title letter.

6. What if your client cannot close a transaction for lack of the necessary $1500 in closing costs? (Assume that the client is instructed to bring a certified check to the closing but is not told the exact amount of the closing costs; this problem then becomes realistic and commonplace.) Is it proper for you to advance this amount to him?

**Explanation:**   There are some bar opinions to the contrary, but if an attorney knows the client is capable of making repayment, she might volunteer to become an escrow agent for purposes of seeing that the necessary sum is advanced and properly dispersed at the closing. Advancing the money is probably not the equal of stirring up litigation, unless the attorney knows or has reason to know that the client is not good for the loan.

# A Procedural Note

Notice the mechanics of a grievance procedure against an attorney. The complaint is made initially to the bar association, which makes a finding and, if the finding is adverse to the attorney, seeks to impose a sanction. Judicial review follows, either as a matter of confirming the sanction or because the attorney appeals.

Sanctions often involve little more than a reprimand. Why so light a touch? Professional liability insurance (often known as errors and omissions insurance) policies normally have exclusions from coverage for fraud, so the court is unlikely to paint too grim a picture of the attorney's conduct because such a portrayal may trigger the exclusion.

More generally, notice that the disciplinary strictures involved are written in a general fashion so as to be applicable to all areas of law practice. For that reason, they may be difficult to apply to a particular area of practice, such as real property transactions. And exactly who wrote them? Any particular segment of the bar? The big-firm, well-heeled segment? See Shuchman, Ethics and Legal Ethics: The Propriety of the Canons as a Group Moral Code, 37 Geo. Wash. L. Rev. 244, 252, 267 (1968).

# A Final Note

Practically every state's real estate licensing statutes for brokers exempt attorneys from provisions regulating the conduct of real estate brokerage. In addition, some state and local bar associations permit attorneys to function as real estate brokers in the same transaction in which they participate as attorneys. Such dual functions compound the issues already discussed here because the broker, too, is subject to professional obligations and some fiduciary duties. Mortland, Attorneys as Real Estate Brokers: Ethical Considerations, 25 Real Prop. Prob. & Tr. J. 755 (1991).

# 3

## Real Estate Brokers

## The Brokerage Business

The first person any prospective vendor of real property is likely to consult is a real estate broker. Today a broker is likely to specialize in gathering listing agreements for property or in selling particular types of property — residential or commercial, sales or rentals, and so forth. An agreement to employ a broker is called a listing agreement. A short form of such an agreement is presented below. It is often promulgated in a standard format by the local trade group representing brokerage firms. In some but by no means all jurisdictions, this agreement must be in writing.

For his services, the broker receives a commission computed as a percentage of the selling price of the property. Because the broker is normally employed by the vendor, he is usually considered to be the agent of the vendor in the subsequent transaction; but there is no law against the purchaser hiring a broker, either to search for property of a specific type or to represent her during the course of a transaction. Each party to a commercial lease, for example, often hires a broker to oversee the course of the transaction. In this chapter, we will deal with the broker's role in the purchase and sale of real property.

An agent or broker usually employs associate agents or brokers, often known as salespersons, who do most of the actual selling, often for a set percentage of the commission. Often the listing broker is not the selling broker or salesperson, which sometimes causes the prospective purchaser to think that the selling broker, salesperson, or firm is working for her. Not so. The selling broker is typically the sub-agent of the listing broker, and the selling salesperson is the sub-agent of the selling broker. Confusing perhaps for the purchaser, but think of it this way: The vendor is the principal, the listing broker is her agent, the selling broker is the sub-agent of the listing broker, and so on until the final contact is made, by the ultimate sub-sub-agent of the vendor, with the purchaser. The relationships form a chain of agency and subagency reaching to the purchaser, who is (legally) on her own. For purchasers, one cannot lay too much stress on those last three words — on her own. Hopefully, too, she is on her guard, warily evaluating the words of the broker or salesperson presenting the properties and describing their features. Some commentators have found this arrangement misleading when viewed from the position of the prospective purchaser. Do you?

# EXAMPLES AND EXPLANATIONS

1. The owner of Blackacre is anxious to sell this choice parcel of real property. Real estate broker B tells her that P is interested in purchasing it and that B would be happy to have a listing for it. "Forget it," says the owner, who nonetheless does not forget what B said about P. The owner negotiates directly with P for the sale of Blackacre and then executes a contract of sale to transfer Blackacre to her. Can B recover anything for the information that he gave the owner?

**Explanation:**   No. Only if the owner and B had a prior relationship of mutual trust and confidence or if the owner expressed a desire to help the blurting broker in his business would B have even a chance of a recovery. There is no basis for an implied contract, and no written one exists either. In some jurisdictions, the special statute of frauds for listing agreements would also be a bar to B's recovery.

The obvious answer is that B had not obtained a listing of the property before blurting out the information that is the broker's stock in trade.

# The Listing Agreement

## *Generally Defined*

A listing agreement is the real estate broker's employment contract. It is typically reduced to writing. Indeed, a writing may be required either by a special-purpose statute of frauds for such agreements, or by regulation of the state regulatory agency in charge of broker licensing and supervision. With such requirements in force, it is also likely to appear on a standard and preprinted form issued by the local brokerage board or trade group. Consider the following, quite typical document:

## LISTING AGREEMENT

I, Victor Vendor, agree to *employ the services* of _____,
a real estate broker duly licensed in the State of _____, to

list my real *property known as* _____ with him, and to permit
him to *sell* that property.

   This listing *begins* on _____, 19_____, *and ends* at midnight
on _____, 19_____. During this period, I promise to accept offers
to sell the property for a *total price* of $_____, payable as follows:

_____

   I agree to pay a commission of *6 percent* of the total selling price when
the property is sold by *the undersigned, or any other broker.*

   This    agreement    is    executed    on    _____,    19_____,
at _____, _____.
            *city*                                 *state*

_____             _____
*Broker*                                            *Vendor-Owner*

   *Employ the services?* What does that refer to? More particularly, what is
it that the broker is promising to do? We know that the owner is promising
a commission for whatever-it-is, but what is it? At a minimum the broker is
making a promise to expend reasonable effort, in good faith, to procure
an offer meeting the prospective vendor's terms. Beyond that, the listing
agreements one typically sees are not specific. This raises the question of
whether, at the listing's inception, it is a unilateral or bilateral contract. If it
is the former, it is not binding on either party until the effort is expended — a
de minimis effort won't do.
   Why don't listing agreements have more detail about the broker's efforts?
Because in some instances — and from the broker's hopeful perspective — a
phone call will line up a purchaser. In others, a month of open house Sundays
won't do the job. In other words, the broker is playing the odds, hoping
that over the whole of her accumulated inventory of unsold, listed properties,
some will sell each month.
   Perhaps the services required of the broker should be spelled out in a
listing agreement. A broker can be required to put a "for sale" sign on the
property, advertise its availability for purchase, show the property at agreed
times, and even accept a deposit (or earnest money) or a down payment in
an agreed amount. Some of these things the broker will want to do anyway
without being required to do so. A "for sale" sign, for example, really advertises the broker's firm — the more of them appearing around town, the better
for the firm. Even though the broker will want to do most of these things,
some things a vendor may want to do: holding the deposit, for example. Is
it a good idea to let the broker do that?
   *Property known as?* Will a legal description of the property be needed to
fill in this blank? This is a contract for personal services. It is not a contract

or a conveyance of real property, so the legal description is not necessary. A street address will do. Simply because a legal description is not necessary, however, does not mean that it is not good practice to use one — on the contrary. This agreement is the first of many documents needed to generate a closing of the title. The use of a full description here might flesh out the intent of later documents or more formally be incorporated by reference into those later documents. Each of these documents might then be construed together to establish a conveyance of the property.

What title interest or estate will be sold? Unless it is agreed otherwise, it is presumed that a fee simple absolute in the title will be sold.

*Sell?* This cannot mean literally that the broker is given the authority, via a power of attorney, to convey the property in the name of the owner. No, no — in early cases, in which brokers actually argued this, the courts rejected this notion. But is the property "sold" if a binding contract of sale is executed? Can the legal doctrine of equitable conversion be applied to it? Or is it sold when the title is conveyed, at the closing? Thus in this one simple word lurks the problem of timing the broker's right to a commission, no matter what its amount. A bit of drafting advice: Make sure the timing is clear!

In most jurisdictions, if the offer meets the terms of the listing agreement, the making of the offer is the time at which the commission becomes due. There is no need for a contract of sale. But is this the common meaning of the word "sell"? See Tristram's Landing, Inc. v. Wait, infra page 29 (held that because a contract of sale had conditional language, it was not considered a sale).

*Begins . . . and ends?* That's it!? When the listing ends, it's over? What about the vendor who accepts a qualified offer the next day? What about the vendor who holds off accepting the offer in the expectation of not having to pay the commission? How should this problem be handled? As written, this agreement may stand as an invitation to vendor fraud.

*Total price?* Inclusive of the commission? Of any mortgage on the property? Again, clarify these matters.

*Six percent?* The percentage is seldom preprinted on a brokerage board standard form. It is something that the listing broker hastens to supply. Consent agreements in several antitrust actions brought by the federal government in the 1970s prevent preprinting of the percentage. Some judicial opinions have inferred that a "usual and customary" fee is intended when this portion of the agreement is left blank. Negotiation over the fee is possible but, as an empirical matter, is seldom undertaken.

*The undersigned, or any other broker?* What type of listing is this anyway? Consider the section that follows.

## The Types of Listing Agreements

Listing agreements typically fall into one of three main types: (1) the open listing, (2) the exclusive agency listing, and (3) the exclusive right to sell. An open listing is a broker's authority to procure an offer but reserves the owner's right to sell the property herself or to authorize other brokers to procure offers too. An exclusive agency listing is again a broker's authority to procure an offer, but it denies the owner the right to deal in a similar way with other brokers without paying the first broker the agreed-on commission. An exclusive right to sell listing has the same effect as an exclusive agency but, in addition, denies the owner the right to sell the property herself without incurring liability for the commission. Each of these three types of listings increases the number of situations that entitle the broker to collect a commission and, concomitantly, restricts the number of situations that assign the owner liability for the same.

There are other types of listings as well: The net listing is one. Here the broker agrees to accept as his commission any portion of the purchase price over an agreed-on figure. A considerable number of states have prohibited this type of listing.

The following problems will help you sort out the three main types of listings.

# EXAMPLES AND EXPLANATIONS

2a. V lists her property with real estate brokers B1, B2, and B3 for sale at $100,000. B1 produces a customer at that price; B2 produces a customer at $110,000. V refuses to execute a contract of sale with B1's customer but does so with B2's customer. That latter customer suffers financial losses and cannot close the transaction. B3 then produces a customer at $95,000. V executes a contract with B3's customer and closes this transaction. All three brokers invoice V for a commission. What type of listing is involved here? And who should V pay? (This problem comes from Casner & Leach, Property 700 (3d ed. 1984).)

**Explanation:** Because the type of listing is not identified, the listing is presumed to be an open one. As to who V should pay, all three. B1 because she first produces a customer satisfying the known terms of the listing. B1 is the only broker with whom V has a duty to deal, but V goes on and signs a contract with B2's customer. The contract is the best evidence that B2's customer is a presumptively suitable purchaser, which entitles B2 to his commission. B3's customer has the same status, only more so: That customer closes the transaction.

2b. Would your answer change if B1 did not hold a real estate broker's license? Turns out to be a salesperson?

**Explanation:** Yes. A broker's license is a precondition to filing suit for a commission. In re Kun, 868 F.2d 1069 (9th Cir. 1989). Further, salespersons hold licenses that contain a condition — that is, they generally cannot sue for a commission on their own behalf; rather, the broker who supervises the salespersons must sue on their behalf.

2c. Would your answer change if B2 had agreed to share his commission with B4, an unlicensed broker?

**Explanation:** Yes, in many states. Agreeing to share a commission with an unlicensed person is grounds for denying the commission entirely, even to a properly licensed broker.

2d. Would your answer change if B3's customer proposed that V syndicate the property and sell the resulting limited partnership shares in it to the customer?

**Explanation:** Yes. A limited partnership interest is personal property, not real property. A broker may only deal in realty as defined in the regulatory code, and when the broker steps beyond the bounds of code-authorized conduct, he or she forfeits the commission. A contrasting case might be a corporate vendor listing its real property assets for sale, then transferring a controlling interest in the corporation to a prospect produced by the broker; in this situation, a commission would be due.

3. V orally agrees to list her farm, Blackacre, with B, who then advertises the farm for sale and makes contact with several prospects. V then notifies B that she is trying to sell the farm herself and a week later executes a contract of sale with P1. B then produces a contract executed by P2 to buy the farm for a higher price. V and P1 close the first contract. B sues V for a commission. What result?

**Explanation:** Judgment for V. Absent a written listing or an express agreement to the contrary, most courts will construe a listing as open, which has two characteristics relevant here. First, the B-V agreement is an agency agreement but not an exclusive agency — it is not V's agreement to deal with only one broker. Second, in an open listing the vendor retains the right to sell the property herself without liability for a commission. This implied term of the listing is made express by V's notice to B. Finally, as we have seen, the listing agreement, even an implied one, cannot be construed as just an agreement to sell for the highest price offered. A vendor can refuse a contract procured by a broker for many reasons, price being just one of them.

4a. V executes a brief but enforceable[1] listing agreement granting B, a

---

1. Read this phrase "brief but enforceable" — which appears often in this book — as one meaning that you should assume that the contract is enforceable unless the context, the facts presented in the problem, indicate otherwise.

broker, an "exclusive right to sell" V's farm, Blackacre. During the listing period, V executes a contract of sale for the property with P. B sues V for a broker's commission. What result?

**Explanation:** Judgment for V. The negation of the vendor's right to deal with the property, when expressly stated in the listing agreement, results in an exclusive right to sell. However, there is no magic in those four words, standing alone and without spelling out their implication for the vendor. Thus, unless B could show that P came to V through his efforts, V has no liability to B for a commission.

4b. Would your answer change if the listing agreement provides that a commission would be due B if "the undersigned, or any other broker" procured a purchaser for the farm?

**Explanation:** Probably. The negation of V's right to deal with the property is express here, although even more explicit language is possible. What language would you suggest?

4c. Before B procures a purchaser, V leases the farm for the listing period and beyond. Is B entitled to a commission?

**Explanation:** Yes. The broker would be due the commission because V's action here has made the broker's procuring a suitable purchaser impossible. V too must deal in good faith with B, and the execution of the lease is not good faith dealing.

# The Multiple Listing Service

At this point, let's consider how the mechanics of the Multiple Listing Service complicate the three classifications discussed thus far. Who is a listing broker? A selling broker? How do they share the commission?

Often an MLS is organized as a nonprofit corporation and is run by the local real estate brokers' trade group. Its regulations permit member brokers to list properties with the service and to sell any property so listed. For purposes of effecting a sale, then, the MLS amounts to a sharing of listings, although regulations often also permit a broker to attempt to sell the property for which he has procured a listing himself for a short time (72 hours, for example) after the listing is obtained; thereafter, the listing must be submitted to the MLS and shared with other members.

Access to the MLS is limited to its membership, and the MLS usually processes a listing only if it is based on an exclusive right to sell agreement. With the listing is also processed a description of the property.

When a commission is due on a listed property, the listing broker and the selling broker (or their firms) split it. The split is sometimes a 50-50 one, but sometimes it is 40-60, respectively. Further, the commission will be split within the listing broker's firm between the listing salesperson and his broker; and the same further split occurs in the selling firm.

In most urban areas with MLSs, over 90 percent of all residential vendors employing a broker have the listing submitted to the service. Thus the MLS is a pervasive factor in residential sales. A broker would find it difficult to compete for brokerage business if he was not an MLS member. FTC, The Residential Real Estate Brokerage Industry 16-17, 110-112, 145-146 (1983).

# EXAMPLES AND EXPLANATIONS

5a. V executes a brief but enforceable listing agreement with B1, a broker. The agreement is entitled a "Nonexclusive Listing." It has a 90-day listing period. It also reserves a commission for B1 if within a year after that listing period, V sells the listed property "to any prospect produced by B1 within the listing period described in this agreement." B1 produces a customer P, but no contract results within the listing period. Thereafter, V cancels the listing, then lists the same property with B2, who receives an inquiry from P about the property. P purchases the property within a year after the execution of B1's listing. B1 sues V for a commission. What result? See Galbraith v. Johnson, 92 Ariz. 77, 373 P.2d 587 (1962).

**Explanation:**  Judgment for B1. The so-called extension clause is meant to protect against vendor fraud. Such a clause may extend liability for the commission from 90 days to 1 year. However long the extension period, it is always express. It is not intended, however, to keep the broker working beyond the primary term of the listing agreement. As a result, the level of broker effort beyond the expiration can decline markedly; in *Galbraith*, the court went so far as to lift the requirement that the broker be the procuring cause of the sale, so long as his efforts were substantial during the primary term. If the standards applied to broker effort and the procuring cause doctrine are different before and after the expiration date of the listing, the extension clause becomes a separate agreement — or, an agreement within an agreement.

5b. Would this result change if after V cancelled the listing she leased the property to P for two years with an option to buy effective at the end of the lease and, at the end of the first year of the lease, the tenant exercises the option?

**Explanation:**  No. The vendor's fraud on the broker is shown by the terms of the lease with the option, and the benefit that the lease confers on

V is substantially the same as a sale. Thus both to discourage V's behavior and to prevent V's unjust enrichment, the judgment should still go to B1.

5c. Does an extension clause empower a broker who has produced several prospects but has not procured a ready, willing, and able purchaser during the primary term to continue negotiations with any of his prospects during the extension period?

**Explanation:**  No. Edmonds v. Coldwell Banker Residential Real Estate Servs., Inc., 237 Va. 428, 377 S.E.2d 443 (1989). The vendor's right to negotiate and sell the property herself is reestablished after the expiration of the primary term.

6. A listing contract contains a provision stating that the commission is payable inter alia "when the listing owner, for any reason, withdraws the listing during the primary term of the agreement." Before the broker expends any significant amount of effort to sell the listed property, the owner withdraws and the broker seeks to enforce this provision. Can he?

**Explanation:**  Yes. See Blank v. Borden, 11 Cal. 3d 963, 115 Cal. Rptr. 31, 524 P.2d 127 (1974) (en banc). The inclusion of this "withdrawal from sale" clause is an indication that the prospective vendor has a choice. She can either accept the broker's services or withdraw from the agreement. But see Wright v. Schutt Constr. Co., 262 Or. 619, 500 P.2d 1045 (1972) (refusing to follow a California case similar to *Blank* involving a withdrawal from sale clause when the trial court found, as a matter of fact, that there was no reasonable probability of sale within the term of the listing agreement calling for a purchase price of "$200,000 net"; opining that when the broker introduced no evidence of damage, the clause in the context of a broker's suit for a $20,000 commission was an unreasonable penalty; and upholding a judgment for the broker for $1 for breach of the clause).

# The Vendor's Liability for a Commission

The vendor is liable for a brokerage commission when the broker procures a purchaser ready, willing, and able to purchase the listed property on the vendor's terms, unless the vendor and the broker agree otherwise. Realty Assocs. of Sedona Valley v. National Bank of Arizona, 153 Ariz. 514, 738 P.2d 1121 (Ct. App. 1987).

Procuring the purchaser is defined as being the proximate cause of the offer. The broker must set off a chain of events leading to negotiations and the offer. No sale is necessary; only an offer need be made.

How do these rules square with the types of listing agreements presented earlier? An exclusive right to sell listing is in many ways an attempt to avoid the impact of this standard black letter statement of the law.

As to the attributes of the purchaser, ready and willing means being in a state of mind (and compos at a minimum) to make the required offer. Able? That means financially able, not capable of buying for cash (unless the vendor required it in the listing) but appearing to be creditworthy. In a majority of jurisdictions, it is largely for the vendor to decide when a purchaser is ready, willing, and able, up to the execution of a contract of sale. In many jurisdictions, when a vendor executes a contract of sale with a would-be purchaser, this act in itself indicates an acceptance of the fact that the purchaser is ready, willing, and able.

The vendor's terms are typically those stipulated in the listing agreement but are subject to a rule requiring that the broker procure an offer on terms substantially the same as, but not identical to, the vendor's. De minimis variations are permitted. The vendor cannot add conditions after the fact.

## EXAMPLES AND EXPLANATIONS

7. When is a purchaser qualified as ready and willing? As able? Do these occur at the same time, or at different times?

**Explanation:**   The times are different. A purchaser is ready and willing at the time the contract is executed, but is not yet financially able; her mortgage loan must be approved before she can be called able. Thus the latter term refers either to a finding that the purchaser is able at the time of the contract or to an allocation of the risk that the purchaser will be found "unable" later. In a majority of jurisdictions, the risk that the purchaser proves unable to buy rests on the vendor.

8. A contract of sale is executed by the vendor and the purchaser, but during the executory period the purchaser fails to qualify for a mortgage loan called for in the contract. Is the broker due his commission? What if the purchaser was qualified for the loan at the execution of the contract of sale but thereafter suffered financial reverses (through no fault of her own) that render her unqualified?

**Explanation:**   As to the first question, the answer is yes in a majority of jurisdictions. The risk that the purchaser proves unable to buy is on the vendor when the issue is the vendor's liability for a commission. That is, the vendor must make a judgment at the time of the contract's execution that the purchaser is financially able to purchase the listed property. It is also sometimes thought that the vendor's contract rights against the purchaser support this result.

As to the second question, the fact that the purchaser's financial reverses occurred during the executory period means that the vendor could have exercised her judgment as she should have. Thus it is more difficult to allocate this risk to the vendor. Some authority supports the idea that the broker should not obtain a commission in this situation. This authority sometimes exists in jurisdictions that have adopted a new rule governing the vendor's liability for a broker's commission: the rule of "no closing, no commission." We will return to this rule later in the chapter.

9. V agrees in writing to permit B, a broker, to "handle the sale" of Blackacre. B produces a customer, C, with whom V executes a contract of sale for the property. C fails to close the transaction, but B sues V for a commission. What result?

**Explanation:** As a matter of contract interpretation, the quoted phrase can be interpreted as providing that if there is no closing between the vendor and the procured purchaser, the vendor is not liable for the broker's commission. In short, "no closing, no commission" becomes the rule governing the broker's entitlement. As a matter of law, a minority of states beginning with New Jersey have recently adopted such a rule as a matter of public policy and, later in Massachusetts, as a matter of contract law. Under either version of this minority rule judgment goes for V, although if the matter were to be decided under the majority "ready, willing, and able" rule the word "sale" would be interpreted in accordance with prevailing law and found to mean "handle the procuring of a contract of sale"; judgment would then go for B. Language such as that presented to you here has provided the opportunity for a majority rule state to accommodate the purposes of the minority rule.

10. What if the listing agreement states that the commission "is to be paid on the sale," but the parties never discussed what this phrase means? If the broker procures a prospective purchaser who executes a binding contract of sale but later refuses to close, is the listing vendor liable for a commission?

**Explanation:** No, although the case presents (first) a question of fact — what did the parties mean by the word "sale"? — and (second) one of law. Because the evidence on the fact question appears nonexistent, and the contract is construed against the drafter or its beneficiary, the broker, the second issue is a closer one than in the previous Example 9 because the listing agreement might only be defining a time at which the commission is to be paid, not whether it is payable. A Massachusetts opinion, however, rejects this narrow interpretation of the agreement. Amid the language presented, the use of the word "sale" is, the court said, to be given its common meaning and refers to a completed transaction — a closing is required before a commission is payable. Tristram's Landing, Inc. v. Wait, 367 Mass. 622, 327 N.E.2d 727 (1975).

Ellsworth Dobbs, Inc. v. Johnson, 50 N.J. 528, 236 A.2d 843, 30 A.L.R.3d 1390 (1967), is the leading case for the "no closing, no commission" rule. In this case, the facts indicate that the broker clearly brought the parties together, but the purchaser's inability to obtain financing several times postponed the closing until finally the vendor released the purchaser from further liability under the contract of sale. The broker sued the vendor.

The result? Held for the vendor. The court said that the vendor, like most listing vendors, expected to pay the commission out of the proceeds of the closing, and further that the broker assumed the risk that the purchaser's inability to finance the sale would balk the closing. The broker was in the best position to assay the purchaser's financial worth. (This was true on the facts in *Dobbs* because the broker and the purchaser had had prior dealings, and the broker expressly assured the vendor at several points of the purchaser's ability to close the transaction.) In addition, when the purchaser expects to pay for property with the proceeds of a sale of stock, but the stock market drops so that the sale produces insufficient funds, the risk is the broker's. Thus the broker, under the rule of *Dobbs*, bears this risk as a result of his expertise and as a matter of policy — presumably the broker is no expert on the stock market, only the real property market.

The court held:

> When a broker is engaged by an owner of property to find a purchaser for it, the broker earns his commission when (a) he produces a purchaser ready, willing, and able to buy on the terms fixed by the owner, (b) the purchaser enters into a binding contract with the owner to do so, and (c) the purchaser completes the transaction by closing the title in accordance with the provisions of the contract. If the contract is not consummated because of lack of financial ability of the buyer to perform or because of any other default of his . . . there is no right to commission against the seller. On the other hand, if the failure of completion of the contract results from the wrongful act or interference of the seller, the broker's claim is valid and must be paid.

236 A.2d at 855. The court held as it did as a matter of public policy, not as a matter of contract interpretation.

11. Using the two rules on vendor liability for a commission presented so far, consider the following short problem: Vendor and Purchaser execute a brief but enforceable contract of sale, but the purchaser does not complete the purchase because she develops an acute phobia and refuses to leave her present residence. If the broker procuring the purchaser sues for a commission, what result?

**Explanation:** In a ready, willing, and able jurisdiction the vendor's acceptance of the purchaser, evidenced by the execution of the contract with her, signifies the broker's procuring a purchaser and therefore his entitlement to a commission. See Blackman de Stefano Real Estate, Inc. v. Smith, 157 A.D.2d 932, 550 N.Y.S.2d 443 (1990) (holding that when the purchaser develops agoraphobia — an unreasonable fear of open places — the broker is nonetheless entitled to a commission under the ready, willing, and able rule).

In a *Dobbs* rule state, absent evidence that the broker should have known about the illness and its probable effect on the transaction, this is not the type of usual business risk that the broker is expected to assume pending the closing. However, where the *Dobbs* rule is a matter of law, not contract interpretation, the vendor might still have expected to pay the commission out of the proceeds available to her at the closing, so the public policy basis of the *Dobbs* rule remains. Judgment for the vendor.

A caveat, however, should be given. In a state (such as Massachusetts) in which the *Dobbs* rule is adopted as a matter of contract interpretation, the answer may vary depending on the contract, for there the parties to the listing agreement may contract around the rule, and the question becomes whether they have done so.

Some food for further thought: Even if a state adopts the "no closing, no commission" rule, then what if the listed property is condemned or destroyed by fire? Does the broker get his commission then? Wasn't the contract of sale executed on the common understanding that substantially the same property would be in existence at the time of the closing?

And what if property is sold on a long-term installment basis or with a takeback purchase money mortgage? In a *Dobbs* rule state, isn't there still some limit on how long the broker ought to be made to wait to get a commission? With property bought on an installment basis, when the executory period is to last ten or more years, shouldn't the broker obtain a commission once the purchaser has established a track record of paying the installments as they fall due? Should the broker wait until the mortgage is paid off, when the vendor has a remedy in foreclosure for nonpayment?

# The Fiduciary Duties of Real Estate Brokers

Brokers owe certain duties to their principal (that is, their employer, usually the vendor but possibly the purchaser, so here we use the encompassing language of the law of agency). These duties are based on a preexisting relationship of trust and confidence, here normally shown by a previously executed employment agreement — the listing agreement. Fiduciary duties arise with that agreement and, as if attached to it, as implied terms.

A broker owes his principal three fiduciary duties: (1) loyalty, (2) dealing in good faith, and (3) the disclosure of facts material to the principal's acceptance of an offer. The duties of loyalty and good faith dealing are often lumped together. They are most clearly violated when the broker does not forward offers to his principal, reveals the latter's confidences, or engages in self-dealing — that is, buys the property himself or in some other way competes with the principal. However, this duty does not end with the expiration of the listing agreement in the sense that the broker cannot thereafter undercut the principal's position using information gained during the course of the listing.

The duty to disclose facts material to the principal is a mop-up duty breached when the broker does not reveal his violation of his first two duties or in some way mispresents the purchaser's qualities — his readiness, willingness, or ability to contract: For example, while knowing that the purchaser's checks bounce, the broker fails to disclose this to his principal. Likewise, a failure to disclose a fact material to the vendor's view of the transaction violates this third, more encompassing fiduciary duty.

# EXAMPLES AND EXPLANATIONS

12. B holds a valid listing of V's property for sale at $100,000. While showing it to P, who is hesitant to make an offer, B states that "the listing price is $100,000, but offer $85,000 and see what V says." V closes the sale at $85,000, but refuses to pay B his commission when she discovers the foregoing facts. B sues V. In this suit, what result? See Haymes v. Rogers, 70 Ariz. 257, 219 P.2d 339, 17 A.L.R.2d 896, modified on reh'g, 70 Ariz. 408, 222 P.2d 789 (1950).

**Explanation:**  Judgment for B, but on the facts, not as a matter of law. The broker has come very close to breaching his fiduciary duty of loyalty to his principal and a slight variation in the broker's words or the lack of the prospect's hesitancy, might mean a different result. For example, if the broker said that "V has an offer at $80,000, but offer $85,000 and see what she says," the fact that the broker has disclosed a prior offer might make a difference. It seemed to in *Haymes*. Similarly, if the broker said, "the vendor hasn't budged off $100,000, but she desperately needs the listing price to pay for an operation for her mother," the broker might well lose.

13a. B holds a valid listing of V's property. P employs B to search for property suitable for her residence. P expresses an interest in V's property to B in the form of an offer to purchase. B does not forward P's offer to V, but instead buys the property himself and later sells it at a profit. On learning the foregoing facts, P sues B. What result?

**Explanation:**  Judgment for P. Fiduciary duties are not just confined to listing agreements, but are formed from every employment agreement undertaken by a broker. While in the employ of P, B owes P his best efforts to find suitable property, and those efforts may not be diverted for the broker's personal gain. B has violated not only the duty of good faith and loyalty but capped his disloyalty with a failure to disclose self-dealing.

Perhaps the remedy is the most interesting part of this situation. P may impose a constructive trust on B's profits or, if B still owned the property, she might force its conveyance to her. See Funk v. Tifft, 515 F.2d 23 (9th Cir. 1975), noted at 1976 B.Y.U. L. Rev. 513, 12 Idaho L. Rev. 217 (1976) (where the purchaser hires the broker to search for property). Hiring a broker should mean just that — hiring a broker, not a competitor. The public expects brokers not to step out of their professional role, and violating those expectations in a way that leads to self-dealing is one way of defining the reach of a broker's fiduciary duty. In many jurisdictions, the state regulatory code for brokers will provide examples of the duties expected of brokers, and such statutes have been used to define the duty that a broker owes a client in nonregulatory litigation.

13b. The same facts, except that V sues B. What result in that suit?

**Explanation:** Judgment for V. He has a listing agreement on which to base a breach of fiduciary duties: the breach of the duty of loyalty — evidenced by the nondisclosed dual representation and the failure to forward the offer — and the self-dealing — B's buying the property for himself. V need not allege damages for breach of such a duty but can recover the profit from the flipped contract.

13c. The same facts, except that there is no employment agreement between P and B.

**Explanation:** No clear answer. Now P's case is harder to make out. Can P's contract be one implied in law, a quasi-contract? As such it would be one whose subject is the transmittal of offers, rather than one involving the full services of a real estate broker. Brokers should not behave as did B: Their state regulatory codes and consumer protection statutes both may have some bearing on this matter. Isn't it in the public interest to have purchasers as well as vendors police the brokerage trade?

If both V and P can recover from B, what does the judgment for each stand for? Are both recovering the lost profits on the deal? The broker might have been a bad actor, but *that* bad?

14. B, a broker, approaches V, the owner of Blackacre, with the information that someone is interested in purchasing the property. V replies that she does not deal with brokers and does not pay them commissions. B replies that he would get his commission from the interested party, P. Although thereafter V thought that she was selling Blackacre to P, she in fact was selling it to B, who promptly turned around and sold it to P. Discuss V's rights against B.

**Explanation:** Judgment for V, in tort for the misrepresentation and for the interference with a prospective advantage. However, without an intent to deal with B, V has no listing or other employment contract on which to bottom a breach of fiduciary duty, so judgment for B on any express contract claim. What about an implied contract? What reliance interest can V show?

15. B, a broker, has an oral listing with V for the sale of Blackacre, an agreement governed by the law of a state requiring that listing agreements be in writing. B shows the property to P while V is not at home, and P then tells B that she will think about it. P thereafter approaches V directly without telling V that B sent her. V and P negotiate directly, agree on a transaction, and execute a contract of sale. B sues P in tort for interference with a prospective advantage. What result?

**Explanation:** In a tort suit for interference with a prospective advantage, it is no defense for P to say that B never obtained a contract of sale for V. A showing that the broker is the procuring cause is sufficient to show B's reasonable expectation of a commission. However, the fact that V is not obligated to pay a commission because of the oral agreement is a bar to the action unless, for example, the purchaser (1) undertakes any liability for the commission, or (2) realizes that the oral listing is invalid, goes back to the vendor with this knowledge, and renegotiates the purchase price for a lesser amount, reducing it by the amount of the commission the parties supposed was previously due the broker. These latter factors show sufficient intent to defeat the broker's rights that a suit might lie in tort, rather than on the listing.[2]

Fiduciary duties must be grounded in some preexisting relationship of trust and confidence. In the context with which we are concerned here, that relationship is shown by the listing agreement. Hence fiduciary duties are a major source of *vendors'* rights against brokers. They may involve the imposition of affirmative duties to speak and act on the vendor's behalf. In some instances, the broker is a volunteer. A broker who has undertaken to record the contract of sale or a deed must do so or suffer the legal consequences. Occasionally, however, a broker has a duty to investigate and disclose to a vendor facts material to a transaction, even if the vendor does not ask. As we have seen, often such affirmative duties relate to the physical characteristics

---

2. Occasionally in the case law one finds an irate broker, with a valid listing, who receives an offer for the listed property in excess of the listed price, which offer the listing vendor refuses to accept, and so B then takes the contract of sale, executed by the prospective purchaser and then by broker as the V's agent, and records the contract, again supposedly acting as V's agent. In a suit in which a broker who did this claimed a commission, the vendor cross-claimed for a species of tort, an interference with an economic advantage — called slander of title — and won. See Brezina v. Hill, 202 Neb. 773, 277 N.W.2d 224 (1979) (awarding vendor damages). See Chapter 13.

of the property or to information available on public records and documents. For example, a broker may have to disclose the legal consequences of a clause in a contract, and his silence becomes a breach of duty. See Crutchley v. First Trust & Sav. Bank, 450 N.W.2d 877 (Iowa 1990) (failure to disclose the legal effect of a nonrecourse provision in a contract).

Investigation or inspection of material features of the property or the transaction is the prudent course for a broker for another reason as well. The purchaser may be able to hold the broker liable in tort for any misrepresentation made during the course of the transaction. For instance, the broker should investigate the veracity of suspicious information on the multiple listing service factsheet for the property. This is so even if the information is supplied by the broker's principal — the vendor — for a failure to do so has also provided a basis for a broker's liablity. As to the broker's possible liability to a purchaser, we now turn.

# Broker Duties to the Purchaser for Misrepresentations

A representation of fact that the broker knows in some sense (see below) is false, but which is material to a plaintiff's transaction, is made with the intention that the plaintiff will act in reasonable reliance on its truth, and causes the plaintiff injury, may be actionable in one of three forms: as an intentional (or fraudulent), negligent, or innocent misrepresentation.

All states recognize an action for some type of misrepresentation. Not all states recognize an action for each type. An intentional misrepresentation is the most widely accepted and is akin to fraud. Here the broker as a defendant has actual knowledge of the falsity of the representation.

A negligent misrepresentation is based on a broker's constructive knowledge of the falsity of the representation: Here the broker either knew or should have known that the representation was false because he should have investigated the matter. Cases involving constructive knowledge often deal with information on the public records — for example, the zoning status of the listed property, its compliance with applicable building and housing codes, or its status as a flood plain on state geological maps. As in other areas of tort law, a negligent misrepresentation can be made honestly and in good faith but still be negligent because it involves facts that the broker should have investigated.

Finally, an innocent misrepresentation is one that although made honestly, in good faith, and after a reasonable investigation of the facts still turns out to be false. Only a minority of states impose liability on a broker for such a statement because liability in this instance is in effect strict or absolute liability: a decision to put the risk of a misrepresentation on the broker.

A misrepresentation can be either an action or some silence or inaction when there is a duty to act or speak. When a vendor's broker shows the listed property to the purchaser, what duties arise when the attributes of the property are not fully made known to the purchaser? If the vendor and the broker permit the purchaser free access to the property to inspect it, if they make no affirmative misrepresentations, and if they do not conceal any defects in it, or if information about the defect is available from third-party sources, then there is no breach of a duty to disclose. Although there is some split in the cases, silence alone is not actionable as fraud. London v. Courduff, 141 A.D.2d 803, 529 N.Y.S.2d 874, 875 (1988), citing Perin v. Martine Realty Co., 5 A.D.2d 685, 168 N.Y.S.2d 647 (2d Dept. 1957), aff'd, 6 N.Y.2d 210, 190 N.Y.S.2d 995, 161 N.E.2d 210 (1959).

# EXAMPLES AND EXPLANATIONS

16a. When the broker and the vendor inspect the property together, the broker notices that there are signs of water seepage in the attic, indicating a leaky roof. If these two parties do not remove debris concealing the signs of water damage in the attic or do not replace the burned-out light bulbs in the fixtures so that other signs of the water damage are not visible, what recourse does the purchaser have against either or both of the parties after the closing?

**Explanation:**   In the purchaser's action for fraud and negligent misrepresentation, some courts would impose liability for the vendor's silence; but without active concealment, this result is very controversial. See Posner v. Davis, 76 Ill. App. 3d 638, 395 N.E.2d 133 (1979), discussed in Peterson, Tort Claims by Real Estate Purchasers against Sellers and Brokers: Current Illinois Common Law and Statutory Changes, 1983 S. Ill. U.L.J. 161, 163-170.

Setting aside for the moment the difficulties of showing each element of a negligent misrepresentation, the purchaser's chances of obtaining a judgment against both the broker and the vendor increase with active concealment. A failure to change the attic light bulbs is less likely to be culpable than is the concealment of water damage behind debris that is the natural accumulation of stuff in attics and not piled there for the purpose of concealing the signs of the damage.

16b. What if the broker saw the signs of water damage in the attic but relied on the vendor's statements to him that the leaks had been repaired and does not investigate further? He instead remains silent as to the possibility of a leaky roof and passes along false information to the purchaser.

**Explanation:**   The vendor's liability is based on an intentional misrepresentation, the broker's is best pleaded on a theory of negligent misrepresentation. The broker's duty, independent of the vendor, to investigate and disclose defects and material conditions of the listed property is a controversial matter today. Given that the broker has reasonable grounds to investigate the condition of the roof, cases split on whether he has this duty. Compare Herbert v. Saffell, 877 F.2d 267 (4th Cir. 1989) (no such duty, applying Maryland law), noted at 63 Temp. L. Rev. 165 (1990), and Lyons v. Christ Episcopal Church, 71 Ill. App. 3d 257, 389 N.E.2d 623 1979) (no such duty), with Easton v. Strassburger, 152 Cal. App. 3d 90, 199 Cal. Rptr. 383, 46 A.L.R.4th 521 (1984) (duty found on theory of negligent misrepresentation). *Easton* is discussed in 17 Pac. L.J. 327, 336-338 (1987) and 11 Nova L. Rev. 825, 832 (1987). Where it is found, it may arise by analogy to cases in which an agent makes a statement to a third party without a reasonable basis, as might be provided by an independent investigation by the broker, for believing its truth. Johnson v. Geer Real Estate Co., 239 Kan. 324, 720 P.2d 660 (1986) (broker had duty to investigate sewer hookups alleged by vendor to be available, but not in fact available), superseded by statute as stated in Frank v. Weber, 777 P.2d 278 (Kan. 1987). It may additionally be premised on brokers' ethics code provisions, state regulatory statutes for brokers, and state unfair trade practice acts, or, more generally, from a discussion of the broker's expertise in real estate and the need for public confidence in that expertise.

16c. Does the duty to investigate (if adopted in a jurisdiction) extend beyond the time at which the brokerage commission accrues?

**Explanation:** As in many areas in which the law is evolving, courts seek resolutions to cases based on "even though" rationales: Even though there may be a duty, the duty only applies while the broker is at work on the transaction. If the case involved a fiduciary duty, can the broker be held responsible up to the time the commission accrues, but not responsible thereafter? No. So is a broker's duty to investigate likely to extend beyond the time he earns a commission? Probably yes. See, e.g., Turnbull v. LaRose, 702 P.2d 1331 (Alaska 1985) (involving a broker's duty to investigate whether lessees will renew lease in a situation in which lessees did not renew three months after sale). But one opinion does not a national trend or a majority rule make. Take each case as they come — this is torts, after all!

17. What if the garage were subject to periodic flooding, and both the broker and the vendor know of the fact but neither discloses it?

**Explanation:** If the information about the flooding is available elsewhere — from public geological survey maps, for example — or is observable, not concealed or undisclosed in answer to a purchaser's question, it is arguable that neither vendor nor broker is liable. Craig v. ERA Mark Five Realtors, 509 N.E.2d 1144 (Ind. App. 1987) (no duty to investigate zoning of property described as multifamily on an MLS property factsheet). This result might change if (again) the court recognizes a duty to disclose anything affecting the habitability of the premises — that is, anything that might become the subject of the implied covenant of habitability in other types of suits. Analogous rules, to the effect that recent, undisclosed rises in tax assessments or recent zoning changes affecting the property need not be disclosed, reinforce this result; there, the availability of tax and zoning records to the public makes the information in these records accessible to the purchaser. But this is no answer because what is accessible to a purchaser is likely to be even more accessible to the broker and become, just because of the accessibility of the public record, a basis for imposing a duty on the broker to know what's in that record.

18a. What if the foundation slab for the house was cracking, and the cracks were discovered by the vendor but not disclosed to the broker, when prior to the listing the broker advised and the vendor installed new wall-to-wall carpeting?

**Explanation:** Here the vendor's concealment is intentional. Presumably, too, the vendor would have minded if in the course of inspecting the property the purchaser rips up the wall-to-wall carpets to get a look underneath. Today in many jurisdictions, there would be a duty on the vendor to disclose. Perhaps a listing broker, with an opportunity to inspect and appraise the property, would be liable as well. However, if the MLS sheet reported that the property was "in good repair," a selling broker may not be jointly and severally liable. The more outrageous and intentional the vendor's concealment of the defect is, as to both the purchaser and the broker, the less likely the broker will be held liable for an innocent misrepresentation. But see Bevins v. Ballard, 655 P.2d 757 (Alaska 1982) (duty found: broker liable for even an innocent misrepresentation when repeating vendor's false information about the capacity of an unfinished well).

18b. Same facts. However, what if the broker knew, but the vendor did not know, of the defective slab?

**Explanation:** The broker is liable for the misrepresentation on the basis of actual knowledge, the vendor on the basis of imputed knowledge. The knowledge of the agent can be imputed to the principal. See C. Goforth, Sales of Structurally Defective Homes: The Potential Liability of Sellers and Real Estate Brokers, 41 Okla. L. Rev. 447, 455 (1988). Has the broker here violated a fiduciary duty to disclose the defect? Probably, so that the ultimate pocket for payment of any judgment will be the broker's.

19. B, a broker with a valid listing to sell V's residence, shows it to P but does not disclose that radon seepage from the ground under the property affects the airspace within the residence. V and P close the transaction, but

after having the property tested, P sues V and B to rescind the sale. What result? What other causes of action should P include in her complaint?

**Explanation:** V is liable for nondisclosure of the condition, but is B? The defect here is not in the physical condition of the listed property, but its "habitability" broadly defined is nonetheless affected by the radon. If the misrepresentation on the broker's part occurs after an inspection and testing of the condition of the property, then there is no negligence on the broker's part. However, if it results from the broker's knowledge and expertise about intangible conditions in the area that affect the property, there may still be an innocent misrepresentation.

In some jurisdictions, the issue becomes how to use the existing case law and particularly the cases relating to housing quality and the warranty of habitability: Is this situation like cases relating to the physical condition of the property, or is it like the cases relating to public documents — zoning changes, flood plain maps, and so forth — matters of public record that both the purchaser and the broker should be aware of? See Chapter 12. Radon seepage is not a condition that affects a region's properties in a similar way; that is, there are "hot spots" and "clean spots" in any region, so the broker who sold neighboring property might have guilty knowledge that other brokers might not possess. Similarly, the seepage results from interaction with the construction techniques used. Thus this is a case in which the complaint should sound in negligent misrepresentation, rather than a breach of fiduciary duty.

20. B, a broker with a valid listing to sell V's residence, shows it to P. But when asked, B does not disclose that V is dying of AIDS. V and P close the transaction, but on learning of V's illness P sues V and B to rescind the sale. What result?

**Explanation:** No rescission because the facts not disclosed are immaterial to the transaction. One does not become infected with the AIDs-related viruses by entering on the listed property — and certainly not by purchasing it. A few states have legislated specifically on this matter, which indicates that the issue is not everywhere an open and shut matter; certainly emotion and controversy surround it. If the contract is not rescinded, another issue, open so far as the case law is concerned, is whether B is liable to have the amount of his commission set off by the litigation costs incurred by V.

21. What if the broker innocently made a misrepresentation of fact, say, about the adequacy of the legal description for the property as represented by the vendor, or about other legal aspects of the transaction for which the vendor could be held responsible?

**Explanation:** Here the broker would not be liable, although the vendor may be liable for rescission or damages. Hoffman v. Connall, 108 Wash. 2d 69, 736 P.2d 242 (1987). The broker is not a legal expert and so is without a duty to independently investigate the applicable law.

# Administrative Regulation of Brokerage Activities

The complaint that fails against a broker in court may be sufficient in a regulatory forum. In each state, real estate brokers are licensed and governed by a statute setting out grounds for revocation of that license. This statute is implemented by an administrative body, often called a Real Estate Commission. For example, see Cal. Bus. & Prof. Code §10177(c) (West 1987); Wash. Rev. Code Ann. §18.85.230 (West 1989). More generally, "making substantial misrepresentation or false promises or suppression, concealment, or omission of material facts" is grounds for an administrative investigation into a transaction conducted by a licensee in Texas. See Tex. Rev. Civ. Stat. Ann. art. 6573a §16(1) (Vernon 1969). Scienter is usually a requirement of these statutes, but they can, at the same time, be very general. For instance, "untrustworthiness" is sometimes a ground for revocation of a license.

Whether a private cause of action arises to enforce the standards imposed on brokers in these statutes is a question on which the courts addressing the issue have split. Obviously the standards are derived from the usages of the brokerage trade, but because their enforcement is here placed in administrative hands, some courts have restricted their enforcement to that agency's procedures.

# A Real Estate Broker's License

Receiving compensation for "buying, selling, or exchanging real estate of and for another, or offering for another to buy, sell, or exchange real estate" requires a broker's license. Even attempting to perform such services in one transaction — without any further activity indicating a course of conduct — requires a license. Fla. Stat. Ann. §475.01(3) (1989); Va. Code Ann. §54-730 (1979) (a typical definition of brokerage activity). Listing, negotiating, or advertising in the course of such activity is also usually prohibited without a license. Nev. Rev. Stat. §645.030 (1989); Wash. Rev. Code Ann. §18.85.010 (1989). Without a license, a broker or one attempting to offer brokerage services cannot collect a commission — at least not in court — and is denied a quantum meruit recovery as well. See, e.g., Mass. Ann. Laws ch. 112, §87RR (Law. Coop. 1985). A licensee is generally prohibited from splitting a commission with any unlicensed person. Tex. Rev. Civ. Code Ann. art. 6573a, §14(a) (Vernon 1990). Although occasional cases permit a finder's fee to an unlicensed person, the trend is to strictly construe the regulatory statutes in this area.

Before obtaining a broker's license, a person must often work for a broker for a period of time and, increasingly, satisfy educational requirements as well. While working in this apprentice capacity, the person may hold a real estate salesperson's license. While a salesperson, one works under the direction and authority of a broker but may not sue or collect a commission in one's own right. See, e.g., Colo. Rev. Stat. §12-61-103(5)(a) (1985).

Each licensing statute contains numerous exemptions, often for persons acting pro se, certain banks and trust companies, and fiduciaries — and attorneys. See, e.g., Fla. Stat. §475.011 (1989); Pa. Cons. Stat. Ann. §455.304 (Purdon Supp. 1990). These exemptions permit the exempted parties to engage in activities that would otherwise be subject to regulation. They do not necessarily permit the charging of a commission when those activities are undertaken.

# 4

## Contract Risk of Loss

In a majority of American jurisdictions, the courts have adopted the English rule that absent an express provision of the contract the risk of loss of the property during the executory period of a contract of sale for real property is on the purchaser. This is a rule that applies to a fortuitous loss, not one for which a party to the contract is responsible. See Ramsey, Executory Contracts for the Sale of Land: Australian and United States Comparative Approaches to Risk of Loss, 22 Real Prop. Prob. & Tr. J. 581 (1987) (a good recent summary of the law). The rule applies even if the purchaser is not in possession of the property during that period, but is subject to the rule that the vendor must be able to convey marketable title, even if the purchaser has already gone into possession. The ability of the vendor to convey marketable title is important because the contract must be one capable of enforcement in equity by specific performance by the vendor. His ability to enforce the contract is the basis for his shifting the risk to the purchaser. The rationale for the majority rule is found in the equitable principle that regards the contract as performed: "Equity regards as done, what ought to be done."

At the same time, if the vendor has insured the property, then he will often be found to hold the proceeds of the policy in trust for the purchaser. This is one way of ameliorating the unexpected effect of the majority rule on the purchaser, who often will not have anticipated the need for insurance on the property during the executory period. This trust theory is also a way around the rule that an insurance contract is personal to the parties to it. Thus this theory looks like an attempt to fashion a correct rule out of two incorrect ones.

The majority rule on this risk is made for the contract that has no provision about the risk of loss. None of the foregoing says that the drafters of a contract of sale should rely on it. It is a court-made rule, and litigation may be required to establish its applicability to the particular situation — and to a particular contract. The same is true for the purchaser's rights in the

43

vendor's insurance. Better to have the vendor endorse his policy for the benefit of the purchaser during the executory period or while the purchaser procures his own insurance. Better yet to have the purchaser named as an insured party in the vendor's policy. See Ramsey, op. cit., at 594.

# The Doctrine of Equitable Conversion

It is often said that the majority rule depends on the equitable conversion of the property. This occurs at the signing of the contract. After that, the vendor (1) holds the legal title to the property in trust for the purchaser, and (2) also holds a lien for the amount of the purchase price. Lawyers Title Ins. Corp. v. Wolhar & Gill, P.A., 575 A.2d 1148, 1153 (Del. 1990). Thus this doctrine regards the purchaser as the owner of the property and as a debtor for its purchase price, and the vendor as a trustee of the title, held for the purchaser, and a creditor for the price. This doctrine arose first in cases in which the vendor died during the executory period, and equity, through a decree of specific performance for the purchaser, found that the contract was performed by the vendor during his life; nothing more needing to be done except to convey the title, equity regarded the transaction as closed. Neither could (in a state in which a marital estate attaches at the time of death) the vendor's spouse claim dower or curtesy in the property when the vendor died during the executory period — the vendor did not have a sufficient interest in the property (was not "seised" of the property, said the common law) when he died.

The doctrine works on a completed, enforceable contract of sale. It does not work on an option to purchase real property — it is said that the option "works" no equitable conversion. If the purchaser improves the property during the executory period, the vendor cannot enjoin the removal of the improvement because the vendor's lien on the property for the purchase price is measured at the time the lien arose — that is, at the time of the execution of the contract, not thereafter. If the property contracted for is timberland, the vendor could enjoin the purchaser's removal of the timber during the executory period for the same reason. The value of the timber measures the value of the lien for which the vendor bargained, and if that value is impaired, the vendor can get an injunction. (In some states, the impairment of value will have to be sufficient to put the remaining value of the property below the unpaid purchase price before the vendor can have an injunction.) Based on the doctrine, the purchaser can also sue the vendor for waste during the executory period.

However, the doctrine does not give the purchaser all the benefits of ownership right away. Absent a contract provision to the contrary, the purchaser is not entitled to the rents, profits, and other benefits of the use of the property. The vendor gets the rent up to the closing. And during the executory period, the vendor is responsible for real property taxes up to the time that the purchaser takes possession.

The emphasis on the doctrine of equitable conversion, however, permits the risk of loss (considered as the subject of a separate (implied) provision of the contract) to be shifted to the purchaser immediately on the execution of the contract. It also shifts the benefits to the purchaser as well. The purchaser, having the benefit of the doctrine of equitable conversion, also has the attendant risks. What if minerals are discovered on the property during the executory period, and at the time of the destruction, the risk of loss is on the purchaser? The person bearing the risk of loss should in fairness also receive the benefits of the appreciation in value. Further, that appreciation, occurring during the executory period, is generally not a reason to deny a purchaser specific performance of the contract. So there may be benefits that modify the harsh effect of the majority rule — at least in a rising market.

Think about the modern contract of sale. How does the doctrine of equitable conversion work in practice? In a word, badly. The enforceability of the contract defines the time at which the risk shifts to the purchaser. Only at that point does the doctrine apply to the contract. The modern contract, loaded with contingencies or "subject to" clauses, is in this regard seldom capable of specific performance much before the closing. Only then will the contingencies, material to the closing and thus a precondition to it, be satisfied. The doctrine, and by extension the risk of loss rule, comes into play when there is a contract in which the contingencies are satisfied. Only when they are is the contract capable of specific performance. That is, this equitable action will not lie if the defendant cannot obtain all that he expects the contract to provide and if the plaintiff cannot perform it.

# EXAMPLES AND EXPLANATIONS

1. In a majority rule jurisdiction, and after the destruction of property, the vendor may argue that, even though the contract had unperformed contingencies, they are immaterial to the contract. If there is some doubt as to the materiality of the contingency to the question of risk of loss, how can a purchaser in a majority rule state further protect himself?

**Explanation:**    There are several methods. (1) By expressly negating the rule by contract. (2) By requiring the vendor to restore the premises by the time of the closing should they be destroyed during the executory period of the contract. (3) By bargaining for a credit against the purchase price due at the closing in the amount of the value of any improvement destroyed. How will that value by determined? Choose one: (a) the replacement cost of the improvement, or (b) the proceeds of the insurance policy held by the vendor on the improvement. From the purchaser's perspective, the vendor's assignment of the proceeds may be insufficient. The purchaser does not know when or if the company will pay, what defenses the insurer has against its insured, etc. (4) By the use of an escrow as a closing device. Do you see why this helps the purchaser's position? The escrow makes the satisfaction of all contingencies subject to the passage of title. Some of these solutions can be used either singly or in combination with others.

By the way, beware of the halfway drafting solution. From the vendor's perspective, he should not try to let an "as is" clause stand for a shift in the risk of loss. Neither should a purchaser rely on his forfeiture of the contract to imply that the vendor retained the risk of loss.

# Criticisms of the Majority Rule

Much criticism has been aimed at the majority rule. First, because equitable conversion is a fiction it depends on the availability of specific performance, not the other way around. Majority rule courts reason from the doctrine to the remedy and are headed in the wrong direction. Second, the implied condition on risk of loss (however it allocates the loss) is itself based on a more fundamental (and also implied) point: That is, the contract was executed on the assumption that the property is a fair consideration for the purchase price, so after the property is substantially destroyed, the exchange is no longer fair and should not be enforced in equity by specific performance. The practical result is that the contract should be viewed as a nullity and the parties should negotiate it again.

This second criticism of the majority rule is in fact the basis for the minority American rule — the so-called Massachusetts rule. This minority rule holds that, absent a contract provision to the contrary, the risk of fortuitous loss of the property during the executory period is on the vendor.

The minority rule rests on two rationales: first, that the destruction of the property results in a failure of consideration in the contract, and second, that the contract itself contains an implied condition that the contract would not be enforceable in the event of substantial destruction. See Anderson v. Yaworski, 120 Conn. 390, 181 A. 205 (1935) (adopting the minority Massachusetts rule), noted in 49 Harv. L. Rev. 497 (1936), 36 N.Y.U.L.Q. Rev. 492 (1936), 30 Ill. L. Rev. 809 (1936).

In a minority rule state, is specific performance with an abatement in the purchase price available to the purchaser? Shouldn't the contract become a nullity and the parties free to renegotiate a new contract? Anytime the court is asked to grant an abatement, they in effect are rewriting a crucial term in the contract — the price term. They should do that carefully, only when they have some basis to tell what the parties would do in this situation. Isn't forcing the parties back to the negotiating tables better than having the court rewrite the old contract? If abatements are permitted, what is the amount of the abatement? Should the price be abated down by the amount of any insurance claim, the replacement cost of the property destroyed, or the contract price of the destroyed property? For a discussion of this issue, see Burack v. Chase Manhattan Bank, 9 A.D.2d 914, 194 N.Y.S.2d 987, 988 (1959) (permitting an abatement for the actual value, not necessarily the replacement cost, of the property destroyed).

Despite the criticism of the majority rule, as well as the adoption of the minority rule in a substantial number of states, the majority rule has survived. Its survival is explained perhaps because a bright line is needed and the rule at least supplies that, as well as a basis on which the vendor and purchaser can plan their relationship during the executory period. Why didn't the common law formulate the minority rule instead?

Which party to the contract — vendor or purchaser — is the most efficient risk bearer? Often the answer will be the party in possession. Possession gives the possessor knowledge about the property, making that party the most efficient risk avoider.

## The Uniform Vendor Purchaser Risk Act

The most sensible rule is often said to be that of Professor Williston, the drafter of the Uniform Vendor Purchaser Risk Act. This act has been adopted in 11 states, including New York and California. For a brief review of New York cases, see K. Holtzschue, Real Estate Contracts 104-106 (1986). The act provides as follows:

> Any contract hereafter made in this State for the purchase and sale of realty shall be interpreted as including an agreement that the parties shall have the following rights and duties, unless the contract expressly provides otherwise:
>
> (a) If, when neither the legal title nor the possession of the subject matter of the contract has been transferred, all or a material part thereof is destroyed without fault of the purchaser or is taken by eminent domain, the vendor cannot enforce the contract and the purchaser is entitled to recover any portion of the price he has paid.
>
> (b) If, when either the legal title or the possession of the subject matter of the contract has been transferred, all or any part thereof is destroyed without fault of the vendor or is taken by eminent domain, the purchaser is not thereby relieved from a duty to pay the price, nor is he entitled to recover any portion that he has paid.

The rationale behind this statute is that the party in possession of the property is in the best position to safeguard it, minimize any damage, and in general know what happened. Its complementary rationale is that, once the purchaser takes legal title, he has had sufficient time to safeguard his interest by procuring insurance and arranging for repairs.

Consider the following questions, which might arise under the act. These questions are reviewed in Ramsey, Executory Contracts for the Sale of Land: Australian and United States Comparative Approaches to Risk of Loss, 22 Real Prop. Prob. & Tr. J. 581, 586 (1987). In each, assume that there has been a destruction of the property so substantial that the act applies.

# EXAMPLES AND EXPLANATIONS

2.  Does the act only apply to contracts of sale, or do documents without that title come within its scope?

**Explanation:**  The act should apply to any document functioning like a contract of sale. The answer should not depend on the title on the first page. Examples of documents with similar legal effects are an option to purchase contained in a lease, a freestanding option, or an installment land sales contract (or contract for deed, as it is called in some regions). An installment land sale contract functions like a contract of sale, but an option often does not: It is more like a contract to make a contract, and this limits the remedies available to its holder — specific performance, for example.

3.  Why does the act permit the parties to contract out of its terms if its rules are so sensible? Is it sensible to contract out of the act partially? Might the parties to a contract opt out for condemnations, but not for other types of destruction? (Why are destruction and condemnation treated the same in the act? They present very different threats to the stability of the contract relationship.)

**Explanation:**  The first paragraph of the act makes an assumption about the general or presumed intent of the parties to the contract. This, by negative implication, says that the act is not intended, as a matter of law or public policy, to read its rules on risk of loss into every contract, overriding a provision of the contract to the contrary. However, it might be sensible to limit the effectiveness of the act to residential contracts and leave commercial contracts (however defined) to the negotiations between the parties, or to the common law.

So the general question is, are the act's provisions rules of law or presumptions about the intent of the parties? Unless the parties contract around the terms of the act, those terms are presumed to constitute their intent as to the matters covered by the act.

4.  What if the vendor has the property rented to a third party during the executory period and either the contract never mentioned which party was to receive the rents during that period, or the contract assigned the rents to the purchaser?

**Explanation:** The basic question is whether the legal title and possession must be actually transferred. If not, the right to receive the rents is the right to receive the profits of title and possession, so in the former instance, §(a) applies, but in the latter, §(b) applies.

5a. What if the vendor and the purchaser agree that the purchaser is to have the right to possession during the executory period? The vendor moves out, but P never moves in, when a fire destroys the property. Who has the risk of loss?

**Explanation:** What is "possession"? Is it actual possession? Constructive possession? Possession given under the color of the contract? Or, here, a contract right to possession, whether or not exercised? Rego Crescent Corp. v. City of New York, 37 A.D.2d 737, 323 N.Y.S.2d 994 (1971), aff'd mem., 32 N.Y.2d 906, 300 N.E.2d 435 (1973) (held that even though neither legal title nor possession was actually transferred, the entry of an order for the vendor granting him specific performance was sufficient to invoke the provisions of §(b)). *Rego* argues for a definition of possession broader than just actual possession. But see Note, Vendor and Purchaser: Possession to Satisfy the Uniform Vendor and Purchaser Risk Act, 28 Okla. L. Rev. 455, 457 (1975) (suggesting that a mere right to possession is insufficient to become a transfer of possession under §(b)).

5b. Assuming that neither legal title nor possession (however defined by local law) has been transferred at the time of a substantial destruction by fire, must the purchaser, to avail himself of the remedies in §(a), claim those remedies by the closing date when the contract makes the time for a closing "of the essence"?

**Explanation:** No, he has a reasonable time to claim the remedy. See Stork v. Felper, 85 Wis. 2d 406, 270 N.W.2d 586 (Ct. App. 1978).

6. Under what circumstances would a court give an abatement in the purchase price but award specific performance, even though the improvement has been totally destroyed by fire during the executory period?

**Explanation:** Among states adopting the UVPRA, there is a conflict in the case law on this point. See, e.g., Skelly Oil Co. v. Ashmore, 365 S.W.2d 582 (Mo. 1963), which presents this situation, and Dixon v. Salvation Army, 142 Cal. App. 3d 463, 191 Cal. Rptr. 111 (1983) (denying a purchaser specific performance with the abatement under §(a) of the UVPRA and contrasting this result with the New York cases); for a general treatment, see Ramsey, op. cit., at 593-594. The basic question is, does the act provide the exclusive remedies for the situations within its scope? Can the purchaser have an action for specific performance when subsection (a) applies and his only express remedy is the recovery of installments paid under the contract? In New York he can, but in California he cannot. In New York, the courts note that the act does not repeal the purchaser's other remedies, and where specific performance with an abatement in the price is one such remedy, the purchaser should not be denied it by negative implication; in California, the purchaser is denied specific performance by negative implication.

7. The act requires that the property be destroyed without fault of the party walking away from the contract. What if the purchaser has not made a good faith effort to satisfy the terms of a financing contingency clause at the time of the destruction? Who then has the risk of loss?

**Explanation:** The act's terms expressly consider fault only in the context of causing the destruction. Good or bad faith in carrying out the contract is not such fault as would affect the provisions of §(a), but the act does not prohibit and so does not preclude other remedies, such as the vendor's action for damages on the contract in this instance.

Now for some other definitional problems.

8a. What is "destruction"?

**Explanation:** The word includes a fire, a flood, an earthquake, and a landslide, but what about vandalism? Onondaga Sav. Bank v. Wagner, 101 Misc. 2d 109, 420 N.Y.S.2d 657 (1979) (holding that destruction includes the results of vandalism). Some courts have interpreted the word expansively. See Sprouse v. North River Ins. Co., 81 N.C. App. 311, 344 S.E.2d 555 (1986) (judicial sale also included). In each case, these things result in destruction of the vendor's ability to sell, but a judicial sale does not result in physical destruction. In the same vein, a related question is what is a "material" destruction? It can either mean "material" to the contract or to the identity of the property. Because of the difficulties involved, New York courts have tended not to distinguish between nonmaterial and material destruction. Considering the intent of the act's drafters, the meaning of this word should probably be confined to the physical destruction of the property.

8b. What is a "transfer"?

**Explanation:** It either refers to a closing or to a right given under a contract that is subject to specific performance. The former is the likely plain meaning of the word in its context — "transfer of the legal title" (as opposed to the transfer of an equitable interest created in the purchaser by a contract of sale).

8c. And, finally, what is a "taking by eminent domain"?

**Explanation:** Following the lead of the previous answer, the phrase probably refers to a completed condemnation, rather than a pending one. Creative Living, Inc. v. Steinhauser, 78 Misc. 2d 29, 355 N.Y.S.2d 897 (1974), aff'd, 47 A.D.2d 598, 365 N.Y.S.2d 987 (1975) (so holding).

That the terms of the statute need further definition is only to suggest that the drafters of contracts in the states adopting the act should supply them. But if they do, have they "agreed otherwise" and put themselves beyond the reach of the act? Hopefully not, not if their intent was to flesh out the agreement that the Act assumes they meant to make.

## Insuring the Property during the Executory Period

What's the practical answer to all of these problems? In a word, insurance. At the start of the executory period, and particularly when the property is insured, the vendor will usually carry it. His policy will typically be required by a lender-mortgagee. Keeping this policy in effect during the executory period is probably, in the small transaction, the simplest method of handling the risk of loss problem. Either the purchaser is named an "insured party" in the vendor's policy or the vendor can add an endorsement to the policy giving the purchaser the right to share in any proceeds.

What is the difference between these two methods? Naming the purchaser as an insured party gives the purchaser the right to participate in the settlement of the claim; not so if the policy is endorsed for his benefit. This latter method leaves the vendor with the sole right to settle the claim but gives the purchaser the right to share the proceeds of that settlement. From the purchaser's perspective, then, naming him as an insured party is preferable.

If neither method is used, then the party suffering the loss under the rules is left to the mercies of equity — in particular, to the operation of the equitable doctrines of subrogation and constructive trusts. Those doctrines, present in the case law of many jurisdictions and used in tandem with the doctrine of equitable conversion, result in a blurring of the crisper distinction between majority and minority rules in this area of law. For example, although an insurance policy is a personal contract for the benefit of the named insured party — whether vendor or purchaser — this fact alone does not prevent equity from imposing a constructive trust on the proceeds of the policy, once received by the insured, for the benefit of the party found to have the risk of loss, while still holding that the claim is personal to the insured. Thus the vendor might hold the proceeds of a policy in trust for the purchaser if the latter has the risk of loss. (In 15 states, the vendor is the purchaser's trustee when the latter bears the risk.) Perhaps too, this theory also works in reverse: that is, that the purchaser might hold the proceeds in trust for the vendor, who in a minority rule state, or by agreement, might have the risk of loss. Of this, more later.

Often an escrow of the insurance policy is a useful device for implementing any such trust if it is sufficiently clear under local law, or the parties desire to make it so by agreement.

# EXAMPLES AND EXPLANATIONS

9. If, in a majority rule state, the purchaser bears the risk but the vendor holds the policy, should the purchaser reimburse the vendor for premiums paid to the insurer during the executory period?

**Explanation:**   No, not if no loss has yet occurred because the trust arises only when the vendor receives the proceeds of the policy, not before. The policy remains the vendor's personal contract with the insurer. However, once a loss occurs and the vendor has the right to make a claim, the answer might change if the equitable theory of the constructive trust is followed to its logical conclusion. Sometime after a loss occurs, the purchaser has the benefit of the insurance and should reimburse the vendor for the premiums. The trustee is then entitled to reimbursement for the reasonable expenses of maintaining the res (the policy) of the trust. Some courts might not maintain the distinction between the policy and the proceeds and, in such courts, the court might find that the trustee has the right to set off the premiums when, as things turn out, the purchaser receives the benefit of the policy in the form of proceeds. Vendor and purchaser might usefully execute an agreement on this point and not leave it to the operation of equity.

10. In a majority rule state, what if the vendor has the policy, but, after an insured loss occurs, will not negotiate the claim with the insurer: Can the purchaser, as the beneficiary of a constructive trust, compel the vendor to do so?

**Explanation:**   Yes, although the earlier distinction between the policy as a personal contract of the vendor's and the proceeds as the res of a trust is harder to maintain in the face of such recalcitrance. Cf. Dubin Paper Co. v. Insurance Co. of North America, 361 Pa. 68, 63 A.2d 85 (1949) (holding that when a vendor settled the claim but returned the proceeds, the purchaser could sue the insurer to compel the issuance of the proceeds again, but this time to him (the purchaser)).

11. Now a harder question. What if the purchaser has the insurance during the executory period, but the vendor is found to bear the risk of loss when a claim arises: Can the constructive trust theory work in reverse?

**Explanation:**   Probably it cannot. Sometimes the doctrine of equitable conversion is premised on a rationale using the language of constructive trusts. When this linkage is present in the case law, the vendor is a trustee of the title for the benefit of the purchaser during the executory period and, after the contract of sale, is subject to specific performance.

Put the issue this way: Should this "title trust" become the basis for the "proceeds trust" as well? Perhaps logically, but the result is not compelled. The vendor might hold the title in trust, but the fruits of the property, such as its rents, have been held not to be subject to a trust. On this authority, the proceeds of the property could be separately dealt with for the benefit of the vendor.

A second theory might reach the same negative answer. That is, a principle of mutuality favors permitting the vendor to secure the purchaser's insurance proceeds. However, recalling your first-year contract law will tell you that the applicability of the principle of mutuality has been narrowed in recent decades.

Finally, as a matter of the expectations of the parties, the vendor might expect to be named as the purchaser's trustee after agreeing to sell the property, but would the purchaser have the same expectation after agreeing to buy, or would he expect to insure only his own interest in the property, knowing that both vendor and purchaser will have a separate interest in the property during the executory period?

12. If the vendor has overinsured the destroyed property for an amount greater than the contract price would call for, does the vendor hold all the insurance proceeds in trust for the purchaser, or just that portion of the proceeds needed to satisfy the contract?

**Explanation:**    The latter. The subject of the trust is the amount that the vendor needs to perform his obligations under the contract.

# 5

## The Statute of Frauds in Real Property Transactions

## Introduction

The Statute of Frauds provides that agreements (read the term broadly to include not just contracts of sale, but installment sale contracts, and even, in some jurisdictions, options to purchase) for the sale of real property "shall not be enforced unless they are in writing and signed by the vendor." Hostetter v. Hoover, 378 Pa. Super. 1, 547 A.2d 1247, 1250 (1988). Under this wording, when the purchaser is the defendant there must be proof that a contract was created, but there is no need for the purchaser to sign it as a precondition of its enforcement.

More commonly, perhaps, the statute requires that "the party to be charged," meaning the party sued on it (the defendant, whether vendor or purchaser) must sign it. Such statutes are more closely patterned on the English Statute of Frauds. See Smith v. Boyd, 553 A.2d 131, 132 (R.I. 1989); and see generally E. A. Farnsworth, Contracts §6.1, at 370 (1982). When the statute is cut from this pattern, the defense must be specifically pleaded as a defense; a failure to plead it waives the statute as a defense, and a general denial as to the existence of a contract is insufficient to raise the defense.

The original English statute, enacted in 1677, provided more generally in part that all interests and estates in real property

> made or created by livery of seisin only, or by parol, and not put
> in writing, and signed by the parties so making or creating the
> same . . . shall have the force and effect of leases or estates at will
> only.

Statute of Frauds, 1677, 29 Car. 2, ch. 3, §4.

Here the party making or creating the interest must sign the writing. This usually will be the vendor, but it can be the purchaser if an easement, other less-than-fee interest, water rights, or a mineral estate, for example, are the subject of a regrant (from purchaser to vendor) in the same document. In a state with a statute patterned on this feature of the English statute, then, it is prudent to have both parties "execute" the agreement by signing it.

The statute was enacted in the wake of the 1666 Great Fire of London. The fire played havoc with real property titles in that city. Property deeds burned in the houses consumed by the fire, leaving the inhabitants to quarrel with their neighbors over boundaries and other matters. All the controversies following hard on these quarrels produced the feeling, in the wake of a crisis of fraudulent claims, that something had to be done to prevent perjury based on alleged parol transfers of property. Reformers said that the remedy for this crisis was enrollment of deeds (something like recordation as we know it). They had been saying much the same thing since the Parliamentary debates over the Statute of Uses in the 1530s. As attorneys found conveyancing uses for the statute, as well as ways around it, fraud became a greater and greater problem. Nonetheless, Parliament and the large landholders in the city and around the shires balked at the idea of recordation because they did not want to reveal the extent of their holdings. A compromise between the reformers and these interests was embodied in part in the statute's §4. A writing requirement, with a voluntary recording system, was the quid pro quo. This history is interestingly reviewed and recited in Hamburger, The Conveyancing Purposes of the Statute of Frauds, 27 Am. J. Legal Hist. 354, 364-375 (1983).

All of the states have adopted the Statute of Frauds, or some portion of it. Note, The Doctrine of Equitable Estoppel and the Statute of Frauds, 66 Mich. L. Rev. 170, 170-171 (1967). Often the statute appears in the following form:

> No action shall be brought . . . whereby to charge any person
> upon an agreement or promise upon the sale of any interest
> in real estate, unless the promise or agreement upon which such
> action shall be brought, or some memorandum thereof, shall
> be in writing, and signed by the party to be charged. . . .

R.I. Gen. L. §9-1-4 (1985). See also Ind. Code §32-2-1-1 (1976); Tenn. Code Ann. §29-2-101 (1980) for other "no action" versions of the statute.

Notice the words "writing" or "memorandum" are not defined. Sir Matthew Hale (1609-1676) produced one of the first drafts of the statute in 1670, and his version of §1 provided: "That it be enacted, that no Estate pass . . . without Deed. . . ." Hamburger, 27 Am. J. Legal Hist. at 365 n. 52. Assuming that deeds were in standard form at the time, that is certainly specific enough. However, the statute, as enacted in all states, is not so specific. Commonly, however, the writing needed to satisfy the usual statute has come to mean one of two things:

1. a document with the names of the parties, an identification of the property, the title to be conveyed, and the price, and the signature of the party to be charged;
2. a document, with the material terms of the transaction, and signed by the party to be charged.

Often the second version of the Statute's requirements incorporates the first, but also included other "material" terms.

Sometimes the price term is left unspecified, but an appraisal procedure is agreed on as a means of arriving at the purchase price. This is sufficient to satisfy the statute. See Cobble Hill Nursing Home, Inc. v. The Henry & Warren Corp., 74 N.Y.2d 475, 549 N.Y.S.2d 920, 543 N.E.2d 203 (1989), reh'g denied, 75 N.Y.2d 863, 552 N.Y.S.2d 925, 552 N.E.2d 173 (1990) (finding sufficient an objective standard without the need for further expression by the parties); cf. Thurlow v. Perry, 107 Me. 127, 77 A. 641 (1910) (holding writing insufficient when a prior oral agreement as to amount of purchase price was not specifically incorporated into later writing "to buy your place as agreed"). Sometimes the identity of the purchaser is unknown when a vendor throws out an offer to deal with anyone meeting her terms unconditionally. A court should be very careful in finding that the vendor intended to deal with just anyone because the resulting agreement would lack mutuality, or the vendor might change her mind or require additional terms before hearing of the acceptance of the offer. Irvmor Corp. v. Rodewald, 253 N.Y. 472, 171 N.E. 747, 748, 70 A.L.R. 192 (1930) (discussing this situation, Cardozo, J., states: "There is nothing more than an offer lanced into the void").

Now ask yourself, is the second version of the statute a good idea? The answer has to be no because if the law does not have a very bright-line idea of what satisfies and does not satisfy the statute, parties will be encouraged to think up material terms after the fact, and many will use the statute as a means of evading transactions to which they would otherwise be bound. That hardly carries out the purposes of the statute. For the basis of the second version of the statute in one state, see N.Y. Gen. Oblig. L. §5-703 (McKinney 1978), interpreted in Lupoli v. West Hills Neighborhood Assocs., Inc., 140 A.D.2d 313, 527 N.Y.S.2d 818, 819 (1988), and Tamir v. Greenberg, 119 A.D.2d 665, 501 N.Y.S.2d 103, 105 (1986) (both cases require that all material terms of the contract be set out).

Nevertheless, in jurisdictions adopting the second version, the resulting rules can be stated as follows: If the parties agree to a term of the contract and it is not incorporated into the memorandum, that document is insufficient and does not satisfy the statute. If the parties did not discuss a term, and the resulting memorandum is silent as to that term, a court can imply a reasonable, or customary, term on the same subject. This result is based on what the court finds that the parties would have done had they discussed the subject.

Such a finding might be made even for the most basic of terms — for example, the price or title to be conveyed. If the parties discussed a term, but did not reach agreement on it, then what's a court to do? Now, of course, we are brought back to the evidentiary uncertainties and temptations raised against this second version of the statute at the outset. To avoid these problems, it is better, therefore, to leave this second version to situations in which the parties agree that they either did, or did not, discuss the term.

The required memorandum may be more than one document, so long as all the documents taken together include all required or material terms and are signed, or are incorporated into a document signed, by the party to be charged. What if a vendor accepts by telegram or fax machine? On proper proof, such a "signature" should suffice.

An option to repurchase, contained in an otherwise sufficient writing, but not signed by the purchaser-optionor, has been upheld against a charge of violating the statute so as to uphold the option. See, e.g., Scutti Enters., Inc. v. Wackerman Guchone Custom Builders, Inc., 153 A.D.2d 83, 548 N.Y.S.2d 967 (1989), appeal denied, 75 N.Y.2d 709, 555 N.Y.S.2d 692, 554 N.E.2d 1280 (1990). Such a result can be justified either because an option works no equitable conversion and thus is not a transfer of real property, or because the optionor by accepting the deed is estopped from denying the option. The latter reason, however, shows that we are close to the boundaries of what the statute permits; it involves equitable estoppel, an exception to the statute dealt with later in this chapter.

Whatever type of writing is required, it need not be delivered to satisfy the statute. The delivery adds nothing to achieve the purposes of the statute. Rulon-Miller, III v. Carhart, 544 A.2d 340, 342 (Me. 1988). The purposes of the statute are evidentiary, and the statute requires no more evidence than a writing. Indeed, the writing, when not having the essentials dictated by the statute, may be used to show an intent not to contract. Such a writing may have been intended to deny the existence of a contract, as when the party signs a letter of intent to make a purchase and sale later.

# EXAMPLES AND EXPLANATIONS

1.  O agrees orally that P can purchase Blackacre from her for $100,000. Later O denies that she agreed to sell and points to the lack of a written agreement with P as proof that she did not intend to sell. O consults you for advice. What do you say to her?

**Explanation:**  Shouldn't an option to purchase real property be in writing and satisfy the Statute of Frauds? An option is an agreement to enter into a contract of sale. A contract of sale creates an interest in real property. An option is therefore an agreement to create an interest in real property in the future and should be written so as to satisfy the statute on that account.

Combs v. Ouzounian, 24 Utah 29, 465 P.2d 356 (1970). What can an option be but an invitation to an expensive lawsuit otherwise? Measuring them against the requirements of the statute is itself a way of preventing fraud, promoting certainty in transactions involving real property, and encouraging parties to think out the terms of such transactions. Exceptions to the statute should be permitted only with a clear indication that the equivalent of a contract will be enforced between the parties.

# Listing Agreements and the Statute

In many states, statutes require that listing agreements be in writing. The listing is technically a contract for the personal services of the broker and so arguably falls outside the purview of the usual Statute of Frauds. However, on the level of practical result, the listing is likely to lead to a transfer of real property and will control some of the terms of that transfer. So some states have enacted special purpose statutes that require a written listing. In other states, a writing is required because of a regulation of the Real Estate Commission or other state agency regulating the licensing of brokers. And in the rest of the states, the listing agreement remains beyond the reach of the statute, even though this might be unwise as a matter of policy. See generally D. B. Burke, Real Estate Brokers §2.3 (2d ed. 1992).

# Exceptions to the Statute

The courts have fashioned two types of exceptions to the statute. Both are designed to carry out its purposes and prevent the statute from itself encouraging fraud. These two exceptions are the doctrines of (1) part performance, and (2) equitable estoppel.

It should be noted that the first doctrine (the most common exception recognized in this country) is really a black letter version of the second and that, historically, the first developed out of cases recognizing the second.

Equitable estoppel requires that the purchaser reasonably rely on a transfer insufficient to meet the requirements of the statute, to her detriment. Often this means that there must be some, albeit insufficient, writing, and that the purchaser pay some money or incur some liability (take out a loan, perhaps) in reliance on the document's validity. See, e.g., Baliles v. Cities Serv. Co., 578 S.W.2d 621 (Tenn. 1979) (involving the defendant's aid to a plaintiff purchaser with an insufficient writing in securing a construction loan), noted in 10 Memp. St. U. L. Rev. 107 (1979); and see generally Note, The Doctrine of Equitable Estoppel and the Statute of Frauds, 66 Mich. L. Rev. 170 (1967). Equitable estoppel also arises from the conduct of a party — through speech, silence, action, or inaction — by which a party secures some benefit. *Baliles,* supra (where the benefit would have been the defendant's obtaining the lot improved with the proceeds of the construction loan). Moreover, this doctrine scrutinizes the conduct of both parties, not just the purchaser's.

Part performance generally requires that (1) the purchaser take possession of the property (in some states exclusive possession is required), and (2) pay all or part of the purchase price, and/or (3) improve the property in some way. The first element of this doctrine applies in all states recognizing the doctrine. As to the second and third elements, they are sometimes both required but sometimes only one of them is required.

Thus, the four versions of the part performance doctrine are

1. possession,
2. possession plus payment,
3. possession plus improvements, and
4. possession plus payment and/or improvements.

See 3 American Law of Property §11.7 (A. J. Casner ed., 1952). Because there are several versions of this doctrine, you should beware of generalizations about it. The courts are straining to use it equitably, and that effort may produce results in any one jurisdiction that defy a concise black letter re-statement.

This doctrine was first recognized only 23 years after the enactment of the statute. Lester v. Foxcroft, 1 Eng. Rep. 205 (H.L. 1700). All but four states recognize the doctrine. Tibbs v. Barker, 1 Blackf. 58 (Ind. 1820). Many state legislatures have codified it. Only Kentucky, Mississippi, North Carolina, and Tennessee do not. In those states, equitable estoppel is the principal exception to the statute.

The first element of the part performance doctrine is thought to provide the same evidence as would a writing, and the second and third are thought to incorporate or black-letter the reliance element of equitable estoppel.

> As a general rule, the effect of the Statute is to render oral contracts for the sale of real property unenforceable, although not invalid. Therefore they cannot be specifically enforced, although they may possibly form the basis of an action to recover damages.

*Hostetter,* 547 A.2d at 1250.

# EXAMPLES AND EXPLANATIONS

2. Ask yourself, why is the distinction just quoted made?

**Explanation:**   One instance in which the distinction might apply, is where the purchaser makes an improvement to the property that is readily compensable in money. Where it is not, then the doctrine of part performance is applied. This makes the statement quoted the basis for a restricted statement of that doctrine. This distinction is generally recognized. E. A. Farnsworth, Contracts, §6.9, at 422 n.11.

3. Is an agreement that is not in writing but is admitted in court in sufficient detail to satisfy the statute binding on the parties thereafter?

**Explanation:** Yes, in Rhode Island — and probably elsewhere, although the case cited is the sole presentation of this issue. The judicial record itself becomes the writing, and this result is based on the court's need to be able to enforce its judgment. Smith v. Boyd, 553 A.2d 131, 133 (R.I. 1989).

4. Is an agreement to settle litigation over a balked purchase and sale, when made by an attorney with a general authority to settle, sufficient compliance with the statute?

**Explanation:** Yes, in New Hampshire. See Halstead v. Murray, 130 N.H. 560, 547 A.2d 202 (1988).

Of the two exceptions, equitable estoppel is the one likely to apply to the greater number of factual situations. This is so because it applies not just to actions involved in taking actual possession but to any action constituting detrimental reliance, whether or not the expense improves the property itself. Architectural fees evince detrimental reliance, whether or not the architect's plans are ever used on the property. So does procuring a mortgage. Estoppel arises from the conduct of a person, whether or not the conduct occurs on the land. On the other hand, part performance is shown by what happens on the land.

Finally, the parties to an agreement whose terms must comply with the statute cannot modify the agreement without again complying with the statute. What is required to be in writing in the first instance cannot be altered by parol evidence — true in most, but not all, states. In some states, the modified agreement is judged according to whether or not, as modified, it is of a type that is subject to the statute. If not, then the modification need not be in writing.

# A Concluding Note

No discussion of the requirements of the Statute of Frauds should be confused with a discussion of the needs and requirements of your clients in a transaction. Generally, it is good practice to memorialize all of the terms they wish in a written contract of sale, whether or not those terms are required by the statute. Getting all the terms of an agreement into a written document is preferable to leaving them to the vagaries of your client's memory.

# 6

## Contract of Sale Conditions

The period of time between the completion of a contract of sale for real property and the closing is known as the executory period. It often commences when the broker fills in the blanks on a standard form contract of sale. But no matter who fills in such blanks, it starts when the parties sign or "execute" the contract.

Don't let the quoted term confuse you, for we are using the term "executory" in a different sense here. The executory period is the time when the contract of sale is not yet fully performed — it is, in this sense, "unexecuted." So perhaps we should refer to the period as the "unexecutory period."

At a minimum, the executory period is the time when the purchaser applies for a mortgage loan, has the property inspected and appraised, and deals with attorneys searching the title and determining its marketability. All this cannot be done overnight. The usual executory period is between 45 to 90 days long.

As you read this chapter, consider the following letter as an executory contract of sale.

September 7, 19____

Victoria Vendor
Blackacre Farm
Myerstown, MD

Dear Vivi:

Thank you for walking the bounds of your farm with me over the holiday weekend. I intend to purchase it and with this letter make the following offer to purchase. Your acceptance of my offer can be indicated by signing the line after my signature.

The price is $500,000, or $10,000 an acre. Enclosed is a check for $25,000, tendered as a down payment, to be credited toward the full price, which is payable as follows:

—     $75,000 upon the offer of title proof,
—     $400,000 payable as the proceeds of a first deed of trust.

I will make application to the Myerstown Federal Savings Bank for a $400,000 loan, to be secured by an appraised first mortgage lien upon the farm, at a satisfactory, conventional rate of interest, for a term of 20 years.

I want to be in possession by Christmas. Settlement shall occur by December 15, 19____, at a place mutually agreeable to both of us and subject to the following four conditions:

1.  Title to Blackacre shall be insurable and marketable of record. Proof of title shall be in a form acceptable to my attorneys, Ketchum & Skinner.
2.  The property is rezoned to permit my home office as a real estate broker.
3.  A survey is done indicating that the boundaries of Blackacre are more or less as we saw them over the weekend.
4.  The sale of my house in town is completed, with the proceeds free and clear.

If these conditions are not met by the closing date, I reserve the right to recover my deposit and withdraw from all my duties undertaken here.

I am delivering this letter to you by hand so you will know my terms, but I am also giving a copy to my attorney, Jim Skinner, for review. Give him a day or two to review it; he will be in touch.

With best wishes for your move to California.

Very truly yours,

Peter Purchaser

This ____ day of September, 19____, I have read and accept the terms and conditions of this letter.

_____

Victoria Vendor

As the above contract clearly indicates, the modern contract of sale for real property is replete with contingency clauses, often known as "subject to" clauses — as in "the closing of the title involved in this transaction is subject to" or "only to be held when the following conditions are met." Thus the contingencies become preconditions to a closing. A precondition is an event not certain to occur which, unless its occurrence is waived, excuses further performance of a contract. Restatement (Second) of Contracts §224 (1981). As we have seen in the materials on risk of loss, such preconditions also serve, so long as they remain unfulfilled, to postpone the time at which the doctrine of equitable conversion attaches to a contract.

## "Subject to Financing" Clause

Perhaps the most-litigated contingency clause is a "subject to financing" clause, in which the purchaser agrees to close only after he has applied for and received a lender's commitment for a type of mortgage financing outlined in the clause. This type of clause is generally of benefit to the purchaser; he can thereafter waive its benefit, as for example by agreeing to close with cash instead of the proceeds of a mortgage loan. Ross v. Eichman, 129 N.H. 477, 529 A.2d 941 (1987) (waiver of benefit of clause effective when given to vendor's broker), on later appeal, 130 N.H. 556, 543 A.2d 427 (1988). However, the clause may arguably benefit the vendor as well, as where the vendor argues that it assures him of the purchaser's financial ability to close the transaction; therefore the purchaser's waiver may not always remove the clause from the contract.

The usual material terms of this type of clause are: (1) the amount of the mortgage loan to be obtained, (2) the term of that loan, stated as a minimum term acceptable to the purchaser, and (3) the maximum interest rate acceptable to the purchaser. These three terms are necessary to avoid a charge that the clause is void for vagueness, indefinite, or ambiguous in its provisions. Such a finding would result in the parties being able to rescind the contract, and rescission will require the other party to tender back any benefits received under the contract, including the purchaser's deposit.

However, less is sometimes made to serve. The third paragraph of the letter at the beginning of this chapter has the first term, a vague reference to the second, and part of the third, so the acceptance letter back will have to provide more. The problems that follow this section explore how and when this is so.

Other terms might include a maximum amount payable in closing costs on the loan, a maximum amount necessary to satisfy the lender's requirements for a mortgage escrow account for real property taxes and property hazard insurance, and a maximum amount necessary each month to repay the loan. See Nodolf v. Nelson, 103 Wis. 2d 656, 309 N.W.2d 397 (Ct. App. 1981).

Executing a contract with a subject to financing clause, the purchaser undertakes the implied obligation to make a reasonable effort to obtain the outlined financing. Proctor v. Holden, 75 Md. App. 1, 540 A.2d 133, cert. denied, 313 Md. 506, 545 A.2d 1343 (1988) (holding that filing application before execution of contract counts toward fulfilling obligation under later-executed contract). Often it is held that the vendor may, but need not, search for the purchaser's financing too. The vendor may not, as a result of his search, force the purchaser to accept financing not called for in the clause.

Of course, much depends on the words of the clause. Some examples follow in the problems.

# EXAMPLES AND EXPLANATIONS

1a. Vivi (V) and Peter (P) executed a brief contract of sale for Blackacre for $375,000. The contract provides in part "if P is unable to obtain this loan [described below] within 60 days from this date, P's deposit will be returned to him in full." The contract is otherwise enforceable.

The contract is further conditioned on P's ability "to borrow $300,000 at a conventional, fixed interest rate of 10 percent, for 20 years." The parties reduce the contract price in the contract to $350,000 but do not otherwise change the terms of the contract. P files one mortgage loan application. In response to this application, the lender appraises the property at $321,000 and offers a mortgage loan whose principal amount is $250,000 and whose interest rate is 10.25 percent. Ninety days after the date of the contract's execution, P requests the return of his deposit. V refuses. P sues V for its return. What result?

**Explanation:** Judgment for V, who is entitled to keep the deposit at this point. V has at least three arguments to make. First, V will argue that the risk of not procuring the required loan is with P.

Second, V can reasonably argue (considering the declining contract prices that this transaction reflects) that the reduction in the purchase price implicitly amends the subject to financing clause, reducing the principal of the required loan to an amount bearing the same loan-to-price ratio as $400,000 is to $500,000 — 80 percent — or $375,000 is to $300,000 — 83 percent. The one lender to whom P applied comes close — 78 percent. V should argue that P has a duty to keep trying.

Another negotiating posture suggests itself. If V offers to make up the difference with a second mortgage loan, P will have the financing he contracted to take. If V takes this route, he can offer a loan with an 80 percent loan-to-price ratio, or he can offer a second mortgage that, when added to the lender's, provides financing in an amount $75,000-100,000 below the contract price. There is, however, authority holding that P does not have to accept V's offer of a loan. Gardner v. Padro, 164 Ill. App. 3d 449, 517 N.E.2d 1131 (1987) (holding that vendor is not a "lending institution" stipulated in clause). However, this offer will tend to show P's good faith.

Third, as to the interest rate, V can argue that P's application to only one lender cannot establish a conventional interest rate. Courts have validated subject to financing clauses that provide for financing "at prevailing conventional rates and terms." See, e.g., Grayson v. LaBranche, 107 N.H. 504, 225

A.2d 922 (1967) (holding purchaser excused after filing two applications, which were rejected, under clause stating "this agreement is contingent on the buyer obtaining a conventional mortgage of _____ at his terms"); Reese v. Walker, 6 Ohio Op. 2d 55, 151 N.E.2d 605 (Cincinnati Mun. Ct. 1958) ("contingent upon securing necessary financing"). Such language applies to all the terms of the financing, not just the interest rate. Cf. Gerruth Realty Co. v. Pire, 17 Wis. 2d 89, 115 N.W.2d 557 (1962) (holding a clause stating "contingent upon the purchaser obtaining the proper amount of financing" indefinite and the contract void, entitling the purchaser's to have vendor's suit to enforce a note for the deposit dismissed).

How are such rates and terms to be ascertained? In a majority of jurisdictions the answer is, through the good faith, reasonably diligent efforts of the purchaser. See, e.g., Betnar v. Rose, 259 Ark. 820, 536 S.W.2d 719 (1976); Phillipe v. Thomas, 3 Conn. App. 471, 489 A.2d 1056 (1985); Anaheim Co. v. Holcombe, 246 Or. 541, 426 P.2d 743 (1967). Such an effort becomes the subject of an implied covenant attached by many courts to this type of clause. If the purchaser makes a good faith effort to obtain financing and the transaction does not close due to the vendor's default, the purchaser will recover his deposit; on the other hand, when no good faith effort is made, the vendor not otherwise in default may retain the deposit. In contrast to a finding of the clause's indefiniteness, only one of the parties, the nondefaulting one, will "win" the deposit when the good faith covenant is at issue.

Another answer is that, for purposes of fleshing out the contract as to this term, P becomes, upon the execution of the contract, V's agent for the purpose of establishing what a conventional interest rate is. Here the good faith covenant is an implied term of this agency. This argument may at first seem strange to you: Why should parties who are in an adversarial relationship when negotiating a contract suddenly become principal and agent for purposes of carrying it out? The answer lies in their mutual interest in implementing the contract and the narrowness of the scope of the agency. As an agent, P owes a fiduciary duty of acting in good faith for the principal. This duty is breached when only one financing application is filed; an application must be filed with a reasonable number of lenders and until P does this, or else shows why one application is a reasonable number, he is in breach and not entitled to his deposit. Osten v. Shah, 104 Ill. App. 3d 784, 433 N.E.2d 294 (1982); Liuzza v. Panzer, 333 So. 2d 689 (La. App. 1976).

In *Liuzza,* the purchaser argued that the purpose of the clause was to provide a third-party appraisal of the property, but if that was the case, the court found that this purpose was not expressed clearly. See also Savich v. Ruiz, 32 So. 2d 415 (La. 1947) (Louisiana is the state in which this purpose for the clause is most clearly stated).

V also has the option of dickering with his offer of a second mortgage loan, lowering the interest rate on it until an effective overall rate of 10 percent is achieved when both the lender's and V's loans are considered together. The parties have lots to talk about here — and they should keep talking with a settlement of this suit in mind.

1b.  Would the result change if the contract called (as did the letter, op. cit.) for P's filing one loan application with a named conventional mortgage lender?

**Explanation:**   No, arguably because once the agency is created its duties can supersede the contract's words, which in any event can be taken to mean that the agent has a duty to apply not just to the lender named but also to lenders like the named one. This rule will depend, however, on a showing of the parties' intentions in this regard. The support for such a view is not overwhelming (but you meet the case in many law school casebooks). See Kovarik v. Vesely, 3 Wis. 2d 573, 89 N.W.2d 279 (1958).

1c.  If the contract did not contain all of the definitive material terms for the loan, what would be the legal effect of establishing the purchaser as an agent?

**Explanation:**   Then the filing of a loan application has the effect of providing material terms for the contract. These terms are filed on behalf of both the vendor as a principal and the agent on his own behalf. The application, agreed to by both parties, can then be incorporated into the contract for two purposes: to satisfy the Statute of Frauds and to supply material terms for the contract.

1d.  If the contract, in the clause quoted in the lead paragraph, stated that "if V or P" but otherwise was the same, would your result change? Could V use such language to authorize his extending a loan to P?

**Explanation:**   In all of the problems so far, the vendor and the purchaser are bound to the agency agreement at the time of execution. Here the agency is a mutual one in the sense that either party becomes the agent of the other for the purpose of obtaining financing. This addition, however, is superfluous. Nothing prevents the vendor from offering a loan to the purchaser in the preceding problems after learning the terms for which the purchaser filed. And the purchaser who refuses to accept such a loan may run afoul of his good faith duty. This argues strongly for the agency theory articulated above, for consider the alternative: If there is no agency, or if it is not mutual, the inclusion in a contract of a subject to financing clause that only P can satisfy, gives the whole contract an illusory quality; P can walk away and wait for V to sue him on his covenant of good faith.

When V has P's covenant of good faith — and nothing else — the lesson for the vendors of the world may be to increase the amount of the deposit that can be retained in the event of the covenant's breach. In one jurisdiction, the Supreme Court has held that, once a mortgage commitment is obtained, the purchaser-borrowers are under a duty not to hinder the closing on the mortgage loan. Bruyere v. Jade Realty Corp., 117 N.H. 564, 375 A.2d 600 (1977) (holding that when the commitment was withdrawn because of the purchasers' divorce, the covenant was breached).

2. V and P execute a brief contract of sale for Blackacre. The contract conditioned the closing on "P's obtaining satisfactory financing." Is this contract unenforceable on account of this language? What other language might be substituted?

**Explanation:** "Available financing" would be better. That is a standard subject to verification in the marketplace and, further, does not depend on the personal satisfaction of the purchaser with the financing. Brack v. Brownlee, 246 Ga. 818, 273 S.E.2d 390 (1980) (holding that "subject to purchaser's ability to secure adequate financing" was not lacking in mutuality as to prevent specific performance). An objective, rather than subjective, standard for fulfilling the contingency is more likely to pass judicial muster on issues such as indefiniteness and mutuality of obligation; moreover, the purchaser's good faith in satisfying the subjective standard is likely to become an issue. "Satisfactory" financing makes the contract resemble an option. See Temkin, Too Much Good Faith in Real Estate Purchase Agreements? Give Me an Option, 34 Kan. L. Rev. 43, 58-59 (1985). Breach of P's covenant to exert a good faith effort to find financing provides grounds for V's retention of the deposit; on the other hand, if the law finds that the clause is indefinite and the contract is void on that account, both parties can walk away from it — and the deposit will have to be returned.

3. V and P execute a brief contract of sale for Blackacre, but the contract provided for a closing only after "P obtains a firm mortgage commitment." After searching for a mortgage loan, P obtains a commitment that requires that P have the proceeds of the sale of his present residence in hand, in an amount not less than $100,000. Can V compel P to go through with the transaction?

**Explanation:** No. The commitment is not "firm" and the precondition for the closing is not met. P cannot be compelled to proceed further. McKenna v. Rosen, 239 N.J. Super. 191, 570 A.2d 1277 (App. Div. 1990); but see Farrell v. Janik, 225 N.J. Super. 282, 542 A.2d 59 (Law Div. 1988) (holding that the word "firm" in this context is redundant, but also holding that condition in mortgage requiring purchasers to receive a certain amount for their existing residence did not satisfy the contingency in their contract and that purchasers were free of further liability on the contract when it proved impossible to sell at the required price).

## "Subject to Sale of Prior Residence" Clause

On the other hand, a contract condition making a closing "subject to the sale of the purchaser's existing residence," is not a statement that the purchaser will not close without being able to use the proceeds of that sale to reduce his mortgage loan amount used to finance a new residence. See Agnew v. Stitch Assocs., 3 Conn. Cir. Ct. 336, 214 A.2d 134 (1965) (suit by purchasers for return of deposit). Similarly, the statement in a contract that a further deposit will be paid at the time the purchaser's existing residence is sold does not make the prior sale a precondition of the closing on the contract for the purchaser's new residence. George v. Oswald, 273 Wis. 380, 78 N.W.2d 763 (1956) (where the purchasers repudiated the contract before the expiration of the period during which the old residence was to be sold). Without a clear expression of intent, then, the sale of a prior residence is not a material term of the subject to financing clause in a purchaser's contract of sale for a new residence.

In the letter at the beginning of this chapter, the clause requiring "the sale of my house in town," and the phrase "with the proceeds free and clear" will not be read together as a part of the subject to financing clause. Any relationship between the various provisions will have to be clearer to create a contract "subject to the sale of a prior residence."

## "Subject to Existing Mortgages" Clause

A related topic is presented by a provision that the closing is "subject to existing mortgages." What does this mean? Is the price term in such a contract definite? It is not unless the parties have provided whether or not the purchaser is to take the title after assuming liability for repayment of those mortgage loans. When such liability is "assumed," this is the traditional way of saying two things: first, that the purchaser has taken title to the property subject to the existing mortgage lien, and second, that the purchaser has undertaken personal liability on the note for the existing loan. If the title is taken "subject to" an existing mortgage, that usually means that the purchaser accedes to the first proposition just explained, but not the second.

No matter what the purchaser's liability, a severable issue is whether the seller is released from his liability by the assumption. A mortgage lender is generally under no obligation to release a selling mortgagor upon a purchaser's assumption. Such a release is likely to occur today only if the purchaser agrees to pay the mortgagee a higher rate of interest than the vendor has been paying; it amounts to a novation of the original mortgage agreement.

## EXAMPLES AND EXPLANATIONS

4. What if the vendor is not personally liable on the existing mortgage, but instead of assuming the mortgage, took title subject to it and later convinces his own grantee purchaser to assume this liability?

**Explanation:** There is a split of authority on the issue of whether, before a mortgagee can proceed directly against an assuming grantee, it must prove that the vendor was personally liable as well. There is a title view and a contract law view of this problem. Some courts take the view that, if the vendor has no liability, he cannot pass any on, to his own purchaser. However, other courts (most recently) take the view that if the vendor and the purchaser intended to benefit the mortgagee, the latter is the third-party beneficiary of their contract.

## "Subject to Rezoning" Clause

If the purchaser needs a rezoning of the property, the contract should make the closing conditional on obtaining the needed change. Otherwise the law presumes that the parties have contracted for the property in light of the present zoning, and the purchaser will bear the risk that the zoning regulation does not permit the future use that he wishes to make of the property. The contract should specify the type of use permissible after the rezoning is obtained.

If the zoning ordinance applicable to the property subject to a contract of sale is changed during the executory period, judicial opinions divide on whether the parties are excused from the performance of the contract or are presumed to have contracted with the knowledge that the zoning might change. The latter view sometimes rests on the doctrine of equitable conversion reviewed in Chapter 4. The former depends on contract theory: If the parties are deemed to have contracted in light of existing law, without at the same time allocating the risk of a change in it, the continuance of that law becomes an implied condition of the contract. You can take your pick; there are two well-established theories for this situation.

There is a need for an express provision of the contract to allocate the risk of an unforeseen change in zoning during the executory period. The need is acute when the purchaser proposes to change the use.

## EXAMPLES AND EXPLANATIONS

5. A city publishes a notice of a rezoning hearing affecting the permitted uses of Blackacre. Several days later, V and P execute a brief but enforceable contract of sale for Blackacre. At the hearing, the use of the land that P proposes for Blackacre is changed from a permitted use to one that requires a special exception. The effectiveness of the use change relates back to the date of the notice of the hearing. The V-P contract is silent on the allocation of the risk of a rezoning. P sues V to rescind the contract. In this suit, what result?

**Explanation:** Judgment for V. The risk of a rezoning during the executory period is with the purchaser. This is the traditional rule. Some courts say, well, the risk shouldn't be on the vendor — after all, what control has he over the local legislature responsible for the ordinance? That the purchaser has no control either is the ready reply to that line of argument. But, say the courts adopting this view, the purchaser is in the best position to know the use that he plans to make of the property and whether or not that use is permitted by the ordinance.

Similarly, in the case of the letter at the beginning of this chapter, a real estate broker should know in which zoning districts she can maintain a home office. Thus the purchaser is correct in making rezoning (if that is necessary) a precondition of the closing if necessary.

6. Same facts as in the previous problem, but in addition, V knew that P wished to use the property in a way possible at the time of the execution of the contract but impermissible after the rezoning without a hearing to obtain the special exception.

**Explanation:**   Judgment for P, on the grounds of a mutual mistake of fact. The facts underlying the traditional rule are distinguishable from this case. See Dover Pool & Racquet Club, Inc. v. Brooking, 366 Mass. 629, 322 N.E.2d 168 (1975); see generally Restatement (Second) of Contracts §§151-152 (1977), and accompanying illustrations and comments.

# "Subject to Attorney Review" Clause

The bar has long argued that attorneys become involved in the typical residential purchase and sale transaction only when they can't be of much help to either party — the reason being that by the time they are involved, the rights and duties of the parties have been fixed by the terms of the contract of sale. One remedy for this situation is the insertion in standard form contracts of an attorney review clause. Under the terms of such clauses, the parties are given the right to seek legal advice within a certain time of the execution of the contract, and the attorney whose advice is sought is given the right to disapprove the contract, rendering it null and void.

The terms of the clauses used in this fashion vary considerably. Sometimes the contract binds the parties if not disapproved within the time set; sometimes the attorney's approval must be express before the contract becomes binding. Compare Nelson v. Ring, 136 A.D.2d 878, 524 N.Y.S.2d 544 (1988) (attorney approval required), with Levison v. Weintraub, 215 N.J. Super. 273, 521 A.2d 909 (App. Div. 1987) (three-day period for disapproval provided); and see generally, Annot., "Construction and effect of clause in real-estate contract contingent upon approval by attorney for either party, 15 A.L.R.4th 760 (1982).

These clauses, however, do not give the parties themselves the right to repudiate the contract unilaterally during the review period. Zapanta v. Isoldi, 212 N.J. Super. 678, 515 A.2d 1298, 1306 (Ch. Div. 1986). (Although nothing prohibits the parties from writing a provision to this effect.)

It is important to remember, when considering these clauses, that they are routinely used in only a few jurisdictions and that the brokerage trade groups are likely to resist their use. In the letter at the beginning of the chapter, the vendor would be well advised to hold the purchaser's letter for two days and then check with the purchaser or the attorney to see if the attorney approved before accepting the purchaser's terms. The purchaser may have been saying that in two days' time, but not before, the offer would be a firm one.

Consider the situation in New Jersey. In the mid-1960s, the state bar and the state brokerage board engaged in litigation over the brokers' alleged unauthorized practice of law. The discovery stage of the case dragged on into 1980, when it was settled by consent. See N.J. State Bar Assn. v. N.J. Assn. of Realtor Boards, 93 N.J. 470, 461 A.2d 1112, modified, 94 N.J. 449, 467 A.2d 577 (1983). The consent decree requires that the board place in bold, ten-point type, the following statement at the start of the board's standard form contract of sale, which is in widespread use in the jurisdiction:

**THIS IS A LEGAL DOCUMENT. IT CREATES RIGHTS AND DUTIES ABOUT WHICH YOU MAY NEED LEGAL ASSISTANCE. YOU HAVE THE RIGHT TO CONSULT AN ATTORNEY FOR THREE BUSINESS DAYS FROM THE EXECUTION OF THIS DOCUMENT. UPON THE ADVICE OF AN ATTORNEY, YOU HAVE THE RIGHT TO REVOKE THIS AGREEMENT WITHIN THAT TIME.**

In effect, this provision creates a right of rescission. In whom is this right created? The "you" could refer to either the vendor or the purchaser, although the purchaser is the most obvious beneficiary: It gives him a three-day cooling off period after the contract's execution. In general, the three-day period is also intended to provide professional review of the contract. The three days, then, probably would not include weekends and holidays. The parties could agree to extend the three-day period but not to shorten it.

# EXAMPLES AND EXPLANATIONS

7. If the purchaser executes the contract first, and four days later the vendor accepts the offer that it contains, may the purchaser, upon an attorney's advice, revoke the contract two days after the acceptance?

**Explanation:** There is no clear answer. In many cases the broker will hold the contract or deliver it, and a rule running the three days from the time the contract is delivered to the broker would make sense. See Denesvich

v. Moran, 211 N.J. Super. 554, 512 A.2d 505 (App. Div. 1986) (reciting New Jersey law and requiring the attorney to notify both the other party and his or her broker).

8. Two days after V and P together execute a contract, P's attorney advises him to revoke it. V inquires as to the reason for the revocation, and P's attorney gives no reason. May P still revoke?

**Explanation:**    Yes. P's attorney is entitled to remain mute and ground her muteness on the attorney-client privilege. In some of the cases involving such facts, the attorney is assigned a duty to the parties to provide advice in good faith, but the burden of showing the attorney's bad faith is on the complaining party. Cf. Indoe v. Dwyer, 176 N.J. Super. 594, 424 A.2d 456, 15 A.L.R.4th 760 (Law Div. 1980).

9. Two days after V and P execute a contract, V is advised to rescind and thereafter resells the property for a higher price. Can P get specific performance of the contract?

**Explanation:**    No. Trenta v. Gay, 191 N.J. Super. 617, 468 A.2d 737 (Ch. Div. 1983). However, V himself would be well advised to follow carefully the contract mechanism for giving notice of the disapproval to the other side. Denesevich v. Moran, 211 N.J.Super. 554, 512 A.2d 505 (App. Div. 1986) (holding that notice to broker is insufficient when contract requires the purchaser to give notice to both the broker and the opposite party).

10. Two weeks after V and P execute a contract together, P delivers a signed waiver of the contract's subject to financing clause. The waiver was prepared by the broker. Does the attorney review provision apply to the waiver document?

**Explanation:**    Yes. If the clause applies to broker-prepared contracts, it should also apply to broker-prepared modifications of those contracts — but only then permitting rescission of the modification, rather than the original contract. Freedman v. Clonmel Constr. Corp., 246 N.J. Super. 397, 587 A.2d 1291 (App. Div. 1991).

# Marketable Title Clauses — Express and Implied

Implied in every contract of sale is a condition that at the closing of the transaction the vendor will produce evidence that his title is marketable. A marketable title is one that is free from reasonable doubt, free of the possibility of litigation, and that a reasonable and prudent purchaser would accept. This implication is the product of the state's interest in cleansing real property title from encumbrances at the time of each and every closing and in the liquidity of the titles subject to its jurisdiction. This doctrine frees up the fee and enhances the purchaser's freedom to deal with the property during his tenure. Unlike some other legal doctrines that are based on strong public policies, the benefit of this doctrine can be waived by the purchaser. (Some encumbrances may be of no concern to particular purchasers and the benefits to them of certain encumbrances, such as utility easements, must be considered as well.) The doctrine also prevents the purchaser and his attorney from flyspecking the title — objecting to minor encumbrances that in fact do not cloud the title as a way of avoiding the closing. The vendor has the burden of proving the title marketable, although in many regions of the country the purchaser may actually pay for the title search and examination.

In some regions of the country, the mechanics of showing a title to be marketable work like this: First, the vendor produces his evidence of title; second, the purchaser examines the evidence. Elsewhere, the purchaser assembles the title evidence from the public records and then examines it. No matter how the evidence is produced, it is the purchaser's obligation to object to any defects in the title and to have the vendor cure them by the time of the closing. If a defect is not objected to and cured by then, it is waived by the purchaser.

# EXAMPLES AND EXPLANATIONS

11a.  V and P execute a brief but enforceable contract of sale calling for V to deliver to P a "merchantable or marketable title" to Blackacre at the closing in exchange for $100,000. Thereafter, during the executory period the abstract of title presented to P's attorney contains a break in the chain of deeds coming down to V. The break is a probate court decree. Is V's title marketable?

**Explanation:**   Yes. It is marketable, as well as marketable of record.

11b.  The abstract shows that V's title relies on a true and correct affidavit showing adverse possession in V's predecessor. Is V's title marketable?

**Explanation:**   No, not on the basis of an unproven affidavit. A judicial decree would establish a link rendering the title marketable. However, a title depending on adverse possession, but provable as such, is generally considered marketable. Conklin v. Davi, 76 N.J. 468, 388 A.2d 598, 601 (1978). It is not, however, marketable of record.

11c.  The abstract shows that the title is subject to a unsatisfied mortgage with a 20-year term and a $20,000 principal amount. The mortgage was executed a decade ago, but the holder of the mortgage lien cannot be located. Is V's title marketable?

**Explanation:**   No. The mortgage lien could be foreclosed anytime within its term, plus whatever time the applicable statute of limitations for mortgages provides. When the term of the mortgage is 20 years, the mortgage is still enforceable, and only a year into the repayment schedule, the mortgagee has ample time to show up and demand the payments due.

11d.  If in the problem above the mortgage were executed 60 years ago, would your answer change?

**Explanation:**   Yes. The probabilities are that the mortgage is now unenforceable by an action in foreclosure. The mortgagee has probably abandoned or waived enforcement of the lien, and the statute of limitations has probably run on its enforcement. A finding of marketability requires no more than a reasonable degree of freedom from litigation; it is not a guarantee to the purchaser that no litigation will occur or an encumbrance exists.

11e.  The abstract shows a power line easement running along one boundary of Blackacre. Is V's title marketable?

**Explanation:**   Yes. An easement located on the property renders it unmarketable unless it is at the same time beneficial to the property. So although the title is technically unmarketable, this is likely not to be objected to. The same rule is sometimes applied to easements that are visible, common in the jurisdiction, or otherwise implicitly accepted by the purchaser. What if the easement ran through the property? Now the title is both unmarketable and not likely to be beneficial. What if the easement reduced its fair market value to $90,000? (Same answer.)

11f.  The abstract shows that a mechanic's lien for $5000 has been filed on Blackacre. Is V's title marketable? If not, what is P's remedy?

**Explanation:**   No. The title is unmarketable, but the remedy is a simple escrow established at the closing in an amount sufficient to prevent the lien from being foreclosed.

11g.  Would your answers to any of the foregoing questions change if the contract called for "an insurable title"?

**Explanation:**   No. This title standard is generally taken to mean marketable and insurable — marketable, as that basic title call is incorporated by implication into every contract of sale, as well as insurable with a title insurance policy customarily used in the jurisdiction. Conklin v. Davi, supra, 388 A.2d at 602.

11h.  How about if the contract called for "a marketable and insurable title"?

**Explanation:**   No. The second adjective adds nothing. It does imply, however, that the title insurance policy called for will contain the usual coverage and the usual exclusions and exceptions, and be issued at regular premium rates. Conklin v. Davi, supra. Thus the word "insurable" in the letter at the beginning of this chapter adds nothing to the purchaser's legal protections. The title insurer will provide coverage for unmarketability in many jurisdictions, and if the title is unmarketable it will not provide title insurance.

11i.  If the contract called for "a title insured by the XYZ Title Insurance Corporation"?

**Explanation:**   There is nothing wrong with this title call as a matter of law. Indeed, because in many regions standardized contracts of sale are printed by title insurers, the inclusion of a named title company is likely. A decade ago, the name might be printed as a part of the standard language in the contract, but today a blank is likely so that the name can be inserted. It is advisable for a party to test this inclusion, however, to make sure that another, equally reputable title insurer would be acceptable as well. If another is not, then the possibility of a business tie-in with the named insurer should be considered — and avoided — by the party to whom the suggestion is made.

11j.  Would your answers change if the contract called for V to deliver a quitclaim deed at the closing?

**Explanation:**   No. A provision in a contract of sale calling for the use of a quitclaim deed at the closing is not a waiver of an implied (by law) obligation that the vendor produce a marketable title at the closing. A purchaser should not be held to have waived such an important protection unless he does so clearly. By definition, a quitclaim affects the vendor's warranties but need not affect the standard of marketability of the title that the vendor must produce.

12.  V and P execute a brief but enforceable contract of sale for Blackacre. The contract calls for V to deliver a fee simple absolute to P "subject to easements of record." During the executory period the adverse user of an undocumented easement over Blackacre ripens into adverse possession. Is V's title marketable?

**Explanation:**   Title by adverse possession is generally a marketable title if the proof required to establish it is available to the purchaser. However, this rule is for the benefit of the holder of the dominant estate benefiting from the easement. It does not apply here. The purchaser of the servient estate should not be forced to buy a lawsuit. Marketability is shown at the closing, and here the title will then be burdened with the easement. Title is unmarketable and purchaser need not accept it, absent an agreement to the contrary. Whether or not the "subject to easements of record" language is an agreement to the contrary is a matter of contract interpretation. The language means "subject to easements existing on the record as of the closing date." An easement arising by adverse possession is not one evidenced on the public records; rather it arises through the actions of the adverse possessor. Purchaser therefore has not agreed to accept it. Finally, suppose that the easement were reduced to judgment by the closing date. Would the judgment be "of record"? The vendor who encouraged that it be put on record this way is subject to a charge of acting in bad faith. The lesson for the parties is the need for further drafting on this subject.

13. V and P execute a brief but enforceable contract of sale. What if the contract calls for a fee "subject to leases," and during the executory period V's lease to L runs out and V renews it for another term? Is V's title marketable?

**Explanation:** A tougher case, but here not only is the vendor sleeping on his rights during the executory period (that was true in the last problem too), but he is actively creating encumbrances on the title. This is a slander of title on the purchaser's equitable interest in the title. Vendor's title is unmarketable because the purchaser need not accept a title subject to the lawsuit he would have to bring, for slander of title, against the vendor. The contract at a minimum should permit a purchaser to review leases entered into during the executory period.

# Marketable Title and Environmental Liens

For purposes of the doctrine of marketable title, an encumbrance rendering a title unmarketable is a broad concept, including any estate or interest in real property that might render the title subject to a reasonable doubt or prospect of litigation. When a toxic substance is discovered on property, its clean-up can be ordered by the government's environmental regulators. When a clean-up in not accomplished in this manner, the government itself may clean up the property, and its clean-up costs can be recovered from an owner of the property and any operator of a business or use on it. To enforce this recovery, the government has a lien on the property. 42 U.S.C.A. §9607(1) (1991). Strict liability is imposed on "owners or operators" of property for the amount of the lien. This lien is sometimes called a superlien because it takes its priority not on a first in time, first in right basis but is superior to preexisting liens. When that property is subject to an executory contract for its sale, the contract purchaser is entitled to the protection of the doctrine of marketable title or any contract remedy that he has negotiated and included in its provisions.

Marketability is a title concept. It is not concerned with the physical attributes of the land. However, marketability is concerned about the possibility of litigation over the title: The purchaser of real property is not, under the doctrine of marketable title, to be compelled to buy a lawsuit. Moreover, the doctrine is concerned not with the outcome or results of litigation, but its prospect. Myerberg, Sawyer & Rue, P.A. v. Agee, 51 Md. App. 711, 446 A.2d 69, 72 (Spec. App. 1982).

The doctrine thus has two concerns: (1) with the existence of an encumbrance affecting the title as well as the reasonable possibility of litigation, and (2) with distinguishing between land use and land title matters. These two concerns come into conflict when considering the possibility of environmental clean-up liens. When toxic substances are discovered during the executory period, the presence of toxic materials on the land only affects the physical attributes and use of the land, not the marketability of the title to it. Only when the environmental lien is filed on the public records will the marketability be affected. Further, once the purchaser becomes an "owner" and the government has cleaned up the toxic site, he may be subjected to litigation to enforce the lien. Harbeson, Toxic Clouds on Titles: Hazardous Waste and the Doctrine of Marketable Title, 19 Envtl. Aff. 355 (1991).

Most of the current authorities hold that the presence of hazardous or toxic substances on property subject to an executory contract is not a defect or encumbrance on the title, such that the purchaser might invoke the doctrine to avoid taking the title. In re Schenck Tours, Inc., 69 B.R. 906 (Bankr. E.D. N.Y.), aff'd, 75 B.R. 249 (E.D.N.Y. 1987) (holding that purchaser forfeited $225,000 deposit). Neither can a purchaser invoke an express warranty or contingency in the contract to the effect that the land use be permitted under applicable land use controls. Cameron v. Martin Marietta Corp., 729 F. Supp. 1529 (E.D.N.C. 1990). Nor can a title insurer be subjected to liability under the provisions of a title insurance policy. South Shore Bank v. Stewart Title Guaranty Co., 688 F. Supp. 803, 805-806 (D. Mass.), aff'd in memo. op., 867 F.2d 607 (1st Cir. 1988) (finding that title insurance protects against past defects in title).

Given this bleak outlook, purchasers rely on negotiating specific contract provisions that assign the risk of the property being subjected to an environmental lien to one party or another. However, this negotiation is only the beginning, as several types of contract provisions are currently in use.

# EXAMPLES AND EXPLANATIONS

14. Which of the following would you expect would hold the greatest prospect for arguing, on behalf of a contract purchaser, that the presence of toxic substances renders the title unmarketable?

a. A provision that the vendor will hold the purchaser harmless by indemnifying the purchaser if toxic substances are discovered by an environmental audit ordered for the property.
b. A provision that the vendor will purchase property insurance whose coverage extends to the presence of toxic substances.
c. A provision in which the vendor warrants that there are no toxic substances on the property.

**Explanation:**   The answer, of course, is that they all leave open the possibility that the purchaser must accept the title to the property, subject to the vendor's performing the duties specified in the provision. Singly or in combination, they are not as good as a walk-away provision for the purchaser, voiding the contract if toxic substances are discovered. Patterson, A Buyer's Catalogue of Prepurchase Precautions to Minimize CERCLA Liability in Commercial Real Estate Transactions, 15 U. Puget Sound L. Rev. 469 (1992).

15. V and P contract to transfer title to Blackacre, subject to a reassessment and reduction of its local real property taxes. Toxic substances are discovered on the property during the executory period. P argues that he will take the title only if the assessment is reduced by the amount of the clean-up costs. Do you agree?

**Explanation:**   No. If state or federal law requires the clean-up, the cleaned-up property is a minimum condition of its sale; the personal liability of the vendor and its sales price are not reduced thereby. Inmar Assocs., Inc. v. Borough of Carlstadt, 112 N.J. 593, 549 A.2d 38 (1988). The liability for a clean-up does not reduce the sales price and the assessed value of the property.

# "Time of the Essence" Clause

Traditionally, time was of the essence in a contract of sale involved in a cause of action at law. Thus, in an action for damages for nonperformance of a contract, a call for a closing on a certain date is sufficient to make damages available from the party not ready to close on that date when the party seeking damages tenders whatever performance is due at the closing, unless that performance is excused, e.g., by the nonperforming party's anticipatory repudiation. Cohen v. Kranz, 12 N.Y.2d 242, 238 N.Y.S.2d 928, 189 N.E.2d 473 (1963). See the letter at the beginning of this chapter (pages 63-64). Further, the use of the phrase "time is of the essence in this contract" means that each action required in the contract's provisions shall be performed promptly at the time or date specified.

However, in equity, time was not of the essence unless expressly made so in the contract or implied from circumstances available to interpret the contract. Time not being essential in equity, a standard of reasonable diligence is substituted. Thus, specific performance is available to a purchaser, even after the date fixed for performance of some action or the closing in the contract. Such an equitable action is available for a reasonable time after the closing date. Freeman v. Boyce, 66 Haw. 327, 661 P.2d 702 (1983).

Today, in both legal and equitable actions, time is not of the essence unless the contract expressly stipulates this or necessarily implies it, or unless the actions of the parties imply it as well. Tannenbaum v. Sears, Roebuck & Co., 265 Pa. Super. 78, 401 A.2d 809 (1979). Thus a failure to perform or close on a stipulated date is not, per se, a breach of the contract actionable by the nonbreaching party. 401 A.2d at 813. Delays are frequent in real property transactions, and a later performance might well be found to be substantial performance. This being so, one wonders whether parties to a contract are wise when they do make time of the essence, and further whether the law isn't wisely formulated when it fails to infer that time is essential in many situations lacking a clear intent by the parties to make it so.

If no time is set for a closing, a reasonable amount of time is implied. Ridge Chevrolet-Oldsmobile, Inc. v. Scarano, 238 N.J. Super. 149, 569 A.2d 296, 300 (1990). However, a contract lacking a time is of the essence clause is no excuse for a party's not closing on the day and at the time named in the contract. The reason for the nonperformance is for the trial judge sitting in equity; he must review its reasonableness. Mouat v. Wolfe, 150 Vt. 637, 556 A.2d 99, 101 (1989) ("Where time is *not* of the essence, the buyer who tenders payment late *may* bring a suit in equity, depending on the reasonableness of the delay, to compel delivery").

In a contract of sale silent as to time, the rule of reasonable diligence applies in two situations. First, the contract may set a date for closing, but when that date is past either of the parties can make time of the essence, in both law and equity, by a clear notice setting a future closing date, reasonably distant from the time of the notice. Thus, even when the parties to a contract postpone a closing twice but thereafter agree to make time "of the essence" for a third closing, the mere use of those words persuaded one court to make it so and to refuse to examine extrinsic evidence of the parties' intent to determine whether both parties knew the impact of those words. Hart v. Lyons, 106 Ill. App. 3d 803, 436 N.E.2d 723 (1982).

Second, when the contract is silent on a closing date, either party during the executory period may call for a closing within a reasonable time.

# EXAMPLES AND EXPLANATIONS

16. What if a contract of sale contains a strict forfeiture clause providing that "this contract is null and void and the purchaser's equity in the property

is forfeited if the closing is not held within sixty days"? Is time of the essence in this contract?

**Explanation:**    From the strictness of the forfeiture, a court might imply that time is of the essence. Hence the contract of sale with such a clause may provide a basis for implying that the parties have agreed to make time of the essence. You may be sure, however, that if the purchaser believes otherwise, he will comb the contract for language indicating that the forfeiture is not as strict as it first seems.

17.  In a land market in which prices are falling, a farmer agrees to sell his farm to a developer. The contract of sale calls for a closing within three months. After three months and one week, the developer has not closed the deal. Is time of the essence in this contract?

**Explanation:**    Here the essentiality of the time of the closing can be implied from the market circumstances surrounding the contracts. Time may be of the essence if by holding it so, a court could prevent the developer from waiting to make a better deal with the farmer. See Kasten Constr. Co. v. Maple Ridge Constr. Co., 245 Md. 373, 226 A.2d 341 (1967); Doering v. Fields, 187 Md. 484, 50 A.2d 553 (1947).

18.  A contract provision states that a failure to make any one of two executory period deposits on the date named "is essential to the performance of this contract" and, when the purchaser fails to make any one of these, the sums so far on deposit are forfeited to the vendor. Purchaser makes the first but not the second; thereafter, purchaser brings an action for specific performance of the contract. May he have a decree in specific performance?

**Explanation:**    Yes, but only if he is willing to put all of the purchase price in readiness, even in escrow with the court, to fulfill his contract obligations. The chancellor will also require that the purchaser pay the full purchase price, without any credit for the first deposit. After all, the first deposit is forfeited under the terms of the contract. However, as to the closing date, that (so far as the facts above indicated) has not been set, so the closing date is not of the essence in this contract; therefore the equitable rule of reasonable diligence controls, and the decree of specific performance can be issued respecting that rule. Decree for purchaser, without any abatement of the purchase price for the first deposit paid.

19.  V and P execute a contract of sale that provides in part as follows: "Settlement within thirty days or as soon thereafter as a title report is delivered to the purchaser and reviewed. If the purchaser fails to close, the deposit herein *may* ["may" was deleted and "shall" inserted in its place] be forfeit *at the vendor's option* [the four italicized words were deleted], in which case

purchaser is relieved of further obligation under this contract." After the title report is delivered, reporting a fee simple absolute in the vendor, purchaser refuses to close. V sues P for damages. What result?

**Explanation:** Judgment for P. The changes in the form contract indicate that the parties intended that the agreement become an option to purchase, by which the vendor agrees to take the property off the market for a certain time in consideration of the deposit paid by the potential purchaser. In an option, no equitable conversion is worked at the execution of the document; the purchaser acquires no equitable interest in the property and no right to have the option specifically performed. Although legal rights may be inferred from its provisions — that is, a party in breach may be liable for contract damages — P, as the optionee, bought the right to walk away from the transaction without further liability. This is consistent with an option. Brown, An Examination of Real Estate Purchase Options, 12 Nova L. Rev. 147 (1987).

At law, in an action for damages, time is of the essence. This supports the inference that V gained the right to be free of P's claims after the time during which V agrees to hold the property off the market. Moreover, in an option, time is of the essence because it is what is bargained for. The optionee must exercise his rights within the option period, and P did not do so here. Schlee v. Bryant, 247 Md. 689, 234 A.2d 457 (1967).

Once exercised, the optionee's rights become those of a contract purchaser. He holds an equitable interest and, in equity, time is no longer of the essence. The purchaser has a reasonable time to close the transaction, regardless of the call for a closing within a reasonable time of the title report's issuance.

## Acreage and Price Terms

When the purchase price in a contract of sale for real property is stated in gross, the risk of a deficiency in the acreage contained within the legal description or described in the contract is on the purchaser. The statement of the price in gross indicates that the purchaser regards the acreage as immaterial to the closing. Including the term "more or less" after the stated number of acres in the legal description is a bad idea from the purchaser's perspective; its inclusion tends to throw the risk of a deficiency on the purchaser. Marcus v. Bathon, 72 Md. App. 475, 531 A.2d 690, 694 (1987), cert. denied, 313 Md. 612, 547 A.2d 189 (1988). When the sale is in gross, the purchaser is not entitled to an abatement in the purchase price to take account of the deficiency before closing.

On the other hand, if the price is stated on a per acre basis, the risk is on the vendor; the statement of the price per acre indicates that the purchaser regards the acreage as a material term of the contract. If the acreage deficiency is substantial and a price per acre is stipulated, the purchaser can decide to reduce the price proportionately and sue for specific performance at the abated price. Might he also sue for reliance damages? Rescind the contract and avoid the closing altogether? These alternative remedies are suggested in the probable order of difficulty in obtaining them. See Hinson v. Jefferson, 287 N.C. 422, 215 S.E.2d 102 (1974) (pointing out that here rescission must be based on a mutual mistake of fact). If the vendor has already received more money than the acreage warrants, the purchaser's cause of action lies in contract for damages.

If the price is stated in gross but the parties agreed to compute it on an acreage or area basis, parol evidence is admissible to show the true nature of the transaction. The contract, after all, is not inconsistent with the area computation, and parol evidence can explain how the parties arrived at the price. Use of parol in this manner should be particularly useful when urban commercial space is involved and the price is computed on a per square foot basis. Similarly, the sale of land in a residential subdivision may be on the basis of the number of buildable lots or parcels involved.

Any representation of the vendor as to the acreage will often change the results of these rules. See Fireison v. Pearson, 520 A.2d 1046 (D.C. App. 1987). The same is true as to vendor's representations about boundaries. Chapman v. Rideout, 568 A.2d 829 (Me. 1990). See generally Restatement (Second) of Torts §552(1) (1977) (stating the elements of negligent misrepresentation).

# EXAMPLES AND EXPLANATIONS

20. In the letter at the beginning of this chapter, the price is stated in both acreage and gross terms. It is implied that dividing the latter by the former will compute the acreage contemplated by the purchaser. However, will such an implication of the acreage in an offer give rise to a warranty by the vendor that the farm contains 50 acres?

**Explanation:**   Not likely. The purchaser must clearly indicate reliance on either one price or the other in the offer or the contract. Here this result is particularly likely because the purchaser inserted a contingency in the offer relating to a survey. The results of the survey will have to be reviewed by the purchaser before closing, and if the legal description produced by that survey fails to encompass 50 acres, the purchaser closes this transaction at his peril.

21. V and P execute a brief but enforceable contract of sale for Blackacre. The purchase price is $100,000, and the contract describes the property as "containing 1000 acres, more or less." In fact Blackacre contains 900 acres

and therefore is worth only $90,000. Can V obtain specific performance of the contract? Can P?

**Explanation:**   It depends. If the purchase price was negotiated on a per acre basis, the acreage is a material term of the contract, and V cannot get specific performance or, at best, can get specific performance subject to an abatement in the price. If P shows acreage material to the contract, then he can get specific performance with an abatement, unless the vendor can show that it was an "all or nothing" transaction. The latter situation is unlikely here because of the more or less language in the contract. That language also indicates, nothing else appearing, that acreage was not material to the whole deal, which means that either V or P can have specific performance, but without any abatement in the price.

# Housing Inspections

Often these days a purchaser will make the contract contingent on the inspection of the property by a private housing inspector. See Hanscom v. Gregorie, 562 A.2d 1232 (Me. 1989) (holding that a contract contingent on an inspector's finding no "substantial defects" in improvements left decision as to substantiality to the inspector); Electronic Realty Assocs., Inc. v. Lennon, 94 Misc. 2d 249, 404 N.Y.S.2d 283 (Sup. Ct. Dutchess County 1978), modified, 67 A.D.2d 997, 413 N.Y.S.2d 728 (1979) (finding that providing the inspection with a warranty is not insurance subject to state regulation). The inspector will examine the condition of the property's improvements, particularly the heating, air conditioning, plumbing, and electrical systems, as well as the roof, foundation, walls, and basement. Because of the broad scope of the inspections, the inspector's finding that the property is unsatisfactory in some respect gives rise to a mutual right to rescind the contract, rather than a right to sue for damages.

Such inspections are useful to vendors as well, particularly in jurisdictions giving broad reach to implied warranties of habitability and to liability for negligent (and even innocent) misrepresentations as to the condition of the premises. However, the purchaser's use of an inspector will not render the vendor immune from a duty to disclose. Caple v. Green, 545 So. 2d 1222 (La. App. 1989) (holding that, as to termite damage, both the vendor and the inspector were liable); Fox v. Ferguson, 765 S.W.2d 689 (Mo. App. 1989). Having the inspector in, however, does provide the purchaser with one more person to sue.

These inspections result in the issuance of certificates by the inspector. These documents "warrant the statements in the report about the condition of the inspected items are substantially accurate and acknowledge responsibility for substantial inaccuracies." The latter are usually (1) subject to some deductible amount that the purchaser, then usually owner, must spend on repairs before contacting the inspector and invoking the claims procedure set out in the certificate, and (2) only inaccuracies reported within one to two years from the date of purchase or closing. Also excluded from any claim are normal maintenance costs, personal injury damages, consequential damages, or the cost of repairing code violations. If an inspection report describes a code violation, the cost of bringing the property up to code standards is not covered, but if the inspected system fails during the claims period, the fact that the failure was due to a code violation is no defense to a claim.

# A Word on Options

When would you expect to use an option agreement instead of a contract of sale? An option is advisable when a purchaser has reservations about the transaction that cannot be resolved by objective standards incorporated into a contingency clause in a contract. Similarly, perhaps the vendor has agreed to sell the purchaser some of his land, but which portion will be conveyed is unclear; because the conveyed portion cannot be described yet, an option might be used.

Options are also useful for the land developer. She might use an option to assemble large tracts of land, not wanting to be bound by contracts until all parcels in the tract are available to her; in this situation, an option ties up the parcels available early in the assembly process and gives her a time during which to work on the more difficult acquisitions. Further, a land developer having difficulty obtaining financing has time to work out those difficulties if she holds options.

An option is generally an offer to sell, irrevocable for a certain time. (It can be an offer to buy as well, but that is rarer.) Thus the vendor is bound to sell, but the purchaser is not obligated to buy; in this sense, it is a unilateral contract binding the offeror to enter into a contract of sale. Often the contract, unexecuted, is attached and incorporated by reference to flesh out the terms of the offer. Some jurisdictions apply the writing requirement of the Statute of Frauds to an option, although it does not create an interest in real property. Rather, it is only an offer to enter into a contract of sale. Time is of the essence. Traditional contract remedies apply. When exercised, the option will "ripen" into a contract.

# EXAMPLES AND EXPLANATIONS

22. LO executes a valid option with D. Before D exercises the option, but within its term, LO executes a contract of sale with T. What remedies has D?

**Explanation:** In general, D as the optionee will have an action for specific performance of the option. However, T may be a bona fide purchaser, without notice of D's right to purchase, and if T is a bona fide purchaser, T will prevail over D. However, if the problem arises during the LO-T executory period, equity will enjoin the closing. If it occurs after the closing, equity may undo the LO-T transaction. Casting the option in a recordable form is the best method of avoiding this problem; under many recording acts, an option is a recordable document.

# Backup Contracts of Sale

Backup contracts of sale are common in "hot" markets for real property or for popular properties within any market. They are effective when a prior contract is terminated by the parties to it. Thus they are used when more than one purchaser wishes to execute a contract of sale.

How should the contract of sale presented at the beginning of this chapter be modified if it is to be used as a backup? How should each of the provisions discussed here be modified? What other provisions should added? See Akawie, Down to Earth: Practice Tips for the Real Property Lawyer: Special Problems in Residential Real Estate Transactions, 13 Cont. Educ. B. Real Prop. L. Rep. 161-162 (August 1990).

When the primary contract is terminated within a short period of time after the execution of the backup contract, the backup then becomes the primary contract. However, a backup purchaser may wish to set a date certain for termination of his own contract; if this proves unacceptable, then the purchaser should have the right to terminate at any time before receipt of the vendor's acceptance of his contract as the primary one.

Disputes are likely to develop over whether the purchaser should pay a deposit. If so, how much? And how should the deposit be held? Perhaps the check should be in escrow, uncashed until the backup becomes the primary contract. If the backup contract contains contingency and conditional clauses, the time for fulfilling the conditions will run either from the date of the execution of the backup or the date on which the backup becomes the primary contract. But the parties to the backup contract should specify which date controls.

# EXAMPLES AND EXPLANATIONS

23. V executes a brief but enforceable contract of sale with P1 and a backup contract with P2. The primary contract is contingent on the sale of P1's existing residence. The sale of the existing residence falls through. V agrees to waive this condition, but P2 insists that he now has the right to buy V's property. Does he?

**Explanation:**   The issue is whether V and P1 can renegotiate their primary contract. Good drafting should settle this issue expressly, but failing that, the equivalent of the termination of the primary contract is a novation of that contract. Whether the parties to the primary contract intended to create a new contract is a matter of intent. Here, the removal of a condition is not likely to be seen as the creation of a new contract between V and P1. Adding a condition might be. Thus absent some provisions controlling the permitted scope of any renegotiation of the primary contract, the parties to it are given wide latitude to conduct renegotiations. Meadows v. Lee, 175 Cal. App. 3d 475, 221 Cal. Rptr. 22 (2d Dist. 1985).

Perhaps renegotiation involving the primary contract should be grounds for termination of the backup.

# Slander of Title

A person recording a contract of sale with the knowledge that it is unenforceable is liable in an action for slander of title. Slander of title is a tort action requiring the plaintiff to prove that the defendant "uttered a false statement" about the plaintiff's title to real property, which statement resulted in actual loss by the plaintiff. Recording the contract is the utterance; and when the recording is made with knowledge that the recording party does not have an enforceable interest in the property, malice is sometimes presumed by the fact of the recording itself, although in some jurisdictions, actual malice must also be shown. See Rogers Carl Corp. v. Moran, 103 N.J. Super. 163, 246 A.2d 750 (App. Div. 1968). Finally, the necessary loss is indicated by a lost sale.

Thus recording a contract known to be insufficient under the applicable Statute of Frauds, or indefinite in any of its material terms and conditions, or unenforceable for any other reason, would render the defendant — typically the purchaser — liable for slander of title. The defendant need not record, for instead a purchaser could refuse to take title disparaging its marketability and, if the disparagement were publicized in some way, might give grounds for the action as well.

The loss suffered by a vendor when a backup contract's closing is delayed because of the recording is an example of the type of losses that might be recovered in such an action. Peckham v. Hirschfield, 570 A.2d 663 (R.I. 1990). For more on this action, see Chapter 13.

# 7

# Remedies for Breach of a Contract of Sale

The following remedies are available to both vendors and purchasers for a breach of contract of sale of real property:

1. damages,
2. specific performance of the contract,
3. rescission, and
4. foreclosure of a vendor's-vendee's lien.

## Damages

The traditional rule is that upon a vendor's breach of contract, a purchaser of real property is entitled to only nominal damages. Such damages usually are measured by the out-of-pocket expenses incurred in the purchase up to the point at which the vendor breaches the contract. This limited measure of damages is explained historically by the vendor's limited responsibility for the review of her title. She was not expected to know the state of the title — she needed an attorney to inform herself on this matter — so why hold her to pay more than nominal damages when her title proved unmarketable and the purchaser refused it? This traditional rule — also known as the English rule in some jurisdictions or the *Floreau* rule, after its leading English case — applies only when the vendor is in breach and the breach involves a noncurable title defect. It does not apply when the vendor's breach is willful or in bad faith. (We will discuss this rule, and its exceptions, later in this chapter.)

This limited measure of damages is perhaps also explained by the early judicial preference for specific performance of the contract of sale. However, that preference in turn is explained by the limited measure of damages available. (This is a chicken and egg problem for legal historians and will not be discussed further here.) The alternative to the traditional rule of nominal damages is "benefit of the bargain" damages. This latter measure of damages requires that the fair market value of the property be computed. That computation was difficult when real property sales were not as common as they are today. Thus a further explanation for the grip of the traditional rule may lie in the erratic and small markets that once existed for real property.

Whatever the historic preference of the courts, about one-half of the states in this country have gone beyond the traditional and limited measure of damages and award benefit of the bargain damages, plus consequential damages. The benefit of the bargain is the difference between the fair market value of the property and the price reserved in the contract — a.k.a. difference money measure of damages.

Upon a purchaser's breach of contract, vendors are likewise restricted to nominal damages in many, but not all, states. Where benefit of the bargain damages are also permitted, as in California under its Civil Code §3307, it is wise to remember that no such damages exist unless the property's fair market value, on the date of the breach of contract, is less than the contract price, for only then will the difference be greater than zero. Whitney v. Bails, 560 P.2d 1344 (Mont. 1977) (construing a statute identical to California's code provision). (And as a practical matter, that the market value will have to fall substantially before a lawsuit to recover the difference money is worthwhile.)

States permitting a vendor more than nominal damages often permit a vendor to recover consequential damages too. Senior Estates, Inc. v. Bauman Homes, Inc., 272 Or. 577, 539 P.2d 142 (Or. 1975). Consequential damages are those whose proximate cause is, and which flow naturally from, the purchaser's breach. Royer v. Carter, 37 Cal. 2d 544, 233 P.2d 539, 543 (1951). They must be computed as those incurred by the vendor, upon a resale of the property within a reasonable time after the breach. The most common type of consequential damages is the expense of reselling the property. Determining what these expenses are requires a close examination by the purchaser's attorney. Some will have been the vendor's responsibility during the first sale and should not be included. Some will be duplicative expenses incurred by the vendor during the first sale but incurred again on the resale and should be included. (For example, the vendor might be responsible for two brokerage commissions.)

After an unjustified breach of contract by the purchaser, almost all pre-printed contracts will permit the vendor to elect to retain the purchaser's deposit, either as part of a forfeiture of the contract or as liquidated damages. Moreover, many cases hold that, upon the purchaser's default, a vendor may retain the deposit unless she intends to sue for more. If she does not intend to sue for more, retention of the deposit shows her election to stand or rest on the contract. If she does intend to sue, she should return the deposit.

However, as one opinion states: "Courts should be particularly solicitious in protecting from forfeiture the down payments of innocent purchasers of residential real estate." Northeast Custom Homes, Inc. v. Howell, 230 N.J. Super. 296, 553 A.2d 387, 391 (Law Div. 1988). One "cf." citation is all that supports this statement, so beware! See also Stanbenau v. Cairelli, 22 Conn. App. 578, 577 A.2d 1130, 1131 (1990) ("A buyer in nonwillful default can recover monies paid upon the contract and retained by the seller, despite an otherwise valid liquidated damages clause, where the seller has sustained no damages"); Safari, Inc. v. Verdoom, 446 N.W.2d 44 (S.D. 1989) (lowering the deposit when purchasers had difficulty paying higher amount shows court that retention of deposit is not a reasonable preestimate of liquidated damages when vendor attempted to retain deposit); Rosen v. Empire Valve & Fitting, Inc., 381 Pa. Super. 348, 553 A.2d 1004, 1006 (1989) (indicating that contract provisions providing a limited right to a return of the deposit will be liberally construed).

However, when a purchaser agrees to accept a refund of any deposits that she has made "as full settlement upon the vendor's default," the clause is evidence that the parties to the contract intended to bar the vendor from obtaining any additional damages. Nonetheless, the case authorities are split on the issue of whether or not to give the quoted provision this effect. Compare Tanglewood Land Co. v. Wood, 40 N.C. App. 133, 252 S.E.2d 546 (1979) (provision prohibited additional damages), with Melcer v. Zuck, 95 N.J. Super. 252, 230 A.2d 538 (Ch. Div. 1967), rev'd 101 N.J. Super. 577, 245 A.2d 61 (App. Div.), cert. denied, 52 N.J. 498, 246 A.2d 456 (1968) (purchaser enabled to collect benefit of the bargain damages in addition to recovering the deposit).

Keeping in mind the foregoing splits in the authorities, examine the following problems from the perspective of both types of states. The problems are arranged according to who is in breach — vendor or purchaser — and according to the type of remedy sought — damages or specific performance. First, consider some problems concerning whether that ever-present out-of-pocket expense, the purchaser's deposit, is recoverable after the deal goes sour. These problems also start with the assumption of a contract silent on the subject of the vendor's right of retention.

# EXAMPLES AND EXPLANATIONS

1a. V and P execute a brief but enforceable contract for the sale of V's residence. The purchase price is $100,000. P makes a $10,000 down payment but then locates another property that she likes better and refuses to close the V-P contract. What if (in the alternative) V quickly finds another purchaser B to buy the residence. B pays $100,000 for it. P asks you to recover the deposit. Will you take P's case?

**Explanation:** No, not to court. V's sale to a third party at the same price means that she has suffered no loss of bargain damages, so a forfeiture of the deposit by P might arguably make V more than whole. Does P's willful default defeat her recovery? Some courts would say so, but this is only a way to avoid discussing the purpose of the deposit. Some courts go on to describe the deposit as "earnest money" — its deposit with the vendor is the purchaser's guarantee of performance of the contract and of making a good faith effort to close the deal.

The difficulty with such a description is that whatever creates a fear of forfeiture can also be described as a penalty for nonperformance. Thus a guarantee of performance is easily construed as a penalty for nonperformance. (Beware of the certainty of any result in this area. Differing results abound.) However, penalties are not often found in contractual silences. They require intent. Permitting V to retain the deposit is a rough way to measure damages, with something left over to pay V for her nonrecoupable expenses on the V-P contract. A brokerage fee, for example, could be 5-7 percent of the purchase price, and considering the time-value of money, V surely has some damages. A close case, but judgment for P would cost more than the deposit itself. An attorney should test the waters with V but explain the difficulties to P as he goes. See Edwards v. Inman, 566 S.W.2d 809 (Ky. App. 1978) (in a purchaser's suit for the return of a deposit, the court ordered its return subject to a deduction for the defendant vendor's incidental damages, in the amount of a real estate commission, survey costs, and attorneys' fees).

1b. You ascertain that a 10 percent deposit is usual and customary in the area. What difference does this make to P's attempt to recover the deposit? Would your answer be different if P had paid $30,000 down?

**Explanation:** Following the custom and usage in the area lends an air of reasonableness to the amount of the deposit here. Compliance with the local custom may provide V with a way of satisfying the burden of proof on the question of whether the amount was a penalty. However, a complete inquiry into whether the forfeiture of a deposit constitutes a penalty requires

— first, a reasonable preestimate of damages,
— second, bargaining in which something is exchanged for the forfeiture, and
— third, a fair result.

The custom need not be a code word for a reasonable preestimate of damages (an element of V's showing that the deposit was not a penalty); indeed, the local custom shows it likely that no actual preestimate was made. So the presence of such a custom is not conclusive but strengthens V's position. She has an argument that the contract is fair in its result, even if no bargaining over the forfeiture took place. So long as the 10 percent deposit level is not exceeded, the answer given previously would be unchanged. But exceeding the 10 percent is evidence of a penalty and weakens V's right to retain the deposit.

1c. The fair market value of the residence soars after P's breach. P's deposit is the usual and customary one, but P wants it back. Will you take her case?

**Explanation:** No, because P is not looking at the relevant time frame. The measure of damages is taken on the day of the breach, not thereafter, and not even when the vendor benefits in the long run from P's default, as here. Vines v. Orchard Hills, 181 Conn. 501, 435 A.2d 1022 (1980); but see Smith v. Mady, 146 Cal. App. 3d 129, 194 Cal. Rptr. 42 (1983).

1d. V decides not to sell but instead sues P for damages. What must V prove in this action for substantial damages?

**Explanation:** An action for damages will require proof of the fair market value of the property. The measure of damages is the difference between the fair market value of the property and the contract price, both measured on the date of the breach. This is the "difference money" measure of damages. In applying this measure of damages, consider the next several problems.

1e. V is of the opinion that P's refusal to purchase "cost me at least $10,000" and asks you to sue P for damages. Will you?

**Explanation:** Not without further investigation. A suit for damages requires evidence of the fair market value of the property, and V's opinion about the losses suffered does not establish that.

1f. V is offered $130,000 for the residence but decides not to sell. She instead sues P for damages. What result?

**Explanation:** An offer to purchase is not a sale, and the best evidence of fair market value is a sale. Still further evidence is required. Annot., Unaccepted offer for purchase of real property as evidence of its value, 25 A.L.R.4th 571, 584 (1983) (collects the cases).

1g. V exchanges the residence for B's. B's residence has a fair market value of $130,000. V then decides to sue P for damages. What result?

**Explanation:**   An exchange of property is not a sale and can be motivated by many considerations beside the fair market value of the properties exchanged (tax considerations, for example). Still further evidence will be required.

1h.  The fair market value of the property remains stable. V quickly finds another purchaser T willing to pay $130,000. Now will you sue V to recover P's deposit?

**Explanation:**   Yes. Even if P's was a willful default, V's net gain on the resale appears to outweigh any damage arising from P's default. California cases analyze the problem this way. See, e.g., Smith v. Mady, 146 Cal. App. 3d 129, 194 Cal. Rptr. 42 (1983) (holding that a quick, profitable resale not only precludes benefit of the bargain damages for the vendor but also may offset any consequential damages incurred by her). They assume that the property was worth the higher price on the day of P's breach. In some states (for example, New York), courts would still say that P should not gain a cause of action by reason of P's own default, but that seems to admit that forfeiture of the deposit is indeed a penalty — and a steep one under the facts here. Maxton Builders, Inc. v. Lo Galbo, 68 N.Y.2d 373, 509 N.Y.S.2d 507, 502 N.E.2d 184 (1986), noted in 38 Syracuse L. Rev. 471, 479-481 (1987). So beware: What happens in California courts does not represent a universal rule.

A general rule: When the vendor has suffered no damages, the purchaser can normally recover the deposit. In some states, however, the willful default of the purchaser is sufficient grounds for a refusal to return the deposit. If the purchaser refuses to close, the vendor may retain a deposit, reasonable in amount, regardless of what happens after the breach.

1i.  The V-P contract provided that "the down payment will stand as liquidated damages for P's breach and after such breach, the contract shall be null and void." V resells the property for $80,000. This is the fair market value on the day of P's default. V then sues P for damages. In V's suit, what result?

**Explanation:**   Judgment for P. The liquidated damages clause in this contract undercompensates the actual damages, but the implication taken from the use of the clause is that V lowered the amount in exchange for the certainty of recovering that amount. So the clause is upheld and serves to bar the recovery of actual damages. Liquidated damages here imply a bar on the recovery of actual damages and an intention to use the clause as V's exclusive remedy. Fabian v. Sather, 316 N.W.2d 10 (Minn. 1982) (where the contract price was $46,000, with a $1000 deposit, to which the vendor was restricted after a $43,000 resale); Harris v. Dawson, 479 Pa. 463, 388

A.2d 748 (1978) (where the contract price was $60,000, with $100 deposit, to which the vendor was restricted after resale at $54,000), overruled by Bafile v. Muncey, 527 Pa. 25, 588 A.2d 462 (1991); Underwood v. Sterner, 63 Wash. 2d 360, 387 P.2d 366 (1963) (where the contract price was $250,000, with a $25,000 deposit, to which vendor was restricted even though jury returned $50,000 damage verdict). In *Fabian,* the contract permitted retention of the deposit as liquidated damages, but also permitted specific performance instead of retention — damages were unmentioned. In *Harris,* retention of the deposit was permitted "either on account of the purchase money, or as compensation for the damages and expenses to which (the vendor) has been put . . . , as the seller shall elect . . . and in the latter case, the contract shall become null and void. . . ." In *Underwood,* the contract provided that "the earnest money shall be forfeited as liquidated damages unless the seller elects to enforce this agreement." The last case is perhaps the weakest, but here the court views the remedies provided as being "in the alternative."

1j. The contract contains the same liquidated damages clause, but V's resale is for $130,000. This is the fair market value on the day of P's default. P sues to recover the deposit. In this suit, what result?

**Explanation:** If the case law of a jurisdiction indicates that its courts will only look at the subjective intention of the parties in their negotiations, the judgment will go for V. However, here P may win on the merits because she can show that the liquidated damages clause overcompensates V for the default. Even if it is a reasonable preestimate and was bargained in good faith, the result is unfair. When examining a liquidated damages clause, a court may be called on to look not only at the procedures used to formulate it but also at the fairness of the bargain it strikes. It is on the latter count that this clause would be found wanting.

1k. V sues P for specific performance. Will you take V's case? Will you more readily take the case if the property is a condominium?

**Explanation:** But wait! Before you answer that question, consider the following section.

# Specific Performance

From an early date, English and American courts granted purchasers of real property specific performance when the plaintiff could show: (1) a contract of sale, binding and enforceable between the parties to it, (2) that the plaintiff was capable of tendering performance (usually this means tendering the purchase price), (3) that there is no reason why equity should not enforce the contract (for example, the price and other provisions in it are fair); often this third element was also shown by the fact that the contract involved mutual rights and duties, and (4) that the plaintiff does not have an adequate remedy at law. The fourth element often involved a showing that damages would be difficult to measure. As we have discussed early on, this might typically be the case, and in some jurisdictions a presumption for specific performance as a preferred remedy arose.

A decree in specific performance was often accompanied by an abatement in the purchase price. Merritz v. Circelli, 361 Pa. 239, 64 A.2d 796, 7 A.L.R.2d 1325 (1949) (citing this rule as applicable only to the vendor's inability to convey the title that he contracted to give the purchaser). Here the purchaser has the right to whatever the vendor can convey, and the abatement was measured by the cost of curing the defect. Id.

Notice that this measure avoids putting the court into the business of computing the fair market value of the property. Going to equity makes the purchaser equate that cost with the value of title defect. Otherwise, the purchaser, given only nominal damages in the law courts, could go to equity and obtain specific performance upon payment of the price less the value of the defect. With the defect measured in terms of its effect on the fair market value, purchasers would obtain by going through with the deal in equity, a kind of benefit of the bargain denied in an action for damages. When the cost of curing the defect is the same as the effect of the defect on the fair market value, however, it is no wonder equity provided the preferred remedy in this area of law for so long.

Further, specific performance, being an equitable remedy, is granted only as a matter of judicial discretion. That is, it is not granted when doing so would itself work an injustice. For example, it is not granted when the subject matter of the contract is destroyed or the contract is rendered impossible to perform — for instance, when the improvements on the property are a large part of its value and are destroyed by fire. Merritz v. Circelli, supra (refusing specific performance to a purchaser when the purchase price of unimproved lots was $12,500, but the cost of installing sewer service would be $8,500).

# EXAMPLES AND EXPLANATIONS

2. V and P execute a brief but enforceable contract for the sale of V's residence. The purchase price is $100,000. P makes a usual and customary $10,000 deposit, or earnest money. V defaults and P asks that you sue V for specific performance of the contract. Will you?

**Explanation:** Specific performance is an equitable action. The party seeking it must be capable of tendering performance: "He who seeks equity must do equity," said the chancellors in this regard. This means that the contract of sale must be legally enforceable, with adequate consideration and a mutuality of obligation. There must also be an adequate basis for equitable relief, which means that there is no adequate remedy "at law" (meaning, usually, in an action for damages). Griffin v. Zapata, 570 A.2d 659 (R.I. 1990).

Equity courts put this latter requirement into black letter law by saying that real property was unique, and so specific performance was the remedy preferred over damages because damages were impossible to measure. See Estate of Younge v. Huysmans, 127 N.H. 461, 506 A.2d 282, 285 (1985) ("Specific performance is ordinarily granted to enforce a contract of sale of real property, unless circumstances make it inequitable or impossible to do so"). Maybe this was appropriate when the English gentry were purchasing and selling land; a transfer then was so rare as to become a societal event of some consequence. However, the black letter persists long past the need for it.

On a practical level, specific performance works better for P than it would for V. Why? Because P wants the property, whereas V made a deal to exchange the property for money. As to P, the transaction is unique: If the closing occurs, P gets that property. However, if V's residence is a condominium (legally, the air rights in a building) or a home in a subdivision laid out cookie cutter fashion on the land, a contract to purchase it is arguably not unique and does not deserve specific performance. (This is a conclusion reached in only a minority of states, but in the rest there is seldom a contrary holding.) To avoid this result, P might allege that she got a good deal in the contract with V, and so the transaction is a unique one — uniquely beneficial. P runs a risk in alleging this. This is so because V may respond that the deal is not fair to her in some way. P overreached, and so V should not have to render specific performance. Remember that the contract must be for adequate consideration — read that as fair consideration and you will see that "the party seeking equity, must do equity." Only the fair deal gets the chancellor's decree in specific performance. Thus P is presented with what is called the "just price" dilemma in assessing the chances of specific performance.

P also has to keep the contract of sale legally enforceable, thus binding on V. In the context of bringing an action for specific performance, this means that P will have to tender her side of the bargain. What does this mean? That P will have to tender the purchase price if that was called for at the closing. In this age of mortgages, in which cash sales are rare, this means that P will have to pursue her mortgage application, get a commitment to lend, and be ready to close. No small job! See Steiner v. Bran Park Assocs., 216 Conn. 419, 582 A.2d 173 (1990) (holding that upon the vendor's default, purchaser seeking specific performance is not excused from showing his financial ability to perform contract). This is P's "tender dilemma." Will the lender go along? If P gets the lender's cooperation, she brings her action with the equities on her side; she has shown that she is willing to go to considerable trouble to pursue the action. Thinks the chancellor, P must really want this property! Assuming that P has not acted unfairly toward V, she probably will get it.

3. All of which brings us back to the question with which we ended the previous section: Can V get specific performance on the same deal with P?

**Explanation:**   If P can have specific performance, why shouldn't V have the same type of decree? A principle of mutuality supports the result. Both parties to a contract should have the same arsenal of remedies available to them so that the law is neutral as between them. Some states would give V this remedy, with no more analysis than just presented. Other states, however, would inquire further: If V was willing to take money in exchange for the land, then why shouldn't she deal with any person willing to pay the price? Why should a court go further and force through the transaction with an unwilling P? After all efforts at a resale, V will still have an action in damages against P if the efforts are unsuccessful or only partly make V whole. This further inquiry would deny V specific performance. Centex Homes Corp. v. Boag, 128 N.J. Super. 385, 320 A.2d 194 (Ch. Div. 1974) (denying specific performance to a developer of a high-rise condominium seeking the remedy against a purchaser who defaulted on a contract to purchase a unit), noted in 48 Temp. L.Q. 847 (1975).

In further support of the vendor's right to specific performance, it has been suggested that the difficulties of gathering information about market prices and conditions would justify, in some real estate markets, extending the remedy to vendors. This might be just another way of saying that damages may be too expensive or difficult to calculate or, once calculated, unreliable. On the other hand, in a mass market specific performance would not lie for vendors, market information being more easily obtained. See Kronman, Specific Performance, 45 U. Chi. L. Rev. 351, 355-364 (1978).

Nonetheless, one court persists in substituting an action at law for damages, even when the result is the same. See Trachtenburg v. Sibarco Stations, Inc., 447 Pa. 517, 384 A.2d 1209, 1212 (1978) (calling an "assumpsit action at law for the purchase price and other damages," "the functional equivalent of specific performance" and promising to use equitable principles in aid of the action at law).

4. In the previous transaction, what if V has the benefit of a very high contract price — say, $30,000 above fair market value? Can V have specific performance?

**Explanation:**   Yes, if V can show that the transaction is unique to her and P cannot show that V overreached or was unfair in some way.

5. What would increase V's chance of getting a decree in the specific performance action?

**Explanation:** An allegation that he is land-poor (lacking in other assets) or needs the proceeds of the sale for some purpose disclosed to P. Finley v. Aiken, 1 Grant, Cas. 83 (Pa. 1855) (granting specific performance where the vendor was seeking delivery of a mortgage).

6. What if V's contract calls for a series of deposits payable by the purchaser during the executory period but, upon the nonpayment of any of these, provides that "the deposits shall be forfeited and this contract of no further effect." Can V, upon the purchaser's nonperformance, retain the deposits thus far paid but still sue for specific performance?

**Explanation:** The forfeiture clause will not per se preclude the action, but the clause, with its no-effect corollary, is some evidence that the parties intended it to preclude specific performance. Martin v. Dillon, 56 Or. App. 734, 642 P.2d 1209, 1211 (1982) (denying vendor specific performance on a contract with the clause quoted, for purchase and sale of a $130,000 residence when the deposits paid-in totalled $2000).

7. If a contract is insufficient for specific performance, may a purchaser sue on it for damages nonetheless?

**Explanation:** No, not in McMichael Realty & Ins. Agency, Inc. v. Tysinger, 155 Ga. App. 858, 273 S.E.2d 228 (1980) (holding that the same standard of definiteness for a contract applies in both suits for specific performance and damages when the legal description of the property, reading "a house and ten acres of a forty-acre tract owned by vendor," is defective).

# The Damage Remedy for a Vendor's Default

## *Nominal Damages*

The willful-nonwillful default distinction, mentioned earlier, grew out of cases in which the vendor's title proved unmarketable or otherwise failed, with the result that the transaction could not be closed because of the *vendor's* default in delivering the title promised in the contract. In these situations, the purchaser could only recover nominal damages — the expenses she was "out of pocket." Underlying this nominal measure of damages is the idea that, absent some fraud or misrepresentation on the vendor's part, she is not responsible for knowing the state of her title; that is a matter for an attorney to investigate. Moreover, the vendor could not make the title good, so why hold her to a futile act? Floreau v. Thornhill, 2 W.B. 1078, 96 Eng. Rep. 635 (1776) (involving a sale of a leasehold).

When the vendor is unable to deliver a marketable title and the transaction fails to close on that account, the purchaser may claim that she obtained the cash to put up the down payment and/or the purchase price from the sale of securities, which since the breach have risen in value. After the default, the purchaser is left with depreciated cash and no property. She claims that it is not fair to permit her only nominal damages. These facts are the very facts in *Floreau*.

The nominal damages rule makes sense in an era of stable property values and short executory periods. Recently, fluctuating values and long executory periods characterize real property markets in this country, so why apply the English rule? One answer often given is that when title fails and neither vendor nor purchaser is responsible, the rule carries out the contract principles of mutual mistake and impossibility of performance.

### Substantial Damages

However, many states have adopted a benefit of the bargain, substantial damages measure. Upon the vendor's breach, the purchaser is entitled to the damages measured by the difference between the contract price and the fair market value of the property on the day of the breach. In states adopting this substantial damages rule, benefit of the bargain measure of damages and nominal, out-of-pocket damages are available too. In such states, the *Floreau* rule might be seen as a limitation on the purchaser's right to substantial damages when the vendor's breach is not due to bad faith or (more narrowly still) is the result of a title defect over which the vendor has no control and cannot cure. See, e.g., Beard v. S/E Joint Venture, 321 Md. 126, 581 A.2d 1275 (1990).

## The Damage Remedy for a Purchaser's Breach

Likewise, upon a purchaser's breach, the vendor is often confined to recovering nominal damages. Hers is the relatively easy task of finding another purchaser. In some states, she is entitled to the amount of the difference between the contract price and the fair market value of the property, measured on the day of the breach. Royer v. Carter, 37 Cal. 2d 544, 233 P.2d 539 (1951) (where the contract price was $24,000 and, after a contract default, the vendor resold for $18,500); Sheppard v. Fagan, 94 Ill. App. 3d 290, 418 N.E.2d 876 (1981). Thus the vendor will have no damages unless the fair market value is less than the contract price, except for her out-of-pocket expenses. In addition, the vendor may recover the expenses that are (1) incurred in any resale, (2) duplicative of the expenses of the original sale, and (3) reasonable in amount. The expenses for maintenance and upkeep of the property from the date of breach to the date of the resale are not recoverable. Rowan Constr. Co. v. Hassane, 17 Conn. App. 71, 549 A.2d 1085, 1090 (1988), aff'd, 313 Conn. 337, 567 A.2d 1210 (1990) (holding that the vendor cannot receive mortgage interest and tax payments made after the date of the breach). Thus a vendor's damages equal the value of the purchaser's unperformed promise, less the savings vendor has at any resale.

The resale price is evidence of the fair market value. It may even be prima facie evidence of that value in some jurisdictions. However, as discussed with regard to a vendor's measure, it is still subject to full proof of that value. In a falling market, for example, a purchaser will not want the fair market value established by this resale price alone. In a steady market, there will be no benefit of the bargain damages, or at least they will be slight compared to the difficulties and costs of proof, which is why vendors often want to retain the deposits paid by purchasers.

Is this fair? The vendor is only going to use this damage remedy in a sharply falling market, and here purchasers may well be hard to come by. After all, a falling market is often accompanied by hard times generally. Maybe we should admit that fair market values in a falling market are very difficult to measure and agree to measure the vendor's damages as of the date of the resale, assuming that the purchaser cannot show that an unreasonably long time has passed between the date of the contract and the resale. See Kuhn v. Spatial Design, Inc., 245 N.J. Super. 378, 585 A.2d 967 (App. Div. 1991) (finding that a vendor's damages are measured by the difference between the value of the house on the date of the contract and the value at the date of resale). Notice, however, that under *Kuhn,* the vendor gives up the certainty of the contract price and has to establish the fair market value on two dates instead of one.

# EXAMPLES AND EXPLANATIONS

8. V and P enter into a contract of sale for V's residence. The purchase price is $100,000. The title search discloses that V has granted an interest in the property that interferes with P's plans for the property. What if that interest is an easement over the backyard? A "residential use only" covenant that prevents P from having a home office?

**Explanation:** In both situations, it is V who has granted the interest making the title unmarketable. Because under the rule in *Floreau* V is responsible for the decrease in value, P should recover, in an action for damages, the benefit of her bargain, or difference money: in this case, the difference between the fair market value of the property with and without the easement, both measured on the day of the breach (which is the day the contract was executed when the transaction has not been closed). Establishing this difference money probably will require expert opinions by appraisers, and the trial is likely to wind up as an expensive "battle of the experts" in front of a jury or the trier of fact. In contrast, specific performance may be the least costly remedy.

In a jurisdiction in which easements are conveyances of an interest in real property and covenants are executory contracts or promises, they may have different effects on the marketability of the title. Whatever these substantive differences are, the remedial consequences of the conveyance-contract distinction are unimportant today.

9. Suppose that in the problem above V does not have title to the residence when the contract is executed, but in fact only has an option to purchase it. What if the optionor defaults or V defaults on the option? What measure of damages can P thereafter recover from V?

**Explanation:** In both cases, V has misrepresented the state of the title by executing the contract with P, unless there was disclosure to P of V's status as an optionholder. In every contract of sale, the vendor makes a representation, implied by law if not express, that she will convey a marketable title to the purchaser at the closing. Luette v. Bank of Italy Natl. Trust & Sav. Assn., 42 F.2d 9 (9th Cir.), cert. denied, 282 U.S. 884 (1930).

That V's default on the contract was not willful when the optionor defaulted, but was when V herself defaulted on the option, makes no difference. However, in the first set of circumstances V has a cause of action for damages against the optionor, and because of this "action over" we shouldn't object to giving P difference money damages. In the second situation V brought this trouble on herself and doesn't deserve much sympathy. In both cases, V takes upon herself the risk that she will not fulfill her obligation to have a title at the closing. Moreover, because she only has an option, V could not yet know whether the title she will obtain is a marketable one. Judgment for P for substantial damages.

10. What if V loses part of her backyard to an adverse possessor during the executory period of her contract with P?

**Explanation:** *Floreau* does not apply. The vendor's sleeping on her rights caused the loss of title, and P should get more than nominal damages for V's omissions, as well as for fraud and misrepresentations; the effect of all three is the same as far as P is concerned. Smith v. Warr, 564 P.2d 771 (Utah 1977).

11a. Same facts as in Example 8, but in addition B offers V $130,000 for the residence. What if P finds out about B's offer before V and B both execute a contract of sale? What can P do at this point?

**Explanation:** P can enjoin V's proceeding further with B and also obtain a decree in specific performance. (This is a classic case for specific performance.) The offer is not evidence of fair market value, and so the damage remedy is inadequate on this basis.

11b. V decides not to sell. What can P do at this point?

**Explanation:** P can get specific performance or bring an action for damages. The choice belongs to P. Because the change of mind on V's part indicates a willful default, more than nominal damages — that is, difference money damages — are available to P.

11c. P finds out about B's offer after V and B execute a contract of sale. What now?

**Explanation:** Specific performance is still available to P. P's prior contract takes precedence over B's. Also available is a temporary restraining order or injunction against V and B closing the second contract. (Query whether a lis pendens, filed with P's specific performance action, would do as well.) The court would grant the order, or issue the lis pendens, to protect its own ability to enforce its decree should P prevail.

11d. What if P doesn't find out about the V-B contract of sale until after V closes this contract with B?

**Explanation:** Now specific performance is unavailable if B is a bona fide purchaser; an action for damages is then P's only remedy. In this action, the sale to B is good evidence of the fair market value of the residence, but more evidence of comparable transactions will be needed to establish that value for the trier of fact. P will get her deposit back, as well as the expenses that she is out of pocket, subject to a caveat to the effect that those expenses are reasonable in amount.

If B is not a bona fide purchaser, then P can elect between the action for damages and specific performance. The decree in specific performance will declare B's title subject to the equities of P's contract, void that title, and transfer it to P.

12. V and P contract for the purchase and sale of V's residence. After a willful default by P, V resells the property and with the proceeds makes a down payment for a new residence. V finances her new residence at a time when the mortgage interest rate has risen two percentage points. V then, in an action for damages, attempts to recover additional financing costs that she incurs in financing the purchase of a new residence after the resale of the property originally contracted for by P. Will she be successful?

**Explanation:** The vendor's damages must be reasonably foreseeable.

Hadley v. Baxendale, 9 Exch. 341, 156 Eng. Rep. 145 (1854). Foreseeability, however, is a question of fact, so there is no clear answer here. For a case denying V recovery, see Gryb v. Benson, 84 Ill. App. 3d 710, 406 N.E.2d 124 (1980) (vendor's additional finance costs are not recoverable). However, vendors have been made responsible for the costs of increasing mortgage interest rates. See Example 13, infra.

## Defining Substantial Damages

Finally, consider what type of damages are available in states that reject the rule of *Floreau* as a limitation on further damages and instead permit both out-of-pocket expenses *and* difference money or benefit of the bargain damages. See Basiliko v. Pargo Corp., 532 A.2d 1346 (D.C. App. 1987) (rejecting *Floreau*). Remember that we are now talking about approximately one-half of the states when considering an expanded measure of damages.

# EXAMPLES AND EXPLANATIONS

13. Purchaser P secures a mortgage commitment with an 8 percent rate of interest. Vendor V breaches the contract and does not close the transaction. The commitment expires, and P's later commitment, secured for a postponed closing, contains an interest rate of 11 percent. P wants V to pay for the difference in the costs of the resulting mortgage and asks you to represent her in this matter. Will you?

**Explanation:**   Yes. Such additional *purchaser's* damages have been held reasonably foreseeable. P can recover the difference in her monthly mortgage payments extended over the likely term during which the loan will remain unpaid. Proof of the likely term is a question of fact. P will bear the burden of showing its length — probably around a decade. Donovan v. Bachstadt, 91 N.J. 434, 453 A.2d 160 (1982). How will the damage award be paid? A lump sum is preferable, but periodic payments on a monthly or annual basis eliminates the possibility of overpayments to P, who may, after all, decide to repay a loan for any number of reasons. In the alternative, V could purchase an annuity yielding the annual difference in mortgage costs and retain the right to the principal amount. Often V will take an amount sufficient for this purchase from the closing proceeds, although V will typically need these to purchase a new residence.

It is unclear whether this award represents general or consequential damages. If the latter, P will have to show the foreseeability of the damages. This foreseeability might be shown by the widespread press coverage given mortgage interest rate changes.

The difficulty of awarding this remedy gives yet another rationale for limiting damages to a nominal amount.

What other consequential damages are available? What if P has valuable rose bushes in her present garden and loses the opportunity to transplant them to V's garden? Foreseeability here would be more difficult to show unless V has knowledge of P's plans. P's loss of a profitable sale of her existing home would make an easier case.

14. Same facts, but the damages concern rising construction costs for a residence to be built on V's unimproved land. Same result?

**Explanation:**   For some reason, substantial damages have long been awarded purchasers in this situation and they are measured by the difference between the construction contract available on the day of the breach and that obtained at the time of the balked closing. If P were to buy another ready built residence instead, the difference money between the cost of financing the house she was to build and the house she bought, would measure her damages.

15. Same facts, but the commitment to lend was made initially by V. Same result?

**Explanation:**   Yes. However, the remedial possibilities in V-P litigation are now broader. Why not give specific performance of V's promise to lend the money, or give specific performance with an abatement in the purchase price equal to the damages?

16. Same facts, but this time V resells to G at a profit. When closing her transaction, G was aware of P's situation. Will you as P's attorney seek to join G as a third-party defendant in the V-P litigation?

**Explanation:**   Yes, you might if V is judgment proof, but otherwise, why not seek to recover V's profit from her and use the resale as one measure of the damages? If you can still add a tort claim to your complaint, however, then a suit against G may have some additional advantage. The tort claim against G is for her interference with a prospective economic advantage — interference with the closing of the V-P contract.

No matter whether the rule of a jurisdiction permits the recovery of nominal or substantial damages, a purchaser can often recover for any improvements made during the executory period. Some jurisdictions limit such recoveries to the amount by which such improvements increase the fair market value of the property, so not all purchasers can recover the costs of such improvements. In this limitation, however, can be discerned the rationale for recovery: that otherwise a defaulting vendor will be unjustly enriched and the recovery is, in effect, the foreclosure of a lien for the amount of the improvement.

17.  V and P contract for the purchase and sale of V's property, Blackacre, but, in a jurisdiction permitting substantial damages, V willfully defaults. P then incurs costs preparing Blackacre for her move to the property. Later, upon V's petition, V is adjudicated bankrupt and her assets, including Blackacre, are subjected to the jurisdiction of the bankruptcy court. The court-appointed trustee in bankruptcy lawfully repudiates the V-P contract, which leaves P with a damages action. When P appears before the trustee and attempts to recover the move-in costs incurred after the default, V resists, saying that the contract damages are measured at the date of the breach, not thereafter. What does P reply?

**Explanation:**   P's reply is that the date on which the contract was repudiated in the bankruptcy court is a further breach, and damages up to that point are recoverable. That P continued to incur expenses shows that she wished to proceed with the contract, and V's actions prevented this by denying P an action for specific performance. That denial is a further default on the contract, and damages should be measured as of the time P lost this legal remedy. Beard v. S/E Joint Venture, 321 Md. 126, 581 A.2d 1275 (1990) (holding that benefit of the bargain damages could be measured as of the date specific performance becomes unavailable due to the vendor's bankruptcy). This is only one case, but it surely is sensible to say that a purchaser should be given an opportunity to show that an item of damages is related to the particular action alleged to be a default, or that the vendor has the burden of showing that the purchaser acted unreasonably in continuing to go ahead with her move after the vendor's first default.

# 8

## Remedies for Breach of a Contract of Sale (continued)

## Rescission

Rescission is the unmaking of a contract. It is a cause of action for the cancellation of a document (here, a contract of sale) by one of the parties to it. In many jurisdictions, it is unclear whether this is a legal or an equitable remedy. The grounds for cancellation are mutual consent to the cancellation, execution of the contract under a mutual mistake of fact or law, fraud, undue influence, duress, a failure of consideration, or occasionally, some statutory ground (such as under a consumer protection statute that permits a cooling off period during which a party can cancel the contract). Gartner v. Eikill, 319 N.W.2d 397, 400 (Minn. 1982); Hilton Hotels Corp. v. Piper Co., 214 N.J. Super. 328, 519 A.2d 368, 372 (Ch. Div. 1986) (equitable remedy granted for original invalidity of contract, fraud, failure of consideration, or a material breach or default); Moonves v. Hill, 134 Vt. 352, 360 A.2d 59, 60-61 (1976) (involving mutual mistake of fact about the acreage sold in gross).

One ground for rescission — a failure of consideration — sometimes does not apply to both parties, for example, as when a substantial portion of the property is destroyed. Remember, however, that destruction is only of the vendor's consideration. The purchaser's consideration is the price, and that's still extant. So this ground only works for the vendor. A contract, then, has to provide that destruction permits rescission, when the risk of loss would otherwise fall on the purchaser, for this remedy to work for the purchaser.

Early election between rescission and damages is not, under modern rules of pleading, necessary, but for tactical reasons, the facts required to prove damages are likely to be antithetical to those that show rescission. Filing for damages affirms the contract and is itself an election not to pursue rescission. To avoid this effect, the trial must proceed in stages — rescission first, then, if no rescission is found, a trial on the damage cause of action follows. In the close case, this emphasizes that rescission is effective when decreed by the court, not when the facts on which it might be based occurred.

A precondition to bringing an action for rescission is an offer to restore the opposite party to the condition in which he was prior to the contract. Khabbaz v. Swartz, 319 N.W.2d 279, 282 (Iowa 1982). This follows from the maxim that he who seeks equity, must do equity and from the sequence of complaints and petitions available to undo a transaction; for example, an action for restitution, or foreclosure of a vendor's or vendee's lien, follows a decree or judgment for rescission. For the purchaser, this means giving any rents of the premises back to the vendor. Metcalfe v. Talarski, 213 Conn. 145, 567 A.2d 1148, 1151-1152 (1989) (requiring purchaser to repay rents actually received, but not value of use and occupancy). For the vendor as plaintiff, this means giving back the portion of the purchase price already paid. For the low-income purchaser seeking rescission, this can be a burden. In his case, good pleading can make it clear that the offer to restore is effective when the decree or judgment is rendered, not when the cause of action is brought. Where the parties "cannot be returned to the ground on which they stood," rescission will be refused. *Hilton Hotels,* supra, 519 A.2d at 372-373.

Rescission based on a contractual right is assignable and goes with the contract; if, however, the rescission is based on fraud, and so its proof lies in facts extrinsic to the contract, the cause of action is less likely to be assignable.

# EXAMPLES AND EXPLANATIONS

1. A vendor, V, sues to rescind a contract of sale because the purchaser, P, knew that the property sold contained minerals unknown to V that V did not intend to sell. V asks for a jury trial. Should he get it?

**Explanation:**   If the suit is to prevent the unjust enrichment of the defendant, the action looks equitable in nature. In equity the judge sits as the trier of fact. No jury trial. Bonnco Petrol, Inc. v. Epstein, 115 N.J. 599, 560 A.2d 655, 662 (1989).

2. Purchaser sues to rescind his purchase contract but has had possession during the executory period and wants payment for improvements made to the property during his possession. Will the issue of the value of the improvements reach a jury?

**Explanation:**   Yes, because this compensation (really a part of the restoration duty) makes the action look like an action for damages — a legal cause of action — for which a jury is available.

3. V executes a brief but enforceable contract with P for the sale of Blackacre for $100,000. P gives V a deposit in the form of a certified check for $10,000. P then refuses to go through with the contract. In a falling market, may V retain the $10,000?

**Explanation:**   Subject to proof of facts about the purpose of the deposit, P's refusal to perform is an abandonment of the contract, and if V acquiesces, the rescission is completed by mutual consent. The duty to restore applies, but arguably only if and when P sues for rescission and obtains a decree against V. In a falling market, however, V cannot be restored to his status quo ante without retention of some of the deposit — how much depends on the fair market value on the day of the breach. In this case, where one party is in breach, the duty to restore might be applied to put the parties as they were on the day of the plaintiff's breach. In any event, in a falling market for Blackacre, the purchaser can likely go out and find comparable property at a lower price than that paid for Blackacre.

4. V executes a brief but enforceable contract of sale for Whiteacre to P for a purchase price of $100,000. P goes into possession and, at the same time, makes a deposit of $10,000. P then makes installment payments totalling $50,000 when V says that he will not close the transaction because a better offer has come along at a higher price — $120,000. What is the measure of P's recovery if he sues in rescission?

**Explanation:**   Whatever P has paid in thus far — $60,000 — plus the costs of carrying the property for the time during which he was in possession. Carrying costs might include repair-maintenance costs, insurance premiums, taxes, and capital value of any improvements made to the property. In some jurisdictions, P might also be entitled to $20,000 for benefit of the bargain damages. Here these are damages for the lost opportunity to sell Whiteacre himself at the increased fair market value, shown in part by the higher price — certainly some evidence of the fair market value of the property on the day of the breach. Think of this last element of P's recovery as compensation for the lost development or appreciated value of the property after the date on which the breach occurred.

Are you mystified by the "opportunity cost" damages given above? So am I, if the damages are consequential ones, flowing from the contract that a purchaser seeking rescission rejects. The presence of this development value means that it is going to be difficult to restore the parties to "the ground on which they stood" — their status quo ante. However, you could think of these damages instead as flowing from a tort, a business tort of interference with a prospective advantage. This requires delicate pleading because it is a tort bottomed on a contractual duty.

5. Must the plaintiff in the previous problem surrender the property when filing the complaint?

**Explanation:**   No. His offer to surrender can be conditional on the defendant V giving him his due.

# Vendor's and Vendee's Liens

Upon the execution of an unconditional contract of sale, or at the time during the executory period when all conditions have been satisfied, there arise two types of equitable liens for the benefit of the vendor and the vendee respectively. They are implied; provision for them need not be express in the provisions of the contract. They are inchoate; they need to be exercised or perfected to attach to the property. They are subject to being perfected through an action to foreclose them. Such an action is everywhere regarded as an equitable one.

Treating the title as subject to these two types of liens, then, achieves much the same result as would an action for specific performance, but it does not invoke the various doctrines conditioning a decree in specific performance.

## Vendee's Lien

This is an equitable lien for the benefit of the purchaser for any payments made under the contract. It attaches to the real property subject to the contract. For the purchaser, it arises during the executory period when the vendor refuses, without excuse, to close the contract.

This lien is generally assignable, insurable, and survives the titleholder's bankruptcy because it attaches to the property and does not create a personal liability in the party owing the price. It must be exercised or perfected before the vendor conveys the title to a bona fide purchaser, a person who pays value and accepts the title in good faith, without actual or constructive notice of the lien, or without any fraud, collusion or participation in the foregoing transaction. Such a purchaser cuts off the lien.

# EXAMPLES AND EXPLANATIONS

6. If a purchaser pays insurance premiums and taxes during the executory period, may he foreclose a lien for these carrying charges?

**Explanation:** Yes. The contract controls the scope of the lien. Its subject can be either payments of money or other services if the contract obligates the purchaser to make these payments or render services benefiting the property.

7. Must the purchaser be in possession when making the payments in the previous problem?

**Explanation:** No. The purchaser needs no special equities to assert the lien. The only precondition to it is his contract status.

8. If the purchaser makes payments, takes possession, and makes improvements to the property, may the cost of the improvements be recovered in the foreclosure of the lien?

**Explanation:** Only if the contract is the basis for the purchaser's possession and, in some other cases, only if the improvements themselves are called for in the contract.

9. Must the contract satisfy the Statute of Frauds to be the basis of this lien?

**Explanation:** No. The lien is equitable, so legal requirements for the contract are not a precondition to its assertion.

Likewise, the purchaser does not have to show that his legal remedies for damages are inadequate; the rationale is that a purchaser performs the contract pro tanto with each and any payment and is asserting, through the lien, an equitable interest pro tanto in the vendor's title. If the vendor is a concurrent holder of the title, the lien is assertable only against the vendor's interest in it. This lien rests on a theory of proportionate equitable conversion. Its assertion is inconsistent with rescission.

10. Is the assertion of the lien also inconsistent with a suit for damages for substantial or benefit of the bargain damages?

**Explanation:** No. Foreclosing the lien does not provide this type of damages. Reimbursement for payment is the object of the foreclosure.

11. P has a vendee's lien against V's title to Blackacre but does not foreclose it until V conveys the title to P1, a bona fide purchaser who has no notice of the lien. Can P now foreclose the lien against P1's title?

**Explanation:** No. P1 is a bona fide purchaser and cuts off the lien. However, if the proceeds of V's sale can be identified, the lien attaches to those proceeds.

12. What if a vendor takes out a mortgage loan in exchange for a note and mortgage in favor of the Greenville Savings and Trust Bank, while the vendee has an unperfected vendee's lien? Which of these liens — the mortgage lien of the bank or that of the vendee's — has priority?

**Explanation:**   The purchaser prevails, unless the bank is a bona fide purchaser. If the bank is a bona fide purchaser, its lien has priority.

13. What if, in the previous problem, the bank took the mortgage lien to secure a prior, unsecured debt. Would that change your answer?

**Explanation:**   Yes. In most real property matters, an antecedent debt is not "value" for purposes of defining a bona fide purchaser. But see Valley Vista Land Co. v. Nipomo Water & Sewer Co., 266 Cal. App. 2d 331, 72 Cal. Rptr. 181 (1968).

## Vendor's Lien

This lien secures all or any portion of the purchase price for the benefit of the vendor. It usually arises at the closing or conveyance by the vendor. It may also arise before the closing, as when it attaches to the purchaser's equitable interest under a long-term installment land sale contract, or in jurisdictions where contracts of sale are recordable and the vendor might bring foreclosure to eliminate the contract interest of the purchaser as a cloud on the vendor's title. However, to arise before the closing, it would have to attach to a contract interest of the vendee capable of performance — in other words, a contract with all contingencies and conditions satisfied — and subject to the doctrine of equitable conversion. A majority of states recognize such a lien.

It is usually an implied lien, although it has been made express by statute in some states (such as Texas). When the vendor sells both real and personal property using one contract for both types of property that names a price that does not attribute a portion of the purchase to the realty, a court may refuse to foreclose a vendor's lien because of the difficulties of attributing or a fear of rewriting the contract's price term. Likewise, when the vendor has taken a mortgage lien from the purchaser, the equitable lien may be found to have been waived by the vendor's acceptance of the express lien in the mortgage documents.

Refusing to imply the lien in both these situations is justified when the vendor, who at a closing has had the opportunity to insist on a mortgage lien, does not do so. If the vendor wants the protection of a lien, he can ask for it. There is no reason to distinguish between such an inattentive vendor and the purchaser's other, unsecured creditors. Indeed, in some states a lien is not implied, either by judicial decision or by statute, in this situation.

Where recognized, a vendor's lien is assignable, insurable, and survives the vendee's bankruptcy. A bona fide purchaser cuts it off.

# EXAMPLES AND EXPLANATIONS

14. V executes a valid contract of sale for Blackacre with P for a purchase price of $100,000. P gives V a $10,000 deposit and a note for $10,000, both credited in the contract toward the purchase price. The contract also provides that P will secure a mortgage loan for $80,000 from the Greenville Federal Savings Bank. P informs V that the bank has agreed to make the loan in exchange for a note and mortgage. Both the title and the loan transaction are closed. P defaults on both V's note and the Greenville loan. V brings a foreclosure action to enforce a vendor's lien, and the bank brings a similar action to enforce the mortgage lien. These actions are joined. Which lien has priority?

**Explanation:** A close case. Some authority holds that the mortgagee bank has priority. V knew of the lien, and his not insisting on priority over it at the closing might be construed as a waiver of priority. Moreover, and more broadly, his acceptance of only the note and thus an unsecured creditor's status as of and after the closing might mean waiver of the right to assert a vendor's lien, no matter what its priority. On the other hand, the existence of the note is not inconsistent with the existence of that lien. The latter merely adds a remedy for enforcing the former. V might have been counting on the lien all the more when he accepted the note alone. In addition, the bank knows of V's existence and, in a jurisdiction recognizing a vendor's lien, should check to see that the purchase price is paid in full before closing the loan transaction; not doing so might deny it bona fide purchaser status as to V. V's lien here functions as would an equitable mortgage.

Because this is a prototypical transaction, you can see that vendor's liens are the subject of much controversy. Liens on title should be in writing; the danger otherwise is that vendors will conceal from unsuspecting purchasers their right to such a lien. Undocumented interests in real property are not, and should not, be favored. Perhaps they should be abolished.

## A Final Word (of Caution)

Remember that both vendor's and vendee's liens are creatures of equity and thus are subject to discretion in their imposition. They are not a substitute for good, preventative legal planning and drafting. They exist to provide remedies when no other remedies are available. For example, if a real estate broker, working for a vendor, deceives that employer and purchases the property himself for resale at a much higher price, the broker will have violated a fiduciary duty to V. An action by V to foreclose a vendor's lien, resulting in a foreclosure sale at the higher price, seems an appropriate remedy.

# 9

## Closings: Deeds and Escrows

## The Closing

The end of the executory period is known as the closing or the settlement. It might as easily be called the transfer of the title, for it is the time when the last steps in the transfer of the title are completed: The check for the purchase price is exchanged for the deed to the property. In many areas of the country, it is a ceremony that both the vendor and the purchaser attend. The ceremonial aspects of a modern closing are an outgrowth of the enfeoffment with livery of seisin — the ceremonial handing of a twig or bit of soil from vendor to purchaser — providing evidence of the transaction and actually delivering the deed as well. Today it is the time when final documents are reviewed by the parties and their attorneys or other representatives. Often the broker attends too because he expects to take away a check for the commission, paid out of the sale proceeds received by the vendor at this time.

In some jurisdictions, the parties meet and the closing takes place in an attorney's office — this is often the case in New England — or at a title insurance or escrow company. Sometimes, as in Massachusetts, it takes place at the public records office so that the deed can be recorded immediately by the purchaser.

In states in the Pacific West and in the Southwest, the parties do not meet face to face. There, the final steps — indeed, all the steps necessary to satisfy each and every condition in the contract of sale — are overseen by an escrow company that, when the final steps are to be taken, clears the check for the purchase price, delivers the deed to the purchaser, and distributes the proceeds of the sale to the vendor and others.

No matter how a transaction is closed, the crucial document for the purchaser is the deed to the property. Its recitations and component parts should therefore become very familiar, almost second nature, to you.

# The Components of a Deed

A deed usually contains four parts: (1) the premises, which includes the granting clause; (2) the habendum, including the warranties; (3) the execution, including the attestation clause; and (4) the acknowledgment. The first and third parts of the deed are necessary for the document to be a legally effective conveyance between the parties to it. You should be able to break down each deed into those four parts and, in the course of doing that, examine each component.

Deeds can either be short or long form deeds. Short form deeds are statutory creatures, and as such they contain words of art that the statute authorizing them defines — that is, the statute provides in part that the word "grant" used in the short form means that certain warranties to title are given by the vendor, whether or not the deed actually contains such warranties. Thus short form deeds omit the habendum, to the extent that it is sometimes in part a repetition of the granting clause found in the premises, and incorporate many of its warranties into the granting verbs. 3 American Law of Property §12.47 (A. J. Casner ed. 1952).

Unaided by statute and left to themselves, conveyancers are prolix. They use many words when one would do, particularly if the purchaser is their client and they want to *make sure* that he gets the full fee simple absolute. Moreover, they have a tendency to copycat forms.

Thus although the word "grant" may suffice as a legal matter, the conveyancer may say that "the grantor . . . *gives, enfeoffs, grants, bargains and sells,* as well as *leases and releases, surrenders, remises, yields up, alienates, confirms, assigns, covenants to stand seised of, quitclaims,* and *conveys* . . . to the grantee."

How many of these words actually refer to a transfer of title by use of a deed? Actually, only one — convey — makes such a reference to what we today know as a deed. Some others — the lease and release and the surrender — were customarily executed with a deed. Most of the others refer to other, more ancient forms of conveyancing.

*Gives?* That verb refers to the operative word in a charter of enfeoffment.

*Enfeoffs?* This is the handing over of the fee simple absolute in the quaint ceremony known as livery of seisin, in which the transferor picks up the proverbial twig, clod of earth, or peppercorn and hands it to the transferee.

*Grants?* If an interest was incapable of livery, as with an interest that is nonpossessory (for example, an easement), then it was granted the transferee.

*Bargains and sells?* What the gentry in the remoteness of their London townhouses did to transfer real property, without going on the land, without standing before the witnesses to the livery, and so perhaps in secret. These verbs, in this sequence, refer to the making of a contract of transfer that a court of equity will enforce and more, execute under the Statute of Uses.

*Leases and releases?* A popular form of transfer just after the Statute of Uses. The transferor leases a term for years to the transferee and thereafter releases his reversion to the same person. After the release, the transferor has handed over her simple absolute. What more could she do? Nothing! Although not a transfer subject to the Statute of Enrollments, its virtue lay in that it also did not require livery because it was recognized in equity without that ceremony.

*Surrenders?* The giving up of a less than fee interest — usually for life or for years — so that it merges into the following future interest, either a remainder or a reversion. A surrender was usually by deed but could also be by operation of law.

*Remise?* This includes both surrender (see infra) and a release of rights in the real property.

*Yields up?* In the feudal system, one yielded up service to the lord of the manor. Examples were knight service, later giving way to money tributes; or a duty to work the lord's fields, on the roadways of the parish, or on the parish church. Thus the word came to refer to the transfer of the obligations on the transferor. Often in leases the lessee "yields and pays" the reserved rent.

*Alienates?* A reference to the transferor's giving up her power to dispose or deal with the real property. It is also the disposition of the transferor's title to one heretofore alien to it.

*Confirms?* A recognition that if the transferor has created voidable rights by the transfer, such creations are made absolute by the use of this word.

*Assigns?* The use of this word in a deed references the assignment of any causes of action necessary to protect the property of the transferee.

*Covenants to stand seised?* This means "promises to defend the seisin of the transferee." It is another form of transfer possible after the Statute of Uses and is used often in intrafamilial transactions in which the consideration was love and affection, rather than money.

*Quitclaims?* An American invention, the quitclaim conveyance grew out of the release and came to mean that the transfer is an "as is" transaction in which the transferor says in effect "I'm not sure what I have, but whatever it is, I give it to the transferee." The quitclaim is much used in the United States in the absence of attorneys, as well as by attorneys when less than a full fee simple absolute is conveyed or when title defects have arisen and are to be cured with the conveyance of the present deed.

*Conveys?* As previously stated, this is a reference to the use of a deed.

So much for the verbs used in the granting clause. Some Eastern and Southeastern state statutes (and good drafting practice) require that the source of the title conveyed in the deed be indicated by book number and page on the public land records. Once found, this information is inserted just after the granting clause, with the words "Being the same interest, title, and estate that John Doe conveyed to the" vendor at Book #____, page ____.

The other three parts of the deed use their own distinctive language as well. For example, the habendum clause usually begins with the words, "To have and to hold, . . . together with (all improvements, later acquired improvements, mineral rights, and so forth)." (Does the language sound familiar? It is also used in the liturgy traditional in Christian marriage ceremonies.)

The habendum usually includes warranties or covenants of title. Of these more later.

The attestation clause typically begins with the language "In Witness Whereof I (we) have set our hands and seals." Signatures follow this phrase, with the initials "L.S." under the signature line. L.S. stands for legilis sigli — Latin for legal seal. A seal is unnecessary in many states today, eliminated by statute.

The last part of a deed is not necessary for the validity of the deed as between the parties. This is the vendor's acknowledgment of the deed as her free and voluntary act. Completion of this part of the deed is necessary for recordation of the document, not (again) to make the document valid between the parties to it. Many states have adopted the Uniform Recognition of Acknowledgements Act, codified, for example, in Va. Code Ann. §§55-118.1 to 118.9 (1974).

In addition to these parts of the deed, some state statutes require that the preparer of the deed so indicate and sign the deed.

Here is a short, early, and somewhat quaint English deed. Disentangle its parts:

## EARLY SHORT FORM DEED

Know all men by these presents, that I, William Penn, of Warminghurst, in the County of Sussex, have had and received of and from Philip Ford, merchant, the sum of £100 of lawful English money, which sum is the consideration for the purchase of 5000 acres of land in Pennsylvania mentioned in one pair of indentures of bargain, sale, and release thereof, bearing the same date as this deed and made between me, William Penn, and Philip Ford, and for this £100, I, William Penn, do hereby for my heirs and assigns, release, remise and quitclaim to Philip Ford, his heirs, executors, administrators and assigns, each and every of them, the same 5000 acres of land.

Witness my hand, this 14th day of July, anno domini 1681 . . . .

_____

William Penn

Sealed and delivered in the presence of

_____        _____

Witness                                                                Witness


_____

Witness


Two questions about this document. What is an indenture? Why was the indenture executed separately?[1] The operative words of grant are "release, remise, and quitclaim." William Penn was using popular and then-current words to confirm the earlier deeds in the wake of later events, perhaps arising out of the receipt of the consideration.

# Deed Warranties

A earlier reference to warranties requires further explanation. Warranties are classified in two ways. First, they can be either special or general warranties. A special warranty is a statement by the vendor that the estate transferred is not otherwise than as stated in the granting clause and the premises because she herself has not encumbered that estate. Special warranties are the norm in deeds around Washington, D.C. A general warranty carries the same message except that the vendor warrants that neither she nor any of her predecessors in title have encumbered the estate.

---

1. These two questions can be answered together. The dual documentation of William Penn's transaction emphasizes an often-forgotten fact about our system of conveyancing. That is, most deeds are drafted so that they memorialize a past transaction; they are, in other words, evidence of that transaction, but they are not the transaction itself. The definition of an indenture reenforces this. Written on sheepskin, parchment, or paper, it is a common law form of deed on which words of the deed were twice written — once on the top half of the deed and again in the bottom half. This two-part document is called a chirograph, and the word "chirographum" (the Latin form) was written in capital letters between the halves. Then the two halves were indented, cut with a ragged or serrated edge, so that the word in Latin was cut in two. Each party to the transfer of title could take away a copy of the deed as evidence of their transaction. Thus could the sheepskin be put back together in case of a dispute.

Underlying this evidentiary function of this early deed is the notion that vendors don't guarantee that they own the title that they sell. They only offer their purchasers their title evidence, presumably the best that they can muster. However, proof of that title awaits litigation over it — although that litigation will confirm rights only against specific individuals and specific interests. The common law tradition, as well as our constitutional guarantees of due process, are the reason for this limited effect.

Special and general warranties are routinely given by vendors. They are seldom bargained for or withheld, although why this is so is unclear and the origins of the practice lost.

Second, warranties can be either present or future warranties. The three present warranties are a warranty of title, of seisin, and against encumbrances. A title defect can be waived at the closing and excepted in the deed. A defect presented to the purchaser but not objected to may be deemed waived at the closing. If not waived, the defect covered by a present warranty is said to be broken, if at all, at the closing and must be asserted during the period of limitation running from the date of the closing. This limited life serves to magnify the importance of the closing and forces the purchaser to investigate the status of the title beforehand. As a rationale for present warranties, however, it ignores the effect of statutes of limitations, which start to run at the closing but continue a purchaser's ability to claim a breach of warranty on account of the defect for the statutory period thereafter.

Future warranties are two in number. The first is a warranty of quiet enjoyment. This gives the transferee the right to enter and remain on the property free of ouster by the transferor or any person claiming through her, bona fide purchasers excepted. The second is a warranty for further assurances. This is the promise of the transferor to do such things as are necessary to put the transferee in possession of the title warranted. This last warranty is often known as the English warranty and not often used in the United States (except in jurisdictions where it is customarily used, as in Virginia). There were formerly at least three future warranties, but only the two just discussed survive and are in common use today.

Minor differences in these definitions exist from state to state. The two classifications just outlined also encounter certain difficulties. For example, what of a mortgage only discovered after the closing? The present covenant against encumbrances provided initial protection against such an interest. But if a later-discovered interest is not asserted, the statute of limitations could have run on a present covenant, and the nonassertiveness of the holder means no breach of the quiet enjoyment warranty — and therefore no remedy under any type of covenant for the purchaser. Similarly, the assertion of rights by the undisclosed mortgagee may breach the covenant against quiet enjoyment long after the statute has tolled on the present covenants.

More generally, consider whether it makes any difference that these warranties are sometimes referred to as covenants. Warranties? Covenants? What's the difference? In some regions, a covenant for quiet enjoyment is called a covenant of warranty. But it may provide more than the usual covenant would give, for it is a covenant that promises that the facts of possession are such as they appear to be.

As previously noted in the discussion of deeds, some states have enacted statutes that incorporate certain of the covenants or warranties into the verbs used to grant or convey the title. A reference in Virginia to "English covenants of title" incorporates a covenant of the right to convey, of quiet enjoyment, and for further assurances. Va. Code. Ann §§55-70 to 55-74 (1974).

The burden of proof with regard to a present covenant can vary according to the type of covenant involved. The grantee must allege a breach of the covenant of seisin and the right to convey, but thereafter the grantor has the burden of proof. For the covenant against encumbrances, the rule is sometimes different because the grantor may not have created the alleged encumbrance, and the grantee then has the burden of proof to show the breach of this covenant.

The measure of damages for a breach of a present covenant, in the case of the covenant of seisin and right to convey, is a fraction of the purchase price, representing the percentage of the price for which title failed. This is a rescission measure of damages; that is, the warrantor must give back a fraction of the price she received, in proportion to the failure of the title. For the covenant against encumbrances, it is the cost of removing the defect if that is possible with the payment of money, and when it is not possible, it is the fair market value with and without the encumbrance, fixed at the time of the covenant's breach.

For a future covenant, the measure of damages is the difference between the fair market value of the property as the deed purported to convey it and as received, and fair market value is measured at the time of the ouster. In each instance, the recited purchase price received by the vendor giving the covenant provides an upper limit on damages. Attorneys' fees are sometimes recovered in a successful action based on a breach of a future covenant.

# EXAMPLES AND EXPLANATIONS

1. Are the present covenants implicitly assigned with each successive transfer of the same property?

**Explanation:** No in most states, yes in others. The American majority rule is that present covenants are not assignable. This rule stems from the fact that a cause of action was not assignable at common law. While this explains the genesis of the majority rule, one might ask: What justifies the rule today? Today each grantor is presumed to have made her own bargain over covenants and should not be held to have liabilities granted in the course of particular negotiations, transferred to other, unknown parties. Thus each covenantee-grantee can sue her immediate grantor-covenantor but not grantors remote to her, those further up the chain of title.

In a minority of states (the leading cases are from Iowa at the turn of the century), the cause of action on the covenants (but not the covenants themselves) is deemed assigned with each successive transfer of the title. But note, the covenant "runs with the title," not the land — no grantee has to take possession to gain the benefit of this implied transfer; taking the title is sufficient. This assignment means that the last assignee-grantee, though remote from the grantor giving the covenant, is the one with the right to sue the breaching grantor. This has the advantage of preventing a line of lawsuits back up the chain of title: Only the present holder of the cause of action, the latest grantee, can sue the breaching covenantor. It often has the disadvantage of lengthening the time of that covenantor's exposure to liability.

2a. Assume that the Statute of Limitations for real property matters is six years. In a jurisdiction permitting the assignment of present covenants, when does the statute run when the first covenantee's prior link in the chain is three years long?

**Explanation:**   The assignment is really of the right to sue the covenantor, and it runs to a remote grantee for a three-year period.

2b. In a jurisdiction permitting the assignment of present covenants, can a mesne or interim holder of the title sue her vendor if a true owner ousts her purchaser from possession?

**Explanation:**   No. If the covenant has been assigned by its beneficiary to her purchaser, that purchaser has the right to sue and the interim title-holder (the original beneficiary) no longer has it. That purchaser must now sue the remote vendor liable on the covenants. The original beneficiary cannot.

3. If a chain of title is subject to a latent defect, such as a forgery, do the covenants run down the chain in a minority rule state if the deeds in the chain are void?

**Explanation:**   The latent defect destroys the estate of each grantee in turn, but if it also destroys the covenants as well, the covenants would not be available when most needed and just when the parties probably intend them to be used. Some courts thus regard the covenants as corollary agreements, not dependent on the validity of the underlying document. To enforce the covenants, privity of estate between the holders of the covenants is not required. However, if any grantee knew of the presence of the true owner, estoppel may be invoked against her enforcement of the covenant.

4. What if the deed with the breached covenant recites a purchase price of $100,000, but in fact the vendor received nothing for the deed?

**Explanation:**   The immediate grantee is estopped from asserting any damages for a breach of covenant or from claiming more than the price actually paid. A remote grantee might be similarly estopped in a minority rule state on the theory that when the implied assignment of covenants is made, it is subject to any defenses the vendor might have. Here, however, when the remote grantee relies on the record, this seems unfair, unless there is a release of liability from the immediate grantee on the record as well. (The release puts the remote grantee to the duty of inquiring into whether the purchase price might have been rebated in exchange for the removal of the grantee's covenant protection.)

# The Delivery of Deeds

A deed must be delivered to be effective. A delivery requires an intent to deliver the deed, as well as the actual, physical delivery, or manumission, of the deed.

Proof of delivery is a matter of gathering evidence extrinsic to the document itself. A delivery requires evidence of (1) the physical presentation of the deed from vendor to purchaser with (2) the vendor's intent to create a present interest in the purchaser at the time of the document's execution and presentation to the purchaser.

Delivery has three functions: (1) it makes the grantor aware of the serious consequences of the transfer of title, thus functioning as a protection for the unwary grantor; (2) it provides evidence of the transfer to the grantee and often to third parties; and (3) its ceremonial aspects mark the beginning and end of rights in the property, as did the ceremony of livery of seisin at common law.

Only an irrevocable delivery is effective. The grantor must put the control of the deed beyond her power and control. A grantor's placing the deed in her safety deposit box will not be an effective delivery. Putting it in a box, giving the box to the grantee, but retaining the key to it, is equally ineffective. A physical handing over is required in most cases. Giving the key to the box is probably not a substitute for delivery of the deed, until the grantee actually uses the key and removes the deed from the box. (If the box were big and heavy, the result might be different, as then the delivery of the key is all the more equivalent, from the grantor's point of view, of delivery of the deed.) After obtaining the deed, a grantee who returns the deed to the grantor for safekeeping, may not intend to alter her right to the deed but subjects herself to the hazards of proof about the grantor's intent.

Neither can the grantor give the deed to her agent, with instructions to deliver it to the grantee, and expect the delivery to be complete at the time the instructions are given; the agency itself implies the right to direct the agent. For example, giving the deed to the grantor's attorney is ineffective as a delivery. This result might change when the agent is a dual one or when, on the way to deliver the deed, the agent recorded it. A recording raises a strong presumption of delivery, and for the purpose of preserving the value of the public records, this presumption is sometimes said to be irrebuttable. In all other instances, only when the deed is actually delivered by the agent has it been delivered.

Acceptance of the deed by the grantee who benefits from the delivery is presumed and so rarely is the subject of litigation.

In a majority of jurisdictions, a condition on delivery to the grantee, not written into the deed actually delivered to the grantee, is ineffective — the conditions are ignored once the delivery is complete. To maintain such a condition in force, delivery must be to a third party, such as an escrow agent. However, a condition that is written into the deed itself (and not in some other document) survives its delivery to the grantee.

When a deed with blank spaces on it is physically delivered to a grantee, the grantee can complete them when doing so accords with the grantor's intent. Here there is a physical delivery, but an intent to deliver must be established.

Courts have established four presumptions to deal with problems of delivery. All of them are rebuttable. First, the deed in the possession of the vendor is prima facie not delivered. Second, the deed in the possession of the purchaser is prima facie delivered. Third, recording the deed is usually prima facie evidence of the vendor's delivery. Fourth, acceptance by the purchaser is presumed.

# EXAMPLES AND EXPLANATIONS

5. V prepares a deed of Blackacre to P. The deed is valid on its face. V gives the deed to P on condition that P pay V $100,000. P does not pay as required. What can V do?

**Explanation:**  This deed has been delivered and the condition voided by the delivery. V can assert a vendor's lien for the purchase price on Blackacre, but the deed has transferred its title to P.

6. V prepares a valid deed to Blackacre, leaving the space for the grantee blank but intending later to convey the property to P. V gives the deed to P, telling P to have her attorney review it. After further negotiations for the sale of the property fall through, P inserts her name and refuses to return the deed. Can V force its return?

**Explanation:**  Yes. V did not intend to deliver the deed, so the delivery is ineffective. In a declaratory judgment action, V is entitled to have the delivery held void. In an action for slander of title, V is also entitled to judgment for whatever damages P has caused.

7. V prepares a deed of Blackacre, valid on its face, to P. V gives the deed to P's attorney for review. The attorney records it and sues V for ejectment. What can V do?

**Explanation:**  V is entitled to have the deed declared void. Two deliveries are required, and only one has occurred. The deed has not been effectively delivered.

# The Doctrine of Merger

The undertakings in the terms and conditions in a contract of sale last only so long as the contract remains executory, and when a deed is accepted as called for in the contract, the contract terms are merged into the deed. Contractual obligations dealing with the title are normally expected by the parties to be performed by the closing or else become a component of the deed. This is particularly true with question of title: The contract calls for a vendor to convey a marketable title, but when the purchaser accepts a deed for less at the closing, the contract provision on the title is merged into the deed. When the risk of loss is on the vendor during the executory period, acceptance of the deed has a similar effect. So, at the closing and with the acceptance of a deed, the risk of loss, and the risk of the later discovery of an encumbrance, falls on the purchaser.

The doctrine of merger is usually a protection for the vendor and discharges her from further liability on the contract. However, when the deed provides greater protection than the contract did during the executory period, the doctrine protects the purchaser as well. Reed v. Hassell, 340 A.2d 157 (Del. Super. Ct. 1975) (where the purchaser uses the doctrine to impose title requirements narrower in the contract but broadened in the vendor's deed).

Only the contract is merged into the deed; if the parties have an "ancillary" agreement, it is not merged. Quite often such ancillary agreements concern aspects of the physical condition of the property. How does one tell whether an agreement is an ancillary one? Ask where the agreement would fit into the components of the deed presented at the beginning of this chapter. Ask, for example, whether or not an agreement that "the air conditioning is in good repair" would be included in a deed. If it would not, as is likely in the example, the agreement is ancillary and is not merged. Ask too if the agreement is necessary for the deed to be effective. If not, the agreement is an ancillary one. For example, a restrictive covenant is not necessary for the passage of the title in the deed; rather, it concerns the use of the property, not its title. In addition, implied warranties of habitability in the contract are usually not merged into the deed. See generally Berger, Merger by Deed — What Provisions of a Contract for the Sale of Land Survive the Closing?, 21 Real Est. L.J. 22 (1992).

# Negligent Preparation of a Deed

In preparation for a closing, an attorney is likely to prepare a deed to present to the purchaser. Its preparation is undertaken, however, for the attorney's client, the vendor. May an attorney for the vendor be liable to the purchaser when one of the deed's provisions was defective?

In Collins v. Binkley, 750 S.W.2d 737 (Tenn. 1988), the answer was yes. There an acknowledgment failed to contain the words "with whom I am personally acquainted." These words were necessary to make the deed recordable. The deeds were in fact recorded, but the vendor then filed for bankruptcy and in bankruptcy was able to void the deed. The purchaser then sued the attorney, and in this suit the attorney was held liable for the damages that purchaser suffered.

Notwithstanding the lack of an attorney-client relationship, the purchaser's use of the deed for recording was foreseeable, and the attorney has a professional responsibility to prepare an effective deed that the purchaser can record. The lack of privity between the vendor's attorney and the purchaser is, here as elsewhere, no bar to the purchaser's suit.

# 10

# *Escrows and Escrow Instructions*

## Escrow Practice

A deed delivered to a person other than the grantee, with instructions to that person to deliver it to the grantee upon the performance or happening of some condition, is said to have been placed "in escrow." Thus a traditional escrow is a mechanism for the delivery of a deed in two steps: first, to the escrow agent,[1] and second, to the grantee.

In many states in the western United States, the use of escrows is commonplace in all types of real property transactions. They are used for both residential and commercial transactions and replace the formal ceremony known as a closing in the Eastern and Midwestern regions of the country.

In the West, however, "going into escrow" refers not just to the delivery of a deed. It also refers to a vendor's and purchaser's setting up a procedure by which the agent oversees the completion of the many steps required to exchange both a deed for the purchase price and a mortgage lien for the purchase money loan proceeds. The escrow is here a mechanism to close both the title and the mortgage transaction simultaneously. An escrow agent's employment agreement is commonly known as the escrow instructions.

These instructions authorize the agent to accept for deposit, in the title transaction: the documents showing compliance with the various contingencies and "subject to" clauses in the contract of sale, the deed

---

1. "Escrow agent" is an imprecise term because the law of agency does not explain all of this person's rights and duties. Nonetheless, the term is widely used to indicate a person who has agreed to carry out the parties' contract of sale according to their previously agreed-on instructions.

executed by the vendor, and the payment of the purchase price by the purchaser. In the mortgage transaction, an escrow agent is authorized to accept: a note and mortgage lien from the purchaser for the lender, documents outlined as necessary preconditions of a mortgage loan, and finally, the mortgage loan proceeds from the lender. All of the documents, checks, and payments required for a closing pass through the hands of the escrow agent. She discharges all liens affecting the marketability of the title, pays for the services rendered in the course of the transaction, and finally disburses the proceeds.

Escrow instructions usually contain both general provisions and those tailored to the particular transaction. The former often state the agent's accounting practices and responsibility for funds. Generally the instructions are not subject to the jurisdiction's Statute of Frauds but are customarily written nonetheless.

There are many reasons why the parties to a transaction might consider using an escrow agent instead of closing the transaction themselves. The agent is often an expert at handling such transactions. Using the escrow avoids a face-to-face closing, and this might be expedient when the vendor is moving some distance away, or the purchaser is moving into an area from a distance. When there are questions about the state of the title, an escrow agent can be instructed to have an updated search performed just before recording the deed, or to record it only after all liens and encumbrances are paid off.

If routinely handled, an escrow is a two-step delivery process for the title. First, the deed is handed to the escrow agent, and second, the agent delivers the title deed to the purchaser when all the conditions in the contract and the instructions are performed. However, the second delivery is deemed effective as of the date the deed is deposited in the escrow agent's account. This is the doctrine of "relation back": the effectiveness of the deed is measured by the date of the first delivery. This legal fiction cuts off intervening interests. The death, incompetency, or insolvency of the vendor does not destroy the validity of the second delivery.

A valid escrow requires two things: (1) a valid and binding contract of sale, and (2) escrow instructions in which the vendor does not reserve the power to recall the deed in the escrow account, absent a breach of the contract or the instructions by the purchaser. As to the first requirement, today a line of authority holds that the instructions, if complete in themselves or as augmented by other documents, can suffice for a contract of sale; thus the possibility of going directly to escrow exists in some states. The second requirement is that of irrevocability, which should not be confused with contract conditions and contingencies. A conditional deed may be put irrevocably into an escrow and the completion of the escrow awaits the fulfillment of the contingencies.

The escrow agent should be a third party, independent of the vendor; if the agent were the vendor's agent, the delivery of the deed into escrow would not put the deed beyond the vendor's control. If, on the other hand, the agent were the purchaser's agent, the rule that conditional delivery to a grantee vests title in the grantee unconditionally would mean that the conditions in the contract of sale could not be enforced.

Once the contract of sale is binding and the escrow created by instruction of the parties, the vendor's placing the deed in escrow puts his ability to deal with the title further on hold. If he marries thereafter, no marital rights will attach to the title. Likewise, the vendor's creditors will not be able to enforce a judgment against the escrow. (This fact may greatly benefit purchasers if the vendor is in poor financial health.) Neither will a vendor be able to make a will devising the escrow. And, if the vendor dies, the deed already in a valid escrow will be beyond the reach of his estate. (The doctrine of equitable conversion reaches the same result for a conveyance without an escrow. See Chapter 4.)

Consider if you will the following, bare-bones escrow agreement between the parties to the contract at the beginning of Chapter 6.

## ESCROW INSTRUCTIONS

This agreement is made between *Vivi Vendor* and _____, escrow agent, on this \_\_\_\_\_ day of _____, 199\_\_\_\_.

Vendor has agreed to convey, and *Peter Purchaser* has agreed to purchase, Blackacre Farm, Myertown, Maryland by contract dated September 5, 19\_\_\_\_, and described as follows:

[legal description inserted here]

being 50 acres, for a price in gross of $500,000 and free of encumbrances except as are set out in the preliminary title report of Title Guaranty Insurance Co., Mooers City, delivered to the escrow agent at the start of the escrow.

Vendor and Purchaser agree to deliver irrevocably all forms and instruments necessary to close this escrow by December 5, 19\_\_\_\_.

Vendor shall deliver a special warranty deed to the property upon request of agent, and Purchaser shall deliver all monies necessary to complete the purchase, including all prorated adjustments and closing costs appearing on Form HUD-1, revised July 1985.

Vendor and Purchaser agree to release agent from all claims arising under this agreement, except for claims based on the fraud and gross negligence of the agent. Agent shall have a lien on all funds on deposit to secure payment of its fee.

Agent's fee shall be _____ percent of all monies on account.

Executed at _____ on _____

_____
Vivi Vendor

_____
Peter Purchaser

Compare this set of instructions with the contract of sale at the beginning of Chapter 6. If the provisions of the contract are inconsistent with the instructions, which will prevail? Generally the instructions are written later in time than the contract is and, being the latest evidence of the parties' agreement, will prevail. The instructions may prevail for an additional reason: they often are more detailed than the contract and therefore fill in the contract's gaps and silences without necessarily being inconsistent with it. If the two documents can be read in harmony, the courts are likely to do so. If clear inconsistencies do appear, the terms of the instructions control those in the contract. If the instructions merely flesh out the contract, the two documents will be read harmoniously.

# EXAMPLES AND EXPLANATIONS

Which of the terms of the escrow instructions (on page 129) conflict with those of the contract (on pages 63-64)? Consider the following items.

1. Is the instruction regarding the preliminary title report a modification of the contract's provision for a marketable title?

**Explanation:**   The instruction's reference to the preliminary title report has the effect of accepting all encumbrances mentioned in the report, whether or not they affect the marketability of the title. In a preliminary report, the title searcher for the insurer will list all encumbrances, whatever their effect on the title to be insured. Further negotiations should occur to make sure that the encumbrances rendering the title unmarketable are not accepted by the purchaser executing these instructions.

2. When will the closing be held? The contract calls for a date certain, but is time made "of the essence" in this contract? Is that aspect of the contract modified by the instructions?

**Explanation:**   The instructions advance the date of the closing by ten days, from the 15th of December in the contract, to the 5th in the instructions.

Probably a typo, but the instructions are the last agreement of the parties on this matter, so if the instructions and the contract conflict, the former will control. When considered with the next paragraph of the instructions, its terms can be said to make time of the essence with this change — and the date for the closing will become December 5th unless the parties change the terms of the instructions.

3. What other problems do you foresee if these instructions are not modified?

**Explanation:** Perhaps the most important terms not yet included in the instructions would (1) incorporate the contract of sale into the terms of the instructions, and (2) give the agent express authority to oversee the performance of the terms and conditions of the contract.

A second matter concerns the relationship of the acreage and the price. Here the acreage is stated, as it was not in the contract (there two prices were named, one in gross and the other on an acreage basis). So the ambiguity in the contract persists here; taken together, however, the addition of the instructions to the sheaf of documents evidencing this transaction shows that the acreage is a concern of the purchaser. Moreover, a statement of the price in gross is not inconsistent with this concern. Thus the vendor should inquire about the impacts of an acreage deficiency on the transaction, a survey should be ordered, and the procedure for the agent's handling of the survey should be added to the instructions.

4. When is the escrow effective? In other words, when does the escrow agent have authority to act for the parties? When does that authority end?

**Explanation:** The receipt of the preliminary title report is the start of this escrow, and that may be too late. Unless the parties mean to see and review the state of the title before going into escrow, this provision should be modified so that the agent can act for the parties as soon as the agreement is executed. Probably the termination of the escrow should not be a date certain but an event certain, such as the satisfaction of the last performed contingency in the contract of sale.

5. Escrows must be irrevocable. Is this one?

**Explanation:** Arguably not, at least not yet. The start of the escrow may be the delivery of the preliminary title report, and the parties should clarify this matter.

6. Who bears the risk if the escrow agent embezzles the funds on deposit with her? If she goes bankrupt?

**Explanation:** Until the title is ready in escrow for delivery to the purchaser, the risk of the agent absconding with the funds on deposit lies with the purchaser. Up to that time, the purchase money in escrow was awaiting title and so was still subject to the purchaser's direction and control. After the title is proven and the deed is put in escrow, the risk lies on the shoulders of the vendor.

7. The escrow agent has duties to both parties? If the agent notices that the purchaser's check for the earnest money deposit bounces, must she inform the vendor?

**Explanation:**   Generally, yes. However, while fiduciary duties are sometimes imposed on agents, don't count on such duties in every situation. Escrow agents are often said to be capable of "merely ministerial acts" in implementing the escrow instructions. Lee v. Title Ins. & Trust Co., 264 Cal. App. 2d 160, 70 Cal. Rptr. 378 (1968) (failing to notify party that the amount of the lien was more than the loan proceeds gives rise to no liability for the agent). For example, if the purchaser proves to be without the financial ability to complete the sale, must the agent disclose this? When must this disclosure be made? When the first mortgage loan application is denied? The second? Third? If a signature on an amendment to the instructions does not match the signature on the original instructions, should the agent inform the opposite party? Lee v. Escrow Consultants, Inc., 210 Cal. App. 3d 915, 259 Cal. Rptr. 117, 123 (1989) (holding that an agent has a duty to verify signatures).

## Misdelivery from Escrow

When a deed is delivered to a purchaser before the latter has performed a condition of the escrow instructions or the contract, the prevailing view is that the deed is void. Similarly, when a forgery of the vendor's signature is involved or fraud is involved in the execution, the deed delivered is void. Thus when the purchaser obtains a deed out of escrow without proper delivery by the agent, the deed is void and the vendor is entitled to its cancellation.

However, in some situations the deed that is misdelivered by the agent is said to be voidable, not void. The difference here, as in other situations, is that the voidable deed becomes good in the hands of a bona fide purchaser, whereas a void deed is no good no matter into whose hands it falls.

A breach of fiduciary duty by the agent in misdelivering the deed results in a voidable deed; so does a mistake of fact, duress, or undue influence on the vendor, involved in the establishment of the escrow. These things result, when followed by a misdelivery, in a voidable deed. Here the vendor meant to establish the escrow and deliver the deed into it and suffers the consequences when the alternative is to visit a loss of the title on a bona fide purchaser.

The rationale for finding a deed voidable often sounds like a characterization of the facts as estopping the vendor from denying the bona fide purchaser's title, rather than an examination of the purchaser's bona fides — and in truth, a little estoppel and an innocent purchaser are the best arguments for characterizing the deed as a voidable one.

Thus, on the one hand, when the deed is stolen from the escrow, the deed is void, but when there is an inadvertent misdelivery of a deed by the agent out of escrow, the deed is voidable. The hard cases lie in between such extremes.

# 11

## Deed Descriptions

In the states that were originally British colonies or were carved out of their territory (Maine, Vermont, parts of Ohio, West Virginia, Kentucky, and Tennessee), conveyances are described by metes and bounds. In the rest of the country (Texas and parts of California excepted), the legal description of real property begins on the macro level, with the Jeffersonian or rectangular survey.

## The Rectangular Survey

Surveyors began this survey (long ago) by establishing a *principal meridian* — a north-south line — established by compass (magnetic compass before 1881 and solar compass after that). The first meridian used was the western boundary of Pennsylvania. There are 35 new principal meridians in the United States, 6 with numbers and the rest named. The locations of most are arbitrary. See Figure 11-1. Each meridian intersects with a *base line,* running east and west. Think of these 2 lines as the x-y axes familiar to you from high school geometry.

Parallel to the principal meridian, running north and south, are *range lines*. Six miles apart, the range lines form 6-mile strips called *ranges*. Parallel to the base line, and also 6 miles apart, are *township lines*. The 6-mile strips bounded by the township lines are called *townships,* as are the 6-mile squares formed by the intersection of range and township lines. See Figure 11-2.

Each township is located between 2 parallel lines, known as *standard parallels,* extending out from a principal meridian in an east-west direction. With reference to the x-y axes of the standard parallels and ranges, particular townships are found by combining "Township 1, or 2, North or South" and "Range 1, or 2, East or West" of a principal meridian. Thus Township 30 North, Range 5 East, is 30 townships north of the base line, and 5 ranges east of the principal meridian in question. Only one such township exists.

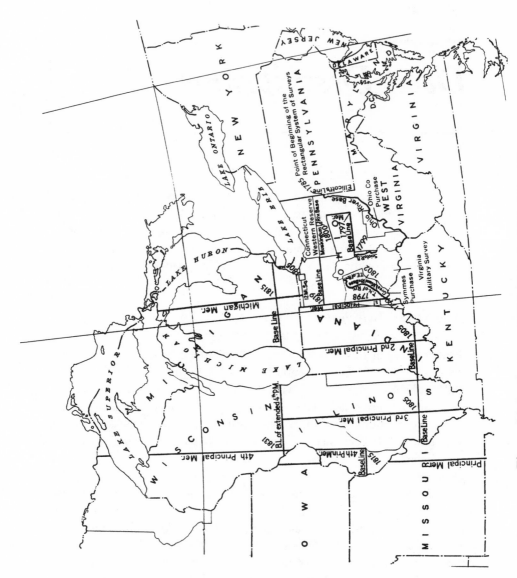

Figure 11-1　Section of U.S. Principal Meridian Map

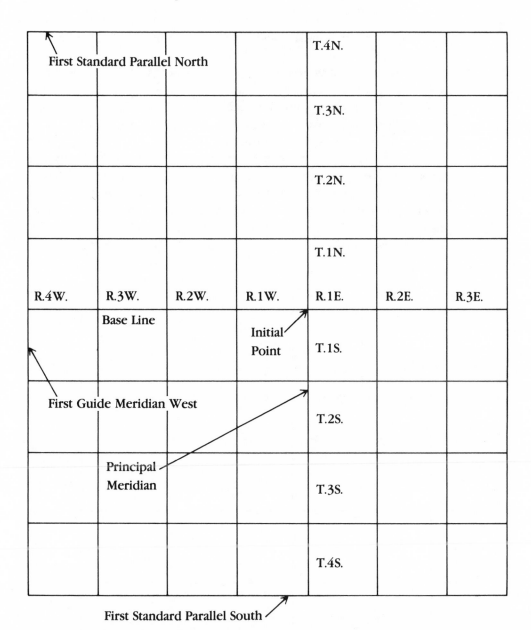

**Figure 11-2   Principal Meridian and Base Line, Showing Townships and Ranges**

From this larger grid (Figure 11-2), the land is divided into sections of 1 square mile each. Thirty-six sections form one 6-square mile township. The sections are numbered from 1 in the northeast corner, running across the top, to 6 in the northwest corner, with 7 just below, 8 to the right, and so on to 12 on the eastern boundary, dropping down to 13 just below it, running back to the western boundary, and so on, until reaching 36 in the southeast corner of the township. See Figure 11-3.

To describe land under this survey, the smallest unit of land goes first and builds to a reference to the principal meridian used in the region. Thus Section 12, Township 5 South, Range 2 West, Salt Lake Meridian — or Sec. 12, T5S, R2W, Salt Lake M. — describes land in northern Utah.

Township sections can be further divided into quarters. When only a part of a section is conveyed and that part is rectilinear in shape, the description reads: "the NW 1/4 of the SW 1/4, of Section 12." See Figure 11-4. If a smaller parcel is conveyed, or if it is not rectilinear, a metes and bounds measure must be used in addition to the rectangular survey description, usually preceding that description in the deed; or, a smaller parcel might be referred to as a numbered parcel in a platted subdivision. None of the above,

| 6 | 5 | 4 | 3 | 2 | 1 | |
|---|---|---|---|---|---|---|
| 7 | 8 | 9 | 10 | 11 | 12 | |
| 18 | 17 | 16 | 15 | 14 | 13 | Range Line |
| 19 | 20 | 21 | 22 | 23 | 24 | |
| 30 | 29 | 28 | 27 | 26 | 25 | |
| 31 | 32 | 33 | 34 | 35 | 36 | |

Township Line

**Figure 11-3   A Standard Township, with Sections Numbered in the Typical Order**

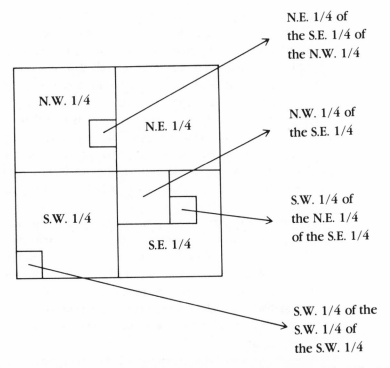

**Figure 11-4   Quarter Sections of Sec. 12, T5S, R2W, Salt Lake M.**

however, is a substitute for incorporating a statement of the city, town, or village, and the state into a description. Otherwise, a mistake in the rectangular survey description can land you in an adjoining state (or, if on the coast, in the ocean!).

## Preferences among Conflicting Elements of a Metes and Bounds Description

As discussed previously, the first two sections of a deed are the premises, followed by the habendum clause. Between these two sections generally appears the legal description of the transferred property. The deed description must identify that property with reasonable certainty.

When the elements of a description are internally inconsistent, boundary descriptions are controlled by a well-established order of priorities of preference: Monuments, courses, distances, and quantity prevail in that order, unless it produces absurd results. Thieriault v. Murray, 588 A.2d 720, 722 (Me. 1991). A monument is generally a stake in the ground, left by the last surveyor to work out the description. The physical disappearance of a monument does not defeat its priority if it can be reestablished by the survey-or's field notes or other evidence. If the surveyor makes a mistake and the monument is wrongly located, the monument as located on the ground is preferred to its true location, particularly if relied on. A monument established before the date of the deed, and referred to in it, is preferred to a monument later established. In this connection, it is often said that natural monuments control artificial ones. An artifical monument is one that either calls for a change in courses with reference to adjoining property later established by survey, or is a natural monument set in the ground after the deed is given (one that uses the description and so relies on it). If there are two conflicting surveys of adjoining property, the one in existence at the time of the deed controls.

"Courses control distances." This is true in most, but not all, states. This means that a boundary line need not stop at a certain distance when the direction it is given would take it further, to a monument further on. More-over, "to" used in this sense is a word of exclusion. "To the old oak tree" means "to this side of the old oak tree," not to its center or far side. Both courses and distances yield to monuments. "First courses control last courses." If the error cannot otherwise be isolated, the last course described often absorbs the error.

The rule of reasonable certainty is judge-made law. In most states, the rule is the same for both contracts of sale and deeds for real property, so it is best to incorporate the fullest available description into a contract of sale. However, the state of Washington requires that a legal description be used in the contract. Is this a good rule? Washington state courts formulated this rule as an interpretation of the state's Statute of Frauds. In this case, however, the statute may work a greater fraud than it would otherwise.

The rule of reasonable certainty is usually not a problem in states using a rectangular or other governmental survey, but in the former colonies (and Texas) it presents a somewhat greater problem. If a person is about to sell real property, she should have her tax assessment reference number, lot and block number, or title insurance policy handy so that she can incorporate the description by reference into any contract executed during nonbusiness hours. If these are not available, the book and page number in the public records where the last recorded description of the property appears might be used as well.

The rule of reasonable certainty requires that there be a point of beginning to the survey. It further requires that the description close. When abstracting a title, the title searcher will generally omit the premises of a deed when a fee simple absolute is conveyed, naming only the parties to it. However, he will generally copy the description meticulously, compare it with past descriptions, and note any discrepancies. He probably hopes that the same description is used all the way down the chain of title. If not, a resurvey of the property may be indicated. If he finds that a description contained less than a grantor owned, he is generally put to an extra search; for example, he might search the land records past the next transfer date until he is sure that successive grantees held for the period of adverse possession.

# EXAMPLES AND EXPLANATIONS

1. What if a deed description is "such land as the grantor (a living person) owns upon her death"?

**Explanation:** This description is void for uncertainty. The description must be certain at the time the deed is effective, and this description is not. It has a testamentary look to it. However, if a description reads "all the lands unsold to other parties on January 1," this is a definite description because the public records will ascertain the land retained by the grantor as of that date. The extrinsic evidence giving certainty to the description is in the public domain and is customarily gathered by abstractors.

2. What if the description is "the house that Bill now occupies"?

**Explanation:** This may be a valid description. If the property is the only one Bill owns, then the description can be given certainty by extrinsic evidence. However, if that evidence creates ambiguity because, for example, Bill owns two houses in the area, the description fails.

3. What if the description is of the "Joe Brown Farm"?

**Explanation:** This description appears to be one that can be fleshed out by extrinsic evidence. If extrinsic evidence is successfully used, the description is reasonably certain. The use of this evidence creates some corollaries to the general rule. For example, the mention of the city or county in which the property lies may be omitted when the grantor owns only one parcel in that jurisdiction. Likewise, omission of the state in which the property lies is not fatal because the law will infer that the place of contracting or closing is the state in which the property lies. Such omissions are curable, but they are not prudent.

4. What if a legal description in a deed reads "all the land that I now possess"?

**Explanation:** The holdings can be established by extrinsic evidence as of the date of the deed, and so the description is definite. Further, there is no ambiguity patent on the face of the deed to render a description uncertain. Remember, latent defects are cured by extrinsic evidence, patent ones are not.

5. What if the description is "part of lot two"? Which part? What shape?

**Explanation:**  This description is indefinite and patently ambiguous. A description that reads "one and a half acres in the northwest corner of lot 2" is similarly ambiguous. There would have to be some customary shape for the subdivision lots in the region for this description to be valid. The Jeffersonian survey (if used in the region) might provide such a customary shape, but otherwise this description fails.

6. How about a description reading "the north side of lot 2"?

**Explanation:**  Courts have held this to mean that the northern one-half of the lot is conveyed. This is a rule of law, not a matter of the intent of the parties. Most of the questions that arise regarding deed descriptions are questions of fact and for the trier of fact.

7. What if the deed says "to A and her heirs, that certain parcel, being one-half of my estate Blackacre"?

**Explanation:**  Here the "one-half" does not describe a certain acreage, so the description is patently ambiguous and fails. If the vendor and purchaser are tenants in common with regard to Blackacre, another problem arises because this description on its face does not describe an undivided one-half in the whole of Blackacre.

8. What if the description is of the "western 50 feet" of a lot?

**Explanation:**  There may be no problem if extrinsic evidence shows that the lot is either a square or rectangle. If the lot is irregularly shaped, however, a problem arises. Similarly, a reference in a description to 50 feet of frontage on a street will imply a rear line of the same length, but unless the property is (again) a square or a rectangle, courts cannot make that implication. How are these problems resolved? They are generally resolved by a presumption that the grantor intended to convey away the larger of the two possible acreages. This is a matter of construing the deed against the grantor. Armed with this rule of construction, there is a latent ambiguity in the deed, and the trial court should admit extrinsic evidence to explain it. If that evidence is conflicting, however, the court will be unable to establish the intent of the parties to the transaction. In many deed description cases, that intent will have receded so far into the past that it will be impossible to establish. In this situation, the courts are likely to reject the extrinsic evidence because of the improbability of its being credible and instead rely on the paper record, on which present-day grantors and grantees most often have to rely.

# Monumentation and Surveying

What if a surveyor running a metes and bounds description makes an error and his plat plan or field notes conflicts with the marker he leaves on the ground? Which controls? If the marker is in its original position, it controls because judicial emphasis in this area is on what the surveyor did, not what he meant to do. This encourages reliance on the facts of possession (which after all creates rights superior to the record) and prevents overlaps or deficiencies on the ground. So when the original monument can be established, it prevails over a plat. But if the plat conflicts with the field notes of the surveyor and no monument can be found, the field notes control because they show what the surveyor did; the plat is then regarded only as a copy of the notes. If there is a conflict between the original monument and the notes but the plat has been recorded in a state that conveys according to a plat reference, here the plat controls and inconsistent evidence is inadmissible. However, in these states this rule is not carried forward to its logical consequence to permit the plat to control over misplaced monuments. The monuments as placed still control.

If a monument is lost, it may be reestablished by witnesses, fences, sworn affidavits, and so forth. A lost but remembered monument may be established by extrinsic evidence. Once established, it must be put back where it was, even if it had been misplaced on the ground by surveyor error. If a monument is lost and no extrinsic evidence is available to reestablish it, the courts then go to the nearest two existing monuments and measure the distance between them, dividing the line proportionately to fix the point lost. This rule has the effect of containing errors within the smallest possible land area. In some situations, however, a deficiency in the legal description may be prorated, as where there are more than two lots and a deficiency in the frontage measurements between two monuments encompassing all of the lots is in dispute.

# Tagalong Words in Deed Descriptions

Many deed descriptions contain the words "more or less" at their end. Is this a good idea? These words either mean that some deviation from the legal description is to be permitted (and the parties should then agree on how much) or they are an allocation and assumption of risk of a deficiency. The risk will generally be assumed by the person taking the deed — that is, the purchaser. In some states, these words are not part of the description; rather, they control it. Whether they indicate an allocation of risk of a shortage in the description or a rule of substantial deviation is a matter for local law to be determined from the whole contract or the intent of the parties; for example, unless the sale is on a per acre basis, the purchaser has likely assumed the risk of any deficiency.

When added to the deed description at its close, an accurate statement of the amount of acreage can supply missing boundaries and close the descriptions that don't otherwise close. So if you have an accurate idea of how much acreage is involved in a sale, it is a good thing to include an acreage statement at the end of the description.

What about the words "to or along" a named street? At common law, this meant that the grantee took to the middle of the street. This was a matter construing the deed in favor of the grantee and assumed that the grantee receives ownership of the street from her vendor. If the boundary were a stream, the result is the same. At common law, the grantee takes to the thread or middle of the stream. If a lake or pond were involved, however, a different result obtains. The lake is not cut into triangular parcels, but a purchaser takes to the low water line of the lake.

To litigate a boundary dispute, does the plaintiff have to have title? The answer in most states is no. The plaintiff's proving title puts an extra burden on her just being a plaintiff, and this seems unfair. Where the pleadings establish the litigation as a boundary dispute, the plaintiff does not have to prove title to reach the boundary claim. Possession is sufficient. This rule originates in the notion that a boundary dispute is really a trespass action. In some states, like Texas, the cause of action is appropriately entitled trespass to try title, but the same result would be reached today in states in which a quiet title action or an ejectment action is used.

# 12

# Implied Warranties for Housing

Implied by law in every contract of sale for the purchase of residential property from a professional builder-vendor is a warranty that the house is constructed in a skillful manner, is free of material defects, and is fit for its intended purpose and habitable. Caceci v. DiCanio Constr. Corp., 72 N.Y.2d 52, 530 N.Y.S.2d 771, 526 N.E.2d 266 (1988); see generally, Powell, Builder-Vendor Liability for Environmental Contamination in the Sale of Residential Property, 58 Tenn. L. Rev. 231, 236-244 (1991). The builder-vendor cannot exculpate himself from this warranty, nor can the purchaser waive it, because it arises by operation of law. This implied warranty of habitability has been the product of judicial decisions in many states; a few state legislatures have created the warranty by statute. See, e.g., Md. Real Prop. Code Ann. §10-203 (1981); Va. Code §55-70 (1981). But the overwhelming majority of states (more than 40) have the warranty in some form. See Grand, Implied and Statutory Warranties in the Sale of Real Estate: The Demise of Caveat Emptor, 15 Real Est. L.J. 44, 45-49 (1986); Shedd, The Implied Warranty of Habitability: New Implications, New Applications, 8 Real Est. L.J. 291 (1980).

The theory of such a warranty is that it arises as an implied term on the contract to purchase the residence and is not thereafter merged into the deed to the real property underlying it. The professional builder's expertise (particularly relative to his purchaser's), his better position to prevent defects, the expectations of the parties, the prophylactic effect of the warranty in discouraging sloppy building practices, the provision of parity of remedies in sale of real as well as personal property, and the ability of the professional to bear the risk of defects — all have been cited as rationales for imposing this warranty on builders. In sum, it might be said that the builder's liability is extracontractual.

The definition of what constitutes habitability varies from state to state. In every state, it extends to the major structural elements of a house; in some states, the case law extends it to the lot, particularly if the lot has been filled, compacted, or the drainage or soil condition affects the house itself. See, e.g., Jordan v. Talaga, 532 N.E.2d 1174 (Ind. App. 1989); see generally Powell, supra, 58 Tenn. L. Rev. at 244-253. Thus when a builder purchases a finished lot — meaning one that has been grubbed, graded, and cleared, or generally prepared for the construction of a structure on it — a house builder can have a cause of action against the vendor-developer of the lot. Expertise is a relative matter in this regard. See Jordan v. Talaga, supra (involving a successful suit by a builder-purchaser using implied warranty theory when the lot turns out to have severe drainage problems).

This warranty survives the closing because it is considered collateral to the deed. (By contrast, title problems are instrinsic to the deed.) This legal result is realistic in large part because the housing defects that are the subjects of disputes over it are not discovered until well after the closing. The statute of limitations thus runs from the date of the defect's discovery, rather than the closing on the property.

Courts generally agree that the warranty is waivable by the warrantee and disclaimable by the warrantor, although the disclaimer must be clearly stated and understood. Perhaps, however, it would be better to say that no court has found a disclaimer is void as against public policy; however, they are not favored.

# EXAMPLES AND EXPLANATIONS

Assume in each of the following problems that the events occurred in serial fashion.

1. V and P close on the sale of a new wood-frame house built by V in the course of his business. P inspects the house before the closing. Thereafter, P discovers that much of the veneer of the drywall will need replacing. Can P recover the cost of the replacement from V?

**Explanation:**  No. The condition of the drywall veneer is a patent feature of the house, that is, visible to P upon reasonable inspection (as opposed to a latent one — one not detectable upon inspection). The implied warranty of habitability does not apply to patent defects; instead, the defects covered must be latent and so not visible upon a reasonable inspection. Unless P can show that he did not have the opportunity to inspect, the implied warranty does not apply.

2. While replacing the drywall, P discovers that the studs are 18 inches apart and that the framing appears to sag between the studs. (Fourteen inches is the industry standard in the region.) P asks you to recover the cost of

bracing the frame or the loss incurred from the house's decreased fair market value. Will you?

**Explanation:** Yes. This defect indicates poor workmanship on a major structural feature of the house by a builder-vendor (someone who should know that the standard distance between the studs on a new wooden frame house is 14, not 18, inches). The warranty applies and gives P the cost of bracing the frame or the decrease in market value. Abney, Determining Damages for Breach of Implied Warranties in Construction Defect Cases, 16 Real Est. L.J. 210 (1988). V may object that the distance between the studs is discoverable through the use of a magnetic device that locates the nails in the studs and that is available at most hardware stores for under $10. To no avail: The device does not affect the patent-latent distinction of the common law in this area.

3. V offers to brace the frame, but P insists that he is entitled to recover the decrease in fair market value and states that until V pays, V will not be permitted to brace the framing. Will you support P's position?

**Explanation:** No, advise against this. Advise instead that V be allowed to perform the bracing to prevent the structure from sagging further. P's insistence is probably based on a belief that if the lesser-cost bracing is done, V's attention will wander. However, his insistence prevents the mitigation of V's damages. To the extent that the implied warranty case law rests on tort principles, mitigation is not required (mitigation of damages being a contract principle); to the extent that it rests on principles of implied contract, mitigation is required. See Wawak v. Stewart, 247 Ark. 1093, 449 S.W.2d 922 (1971). The lesson is that an implied warranty is a hybrid of tort and contract law, making P's position a risky one; indeed, deterring such an insistence is one reason why the lesser measure of damages, as between the cost of repair or the decrease in the fair market value, may be preferable.

4. After the closing of the V-P transaction, P discovers that the wood in the cabana alongside the swimming pool turns out to be rotten and has to be demolished. Can P recover for this situation?

**Explanation:** No. The defect must go to the habitability of the property, which refers to the condition of the major structural features of the house; the cabana is superfluous as far as the habitability of the house is concerned. When the property has features that provide more than a habitable structure, the implied warranty is not applicable to those features.

Assume in the following problems that the events occurred in the alternative.

5. V and P close on the sale of a house in January 1993. The following July, P realizes that the air compressor and ventilation system for the air conditioning lacks the capacity to cool the house. Overhaul of the air conditioning will cost $5000. P asks you to recover $5000 from V. Will you take P's case?

**Explanation:** There is no mention here that V is a builder-vendor, so the implied warranty of habitability may not apply. See Gaito v. Auman, 70 N.C. App. 21, 318 S.E.2d 555 (1984), aff'd, 313 N.C. 243, 327 S.E.2d 870 (1985), and noted, 21 Wake Forest L. Rev. 515 (1986) (where a builder-vendor was sued and found liable under similar circumstances). However, recent cases have considered whether the nonbuilder vendor of a residence ought not to warrant that the house is suitable for its intended purpose. See, e.g., Johnson v. Davis, 480 So. 2d 625 (Fla. 1985), noted in 14 Fla. St. L. Rev. 359 (1986). Here, the wintertime closing indicates that P's reasonable inspection of the premises might include turning the air conditioning on but not running it for any prolonged period. Therefore, V had knowledge about the air conditioner's capacity not disclosed to P, and the spirit of the implied warranty — with its no-ability-to-inspect rationale — would be carried out by imposing liability on V; however, another rationale for the implied warranty is that the builder-vendor has the expertise to fix the defect, and that is not the case here. On balance, judgment for P is likely, so you should take P's case. Compare Park v. Sohn, 89 Ill. 2d 453, 60 Ill. Dec. 609, 433 N.E.2d 651 (1982) (where the court held that the defendant need not be a full-time professional builder to be liable, in a situation in which defendant had built one house prior to the defective one, but subsequently built six more) with Stevens v. Bouchard, 532 A.2d 1028, 1030 (Me. 1987) (where the court declined to impose liability like builder-vendor liability "on the seller of every existing home" because "the owner of an older home stands in a much different relation to that property than does the builder-vendor of a new residence").

6. V and P close the purchase and sale of V's house. V is the builder-vendor of the house and has lived in it for two years. After the closing, P discovers that the water coming from the tap is not potable and asks you to take his case. Will you?

**Explanation:** The fact that V has lived in the house should not affect the applicability of the implied warranty; indeed, it should give V all the more knowledge about the quality of his workmanship and heighten his duty to disclose the defect. Mazurek v. Nielson, 42 Colo. App. 386, 599 P.2d 269 (1979) (builder-vendor attempted to sell but was unsuccessful and moved in himself). As to this particular defect, it does not involve the physical condition of the improvement. If the water comes from a public utility line,

P's remedy is against the utility, and P is in the best position to provide the information on water quality to the utility. If the water comes from an on-site well, P must evaluate whether V's work in drilling the well affected its quality; if not, perhaps P is in the best position to bring a nuisance suit against any neighboring polluter. But see McDonald v. Mianecki, 79 N.J. 275, 398 A.2d 1283 (1979).

In general, that a person who, in other respects, is a builder-vendor constructs a house for himself, should not by itself prevent liability for the implied warranty. If it were otherwise, the likelihood of vendor fraud is too great. Builders might fabricate transactions as concerning their personal residences.

7a. A builder-vendor constructs a small, ornamental fishpond in the sideyard of a house. The pond is cement and not attached to the house itself. The fourth owner of the house has a four-year-old who trips on the cement edge, falls forward into the water, hits his head on the bottom, and suffers severe brain damage. Is the builder-vendor liable?

**Explanation:** The builder-vendor may well be liable; the remoteness in time or title does not, standing along, cure the potential of the defect for grave mischief.

7b. What if the second owner of the house had the pond built, but otherwise the facts were the same? Would that owner be liable for the injuries?

**Explanation:** The answer was no in Preston v. Goldman, 164 Cal. App. 3d 1135, 210 Cal. Rptr. 913 (1985), rev'd, 42 Cal. 3d 108, 227 Cal. Rptr. 817, 720 P.2d 476 (1986), noted in 17 S.U. L. Rev. 23 (1987). Note, however, the extent to which the improving owners had to go to free themselves of liability.

8. V and P execute a brief but enforceable contract for the sale of V's house. P asks B, V's broker, if the house has termites. B answers that it has been regularly inspected for termites. V tenders P a ream of papers showing the major expenditures on the upkeep of the house. After the closing, P realizes that the property is infested with termites and that the property has not only been inspected, but also has been treated for termites by V. The bills for the treatments were tendered to P among the expenditure records. P asks you to recover the costs of exterminating the termites. Will you take his case? See Cohen v. Blank, 359 Pa. Super. 93, 518 A.2d 582 (1986) (in an action for a broker's misrepresentation that a parking space was sold along with a townhouse, the court held that the vendors were liable for the fair market value of the parking space, even when the vendors were unaware of the broker's representation to the effect that the space was included in the townhouse sale). What if the vendor had answered P's question, while the

broker tendered P the expenditure records? Kantor v. Norwood Group, Inc., 127 N.H. 831, 508 A.2d 1078 (1986).

**Explanation:**   Recent cases have held vendors liable for the active misrepresentations of an agent like B. The fact that V was willing to disclose the treatments makes him innocent of any misrepresentation himself, and the fact that the agent's misrepresentation was passive may further distinguish the recent cases. However, if the result for P is the same misleading impression of the transaction, the type of misrepresentation — whether it is active or passive — should not matter. V is liable for the cost of exterminating the termites. If it was V who did the misrepresenting, V would not be able to make B jointly liable with him.

# Measuring the Damages for the Implied Warranty's Breach

The theory on which the case is pleaded makes a difference here. Most courts have treated damages for breach of this warranty as a species of contract damages and granted damages for the economic loss to the value of the defective structure. Cosmopolitan Homes v. Weller, 663 P.2d 1041 (Colo. 1987). Damages thus include the loss of value, the expenses of dealing with a defective structure (including the cost of repair), and the loss of expected use of the property. However, if the cause of action is treated as one lying in negligence, then economic losses may not be recoverable unless there is personal injury or some unsafe and dangerous condition likely to create such an injury. Council of Co-Owners Atlantis Condominium, Inc. v. Whiting-Turner Contracting Co., 308 Md. 18, 517 A.2d 336, 344 (1986).

It seems unwise to restrict the measure of damages and reject proof of economic loss as some courts have. Injury both to one person and to one person's property inflict losses, and in any event, why should the law penalize those who wish to prevent an injury? Persons who anticipate and act to prevent injury should be in the same position as those who fail to anticipate it and suffer. Barnes v. Mac Brown & Co., 264 Ind. 227, 342 N.E.2d 619, 621 (1976).

The loss of value can be measured either by the decrease in the fair market value of the defective structure or its replacement-repair cost. The cases split on which measure is proper. Sometimes the split is even intrajurisdictional. However, the greater weight of authority stands behind using the cost of repair, unless economic waste would result. Abney, supra, 16 Real Est. L.J. at 214. The possible rules using the two measures can include (1) both of them; (2) either of them; (3) the lesser of them; or (4) the repair cost, unless economic waste is present, in which case, the decreased value. Abney, supra, 16 Real Est L.J. at 216-218. Economic waste is present when the cost of repair is disproportionately large in comparison to the loss of value. It is little more than permission to the builder to upset the judicial preference for repair costs by presenting proof that repairs are too costly in view of the benefit the purchaser would receive from them. In such cases, the courts permit decreased value as the measure of damages.

Can attorneys' fees be recovered in the successful action? The answer is yes in some states with a statute giving such fees in the successful contract action. So, in such states, if the action on the implied warranty is one for breach of a contract, then attorneys' fees can be recovered.

In general, there is a duty on the part of the person claiming the benefit of the warranty to mitigate damages. Again, the assumption seems to be that the action on the warranty is one lying in contract. Wawak v. Stewart, 247 Ark. 1093, 449 S.W.2d 922 (1971).

# EXAMPLES AND EXPLANATIONS

9. V and P close the purchase and sale of V's house. Thereafter P realizes that five years ago the house was the site of a gruesome multiple murder. P asks you to recover from V or V's broker damages for the nondisclosure. Will you take P's case?

**Explanation:**   Except for one California case, damages for emotional distress have not been recovered. These sound in tort. See Reed v. King, 145 Cal. App. 3d 261, 193 Cal. Rptr. 130 (1983). The *Reed* case involved the facts presented here but was appealed on a motion for summary judgment. The court held that P should be permitted an opportunity to prove that the fact of past crimes decreased the fair market value of the property. You should take the case but encourage its settlement because the proof required will be difficult, costly, and seem novel to a jury. If the case law goes the right way, a nonjury trial is preferable.

10. V and P close the purchase and sale of V's lot, on which V (a builder-vendor) will construct a house for P. The lot is limited by a binding covenant to use as a single-family residence, but after the closing P discovers that a septic tank could not be installed on the property. What remedy does P have against V? How would your answer change if the closing had been on a house and lot?

**Explanation:**   See Hinson v. Jefferson, 287 N.C. 422, 215 S.E.2d 102, 111 (1975) (extending an implied warranty of habitability to this situation and rejecting mutual mistake of fact). However, in some courts the fact that this defect does not affect the physical condition of the residence might make a difference because the warranty does not cover the land itself. P's case is stronger when the house is complete and then sold with the land on which it sits.

# The Problem of Subsequent Purchasers

As of 1989, ten states have extended the protection of an implied warranty of habitability to second or subsequent purchasers of residential property. About a dozen states (including some of the ten states extending the implied warranty) permit a similar suit based on a theory of negligence. Three states and the District of Columbia permit strict liability as a theory. Three states have denied subsequent purchasers these remedies against the builder-vendor. Cherry, Builder Liability for Used Home Defects, 18 Real Est. L.J. 115, 139-141 (1989). Most of these cases were decided well after the establishment of the implied warranty in the law of the jurisdiction, during the decade 1976-1985. Because of the subsequent purchaser's lack of privity with the builder-vendor, seven states have denied the remedies extended by an implied warranty of habitability, but use some or all of the other remedies, particularly negligence. Note, Latent Defects: Subsequent Home Purchasers Beware, 40 S.C. L. Rev. 1017, 1021 (1989).

# EXAMPLES AND EXPLANATIONS

11. Where the time of the first purchaser as owner is brief — less than one year — the courts have extended the implied warranty to the second owner. Redarowicz v. Ohlendorf, 92 Ill. 2d 171, 65 Ill. Dec. 411, 441 N.E.2d 324 (1982), discussing and summarizing the cases on this question to the date of the opinion. What if a defect is discovered 30 years later? Is the builder-vendor still liable?

**Explanation:** Yes, if the implied warranty action was one for strict liability. The builder-vendor would be best able to bear the risk of the defect after producing many units of a product, and so would become an insurer of a defect-free product. However, some builder-vendors of housing produce only ten or so "products" per year; although insurance is available, it will be expensive if the liability is unending. Thus there are some strong arguments for not considering an action to enforce the implied warranty as one in strict liability. (If the courts had intended that, they could have said so, and most did not.)

On the other hand, if the cause of action were viewed as one for strict liability, the applicable statute of limitations would be shorter — as tort limitations are generally shorter than those applying to contract or property causes of action.

If strict liability was the theory of the action, then the purchaser could recover for the decrease in the fair market value attributed to the defect. Maybe a neighbor could recover a similar amount, measured by the decrease in her fair market value attributable to her living next to a defective house? These exciting possibilities may be reasons not to analogize the implied warranty action to strict liability. The builder's work, on which the warranty is based, should remain the key to it, or else the builder's insurance premiums will rise higher still.

12. If second purchasers are covered, then what about installment land sale purchasers? Tenants? Lenders? Adverse possessors? Must there be in the plaintiff, if not an interest identical to the first purchaser's, one that is substantially similar?

**Explanation:** This would impose a type of privity of estate requirement, as an element to bringing the action on the implied warranty. Is this wise? Recognizing the second purchaser as a proper plaintiff is to eliminate privity of contract as an element of the action. Should privity of estate be eliminated as well? Those not in privity of estate will have someone else to sue, and that intervening party may be the most efficient litigator against the builder — being in possession of the facts, with sufficient incentive to sue, and so forth — whereas the intervening vendor has moved away, often out of the jurisdiction.

13. What if the first purchaser accepted a disclaimer of suitability for the plumbing, but a subsequent purchaser took title and possession of the property without notice of this disclaimer and later attempted to convince the builder-vendor to fix the plumbing?

**Explanation:** The inability of a builder to protect himself by contract has been cited as a reason not to extend implied warranty protection to a subsequent purchaser. Crowder v. Vanderdeale, 654 S.W.2d 879, 883 (Mo. 1978), noted in Cherry, Builder Liability for Used Home Defects, 18 Real Est. L.J. 115, 136-137 (1989) (suggesting, however, that the builder's only real protection is to construct a defect-free residence; the appendices to this article collect the cases and statutes relevant to the subsequent purchaser issue). The builder need not perform the repair.

14. What is the applicable statute of limitations — the one applying to tort, contract, or property causes of action? See Cherry, supra, 18 Real Est. L.J. at 133-136. When does the statute start to run?

**Explanation:** In jurisdictions that accept the discovery rule for the warranty, the statute will not begin to run until the defect is discovered or should be discovered by a reasonable inspection. If this is so, the defects that appear only once the subsequent purchaser is in possession makes the subsequent purchaser the first person to have the cause of action created by the warranty. Hermes v. Staiano, 181 N.J. Super. 424, 437 A.2d 925 (1981). This procedural wrinkle in some of these cases obviates the need to distinguish between first and subsequent purchasers.

# Disclaiming the Implied Warranty

A disclaimer of the implied warranty, if specific, conspicuous, and mutually agreed-to by the parties, is effective.

The required specificity avoids language such as an "entire agreement" clause might contain; stating that the contract contains the entire agreement between the parties is not specific enough. As a matter of fact, it shows, ipso facto, that the parties did not bargain over the implied warranty. Although an "as is" clause is an effective disclaimer in some jurisdictions, in others it is still not specific enough: it is either an acknowledgment of the present condition of the property, without consideration of the legal consequences of that condition, or is a disclaimer, which applies only to patent, but not latent, defects.

The conspicuousness required of a disclaimer has to do with the size of the type, the typeface, or the color of the print in which the disclaimer appears.

The mutuality required of a disclaimer agreement may be the result of varying amounts of discussion: (1) the vendor's drawing attention to the agreement, or (2) a knowing, informed waiver of rights, or (3) a general discussion of the rights, including any express warranty extended in lieu of implied one. On the other hand, a specific, unambiguously worded, conspicuous disclaimer may carry the inference of a mutual agreement. See Abney, Disclaiming the Implied Real Estate Common-Law Warranties, 17 Real Est. L.J. 141 (1988); Powell, Disclaimers of Implied Warranty in the Sale of New Homes, 34 Vill. L. Rev. 1123 (1989).

# EXAMPLES AND EXPLANATIONS

15. The contract of sale provides that "the purchaser enters into this contract in full reliance upon his independent investigation and judgment." Does this clause disclaim the implied warranty?

**Explanation:**   No, certainly not as to latent defects. By definition they cannot be investigated. See Wagner v. Cutler, 757 P.2d 779 (Mont. 1988) (a negligent misrepresentation case, but suggesting that the answer is no). This "investigation" clause does not meet the specificity requirement previously discussed. It should be strictly construed.

16. The contract of sale provides that "the property is sold as is." Does this clause disclaim the implied warranty?

**Explanation:**   "As is" has a commonly accepted meaning and so the specificity requirement might be met. Mutuality of agreement would then be dispositive to the outcome of the case. See Melody Homes Mfg. Co. v. Barnes, 741 S.W.2d 349 (Tex. 1987) (sliding over this question with the statement that the purchaser has an obligation to read what he signs and holding that contract language stating that there are "no warranties, express or implied" is sufficient to disclaim the warranty).

17. When builder-vendor V gives an express warranty, is the implied one negated?

**Explanation:** Generally not. Wingfield v. Page, 278 Ark. 276, 644 S.W.2d 940 (1983). These warranties are regarded as cumulative unless it is clear that the parties intend otherwise. The implied warranty is here regarded as a minimum protection, unless it is expressly waived by the warrantee. Where, however, the express warranties are expressly bargained for and become provisions of the purchaser's contract, a negation of the implied warranty may be in order. Implied warranties arise, in the minds of many, to protect those who do not — or don't know enough — to bargain on the matter.

## Lenders' Liability for Implied Warranties

The court in Connor v. Great Western Sav. & Loan Assn., 69 Cal. 2d 850, 73 Cal. Rptr. 369, 447 P.2d 609 (1968), held that a lender has a duty to protect the purchasers of newly built residences from structural defects. The defect involved was a cracked foundation caused by soil expansion around the new construction. The Association found liable in this case, however, had gone well beyond the business of lending money as it is usually conceived: It had accepted the developer's financial statements and corporate accounts without inquiry, accepted the use of canned architectural plans and specifications without checking their suitability for the site, bankrolled the developer's land purchases by holding the title to the land itself, and agreed to become both the construction and the permanent lender for the project. Further, neither the lender nor the developer had any experience in the county in which the subdivision project was to be located — in fact, the developer had been a haberdasher up to that point in his life.

Subsequent cases have cited *Connor* to distinguish it; in more recent attempts to use its holding as authority, one or another element of the lender's involvement with the developer has been lacking. Christiansen v. Philcent Corp., 226 Pa. Super. 157, 313 A.2d 249 (1973). So the precedential value of *Connor* has been limited. Annot., Financing agencies' liability to purchaser of new home or structure for consequences of construction defects, 39 A.L.R.3d 247 (1971 and Supp. 1989); see, e.g., Bradler v. Craig, 274 Cal. App. 2d 466, 79 Cal. Rptr. 401, 406 (1969) (refusing to extend lender liability to subsequent purchasers unless the lender steps out of its usual business role of lending money).

In addition, the California legislature has reversed the holding of *Connor* by a statute immunizing a lender from losses flowing from the breach of the due care liability imposed there, "unless such loss or damage is a result of an act of the lender outside the scope of the activities of a lender of money or unless the lender has been a party to misrepresentation with respect to such . . . real property." Cal. Civ. Code §3434 (West 1970), discussed in Gutierrez, Liability of a Construction Lender Under Civil Code Section 3434: An Amorphous Epitaph to *Connor v. Great Western Savings & Loan Association*, 8 Pac. L.J. 1 (1977).

The inquiry of whether the lender has stepped outside its normal business is more fruitful than an inquiry into the degree of control exercised by the lender. In fact, the prudent lender will inquire and review almost all aspects of a development project; the law wants to provide incentive for such a review. Comment, Indirect Liabilities of Construction Lenders in a Development Setting, 127 U. Pa. L. Rev. 1524 (1979). A lender may inspect the project as construction proceeds, but for his own purposes, and absent evidence that it knows of a vendor's breach of warranty, should not be liable for an implied warranty.

# EXAMPLES AND EXPLANATIONS

18. A lender makes a loan secured by a mortgage lien on real property to be developed, with the loan proceeds, into a shopping center. The return on the money loaned is stated as a small percentage of the rental income of the center. The developer-borrower defaults on the loan and offers the lender, in lieu of foreclosure of its security lien, a deed to the center. The lender accepts the deed. Is the lender then liable to tenants in the center for structural defects causing damage to their tenancies?

**Explanation:** No. There is no liability when the lender exercises a remedy provided by a usual and customary mortgage document. Foreclosure is the usual remedy for a loan default. Therefore, the lender here has not stepped out of its moneylending business. Its rate of return may or may not be the usual and customary one in some markets, but that rate is irrelevant to whether or not it can accept the deed in lieu of its standard remedy for a default. Smith v. Continental Bank, 130 Ariz. 320. 636 P.2d 98 (1981).

Moreover, the lender's acceptance of the deed in lieu of asserting a traditional remedy like foreclosure encourages settlement of matters that would otherwise become the subject of litigation. A judicial interest in preventing crowded dockets suggests that the deed be accepted without liability, for to require a lender to foreclose in order to shield itself from liability burdens the courts. It may also discourage lending and penalize the lender in the regular conduct of its business, so the lender who sells property as received by a deed in lieu should likewise incur no warranty liability. Kennedy v. Columbia Lumber & Mfg. Co., Inc., 384 S.E.2d 730, 734 (S.C. 1989).

However, if the lender receives the deed and then completes the improvements on the structure, implied warranty liability may arise for the portions of the structure completed by the lender; or if the lender gives express warranties on its work, or is aware of defects and conceals them, or becomes highly involved with a builder completing those portions (*Connor* again), lender liability may result.

## Implied Warranties for Commercial Real Property

Finally, consider whether the factors giving rise to an implied warranty in the sale of residences do not also apply to the purchase and sale of commercial properties. Powell & Mallor, The Case for an Implied Warranty of Quality in Sales of Commercial Real Estate, 68 Wash. U.L.Q. 305 (1990) (arguing for the extension of such a warranty).

Unloosed by judicial decree, the implied warranty of habitability has been difficult to contain. Its uncertain legal reach has prompted some states to enact warranty statutes codifying its rules. In New Jersey, the state provides for the registration of builders and requires registered builders to contribute to a compensation fund for defects. N.J. Stat. Ann. §§46:3B-1 et seq. (West 1985) (two years for mechanical system defects and ten for structural defects), discussed in Catalina, Home Buying: The Demise of Caveat Emptor in New Jersey, 7 Real Est. L.J. 158 (1978). Such statutes are justified by the building industry as a method of limiting liability for the small, thinly capitalized builder — who after all (the industry says) accounts for the majority of builders. A similar program of private insurance for defects is managed by a corporate subsidiary of the National Association of Home Builders, a trade group for builders. It is called the Home Owners Warranty (HOW) Program. It provides for a complaint mechanism for owners and favors arbitration of claims.

# 13

## Slander of Title

## Elements of Slander of Title

Slander of title is a misnomer. Unless you regard a land title as the personification of a person, it cannot literally be slandered, and the law of slander is not involved in what is traditionally called "slander of title." Slander of title is actually a species of the tort of interference with a contract or with an economic or prospective advantage. It might better be called the tort of injurious false statements.

Slander of title was early recognized as an oral disparagement of a plaintiff's title. Thus the "slander" involved must be taken to mean an injury or deprecation of some type. Today a deprecating remark about either the physical qualities or the title of real property that interferes with an ongoing or prospective sale or lease transaction can become a basis for this action.

Slander of title, then, is the uttering, making, or publication of an unjustifiable and false statement about a title that deprives the plaintiff of a beneficial relationship with another, the benefit of which would otherwise have been hers. Beane v. McMullen, 265 Md. 589, 291 A.2d 37 (1972); Prosser & Keeton, Torts 962-963 (5th ed. 1984). An escrow agent does not, for example, publish a statement about the title in carrying out escrow instructions, though the statement may be false.

In many states, actual malice on the defendant's part is an element of the tort; that is, the defendant must have intended to injure or annoy the plaintiff. Howarth v. Ostergaard, 30 Utah 2d 183, 515 P.2d 442, 444 (1973). Sometimes, however, malice can be implied from the defendant's actions, as when the disparaging statement is the result of recording a document. In all states, then, it is an intentional tort.

In addition, special damages arising out of the defendant's interference in the transaction are everywhere an element of this tort. Den-Gar Enter. v. Romero, 94 N.M. 425, 611 P.2d 1119, 1124 (Ct. App. 1980). As to the element of special damages, the courts have proceeded to define it in a tortuous case-by-case, loss-by-loss manner; what is meant generally is thus unclear. Special damages are pecuniary, but a definition of their source awaits a plaintiff's request for recompense. They might include the impairment of a property's value or the expenses of counteracting the statement, including litigation costs when, for example, a quiet title action is necessary.

Assertions about the state of the title involved in a transaction can be made in many ways. Examples are a broker's remark about a broken water heater that is, in fact, not broken; a false report by an abstractor that is shown to a bank that thereby refuses a loan; or a nonexistent interest reported as an exception on a title insurance policy and shown to a purchaser. And any false or nonexistent encumbrance on a title can be recorded, and so published in a way in which it will be hard for the recording party to deny intentional action. For instance, a broker looking to make sure a transaction closes, has been known to record a contract of sale. See, e.g., Brezina v. Hill, 202 Neb. 773, 277 N.W.2d 224 (1979) (broker recording contract of sale); Continental Dev. Corp. of Florida v. Duval Title & Abstract Co., 356 So. 2d 925, 927-928 (Fla. App. 1978) (title company filing mechanic's lien for title work, held improperly and maliciously filed).

# EXAMPLES AND EXPLANATIONS

1. A statute of limitations problem: If the false document is recorded, does the statute run from the date of recordation, or is the action available continuously thereafter, running from the date of recordation so long as the document remains on the public records?

**Explanation:** The cases are split on this issue. Compare Hosey v. Central Bank of Birmingham, 528 So. 2d 843 (Ala. 1988) (applying the statute for slander and holding that the statute runs from the date of filing, but not continuously), with Green v. Chamberlain, 60 So. 2d 120 (La. App. 1952) (holding the action a continuous one so long as the document is of record). Reframing the issue slightly may give way to better analysis of it. This is a tort: the action lasts so long as the defendant falsely claims or disparages the title. The time during which the document is on the record is one way of measuring its duration, absent further proof, but if the defendant does not claim an interest in the title, the action is tolled and the statute runs from the date of the last claim.

## The Measure of Damages

The measure of damages creates some confusion. Often the transaction interfered with is a contractual one, so some states (are misled and) apply a contract measure of damages. This gives the plaintiff what she would have obtained in an action for breach of the contract interfered with, but it limits damages to those contemplated by the contracting parties, one of whom is not a party to the main action.

Others apply a tort measure. Then the plaintiff is entitled to proximate or foreseeable damages, as in a successful negligence action.

A third measure is to give foreseeable damages, plus unforeseen expenses, plus damages for mental suffering, and in appropriate cases, punitive damages as well. This third approach is the most often used. See, e.g., Rite Aid Corp. v. Lake Shore Investors, 298 Md. 611, 471 A.2d 735, 44 A.L.R.4th 1063 (1984). Punitive damages are most often awarded when a defendant records a document reflecting a nonexistent interest or encumbrance on a title, with the result that a prospective transaction is delayed or does not close.

The weight of judicial opinions evaluating this tort favors a tort measure because of its intentional nature and the need for the defendant to justify her statement by way of defense. Restatement (Second) of Torts §774A (1979) (giving a successful plaintiff damages measured by her pecuniary loss, consequential damages legally caused by the defendant, as well as emotional losses and actual harm to reputation reasonably expected to result from the interference). For cases adopting the Restatement view, see Bean v. Johnson, 279 Ark. 111, 649 S.W.2d 171 (1983); Tose v. First Pennsylvania Bank, N.A., 648 F.2d 879 (3d Cir. 1981).

# EXAMPLES AND EXPLANATIONS

2. A defendant's actions give rise to a third party's breach of a contract of sale that is clearly unjustified under the contract. As a result the plaintiff has a cause of action for breach of contract against the third party, as well as a slander of title action against the defendant. Can the plaintiff sue the third party in contract, and then the defendant for slander of title?

**Explanation:** Yes. Whether the measure of damages lies in contract or tort, or the jurisdiction has adopted the Restatement view, the plaintiff's measure of damages is not affected; that is, the defendant is liable for the damages, even though the third party is also liable. However, the plaintiff may not actually recover the same damages twice. If the third party is successfully sued for breach of contract and in fact pays contract damages, the plaintiff may not recover them from the defendant as well; in this situation, the defendant will pay tort and Restatement damages over and above the contract measure already recovered. See Restatement (Second) of Torts §774A(2) (1979).

# 14

## Recording Acts

Every state has enacted a statute establishing the office — usually a part of local or county government — for the receipt and maintenance of documents relating to the transfer and ownership of titles to real property. Even civil law Louisiana has such a statute. The public official in charge of this office is generally known as the Recorder of Deeds, or sometimes the Register of Deeds. The documents presented to him are thus "recorded" and thereby become "public records" — that is, they are maintained for and accessible to the public at large.

The legislative objective in enacting recording acts is to encourage purchasers to put their deeds and other ownership documents on the public record. One consequence for a purchaser is that, once on the record, the recorded copy provides notice to others that the purchaser holds the title or interest referred to. By statute, the notice effect of the recording is the same whether or not the third party actually knows of the recording — that is, the third party has "constructive notice" of the recorded document. The flip side of this effect is that persons can rely on the record and safely ignore the threat of unrecorded matters of which they have no other, actual notice. Another consequence of recording is that, again by statute, the document is thereafter self-proving — that is, it becomes admissible in court without further proof (although it still is subject to challenge there). Thus the recording acts provide the grist for determining which of two or more conflicting titleholders have priority, as when the same interest or property is sold more than once.

The protection of subsequent purchasers is the main purpose of the acts. They, however, must qualify for the protection by meeting the acts' requirements. Their principal protection is derived, not only from what the recording act states, but by searching the public records and saving themselves from unwise investments in real property subject to prior interests that would defeat their plans for the property. Incidentally, the acts also preserve the history and state of a title by giving everyone an incentive to record and protect their interests in turn, by giving purchasers subsequent to them notice of it. In this sense, the notice provided by the acts is prospective, and when the protection of the act is given, it is not thereafter taken away by another conflicting claimant thereafter recording a prior conveyance.

This conflict is a zero-sum game: Someone wins the title, and the loser (or losers) are relegated to a suit for damages. To the extent that conflicting titles and interests are not prioritized by the acts, the common law rule concerning them controls. So let's review the common law first.

## The Common Law Rule: "First in Time, First in Right"

The common law for determining the priority of title between two persons sold the same property interest was first in time, first in right. Thus if O conveys to A and then conveys the same real property to B, A's title prevails over B's. In this way, we say that A has priority of title over B. A better statement of the rule might be prior in time, prior in right. How does that rule apply to the following situation?

## EXAMPLES AND EXPLANATIONS

1a. O contracts to sell Blackacre to A, who does not record. O then conveys Blackacre to B, who pays a deposit but also does not record. So what happens when neither of two conflicting purchasers record in a state (like every state) with a recording act?

**Explanation:**   Under the common law rule, B has priority and thus his title prevails over A. The common rule applies as between legal interests, but in this case only the conveyance (the very word says to the legal mind that a deed was used) to B was a legal one; the contract to A creates an equitable interest in A as a transferee of the property. So B now has priority, but that can change. In this situation, A and B might race to otherwise complete and record their transactions, and the first to do so prevails. For example, if B closes his transaction, takes a deed from O and records that, B then cuts off A's interest if, when B records, A hasn't yet paid O the purchase price. (In any case, the inferior interest is left to his rights and remedies against O, if any.)

Based on the answer that common law judges gave to the preceding problem, it is not strictly true that the rule was based on the idea that if O transferred the property once, he could not thereafter transfer the same interest again — often it was said that O had nothing to give after giving it away once. That is only true if interests of the same type (legal and legal, or equitable and equitable) are transferred to different persons.

1b.  If B receives a contract, not a deed, who would prevail?

**Explanation:**   A would. If both of the conflicting interests are equitable, the first in time prevails. If both A and B have executory contracts for
the purchase and sale of Blackacre, they will be involved in a race to close
their transactions, and the first to do so prevails. Thus A prevails, for now.
But the priority as of now could change if B continues to run and wins the
race.

The common law rule applies in all states, absent the applicability of the
state's recording act. That is a big proviso, one that often swallows the rule.
But the rule is worth remembering nonetheless.

# The Recording Acts: "First to (Validly) Record, First in Right"

There are three types of recording acts: race, notice, and race-notice acts. In
a race jurisdiction, the first to record is first in right. This result obtains even
when the purchaser who first records, takes with notice (meaning actual
knowledge of a properly executed document) of the prior transfer. Thus the
knowledge of the winning transferee is irrelevant. The objective of such acts
is to promote the use of the public records and give them certainty. The
following statutory language is typical of a race statute:

> No conveyance of real property is valid as against a purchaser, but
> from the time of its recordation.

Few states today have race statutes. Louisiana and North Carolina have
one generally applicable to conveyances; Pennsylvania and Arkansas have one
applicable only to mortgages. Can you see why a state might prefer this type
of recording act when dealing with claims between mortgagees?

A notice recording act protects the subsequent purchaser who is a bona
fide purchaser (BFP). A BFP is one who takes his interest without either
actual or constructive notice of the prior transfer and pays value for the
interest. The value paid must be real, as opposed to a legal consideration or
an executory promise; it must be new or present value, as opposed to past
consideration; and it must be adequate, meaning a substantial amount of the
fair market value of the interest taken. In a notice state, a subsequent BFP
prevails over a prior unrecorded transferee, regardless of whether or not he
records first. If the prior transfer is recorded, the subsequent purchaser cannot
become a BFP. Why? Because the prior recording gives by law constructive
notice of the interest whose instrument is recorded. Twenty-one states have
this type of recording act today. They typically read as follows:

> No conveyance of real property shall be valid against subsequent
> purchasers without notice, unless that conveyance is recorded.

Historically, this notice type of recording act replaced the race statute of some states; the legislatures recognized the fact that the winners of the race to the courthouse were arriving at the recorder's offices with a malicious gleam in their eyes. The trouble with their reform was that the change in the law protected the lazy — those later purchasers protected by the notice act had little incentive to record. They had only to remain subsequent purchasers. This did not promote use of the records, and their certainty was diminished to that extent.

With the defects in notice statutes in mind, 25 states and the District of Columbia amended their acts still further. They enacted race-notice acts. In these jurisdictions, the protected class of subsequent purchasers is narrowed. To come within it, a subsequent purchaser must not only be a bona fide purchaser, as in a notice act state, but must also be the first to record, as in a race act state. Friendship Manor, Inc. v. Greiman, 244 N.J. Super. 104, 581 A.2d 893 (App. Div. 1990) (charging purchaser with constructive notice).

The following statutory language is typical of a race-notice statute:

> Every conveyance of real property which is not recorded is void as
> against any subsequent purchaser, in good faith, of the same
> real property, whose conveyance is first recorded.

Remember that when litigation occurs between prior and subsequent transferees of the same property, the issue is priority of title. The effectiveness of the deed or other conveyance, as between the parties to it, is not usually the issue. The recording acts do not affect the validity of the documents; they do not render them ineffective as between the parties.

No one disputes that the titleholder who conveys the same property twice is a bad actor and perhaps liable for fraud or misrepresentation. Such a suit is based on the deed given by the holder. If the prior transferee loses the recording act litigation, the holder's misrepresentation in his use of the deed involves an implied promise not to sell the same property again, not to empower a subsequent purchaser to defeat the prior purchaser's interest. If the subsequent purchaser loses, the misrepresentation involves the status of the holder's title. In either event, liability would follow.

The recording acts (of any type) put state legislatures in the unenviable position of choosing which of two parties is going to lose the title that both thought was conveyed and that both expected to receive. Usually both parties are innocent. Hard choices are involved, but clear rules are needed if the conveyancing system is to work smoothly.

# EXAMPLES AND EXPLANATIONS

2a.  O conveys to A, who does not record. Then O conveys to B, a BFP who does not record. O then conveys to C, also a BFP. The applicable act is a notice statute. Who prevails?

**Explanation:** This is the horror story of subsequent purchasers in notice states. B would be a subsequent purchaser protected by the act, except for the fact that O conveyed to a person subsequent to him. If that latter person is a BFP, then he latter becomes the protected party. If O was a bad actor to start with, the fraud he perpetrated once likely won't stand in his way (unless B threatens him with mayhem). Thus in a notice state, it is not strictly speaking true that B has no incentive to record.

2b. What if A paid $10,000, B paid $5000, and C's deed recited that its consideration was "love and affection, and $1 paid in hand"? Now who prevails?

**Explanation:** C prevails if he can show that he is not a donee and is a BFP. Donees do not prevail even though they promptly record, except in Colorado. If C is a donee, then B prevails. B prevails (if he does) regardless of the fact that the fair market value of the property is $10,000 (what A paid). A donee is not a BFP. A BFP must pay something more than nominal damages. "Love and affection" does not qualify C as a BFP. Neither does $1, particularly when the value-to-payment ratio is apparently 10,000 or 5000 to 1. Although C may be able to show that love and affection involved the provision of something more tangible of value, B will prevail if C cannot make that showing.

3. O conveys to A, a donee, who does record. O then conveys to B. Which party prevails?

**Explanation:** A prevails, not as a donee, but because his recording is constructive notice to B, who cannot thereafter become a BFP exactly because he has constructive notice of A's conveyance. B will be treated as if he had searched the title, found A's deed, and thus gained notice of it. Otherwise, B's actions are not the sort that the recording acts wish to encourage. Why, after all, encourage people to be willfully ignorant? The recording acts do not prohibit transfers to donees. (They might not protect them much, as in the prior problem, but that's another matter.) Imagine where intrafamily conveyancing would be if it were so! Finally, it makes no difference whether the first transferee is a BFP or not — it is the subsequent purchaser who, under notice and race-notice acts, must qualify as a BFP.

# "For Value"

Some recording acts provide that the subsequent purchaser "for valuable consideration" is protected by the act (if he meets the act's other requirements). When this proviso is not express in the act, the provision is usually implied by the courts. The subsequent purchaser's reliance on his grantor's clear title causes him no injury until he pays value. Taking the title as a donee causes the subsequent purchaser no injury; it is only when that purchaser subsequently pays the purchase price that he suffers injury. To qualify as a subsequent purchaser "for value," one must pay more than nominal consideration. How much more? The answer is often unclear, and indeed judges are probably hesitant to make the lines too bright. Let's suggest here that more than earnest money or a contract down payment be made; otherwise, a court can use the contract itself as a guide in putting the subsequent purchaser back in his place, status quo ante. Reasonably adequate consideration is required of the subsequent purchaser. See Alexander v. Andrews, 135 W. Va. 403, 64 S.E.2d 487 (1951) (finding that a payment of $1000 for property valued at about $4000 is inadequate, but that $1000 plus an agreement to care for and bury the grantor was adequate).

# EXAMPLES AND EXPLANATIONS

4a.  O conveys to A, who does not record and pays less than full market value. O then conveys to B, a donee, who records. Who as between A and B prevails?

**Explanation:**   Under all types of recording acts, judgment will go for A (again, except in Colorado). Eastwood v. Shedd, 166 Colo. 136, 442 P.2d 423 (1968), interpreting Colo. Rev. Stat. §38-35-109 (1973). Subsequent donees don't win, even when they record promptly to protect their interests. They don't pass the harm threshold, and defeating their interests restores the status quo ante of the whole messy situation.

4b.  Same facts, except that A paid full value and B, no longer a donee, paid enough to believe that he was getting a good deal but not so little as to become suspicious that O had previously conveyed.

**Explanation:**   Judgment for B. Courts do not inquire too closely into the consideration for a conveyance once past the threshold at which B passes for a BFP. Only if B has actual knowledge of the prior transfer would the result change.

4c.  Same facts, except that B takes title as a donee and then goes into possession, improving the property.

**Explanation:**   Most courts require that B pay the purchase price, or contract with a third party to pay it (for example, take out a mortgage loan from a bank), to satisfy the requirement that the class of purchasers protected by the statute take title "for value." The detriment that B suffers by expenditure of time, effort, or money for the improvement can be compensated with a lien on the title, measured by the addition of fair market value or the cost of labor and materials. Lown v. Nichols Plumbing & Heating, Inc., 634 P.2d 554 (Alaska 1981).

4d. Same facts, except that B takes title and records his deed, but mortgage financing problems prevent the closing of a mortgage loan at the same time, so that B holds the title not having paid any of the purchase price. Between the title and the mortgage closing, A records. B's deed recites a substantial consideration, but the deed is held in escrow pending delivery when financing is arranged.

**Explanation:** An unusual situation, but there are cases decided on these facts. Unfortunately, they are split as to the result. Giving B judgment is supported by a policy of penalizing A for not promptly recording. On the other hand, A can argue that B has not yet qualified himself for statutory protection. So long as doubt remains on that issue, B should search the record again before making payment, and his search should stop only on the date payment is made and statutory protection achieved. A's argument rests on the premise that B's lack of notice is insufficient when he has suffered no injury as a result. B's response is that it is A who should be charged with notice of documents on record at the time of his recordation and that he should not be charged with two checks on the record.

Judgment for B.[1] A's recording affords no notice to someone who has already recorded, and meanwhile B has contracted to pay the consideration through mortgage financing and the escrow. Compare *Lown,* supra, with Lowden v. Wilson, 233 Ill. 340, 84 N.E. 245, 249 (1908). More to the point, value should be measured at the point of taking one's estate or interest in the property, not thereafter. Once taking the title, B is entitled to arrange to contract to pay — just as he would be entitled to turn around and transfer the title for value. The court should protect his right to alienate and can do so only if it protects his right to secure his title too.

# Subsequent Purchasers

A subsequent purchaser includes any person taking a deed to real property, mortgagees (either as purchasers of a mortgage lien or by specific reference), but not (unless expressly mentioned) lessees. Often leases with a term of three years or more are expressly made recordable, but for these purposes, a

---

1. For a contrary but well-articulated view, see Mattis, Recording Acts: Anachronistic Reliance, 25 Real Prop. Prob. & Tr. J. 17, 56-62 (1990).

lease may be regarded as a transfer of possession, rather than a conveyance or else a transfer not "for value" as we have previously discussed that term.

The term subsequent purchaser also, and often expressly, includes a person paying a portion of the agreed purchase price under an otherwise enforceable contract of sale for real property.

# EXAMPLES AND EXPLANATIONS

5. In a state in which contracts of sale are recordable, O conveys to A, who does not record, and then contracts to sell to B, a BFP who pays a down payment and records. Who has priority of title?

**Explanation:**  Judgment for B, but the court should condition the granting of title upon B's payment of the outstanding portion of the purchase price to A. O is estopped to protest this condition, and A is assigned O's rights in the contract, unperformed at the time B learns of A. Mitchell v. Dawson, 23 W. Va. 86, 88 (1883).

## Judgment Holders as Protected Parties

Some (about one-half) of the recording statutes expressly provide that subsequent judgment lien creditors are protected. Subsequent creditors, as such, are not protected; it is only when a creditor reduces a debt to judgment that the issue arises of how to treat the judgment lien created when the judgment is docketed or entered on the court records.[2] See generally, Schechter, Judicial Lien Creditors Versus Prior Unrecorded Transferees of Real Property: Rethinking the Goals of the Recording System and Their Consequences, 62 S. Cal. L. Rev. 105 (1988).

# EXAMPLES AND EXPLANATIONS

6. Suppose O conveys to A, who does not record but who pays value sufficient not to put him on notice of any difficulties with O's title. B then

---

2. The law governing judgment lien creditors is state statutory law. Many state statutes provide that a state court's granting a judgment itself creates a general lien on all of the debtor's real property (as defined by state law) in the county in which the judgment is rendered. Other state statutes provide that docketing of the judgment in the county in which the debtor has real property creates the lien. In the former category of jurisdictions, the creditor need do no more than secure the judgment; in the latter, the creditor has to do more, that is, he must have the judgment docketed in the appropriate book of judgments, under the name of the debtor named in the judgment. In Alabama, Georgia, and Mississippi, a judgment lien reaches both real and personal property; in California, business personal property is reached. Federal court judgments are subjected to the rule of the state in which the federal district court sits, except that federal court judgments cannot be treated more stringently than a state court's. See 28 U.S.C. §1962. Out-of-state judgment creditors must generally bring an action to enforce the judgment of another state's courts.

obtains a judgment lien, which is docketed before A records his conveyance. Who prevails?

**Explanation:** In some states it is held that a judgment lienor does not fall within the class protected by the recording act because he has not paid value in reliance upon O's title to his real property. Judgment for A on that account; even though A was not the first to record, he was the first to record "for value," meaning value given on account of the real property. The arguments for B would involve interpreting the phrase "subsequent purchaser" to include B — quite a stretch! (Although there are cases doing just that). Check local law and the wording of the statute on this.

7. In a jurisdiction in which subsequent purchasers encompass judgment lienors, does B, a person who records a mortgage taken to secure or in exchange for a preexisting debt, prevail over A's prior unrecorded mortgage or deed?

**Explanation:** The weight of authority says that a lien creditor like B has not relied on the records in extending the initial loan or credit that created the debt and so is not a creditor protected by the act (of any type). B must show himself to be one who in the initial credit transaction customarily searches and relies on the public records. In addition, the execution of the mortgage in exchange for the preexisting debt requires some additional consideration if the mortgage transaction is to avoid the charge that the lien creditor did not take his interest in the property "for value." A preexisting debt is not "value" as required for an effective recording. There must be some additional consideration given at the time of taking the mortgage. See Osin v. Johnson, 100 U.S. App. D.C. 230, 243 F.2d 653 (D.C. Cir. 1957); Gabel v. Drewry's, Ltd., USA, Inc., 68 So. 2d 372, 39 A.L.R.2d 1083 (Fla. 1953). So judgment for A.

While a contrary result might be justified as a means of punishing A, the prior grantee who does not record promptly, the lack of reliance by the subsequent mortgagee B represents a better rationale.

# Bringing the Recording within the Chain of Title

Incorporated into the recording act (of any type) are the practices of the local abstractors or searchers of titles. They search the public records by first chaining the title and then searching for conveyances from the owners forming the chain.

Chaining the title involves a search backward in time. A prospective purchaser knows the name of his vendor. He searches for that name in the index of grantees (or purchasers), and when he finds it he looks across the page for the cross-reference to the name of the vendor involved in the last completed purchase and sale transaction — in which his vendor was the purchaser.

The chaining search then continues by repeating this process, looking for the name of the last-found vendor in the index of grantees. When this process has been repeated enough to find out who held the title for the search period (60 years at common law, but often back to the date the property came out of the public domain), the chain is complete.

Then the search shifts to the grantor indexes, looking for conveyances out of the owners in the chain. This involves a search that goes forward in time, back to the present. The result of this part of the title search is a series of references, by book and page number, to a series of deeds, mortgages, and other documents. The searcher then goes to the books referenced and obtains copies of the documents conveying the title, or encumbering it, down to the present.

# EXAMPLES AND EXPLANATIONS

In the following problems, there is case authority for the results indicated, but there is also often a split in the cases. Purging the title of out-of-the-chain documents has a title cleansing effect, provides abstractors of title with clear rules for guiding their work in the record room, and encourages all transferees to record their documents promptly. In this light, consider the following problems.

7a.  O conveys to A, who does not record. A conveys to B, who records. O then conveys to C, a BFP who does not record. Who, B or C, prevails in a race state?

**Explanation:**   No one wins under a race recording act. A's recording is not within the chain of title that C will search. C will be looking for conveyances out of O and will not, using the records arranged by the names of grantors and grantees, find A's conveyance. A might have priority of title, but not because of the recording act. Rather, A wins because the common law rule prefers his chain of title; it is first in time.

There is authority for the foregoing result (but the cases are not uniform). First to record, under a race statute, is thus interpreted to mean first to effectively give notice by recording. The tension here is that the recording statute in grantor-grantee index states nowhere mentions the need to record within the chain of title.

What should B have done? He should have recorded A's conveyance, and only after that recording put his own conveyance on the record. Then there would be a chain of title leading subsequent purchasers like C to the record of his interest. Bringing one's recording within the protection of the act means recording not just one's own interest but also any interests leading to it.

7b. Same facts, except that the recording act is a notice type.

**Explanation:** C wins under a notice recording act because it requires only that C be a subsequent BFP. He is that and prevails on that account.

7c. Same facts, except that C is no longer a BFP but does record, and the recording act is a race one.

**Explanation:** C wins. He has become the first to record in such a way that his chain of title can be searched; he is the first to validly record. If C still had his bona fides, he would also win in a race-notice state because he would then have done both of the things required by that type of recording act: been the first to record validly and be a BFP.

Sometimes the person protected by a recording act has not fulfilled all of the requirements of the act himself. He then relies on the actions performed by his predecessors in his chain of title. Consider the following examples.

8. O conveys to A, who does not record. B has notice of the O-A conveyance. O then conveys to B, who records. B then conveys to BFP C. Who prevails?

**Explanation:** C prevails in all jurisdictions. In a race state, B is the first to record and his knowledge is irrelevant to his protection. B conveys his priority of title over A in his conveyance to C. Conversely, it is said that C shelters under the right of B to alienate a title superior to A. This rationale is often described as the "shelter rule." The rule is also a recognition that, in this instance, B is permitted to convey a better title than he has. (Violating this basic rule reveals, of course, the weakest link in this analysis and reiterates the fact that, in recording act cases, the courts are forced to choose between two innocents; someone is going to get burned.) In a notice state, C is a subsequent BFP and that qualifies him for protection under the statute. In a race-notice state, C wins again. If he won in the first two types of states, he automatically wins in the race-notice type of state because this third type of statute combines the elements required for protection in the other two. He satisfies the BFP requirement of notice states himself and takes his recording priority over A from the actions of his grantor B, regardless of B's knowledge. C takes free of the taint of that knowledge. (C is often said to be "freed of the equities" that might attach to B in this situation.) See Morse v. Curtis, 140 Mass. 112, 2 N.E. 929 (1885); contra Woods v. Garnett, 72 Miss. 78, 16 So. 390 (1894).

The previous problem is an example of the working of the recording acts through the concept of a chain of title. The mechanics of abstracting a title in a grantor-grantee index is important to the functioning and interpretation of the recording acts, although nowhere mentioned in the acts themselves. Consider the following (a variation on Example 7) in this regard.

9a. O conveys to A, who does not record. O then conveys to B, who does not record. A then conveys to C, who does record. Who prevails?

**Explanation:** In a race state, C's recording is ineffective. B or B's abstractor cannot find it. Either one will be searching the record for conveyances by O, and because they can't find A on the public records, they also can't find C. A race state, then, requires an *effective* recording. In this situation, effectiveness means enabling an abstractor to reach the recorded documents — which can't be done here! In a race state, the first to record between A and B will establish priority of title. Neither has done that, and the common law rule still applies as between A and B. The further question is, should A's common law priority be given to C? The better view is, probably not. This for the reason that, if it is, C will have no incentive to record A's deed, and then his own, to complete the chain of title down to himself. If the recording acts are seen as an incentive to keep the public records in the best shape possible, reflecting the true state of a title, then C should be given every incentive to get his grantor's deed on the record.

In a notice state, B wins if he is a BFP. In a race-notice state, no one is yet protected by the statute.

If a purchaser seeks the protection of a recording act, he must make sure that unrecorded documents in his chain of title are recorded in an order that will enable an abstractor to reach him once the chain of title is established.

9b. Using the same facts, if A recorded after C, that recording would be ineffective in all states. Do you see why?

**Explanation:** A's failure to record before C does puts A's later recording outside the chain of title. A must record first, followed by C, to establish an effective chain.

10. O conveys to A, who does not record. O conveys to B, who does not record. A records. B conveys to C, a BFP who records. What arguments can you make for A and C?

**Explanation:** A argues that C should extend the period of search out of O to the date on which C takes. If he does so, he or his abstractor will discover A's recorded conveyance. C argues that A's failure to record promptly permitted O to convey again and that the title search should be conducted in the usual manner. Title searches would be too expensive otherwise. (If the facts were changed slightly — and if B had recorded, but not promptly — this efficiency argument is diminished. How would a prudent abstractor search C's title?)

11. Would your answers to these problems change if the abstractor used a tract index instead of a grantor-grantee index?

**Explanation:** Yes, if by statute the tract index has the notice-giving, self-proving legal consequences attributed to the grantor-grantee index. Then a subsequent purchaser could not ignore out-of-chain documents; rather, he would have to make a reasonable inquiry into the transaction that the documents purport to reflect, and be on constructive notice of what that inquiry would yield.

However, if the statutes are not clear on the legal effect of the tract index, the answers probably would not change. Even if the title searcher consults a tract index and there finds a document recorded outside the chain of title, the legal effect of seeing the document may be nil. This is so because the legal record often remains the grantor-grantee index, not the tract index. What is recorded there provides the notice with which subsequent purchasers are charged. "Recording outside of the grantor-grantee index, as in the tract index, is recording merely for convenience." Skidmore, Owings & Merrill v. Pathway Fin., 173 Ill. App. 3d 512, 527 N.E.2d 1033, 1035 (1988). What purpose is left for a tract index? Well, remember that it is just that — an index — and, as such, is a useful corrective for the recorder's mistakes in indexing by name. So assuming that the "recording" is within the chain of title, the tract index serves as a check on the name index.

Finally, no matter what type of index is used, what if the formalities required by the recording acts are not met? The acknowledgment may not be valid. Messersmith v. Smith, 60 N.W.2d 276 (N.D. 1953) (held that no constructive notice is imparted by a defectively acknowledged deed). How sensible is such a holding? Not very. To this effect, see Amoskeag Bank v. Chagnon, 133 N.H. 11, 572 A.2d 1153 (1990) (improperly recorded mortgage is sufficient to obligate purchaser to inquire whether properly acknowledged mortgage exists off record); In re Sandy Ridge Oil Co., Inc., 510 N.E.2d 667 (Ind. 1987), noted at 22 Ind. L. Rev. 369, 394-397 (1989) (held that the failure to meet the statutory requirement that the name of the deed's preparer be stated on the document does not destroy the notice-giving effect of its recordation; the requirement, it was found, was intended by the legislature to deter the unauthorized practice of law, not to affect the recording). Finally, some states will have a statute curing defect such as this when the document has been on the record and unchallenged for one to three years. Of such curative statutes, further discussion appears in Chapter 16.

# Circuity of Interests

O conveys to A, who does not record. O then conveys to B, who records first but takes with notice of A's interest. O then conveys to C, who takes without notice of A but with notice of B, and records.

This scenario results not only from a series of voluntary transfers, such as contracts, deeds, and mortgages, but also from a series of involuntary ones (arising out of judgment liens). Under nonrace acts, A, B, and C are each superior and at the same time inferior to each other: A has priority over B, B has priority over C, and C has priority over A. Circuitous priority results: There are more than two liens, and each is inferior to another.

One solution to this problem is to say that here we have a situation that the recording acts are incapable of handling and that therefore the common law controls: First in time, first in right, then, is the governing principle. This solution might be appealing when A's failure to record is due, not to his own efforts, but to the misindexing of his interest by the recorder of deeds.

What should be done? In reaching the preferred solution, assume that the fair market value of the property is $100,000, but that a judicial sale brings only $80,000. That amount ($80,000) is what is available to satisfy all claims. Further assume that A's claim on the $80,000 is $40,000, B's is $20,000, and C's is $40,000, but not all of these amounts can be paid in full.

Now first, take the $80,000 and subtract the amount of the claim about which C had notice. This latter amount is the amount of B's claim, or $20,000. So: $80,000 − $20,000 = $60,000. Sixty thousand is the amount available to satisfy C's claim. C's $40,000 claim falls within this latter $60,000, so C will be paid in full. Hold $40,000 for C.

Second, with the same amount available ($80,000), subtract the amount about which B knew: $80,000 − $40,000 (A's claim) = $40,000. This is more than B's claim of $20,000, so B will be paid in full too. Hold $20,000 for B.

Third, take the remainder and pay A with it. Because $60,000 is now held for payments to C and B ($40,000 and $20,000, respectively), only $80,000 − $60,000, or $20,000, is left to pay A. Thus A will *not* be paid in full; A gets $20,000 or half of his claim.

There is a general principle at work here: Everyone competing for the available fund is paid from that fund, minus the amounts of which each had notice, and the last transferee, as the subsequent purchaser protected in some form by the recording act, is first paid. For a recent use of this method in a personal property case, see ITT Diversified Credit Corp. v. First City Capital Corp., 737 S.W.2d 803, 804 (Tex. 1987), noted at 19 Tex. Tech. L.Rev. 1511, 1518-1522 (1988) (providing a good summary of the various solutions).

This problem of circuity arises in several contexts. The first we have seen. The second is a land development problem in which A is a farmer, holding land that O, a developer, would like to develop. Being thinly capitalized, O agrees with A that A will take back a purchase money mortgage for some portion of the price of the land. O also agrees with A that A in the future will subordinate the priority of his lien to a later construction loan and mortgage lien. This subordination agreement is not recorded. A sells the land to O and takes back this mortgage lien. O then mortgages the land again to B, who knows of A's lien. What B doesn't know, however, is that C, appropriately here a construction lender, makes a construction mortgage to O, takes back a lien, and claims the benefit of the off-record, subordination agreement giving C priority over A. A, B, and C all record their liens promptly.

In some cases, B is paid first, then C, and then lastly A. Sometimes this solution is known as the New Jersey rule. B knew nothing of the A-C subordination agreement and should not suffer for it. C is next preferred because this preference gives him the benefit of his agreement with A, who is left with the residue of the available funds.

Is this fair? To the extent that B is preferred first even though he never should expect to take priority over A, it is not. Also, C has his expectation defeated when he expected to step into A's shoes.

Is there a better solution? Again, yes. Assume that A's claim is $40,000, B's $10,000, and C's $40,000, and that a judicial sale brings $50,000. Then, out of the $50,000 set aside the amount of A's claim, or $40,000; then pay out the $40,000 first to C, up to the amount of his claim, then to the extent there is a balance remaining, pay out the remainder to A. (So far, C will be paid $40,000 and A nothing.) Pay the remainder of the available fund to B, so B gets the remaining $10,000. There is nothing left to pay A any of his claim.

Paying C and A out of A's claim, first set aside, prevents B from getting a windfall from a priority that he never expected to have. However, the subordination agreement is enforced only to the extent that it can be satisfied out of A's claim, of which B knew. Then B is paid, out of the fund available, minus A's claim of which he had notice. This gives B the benefit of the priority that he did expect, irrespectively of the subordination agreement. Then, if proceeds are still available, the subordination agreement is enforced again to the extent of any funds not yet paid out: first to C, as the agreement anticipated, and then to A.

A third context in which circuity is a problem involves mortgages and federal and state income tax liens. For an example see In re Holly Knitwear

Inc., 140 N.J. Super. 375, 356 A.2d 405 (App. Div. 1976). Thus if A is a mortgagee, B holds a state lien, and C a federal lien, the federal lien is superior to a state lien but must be recorded to be effective against mortgage liens previously recorded; and state liens are superior to all recorded mortgages; and A and B record promptly, circuity results again (with the same solution). Can you work it out?

# Indexing

The majority of states hold that the index is not a part of the official record. The consequence of this holding is that a purchaser, recording and thus relying on the records to give notice to subsequent takers, is not responsible for checking the index to find out if the document is properly indexed. Haner v. Bruce, 146 Vt. 262, 499 A.2d 792 (1985), noted in 12 Vt. L. Rev. 283 (1987); see generally Annot., Failure properly to index conveyance or mortgage of realty as effective constructive notice, 63 A.L.R. 1057, 1058, n.12 (1929). Thus in only a few states — Iowa, North Carolina, Pennsylvania, Washington, and Wisconsin — is indexing regarded as the final step in recording and the purchaser given the responsibility of checking the record for mistakes in the index. Compiano v. Jones, 269 N.W.2d 459 (Iowa 1978). How sensible is the majority rule on indexing? See Howard Sav. Bank v. Brunson, 244 N.J. Super. 571, 582 A.2d 1305, 1309-1310 (Ch. Div. 1990) (in this opinion New Jersey takes some tentative steps into the minority rule camp). Doesn't a holding that the recorded but misindexed document imparts constructive notice set off a search for a needle in a documentary haystack?

# Rights of Parties in Possession

A final point. A right to real property manifest by the possession of its holder (or his agent) takes precedence over any right arising under the recording acts. Indeed, remember that the recording acts do not create any rights that would not exist independently of the documents recorded; they only establish a priority of rights. Another way of saying this is that establishing priority of title under the acts is no substitute for a thorough inspection of the property itself. Not only is an inspection valuable to a purchaser interested in the physical condition of the property, but it also will reveal any rights in possession — for example, a tenant who can tell the purchaser of the possessory rights of his landlord, a visible easement across the property, an adverse claimant in possession, or a neighbor adversely possessing land along the boundaries to the property.

The problems that can arise from this inspection can be tough ones. For example, a tenant in possession consistent with a lease does not provide the prospective purchaser with notice of an unrecorded option to purchase the property, which is not a part of the lease itself. And a tenant in common, when in possession, has the right to possession of the whole property, but that is not inconsistent with the rights of other co-tenants who all own undivided fractional shares of the property. An unrecorded prior conveyance by an out-of-possession co-tenant may be effective against the subsequent purchaser who does not track down all the co-tenants and have them execute deeds of their interest to him. What if the spouse of the record owner is in possession? Today one can't assume that this possession is consistent with the record without some further inquiry.

Mark Twain loved cats and insisted that each home should have at least one. "A home without a cat may be a perfect home, perhaps," he said, "but how can it prove title?"

# 15

## Title Searches, Abstracts, and Title Insurance

## Abstracts of Title

An abstract of title is the result of the title search. It is the title searcher's written memorandum and work product. As such, it is a summary of the documents comprising the chain of title, as well as any liens or encumbrances on that title, all arranged in chronological order. See Root, An Abstract of Title, 14 Am. L. Reg. 529 (1875) (for a detailed definition). Each document noted in the abstract is called a link in the chain of title, and the links, taken together, constitute the chain going back in time for the period of the search. In many jurisdictions, an abstractor works in the public records office (or offices) to compile the documentary material that goes into the abstract. When a title insurance company compiles an abstract, it often uses documentary materials in its own possession, together with its own indexes; thus it does not rely wholly on the public records. Rather, some larger title companies, singly or in combination with other companies, daily copy or "take off" the public records customarily searched in the jurisdiction, and the "take-offs" become the company's "title plant."

Once the abstract is compiled, it is reviewed, often by an attorney, and often by an attorney approved or employed by a title insurance company, which issues a title insurance policy using the abstract as a basis for drafting the exceptions to coverage in the policy. An attorney in private practice issues a certificate of title. Warvelle on Abstracts, ch. 32, at 615-655 (4th ed. 1921). When a title insurance company employs in-house abstractors, it compiles a preliminary report on title, showing the interests that it will list as exceptions to coverage. Such a report functions in many regions today as an abstract and gives the parties notice of the less than fee interests to cure or deal with in other ways, before the closing.

For examples of title review problems in particular states, see Fishman, The History of a Maryland Title: A Conveyancer's Romance Renewed, 42 Md. L. Rev. 496 (1983); Kubicek & Kubicek, Selected Topics in Examination of Abstracts of Title, 26 Drake L. Rev. 1 (1976); Mazel, Two Perspectives on the Real Estate Title System: How to Examine a Title in Virginia, 11 U. Rich. L. Rev. 471 (1977); Tyler, Pitfalls in Title Examination, 35 Mass. B.Q. 20 (1950).

# EXAMPLES AND EXPLANATIONS

1. What if in the course of reviewing the policy, you discover that in one document in the chain of title, there is a nine-month elapsed time between the date of the deed and the date of recording?

**Explanation:** The delay in recording is suggestive of a conditional delivery, and inquiry of the parties about the condition is in order.

2. What if you discover that the grantee in one deed in the chain is Billy Joe Barton, but later, as a grantor, the name on the deed is William Barton?

**Explanation:** The doctrine of idem sonens states that like-sounding name variations between the name of a person taking title as a grantee and a name used as the next grantor in the chain of title do not render the title unmarketable. The cure is an affidavit to the effect that the different names were used by one and the same person. See J. I. Case Credit v. Barton, 621 F. Supp. 610 (D. Ark. 1985).

3. V agrees to sell Blackacre to P. V employs an abstractor, A, to search the title. At the closing, V delivers to P an abstract of title produced by A. P immediately presents the abstract to a mortgage lender M and requests that it be used in conjunction with her application for a loan secured by Blackacre. The abstractor fails to disclose another prior mortgage on Blackacre.

Two years later, P applies for a second mortgage and again presents the abstract to a mortgage lender M1. M1 loans P money for home improvement in return for a note and a mortgage lien on Blackacre. Later still, P attempts to sell Blackacre to P1. P again presents the abstract. P1 accepts it and the P-P1 transaction is closed.

Do P, M, M1, and P1 all have a cause of action against the abstractor? If so, what is the measure of damages in each action?

**Explanation:** To bring a cause of action against an abstractor of title, P, M, M1, or P1 will have to show that she is (1) in privity of contract with A, or (2) that the use made of the abstract was reasonably foreseeable on A's part. Privity of contract is the traditional, once universal rule, but has given way in recent cases to a rule of reasonable foreseeability. P is certainly within the ambit of foreseeability, and so is M, although many cases involving a mortgagee will probably also involve mortgages that were executed contemporaneously with the closing of the title, and so the lapse of time cannot be too long for M to prevail. The longer the intervening time, the less likely it is that the use of the abstract is foreseeable. Thus M1 and P1 may have difficulty bringing a cause of action. The following case discusses this issue and the damages question.

# Abstractors' Liability

In Williams v. Polgar, 43 Mich. App. 95, 204 N.W.2d 57 (1972), aff'd, 391 Mich. 6, 215 N.W.2d 149 (1974), noted at 21 Wayne L. Rev. 139 (1974), an installment land sale contract purchaser brought suit for negligent misrepresentation against an abstract company. The purchaser had had a prior abstract recertified when first undertaking to purchase property, and had it recertified periodically. The abstract had first been compiled in 1926, but then, and subsequently, failed to include proceedings widening an abutting street. Twelve years after taking possession under the contract, the plaintiffs brought suit.

The Michigan Supreme Court held that the plaintiffs had stated a cause of action for negligent misrepresentation and that the cause sounded in tort, so that the first issue was to establish that the abstract company owed the plaintiffs a duty. To resolve this issue, the plaintiffs had to be one of a protected class of persons who the abstract could foresee would rely on the abstract issued (in the normal situation in Michigan) to the vendors. The court found that the purchasers were within the zone of foreseeability. Finally, the court held that the statute of limitations on the cause of action ran from the time of the discovery of the omission in the abstract, rather than (as a majority of courts had previously held) from the time the abstract was issued. The court saw no danger of unmanageable liability for the abstract resulting from its holding: the limited numbers of parties to any real property transaction precluded such a possibility.

For a case adhering to the majority rule on the statute of limitations, see Anderson v. Boone County Abstract Co., 418 S.W.2d 123, 34 A.L.R.3d 1111 (Mo. 1967). For attorney liability cases for negligent examination of an abstract, see Annot., Attorney's liability, to one other than his immediate client, for consequences of negligence in carrying out legal duties, 45 A.L.R.3d 1181, 1200-1202 (1972).

The litigation in the *Williams* case went on and on. See Williams v. American Title Ins. Co., 83 Mich. App. 686, 269 N.W.2d 481 (1978) (affirming an award for consequential damages for demolition and relocation of building).

Thus an abstractor today is generally liable not only to the party for whom the abstract is prepared, but also to those who did in fact or who would foreseeably rely on the abstract. Negligent misrepresentation, however, is no picnic for plaintiffs: There are numerous elements to the tort, all of which must be proven by the plaintiff.

# Regulation of Abstractors

Many states' statutes govern the type of bond an abstractor must post before conducting business, the type of real property records that must be maintained, and the expertise of the abstractor as determined by testing and educational requirements. Eckhardt, Abstractor's Licensing Laws, 28 Mo. L. Rev. 1 (1963).

# Title Insurance

## *The Policy*

Title insurance policies[1] insure "against loss or damages, not exceeding the amount of insurance stated in Schedule A, plus costs, attorneys' fees, . . . sustained or incurred by the insured," by reason of (1) the title to the estate or interest described in Schedule A "being vested otherwise than as stated"; (2) a "defect . . . on such title"; (3) "lack of a right of access to and from the land"; and (4) the unmarketability of the title. For the policy, the holder pays one premium, for which she obtains coverage for as long as she holds the insured title, and even beyond, in the situation in which she is asked to make good on the deed warranties that she gives as a vendor of the insured title.

Schedule A is the first of three component parts to a title policy. It defines the estate or interest that the policy insures. It is a statement of

---

1. The phrases quoted in this and subsequent paragraphs are found in the owners and lenders policy forms issued in 1970 and 1990 by the American Land Title Association (ALTA), the major title insurers' trade group.

coverage. What Schedule A gives, however, the second component, Schedule B, limits, for it is a statement of the results of the title search. Thus, if the search uncovers defects on the title, they are recited as exceptions to coverage in Schedule B. With these recitations, the insurer can do a great deal to limit its risk of having ever to pay a claim. It is the functional equivalent of an application for insurance used in other types of insurance. The information it contains is used to assess the risk of issuing a policy. Often this schedule contains preprinted, standardized exclusions from coverage as well.

A third component of the policy is its "Conditions and Stipulations," covering such topics as the insurer's duty to defend the insured title, the procedures for making a claim and defining a loss, the measure of damages, and other subjects.

In all, title insurance has three aspects. It is an indemnity agreement (not a guarantee of the status of the title); it is litigation insurance; and, perhaps above all, it involves the hiring of experts in title matters. Make sure that you can trace these aspects of the policy through its provisions. In particular, as to the second, notice the differences between the 1970 and 1990 ALTA policies.

As to the first (indemnity) aspect of the policy, the policy should be seen as looking both backward and forward in time. Its two faces pivot around the date of the policy. One face looks back, to determine the facts and the interests that the policy both insures and excepts. The other face looks forward into the future, after the date of the policy, to await the assertion of a claim adverse to the insured title. This aspect of the policy has an impact on the measure of damages as well. Only losses that are "actual" and "sustained or incurred" are insured. (With this aspect in mind, would you advise a client who has just inherited or been given property to have her title insured?)

The second, litigation component is triggered by the insurer's duty to defend the insured title. This duty is sometimes analogized to the title covenants in a deed. This analogy, however, is of limited value. The duty to defend is broader than the duty to pay a claim. Because the duty must be performed before the duty to pay becomes clear, the insurer will often have to defend in instances in which it ultimately will not have to pay, as for example will be the situation when its defense is successful.

The third component of the policy is a matter of the expectations of the insured. Nowhere in the policy does the insurer undertake to make a search of the title, but why else would many insureds be interested in a policy? Don't the exclusions define the extent of the search and force the insured when applying for insurance to disclose facts that will aid the searcher? (Indeed, in what situations would you advise a client to obtain title insurance when the title has already been searched by an abstractor and examined by a competent attorney?)

The following, short-form policy is typical.

# OWNER'S POLICY OF TITLE INSURANCE

Subject to the exclusions, exceptions, and conditions later appearing, The Blank Title Insurance Company insures *as of the date of the policy,* against *loss or damage* not exceeding the amount of insurance shown herein, and costs, attorneys' fees and expenses which the Company may become obligated to pay, *sustained or incurred* by the insured by reason of:

1. *title to* the estate or interest described in Schedule A being *vested otherwise* than as stated therein; or
2. any defect in or lien or encumbrance on such title; or
3. lack of a right of access to and from the land; or
4. the unmarketability of such title.

## *SCHEDULE A*

Policy No.: _____

Date of Policy: _____

Amount of Insurance: _____

Name of Insured: _____

Estate or Interest Insured: _____

Description of Land: _____

## EXCLUSIONS FROM COVERAGE

1. Any law, ordinance, or *governmental regulation* (including but not limited to housing or building codes and zoning or subdivision regulations).

2. Rights of eminent domain or governmental rights of police power unless notice of the exercise of such rights appears in the public records at the date of this policy.

3. *Defects,* liens, encumbrances, adverse claims, or other matters (a) *created, suffered, assumed, or agreed to* by the insured; (b) *not known to the Company and not shown on the public records, but known to the insured* at the date of the policy or at the time the insured took the estate or interest insured; (c) resulting in no loss or damage to the insured; (d) attaching or created subsequent to the date of this policy.

## *SCHEDULE B*

The Company does not insure

1. rights or claims of parties in possession;
2. what an accurate survey would disclose;
3. easements not shown on the public record;

4.   mechanic's liens;
5.   taxes not yet liens on the date of this policy;
and [here are noted the results of the title search].

## CONDITIONS

The coverage of this policy continues so long as the insured retains an estate or interest in the land or has liability by reason of covenants of warranty, provided that coverage shall not continue in favor of any purchaser from the insured of such estate or interest.

The Company, at its own cost and without undue delay, shall *provide for the defense* of the insured in all litigation consisting of actions or proceedings against the insured to the extent that the litigation is founded upon an alleged defect, lien, encumbrance, or other matter insured against by this policy, provided the insured notifies the Company promptly in writing of such litigation. The Company has the *right* to prosecute any action or proceeding *to establish* the title as insured, whether or not liable hereunder. Whenever the Company interposes any defense or brings any action or proceeding to establish the title as insured, the Company may pursue any such litigation to final determination and reserves the right to conduct all appeals from any adverse judgment or order. The insured shall cooperate with the Company in any such litigation and appeal.

The Company shall have the option to pay or settle any litigation, action, or proceeding for or in the name of the insured or terminate all liability to the insured by payment of the amount of the insurance shown herein, together with the payment of all costs, attorneys' fees, and expenses incurred up to the date of payment.

The Company's liability under this policy shall in no case exceed the least of (a) the actual loss of the insured, or (b) the amount of insurance stated in Schedule A, payable within 30 days after the amount of loss or damage is definitely fixed.

No claim under this policy is maintainable (a) if the Company removes the defect, lien, or encumbrance or establishes the title as insured, or (b) until there is a final determination and disposition of all appeals adverse to the title, or (c) for liability voluntarily assumed by an insured in settling any claim or suit without the prior written consent of the Company.

All payments under this policy or another policy insuring any mortgagee of the insured title reduces the amount of insurance pro tanto. Whenever the Company settles any claim under this policy, all right of subrogation shall vest in the Company, which shall thereafter be entitled to all rights and remedies which the insured would have had with respect to the insured title. This policy is the *entire contract* between the insured and the Company and any claim for loss or damage, whether or not based on negligence, shall be restricted to the provisions, conditions, and stipulations of this policy. Notice of loss or claim required by the policy shall be sent in writing to the principal place of business of the Company, _____.

## Policy Highlights

Title insurers give some of the phrases of the policy particular meanings or a particular emphasis. Consider the following phrases.

*Insures as of the date of the policy.* This phrase emphasizes the risk elimination aspect of title insurance. The insurer does not insure future events or nonevents. This type of insurance is unlike health, accident, or life insurance. It looks into the past, not the future: it reflects the state of the title as of the date of the policy. The "description" of the insured title in Schedule A (referred to in the first statement of coverage) reenforces this notion, and exclusion 3(d) provides the mirror image of this phrasing.

The date of the policy is not necessarily its date of issuance. In many regions of the country, it is issued after the closing and after the insurer has had a chance to perform a last-minute search for documents both affecting the insured title and recorded up to the time the deed is filed for record. This can be many days after the closing, but the policy might still be dated either as of the closing or the date on which the bring-down search is completed.

*Against loss or damage . . . sustained or incurred.* These phrases serve to emphasize the indemnity aspect of the policy. If the insured title is encumbered by an interest covered (and not excepted or excluded) by the policy, the encumbrance must result in a loss to the insured. Often this means that the encumbrance must be asserted, rather than merely discovered to exist. Exclusion 3(c) mirrors this phrasing.

*Title to.* Notice that in the statements of coverage the references are to the title to an estate or interest, any defect or lien on the title, or a right of access. The insurer is taking pains to emphasize that the land, or possession of the land, is not insured — only title to an interest in the land is covered. The first three standard exceptions, shown here in Schedule B, reenforce this point: the "rights of parties in possession," "what an accurate survey would disclose," and "easements not shown on the public record" are not insured.

*Vested otherwise.* This phrase, found in the first statement of coverage in the policy, has two meanings. Primarily it is a reiteration of the requirement of a loss or damage. That the insured title is not as described is insufficient for a claim; the title must also be "vested otherwise," meaning that it must exist in someone other than the insured — a someone who is presumably capable of asserting it as well. Secondarily, the phrase is also taken as a negation of the requirement of an insurable interest in the insured. Insurers sometimes attempt to argue that if the title or interest insured never was in the insured then there never was any coverage. Title insurance is thus a policy issued against the possibility that the insured may be found to lack the insurable interest that she was thought to hold. The idea of an insurable interest does not fit well with it.

*Exclusions for . . . governmental regulations,* as well as rights of eminent domain and the police power, all contained in the first two exclusions, makes the fundamental point that only private interests are insured. Assertions against the insured title based on public rights are excluded. Notice, however, that some public rights are excluded categorically; those related to building and housing codes, zoning, and subdivision regulations are examples. Others, such as those based on eminent domain and the police power, are excluded, unless exercised and appearing of record — in which instance, they can be searched for and discovered in the course of a title search.

*Defects . . . created, suffered, assumed, or agreed to.* This is the broadest, perhaps the most litigated of the exclusions from coverage. It is in part a reiteration of the principle stated in the Conditions, to the effect that "liability voluntarily assumed" by the insured in settling a claim without prior consent of the insurer creates no coverage. Here, however, the objective is to prevent the insured from creating a defect on the insured title and then basing a policy claim on it. An actual intent is necessary on the insured's part. If the defect is the unintended legal consequence of the insured's act, the exclusion does not apply. However, the cases often treat this string of verbs as if they have different — and increasingly broad — meanings. With this in mind, the phrase "defects . . . and other matters" may also be given generous meanings, and the doctrine of ejusdem generis may not apply. Remember that exclusions in any policy of insurance, not just title insurance, are to be narrowly construed, particularly so when they defeat the expectations of the insured.

Will this exclusion, known as Exclusion 3(a), prevent the insured from recovering on a defect arising because of faulty closing procedures at the insured's own closing?

*Defects . . . not known to the Company and not shown on the public records, but known to the insured.* This is the second most-often invoked exclusion; here insurers eliminate from coverage those defects for which no search of the public records can be conducted but of which the insured knows when the policy is issued.

The *Conditions* generally commence with a series of definitions. They make plain that the insured's coverage continues indefinitely. This is not term insurance. However, the coverage cannot be assigned, except as expressly permitted by the policy, to any purchaser of the insured. Once the insured sells the insured title, the policy is converted into coverage for any further liability that the insured may have for warranties given in the deed or other document by which the sale is accomplished. Thus only this warranty coverage survives the sale of the insured title by the insured.

The Conditions contain a *duty to defend* the insured title, as well as the *right to establish* it. The words are litigation-oriented, but they extend to an administrative proceeding as well. If there is a right to establish the insured title, there may also be a duty to establish the title. A principle of mutuality supports such a duty. However, this duty, once undertaken, can be pursued through all appeals. A condition in the policy 7(b), reiterates this principle. A good faith duty to settle the claim (not express in the policy) may in many cases result in speedier settlements of the dispute for the insured. Once undertaken, any litigation is in the insurer's hands. Successful litigation is, in these conditions, clearly an alternative to payment of the claim. The insured cannot have both payment of the claim and the title as insured — that would be a windfall to her. Payment of the claim gives the insurer a subrogation right to any entitlement previously held by the insured.

The policy attempts, through an *"entire contract* or agreement" clause, to restrict any claim based on negligent abstracting or title search. This attempt has been largely unsuccessful. Tort claims for defective searches are often (not always) allowed.

# EXAMPLES AND EXPLANATIONS

4a.  In the following examples involving a title insurance policy, assume that O purchases a 1970 ALTA owner's policy that has a policy date the same as the date on which O closed the purchase of the interest. Assume that the interest insured in the policy is a fee simple absolute, unless otherwise noted.

O purchases a subdivision lot. The lot is in a subdivision for which a plat was never filed. Does O have a claim under her policy?

**Explanation:**   No. A title to the lot can be marketable in the legal sense, but without fair market value in the economic sense. See Hocking v. Title Ins. & Trust Co., 37 Cal. 2d 644, 234 P.2d 625 (1951) (involving a lot in Palm Springs left without legal access because of an improperly filed plat).

4b.  The lot turns out to be surrounded by a trackless swamp and is accessible only by four-wheel vehicles. Does O have a claim for the lack of access to the lot?

**Explanation:**   No. The policy insures that there is a *right* of access to the lot, not that a low-slung car can reach it without damage. This is title insurance, not property insurance. See Title & Trust Co. of Florida v. Barrows, 381 So. 2d 1088 (Dist. App. 1979).

4c.  O purchases a house and lot along with a title policy. Five years after moving in, O discovers that one of the deeds in her record chain of title was executed by a man adjudicated incompetent three years before the date of execution. Does O have a claim against the insurer?

**Explanation:** Yes. See Citicorp Sav. Bank of Illinois v. Stewart Title Ins. Corp., 840 F.2d 526, 531 (7th Cir. 1987).

4d. Same facts, but the adjudication of incompetency takes place after the date of the policy. The finding of incompetency, nonetheless, is based on facts occurring before that date. Does O have a claim against her insurer?

**Explanation:** Yes, O still has a claim.

4e. Same facts, but O has notice of the incompetency proceedings and does not disclose what she knows to the insurer. Does she have a claim against the insurer?

**Explanation:** This hypothetical presents an Exclusion 3(b) question. O still has a claim because the proceedings are a public record of which the insurer also knows.

4f. O purchases and insures a 99-year leasehold on a condominium unit in a large resort subdivision. O agrees not to occupy the unit for more than one week per year and to permit a development company to manage the unit, along with all other units, and share pro rata in the profits from the rentals of all units. Ten years later, the creditors of the resort force it into bankruptcy. The trustee in bankruptcy seeks to evict O for nonpayment of maintenance fees. Does O have a claim against her insurer?

**Explanation:** No. The policy does not insure against the risk of bankruptcy as such but may insure against a bankruptcy court finding that the insured title or interest is invalid. First National Bank & Trust Co. of Port Chester v. New York Title Ins. Co., 171 Misc. 854, 12 N.Y.S.2d 703 (Sup. Ct., Westchester County, 1939) (holding that the invalidity of a mortgage as a preference was a defect in title insured by an insurer). Bankruptcy is a business, not a title risk. Maintenance fees in a condominium are given priority over the interest insured as a leasehold.

4g. Same facts, except that the trustee argues that the leasehold interest insured was really an equity contract, subject to the securities laws, and O is not the holder of an interest in real property, but an investor in the resort. Does O now have a claim against her insurer?

**Explanation:** Yes. The question of whether the policy insures against the risk of bankruptcy is unchanged; it does not. However, the resort-wide management of the units for the owners is a violation of the securities laws, and the trustee has authority to recharacterize the leaseholds as "equity" interests in the resort — the securities law equivalent of shares. Thus when the policy was issued, the interests insured were not leaseholds and were unmarketable as such. O does have a claim. See Allison v. Ticor Title Ins. Co., 907 F.2d 645 (7th Cir. 1990).

Title insurance policies are issued in two forms: One standard policy is issued to owners and another to mortgage lenders insuring the priority of their lien. As between the two policies, there are differences in coverage. Think about whether an insured lender must foreclose before making a claim. How feasible is that in the context of the national secondary market for mortgages?

4h.  O wishes to refinance her residential mortgage. ME1 holds a mortgage lien on the premises. O approaches ME2 about a new lower-rate loan and mortgage. ME2 agrees to extend the new loan to O. An escrow account is established by ME2 with a subsidiary of a title insurer to pay off ME1's old loan, release ME1's lien, transfer a new lien to ME2, and insure ME2's lien priority. ME2 pays the proceeds of its loan into escrow, ME1 receives the escrow agent's check payable to it to release its lien and deposits the release of lien into escrow; ME2's title policy is released from escrow; the check payable to ME1 is returned for insufficient funds. The escrow agent goes bankrupt. Does ME2 have a claim against the insurer?

**Explanation:**   No. The risk of loss through default lies with the new mortgagee ME2, who established the escrow. Moreover, at the time of default, the agent held the funds for ME2, not ME1. (It held them for the latter until ME1 submits the release of lien to the agent, but at the point ME1 has completed its escrow obligations, the funds were held in ME2's name.) See Jones v. Lally, 511 So. 2d 1014 (Fla. App. 1987). However, the resolution of the risk of loss issue does not answer the question of whether, even when ME2 has this risk, it is also a risk covered by the title insurer. Let's argue here that the risk of insolvency of the agent relates to separate functions — insuring and escrowing the title — and should be separately treated, unless the insurer agrees to hold harmless those of its insureds using its escrow services.

## Measuring the Damages of the Policyholder

In situations involving a partial failure of title, an insured is entitled to either (1) the actual loss caused by the defect, or (2) the difference between the fair market value of the title with and without that defect, whichever is less. In instances of a total failure of title, the insured is entitled to the fair market value of the title that she thought she had. The amount of the policy serves as an upper limit on the insurer's liability under the policy and is subject to the requirement that the insured show the loss or damage.

The traditional date for measuring damages is the date of the closing on the insured title, but reliance damages have also been awarded when the insurer knows that the property, title to which is insured, is to undergo development of some type; thus damages have also been measured on the date on which the title defect limiting development is discovered.

# EXAMPLES AND EXPLANATIONS

5. O starts to develop land but discovers an easement across it. The insurer admits that its title searcher missed this interest when conducting the search but argues that the value of the easement is measured as of the date of the policy, not the date of the easement's disclosure. On this argument, what result?

**Explanation:** Compare Overholtzer v. Northern Counties Title Ins. Corp., 116 Cal. App. 2d 113, 253 P.2d 116 (1953); Hartman v. Shambaugh, 96 N.M. 359, 630 P.2d 758, 761-763 (1981) (preferring the date of discovery of the defect), with Glyn v. Title Guaranty & Trust Co. of New York, 132 A.D. 859, 117 N.Y.S. 424 (1909). The modern view is that the date on which the defect is discovered is the date for measuring the damages.

6. Same facts as in Example 4f above (the resort condominium problem), but the insurer argues in addition that the bankruptcy has made the leaseholds valueless, and the measure of damages should be their value as of the date of the claim. Will the insurer prevail with this argument?

**Explanation:** In a falling market that, as here, hits bottom at a value close to zero, the modern view may result in a claim with a very low monetary value. However, cases like *Hartman,* declaring that the date of discovery is the one on which damages are measured, is an example of a rule seeking indemnity for the insured who has started to develop the property and relied on the title permitting that development. When the insured has committed herself to a mortgage on the leasehold, she in effect has used the title as would any developer, as a source of funds. She remains liable to repay that mortgage loan, and the title insurer, if otherwise liable, should pay as of the time of the closing on her purchase and that loan. Cf. Rocco Enters., Inc. v. Continental Casualty Co., 702 F. Supp. 596 (D. W. Va. 1988); Safeco Title Ins. Co. v. Reynolds, 452 So. 2d 45 (Fla. App. 1984).

In some cases, however, recovery of damages measured by the value of the leasehold on the purchase date does not preclude a showing of economic loss — that is, damages including loss of profits on rents for the unit. See Native Sun Inv. Group v. Ticor Title Ins. Co., 189 Cal. App. 3d 1265, 235 Cal. Rptr. 34, 37-38 (1987) ("lost rents are recoverable because the plaintiff was able to show that in the absence of the defect he would have been able to collect rent on the four houses in dispute"). Damages caused by the defect in the title are compensable, no matter what the date on which the defect is measured. See generally Lifland & Wells, Title Insurance and the Measure of Damages, 15 CEB Real Prop. L. Rep. 125-127 (Apr. 1992) (reviewing the rules and collecting California cases).

# 16

## Model Marketable Title Act and Curative Statutes

## Model Marketable Title Act

In the early 1960s and nearing retirement, Lewis Simes, long a professor at the University of Michigan, wrote a statute based on the earlier work of a colleague, Ralph Aigler. This statute has become the most widely adopted reform of American conveyancing proposed since the 1930s. It is now adopted, with some modifications, in 17 states.

The purpose of this statute is to eliminate long chains of title; to cleanse a fee simple absolute of less than fee encumbrances; to define the length of time during which a title must be searched; to fill gaps in the title-cleansing aspects of statutes of limitation, which cannot extinguish nonpossessory interests, future interests (until they are possessory), or interests owned by those under a disability; and, finally, to force holders of otherwise time-barred interests to record a notice of them in the recent public real property records.

This is a tall order. It is accomplished without extinguishing or curing defects in the title documents remaining to be searched or without declaring the legal effectiveness of those documents. Moreover, in some states, the purposes in view for these statutes will be hard to achieve all at once. In states carved out of the public domain, for example, long chains of title will not be routinely eliminated when the interests of the United States are exceptions to the statute's main provisions.

A shortened version of the text of Simes's effort follows.

# MODEL MARKETABLE TITLE ACT

*Section 1.*    Any person having an unbroken chain of title of record to any interest in land for 40 years or more shall be deemed to have a marketable record title to such interest, as defined in Section 8 and subject to the matters stated in Section 2.

*Section 2.*    Such marketable record title shall be subject to:

(a) All interests and defects which are inherent in the muniments of which such chain of record title is formed; provided, however, that a general reference in such muniments to easements, use restrictions, or other interests created prior to the root of title shall not be sufficient to preserve them, unless specific identification be made therein of a recorded title transaction which creates the interest preserved.

(b) All interests preserved by the filing of proper notice or by possession by the same owner continuously for a period of 40 years or more.

(c) The rights of any person arising from a period of adverse possession, which was in whole or part subsequent to the effective date of the root of title.

(d) Any interest arising out of a title transaction which has been recorded subsequent to the effective date of the root of title from which the unbroken chain of title of record is started; provided that no interest extinguished by Section 3 shall be revived.

(e) The exceptions stated in Section 6.

*Section 3.*    Subject to the matters stated in Section 2, such marketable record title shall be held by its owner and shall be taken by any person dealing with the land free and clear of all interests whatsoever, the existence of which depends on any act, transaction, event, or omission that occurred prior to the effective date of the root of title. All such interests, however denominated, whether legal or equitable, present or future, whether such interests are asserted by a person who is sui juris or under a disability, within or without the state, natural or corporate, private or governmental, are hereby declared to be null and void.

*Section 4.*    Any person claiming an interest in land may preserve it by filing for record during the 40-year period immediately following the effective date of the root of title of the person whose record title would otherwise be marketable, a notice in writing, setting forth the nature of the claim. No disability or lack of knowledge of any kind on anyone's part shall suspend the running of this 40-year period. A continuous 40-year period of possession, during which no title transaction appears of record in this chain of title, shall be deemed the equivalent of a filing under this section.

*Section 5.*    The notice shall contain an accurate description of the land affected, which is at least as full as the description in any recorded instrument on which the claim is founded. It shall be filed in the records of the county in which the land is situated, entered in the records in the same manner as other recordable transactions, and indexed both by the name of the claimant in the grantee index and by legal description.

*Section 6.*   This act shall not be applied to bar any lessor or his successor as a reversioner of his right to possession on the expiration of any lease; or to bar or extinguish any easement clearly observable by physical evidence of its use; or to bar any right, title, or interest of the United States, by reason of failure to file notice as required by Section 4.

*Section 7.*   This act shall not change or modify any applicable statute of limitations.

*Section 8.*   Definitions

(a) "Marketable record title" means a title of record, as indicated in Section 1, which operates to extinguish such interests existing prior to the effective date of the root of title, as are stated in Section 3.

(b-c) "Records" includes probate and other official public records, as well as records in the registry of deeds. Recording, when applied to court records, includes filing.

(d) "Person dealing with the land" includes a purchaser of any estate or interest therein, a mortgagee, a levying or attaching creditor, a land contract vendee, or any other person seeking to acquire an estate or interest therein, or impose a lien thereon.

(e) "Root of title" means that conveyance or other title transaction in the chain of title of a person, purporting to create the interest claimed by such person, upon which he relies as a basis for the marketability of his title, and which was the most recent to be recorded as of a day 40 years prior to the time when marketability is being determined. The effective date of the "root of title" is the date on which it is recorded.

(f) "Title transaction" means any transaction affecting title to any interest in land, including title by will or descent, title by tax deed, or by trustee's, referee's, guardian's, executor's, administrator's, master's, or sheriff's deed, or decree of any court, warranty deed, or mortgage.

A marketable record title protected by this act can consist of a chain with a single link. If O conveys to A who records in 1949, A will in 1990 have the protection of the act. The 1949 conveyance is the root of title and the single link in the chain of marketable record title. On the other hand, if the O-A 1949 conveyance is not recorded until 1959, A will not gain the protection of the act until the year 2000 because the recording is what establishes the root of title, and that has been moved forward ten years by the failure to record for that time.

A marketable record title is more likely to have more than one link. If O conveyed to A who records in 1949, A to B who records in 1950, and B to C in 1960, but C does not record and conveys to D in 1970, the break in the chain of recording denies D a marketable *record* title until such time as the chain of title is one completely of record — even if the unrecorded transaction can be proven by extrinsic (meaning here, outside the public records) evidence. A person seeking the protection of the act must have unbroken record title back to, but also including, the root of title. See generally Iowa Title Standards Committee, Iowa Bar Association, The New Iowa Land Title Examination Standards, 34 Drake L. Rev. 589, 664-672 (1985).

Section 2 of the act defines some interests to which a marketable record title is subject. Thus, if the root of title states that the title transferred is "subject to all easements and covenants of record," the title searcher has no duty to go back, past the root of title, to ascertain what these interests might be. The lack of a specific reference, in a book number and page, is fatal; only a specific reference preserves them. Semachko v. Hopko, 35 Ohio App. 2d 205, 301 N.E.2d 560 (1973), noted at 23 Clev. St. L. Rev. 337 (1974). However, a reference in the root of title to a preexisting easement conveyed by deed recorded in book number 65, page 670, would preserve the easement. See Section 2(a) of the act.

Likewise, interests conflicting with a marketable record title, predating the root of title and recorded during the period of marketability commencing with the date of the root of title, are preserved. So if O conveys to A in 1950 and that conveyance becomes the root, but in 1948 O had conveyed an interest to X in conflict with A's deed, and X conveyed the interest to Y in 1960, Y's interest is preserved. However, if X had waited until 1991 to convey to Y, the interest would not be preserved because it was not the subject of a conveyance within the 40-year period of marketability running from the date of the root of title. See Section 2(d) of the act.

Marketable record title is also subject to persons establishing adverse possession or prescriptive rights (see Section 2(c)), rights held in possession for 40 years, or rights preserved by a notice (Section 2(b)).

See generally Conine & Morgan, The Wyoming Marketable Title Act — A Revision of Real Property Law, 16 Land & Water L. Rev. 188 (1981); Curtis, Simplifying Land Transfers: The Recordation and Marketable Title Provisions of the Uniform Simplification of Land Transfers Act, 62 Or. L. Rev. 363 (1983); Hicks, The Oklahoma Marketable Record Title Act Introduction, 9 Tulsa L.J. 68 (1973); Note, The Indiana Marketable Title Act of 1963: A Survey, 40 Ind. L.J. 21 (1964); Note, The Mechanics of Iowa's Marketable Title Legislation, 22 Drake L. Rev. 326 (1973).

The constitutionality of marketable title acts has been established in several cases. Presbytery of Southeast Iowa v. Harris, 226 N.W.2d 232, 242 (Iowa 1975), cert. denied, 423 U.S. 830 (1977) (holding that the act is no violation of the due process clause); Wichelman v. Messner, 83 N.W.2d 800, 817 (Minn. 1957) (holding act with provision for filing preservation notice constitutional).

At the federal level, the U.S. Supreme Court has not dealt with a case involving a marketable title act, but it has upheld against various constitutional challenges a much more draconian statute. This statute was Indiana's Dormant Mineral Lapse Act. The act provided that a mineral interest unused for a period of 20 years was automatically extinguished, and that the title to the lapsed mineral interest automatically reverted to the holder of the title to the surface, unless the separate mineral interest is preserved by a recorded statement of claim, filed with the Recorder of Deeds. Texaco, Inc. v. Short, 454 U.S. 516 (1982). This statute was upheld under both the due process and the takings clauses of the Fourteenth Amendment. The Court found that the act was similar to recording acts and adverse possession statutes and that its purpose (the encouragement of the development of mineral interests and consolidation of surface and mineral estates) was a legitimate one, outweighing the slight burden of recording a claim periodically imposed on the holder of mineral interests.

# EXAMPLES AND EXPLANATIONS

1. Does the Model Marketable Title Act (beginning on page 196) extinguish an unrecorded party wall agreement made over 40 years ago for a duplex residential structure?

**Explanation:** Section 2(d) would seem to require two things that this agreement does not have: first, that the agreement be linked to a title transaction making up the marketable record title, and, second, its recordation be within the period of marketable title. However, the two other sections (§§4 and 6) suggest that if this agreement can be treated as one involving a visible, possessory interest, then it will be preserved, and marketable record title is held subject to it.

2. Does the act require recordation of a boundary agreement between neighbors established by mutual acquiescence?

**Explanation:** No. Unwritten agreements need not be recorded.

3. Is a reciprocal negative easement, established by judicial decision as in Sanborn v. McLean, 233 Mich. 227, 206 N.W. 496 (1925), valid for no longer than 40 plus years in a state adopting the act?

**Explanation:** To the extent that such an easement arises from the inquiry notice given by the construction of improvements implementing the larger scheme of restrictive easements and covenants in the neighborhood, it might be regarded as a possessory interest covered by §§4 and 6. But to the extent that it is a mistake or gap in the written scheme, it must be filed every 40 years, and if not filed, is extinguished by the act.

4. O executes an installment land sale contract for Blackacre with A. O conveys Blackacre to B, who records his deed. How does the act treat this type of contract?

**Explanation:**  From the definition of a "title transaction" in Section 8(f), it does not appear that an installment contract falls within the definition.

5a. O conveys to A 42 years ago; A records and remains in continuous possession of Blackacre right to the present. Forty-one years ago, B conveys Blackacre to C. B had no prior interest in the property. C records and, one month later, conveys to D. Today D wants to sell to your client. What advice would you give this client? If A had been out of possession for 20 of the last 42 years, would your advice change?

**Explanation:**   Here there are two "roots of title" leading to two chains of marketable record title. This is arguably a situation that the act was not intended to handle, so one might argue that the act is inapplicable. See Exchange Natl. Bank v. Lawndale Natl. Bank, 41 Ill. 2d 316, 243 N.E.2d 193 (1968) (holding that a wild deed cannot serve as a root of title).

The better answer is that this client will have to yield to A's rights under Section 4 of the act, which take precedence over an out-of-possession, but otherwise marketable, record title. If A were out of possession for 20 of the last 40 years and does not qualify for Section 4 rights, then your advice would change and your client's filing a Section 4 notice is in order, but the timing of that notice is unclear. See Marshall v. Hollywood, 224 So. 2d 743 (Fla. App. 1969), aff'd, 236 So. 2d 114 (Fla. 1970) (holding that a wild deed can serve as a root of title and, as such, extinguish the true title). The *Marshall* opinion is discussed in Note, The Marketable Record Title Act and the Recording Act: Is Harmonic Coexistence Possible?, 29 U. Fla. L. Rev. 916, 927-931 (1977).

5b. Could a void tax deed serve as a root of title?

**Explanation:**   If a wild deed can serve as a valid root of title, then in all probability deeds that are, on their face, less certain to convey what they purport to convey — as in the instance of a void tax deed — will probably serve as well. Mobbs v. City of Lehigh, 655 P.2d 547, 551-552 (Okla. 1982). If, however, the reference to a possibly adverse instrument is clearly indicated in the deed so that the title searcher can locate it in the records or with a reasonable investigation, the deed containing such a reference will not serve as a valid root of title to extinguish that adverse interest.

5c. How about a quitclaim deed as a root of title?

**Explanation:** If a wild deed can serve as a root, one would expect that a quitclaim would too. But can such a deed also be a "title transaction" that, after all, must purport to create an interest in real property? Does a quitclaim deed make such a claim? Arguably not. See Wilson v. Kelly, 226 So. 2d 128 (Fla. App. 1969) (holding that a quitclaim is not a valid root of title, which must both describe the land and an interest in it).

6. Forty-five years ago, O mortgages Blackacre to M. O makes regular payments under the mortgage, but the principal is not fully repaid today. Thirty-nine years ago, O conveys Blackacre to A. When should M file a Section 4 notice? What if the act were amended to provide, at the beginning of Section 1, "No action shall be brought affecting the possession or title to real property, except by . . . " (thereafter continuing as in the model act); would this amendment affect your answer?

**Explanation:** Probably the notice filing, if it occurs today, comes too late to preserve the effectiveness of the mortgage. The Section 4 notice must be filed within 40 years of the root of title, and the facts indicate that the root is removed by more than 45 years from the present day. Thus, to preserve M's interest, he would have to file a notice in the public records at least once every 40 years.

An act set up like a statute of limitations would probably yield the same answer.

7. Forty-five years ago, O dies and in his will devises Blackacre "to S for life, remainder to C." The will is duly probated, and S mortgages Blackacre to M a year later. That same year S defaults on the mortgage loan payments, M forecloses on Blackacre, and A buys the property in fee simple absolute at the foreclosure sale. A's interest passes to B. Forty years after taking possession of Blackacre under the O's will, S dies. What does C have? If S had been in continuous possession for 45 years and never mortgaged the property, what would C have?

**Explanation:** Nothing, and the fee simple absolute, in that order. The foreclosure deed is here the "root of title," as defined in Section 8, and the title examiner will not go back in his search past the date of that deed. As to the second question, the possessory right of S asserted over 45 years takes precedence over any marketable record title. See Section 2(b) and Cochran, The Root of Title Concept or How to Use the Florida Marketable Record Title Act, 52 Fla. B.J. 287 (1978).

# Curative Acts

A curative statute is retrospective legislation, reaching into the past to operate on past transactions in order to render valid those transactions that would otherwise be ineffective to do what the parties to the transaction intended. They are enacted to remedy frequently recurring types of defects and irregularities, particularly in the formalities of executing a transaction (often imperfectly understood by the parties to it). In transactions in which the parties' actions are sufficient to disclose their full intent, these statutes confirm that intent.

Other typical effects of such statutes are to authorize that, once cured, the otherwise defective document imparts constructive notice under the recording acts and is admissible as evidence of the transaction. Typical statutes have the following characteritics:

1. They provide an immediate and automatic remedy for a defect and do not require resort to the courts. They should be automatic (operating on documents recorded for a period of ten years, say, and not operating on "all documents on the record on January 1, 1989").
2. They cure all defects of a certain general type: for example, a defective attestation or acknowledgment in a deed; a defective corporate authority to execute a deed; a conveyance by a partnership in partnership name, rather than the names of the individual partners; or, the failure of both spouses to join in a deed and so to release a marital right or homestead right.
3. They exert their effect on documents placed on the public record at a time removed from the recording of the document — not too greatly removed, but not at a time so close to the execution and recording as to encourage carelessness.

Massachusetts and Wisconsin have the greatest variety of these statutes. See, e.g., Mass. Gen. L., ch. 184, §23 (1980).

The following is typical of a curative statute. Consider its text:

> When any written instrument, in any manner affecting or purporting to affect the title to real estate, has been recorded for a period of ten years and such instrument, but because of any defect, irregularity, or omission, fails to comply in any respect with any statutory requirement relating to the execution, attestation, acknowledgment, or recording, such instrument and the record thereof shall be fully valid, binding, and effective to the same extent as if the instrument had in the first instance been in compliance with any such statutory requirement.

# EXAMPLES AND EXPLANATIONS

8. In a state in which a curative statute like the one above is enacted and has been in effect for 20 years, assume that, ten years ago last month,

O conveyed Blackacre, in an unacknowledged deed, to a joint tenancy with a right of survivorship, composed of O, A, and B. This deed is otherwise valid to create a joint tenancy and is promptly recorded. O died one year ago, leaving her widower as her sole heir. Who owns Blackacre today?

**Explanation:**   It depends on whether the defective deed, when "cured" of the defect by the statute, is given the priority it would have had had it not been defective when first recorded, or is given the priority it has as of the time it is cured of its defective feature. There is in general little hesitancy in holding today that the reach of the statute is retroactive and that the deed takes the priority it had ten years ago. If so, the widower loses any interest in Blackacre because his spouse's death activates the right of survivorship, and A and B thus succeed to O's interest in the property. See Dennen v. Searle, 149 Conn. 126, 176 A.2d 561 (1961), noted in 36 Conn. B.J. 642 (1962).

As to this type of defect, moreover, the requirement (of an acknowledgment) is one that is created by statute. What the legislature can create, it can modify — or abolish. On that ground, the retroactive effect of the curative statute cannot be beyond the power of the legislature.

Finally, if the purpose of the curative statute is to do what the parties intended to do in the beginning, why not give the statute the power to correct the defect in what they did, as of the time they intended that the transaction be effective. The intervening interest of the widower is defeated on that basis as well. Watson v. Mercer, 33 U.S. 88 (1834) (Story, J.); Weeks v. Rombaugh, 144 Neb. 103, 12 N.W.2d 636 (1944).

# Title Standards

These are a third type of conveyancing reform often available today. These standards are promulgated by state bar associations and are intended to prevent attorneys from raising minor objections to a title's marketability when mechanisms, statutory and otherwise, are available for cleaning up that title. Twenty-four states had such standards in 1981.

One commonly used title-clearing mechanism is the filing of an affidavit reciting facts tending to prove the title with the deed.

These standards do not have the force of law. They are guidelines. However, in one state, Nebraska, the legislature periodically enacts them as statutes.

An exemplary title standard provides that "inconsistencies in recitals or indications of dates, as between dates of execution, attestation, acknowledgment, or recordations, do not, in themselves, impair marketability." Oklahoma Bar Association Title Standard 6.2, found in Okla. Stat., tit. 16, ch. 1, appendix (Supp. 1988).

What if the date of the execution of a deed is the day after it was acknowledged? The comment on Standard 6.2 cited above permits the examiner to ignore the recitals of dates "as notoriously inaccurate"; "the inconsistency or impossibility of a recited date should not be regarded as vitiating the particular formality involved." Moreover, the comments add, an "Act curative of the formality will eliminate any question as to its date." Thus does a title standard extend the reach of a curative statute.

Another typical standard relates to mortgages on the records that might be presumed stale. Mortgages with a stated maturity date can be presumed satisfied 10 years after that date or, if lacking a maturity date, 40 years after filing. Such title standards have the effect of insulating the conveyancing bar from charges of malpractice when following the practices recommended in the standard.

# 17

## *The Torrens System*

We have been discussing the recording acts and their uses by abstractors and attorneys — but in the eyes of many there is a better way. Instead of just presenting the documents needed to examine the current state of a title, what if references to all the interests encumbering a title were assembled in one place and the title guaranteed to be otherwise unencumbered by the governmental officer in charge of the records? Such a system would be a tract index, an abstract of title, and a guarantee of the title — all reduced to one document. The public records would then present not just evidence of title, but the thing itself. A present-day analogy would be the registration certificate to your automobile.

Such a system would, furthermore, eliminate the need to present a chain of title. The title on the document would present the results of an evaluation of a chain of title, and rather than chaining the title each time the title was transferred, one final title search that resulted in a certificate of title would be guaranteed as the state of the title. That title would then be "registered."[1]

Sound good? Sound possible? Such a system in fact is used in most nations outside the formerly communist bloc, except for the United States. Even Great Britain, the country from which we inherited our system, uses it. So do most of the countries formerly part of the British Empire, although the system is more widespread than that. See Franco, The Legal Insecurity of Land Property in Venezuela: A Case Study of the Registry System, 3 Law. Americas 464, 468 (1971). This system is called the Torrens system, named for a British civil servant and state premier in Australia, Sir Robert Richard Torrens. As a customs collector in Australia, he noticed the way the titles to

---

1. "Registered" is used here to distinguish the process from recording, although in some jurisdictions the recorder is called the registrar of titles. For the present, forget this fact; registration is a reference to a guaranteed title, recordation to the present system of laying title evidence on the public record.

ships were transferred. S. R. Simpson, Land Law and Registration 68 (1976) (perhaps the leading treatise on registration); see also E. Dowson & V. Sheppard, Land Registration (1952); T. Ruoff, An Englishman Looks at the Torrens System (1957); for a good treatise on one country's system, see V. DiCastri, Thom's Canadian Torrens System (2d ed. 1962).

The Torrens system works on three basic ideas: the *mirror* principle, the *curtain* principle, and the *fund* principle. Simpson, supra, at 22; Ruoff, supra, at 9. The *mirror* is the idea that the certificate of title reflects the state of the title at the time of issuance; all interests unnoted on the certificate do not exist. Thus the mirror does not reveal the history of the title; all unused interests are obliterated. Frazer v. Walker, [1967] A.C. 569 (registered owner acquiring his title under void instrument obtains indefeasible or absolute title unless it is subject to some statutory exception, as for fraud, rendering the certificate open to challenge).

The *curtain* principle holds that the issuance of the certificate brings down the curtain on all unnoted interests. All adverse possessors, holders of secret liens, equities, and future interests or estates are bound by the certificate's description of the title. Gibbs v. Messer, [1891] A.C. 248, 254.

Thereafter, they must look, under the *fund* principle, to a guaranty fund for compensation for the loss of any valid, but unnoted interest — even if that interest was in possession at the time at which the certificate was issued. No action for possession (for example, foreclosure, perfection of a mechanic's lien, or ejectment) is thereafter held by the interest holder; thereafter, money from the fund, rather than possession, must suffice. Canadian Pacific Ry. Ltd. v. Turta, [1954] 3 D.L.R. 1 (upholding application of a statute of limitations on claims against the fund by owners unaware of the deprivation of an interest in their title). Compensation by the fund is given on an indemnity basis. McCormack, Torrens and Recording: Land Title Assurance in the Computer Age, 18 Wm. Mitchell L. Rev. 61, 80-89 (1992).

Overall, perhaps the biggest advantage of the Torrens system today is that it makes the public records subject to automation and computerization.

This system still uses contracts of sale and deeds, not as a means of conveyance but usually as evidence that the grantors wish to have a new certificate of title, naming the purchasers as the titleholders, issued by the registrar. Only the issuance of a replacement certificate acts as a conveyance. Transactions must be registered against the title enrolled in the state-operated land title office to be valid and are not valid until registered. See, e.g., Head, The Torrens System in Alberta: A Dream in Operation, 35 Can. B. Rev. 1 (1957). When less than the full fee simple is transferred, the holder of the interest files to have a "caveat" enrolled in the certificate; unless so enrolled, the interest is not valid. Two certificates are in existence: One remains with the registrar and another is held by the current owner. If the current owner resists having her certificate "charged" through enrollment of a less than fee interest, then resort is had to an administrative hearing or judicial review of the dispute, or both.

At one time, 22 states in this country had Torrens systems in place. The first state to adopt the system was Illinois in 1895. The American Bar Association endorsed it in 1916. However, the number of user jurisdictions has dwindled to just a few: to the island of Oahu, Hawaii; to Cook County, Illinois, where counties are permitted to use the system by local option; to the Suffolk and South Shore counties in Massachusetts; and to Hennipen, Ramsey, and Saint Louis Counties in Minnesota, the Twin Cities and the Duluth area.

There are several variations in the way the systems still in use work. Two states, Massachusetts and Minnesota, provide the clearest contrasts. In Massachusetts, the system is administered by the courts; the Land Court, a limited-jurisdiction court, supervises all registrations in an action that resembles a quiet title action. Mass. Gen. L. Ann. ch. 185 (1968). Thus, parcels with title problems are good candidates to be "Torrenized." Also good candidates for using the system are parcels whose acreage is uncertain. The Land Court has high surveying standards. In addition, the system was given a healthy boost with a strong judicial opinion in its favor, an opinion written by no less a light than Justice Holmes while sitting on the Supreme Judicial Court of Massachusetts. See Tyler v. Judges of the Court of Registration, 175 Mass. 71, 55 N.E.2d 812, 51 L.R.A. 433, appeal dismissed, 179 U.S. 405 (1900).

In Minnesota, the system is administrative in nature; attorneys are appointed by system administrators to perform a title search before the issuance of a certificate. Here the system was established before title insurers were on the scene to provide competition, was guided by a strong advocate (one R. G. Patton) in a jurisdiction with a tradition of good local government, and was, as in Massachusetts, the subject of a strong, favorable judicial opinion.

Why did the system dwindle in the United States? First, it had fierce competition from title insurance companies. Second, the guaranty funds have provided inadequate compensation: large claims made during the 1930s depleted them and made the system unreliable and unattractive to mortgage lenders. In California, for example, the system had been widely used in the four counties around Los Angeles, but one claim wiped out the entire fund in 1937. Third, unsympathetic courts rendered decisions making the certificates of title inconclusive. Behind this judicial sympathy for ousted interest holders often lay administrative sloppiness or an unprofessional title search. Fourth, many special-purpose title searches were still necessary in some jurisdictions; for example, searches were often needed to locate encumbrances such as tax liens or to determine the acreage of a parcel. Often such limited searches were made necessary by judicial decisions or by statutory exceptions to the conclusiveness of the registered title. Finally, a pre-New Deal tradition that limited delegations of authority made to administrators — bolstered by the ideas that land titles were a matter for attorneys and the judiciary, and that due process problems with statutory procedures often flawed the system — worried the system during its decline.

Thus the causes of the system's decline were many, but the coup de grace is usually supposed to have been administered by (of all people!) a law professor. Professor Richard Powell's 1938 book Registration of Title in the State of New York was a careful criticism of the system, but it was seen as a sweeping one — and was instrumental in sweeping the system away. Powell was not, however, the only academic critic of the system. See Bordwell, Registration of Title to Land, 12 Iowa L. Rev. 114 (1927).

Powell's book caused a lively debate, reflected in the law reviews of the time. See, e.g., McDougal & Brabner-Smith, Land Title Transfer: A Regression, 48 Yale L.J. 1125 (1939). Since the 1930s, the title insurance industry has matched Torrens supporters with page for page of print. See, e.g., D. B. Burke, American Conveyancing Patterns (1978), and B. Shick & I. Plotkin, Torrens in the United States (1979).

The system, nonetheless, has its present-day defenders. See Bostick, Land Title Registration: An English Solution to an American Problem, 63 Ind. L.J. 55 (1987); Fiflis, Land Transfer Improvement: The Basic Facts and Two Hypotheses for Reform, 38 U. Colo. L. Rev. 431 (1966); Goldner, The Torrens System of Title Registration: A New Proposal for Effective Implementation, 29 UCLA L. Rev. 661 (1982); Janczyk, An Economic Analysis of the Land Title Systems for Transferring Real Property, 6 J. Legal Stud. 213 (1977); Lobel, A Proposal for a Title Registration System for Realty, 11 U. Rich. L. Rev. 501 (1977); McCormack, Torrens and Recording: Land Title Assurance in the Computer Age, 18 Wm. Mitchell L. Rev. 61 (1992). Most of these advocates propose a gradual, noncompulsory introduction of the system by administrative officials with the help of the bar.

Finally, for some excellent summary discussions on comparative conveyancing, see Cribbet, Land Law — The View of Scandinavia, 62 Nw. U.L. Rev. 277, 281-285 (1967); Large, The Land Law of Scotland — A Comparison with American and English Concepts, 17 Envtl. L. 5, 26-28 (1986); Merryman, Toward a Comparative Study of the Sale of Land, II Jus Privatum Gentium 737 (1969); Newman, A Typical House-Purchasing Transaction in the United Kingdom, 12 Am. J. Comp. L. 797 (1967); Rudden, Soviet Housing Law, 12 Intl. & Comp. L.Q. 591, 614-626 (1963).

# PART TWO

---

# *Law of Mortgages*

# 18

## *Mortgage Lenders and Markets*

Up to the 1930s, mortgage capital was distributed in short-term loans, usually payable in interest-only installments until the end of the term, when the total amount of principal outstanding was then due. Terms were not likely to be more than ten years in length, and the so-called balloon payment at the end of the term often meant that the loan was refinanced, rather than repaid.

During the Depression of the 1930s, with its attendant bank failures, the federal government stepped up its regulatory interest in the banking system — most particularly in the savings and loan associations, which were then (and up to very recently) the major providers of residential mortgage capital. These associations had started in the nineteenth century, often as workingmen's mutual aid associations. A person had to be a "member" to obtain a loan from them, but one became a member by holding a "passbook" or having a savings account at the association. The interest rate payable on these accounts, whose transactions were recorded in the passbook, was protected by statute; that is, the rate payable was higher than rates on comparable accounts held with commercial banks. With these higher rates, the associations were sheltered from competition and able to attract deposits which could then become the basis for loans secured by mortgages. The associations were restricted in their geographic lending area and in the type of loans they could make — most of their capital had to be put into residential mortgage loans. In effect, the federal government underwrote the primary lenders of mortgage loans by helping to create a legal environment in which capital was easy to attract.

In some regions, these mortgage lenders were mutual banks: that is, holding an account with them formed the basis for owning shares in the bank. This form of bank was common in the Northeast, particularly in Massachusetts, New York, Pennsylvania, Ohio, and Illinois. The rest of the savings banks were savings and loan associations holding either state or, after the 1930s, federal charters. Many had their deposits insured by the federal government as well; they did not have to hold a federal charter to obtain federal deposit insurance for their accounts.

One by-product of this federal intervention was a wave of standardized mortgage terms: amortized monthly payments, containing a little repayment of principal as well as the payment of interest; level monthly payments; longer terms for repayment; and no balloon payments at the end of the term. See F. Case & J. Clapp, Real Estate Financing 97-123 (1978), and R. Pease & L. Kerwood, Mortgage Banking 44-50, 72-118 (2d ed. 1965), for a description of the system up to the mid-1960s.

This type of federal support — sheltered interest rates and deposit insurance — worked well until the mid-1960s. At that time, however, the system started to fail to attract sufficient capital to meet the nation's housing and building needs. The reason was the availability of alternative investments for the middle-class who, up to this time, had deposited their savings with the associations.

The federal government came up with a new pattern for underwriting the mortgage market. Up to this time, only a small (relatively speaking) secondary market for mortgage loans had existed; that is, some associations, mutual banks, and other private mortgage lenders, when strapped for cash or new loan funds, could sell portions of their portfolio of loans to larger banks. Usually the purchasers in such markets were large commercial banks. F. Case & J. Clapp, supra, at 124-141, provides an overview of this market as a model for federal involvement. The federal government's view is detailed in United States Department of Housing & Urban Development, Background and History of the Federal National Mortgage Association 1-45 (Jan. 1, 1966). A more detailed examination of the switch in roles is provided by Bartke, Home Financing at the Crossroads — A Study of the Federal Home Loan Mortgage Corporation, 48 Ind. L.J. 1 (1972); Bartke, Fannie Mae and the Secondary Mortgage Market, 66 Nw. U.L. Rev. 1 (1971). A well-written, and more popular, version is provided in M. Mayer, The Builders 377-397 (1978).

The federal government created several new types of purchasers in the secondary market. With federal funds it capitalized several quasi-public corporations, with charters authorizing them to buy mortgage loans, pool them in amounts totaling millions of dollars, and then use the proceeds of these pools to pay the holders of securities backed by the pools in which the mortgages are retained. Neat, huh? Investors in the securities would then provide funds for creating new pools, into which mortgages could again be put. On and on, in an endless cycle of floating securities, creating pools, and eventually getting new money into the hands of the primary lenders of mortgage capital to make new loans.

Most likely the borrower-mortgagor would never know that their loan documents have been assigned to a purchaser in the secondary market because the original lender would become the "servicer" of the loan. The monthly mortgage payment would still be sent to the same place but would be passed on by the servicer. Many primary lenders came to depend on the fees received for servicing the loans they had originated. With time, some lenders became servicing specialists.

The names of quasi-public corporations established to support what quickly became a huge secondary market for mortgages are the Government National Mortgage Association, the Federal National Mortgage Association, and the Federal Home Loan Mortgage Corporation. They are known as Ginnie Mae, Fannie Mae, and Freddie Mac, respectively. (For a time, the first two were jointly managed.) Since the early 1970s, these three have been major players in the market for mortgage capital; as we will see, they have also been major forces tending to standardize mortgage note and mortgage lien and deed of trust documents. In this instance, standardization has also meant fairer, more evenhanded treatment of mortgagors.

Ginnie Mae underwrites the markets for subsidized mortgages associated with federal housing programs. Fannie Mae and Freddie Mac underwrite the conventional mortgage market.

At the end of 1989, Fannie Mae held $228 billion in mortgage-backed securities, assembling these pools and collecting and paying out proceeds of the mortgages in the pools accounted for most of its business. Their other business was the result of direct lending, to the tune of about $108 billion. Comparable figures for Freddie Mac were $272 and $15 billion on the same date.

These institutions have helped the mortgage market weather adverse economic conditions. Fannie Mae lost money during the years 1981-1985; in 1981 its net worth was negative, but it was able to continue to borrow both short- and long-term funds.

Another, similar corporation underwrites agricultural loans — the Federal Agricultural Mortgage Corporation, nicknamed (you guessed it) Farmer Mac. It was established in 1987.

The underwriting available from these secondary market purchasers has enabled new types of mortgage lenders to gain a strong position as originators of residential mortgage loans. Often they are corporate subsidiaries of commercial banks and savings banks, but just as often they are stand-alone mortgage bankers — all capable of closing mortgage transactions and servicing mortgage payments without the long-term risk of holding portfolios of 20- to 30-year mortgages.

# 19

## Mortgages

What is commonly referred to as a mortgage is, in reality, two documents. The first is a promissory note, in which the debtor-borrower promises to pay back the loan of the creditor-lender. The second is the document in which the debtor qua mortgagor conveys a lien to the creditor qua mortgagee. In various regions of the country this second document is called a mortgage or a deed of trust. (There are differences between a mortgage and a deed of trust, but in those situations in which the differences have no practical effect on the problems being discussed, the word mortgage will be used.)

Thus, properly speaking, a mortgage is a document conveying a lien. This lien attaches to property improved or purchased with the loan proceeds. The improvement or the purchase is not necessary for the validity of the lien — that is only the typical arrangement.

## The Title Theory of Mortgages

At common law, as the colonies received that law from England, a mortgage was a conveyance of the legal title to the mortgagee (the lender). He was vested with the legal title to the property securing the loan, subject, however, to the condition that the lien could not be foreclosed after the loan was repaid. Some would say that the mortgagee had a defeasible or conditional fee simple absolute: "to the mortgagee so long as the loan is unpaid" — defeasible fee language — or "to the mortgagee, but if the loan is repaid, to the mortgagor" — fee simple, subject to a condition subsequent, with a right of reentry. (Can't you hear your first-year property teacher saying, "I told you so. Future interests *will* prove useful!"?) The mortgagee holds the legal estate, and the mortgagor the equitable one. Barclays Bank of New York v. Ivler, 20 Conn. App. 163, 565 A.2d 252, appeal denied, 213 Conn. 809, 568 A.2d 792 (1989).

In other words, the common law mortgage was very different from a mortgage as we know it today; instead, it was a conditional conveyance. This is the title theory of mortgages. The lingering effects of this theory make for some very unexpected rules of law — unexpected in that they sometimes, in seemingly quirky ways, violate modern expectations.

## The Lien Theory of Mortgages

However, a second theory of mortgages was inherited from England but was used only in that country's equity courts. It is known as the lien theory of mortgages. Under it, the debt was the principal obligation and the mortgage a collateral agreement to secure the debt. In recognition of this theory, the mortgage became a lien on the secured property, not a common law estate in it. It was regarded as personal property of the mortgagee, should he die, for purposes of administering his estate. Meanwhile, the mortgagor is given an equitable estate, called the equity of redemption. This equity has all the attributes of ownership, except that it can be terminated by a proceeding to enforce the mortgage lien. This proceeding is an equitable one and is called foreclosure.

Early in the history of this country's Republic, most states quickly adopted the English equitable or lien theory of mortgages, and the title theory is used in only a few states today. However, the two theories are just that — *theories* — and when applied to particular documents, the distinctions between them become blurry.

## EXAMPLES AND EXPLANATIONS

1. MR executes an enforceable[1] mortgage in favor of ME. C, a creditor of ME, asks you whether he can enforce a judgment against ME by levying against MR's property. What do you say? If C were a creditor of MR, would your answer change? See Sturges & Clark, Legal Theory and Real Property Mortgages, 27 Yale L.J. 691 (1928) (more than you need to know about the distinction between lien and title mortgages, but a fine piece of writing by one of the founders — Sturges — of the legal realist movement).

**Explanation:**   No and yes, respectively, in both lien and title states. A summary of these results and a further example of the lack of difference

---

1. The use of "enforceable" in this chapter means to indicate that, unless the content of a problem expressly indicates to the contrary, the mortgage is enforceable and not subject to hidden defects, such as a failure of delivery or other legal problems not indicated on the face of the document.

between lien and title theories are found in the commonly accepted answers to the following questions:

| Issue | Lien | Title |
|---|---|---|
| Can ME's creditors reach land? | no | no |
| Can MR's creditors reach land? | yes | yes |
| Will a judgment against ME be levied against the land? | no | no |
| Will a judgment against MR be levied against the land? | yes | yes |
| Does the existence of a mortgage determine whether MR's spouse has a marital estate in the land? | no | no |

These results should conform to your own expectations about the relative rights of lenders and borrowers. Now for some problems in which the theory of the mortgage does make a difference.

2. MR executes an enforceable mortgage in favor of ME. MR defaults, and ME begins foreclosure. Can ME go into possession of the land before the foreclosure decree is issued?

**Explanation:**   This is one of the few areas of mortgage law in which it matters whether a lien or a title theory is used. In title states, the mortgagee can gain possession of the land immediately after the mortgagor's default. Think about the analogy to a fee simple determinable in this regard.

In lien states, the right to possession does not arise immediately after default, but later. How much later is the subject of local rules, varying from state to state. In such states, courts often speak of a hybrid or intermediate theory of mortgages. The date on which the mortgagee is entitled to possession can be the date the mortgagee files for foreclosure, the date of the decree in foreclosure, or the date on which the decree becomes final.

In this regard, think about the analogy to a fee simple subject to a condition subsequent: There the right of reentry is not automatic — as it is with a possibility of reverter following a determinable fee — but instead it must be exercised by the mortgagee. The required exercise is not one of self-help, but commences with the filing of a foreclosure suit. See J. Bruce, Real Estate Finance in a Nutshell 8-9 (2d ed. 1985); G. Nelson & D. Whitman, Real Estate Finance Law §1.5 (2d ed.1985); G. Osborne, Mortgages §14-16 (1970); Kratovil, Mortgages — Problems in Possession, Rents, and Mortgage Liability, 11 DePaul L. Rev. 1 (1961).

Two examples from the cases: In Trannon v. Towles, 200 Ala. 82, 75 So. 458 (1917), the court denied a mortgagor's trespass action brought against a mortgagee who took possession of the secured property before default under authority of a title mortgage; and, in Glover v. Marine Bank of Beaver Dam, 117 Wis. 2d 684, 345 N.W.2d 449, 453 (1984), the court stated that a mortgagor under a lien mortgage retains the title and the right to possession until a valid foreclosure.

3. MR executes an enforceable mortgage in favor of ME. The mortgage covenants contain a use restriction on the land. MR conveys the property to X, who does not assume the mortgage. Can ME enjoin X from violating the use restriction?

**Explanation:**    Again, the answer depends on whether the mortgage is governed by a lien or title theory. If lien, then ME and X are not in privity of estate and, because neither are they in privity of contract (the fact of nonassumption makes that certain), there is no link between the interests of ME and X to provide the basis for enforcing the restriction against X. If a title theory underlies the MR-X mortgage, there is still no privity of contract, but there is privity of estate, and the use restriction can be enforced by ME against X. The latter succeeds to MR's title diminished by the conveyance of the benefit of the use restriction, and so X takes title subject to it. If the restriction was important enough to ME that he negotiated for it in the first instance, it is no less important to him after the MR-X conveyance when, as before, the property is security for the mortgage debt.

# The Accumulation of Mortgage Remedies

The history of mortgages is recorded in a series of remedies provided to the lenders, to which the borrowers react in a series of pendulum swings — now swinging in the lenders' favor, then in the borrowers'. This same history is one in which remedies are piled on top of another, so that the most recent ones do not alter or abolish older ones.

Thus, the title theory of mortgages provided for a "law day," or payment date. This was a date on which either payments were due or the conditional title of the lender became absolute. If the mortgagor "doth not pay, then the land which he puts in pledge . . . is gone from him for ever, and so dead." Littleton's Tenures §332 (E. Wambaugh ed. 1903). What if the borrower did not pay on the day the debt was due but had a good reason for not doing so (for example, he was robbed of the payment on his way to the lender's)? Or, what if the lender hid from the borrower? The law seemed to encourage such shady dealings. Or, what if the time and place of payment were unclear? The borrower then went to an equity court and asked that he be granted an *equity of redemption* — the right to pay the loan off after payment day. Often, the practice was for the court to grant a six-month period, running from the date of the decree and during which the mortgagor must pay the debt or else lose the title. Anonymous Case, 27 Eng. Rep. 621 (1740). Once the courts got used to granting one extension, they sometimes granted several such, in a row. Nanny v. Edwards, 38 Eng. Rep. 752 (1827) (noting that three extensions were usual). Such an equity of redemption could not, at the execution of the mortgage, be bargained away. Peugh v. Davis, 96 U.S. 332, 337 (1878).

Once this became a matter of routine right for borrowers, lenders felt insecure in dealing with the secured real property, even after payment day, because the borrower might ask for an equity of redemption. See Novosielski v. Wakefield, 34 Eng. Rep. 161, 162 (1811). To foreclose this possibility, lenders started asking for a decree to confirm their absolute title to the real property; in return they agreed not to pursue the other assets of the borrower further (that is, they agreed not to sue on the note for a deficiency judgment). This confirmatory decree was a decree of *strict foreclosure*. Perine v. Dunn, Johnson's Ch. Rep. 140 (N.Y. 1819). To "foreclose" means to shut out or bar; what is being barred here is the equity of redemption. When we speak today of foreclosing a mortgage, the reference is really not to enforcing the lender's right (which is what many assume it means) but to barring the rights of the borrower in the property. See Note, Power of Sale Foreclosure: What Process is Due?, 36 Ala. L. Rev. 1083, 1084-1087 (1985) (a brief history of strict foreclosure).

Once strict foreclosure was well established, borrowers asked for a *statutory right of redemption*. This referred to the borrower's right to redeem or pay off the debt during a statutory period after the foreclosure decree and receive back a clear title to the real property. The period of statutory redemption is piggybacked onto the process of obtaining the decree. As we shall emphasize in later sections, this right is statutory and not by any means available in all states.

Lenders responded to this change, which they regarded as too borrower-oriented, by inserting into the mortgage document a *private power of sale*. This power enabled them to bypass the judicial process altogether. The power of sale provisions were first used in corporate transactions, but later were incorporated into residential mortgages and became the basis for a deed of trust.

Borrowers responded to this private power with a further petition to the legislature, asking that foreclosure be made a mandatory remedy. As a result, *judicial foreclosure codes* were enacted in every state.

Lenders responded to such codes by elaborating on their private powers of sale and transferring such powers to a trustee who, during the term of the loan, would hold the title and, upon notice of default from the lender, would sell it. If the codes barred the lender from using the power, they did not bar the trustee, who after all was the mortgagor's agent as well. The document creating this trust is known as a *deed of trust*. Do you see its substantive and procedural advantages over a mortgage for a lender?

Some states responded to the deed of trust with several statutory requirements, basically requiring a *judicial confirmation* of the private sale. This response is still going on today.

The pendulum of remedies thus looks like this:

| Advantage to Lenders | Advantage to Borrowers |
| --- | --- |
| the title mortgage | equity of redemption |
| strict foreclosure | statutory right of redemption |
| private power of sale | judicial foreclosure codes |
| deeds of trust | confirmation of sale |

Two caveats about this table are in order. First, remember that this is a historical pendulum; it is not meant as a graphic picture of any state foreclosure code. For instance, in some states today, a power to cure the default is provided before the decree is final. Second, recall again that these remedies are cumulative; that is, the availability of one does not mean that other earlier remedies are denied. Later ones don't repeal early ones.

These remedies all have modern applications: For example, the equity of redemption cannot be waived by a mortgage covenant in the same documents as are executed at the time of the original mortgage transaction. Neither can a mortgagor agree, at the time of the original mortgage closing, to convey the property to the mortgagee after a default in lieu of the mortgagee's bringing a foreclosure action. Both of these covenants would be what the common law called a clog on the equity of redemption, a right available to mortgagors even in the midst of foreclosure. This prohibition against clogging the equity of redemption was seen as a protection of the integrity of the judicial process involved in a foreclosure, as well as a type of consumer protection device.

Even the mortgagee's right to a receiver to manage the secured property and to collect its rents and profits may be seen as a clog on the equity of redemption. The granting of the right to a receiver, in advance of the need for the remedy, will provoke strict judicial scrutiny of the provision when it appears in a mortgage loan document.

# EXAMPLES AND EXPLANATIONS

4. Suppose that a developer D needs construction financing, but the capital market for such financing is tight. A mortgage lender L is willing to make a loan in an amount representing 80 percent of the fair market value of the land plus the improvements that D proposes to construct upon the land, evidenced by a note and secured by a mortgage lien. In addition, however, L proposes that D convey to L an option to acquire a 20 percent interest in the land and the improvements at the completion of construction. D agrees to the conveyance in writing. The loan agreement is executed, the note and mortgage executed, and L disburses the loan principal. But when L exercises his option, D refuses to convey the 20 percent interest. L sues D

for specific performance of D's agreement to convey the 20 percent interest. Will L obtain specific performance of this agreement?

**Explanation:**   Before this question can be answered, a little math is necessary: 80 percent, the loan-to-value ratio used to compute the principal amount of L's loan, and 20 percent, the amount of the interest in the fair market value requested by L, add up to 100 percent. This being so, L is asking that D convey away his equity in the property — the amount of the market value in excess of the loan amount — at the time of the execution of the loan documents (the note, the mortgage, and so forth).

Let's also be sure we know what interest of the borrower is involved. It is the equity of redemption that is involved because the interest is sought by L in the option before foreclosure. Statutory redemption is an interest which in contrast arises only at the time of the foreclosure sale (and then only in states with a statute establishing this right); we are not involved with a foreclosure yet, so statutory redemption is not involved.

Further, the equity of redemption is only valuable if there is a portion of the market value over the amount of the loan available to the borrower like D at the time of the loan. Otherwise, strict foreclosure is possible for L because D's remaining interest has no monetary value.

L is thus asking that the amount representing the equity of redemption be conveyed away at the time of the loan, so that D will have no equity in the property. The issue then is whether the equity of redemption can be conveyed at the same time as the lien. The common law answer was clearly in the negative: Common law lawyers said that the equity of redemption could not be "clogged" or waived in advance of foreclosure. The doctrine prohibiting clogging the equity was in effect a consumer protection measure: Specific performance of L's option on the 20 percent interest is in effect a clog and so is unenforceable when executed as part of the original mortgage transaction. The common law requires later execution of such an option and independent consideration in order to validate such an interest; otherwise D's entire interest in the project is extinguished. If the equity of redemption provides D with an interest in the secured property, then L has clogged it with his option. Thus no specific performance, and judgment for D.

Today, however, there is another point of view. Assuming that consumer protection statutes, usury laws and cases, and doctrine of good faith dealing and unconscionability are in place in the jurisdiction, when there is no collateral advantage taken by L in securing the option, then why should D and L not be permitted to make a deal that suits their circumstances, notwithstanding the ancient doctrine of clogging? If L's interest rate is a conventional one, the usury ceiling is not exceeded, and the option is not an equitable mortgage, there is no clog.

Thus, although two answers are possible, this scenario is likely to be seen as a classic clog on the equity of redemption. The presence of other consumer protections for D should not be seen as an abrogation of his common law rights to avoid foreclosure by exercising his equity of redemption. The common law-property law point of view will probably prevail over one resting on the parties' freedom of contract. But see Licht, The Clog on the Equity of Redemption and Its Effect on Modern Real Estate Finance, 60 St. John's L. Rev. 452 (1986) (arguing the other way).

# Equitable Mortgages

An equitable mortgage is one that the parties intended to have function as a mortgage, but that does not. A mortgage can be equitable because either the form of transfer does not create a lien — rather, it creates less (as, for example, where a contract of sale is executed) or creates more (as, for example, where a deed, absolute on its face, is used) — or because the alleged mortgagor has himself only an equitable interest in the secured property. Thus the question arises: When will a document that is not styled as a mortgage be treated as if it were a mortgage because, in the context of the transaction in which it is used, a court will find that the parties intended that it perform the same function as a mortgage?

In a majority of jurisdictions a deed in fee simple absolute, valid as such on its face, can be shown to have been intended as a mortgage by the parties, shown such by parol evidence, even without the presence of fraud or mistake. However, the burden of proof for such a showing is high — sometimes even a standard of clear and convincing evidence is used. The most satisfactory evidence is, of course, another document showing the parties' agreement; next best would be a completed transaction supporting the idea that the deed was intended to function as a mortgage. The completed transaction is part performance of the intended mortgage transaction.

In many of the reported appellate opinions on equitable mortgages, it is the mortgagor who is seeking the protection of the doctrine, usually to force the so-called mortgagee to foreclose. The exercise of some form of the foreclosure remedy is typically mandatory for mortgages, and the state statutes governing it have many built-in protections for the mortgagor (as we will see in upcoming sections of this and the next several chapters of this book). However, persons wishing to be mortgagees have also sought to use the doctrine. They have a more difficult task. The person seeking to show that a deed, absolute on its face, is really a mortgage is attempting to cut back the reach of the document, and so parol evidence to support his showing is not necessarily inconsistent with the facial contents of the document. (In a lien theory state, there is no prohibition on parties agreeing to execute a title mortgage; and in a title theory state, of course, no prohibition exists.) A person seeking to become a mortgagee is usually attempting to show that a document purporting to do less than create a mortgage actually does more than it says; and parol evidence inconsistent with the agreement is inadmissible.

# EXAMPLES AND EXPLANATIONS

5. O conveys Blackacre by a short-form warranty deed to X. X records. X agrees in writing to reconvey the property after three years, but the agreement is unrecorded. After four years in possession, X refuses to reconvey. Is the agreement to reconvey capable of specific performance? Would your answer change (a) if the agreement to reconvey is oral, or (b) if the deed and the agreement do not cross-reference one another? And (c) if the two documents taken together are construed as a mortgage, what type of mortgage, lien or title?

**Explanation:** Yes, no, no, and it depends. See J. Bruce, Real Estate Finance in a Nutshell 44-45 (2d ed. 1985); G. Nelson & D. Whitman, Real Estate Finance Law §§3.4, 3.5 (2d ed. 1985); G. Osborne, Mortgages §§28, 29 (1970); Cunningham & Tischler, Disguised Real Estate Security Transactions as Mortgages in Substance, 26 Rutgers L. Rev. 1 (1972). In Sears v. Dixon, 33 Cal. 326, 198 P. 19, 21 A.L.R. 499 (1921), the court noted that a deed taken together with a contemporaneous promise to reconvey was to be construed as a mortgage. No specific cross-reference between documents that, taken together, might be said to constitute a mortgage, is necessary in an equitable action like specific performance. There is no prohibition on the resulting mortgage being construed as a title mortgage in any state, and the intent of the parties may show it to be a title mortgage — after all, the parties did use a deed. However, in every state the foreclosure statutes are said to provide a mandatory remedy; this feature of the remedy indicates that the mortgagee's interest in the property is not regarded as vested until the remedy is used and results in a title in the mortgagee (if that is the result). Putting off the mortgagee's title in this way is a good indication of a public policy to prefer the creation of a lien theory mortgage, unless the parties clearly indicated otherwise.

6. P agrees to sell his house and pay the proceeds to his brother, in exchange for a mortgage on the brother's house. P sells his house and pays the proceeds to the brother, who dies before executing the mortgage. P's sister-in-law, the brother's widow, refuses to execute a mortgage. Can she be compelled to do so?

**Explanation:** Yes. The sale of the house is a completed transaction and is part performance of the mortgage transaction. The so-called mortgagee relied to his detriment, and the brother received the benefit of the sales transaction. The sister-in-law's denial of the mortgage results in a type of fraud that equity will not countenance. See Cauco v. Galante, 6 N.J. 128, 77 A.2d 793 (1951). A good review of the law is contained in the opinion in Poultrymen's Serv. Corp. v. Baer, 63 N.J. Super. 163, 164 A.2d 195, 197-198 (Law Div. 1960) (reviewing N.Y. and N.J. cases).

7. If the brother had agreed to use the proceeds of P's house sale to buy a house, would your answer change?

**Explanation:**   No. Tracing the proceeds of the sale of the house in this way provides an example of the common law doctrine of a purchase money mortgage. P in effect said to his brother, "Here, take the proceeds and buy a house." The brother wouldn't be buying the house without P's urging and aid; P motivated the purchase and prevails over later lienholders, even if they had no notice of his interest. So such a mortgage prevails over any later third-party mortgage. This doctrine provides one example of the doctrine of part performance. Stewart v. Smith, 36 Minn. 82, 30 N.W. 430 (1886); G. Nelson & D. Whitman, Real Estate Finance Law §§9.1, 9.2 (2d ed. 1985). (We will see the term "purchase money mortgage" used in other contexts, with different meanings, so be clear on the context when you see this term.)

8. M furnishes materials used in the construction of O's house. M files no mechanic's lien, but after the statutory time for filing the lien has passed, M sues to foreclose an equitable mortgage on O's property. In M's suit, what result?

**Explanation:**   The case authorites are split on this one. The court may regard the mechanic's lien statute as a mandatory and exclusive remedy. However, the statute also shows a legislative policy of benefiting mechanics generally, and the mechanic without a lien typically has an employment contract on which to sue; a successful suit on it will result in a judgment that might be executed against the house in the future. The mechanic added value to O's house, O received the benefit of his materials, and might in equity be compelled to satisfy an equitable mortgage. See G. Osborne, supra, §48; J. Bruce, supra, at 47-48.

In addition, if O sat back and watched while M furnished his materials for the house, estoppel provides another theory to support the imposition of an equitable mortgage on O's property.

9. Mort Gage is negotiating for a bank loan for real estate development. The bank agrees to loan him $1 million, and in consideration for this Mort gives the bank a promissory note for that amount. The bank also requires him to execute a statement that provides "Borrower will not permit or create any lien or encumbrance other than those presently existing on (his residence)

without prior written consent of Bank." Mort defaults on his loan, and the bank seeks to foreclose the interest created by the statement as if it were a mortgage. In the bank's suit, what result?

**Explanation:** This statement is a so-called negative pledge. Such a pledge is a contractual promise not to further encumber Mort's title. The bank, not the mortgagor, argues that the pledge is an equitable mortgage. Its strongest argument is that, upon breach of the pledge, the measure of damages is the amount of the debt in the note, which, when reduced to judgment and levied on, produces a judicial sale of the property — just as would a mortgage foreclosure. The bank, however, hid this legal consequence of the pledge from Mort and so shouldn't benefit from its nondisclosure. If it had wanted a mortgage, it easily could have requested one and didn't do so. See Tahoe Natl. Banks v. Phillips, 4 Cal. 3d 11, 92 Cal. Rptr. 704, 480 P.2d 320 (1971).

Typically, a negative pledge has not been found to be an equitable mortgage. Id.

10. Grammy, an 80-year-old woman, gives Sonny a deed to her farm in exchange for Sonny's agreement to pay the taxes and insurance on the farm and to provide Grammy with "food, shelter, and clothing so long as Grammy lives and the necessities of life to the extent that Grammy cannot provide these necessities for herself." Grammy brings suit to cancel the deed, alleging a breach of the conditions in the deed and Sonny's shattering of her emotional well-being. In her suit, what result and why?

**Explanation:** Judgment for Grammy. See Thompson v. Glidden, 445 A.2d 676 (Me. 1982) (remanding for a new trial, but upholding the validity of this type of equitable "support" mortgage and finding that money as well as emotional support for the elderly are valid types of consideration for it). If Sonny had recorded his deed as soon as he received it, would it be a deed granted "for value" as the recording acts require? At the time, the answer would be no. Consideration for the elderly might also require that this type of transaction be construed liberally in their favor — even if this violates the usual rules of construction.

11. What of the sale-leaseback? It could be an equitable mortgage too when there is a disparity between the fair market value of the property and the sale price, or when the rent in the leaseback is below the fair rental value. If one of the parties to the transaction believes that the courts would find the transaction a mortgage, is that sufficient to make it one?

**Explanation:** No. The parties are entitled to cast the transaction in the form they wish. The intention of the parties (plural, not singular) controls: Otherwise, every transaction could be upset by a dissatisfed party.

# Note and Mortgage Terms

The note, as was discussed at the outset, contains the personal promise of the debtor to repay the loan. It also defines a right to prepay the loan (if the lender wants to extend that right) and prepayment charges. In many jurisdictions, there is no right to prepay unless the note extends it, and then only to the extent defined in the note.[2] Any charges levied on late payments, often imposed after a grace period as passed, are also set out. Often a procedure for giving the debtor notice of a late payment is set out as well, along with a waiver of some common law debtor's rights (for example, presentment, or notice of dishonor) and a statement of joint and several liability for the debt on the part of every debtor executing and delivering the note.

The mortgage (or deed of trust) contains a conveyance of the lien; it is like a deed of the lien in this regard, containing a description of the property securing the debt, followed by a habendum, deed warranties, a testimonium, and an acknowledgment by the debtor. The deed-like aspects of the mortgage are followed by a series of covenants, used uniformly in each state in which a lender does business. These uniform covenants are promises by the mortgagor. They (1) promise prompt payment of the debt; (2) establish a mortgage escrow account for property taxes, insurance premiums, and ground lease payments; (3) settle on how payments will be applied (to late fees, prepayment fees, interest, and principal due, generally in that order); and (4) promise further (5) payment of prior liens, (6) maintainence of hazard and mortgage insurance policies, and (7) not to commit waste. They also give the lender (8) the right to inspect the property and a share in (9) insurance and (10) condemnation proceeds to satisfy the debt. Further covenants give the mortgagee (11) the right to satisfy prior liens, and (12) exercise any and all rights in the covenants without being estopped or waiving any other right or remedy, as well as (13) set out a notice procedure for defaults in the covenants, (14) determine which law controls the interpretation of the mortgage, and (15) set out the severability of each covenant.

# Mortgage Terms

In any mortgage loan there are four provisions crucial to the transaction: (1) the loan amount or principal, (2) the interest rate, (3) the term or duration of the repayment period, and (4) the monthly payment. They are all set out in the note. Once any three of these are set, the fourth can be determined.

---

2. Compare Patterson v. Tirollo, 133 N.H. 623, 581 A.2d 74, 77-78 (1990) (holding that, under the law of negotiable instruments, no prepayment exists in an otherwise silent mortgage), with Maloney v. Furches, 503 Pa. 60, 468 A.2d 458, 461 (1983) (finding an implied right to prepay in otherwise silent mortgage as a matter of promoting the alienation of property).

Up to the 1930s, there was only a trio of crucial terms — the monthly payment was absent from the litany. In the 1920s, payments made during the term of the loan consisted of interest only; the principal was due on the payday in a lump sum know as a balloon payment; often this meant refinancing the loan at that time. Only in the 1930s, through the influence on mortgage lenders of the Federal Housing Administration, and its standardized notes and mortgage covenants, were monthly payments made constant and amortized. Amortization means that each payment contained some repayment of principal and payment of interest, paid on a declining balance as the principal is repaid. In this manner, at the end of the last payment, the loan was completely repaid. Obviously, payment of interest on a declining balance requires that the early payments be mostly interest, which suits the borrower just fine, considering that the interest portion of the payment is deductible from income taxed by the Internal Revenue Code.

Also in the 1930s, two other changes were made in mortgage financing. First, the terms of such loans were lengthened. If 5- to 10-year terms were common in the 1920s, 20- to 30-year loans were common thereafter. Second, interest rates were protected by federal regulation: The interest rates paid on deposits in savings bank accounts were higher than those paid on deposits with other types of banks, primarily commercial banks. As a result, the home ownership rate in this country, expressed as a percentage of all American households owning their dwelling, jumped up from 25 percent in 1890, and 40 percent in the 1920s, to 60-70 percent in recent decades.

The regulatory scheme of the 1930s, designed to shelter the flow of mortgage capital to the residential market, lasted until the mid-1960s, when the federal role was redesigned. With the passbook rate of interest competing against so many alternative investments, the federal government started to underwrite the establishment of a national secondary market for mortgage loans.

# EXAMPLES AND EXPLANATIONS

12. B borrowed $80,000 from L and executed a brief but enforceable mortgage. The interest rate was 10 percent, the term 20 years, and the monthly payment necessary to amortize the loan was $772.02. Two years later, the bank changes its method of computing the interest. B's payment is the same, but the amount of money allocated monthly to reducing the principal is less, so the effective interest rate rises to 10.08 percent and the loan will not be repaid within the 20-year term. B asks you to sue L. Will you take his case?

**Explanation:** Yes, as a class action, certifying as a class all similarly situated borrowers taking out loans during the 2-year period. Silverstein v. Shadow Lawn Sav. & Loan Assn., 51 N.J. 30, 237 A.2d 474 (1968), in which the 360/360 method of computation was changed to 365/350, which means that 365 days worth of interest were due after 360 days. This is the short year swindle. See D. Hapgood, The Screwing of the Average Man 30-31 (1974), a book written just after a spate of litigation on methods of computation. What if the lender disclosed the change while making it? Would that change the outcome of B's suit? Probably not, because it is the unilateral change in the mortgage agreement by the lender that will force the refund of the extra interest payments. Is the change a type of "bait and switch" tactic? It is invalid as such.

13. B borrows $100,000 from L and executes a brief but enforceable mortgage, with a note fixing the monthly payment and the term of the loan repayment. The note also provides for a 10 percent rate of interest, "provided that L may not change the rate of interest except at any time after three years from the date hereof." L notifies B that thereafter the interest rate will be 10.5 percent. B protests the rate increase. What is the basis for his protest?

**Explanation:**   With the monthly rate and the loan term fixed, one court held that the interest rate could not be increased because the collection could not be accomplished without extending the term or increasing the monthly payment, something for which the note did not provide. Goebel v. First Fed. Sav. & Loan Assn. of Racine, 83 Wis. 2d 668, 266 N.W.2d 352 (1978). Only at the end of the term can the increased interest be collected in a balloon payment.

A more draconian alternative holding for *Goebel* is that the interest rate cannot in fact be increased if the increase cannot be accomplished without extending the term or increasing the amount of the monthly payment, contracted for at a certain, level rate to the end of the term of the loan, at which time (it is agreed) the loan is considered repaid. In fact, this broader holding does the lender a favor because, if the lender were to change the interest rate for a first time, doesn't the note lack a material term — a definitive rate of interest? Without such a term, what happens to the note and to the underlying mortgage? Anything the lender doesn't want to have happen? *Goebel* may be a case the lender wants to lose, to a greater extent than it did.

The loan transaction in *Goebel* closed in 1964, when interest rates were 5-6 percent. The case was litigated when interest rates were about 8 percent. The context for the interpretative issues in the case is important. The lender wanted to increase the return on the portfolio represented by these loans to pay the extra money it found itself paying to attract new deposits. It probably still had these loans in its portfolio and could not sell them into the secondary mortgage market.

As an early attempt to draft a variable rate mortgage, the *Goebel* mortgage and note is a stumbling effort, but later, more organized attempts are inadmissible as evidence of the drafter's intent here.

Because the extent, amount, and method of calculation of the interest rate increases is unclear, how certain is it that a junior lender, checking the public records, will be able to ascertain just how much of the value of the property is likely to be mortgaged through this instrument? If the junior gets no notice of the extent of the senior mortgage, then can the priority of the senior lender be secure? The answer is no; that, as to the extent of the increase liability, the senior lender may take a priority inferior to the junior who becomes a protected, subsequent purchaser under the applicable recording act.

The *Goebel* opinion stresses that the provision for increasing the interest rate is not surplusage because the lender can collect the increased interest at any prepayment — total or partial — of the loan (and most mortgage loans are in fact wholly paid off before the end of the term of the loan), or at any acceleration of the loan worked by a due-on-sale clause. Or, again, the clause could be used when interest rates decline. And, even so, there is no provision at all for collection of the interest rate increases if the loan "goes to term."

In the situations in which the lender can collect the increases in the interest rate, there most probably will be a sale or refinancing involved. In these transactions, the increased interest will be collected from the proceeds of the sale or refinancing. In effect, the loan agreement in this case has been turned into a mortgage in which the lender shares in the appreciated fair market value of the secured property — a shared appreciation mortgage.

Several issues arise. If the loan is not assignable, won't may borrowers just not prepay? But assuming that the prepayment is permitted, how about the lender's collecting a balloon payment of accrued interest at the end of the term. Or increasing the interest component of the the monthly payment, even to the point of making that payment all interest? (The mortgagor's tax accountant would like this solution, at least in the short term.) Then the principal would have to be collected at the end of the term. However, even this is not likely to satisfy the lender. It wants the income flow from the mortgage loan, not the right to bigger prepayment penalties, balloon payments, or restructured monthly payments.

Indeed, the lender has bargained for an interest rate that reflects a profit on a declining principal balance. Each month, the borrower pays interest in the loan and some principal, so that at the end of the term, the loan is completely repaid. In the beginning of the loan, most of the payment is interest; toward the end, most is principal. Why is the payment schedule structured in this manner? Some would say that the Internal Revenue Code holds the mortgagor's answer (remember that the interest portion of the payment is tax deductible). The mortgagee's answer is its interest in a slowly declining principal as the basis for its interest payment.

Another type of answer altogether would say that understanding the way the interest rate is calculated explains the underlying intent of the parties to the mortgage loan. The rate of return is calculated backwards, making the assumptions (1) that an alternative investment would yield this rate, and (2) that the money for that alternative investment is available only as the principal is repaid, so that the mortgagee is assumed to be engaged (but is not in fact engaged) in a continuous process of reinvestment of the loan principal as each payment is made. To real property investors, such a rate is known as the internal rate of return. (It is often used in partnership prospectus tables.) In summary, the mortgagee was arguing that the interest rate provision of the note should be given primacy over the other members of the quartet. The *Goebel* opinion rejects this notion and treats all equally. Balloon payments aside, the provisions for the increase in the interest rate come very close to being surplusage.

# Alternative Mortgage Instruments

Alternative mortgage instruments, or AMIs, were drafted in the 1970s as alternatives to fixed interest rate instruments. There are many types, but they have a common genesis in (1) the credit problems experienced by mortgage lenders themselves during the seventies, (2) the lenders' desire to update their portfolios for marketing purposes, and (3) the impact of inflation, which ate up the profit margins on lenders' fixed rate porfolios during that same decade.

The first type of AMI was the variable rate mortgage. Stormy congressional debate of legislation and regulations authorizing this type of mortgage for use in Federal National Mortgage Association and Federal Home Loan Mortgage Corporation secondary market purchase programs prompted lenders to fall back on rigorous enforcment of due-on-sale covenants.

Generally, AMIs are created by redrafting the covenants of a note, rather than changing the provisions of the mortgage; in most cases, these changes form a contract on the borrower's part to pay a higher interest rate upon the happening of some event or contingency. In a variable rate mortgage, for example, the interest rate floats, up and down, according to some predetermined index spelled out in the note's covenants. State legislatures, and the Congress, responded to the idea of a free-floating rate with limitations on any one change: for example, limitations on the amount the monthly payment can change, or a ceiling on the interest rate changes on any one change or over a number of years. So limited by federal regulation and the legislatures of several states, the variable mortgage became known as an adjustible rate mortgage, or ARM. Usually the interest rate of an ARM loan is stable for the first two or three years of the term, and then may be adjusted at six-month intervals thereafter. For the borrower, the amount of future monthly payments are not known at the closing. Federal regulations today govern many of the provisions of an ARM taken as customary in the industry.

Some AMIs were designed particularly for certain demographic groups within our society. The reverse annuity mortgage, or RAM, for example, is designed to advance the loan proceeds in installments to the elderly who are "land-rich, cash-poor" — who, in other words, own their homes outright, having paid off their purchase money mortgages long ago, but who are short on income after retirement. The RAM provides them an annuity, resulting in a lien growing in value, up to a preset amount, which can be recouped out of the mortgagor's estate after their death. It is, in the language of the next section, a mandatory, future-advance mortgage.

Another AMI, the graduated payment mortgage, or GPM, is intended to be a mortgage without a level series of amortized repayments; rather, the GPM is paid off in a series of payments that rise over the term of the loan — low at first, so low perhaps that no principal is amortized, but building as the income of the mortgagor rises. This mortgage is intended for the youthful, first-house purchaser, or for the low-income segment of the population. A mortgage loan that defers interest, principal, or both in some prearranged way is a variant of a GPM. GPMs have had limited success because of difficulties in selling pools of them into the national secondary mortgage market.

To solve the problem of fluctuating interest rates, without using the short periods of readjustment used in an ARM, what about rolling over the outstanding loan principal at three- or five-year intervals? This is the idea of the roll-over mortgage, the ROM. Thus the ROM has a long-term payment schedule but an interest rate that is renegotiated at intervals. Sometimes the refinancing is obligatory, sometimes optional, with the mortgagee. When ROMs are optional, they are like the balloon payment mortgages of the 1920s.

Lenders often wish to share in the appreciation in the fair market value of the secured real property. In exchange for a reduced interest rate, borrowers are sometimes willing to let them do so. This willingness results in a shared appreciation mortgage, or SAM. What drafting problems can you foresee with a SAM?

# Future Advance Mortgages

In mortgages and deeds of trust, after providing that the instrument secures the principal amount of the debt disbursed at the loan closing, the following provision often appears:

> also secured by this mortgage are all future advances and indebtedness of the borrower up to the maximum amount of $10,000. Such sums as are advanced in the future are to be used by the borrower for the improvement, renovation, and rehabilitation of the property described in this instrument. Such advances will be made upon the presentation of executed job orders for the improvement, rehabilitation, and renovation of the subject property.

With this clause a mortgagee is attempting to gain priority for any future advances made to the borrower over intervening lienors — that is, lienors who file (say) mechanic's liens after the date of recording of the initial mortgage but before the date on which the advance is to be made. If the clause binds the lender to advance the money, and a lawsuit might result if the advance were withheld, the lender has obligated himself through this clause to make the advance. Obligatory advances generally gain a priority over intervening lienors, and such liens are subordinated to the obligation stated in the initial mortgage.

In a majority of states deciding the question, the mortgagee is protected for all future advances up to the time at which he has actual notice of intervening liens later recorded. See Note, 21 Okla. L. Rev. 79, 79-80 (1968). No constructive notice is charged to the mortgagee through the recording acts. Note, 47 Iowa L. Rev. 432 (1962). And in most states, no payment schedule is necessary to enable the mortgagee to assert that his advances have the character of an obligation.

In such jurisdictions, if the advance is made under progress payment schedules, it becomes obligatory by definition. When a future advance mortgagee is committed under a recorded mortgage to lend a specific sum, or up to a specific sum, and once several advances are made, with more to follow to complete the lender's agreement, the majority of courts treat the transaction as a continuous one, and neither actual or constructive notice of intervening liens will defeat the lender's priority. The mortgagee has no duty to recheck the public land records for the existence of intervening liens. Thus, with such obligatory advances, neither actual nor constructive notice defeats the intent of the parties to treat the loan transaction as a continuous one.

In a minority of states, the mortgagee is required to check the records before making each future advance. In such jurisdictions, no advance is deemed obligatory unless the lender first checks the records. In a sense this result is contrary to the theory of the recording acts, which are usually thought to establish prospective rather than retroactive notice.

When a future advance is optional on the lender's part, however, a lender's actual notice of an intervening lien will subordinate the lender's advance to the amount of an intervening lien. In a majority of states, a lender's constructive (not actual) notice of an intervening lien does not defeat the priority of an optional advance. Lincoln Fed. Sav. & Loan Assn. v. Platt Homes, 185 N.J. Super. 457, 449 A.2d 553 (Ch. Div. 1982).

So there are basically two rules governing future advance mortgage clauses. (1) Obligatory future advances have priority over intervening liens. (2) When the advances are optional, they are subordinated to the intervening lien if the lender has actual knowledge of the intervening lienor (the majority rule) or constructive notice of his presence (the minority rule).

The distinction between obligatory and optional advances is a matter of judicial interpretation in most jurisdictions. Optional advances are generally found where, (1) the mortgator abandons the property, (2) the procedure for disbursement of the advance has not been followed by the lender, (3) the advances were made before they were to be paid under the payment schedule (in this case they can later become obligatory at the due date), and (4) the lender represents that intervening lienors will get the advance.

The case law is split in situations in which money is diverted or dissipated by the mortgagor, as where he is a developer with a warehouse account used for several projects. See First Natl. Bank v. Convey Sheet Metal Co., 244 Ark. 963, 428 S.W.2d 293 (1968). Some cases say that in this situation the lender may be required to check the records, and if he finds something there that unsettles him and that litigation would be required to resolve, he can go ahead and pay out on the theory that he should not be put to a lawsuit regardless of his suspicions. Imhoff v. Title & Trust Co., 113 Cal. App. 2d 139, 247 P.2d 851 (1952).

Of course the lender may defend his priority by advancing the money, even though state law would find that the advance was optional, by showing that it was spent to perform his convenanted duties under the mortgage agreement or was an assertion of his right to preserve the encumbered property from waste or deterioration, as where he spends money for tax payments, restoration of the property, or janitorial service. What is required of the mortgagee under the covenants in the agreement is generally determined in these cases by what objectively is necessary to sustain his position. What matters is not what the mortgagee may elect to do personally, but what keeps the value of his security intact.

On the other hand, advances are found obligatory under state law if definite sums to be advanced have been stated on the face of the loan agreement, or if the loan application by the borrower and the loan commitment executed by the lender constitute offer and acceptance so that the lendor would be liable in damages if he did not make the advances.

If the public land records in the jurisdiction are sufficiently accurate so that as a matter of policy the state wants to encourage reliance on them, the future advance clause might be interpreted as the lender's offer to advance the money, but it may not yet constitute an obligation to do so. In the typical case, where construction or improvement of a property is the subject of the loan agreement, the lender will require proof of the work performed and some inspection of it by a qualified individual such as an architect. Only upon presentation of this third party's certification that the work has been performed will the advance actually be disbursed, and in such situations the lender might be construed to have contracted for an optional advance and thus should check the public land records for intervening liens before each advance is made.

In California under a "stop notice" law, this has become routine practice and is certainly consistent with a policy of encouraging reliance on the public records.

Several other states have been dissatisfied with judicial distinctions between obligatory and optional advances. In Illinois, for example, a statute gives the mortgagee an 18-month priority. Ill. Stat. Ann. ch. 30, §37(a) (1975). After this time, constructive notice of intervening liens comes to the lender through the recording acts. After the mortgagee's 18-month grace period, the common law distinction between obligatory and optional advances again takes hold. In a similar vein, the Florida legislature protects the mortgagee for a period of 20 months after the loan closing. See Silver Waters Corp. v. Murphy, 177 So. 2d 897 (Fla. App. 1965). In Maryland, a statute provides a limited priority for maintenance expenses of the mortgagee up to $1500 if the face amount of the debt is not increased. Md. Code art. 66, §2 (1975). In addition, several states have codified the actual notice rule. See, e.g., Cal. Civ. Code §2884 (1975); Conn. Stat. Ann. §49-2 (1975); Ohio Stat. Ann. §1311-14 (1975). One state has prohibited mortgages for future advances unless the advances are mandatory and a maximum is stated on the face of the loan agreement. N.H. Rev. Stat. §479:3-5 (1955). The state of Delaware has achieved the same result by judicial opinion. J. I. Kislak Mortgage Corp. v. Wm. Matthew Builders, Inc., 287 A.2d 686 (Del. Super. 1972), aff'd, 303 A.2d 648 (Del. 1973).

In the Federal National Mortgage Association form Uniform Covenant 3, there is a reference to future advances in the schedule for applying the payments of the borrower. In many situations this reference may not be necessary because, although there is no reference of future advances in the mortgage agreement, all advances extended to the borrower within the principal amount stated on the face of the mortgage are likely to be secured. So if the mortgage was given for $50,000 and had declined to $45,000, the mortgagee could make a $5000 advance to the borrower after the initial loan closing and feel secure that the loan would receive priority over intervening liens. In this limited sense, a kind of revolving credit is secured by the typical mortgage without any mention of future advances.

# EXAMPLES AND EXPLANATIONS

14a. MR executes a brief but enforceable residential mortgage in favor of ME. The mortgage advances MR the purchase money for the secured land and contains the following clause: "also secured by this mortgage are all future advances and indebtedness of the borrower up to a maximum amount of $50,000." MR also agrees with ME that ME will advance MR the full $50,000, in increments of $10,000, as MR builds a house on the land. MR promises to use the whole $50,000 to improve the secured land. ME agrees to disburse the first $10,000 when the foundation is finished. ME later refuses. May MR then compel such a disbursement?

**Explanation:** Yes. It is a mandatory or obligatory advance under the loan agreement. Southern Trust Mortgage Co. v. K & B Door Co., 104

Nev. 564, 763 P.2d 353, 355, n.2 (1988) (when the deed of trust states that "all funds" are "to be deemed obligatory advances," a right to inspect the progress of the construction, when used to verify progress, does not turn an obligatory advance into an optional one). To do so would defeat the purpose of the loan. Dempsey v. McGowan, 291 Ark. 147, 722 S.W.2d 848, 850 (1987). Neither is the answer to this question likely to change when the agreement to disburse was executed later than the agreement to loan.

14b. What if C had filed a mechanic's lien before ME's disbursal?

**Explanation:** ME would have priority over the mechanic's lien, on the same rationale. In addition, consider that C, the mechanic, wouldn't be working and paid — on this job site, anyway — unless the proceeds of the loan are disbursed; those proceeds make his work possible, so C shouldn't complain about ME's priority. Unless the mechanic's lien statute very clearly indicates otherwise, ME should prevail.

14c. Same facts as in 14a and 14b. The MR-ME agreement calls for the second $10,000 disbursement when the first floor is in place. However, ME knows that MR has diverted some of the funds from the first disbursement to improve another lot that MR owns. MR is therefore in default on the loan agreement. C, a mechanic working on MR's improvement, files a mechanic's lien before ME makes the second disbursement. Who has priority as to this second disbursement, C or ME?

**Explanation:** ME, who has made the disbursement as required by the terms of the agreement. MR's default should not — and usually does not — make this disbursement optional. A disbursement made subject to a commitment to disburse is obligatory, not optional. See Kratovil, Mortgage Priority Problems: The New Illinois Mortgage Foreclosure Act and the Impact of the Uniform Acts, 8 N. Ill. L. Rev. 1, 4-11 (1987).

14d. Same facts, but in addition C disputes with ME the payment made by MR to C. Next week, ME makes another advance to MR. State the priority of the mortgage and mechanic's liens.

**Explanation:** Now ME has actual notice of the claim of C. In many jurisdictions, that would turn the obligatory advance into an optional one. ME ought not to have to search for mechanic's liens before making each advance, but here he has more than the constructive notice that the recording acts would provide. Whether or not C files a lien is irrelevant. See J. Bruce, Real Estate Financing in a Nutshell 63-70 (2d ed. 1985); G. Nelson & D. Whitman, Real Estate Financing Law §12.7 (2d ed. 1985); G. Osborne, Mortgages §§113-114 (1970).

# Dragnet Clauses

This type of clause provides that the mortgage secures all present and future debts of the mortgagor, whether or not contemplated at the time of the execution of the mortgage in which the clause appears. Thus it is like a future advance clause but is broader and open-ended — that is, unlimited in amount. Courts often take a cue from this similarity and construe the clause to apply only to future loans originated (as opposed to acquired by assignment) by the same lender. This clause permits the mortgagee to consolidate multiple suits against the mortgagor.

# EXAMPLES AND EXPLANATIONS

15. MR executes a brief but enforceable residential mortgage in favor of ME. The mortgage stated that it "secures all debt now due or hereafter due that ME holds against MR as maker, surety, guarantor, partner or otherwise, whether contracted directly or purchased by ME." MR executes this mortgage on his farm for a loan to finance their farming operations. Later he ceases those operations and secures a mortgage on a residence in town from the same lender, but the farm mortgage is not paid off and released, although it is not in default. What type of transaction will this clause reach? Who has the burden of showing its intended effect?

**Explanation:**   Most courts strictly construe a dragnet clause. The differing purposes of the two loans is sufficient to find that the clause in the first mortgage does not mean that the title to the farm stands as security for the loan on the residence in town or vice versa. Decorah State Bank v. Zidlicky, 426 N.W.2d 388 (Iowa 1988); see also First Security Bank of Utah v. Shiew, 609 P.2d 952 (Utah 1980). The *Shiew* opinion contains a good recitation of the the black letter law on these clauses.

The strict construction of these clauses is necessary because otherwise the clause provides no notice of the extent of its reach. Title searchers and abstractors cannot define the reach of the clause without the strictest construction, particularly as to a search for other transactions between the same parties. See Amos v. Lance, 355 So. 2d 84 (Miss. 1978) (refusing to enforce a dragnet clause in a mortgage foreclosed in one county against property, located in another county, in order to satisfy deficiency judgment), noted in 50 Miss. L.J. 124 (1979).

Some courts even require that the later mortgage refer back expressly to the mortgage with the dragnet clause. (There is a presumption here that if a separate mortgage without a reference back is used, the waiver of the clause is intended.) Moreover, parol evidence is generally admissible to show how the parties intended the clause to function. Canal Natl. Bank v. Becker, 431 A.2d 71 (Me. 1981).

16. If the earlier mortgage with the dragnet clause requires a specific type of foreclosure, is an expressly referenced later mortgage between the same mortgagor and mortgagee for a similar purpose limited to the same remedy?

**Explanation:** Yes. Usually such a clause benefits the mortgagee, but it need not be so. The benefit of the clause can run to the mortgagor as well. For example, if a statutory benefit is given the mortgagor of the first mortgage, then that benefit runs to the mortgagor in later secured loans too.

# Applying for a Mortgage

In the residential mortgage situation, many cases state that the application is an offer, and the commitment letter is an acceptance. That would mean that a contract is established at the time of the commitment to lend.

Consider yet another agreement contained within this contract. The receipt of the application is accompanied by the payment of an application fee, usually for the credit report and an appraisal of the property. The acceptance of the application establishes a contract to process it. See Jacques v. First Natl. Bank of Maryland, 307 Md. 527, 515 A.2d 756 (1986) (finding such a contract). What consideration underlies such a contract? The applicant pays some fees at the filing of the application, seeks the advantage of obtaining a commitment to loan, and forgoes other applications (sometimes). The lender gains the benefit of reviewing this and a flow of other applications in order to accept the best of them, and thus mold the most profitable loan portfolio to meet its business needs. If a contract to process exists, then, a standard of due care and reasonable consideration of the application within a reasonable period of time attaches to the lender's duty to process.

Is the suit to enforce this contract best brought in contract or tort? The Jacques won their case on a negligence claim, but it was a claim for negligent processing of the loan application. Damages included the difference between the costs of financing that they would have obtained, but for the negligent processing, and the higher-cost financing they were obliged to accept.

One case does not make a national trend, but lenders have also been held liable for negligence in the preparation of the documents called for in an application. See, e.g., Larson v. United Fed. Sav. & Loan Assn., 300 N.W.2d 281, 21 A.L.R.4th 855 (Iowa 1981) (negligent appraisal of property).

# EXAMPLES AND EXPLANATIONS

17. H and W, husband and wife, file an application for a residential mortgage. It is accepted by letter, but when the day of the loan closing arrives,

they find that the lender is only willing to lend at a rate of interest 1 percent higher than requested in the application. Can they obtain specific performance of the application and the acceptance letter as a contract?

**Explanation:**   As a general rule, commitments to lend money through residential mortgages are not subject to specific performance. H and W would, however, have a cause of action for damages against the mortgage company. If they wish to bring this cause of action, they should not close the loan. The leading and classic case is Rogers v. Challis, 27 Beav. 175, 54 Eng. Rep. 68 (1859); see also G. Osborne, Mortgages §26 (1970). (There are some cases contra, but they involve commercial mortgages.)

18. M and F are engaged to be married. They execute a contract to purchase a townhouse in joint tenancy and present the contract of sale and an application for a mortgage to ME, a mortgage company. ME denies the application. Upon investigation, M and F discover that it is ME's policy not to lend to unmarried couples. A federal statute, The Equal Credit Opportunity Act, prohibits "discrimination in lending . . . on the basis of . . . sex or marital status." If this is ME's sole basis for its refusal to lend, can ME be compelled to accept the application?

**Explanation:**   Yes. See Markham v. Colonial Mortgage Serv. Co., 196 U.S. App. D.C. 50, 605 F.2d 566, 55 A.L.R. Fed. 448 (D.C. Cir. 1979). The legislative history of the language in the ECOA is clear that it applies only to credit denied married women seeking a loan in their own name. (Can you imagine Congress in the 1970s extending protection to unmarried couples?) The lender argues that the denial was not based on marital status but on just the opposite — the lack of marital status. Rejecting such an argument, a court would have to shift away from the legislative history of the statute and use instead the statute's plain meaning: that the phrase "marital status" must include its negative, the lack of marital status. This looks like equal protection analysis, but this isn't a constitutional law matter. Maybe the court is thinking ahead, looking to fend off a constitutional challenge to a potentially underinclusive statute. After *Markham,* what's next? Group house mortgages? Religious communities looking for a loan? To the extent that mortgage loans are made to unmarried couples, will single women and married women seeking loans not get loans? In tight markets, the two-income couple, married or not, may be the type of mortgagors preferred by lenders.

# Mortgage Escrow Accounts

In the course of applying for a mortgage, mortgagors often agree to put on deposit, every month and with each mortgage payment, money to pay real property taxes and property hazard insurance premiums as they are due. The account maintained by the mortgagee for the purpose of accumulating these monies until they need to be paid out is called a reserve account, or a mortgage escrow account. Distinguish this term from the escrow previously discussed as an alternative to the direct delivery of documents and the face-to-face closing of the transaction. The mortgage escrow has a much narrower purpose.

The maintenance of this account is controlled by the terms of the mortgage or deed of trust. Uniform Covenant 2 of the FNMA-FHLMC mortgage reads as follows:

> Subject to applicable law or to a written waiver by Lender, Borrower shall pay to Lender on the day monthly payments are due under the Note, until the Note is paid in full, a sum ("Funds") equal to one-twelfth of (a) yearly taxes and assessments which may attain priority over this Security Instrument, (b) yearly leaseholds payments or ground rents on the Property, if any, (c) yearly hazard insurance premiums, and (d) yearly mortgage insurance premiums, if any. These items are called "escrow items." Lender may estimate the Funds due on the basis of current data and reasonable estimates of future escrow items.

Thus far, we have an explanation of the types of monies that may be escrowed. Of course, if the jurisdiction's statutes require that the mortgagor be given a choice as to whether or not to maintain an escrow with the mortgagee, that statutory requirement controls. Often when the mortgagor pays down more than the usual percentage of the purchase price (and so is not financing the purchase pro tanto), the mortgagor will be given the option of paying the escrow items himself.

Notice too that the Uniform Covenant puts a maximum on how much of the total annual amount can be collected with any one monthly payment. However, manipulation of the total amount estimated by the lender to be necessary for each item affects the monthly payment; each item can be estimated separately, rather than together as a group. No matter how estimated, the mortgagee is subject to a good faith and fair dealing requirement of the common law.

This Covenant continues:

> The Funds shall be held [in a federally or state-insured institution]. Lender shall apply the Funds to pay the escrow items. Lender may not charge for holding and applying the funds, analysing the account or verifying the escrow items, unless Lender pays Borrower interest on the Funds and applicable law permits the Lender to make such a charge. Borrower and Lender may agree in writing that interest shall be paid on the Funds. Unless an agreement is made or applicable law requires interest to be paid, Lender shall not be required to pay Borrower any interest or earnings on the Funds. Lender shall give to Borrower, without charge, an annual accounting of the Funds showing credits and debits to the Funds and the purpose for which each debit to

the Funds was made. The Funds are pledged as additional security for the sums secured by this Security Instrument.

If the amount of Funds held by Lender, together with the future monthly payments of Funds payable prior to the due dates of the escrow items, shall exceed the amount required to pay the escrow items when due, the excess shall be, at Borrower's option, either promptly repaid to Borrower or credited to Borrower on monthly payments of Funds. If the amount of the Funds held by Lender is not sufficient to pay the escrow items when due, the Borrower shall pay to Lender any amount necessary to make up the deficiency in one or more payments as required by Lender.

Thereafter, this Covenant imposes on the mortgagee the duty to make a prompt refund of all funds on account at the time of the release of the mortgage lien or, when the property is sold, application of all funds on account to satisfy that lien.

The issues that worried many courts in the 1970s was whether or not the language of this Covenant creates a trust, of which the mortgagor is the beneficiary and the mortgagee the trustee. What do you think? Most courts held that no trust was created. La Throp v. Bell Fed. Sav. & Loan Assn., 68 Ill. 2d 375, 370 N.E.2d 188 (1977), cert. denied, 436 U.S. 925 (1978), noted in 7 Real Est. L.J. 163 (1978); Sears v. First Fed. Sav. & Loan Assn., 1 Ill. App. 3d 621, 275 N.E.2d 300, 50 A.L.R.3d 683 (1971); Kronisch v. Howard Sav. Inst., 161 N.J. Super. 592, 392 A.2d 178 (App. Div. 1978) (despite the language of trust, a debtor-creditor relationship was created by mortgage covenant); Annot., Rights in funds representing "escrow" payments made by mortgagor in advance to cover taxes and insurance, 50 A.L.R.3d 697 (1973). However, some held that the mortgagor had contractual rights that amounted to the same thing. Brooks v. Valley Natl. Bank, 24 Ariz. 484, 539 P.2d 958 (1976) (this opinion collects the cases).

What language is relevant to a resolution of this issue? *La Throp* indicates that the mere mention of the word "trust" in an escrow account covenant is insufficient to establish a trust relationship. Most courts agreed, at least sub rosa, that interpretation of the covenant was the dispositive issue.

# EXAMPLES AND EXPLANATIONS

19. If the covenant were to contain a late payment penalty, what does that indicate about the relationship created between lender and borrower?

**Explanation:** The presence of such a penalty tends to reenforce the idea that the account is maintained for the benefit of the lender, and not the borrower; likewise, it negates the idea that the account is a trust fund.

20. What about the language indicating that "the Lender shall hold the funds" and "the Lender shall apply the funds"? What does this language indicate in a trust relationship?

**Explanation:**  These phrases indicate that the lender undertakes a duty in relation to the funds, but they are insufficient to indicate that the lender is a trustee of the funds; however, a contract duty may be found.

21. What if an employee of the mortgagee were to abscond with the funds or is negligent in making the payments for escrow items as due the tax collector or insurer? Does the lender or the borrower undertake this risk?

**Explanation:**  Even though the lender does not have the duties of a trustee, it may have contract duties to the borrower nonetheless, and inadeqate supervision of an employee may give rise to an action for a negligent implementation of a contract duty. Likewise, the lender is an agent of the borrower for paying over funds on account and a failure to pay is a breach of the agency.

What impact on the finding of a debt or a trust would the financial markets surrounding the account have? If the average mortgagor would lose $15-20 in interest at the time the *Brooks* opinion was handed down, but subsequently, in a market in which interest rates were up, would lose $40-50, should that make a difference to the court? No matter what language is relevant, any litigation imposing a trust would have to be brought as a class action to be worthwhile. If passbook rates were to be paid in the typical account, no one individual mortgagor would have sufficient economic incentive to carry the litigation through to judgment. See generally Hines & Baughman, Should Lenders Pay Interest on Mortgage Escrows?, 8 Real Est. Rev. 79 (Fall 1978).

# 20

## *Junior Liens*

When a titleholder mortgages her property twice, the lien given and recorded first is called the senior lien, and that given a second is called a junior lien. Each of the mortgagees holding a lien is entitled to the security in the property for which she bargained at the time of the transfer and recording of their respective liens. This means that a senior lien is entitled to a foreclosure conducted as if the junior lien did not exist. This is accomplished by giving a foreclosure the effect of wiping out any liens junior to the lien foreclosed. This effect means in turn that a title sold at any foreclosure sale will be in the same state as it was when the senior mortgagee bargained for her security. In this way, she gets what she bargained for.

Foreclosure procedures typically involve a title search at some early point in the proceedings. As the result of the search, junior mortgagees are made parties to the foreclosure and receive some of the proceeds of the sale, if any remain after the satisfaction of all liens senior to them. Junior mortgagees and any holder of a junior interest in the property, such as a lease, are necessary parties to a senior foreclosure. In contrast, a senior mortgagee or other interest holder is a proper, but not a necessary party, to a junior foreclosure.

In a foreclosure of a senior lien, a junior mortgagee has the same right as a mortgagor to redeem the senior mortgage by paying the outstanding debt due on it. She can also sue the mortgagor for a deficiency judgment if the proceeds of the senior foreclosure sale are inadequate to satisfy the full amount of the debt owed to her at the time her lien is extinguished. Finally, she can purchase the property at the foreclosure sale.

The doctrine of marshalling may further protect the junior lienholder when the mortgagor owns two properties, both of which are subject to the senior lien and one of which is subject to the junior. Under this doctrine, the senior can be compelled to satisfy her debt from the property exclusively available to her. The senior is still entitled to have her debt satisfied first but is limited in the order in which she must seek satisfaction. She must foreclose first on property available only to her. Note, Marshalling: Equitable Rights of Holders of Junior Interests, 38 Rutgers L. Rev. 287, 289 (1986). In a few states, this doctrine is codified. Id. at 290 n.29. The senior and junior interests need not be of the same type for the junior to seek the protection of the doctrine (for example, judgment creditors can use the doctrine against mortgagees, and vice versa). Marshalling is an equitable doctrine, subject to the discretion of the judge, and so is not everywhere seen as a right, although if a junior makes a timely assertion of this doctrine and shows that, first, no prejudice to senior lienholders results and, second, its use would not defeat any statutory rights, it is likely to be used.

Likewise, the junior lienholder is entitled to the security for which she too bargained. The senior mortgagee can neither extend the time for payment, raise the interest rate on the note accompanying the senior lien, nor raise the monthly payments without the approval of the junior. The reason for requiring the approval is that, otherwise, the junior would be less secure than she bargained to be. If the junior becomes less secure, her lien will, in part, become senior (in any later foreclosure) to that portion of the payment of the senior note obligation that diminishes the security of the junior.

What the junior mortgagee cannot do is force the senior mortgagee to foreclose her lien, even if the titleholder is in default on the note or on a covenant in the senior mortgage. The principle is the same. The senior bargained for a remedy and is entitled to choose when and where to use it. She invested money for a certain period of time and is entitled to choose the time to call in that investment.

The junior mortgagee, however, can foreclose her mortgage lien separately from the senior lien. If she does this, she forecloses on the title as it was when she executed her mortgage. That is, the title sold at the foreclosure sale will be subject to any senior lien, and the obligation to pay the senior note will still exist. So the purchaser at the sale gets to step into the mortgagor's shoes on the secured property but also gets the title subject to the senior mortgage. She has no personal obligation to pay the senior debt, but if it is not paid, the senior mortgagee can foreclose and the junior mortgagee in possession, or the purchaser at the junior foreclosure, will lose the right to possession. In effect, the junior mortgagee forecloses on the title existing at the time she bargained for her security, and her foreclosure sale transfers that title along with the rights that the mortgagor has in any foreclosure of any senior lien.

In any foreclosure, questions of priority of title are resolved only to the extent necessary. There is no proceeding that will adjudicate the priority of all liens and other encumbrances attaching to the title. Foreclosure is not a proceeding in rem. To the extent that the proceeds of the sale, however conducted, must be distributed, that distribution will be in accord with the priorities found inter se. When junior liens are wiped out in a senior foreclosure and turned into a right to share in the proceeds, those junior liens are lined up in priority to receive whatever proceeds are available. If the junior is partially satisfied from the proceeds, or a deficiency judgment is otherwise available, the unpaid junior may sue for a deficiency. However, if no proceeds are available for distribution, no priorities will be determined. The junior lienholders left in the cold must enforce their notes against the personal assets of the debtor, no longer a mortgagor as to the wiped-out junior.

Thus the priority of a junior lien will be determined in a senior foreclosure in which the junior is joined as a party, but the priority of a senior lien will not be determined in a foreclosure of a lien junior to it, unless the senior mortgagee joins in the action. These principles are in accord with the relativity of title underlying the common law system of title.

# EXAMPLES AND EXPLANATIONS

1. In a title state for mortgages, O executes a mortgage on Blackacre in favor of M1, and then later executes a mortgage on Blackacre in favor of M2. What interest does M2 take in Blackacre?

**Explanation:** The O-M1 mortgage is the conveyance of a defeasible fee to M1, who holds the title so long as the mortgage loan is unpaid but agrees that, upon repayment, she will reconvey the title to O. If M2's mortgage is executed while M1's is still outstanding, O has conveyed her defeasible equity of redemption to M2, that being the right held by O after the execution of the first mortgage. See J. Bruce, Real Estate Finance in a Nutshell 24-26 (2d ed. 1985); G. Nelson & D. Whitman, Real Estate Finance Law §§10.9-10.15 (2d ed. 1985); G. Osborne, Mortgages §§181, 182 (1970).

2. If O's mortgages in the preceding paragraph were executed in a lien state, what would your answer be?

**Explanation:** Both M1 and M2 hold liens on Blackacre. M1 holds the first lien, superior to M2's. M2 holds a second or junior lien — junior, that is, to M1's.

3. If M2 forecloses in a lien state and purchases at the judicial sale, what is the state of her title?

**Explanation:** M2 takes over O's rights as of the time O and M2 executed their mortgage transaction. That is, M2 gets the title in the condition in which it was at that time. That's what M2 expected to have as security for her loan, and what she gets. So M2 gets possession of Blackacre, with its title encumbered with M1's mortgage lien — again, this encumbrance was attached to the title when M2 made her deal. M2 gets possession, together with the right to pay off M1's loan. She takes title subject to the senior lien but without assuming the personal obligation to pay it.

4. Can M2 force M1 to foreclose? Would your answer change if M1's mortgage were in default?

**Explanation:** No, M2 cannot force the holder of a lien senior to her own to foreclose. M1 bargained for the right to foreclose at a time and place of her own choosing; she cannot be forced to use what she bargained for as an elective remedy. Even if the senior lien is in default, the senior lienor cannot be forced to foreclose. In a few states, when and only when the senior mortgage debt is due, M1 can be compelled by M2 to foreclose her lien.

5. A first mortgagee M1 brings an action to foreclose her mortgage lien. A junior mortgagee M2 with security in the same property is properly joined in M1's action. The mortgagor has a defense to the action that, if properly and timely asserted, would result in the action's dismissal. The mortgagor does not assert this defense but, over M2's objections, consents to a judgment binding M2, in exchange for M1's waiver of her right to a deficiency judgment. M2 in a timely manner, attempts to assert the mortgagor's defense. Should M2 be permitted to assert this defense?

**Explanation:** No. The defense is one relating to the first lien mortgage transaction, to which M2 was not a party. M2 is a poor source of evidence relating to this defense, took her junior lien in the expectation that the senior lien was enforceable, and would otherwise be unjustly enriched (by having the first lien not subject to dismissal). See State Mutual Life Assurance Co. of America v. Deer Creek Park, 612 F.2d 259 (6th Cir. 1979).

6. O executes brief but enforceable mortgages to M1 and M2 in that order. Before a large payment on M1's mortgage comes due, O asks X to make the payment and to pay the outstanding balance of M1's mortgage. M1 agrees to deal with X, and X pays off M1's mortgage. Can X assume M1's lien status over M2's protest?

**Explanation:** Yes. M2 never expected to have, as security for her loan, a title unencumbered by M1's lien. X assumes M1's lien position by virtue of subrogation; X steps into M1's shoes and takes over her rights and duties. Any other result would be a windfall for M2. It is said that X has an "equity of subrogation."

7. If X assumed M1's lien status in the preceding paragraph and foreclosed, what would be the state of the title after the foreclosure?

**Explanation:** M2's lien would be wiped out in X's foreclosure because that is what M1 bargained for and what was transferred to X by M1. M1 bargained for security in a title in foreclosure unencumbered by M2's lien and, M1's remedy being transferred to X, that is what X is entitled to as well.

8. What were M2's alternatives to taking junior lien in the preceding paragraphs?

**Explanation:**   Some alternatives are M2's leasing the property and taking possession (when the rents and profits from doing so can satisfy the debt), buying the property and leasing it back to O (a sale-leaseback), taking a vendee's interest in a contract of sale (giving O an option to repurchase it) or an installment land sale contract, or providing O with wraparound financing, discussed in the chapter on construction financing. See Chapter 30. In addition, the junior mortgagee can take a participating note — that is, one payable in interest and a portion of the rents and profits from the property — or an equity interest in the property as partial repayment of the debt. To avoid the charge that such an interest is a clog on the equity of redemption in the first loan, such an interest in the appreciated value of the property cannot be so large as to result in the mortgagor's being unable to redeem in the senior foreclosure. Thus the value of the junior's interest should be assigned a stated value and be capable of repurchase at any time prior to any (junior or senior) foreclosure. To avoid the charge that it is clog on the equity of redemption of the junior mortgage, it should be in a separate agreement, for a stated sum, and extinguish stated portion of the debt when the interest passes to the junior mortgagee. Barach, A Practical Guide to Equity Participation Loans: Legal Principles and Drafting Considerations, 20 Real Est. L.J. 115, 131-133 (1991).

# 21

## Transfers of the Mortgage

## Assuming Debt versus Taking Title "Subject to"

When a mortgagor transfers his title to property securing a mortgage, the transferee will usually finance the purchase with the proceeds of a new mortgage loan. The new mortgagee will usually require that its lien be a first lien, thereby requiring that the mortgagor pay off the outstanding debt, usually from the proceeds of the sale. When this is not done, the grantee-transferee may take the title of the mortgagor-vendor subject to the outstanding lien of the preexisting mortgage (known as taking title "subject to," a subject we previously discussed in the context of contracts of sale). Taking title subject to, does not oblige the purchaser to pay the debt evidenced in the note, but the property he receives may nonetheless be called on to secure repayment of that debt through a sale by foreclosure, which will extinguish the purchaser's rights in the property. Such a purchaser is, for present purposes, the holder of an interest junior to that of the preexisting mortgagee. Thus the transferee takes title subject to the right to foreclose held by the preexisting mortgagee.

Now for a grantee who assumes the debt. An assuming grantee or transferee is personally liable for the debt; he undertakes to repay the outstanding amount due on the preexisting note. Thus not only does the property remain the primary security for repayment, but the grantee, along with the mortgagor, is also personally liable for repayment as well. When a grantee assumes the debt, he also becomes the primary debtor, the person to whom the mortgagee must look first for repayment. The original debtor becomes a surety, liable to repay when the assuming grantee does not. This requires that the mortgagee consent to the arrangement. When asked to repay, the original debtor is then allowed to turn around and, in turn, ask the assuming grantee for the necessary funds. Yasuna v. Miller, 399 A.2d 68, 73 (D.C. 1979).

# Transfers by the Mortgagor

Let's now use the distinction between taking title to real property subject to an existing mortgage and taking title while assuming an existing mortgage.

If, for example, in the context of a subdivision development, a developer-mortgagor finances the construction of houses with a blanket mortgage loan (in which the lien of the mortgage attaches to all lots in the subdivision) and the purchasers of each house and lot take title subject to the blanket mortgage, which of the purchasers should be foreclosed on first if not all lots are needed to satisfy the debt and the purchasers assert the doctrine of marshalling as a defense?

The answer is that an inverse order of alienation will be used: That is, the last purchasers to take subject to would be the first foreclosed. Viewed from the perspective of the first purchasers in the subdivision, their purchase took place at a time when there was relatively more property to satisfy the blanket mortgage, but the last purchasers had no such cushion.

Would your answer change if each purchaser assumed the developer's loan? Yes, then the chronological order of alienation would control the sequence of foreclosure. Here the first purchaser was facing a potentially large liability, but subsequent purchasers take in reliance on the prior assumptions.

What if some purchasers took subject to, but others assumed? Now one might go down the chronological order of assumptions, then back up the inverse order of "subject to" purchasers, on the theory that the assuming purchasers undertook the greater risk (of personal as well as grantee liability). See generally G. Osborne, Mortgages §§286-292 (1970).

So far we have just been discussing the order in which purchasers might be subjected to foreclosure. How about the later problem of distributing the proceeds of the foreclosure sale? If the whole subdivision is placed in foreclosure, would junior mortgagees, whose loans were secured by individual lots, receive the proceeds of the foreclosure sale in the order they recorded their liens, or should they share ratably in the proceeds, receiving only those proceeds derived from the sale of the lot securing their loan? See Metcalfe & Sons, Inc. v. Canyon Defined Benefit Trust, 318 Md. 565, 569 A.2d 669 (1990) (deciding that the latter course is best).

# EXAMPLES AND EXPLANATIONS

The following problems develop, in their answers, some material that might otherwise be set out in black letter style. But, for once, approaching a difficult problem through a series of hypotheticals seems preferable. So consider the following.

1. MR executes a brief but enforceable note and mortgage in favor of ME. MR conveys to A1, agreeing with A1 that A1 will assume MR's debt

and take subject to the mortgage lien. Does this agreement have to be in writing?

**Explanation:** Most assumption agreements are contained in a deed covenant, and so are in writing. When the agreement and the deed are independent of one another, a majority of courts addressing the question have held that the Statute of Frauds does not require a writing. See, e.g., White v. Schnader, 185 Cal. 606, 198 P. 19, 21 A.L.R. 499 (1921) (stating that the Statute of Frauds does not require a writing in this instance). Under the statute, this is not an agreement to pay the debt of another. The presence of the mortgage muddies the applicability of that section of the original Statute of Frauds. Moreover, the original mortgagor, MR, is still liable to ME; if he were not, the note and mortgage terms would have been changed unilaterally by the MR-A1 agreement and, because ME was no party to this agreement, he is not bound by it. See G. Osborne, Mortgages §255 (1970).

2. Assume the facts in the preceding paragraph. If A1 later contends that the agreement was really an agreement to take Blackacre subject to ME's mortgage lien, will A1 be able to show this? If MR wanted to show that A1 really meant to assume, but that they used the words "subject to" instead, would he be able to show that?

**Explanation:** The parol evidence rule does not prevent a showing that a "subject to" agreement is really intended, but it would prevent a showing that a subject to agreement was really intended to function as an assignment. The rule does not prevent cutting back on the effect of the agreement, but it cannot be used to expand its legal effects. Osborne, supra, §256.

3. Assume the facts in Example 2. If thereafter A1 conveyed to A2, who in turn conveyed to A3 — all grantees assuming the original debt and obligation to ME — can ME go directly against A3 to recover the debt? On what theory or theories?

**Explanation:** There are two theories. First is the derived right or contract theory. This means that the mortgagee ME derives his right by stepping into the shoes of the mortgagor MR, who has the right to go against the assuming assignee for the repayment of the outstanding balance of the loan. The theory is one of subrogation; ME is subrogated to MR's right to seek repayment from the assignee. For an instance of its use, see Somers v. Avant, 149 Ga. App. 515, 254 S.E.2d 722, rev'd, 244 Ga. 460, 261 S.E.2d 334 (1979).

Second is the third-party beneficiary theory. See, e.g., Hafford v. Smith, 369 S.W.2d 290 (Mo. App. 1963). Under this theory, the mortgagee is the third-party (donee or creditor) beneficiary of the series of assignments between the MR and the first assuming grantee or between subsequent assuming grantees.

Which theory is used makes a difference in three instances. Let's add some more facts to the basis problem. See J. Bruce, Real Estate Finance in a Nutshell 95-103 (2d ed. 1985); Osborne, supra, §§261, 262.

The three instances are as follows:

a. Will it make any difference if ME has not yet foreclosed? Yes, because the derived contract theory depends on the enforcement of the rights of the mortgagee. Foreclosure is the vehicle of enforcement, so that, before foreclosure, the mortgagor cannot turn to A1 and ask him to make good on his assumption because he is not yet liable over to ME. Likewise, A1 cannot turn to A2, and A2 to A3. If ME is a third-party beneficiary of the later transactions involving A1, A2, and A3, the latter parties are directly liable to ME, and this direct liability exists preforeclosure. The theory works both ways too (which is another way of saying that it is equitable to use it here). Why? Well, ME is benefited by the assignees' assumptions and they receive some benefit back, through the financing already extended by ME if the assignees purchased the property at a lower price which takes account of the preexisting note and mortgage obligation. In fact, third-party beneficiary theory was developed to give ME options besides foreclosure; as such, it operates, as does foreclosure, as an equitable right.

b. Will it make any difference if A2 takes subject to? Again, yes. Here a nonassuming grantee (NAG) has been inserted into a chain of assuming grantees. The successive liabilities necessary to make the derived contract theory work does not do the job. The result is that ME cannot establish a chain of derived rights that leads to the last, or remote, assuming grantee, the RAG (A3). The RAG is thus off the hook here. What is the result under third-party beneficiary theory? Under this theory there is a possibility that ME will directly sue the RAG. The thinking requires some inferences about why the RAG might, during the course of the transaction in which he takes title, assume a personal liability for which he would not otherwise be responsible. His grantor might consider that he (the mesne grantor) is liable and want to bargain for the transfer of that liability to his grantee. So the purchase price might be adjusted accordingly. Also, the RAG, coming at the end of a chain of title, might be holding title to real property that has appreciated in value. In such a rising market, the risk of holding the title subject to would mean that he has no ability (if he chose) to pay off any default on the note, stave off foreclosure, and thereby preserve his built-up equity in the property, which he might lose in foreclosure. These are inferences about a transaction between the NAG (or his successor) and the RAG. (If the inferences fail to convince, then the idea of a donee beneficiary is a fallback position.) The beneficiary of that later transaction is ME, who then becomes the third-party beneficiary of the later NAG-RAG transaction and so can enforce the remote assumption of the debt by the RAG.

c. What if MR releases A3 from his assumption? Here again, the theory matters. The mortgagee must join in such a release in third-party beneficiary states. Remember that ME is the beneficiary of the later transactions in the

MR-A1-A2-A3 chain of title. If the derived contract theory is used, ME need not join; in such states, ME still has his rights against MR, and it is MR who increases his own liability if he eliminates his "rights over" against A1, A2, or A3.

In Zastrow v. Knight, 56 S.D. 554, 229 N.W. 925, 72 A.L.R. 379 (1929), an extension agreement (extending the time for payment) was executed between the mortgagee ME and the RAG. Does the mortgagor have to join? The answer is yes in derived contract states. The enforcement mechanism for this is the discharge rule. This rule states that the mortgagor who does not consent to a ME-A3 extension agreement is discharged. At common law the discharge was a total one. The mortgagor could not be held liable for any amount of the debt in an action to enforce a deficiency judgment. The majority of cases today hold that he is only discharged in part, that is, to the extent of his prejudice, measured in *Zastrow* by the amount the secured real property fell in value during the extension period.

The answer is no in third-party beneficiary states, but the reasons are not at all clear. It may be that MR, standing as the surety for the RAG, receives a benefit from the extension agreement. The benefit is time. The march of litigation, back up the chain of title through interim grantees, is stalled by the agreement, and MR is given more time to make good on his suretyship obligation. How can he be heard to complain of that? MR is the third-party beneficiary of the extension agreement. That agreement is in effect a ratification by ME of the surety relations between MR and A1, A2, and A3.

A summary diagram of all three of the foregoing instances would look this way:

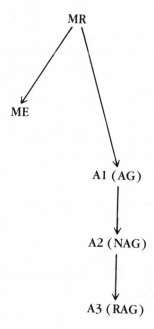

in which

**ME** = original mortgagee

**MR** = original mortgagor, who remains liable on the note after his conveyance to A1

**AG** = assuming grantee, who has taken a deed containing an assumption
agreement or made such an agreement separately

**NAG** = nonassuming grantee, who takes his title subject to ME's lien

**RAG** = remote assuming grantee, who has made his agreement to assume
with NAG, MR, or ME.

Thus there are at least three instances when the theory of the case matters
when the mortgagee sues the last, though not necessarily the remote, assuming
grantee to enforce the debt. Although one state may adopt one or both of
the theories, it is better to see the two theories as equitable adjustments to
the circumstances of the case. Often the derived contract is a jurisdiction's
original theory, and the third-party beneficiary analysis is added later, to do
equity. However, the law is accretive — the third-party beneficiary does not
usually replace the derived contract theory. Although a simpler solution might
be to admit that all is equity here, the trouble with such simplicity is that it
arrives late in the day.

4. FNMA-FHLMC Uniform Mortgage covenants make any of MR's
grantees personally liable for the debt. They take advantage of both derived
contract and third-party beneficiary theory. The former will make everyone
in the mortgagor's chain of title liable up to the NAG, while the latter will
make everyone liable below that point. What about the NAG himself?

**Explanation:**   He is typically liable through being put on constructive
notice under the recording acts and because the mortgage covenants aim at
abolishing the rules of suretyship that would protect him at common law.
See First Fed. Sav. & Loan Assn. of Gary v. Arena, 406 N.E.2d 1279 (Ind.
App. 1980), noted at 15 Ind. L. Rev. 365-366 (1982).

5. MR executes a brief but enforceable mortgage in favor of ME. MR
then conveys to an assuming grantee, P, who in turn conveys to P1, who
understands that he is taking subject to the preexisting mortgage. After the
closing, P1 alleges that an assumption covenant in their deed — to the effect
that P1 "assumes and agrees to pay the note held by ME" — was added after
the deed was delivered. However, there is evidence that P1 did investigate
the outstanding debt on the mortgage note during the course of the P-P1
executory period. In equity, P1 seeks relief from liability under the assumption
covenant. In this suit, what result?

**Explanation:**   P1 is probably bound by the agreement to assume the
repayment of the note, but this result is subject to proof. He should have

checked his deed in this regard. The change in words in the covenant required to assure P1 of only taking title subject to is slight and easily accomplished: P1 would only have to agree "to take title subject to, but not to assume personally," the obligation of MR's note. For the assumption covenant in P's deed to be subject to reformation and removal, P1 will have to show clearly that he and P intended that he not assume the personal obligation to repay. P1, after all, is bringing a fraud action and has a high burden of proof. This burden might best be met by showing an agreement to that effect in the contract of sale executed by the parties; such an agreement might be an ancillary contract not subject to merger in the deed.

In lieu of such evidence, P1 might show that he paid full market value as a purchase price, giving rise to the inference that in this situation he would not have assumed the obligation to repay MR's note as well; if he cannot show that, then the law might imply an assumption agreement, derived from the contract or its price term and enforced by P through rights derived from MR's vendor's lien on the property, or by ME as the third-party beneficiary of that implied, derived contract. See, e.g., Hafford v. Smith, 369 S.W.2d 290 (Mo. App. 1963) (an example of an implied assumption agreement).

Implied assumption agreements are involved in relatively few cases, but *Hafford* provides a good example of such an agreement.

6. Can an assuming grantee of the mortgagor use any defenses that the mortgagor would have used against the mortgagee?

**Explanation:** If the defenses are raised in a foreclosure action by the mortgagee, then the answer is yes in derived contract states but no in third-party beneficiary states. Generally, however, in nonforeclosure suits on the note, the answer is no. That is consistent with deriving the mortgagor's rights from the outcome of foreclosure by requiring foreclosure first. But this result makes one uneasy. Why? Because a mortgagee may obtain the debt or property more easily than he otherwise would have, creating a windfall. However, if the defenses are intent-based, such as a lack of capacity, mutual mistake, or lack of consideration, perhaps the rule is justified, but some policy-based defenses may be important enough to preserve in the hands of assuming grantees. See Osborne, supra, §267; and see Dunning v. Leavitt, 85 N.Y.30, 39 Am. Rep. 617 (1881).

# Transfers by the Mortgagor: Due-on-Sale Clauses

If all or any part of the Property or any interest in it is sold or transferred . . . . Lender may, at its option, require immediate payment in full of all sums secured.

The background of this covenant is worth mention. In the late 1960s and early 1970s, institutional mortgagees found themselves having to borrow in capital markets with unstable (mostly rising) interest rates. Their loan portfolios, however, had low-yield loans. In mortgage banking this problem is known as "borrowing short and lending long" — borrowing with short-term notes and paying off the short-term notes with the income from their (long-term) mortgage portfolio. The difference between the banks' receiving low rates of interest on their portfolio loans and paying high rates of interest as borrowers meant a capital shortage for residential and other types of mortgagors. Mortgagees needed to turn over the loans in their portfolio faster so that the long-term mortgage rate could keep pace with the short-term capital markets the mortgage lenders found themselves in.

The partial answer to their economic problem was the so-called due-on-sale clause; another answer was the variable or adjustable rate mortgage note, discussed elsewhere in these materials. In tandem, then, the lenders hoped that they could recover profitability. In the meanwhile, they often lived off closing and servicing fees.

The due-on-sale clause faced litigation challenges. It was first used in the 1950s and routinely used by the early 1970s, but mortgagors contested its use, typically arguing that the mortgagee was no less secure with the mortgagee's purchaser assuming the obligation to pay the loan than it was currently. There was thus no need for the clause, the argument ran, and its use was unconscionable, a penalty, and/or a restraint on alienation. Most courts responding to such challenges held that the mortgagee could have automatic enforcement of the clause and thus acceleration of the debt. Lake v. Equitable Sav. & Loan Assn., 105 Idaho 923, 674 P.2d 419 (1983) (containing a string citation to these many cases). A few — an influential few — held that enforcement was not automatic and that the mortgagee had to make a showing of insecurity as a precondition to enforcement and acceleration. California was one of these influential few jurisdictions. See, e.g., Wellenkamp v. Bank of America, 21 Cal. 3d 943, 148 Cal. Rptr. 379, 582 P.2d 970 (1978).

In the mid-1970s, then, federal banking regulators proposed preemptive regulations validating this type of clause. The Supreme Court upheld the regulations and gave them preemptive effect. Fidelity Fed. Sav. & Loan Assn. v. De La Cuesta, 458 U.S. 141, 147 (1982). At the end of the same year, the Congress further responded with legislation validating the clause. See 12 U.S.C. §1701j-3 (1987) (the Garn-St. Germain Depository Institutions Act of 1982). The final result of this decade-long activity was the clause at the beginning of this section. Martin v. Peoples Mutual Sav. & Loan Assn., 319 N.W.2d 220 (Iowa 1982); Capital Fed. Sav. & Loan Assn. v. Glenwood Manor, Inc., 235 Kan. 935, 686 P.2d 853 (1984); Gate Co. v. Midwest Fed. Sav. & Loan Assn., 324 N.W.2d 202 (Minn. 1982).

Turn now to the language of the clause itself. Sale or transfer? Garn-St. Germain established some exceptions — some situations in which the lender was not permitted to accelerate the debt. These were taken from clauses permissible under the regulations and often reflected the situations in which the early versions of the covenant had been successfully challenged in court. For example, the creation of a junior lien was not a sale or transfer because the priority of the senior lien was undisturbed. Similarly, a purchase money security agreement for household appliances was excepted; so too, were various intrafamily transfers (including transfers made as a part of a divorce proceedings, or transfers after the death of the mortgagor to members of his family), leases of the property for three years or less or transfers into inter vivos trusts. See 12 U.S.C. §1701j-3(d)(1)-(8).

Not to imply that there is a requirement that Congress be consistent, but is the theory of all of these exceptions the same? Obviously not.

The Garn-St. Germain Act has some interesting provisions. Here are the crucial ones:

> Notwithstanding any provision of the constitution or laws
> (including the judicial decisions) of any State to the contrary,
> a lender may, subject to [contrary laws and decisions applicable for
> an interim or "window" period], enter into or enforce a contract
> containing a due-on-sale clause with respect to a real property loan.

§1701j-3(b)(1). This is the section that provides the mortgagee's basic authority to enforce the clause. Probably the well-advised mortgagee, using the statutory authority here, will standardize its language.

> Except as otherwise provided in [the exceptions discussed
> previously], the exercise by the lender of its option pursuant to
> such a clause shall be exclusively governed by the terms of a
> loan contract, and all rights and remedies of the lender and the
> borrower shall be fixed and governed by the contract.

12 U.S.C. §1701j-3(b)(2). Taken together with the lender's basic authority, this section raises some interesting questions. "Governed by the terms of a loan contract . . . governed by the contract"? This could mean that any reading of the clause is subject only to textual analysis, unaided by the case law of the jurisdiction for which the contract is written. This interpretation of the clause was rejected by one state court in Fogel v. S.S.R. Realty Assn., 190 N.J. Super. 47, 461 A.2d 1190, 1193 n.1 (App. Div. 1983). This federal statute applies alike in states that found such clauses an unreasonable restraint on alienation, as well as for states whose courts upheld the clauses' automatic acceleration provisions — and to the extent that some states used their contract law to invalidate the clause, this interpretation must be intended. However, the reach of the statute into a state's substantive contract law should not be further than necessary to accomplish its purpose. All contract defenses

otherwise continue to apply: Examples are the rules relating to the unconscionability of contracts or to contracts of adhesion.

Who has the burden of proof when enforcing the clause provisions —
mortgagor or mortgagee? On the face of this statute, it is impossible to say.
To the extent that the enforceability of the clause is "governed exclusively"
by its terms, the lender need not show itself insecure after the transfer; and,
assuming that insecurity is relevant at all after the act's passage (a big question
in itself), the mortgagor has the burden of proving that the lender is no less
secure after a transfer. See Weiman v. McHaffie, 470 So. 2d 682 (Fla. 1985)
(holding that the mortgagee need not show insecurity and finding that this
is the majority rule).

And whose law? Is the mortgagee's authority a matter of federal common
law, or of federal courts applying state law? Is the statute, as one commentator
deftly said, in the spirit of *Erie v. Tompkins* or *Swift v. Tyson*? Roberts, Property,
34 Syracuse L. Rev. 371, 374-375 (1983). The controversy over federal
preemptive regulations and the *De La Cuesta* opinion preceding the enactment
of this statute, suggests that the latter opinion controls. But assuming that
the courts are authorized in this statute to develop federal common law rules,
does the statute control the equity powers of federal courts as well? Probably not.

A federal court has the power to hold that enforcement of a due-on-sale
clause along with enforcement of a prepayment penalty is a penalty and that
the lender cannot enforce both together. If the mortgagee accelerates the
debt at his option and then deducts the prepayment penalty from the amount
to be credited toward repayment of the debt, it obtains a double benefit from
a unilateral action. In re LHD Realty Corp., 726 F.2d 327 (7th Cir. 1984)
(holding that a mortgagee cannot accelerate the outstanding debt and concur-
rently levy a prepayment charge). See Stark, Enforcing Prepayment Charges:
Case Law and Drafting Suggestions, 22 Real Prop. Prob.& Tr. J. 549, 554-
555 (1987)

A due-on-sale clause is defined in this act as

> a contract provision which authorizes a lender, at its option, to
> declare due and payable sums secured by the lender's security
> instrument if all or any part of the property, or an interest therein,
> securing the real property loan is sold or transferred with the
> lender's prior written consent.

12 U.S.C. §1701j-3(a)(1). With the definition of the clause, several problems
arise. What if the clause drafted by the mortgagee were mandatory and
automatic? According to the literal reading of the definition, such a clause is
not authorized by the statute: An authorized clause is an optional one, working an acceleration only at the option of the mortgagee. This is a trap for
the unwary mortgagee or its counsel, but note the dangers of textual analysis
unaided by any legal context as mentioned previously. The optional feature
of the authorized clause implies that the acceleration is not self-executing but

is a right that should be elected by the mortgagee, with an appropriate notice to the mortgagor. This notice is not express in the statute but might reasonably be implied from it. Moreover, the acceleration operates when "all or any part of the property, or an interest therein . . . is sold or transferred." When is that? Part of the title is transferred when a contract of sale is signed, but is that a "sale or transfer"? Probably not, unless the mortgagee wanted to trace every one of its borrowers executing a contract of sale, whether or not that contract results in a closing.

> In the exercise of its option under the due-on-sale clause, a lender
> is encouraged to permit an assumption of a real property loan
> at the existing contract rate or at a rate which is at or below the
> average between the contract and market rate. . . .

12 U.S.C. §1701j-3(b)(3). Is this section window dressing? Assumption agreements are not outlawed, but a mortgagee's conditioning approval of a transferee on the current interest rate is not sanctioned either. What if a mortgagor maintains that a mortgagee can disapprove an assumption but not condition approval of a transferee on a higher rate? This argument may be strong if made in the context of an authorized due-on-sale clause appearing in an adjustable rate mortgage transaction. In such a situation, should the mortgagee have to justify his disapproval with a showing that it is otherwise insecure? Arguably so.

# EXAMPLES AND EXPLANATIONS

7. What if a mortgagor with a due-on-sale clause in his mortgage, sells a portion of a large parcel, but retains the rest? The clause, as authorized in the act, provides that it operates on a sale of all or part of the secured property, so it literally applies. But if the mortgagor claims that the retained portion of the property is sufficient collateral for the outstanding debt, how has the mortgagee been harmed by the sale?

**Explanation:** Courts are divided about the result here. The Garn-St. Germain Act provides that "the exercise [of the lenders' rights under the clause] shall be exclusively governed by the terms of the loan contract." Its terms permit enforcement. Frets v. Capital Fed. Sav. & Loan Assn., 238 Kan. 614, 712 P.2d 1270 (1986) ("It is acceptable for a savings and loan association to enforce the due-on-sale clause for the purpose of improving its position in the money market"). *Frets* certainly takes the big picture into account. However, the clause in *Frets* provided that the lender could accelerate "for any reason it deems sufficient." And so the mortgagee had reserved its contract rights to enforce the literal terms of the clause. However, if contract law controls (notice the shift of ground here), some courts conclude that the law of adhesion contracts, unconscionable conduct, and the duty of good faith require that the mortgagee not use the power in this instance. Some courts interested in the judicial process have a further rationale for intervening here; they hold that Congress could not have intended the act to restrict judicial power, particularly its equity powers — if it did, it acted beyond its authority and, as a matter of separation of powers, acted ultra vires.

This controversy will recur whenever debt acceleration is the subject of dispute between mortgagor and mortgagee. Remember that acceleration will not normally be implied — the law assumes that the mortgagee made an investment that he expected to run its full course. Cf. Gonzales v. Tama, 106 N.M. 737, 749 P.2d 1116 (1988) (for an opinion in which the acceleration right was implied); and see, e.g., Graf v. Hope Bldg. Corp., 254 N.Y. 1, 171 N.E. 884, 70 A.L.R. 984 (1930).

As a practical matter, mortgagees will not enforce the clause at the time a mortgagor executes an executory contract for the sale of real property. Too many executory contracts are never closed. As a result, enforcement is not worthwhile. In any event, the notice to the mortgagee of a sale or transfer will come through the public records for real property. A deed will always be recordable; often contracts of sale are not. Thus the mortgagee will not be able to discover that he has the right to accelerate without first checking the records and cross-referencing the recent recordings with a list of its mortgagors. Peoples Fed. Sav. & Loan Assn. v. Willsey, 466 N.E.2d 470 (Ind. App. 1984), later proceeding, Willsey v. Peoples Fed. Sav. & Loan Assn., 529 N.E.2d 1199 (Ind. App. 1988).

8. Would an installment land sale contract (ILSC) be a sale or transfer for purposes of this clause?

**Explanation:**   Courts have divided on this question as well, both before and after the passage of the act. (Regulations issued under the act apply to installment land sale contracts, but where is the authority for that in the statute?) The title under such an arrangement stays in the vendor. The purchaser takes an equitable interest in the property. On that account, there is no sale or transfer of the title. On the other hand, the vendee acquires an equity in the title, and the act covers the sale or transfer of "any interest" in the secured property. However, the equitable interest has the priority of a junior lien, and so one of the exceptions in the act may apply and prevent enforcement and acceleration in this instance. See New Home Fed. Sav. & Loan Assn., 333 Pa. Super. 393, 482 A.2d 625 (1984) (ILSC transfer triggers the due-on-sale covenant, and holding that the court is preempted by the act from considering covenant's validity as an unreasonable restraint on alienation).

9. If an ILSC did trigger the lender's right to accelerate under the clause, would forfeiture of the contract by the vendee's default "untrigger" that right?

**Explanation:**   No. Not in Iowa. Home Fed. Sav. & Loan Assn. v. Campney, 357 N.W.2d 613 (Iowa 1984). When the vendor-mortgagor makes arrangements for other financing, the mortgagee cannot untrigger the acceleration; his decision to accelerate is irrevocable once the mortgagor relies on it to his detriment. In the alternative, when the vendor-mortgagor retains payments after forfeiture and wants to use them to prepay the mortgage, he could probably do so. Similarly, a mortgagee may revoke the decision to accelerate and enforce the prepayment penalty only if the mortgagor has not relied to his detriment on the acceleration decision. In re Adu-Kofi, 94 B.R. 14 (Bankr. R.I. 1988).

10. A mortgagor with a standard due-on-sale clause in a first mortgage executes a second mortgage. The second mortgage is foreclosed. The first mortgagee accelerates the amount due on the first. May he do so?

**Explanation:**   Yes. The exception for junior liens is not applicable because the foreclosure itself is a sale or transfer, albeit involuntary, of the secured property. Unifirst Fed. Sav. & Loan Assn. v. Tower Loan of Mississippi, 524 So. 2d 290 (Miss. 1986).

11. When the due-on-sale clause provides that the mortgagee may accelerate upon any sale or transfer but shall not "unreasonably withhold consent" to the sale or transfer, is the mortgagee entitled to raise the interest rate as a precondition to giving its consent?

**Explanation:**   It can reasonably be argued that the language is intended to allow the mortgagee to evaluate the credit-worthiness of the borrower in order to determine whether the transferee is of equal or better credit-worthiness. In the comparable area of lease assignment case, this is the accepted interpretation of such language. If the transferee's creditworthiness is just as good, then the mortgagee has what his initial bargain was and is not entitled to more. But see Western Life Ins. Co. v. McPherson K.M.P., 702 F. Supp. 836 (D. Kan. 1988) (holding otherwise when the credit of the transferee was not an issue; indeed, the mortgagor was a Bronfman family partnership).

12. Can the benefit of this clause be waived by the mortgagee?

**Explanation:**   Yes. Cooper v. Deseret Fed. Sav. & Loan Assn., 757 P.2d 483 (Utah App. 1988) (in which the mortgagee has knowledge of the sale or transfer for a four-year period, during which time the mortgagor foreclosed a purchaser's interest and tendered mortgage payments to bring the loan in balance).

13. May an accelerating mortgagee also enforce a prepayment charge when the mortgagor pays the debt?

**Explanation:** No, not according to the case law. Rodgers v. Rainier Natl. Bank, 111 Wash. 2d 232, 757 P.2d 976 (1988). It is unfair to have the mortgagee benefit by his own unilateral decision to accelerate. The regulations of secondary market purchasers like FNMA and FHLMC reach the same conclusion. Thus a mortgagee, particularly in a residential loan setting, will have to elect between enforcing any prepayment charge and accelerating the debt. Used in tandem, these two clauses can result in unfairness to the mortgagor.

Does the Garn-St. Germain Act apply to commercial mortgage loans? It doesn't say it doesn't, so it does. Not impeccable logic in all situations, but good enough here. Western Life Ins. Co. v. McPherson K.M.P, 702 F. Supp. 836 (D. Kan. 1988); Eyde Bros. Dev. v. Equitable Life Assurance Socy. of the United States, 697 F. Supp. 1431 (W.D. Mich.), aff'd without op., 888 F.2d 127 (1988); McCausland v. Bankers Life Ins. Co. of Nebraska, 110 Wash. 2d 716, 757 P.2d 941, 81 A.L.R.4th 411 (1988).

14. Would any of the following transfers of the title trigger the mortgagee's right to accelerate the unpaid debt?

14a. To a general partnership in which the mortgagor held an interest and was a partner?

**Explanation:** See Fidelity Trust Co. v. BVD Assocs., 196 Conn. 270, 492 A.2d 180 (1985) (holding that there is no "sale or transfer" here because the mortgagor is both transferor and, surrounded by his partners, transferee, and, assuming arguendo that a transfer is present, the mortgagee is no less secure after it).

14b. To an Illinois land trust in which the mortgagor or his family was the beneficiary?

**Explanation:** Fairbury Fed. Sav. & Loan Assn. v. Bank of Illinois, 122 Ill. App. 3d 808, 462 N.E.2d 6 (1984). The establishment of a trust puts the title in the trustee but is not a transfer to a purchaser; rather, it is the creation of a personal property interest in the beneficiary of the trust — also known as the mortgagor. There is no transfer here as well.

14c. Into escrow for use of the title in a sale and leaseback transaction?

**Explanation:** First Fed. Sav. & Loan Assn. v. Treaster, 490 N.E.2d 1149 (Ind. App. 1986). There is a transfer here: The legal title goes to the purchaser-lessor, and the due-on-sale clause is triggered.

15. Finally, would you expect that a mortgagee would insert a due-on-sale clause in an adjustable rate mortgage?

**Explanation:** No. See Murrey, Due-on-Sale Clauses in Adjustable Rate Mortgages, 12 Real Est. L.J. 229 (1983) (arguing that such clauses should be enforced in that context only upon a showing of insecurity by the mortgagee).

# Transfers by the Mortgagee

The transfer of a mortgage (meaning the mortgage lien) alone is a nullity. This is so because the express purpose of the lien is to serve as security for the accompanying note. The note is never transferred separately. When it is transferred, the mortgage follows it, willy-nilly, even in the absence of an express assignment. As the common law lawyers used to say, the note and the mortgage live and die together.

However, although no express assignment of the mortgage is necessary for it to follow the note when assigned, mortgage assignments are usually in writing. This practice is a matter of prudence on the part of the assignee, who seeks the writing to record it so as to achieve protection against subsequent bona fide assignees. In most states, the assignment of a mortgage is a recordable document, and, on the assignee's part, the practice is to record it.

After an assignment, the mortgagor will want to assure himself that he is making payments on the note to the right party. If the note is nonnegotiable, he can pay the mortgagee anytime prior to the time he has actual notice of the assignment. The assignee's recording does not affect the mortgagor; he need not check the record before each payment. In old cases, he does have a duty to make the mortgagee show him the note when making payment and a duty of inquiry if the note was not produced. Such a duty worked well for the one-payment, common law mortgage, but is ill-adapted to the many, level payments due in the modern amortized mortgage transaction. This duty persists until the final payment is made.

If, however, the note is negotiable, the mortgagor's duty is to demand production of the note before making any payment, and the mortgagor who does not runs the risk of having to pay twice — once to the mortgagee and again to the assignee. The mortgagor is presumed to know the legal effect of what he signed and, when he executes a negotiable note, is presumed to know that the mortgagee will use the authority to assign given in the note.

After an assignment, the mortgagor may want to assert the same defenses that he has against the mortgagee against the assignee as well. Whether or not he can depends on two issues: first, whether the note is negotiable, and second, whether the assignee is a "holder in due course." To take free of a mortgagor's defenses, the assignee must win on both issues. He must both hold a negotiable note and be a holder in due course. First Maryland Fin. Servs. Corp. v. District-Realty Title Ins. Corp., 548 A.2d 787 (D.C. App. 1988) (finding note negotiable, but its holder not a holder in due course). Let's address each issue separately.

## *The Negotiable Note*

Negotiability is the authority to transfer a note for value by endorsement or delivery. Thus negotiability is a type of transferability expressed in a note (or other bill of exchange, check, or promissory note).

# EXAMPLES AND EXPLANATIONS

16. MR executes a brief but enforceable note and mortgage in favor of ME. The note is payable "to ME or to his order." What is the effect of this language?

**Explanation:**  This is the language that renders the note negotiable (that is, transferable to a person who, if a bona fide purchaser for value, takes free of defects in the interest of the transferor). Take any check out of your checkbook: It will have similar language just in front of the payee's name. That language makes the check negotiable, meaning it can be endorsed over to another.

17. If the note in the previous problem said that "this note may be assigned or transferred to any person," what would be the effect of this language?

**Explanation:**  The same. This language is often used in plain language notes. There it is presented as the equivalent of the "or order" phrase.

18. The note in Example 16 contains covenants requiring MR to maintain the premises, not commit waste, and insure the premises. What is the effect of such covenants?

**Explanation:**  "The negotiability of an instrument is not affected by . . . a promise or power to maintain or protect collateral." U.C.C. §3-112(1)(c). The named covenants do not affect the unconditional promise to pay the debt.

19. A note provides that "this note is secured by a mortgage executed contemporaneously with it." What is the effect of such language?

**Explanation:**  This language does not affect the negotiability of the note. See U.C.C. §3-105(1)(e) ("A promise or order otherwise unconditional is not made conditional by the fact that the instrument . . . states that it is secured, whether by mortgage, reservation of title, or otherwise."). On the other hand, language such as "the debtor hereby grants a security interest in the property" would destroy negotiability. See U.C.C. §3-112(1), in which many promises (but not the actual transfer of a lien) affecting collateral are authorized.

20. A note provides that it is enforceable only through the mortgage executed contemporaneously with it. What is the effect of this language?

**Explanation:**   This is so-called nonrecourse language. The mortgagee is to have no recourse against the assets (other than the secured real property) of the debtor. It does not destroy the note's negotiability.

21. The language in the note referred to in the previous example is followed by the sentence: "The terms of said mortgage are by this reference made a part hereof." What is the effect of this addition?

**Explanation:**    It is fatal to negotiability. Holly Hill Acres, Ltd. v. Charter Bank of Gainesville, 314 So. 2d 209, 17 UCC Rep. Serv. 144 (Fla. App. 1975). "A promise or order is not unconditional if the instrument . . . states that it is subject to or governed by any other agreement." U.C.C. §3-105(2). See also United States v. Farrington, 172 F. Supp. 797 (D. Mass. 1959) (a pre-U.C.C. case stating the belief that it is in accord with the code).

22. A note provides for a confession of judgment against the debtor at any time the noteholder selects an attorney for the debtor and directs that attorney to confess judgment. What is the effect of this provision?

**Explanation:**   U.C.C. §3-112(1)(c) permits a confession of judgment. This section encompasses the authority to select the attorney to confess judgment for the debtor. Yet this note provision goes too far: it permits a confession of judgment before the maturity of the debt. In this regard, you should know that a note provision referring to the acceleration of the debt or its prepayment would probably not affect negotiability. U.C.C. §3-105(1)(c). What is the theory here? Provisions that affect the maturity date of the debt do not per se destroy the unconditionality of the promise to pay but merely change the payment day. *Quere,* however, whether a confession of judgment deemed to waive defenses that a holder in due course takes free of is distinguishable from a waiver of all defenses; a waiver that is too broad would destroy negotiability. Geiger Fin. Co. v. Graham, 123 Ga. App. 771, 182 S.E.2d 521 (1971) (in which the court does not discuss this point at length).

These findings of negotiability depend on the code. An early case, reflecting the law of bills of exchange in the nineteenth century, found nonnegotiable a note containing both a confession of judgment and a waiver of the maker's right to have property appraised before it could be sold to satisfy the note. Overton v. Tyler, 3 Pa. 346, 347 (1846) (In this opinion, Chief Justice Gibson made his famous statement that "a negotiable bill or note is a courier without luggage." Nice words, but the Chief Justice was ruling in favor of the holder, not the maker, of the note as he used them. Nonetheless, Gibson's phrase became the verbal skewer to find many a later note nonnegotiable.)

By now, of course, you will have noticed that the code glorifies negotiability. As Grant Gilmore so nicely said, it is "negotiability *in excelsis*." Formalism and the Law of Negotiable Instruments," 13 Creighton L. Rev. 441, 461 (1979) (explaining the need to merge the debt into the debit instrument).

23.  MR executes in favor of ME a brief but enforceable mortgage accompanied by a series of six notes, one of which is endorsed and assigned in writing to A, another to B, a third to C, and all of which are secured by the mortgage and are payable "to ME or order." A default occurs in all three notes, and the security of the mortgage is insufficient to cover the debts in the three notes. How should A, B, and C share the proceeds of any foreclosure? If the notes were endorsed "to the bearer," would your analysis of the sharing arrangement change?

**Explanation:**   The courts would first examine the notes, looking for a contractual agreement to resolve this situation between the noteholders inter se. Failing in that, they would either use a first in time rule, satisfying them in the order of assignment, or else permit all the holders — ME, A, B, and C — to share equally in the proceeds of the sale of the security. The latter is the preferred view. Thus, if the notes are silent on the issue of priority, the priority of each note is equal.

However, even where such equality is the general rule, the endorsement of each note is itself a guarantee of payment by the original ME, so the endorsement provides a partial solution to the priority question: that is, the endorsing original mortgagee goes last. Thus, if ME retains any of the notes, they are repaid after the ones endorsed and assigned.

In addition, when the notes are assigned "to bearer," their satisfaction is premised on an implied warranty of repayment: ME is then estopped to deny repayment and cannot compete with the assignees, who must be paid first for this reason as well.

24.  If in the preceding paragraph, ME, A, B, and C all execute an agreement in which each agrees to share the loan proceeds and each is assigned a certain percentage of those proceeds, will that agreement control the common law rule in the applicable jurisdiction?

**Explanation:**   Yes, the percentage interests will control. Absent an agreement, the four would share pro rata and equally. And, because the agreement represents an opportunity to negotiate over and sort out the status of ME as opposed to the assignees, the agreement, even if silent, makes it doubtful that a court would prefer the assignees over ME.

## Holder in Due Course

The second issue involved in determining whether or not the assignee can take free of the mortgagor's defenses is the status of the assignee. He must show himself to be a holder in due course — one who takes the note for value, in good faith, and without notice that the note has been dishonored or is subject to a claim or defense to it by any person. A holder in due course is the term for the person whom you have met in other contexts as a bona fide purchaser. (It was originally an English term, adopted in this country first by the drafters of the Negotiable Instruments Law, the precurser of the U.C.C.'s Article 3.)

If the note is negotiable and if its holder is a holder in due course, then the assignee takes free of so-called personal defenses that the mortgagor has against the mortgagee: examples are a failure of consideration, breach of a covenant, unconscionable conduct, or fraud. However, even a holder in due course takes the note subject to real defenses, such as a lack of capacity to contract due to infancy or mental incompetency, an illegal purpose in the contract, or an execution of the contract under duress. Real defenses are listed in U.C.C. §3-305(2).

The law develops the same sort of list when distinguishing between void and voidable deeds. Personal defenses are related to the terms of the original transaction between the mortgagor and mortgagee, but real defenses relate to the status of the parties to it.

Real defenses are subjected to a further scrutiny and classified in one of two ways — as either patent and latent. A patent defense is asserted by the mortgagor. A latent defense is asserted by a third party, as when, for example, the marriage of the mortgagor gives rise to a marital right that the spouse can assert. An assignee (whether or not he is a holder in due course) takes free of such a right.

An assignee will not be a holder in due course when he is too closely connected to the mortgagee. The close connection can be shown by the common use of forms by the mortgagee and the assignee, a corporate parent-subsidiary relationship, or a pattern of assignments by the mortgagee. An additional basis for denying an assignee rights as a holder in due course occurs when a statute limits this status. In about 15 states, for example, home improvement notes and mortgages cannot be a basis for holder in due course, taking free of defenses about the adequacy of the work. See the Uniform Consumer Credit Code. Likewise, the Federal Trade Commission by regulation abolishes the holder in due course doctrine in the context of a person's purchase of $25,000 or less of personal, family, or household goods, financed by a third party (not the seller) and secured by a mortgage. However, even the FTC regulation has its limits. See Alvarez v. Union Mortgage Co., 747 S.W.2d 484 (Tex. Civ. App. 1988) (held that the FTC regulation does not preclude the home owner being liable for fraud on the mortgage application).

# EXAMPLES AND EXPLANATIONS

25. MR executes a brief but enforceable note and mortgage on Blackacre in favor of ME, who records and assigns to AE in writing. AE records. MR then conveys Blackacre to GE for value. State the title as between AE and GE.

This problem can be diagramed as follows:

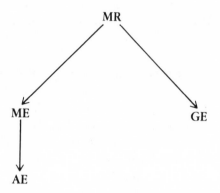

**Explanation:**   As to the state of the title: If the note is negotiable and the AE is a holder in due course, AE's rights attach to GE's title. The recordings are irrelevant, and the rules of negotiability control. If the note is negotiable but the assignee is not a holder in due course, judgment still goes for the assignee. But now the rationale for the prior answer is in the constructive notice given by the recording act.

26. Assume the facts of the previous problem. What if MR tenders payment of the note, but ME and AE refuse it. Is the lien of the mortgage discharged?

**Explanation:**   Yes. The mere tender of payment, when refused by the mortgagee, discharges the mortgage lien, but not the underlying debt. Kortright v. Cady, 21 N.Y. 343, 345 (1860).

27. Assume the facts diagramed in the prior problem, except that the mortgagee ME assigns twice: once, as before, to AE, who records, and then later, to AEE. What is the state and title between the two assignees, AE and AEE?

**Explanation:**   If the note is nonnegotiable, then the recording act priorities control. In this event, AE, having recorded, provides constructive notice to any later assignee like AEE. If the note is negotiable, then the law of negotiable instruments controls, and the holder in due course prevails.

Today the most common assignment of the residential mortgage is made by the original lender who assigns or sells the loan with its documentation to an assignee-purchaser in the national secondary mortgage market. The mortgagee here remains the servicer of the loan and, more important, the agent of the assignee-purchaser. Are the problems that we just reviewed the same in this context? The presence of the agency should give the mortgagor faced with the possibility of a double payment an easier time of it.

28. Curtis conveys Blackacre to Armstrong, who records. Armstrong mortgages his interest back to Curtis, who records the mortgage. Curtis assigned his mortgage to the plaintiff, who does not record the assignment. Armstrong then conveys Blackacre to Curtis, who records, and then Curtis conveys to the defendant, who records. Plaintiff seeks to impose his lien on the defendant's title. Can he? The defendant cannot claim the protection of any type of recording act. What arguments are left to the defendant in a dispute with the plaintiff over priority of title to Blackacre? See Curtis v. Moore, 152 N.Y. 159, 46 N.E. 168 (1897).

**Explanation:**   Defendant can argue that when Armstrong conveyed by deed to Curtis, the same person held both the mortgage and the deed (so far as the defendant can tell) and that the mortgagee interest appeared merged with that in the deed, giving Curtis the full, unencumbered fee simple absolute. Remember the working of the merger doctrine in common law estates — a similar doctrine is at work here. Thus the mortgage is extinguished under the merger doctrine. In addition, some courts would permit the defendant to assume, when examining his abstract of title, that the deed was given in lieu of foreclosure and work a merger on that basis, giving broad effect to the record.

However, many courts would reject an argument based on the merger doctrine and insist that the defendant in *Curtis* has a further duty of inquiry of his grantor. But a grantor like Curtis, making the conveyance with the deed, is in effect already dissembling. Having lied in effect once, why not twice? Why not say that the mortgage and note are destroyed or lost? Even if the defendant asked Curtis for a deed of release, wouldn't the latter supply one? Could the defendant-grantee trust the results of his inquiry? On the face of this record, then, perhaps no duty of inquiry should be imposed.

In Curtis v. Moore, judgment went for the plaintiff: The court cited the rule that the innocent payment by a mortgagor of a negotiable note, to an assignor of the note, is ineffective after the assignment is made, even though the assignment is recordable (as in most states it is) but not recorded by the assignee.

This may be an efficient rule when a mortgagor is making payments; he should demand to see the note as he pays, even if he pays each month and particularly when he makes the last payment and demands a release of the lien. However, when the title is transferred with the lien attached, should not the purchaser be able to rely on the state of the record? In this event, payment to the assignor-mortgagee should bind the assignee until the assignee gives notice of the assignment to the mortgagor. If the payments are made on an installment basis, then perhaps actual notice should be required. If a transfer of the mortgaged title is involved, then a lack of constructive notice through the record should entitle the purchaser to priority. Otherwise that purchaser will pay twice, once in the fair market (unencumbered) value of Blackacre and again to release the lien of the plaintiff, whose failure to record caused the problem in the first place.

# Mortgagee in Possession

Today, when a mortgage document is silent about the mortgagee's right to possession, the mortgagee still has the right to bring a cause of action in waste to prevent the physicial deterioration of the secured property. He may, as a result of a judgment in this action, gain the right to take possession of the property to the extent necessary to prevent waste.

A mortgagee in title states is entitled in theory to possession to secure the debt after the mortgage is executed; in other states, this right arises upon default. However, in lien states, it arises only after foreclosure. Because most states today regard themselves as lien jurisdictions, mortgage covenants often provide the mortgagee with an express right to have a receiver appointed or to possession upon default.

No matter when this right arises, however, the mortgagee in possession must exercise care. He will be responsible not only for the rents and profits actually collected, but also for those that a prudent owner would collect. This prudent owner standard of care applies to the expenditure of funds for operation and maintenance of the property. A mortgagee in possession may have to guard against vandalism on the property but at the same time may have to take care that expenses incurred in guarding it are prudent. See N.Y. & Suburban Fed. Sav. & Loan Assn. v. Sanderman, 162 N.J. Super. 216, 392 A.2d 635 (Ch. Div. 1978). For purposes of environmental statutes on hazardous wastes, the mortgagee in possession may also incur liability for clean-up costs.

When the property is subject to leases, a mortgagee in possession has no right to disturb senior leases (those executed before his mortgage). Why? Because only the reversion of the landlord was bargained for and mortgaged to the mortgagee as security. So long as a senior tenant pays the rent according to his lease and keeps its covenants, he is secure in the possession of his term. He could even prepay the rent according to his rights under the covenants and would be secure from a claim for a second payment by the mortgagee in possession. Absent a special consent provision in the mortgage, the mortgagee in possession would have to evict the mortgagor-landlord and take over his reversion before being able to reach a senior tenant's rent payments.

A junior lessee, on the other hand, will be forced to recognize the mortgagee in possession. He must "attorn" in the language of the common law. Thus a mortgagee will be able to take possession of a junior's leased premises, unless the lessee attorns, and relet because, as to junior lessees, the mortgagee bargained for the security of letting the premises in the future. (Unless he takes possession of the junior lessee's premises, the mortgagee cannot reach the rent.) Thus he can agree on a new lease with an existing junior lessee. The easiest agreement on this score will be to relet at the existing rent to the junior lessee, but in a rising rental market, he may (and probably will) ask for more. Such rents are part of the security for which he bargained when executing his mortgage. See Randolph, The Mortgagee's Interest in Rents, 29 Kan. L. Rev. 1, 5 (1980).

The mortgagee's rights when taking possession are analogous to those of a foreclosing mortgagee. Thus a junior mortgagee in possession has the right to oust nonattorning junior lessees, but no such right with regard to senior lessees. Against the latter, the most that a mortgage gives him is the right to collect the rent due.

## An Assignment of Rents

If there is a post-default pledge or assignment of rents in the mortgage, the mortgagee in possession may collect the rents and apply them to the outstanding debt (and is probably personally liable on the lease provisions as a landlord). A pledge is a bailment, and delivery of possession is necessary to complete it. A bailment is possession for a limited purpose and does not involve a transfer of the mortgagor's title or interest. An assignment does involve a transfer of title, but not possession. However, the assignment is often a present, absolute, and unconditional transfer of the rents, with the mortgagor retaining a license to collect rents until a default. However it is drafted, the rationale for such a clause is in part to make clear that the mortgagee in possession has not taken over the mortgagor's reversion(s) and has not ousted him for all purposes. To do so would give the junior mortgagee's the right to attorn or vacate, and because most leases will be junior to the mortgagee's lien, the prospect of tenants vacating a property is not a happy one. Indeed, in many first mortgage documents, the mortgagee often insists that a future, junior mortgagee become, by subordination or otherwise, junior to all lessees. This is a way of assuring itself that a junior mortgagee either foreclosing or in possession, will not give lessees an opportunity to vacate their premises.

And, no matter that an assignment clause is drafted as absolute and unconditional, the courts have had a tendency to treat such clauses as if they were only security or executory agreements — present transfers of a future interest, if you will — until a default occurs. Such clauses are more likely to be enforced in title, rather than lien, jurisdictions. The effect of such a view in lien jurisdictions is that the mortgagee will have to take some affirmative steps in addition to invoking the clause — such as foreclosing, taking possession, or petitioning for a receiver to be appointed — to secure or execute the agreement in the clause.

# Receiverships

If a mortgagee does not wish to go into possession, he has an alternative — the appointment of a receiver. For a mortgagee, such an appointment has several advantages. First, the receiver can act as a stakeholder when the amounts due are in dispute. Second, a mortgagee in possession has a duty to account, which a receiver does not. Third, the mortgagee in possession is subjected to tort liability from which a receiver can shield him. Fourth, the appointment of a receiver does not terminate existing leases on the mortgaged property because the receiver has duties to both mortgagor and mortgagee and is the agent of both; indeed, the distinction between junior and senior leases can be obviated on that account.

Thus the receiver, being a court-appointed person, is regarded typically as a mutual agent, not as (more important) the agent of the mortgagee. Where the income flow from leases is important to the mortgagee, the possibility that a mortgagee's taking possession will be construed as an ouster of the junior lessees is sufficient to make the mortgagee consider a receivership more desirable than taking possession. And, by the same token, many mortgagees will also consider an assignment of rents clause in the mortgage more valuable than a right to a receivership, and for the same reason: that assigning the rents removes the mortgagee one more step from taking possession.

Thus a junior lessee does not have the right to vacate when the receiver takes over. In most courts that have considered the issue, the receiver is permitted to hold junior lessees to their lease obligations.

Receiverships are equitable in nature. This means, among other things, that a court, in considering a petition for the appointment of a receiver, is not bound by the covenants of the mortgage. Standards for the appointment of a receiver vary from state to state, but a petition for appointment will be heard only after a default.

A mortgagee seeking a receiver must establish (1) a default, and (2) insecurity. Insecurity can mean several things. First, that the fair market value of the property is insufficient to cover the outstanding debt. Second, that the remedies otherwise provided are inadequate: that is, that the mortgagor is insolvent so that the legal remedies on the note are inadequate, that the property securing the debt is threatened with loss or destruction, or that waste is being committed on the property. Union Guardian Trust Co. v.

Rau, 255 Mich. 324, 238 N.W. 166 (1931) (holding that nonpayment of taxes constitutes waste and justifies receiver's appointment). The latter is perhaps the most commonly required element of proof necessary to justify a receivership. Today the grounds for a receiver are little different in title and lien jurisdictions, although perhaps the remedy traditionally has been granted more readily in lien theory states (which means, just about everywhere!).

The rights of a mortgagee to take possession of the secured property depends on the distinction between title and lien mortgages. With a title mortgage, the mortgagee has the right to the possession, rents, and profits of the secured property. With a lien mortgage, that right arises only after a default — at the earliest. Many lien jurisdictions put the mortgagee off until after foreclosure. Grether v. Nick, 193 Wis. 503, 213 N.W. 304, 215 N.W. 571, 55 A.L.R. 530 (1921). A mortgage often, after the granting clause, will include language such as; "together with all . . . rights, appurtenances, and rents." This is insufficient to assign the rents if local law does not permit the mortgagee to have possession or rents before a certain date.

A junior mortgagee is entitled to a receiver when the senior mortgagee has not yet petitioned for one's appointment, even when the senior mortgage contains a covenant currently entitling the senior to a receiver. That senior covenant is viewed as executory until the senior affirmatively acts upon it. Before the senior does so, the junior can have his own receiver collect the rents for him and, once collected, cannot be forced to disgorge them if the senior later has a receiver appointed, although the senior's receiver will then have a superior claim to receive the rents and in effect trumps the junior receiver's right. Sullivan v. Rosson, 223 N.Y. 217, 119 N.E.2d 405, 4 A.L.R. 1400 (1918).

# EXAMPLES AND EXPLANATIONS

29a. MR executes a brief but enforceable mortgage in favor of ME. The security for the mortgage is Officeacres, a large office building. MR also executes a junior mortgage on the same property in favor of MEE. In a title state, is ME entitled to the rents if MR is not in default on the mortgage?

**Explanation:** Yes. ME is entitled to a receiver or to possession upon a showing of good cause (either waste, default, or lender insecurity) upon the execution of the mortgage, so of course he is entitled to file a petition later, at the time of default. See G. Nelson & D. Whitman, Real Estate Finance Law §§4.33-4.35 (2d ed. 1985).

29b. Would your answer be the same in a lien state? If so, how should ME react to the difference?

**Explanation:** The answer would be different. "No" is the answer to Example "a" in a lien state, where the date on which ME is entitled to go into possession or to petition for the appointment of a receiver is (1) the date of default, (2) the date of filing for foreclosure, (3) the date of the decree, or (4) the date on which the decree is confirmed. In a lien state, the mortgagee derives his right to the rents from his right to enforce the lien upon default. At the time of default, he is subrogated to the mortgagor's right to collect the rents — he steps into the mortgagor's shoes. In response to this situation, ME should insist on an express covenant assigning the rents to him on default. Such a clause does not give the mortgagee a right to possession, and an entry to collect the rents may not be made unless a demand for them is first made of the landlord-mortgagor. 1180 Anderson Ave. Realty Corp. v. MINA Equities Corp., 95 A.D2d 169, 465 N.Y.S.2d 511 (1983). Such a clause is one of the covenants distinguishing a commercial mortgage from a residential one. In a lien state, the courts sometimes treat such a covenant as an executory contract, executed upon default. Its subject is a lien on the rents, postponed until default and foreclosure is commenced.

29c. Even if ME is entitled to go into possession, would he want to? What if the leases for the offices in the building were made prior to the execution of ME's mortgage? Would that affect your answer?

**Explanation:** No. ME may not want to run the risks associated with being a mortgagee in possession, particularly if going into possession would constitute an ouster of existing lessees. Here, however, senior lessees cannot be disturbed. Once in possession, the mortgagee is held to the standard of care of a prudent owner. This standard applies to profits he should make and expenses he might reasonably incur.

29d. Will MEE's remedies differ from ME's?

**Explanation:** A junior mortgagee like MEE may have a broader right to a receiver than ME does. He is more likely to be able to show insecurity.

29e. Is the authority of a receiver, pending foreclosure, generally broader or narrower in a lien state than it is in a title state?

**Explanation:** Broader. When the mortgagee files for foreclosure, equity, regarding as done what should be done, will give the receiver broader powers while the action is pursued diligently and in good faith. See Nelson & Whitman, supra, §4.34.

29f. If either ME or MEE has a receiver appointed, how long does the receivership last?

**Explanation:** Until the period of statutory redemption ends, or any decree in foreclosure is absolute.

29g. If MEE petitions for a receiver to hold Officeacres, and the building generates more proceeds than necessary to satisfy MEE's debt (payments), is ME entitled to the surplus? If not, to whom does the surplus go?

**Explanation:** No. He would get more than his bargain if such were the case. The surplus goes to MR. Sullivan v. Rosson, 223 N.Y. 217, 119 N.E. 405, 4 A.L.R. 1400 (1918) (holding that a senior mortgagee is not entitled to the proceeds generated by a receiver appointed as a result of the petition to the court of a junior mortgagee). If the junior mortgagee is diligent in seeking the remedy and the senior is not, why should the senior profit from the diligence of the junior?

29h. If after MR's default in mortgage payments, ME, MEE, and MR work out an agreement on future payments, should the title insurer be a party to the agreement?

**Explanation:** Yes, because the agreement affects each's lien priority. See H. Kane & K. Barrett, Real Estate Workouts — Dealing with Third Parties, in A. Kulkin & P. Roberts, Real Estate Bankruptcies and Workouts 225, 225-232 (1983).

29i. If MR is in possession of one of the offices in the building when the mortgage was given, does MR have to surrender that office to a receiver?

**Explanation:** For an negative answer in a case set in a residential context, see Holmes v. Gravenhorst, 238 A.D. 313, 263 N.Y.S. 738, rev'd, 263 N.Y. 148, 188 N.E. 285, 91 A.L.R. 1230 (1933) (holding that the mortgagor-occupant need not pay a reasonable rent to a receiver, and that neither can the receiver evict the occupant). The mortgagor's partial possession of the secured property decreased the security offered the mortgagee for the debt, and a mortgagee who takes the security on that basis is entitled to no more security than he bargained for.

Further, if the occupying mortgagor agrees to pay rent to any receiver appointed under the mortgage covenants, that may not authorize the mortgagor's eviction for nonpayment of the rent — eviction must await foreclosure. Carlin Trading Co. v. Bennett, 24 A.D.2d 91, 264 N.Y.S.2d 43 (1965), noted in 17 Syracuse L.Rev. 774 (1966).

Receivers are often appointed ex parte — on the sworn affidavit of the mortgagee. Such procedures have been challenged on due process grounds, but were upheld in Friedman v. Gerax, 100 Misc. 2d 820, 420 N.Y.S.2d 247 (1979) (holding that the ex parte appointment of a receiver under judicial supervision, with an opportunity for an immediate hearing on the underlying grounds on which the receiver is appointed, is not unconstitutional).

## Federal Bank Receivers — The Super Receiver

The current frenzy over the failure of savings and loans, long prodigious mortgage lenders, deserves a note here in the context of failed banks taken over and managed by federal regulators that act as receivers until the bank's assets are either liquidated or purchased by another bank. Normally a receiver is a person stepping into the shoes of the mortgagee, and as such, he is bound by the agreements that bind the mortgagee, whether or not they are documented. Not so for the federal receiver!

Most institutional mortgage lenders have deposits insured by the federal government. The two federal insuring agencies are the Federal Deposit Insurance Corporation (FDIC) for commercial banks and (up to 1989) the Federal Savings and Loan Insurance Corporation (FSLIC), now the FDIC, for federal or federally insured savings banks. When a bank fails, the federal agency has two roles. First, it takes over the bank and manages the bank's assets as a receiver, and second, it acts in its corporate capacity to continue its insurance on the bank's deposits as before.

As a receiver, the agency has two primary options. First, it can liquidate the assets of the bank and pay the insured depositors. Second, it can sell the bank's healthy assets (for example, the mortgage loans not in default) to another bank. This sale is subject to two, interrelated conditions: (1) that the purchasing bank assume the obligation to pay the depositors, and (2) that the purchasing bank receive from the agency a sum sufficient to cover the difference between the value of the assets sold and its future obligation to the depositors. The second condition is technically met by the agency's purchase, in its corporate, insuring capacity, of the failed bank's bad loans for an amount sufficient to meet the second condition of sale. Thus the agency (acting as a receiver) sells the bad loans to itself (in its second, insuring capacity) for a sum to be paid over to the purchaser of the failed bank to cover the latter's obligations to depositors.

As a receiver, the federal agency take the loan assets of a bank free of any undocumented secret agreements to which the documented loan might be subject. This doctrine is called the *D'Oench* doctrine. D'Oench, Duhme & Co. v. FDIC, 315 U.S. 447 (1942) (holding that a demand for payment of a note held by a failed, insured bank was not subject to the defense by its maker of an oral agreement that the loan proceeds documented by the note would never have to be repaid). If the note was either designed to deceive the regulators of the bank, or would have that effect, its maker is estopped to deny the demand made. No intent to defraud need be shown. "Rather, the doctrine prohibits all secret agreements that tend to make the [federal agency] susceptible to fraudulent arrangements." Timberland Design, Inc. v. First Serv. Bank for Sav., 932 F.2d 46, 48 (1st Cir. 1991). It is also a protection and a preference for depositors who cannot otherwise protect themselves, over borrowers who can. Id.

The *D'Oench* doctrine applies, as a matter of federal common law, to all federal agencies. Victor Hotel Corp. v. FCA Mortgage Corp., 928 F.2d 1077 (11th Cir. 1991). Its status as a matter of federal law is rooted in policy and estoppel principles, but nonetheless courts have recognized that the doctrine has a statutory basis as well. See 12 U.S.C.A. §1823(e) (West 1989) ("No agreement which tends to diminish or defeat the interest of the Corporation (the FDIC) in any asset acquired . . . shall be valid against the Corporation unless such agreement . . . is in writing ."). See also FDIC v. McCullough, 911 F.2d 593, 598 n.4 (11th Cir. 1990). Section 1823(e) further provides that the agreement must be executed by the institution, and that any person claiming its benefit contemporaneously with the acquisition of the asset be approved by the institution's loan committee or board of directors, and be at all times an official record of the institution. Id., §1823(e)(2)-(4).

The doctrine cannot be invoked by a solvent bank. First Interstate Bank v. First Natl. Bank, 928 F.2d 153 (5th Cir. 1991).

As a receiver, the FDIC can "disaffirm or repudiate any contract or lease — (A) to which the institution is a party; (B) the performance of which the . . . receiver, in the . . . receiver's discretion, determines to be burdensome; and (C) the disaffirmance or repudiation of which . . . the receiver determines . . . will promote the orderly administration of the institution's affairs." Promoting the orderly affairs of the failed institution by disaffirming burdensome contracts, such as mortgage agreements, provides the federal receiver with broad powers indeed. What little case law there is on this section so far suggests that a rule of reasonable business judgment and prudence is imposed on the receiver by this statute.

# EXAMPLES AND EXPLANATIONS

30. When the FDIC takes over the assets of Assets Bank, a loan file contains a written agreement that the mortgagee bank will retain a percentage of the loan proceeds and pay them to C. The agreement is executed by the mortgagor MR, but not by Assets. On the date of the takeover, C is litigating the enforceability of the agreement against both Assets and MR. Is the agreement enforceable against the FDIC as a receiver?

**Explanation:**    No. The knowledge of the FDIC, gained from the file at the time of the takeover, is irrelevant to an application of the doctrine and the statute codifying it. At the time the FDIC acquires the loan as a receiver, the requirements of §1823(e) cannot be satisfied. In addition, whether Assets accepted the agreement cannot be ascertained from the loan file, and so the agreement is a secret one for the purpose of this doctrine. The purpose of the *D'Oench* doctrine is to prevent the regulator taking over a bank from being misled, and an unclear document in a loan file is likely to do so. Twin Constr., Inc. v. Boca Raton, Inc., 925 F.2d 378, 383 (11th Cir. 1991) (discussing Langley v. FDIC, 484 U.S. 86 (1987)).

# 22

## Foreclosures

When mortgage payments remain unpaid after they are due, the mortgagor is in default on the note. After the lapse of a time indicating that payment is unlikely, the mortgagee's principal remedy is foreclosure. The object of foreclosure is the perfection of the lien of the mortgage. It is everywhere the subject of state statutes, very detailed statutes prescribing the procedures that the mortgagee must use. The use of such statutes is mandatory for mortgages and deeds of trust. Notwithstanding the statutory basis of this action, the cause of action is generally regarded as an equitable one.

The mortgagee's filing a foreclosure action is preceded by attempts to collect the amounts in default, first by letters and then by more personal means. Collection procedures are followed by a notice to the mortgagor accelerating the debt if that is permitted by the mortgage covenants.

This acceleration is authorized by a covenant in the note permitting the mortgagee, upon a default in payment, to declare the whole sum of accrued interest plus unpaid principal due and payable. It permits the mortgagee to sue for the whole debt at one time or to collect any part of the debt at once by a personal judgment against the mortgagor.

Such acceleration clauses were inserted in standard-form mortgage documents first in the 1930s to avoid, absent agreement otherwise, two rules of law about mortgage agreements: first, that the mortgagor has no right to prepay. The mortgagee bargained for an investment of a certain length, and he's to have it. The second rule is that the mortgagee has no right to accelerate the debt, absent evidence of anticipatory repudiation. Do either of these presumptions about the mortgagor and mortgagee's agreement make sense today? Arguably not. Such clauses were at first intended to lay a basis for an action by the mortgagee in equity to prevent multiple suits; this action was known as one for the equitable writ of quia timet.

These two rules of law are really legal presumptions; they are repudiated today in few states, perhaps because the documentation for a mortgage usually declares otherwise. Only Pennsylvania has an implied right to prepay, found in a 1983 Pennsylvania opinion. See Maloney v. Furches, 309 Pa. Super. 129, 454 A.2d 1117, rev'd 503 Pa. 60, 468 A.2d 458 (1983). As to the acceleration right, when an acceleration covenant is not express in the mortgage, can't one be implied today?

Foreclosure is an expensive process. The mortgagee would rather spend some money on collection procedures before resorting to it. Thus acceleration is typically used after collection procedures are tried, and, by that time, the mortgagor may be six months to a year in arrears on payments. Thus acceleration may only be used against the chronic defaulter and when a basis for anticipatory repudiation of the whole debt is established by the mortgagee. Standard FNMA-FHLMC mortgage forms often require that a 30-day notice be given by letter before an acceleration. The case law of many states, which provides the legal background for these forms, denies the mortgagor the right to reinstate the debt after the mortgagee accelerates it. However, FNMA-FHLMC standard mortgages permit the mortgagee to recoup the costs of collection upon reinstatement of the outstanding debt and lien. See Uniform Covenant 18 (FNMA-FHLMC Uniform Instrument, Form 3021, Dec. 83). This covenant applies regardless of the time and expense to which the mortgagee has been put. Bergman, A Lender's Guide to Mortgage Foreclosure: A New Look, 22 Real Est. Rev. 43, 44 (Spring 1988).

One court, interpreting a statute requiring that a mortgagee give a mortgagor a 30-day notice before accelerating, held that the notice applied to accelerations preceding a mortgage foreclosure, but not to accelerations preceding a suit on the personal liability in the note. Certified Realty Co. v. Smith, 198 Colo. 222, 597 P.2d 1043 (1979), noted at 52 U. Colo. L. Rev. 301 (1981). This distinction is unfair to mortgagors.

## Graf v. Hope Building Corporation

An acceleration will be enforced according to its terms, absent equitable defenses to its use by the lender. The leading case is Graf v. Hope Building Corp., 254 N.Y. 1, 171 N.E. 884 (1930). The majority in this case set a standard of strict enforcement, over the vigorous dissent of Judge Benjamin Cardozo. Bergman, Strict Acceleration in New York Mortgage Foreclosure — Has the Doctrine Eroded?, 8 Pace L. Rev. 475 (1988) (concluding no, although in other jursidictions Cardozo's dissent has proven persuasive).

In *Graf,* the mortgagee made a $335,000 loan for ten years. The mortgagor made payments quarterly for two years. The note provided for acceleration of the total unpaid debt 20 days after a default in any payment. The mortgagor was a corporation, and its president alone had the power to sign checks for the payments. When about to leave for Europe, the president signed two checks for the next two payments. Just before the first of these payments were due, the corporation was informed of the amount due and found that a corporate employee (slightly) miscalculated the amounts due. The checks were tendered, with a notice that the deficiency would be made up as soon as the president returned from Europe. Which he did, during the 20-day grace period, but he was not informed of the mistake, and on the second day after the grace period expired, the mortgagee began foreclosure.

The majority in *Graf* thought that the acceleration clause was good for all purposes. The dissent thought otherwise, that it was good only to protect the mortgagee against insecurity. For example, it could not be used when the mortgagee waived strict compliance with it, when he evaded payment, and when he assigned the note without notice to the mortgagor that the assignee should now receive the payments. In the face of the letter from the mortgagor indicating that the deficiency would be paid soon, the mortgagee's inaction for the 20-day period is unconscionable and the equivalent of an evasion of payment. What profit, after all, did the mortgagee derive from the foreclosure? If the answer is none, or one disproportionate to the injury to the mortgagor, then the acceleration works a penalty on the mortgagor, and the parties to the loan agreements have made a mutual mistake of fact in forecasting the consequences of their agreement.

"We feel that the interests of certainty and security in real estate transactions forbid us, in the absence of fraud, bad faith, or unconscionable conduct, to recede from the [well-recognized effect of an acceleration covenant] doctrine that is so deeply imbedded in equity." 254 N.Y. at 6, 171 N.E. at 884 (quote from the majority opinion in *Graf*). Judge Cardozo, on the other hand, insists that "[e]quity declines to treat a mortgage upon realty as a conveyance subject to a condition, but views it as a lien irrespective of its form." Id. at 8, 171 N.E. at 886. Then, citing cases when liquidated damage clauses have been struck down, Cardozo states that "a like dispensing power . . . runs through the whole rubric of accident and mistake." Id. at 9, 171 N.E. at 887. When "the default is limited to a trifling balance," "the failure to pay the balance is the product of mistake," id. at 12, 171 N.E. at 888, and "where the mortgagee indicates by his conduct that he appreciates the mistake and has attempted by silence and inaction to turn it to his own advantage," equity should reinstate the debt and the lien. Id. at 12, 171 N.E. at 888. The mortgagee, in Cardozo's view, was avoiding payment, which he must have known he could have for the asking.

Would you suggest that the holding in *Graf* enforcing the note covenant as written and permitting the foreclosure to proceed be limited to defaults in payment, rather than applied also to other types of defaults, as say, a failure on the mortgagor's part to pay real property taxes? By statutes, many state foreclosure codes will permit payment up to a short time before the foreclosure sale, thus qualifying the holding of the majority in this case. An occasional case, decided in New York and elsewhere, ameliorates the harshness of the *Graf* holding. For an antidote to *Graf*, see Bisno v. Sax, 175 Cal. App. 2d

714, 346 P.2d 814 (1959) (an opinion weighing the benefit to the accelerating mortgagee against the injury to the mortgage and relieving the mortgagor of acceleration after a one-day default); see also Kerin v. Udoft, 165 Conn. 264, 334 A.2d 434 (1973); Beal v. Mars Larson Ranch Corp., 586 P.2d 1378 (Idaho 1987). The last two cases find an equitable right to reinstate both the debt and the lien, implying a rejection of the majority in *Graf* whether the acceleration covenant is in the note or the mortgage.

# Soldiers and Sailors Relief Act

Statutory relief from mortgage foreclosure is available to those on active duty in the armed services, as a part of a general immunity from civil process adversely affecting their rights and property. This relief does not extinguish the duties under the note and the mortgage covenants accompanying it, but rather suspends their enforcement for the period of service. The purpose of this immunity is to permit service personnel to give full attention to military duties. See 50 U.S.C.A. §532 (1990). The foreclosure proceeding may be stayed upon motion of the service personnel or a person acting on his or her behalf. Id. §§(2)(a).

# Deacceleration in Bankruptcy

In re Taddeo, 685 F.2d 24 (2d Cir. 1982), held that, after a mortgagee accelerates the debt, a mortgagor filing for bankruptcy under Chapter 13 of the federal Bankruptcy Code (11 U.S.C. §§1301 et seq (1978)) could cure the default and reinstate the debt and the mortgage lien as a part of a plan to reorganize the finances of the bankrupt debtor. Chapter 13 provides a debtor with an opportunity to reorganize her debts, rather than have her assets sold or liquidated to satisfy them. (Liquidation sales occur under Chapter 7 of the code.)

In *Taddeo*, the acceleration preceded the mortgagor's filing for bankruptcy and, under the automatic stay provisions of the code (§365(a)), that filing stayed the mortgagee's foreclosure proceeding: It could not proceed further without violating the stay, and any judgment in foreclosure would thus become a nullity.

The mortgagee was the Taddeo's only creditor, but this fact made no difference to the court.

*Taddeo* has been widely accepted by other bankruptcy courts and in other federal circuits as well. However, there has been much dispute over exactly when the debtor's right to deaccelerate ends. Setting this date is a matter of balancing the costs incurred by the mortgagee against the benefits achieved thereby by the mortgagor. Many courts have decided that the judgment in foreclosure is the date at which the right ends; this date, however, may, under the foreclosure codes of some jurisdictions, be before the sale. The sale is the event that changes the equities drastically, often introducing a third party, the purchaser at the sale, who seeks to gain the title to the property, not the right to receive mortgage payments. The purchaser's presence is often taken as a reason for cutting off the right to deaccelerate at the date of the sale. If acceleration is permitted thereafter, it is only upon the payment of a lump sum representing what the purchaser paid at the sale. However, when the purchaser at the sale is the mortgagee, this reason vanishes, and some courts have refused to terminate the right at the sale date. The debt can still be reinstated and paid as the mortgagee originally agreed to have it paid, in installments. Courts have also refused to end the right when the parties to the foreclosure must get the sale confirmed by a judicial decree, or if the title of the purchaser at the sale is not yet absolute and will not be so until the end of a statutory redemption period; nothing has really changed, these opinions argue, because the mortgagee is still out of possession, and the mortgagor, under the statutory redemption right, is still in possession.

In summary, with acceleration, but no foreclosure judgment, reinstatement of the debt occurs; with a judgment, but no sale, reinstatement follows too; after a sale, the acceleration is curable, but because a purchaser is present now, curing the acceleration is only permitted within the period of statutory redemption and only upon the payment of a lump sum to the third-party purchaser, or in installments to the mortgagee purchaser. See Laurence, At Home with the Bankruptcy Code: Residential Leases, Installment Real Estate Contracts and Home Mortgages, 61 Am. Bankr. L.J. 125, 142 (1987) (summarizing the case law).

## Methods of Foreclosure

The most common method of foreclosure is *judicial foreclosure*. It is available in all states and requires a public sale of the property by a public official. It started in New York in the early nineteenth century and quickly spread around the country, particularly in the Western states. Its purpose is to protect the equity of the borrower in the property. It liquidates the security by a sale inviting, but not always involving, competitive bidding that is intended to obtain the highest possible price for the mortgagor's benefit, although how well it accomplishes that objective is open to question today. It is more consistent with the lien, rather than the title, theory of mortgages. Lansing v. Goelet, 9 Cow. 346 (N.Y. 1827). It is said that the sheriff "cries the property from the steps of the courthouse." The sale is usually conducted like an auction by the official. But see Freyfogle, The New Judicial Roles in Illinois Mortgage Foreclosures, 19 Loy. U. Chi. L.J. 933, 934 (1988) ("No longer must sales be conducted by public auction. . . . Now, brokers can be used, and property can be sold in ways that approximate the usual processes of selling nonforeclosure property," discussing Ill. Rev. Stat. ch. 110, para. 15-1506, 15-1507 (1987)).

The procedural steps in a judicial foreclosure are as follows:

1.  summons and complaint, followed by an answer, other pleadings as necessary, and a motion for summary judgment and a trial;
2.  the appointment of a referee to compute the debt outstanding and to search the title;
3.  the report of the referee;
4.  a judicial order authorizing the sale (sometimes this is a decree nisi, ordering the transfer of title to the purchaser at the sale, unless the sale is for some reason upset) — this is then known as the foreclosure judgment;
5.  notice or advertisement of the sale;
6.  the sale; and
7.  a judgment confirming the sale.

This is only a very general multipurpose description of the process; for example, there will seldom be a presale decree nisi and a judgment confirming the sale afterwards.

The proceeds of the sale are distributed, first, to pay the expenses of the foreclosure; second, to pay the foreclosing mortgagee the outstanding debt; third, to pay other liens that would otherwise be extinguished by the proceeding, in the order of priority established in the order for the sale; and, fourth, to the extent there is a surplus, to pay it to the mortgagor. If the sale proceeds are insufficient to pay the outstanding liens and encumbrances subject to the action, then the mortgagor is liable for the amount of the insufficiency in what is known as an action for a deficiency judgment.

Preparation for this sale includes a search of the title, in order to establish the persons to whom the proceeds of the sale are to be paid and the order in which they will be paid. Thus judicial foreclosure is particularly useful as a remedy when there is some dispute about priority of liens that the searcher and the court can help to resolve.

What is sold at the foreclosure sale? The interest being sold is twofold: It includes both the interest of the mortgagor and the interest of the mortgagee — both borrower's and lender's interests are sold. The purchaser is not necessarily buying a fee simple absolute; rather, the title to be sold is subject to any liens superior to that of the foreclosing mortgagee. Where the creditor has made optional advances, the status of the foreclosing creditors lien may be "split." The presence of such a split in the priority accorded one creditor is another reason to utilize judicial foreclosure.

The mortgagee, however, is a privileged bidder at a judicial sale; she has a "credit bid," for which no cash need be raised and no certified check presented, up to the amount of the outstanding debt of the mortgagor. By this point in the proceedings, this amount will be either certified by the court or incorporated into its presale judgment. Thus the mortgagee does not have to pay cash up to the amount of her lien. Her status as a credit bidder has in practice dampened competitive bidding at judicial sales.

However, the expenses of the foreclosure process itself are paid first, before any lienholder is paid even $1. Thus the sheriff, court officers, and (of course) attorneys go first! Standard FNMA-FHLMC mortgage forms are silent on the question of who pays for the costs of collection, much less those of foreclosure, which means that there is a point when the costs of both collection and foreclosure have risen so high that the mortgagee has more incentive to continue foreclosure through to a final judgment than to settle for some negotiated reinstatement of the debt and the lien.

Thus the decree in foreclosure confirms the lien and title priority of various lienholders. Sometimes, however, it is a decree nisi and is issued before the sale. This type of decree becomes absolute after the sale, unless some objection is raised to the conduct or the results of the sale. On the other hand, sometimes the decree is granted after the sale, and in this instance it confirms the sale.

A bid at the sale is an offer to purchase. It is binding upon acceptance by the official conducting the sale. The successful bidder cannot withdraw her bid after the fall of the auctioneer's hammer; that is the point at which the bid is considered accepted, although a few cases require that a judicial confirmation is the point of acceptance. In re Marriage of Davies, 48 Wash. App. 29, 737 P.2d 721 (1987), noted in Staples, Judicial and Execution Sales in Washington, 24 Gonz. L. Rev. 249 (1988) (one of the few cases permitting a successful bidder to revoke his bid). (But isn't a sale that can be undone by the successful bidder also unlikely to bring out serious bidders or fetch much of a price? And what criteria control bid revocation? Generally a mistake of fact is insufficient.) If a court does order a resale after acceptance of the successful bid, however, any deficiency in the price brought by the later judicial sale may be assessed against the bidder at the first, as damages.

The advantages of a judicial foreclosure are several. First, because the sale is conducted under the supervision of a court, it is less susceptible to abuse and is beyond suspicion. Second, if the sale does not fetch enough to satisfy the amount of the debt, a deficiency judgment is possible in most jurisdictions. Third, any person, including the mortgagee, is permitted to purchase at the sale. (This is not always so when the sale is conducted under a private power of sale.) Fourth and finally, as before noted, this method of foreclosure will resolve conflicts involving the priority of various liens; so, if that is a problem in a particular instance, judicial foreclosure will be the preferred method of foreclosure.

There is, however, an alternative in many states. The next most widely available method of foreclosure is a *power of sale foreclosure*. The sale here is conducted under a mortgage with a power of sale, or a deed of trust (the more commonly used form of security instrument). See Cal. Civ. Code §2924 (West 1987); N.Y. Real Prop. Acts. Law §§1401-1461 (McKinney 1979).

The sale conducted under a power of sale is a private sale in the sense that the party conducting the sale is a private party, not a public official. Otherwise, the sale will look like that conducted in the course of a judicial foreclosure; it will often be an auction sale, advertised in advance as required by state statute. Because this private sale is authorized in a deed of trust, rather than a mortgage, the person conducting the sale will often also be the trustee authorized to do so in the deed.

Power of sale foreclosure was available in only 18 states in 1938, but today it is available in 34 states and the District of Columbia. It is cheaper than judicial foreclosure and takes less time. It has spread rapidly across the country during the years since World War II. Reeve, A New Proposal for a Uniform Real Estate Mortgage Act, 5 Law & Contemp. Probs. 564 (1938).

The first step after the debt has been accelerated is a notice of default to the trustee. That is often recorded on the public records as well. When and if the trustee orders the sale in response to the notice, that order may be recorded as well. Thus at various crucial steps, the records will reflect the exercise of this power.

Today, however, the pattern is for increased statutory controls on this remedy. Three typical requirements are (1) that the property be appraised and a floor bid set, (2) that the sale, privately conducted, not be firm until confirmed by a court decree, and (3) that the mortgagee not be permitted to bid at the sale. Arkansas has recently enacted a statute controlling private sales. See Note, Nonjudicial Foreclosure in Arkansas with the Statutory Foreclosure Act of 1987, 41 Ark. L. Rev. 473 (1988). In one state, Colorado, power of sale foreclosures must be conducted by a public trustee, who is a county employee with jurisdiction over all private power foreclosures in that county. See Note, Foreclosure by Private Trustee: Now is the Time for Colorado, 65 Denv. L.J. 41 (1988).

Why has power of sale foreclosure proven so popular? Its cheapness, informality, and relative speed are definite advantages, but there are some procedural advantages as well. The deed of trust empowers the trustee to hold the lien and foreclose it when given notice of a default by the mortgagee (here known as the beneficiary of the trust). Thus the deed of trust looks like a return to the title theory of mortgages. With a mortgage, the mortgagee must initiate the action in foreclosure to perfect her lien; she has the burden of litigation. With the deed of trust, the burden of bringing litigation shifts to the "mortgagor" (known as the settler of the trust) who must initiate litigation to enjoin the sale from taking place. The shift in the burden of litigation also signals a shift (to the borrower) in the burden of proof. Finally, the trust lasts as long as its purpose — collection of the debt — and no statute of limitations runs against it from the due dates of the loan.

Typically too, the trustee will be an officer of the lender or lending institution. She is nominally the mutual agent of both the beneficiary and the settlor. Generally, a court will not interfere with the exercise of a power of sale, absent fraud, chilled bidding, or other conduct by the mortgagee exercising the power shocking to the court and working irreparable injury to the mortgagor. Caldwell v. Caldwell, 166 Ala. 406, 52 So. 323 (1910) (the early case law for this method of foreclosure often comes from the jurisdictions in the Southeastern United States). In some states, there is no right of statutory redemption following a sale under a private power by a trustee.

The constitutionality of power of sale foreclosures have been litigated extensively. Most of the cases have found that there is no state action and so the due process clause of the Fourteenth Amendment is inapplicable. Charmicor v. Deaner, 572 F.2d 694 (9th Cir. 1978); Northrip v. Federal Natl. Mortgage Assn., 527 F.2d 23, 27 (6th Cir. 1975); Leininger v. Merchants & Farmers Bank, 481 So. 2d 1086 (Miss. 1986); Kottcamp v. Fleet Real Estate Funding Corp., 783 P.2d 170, 172 (Wyo. 1989) (holding that authority given to sheriff, not state, to conduct the sale). But see Turner v. Blackburn, 389 F. Supp. 1250 (W.D.N.C. 1975) (forcing a junior mortgagee to reconvey the title to a mortgagor and finding that the power of the court clerk to enforce by contempt orders the filing of a timely report on the exercise of the power of sale, the clerk's administration of upset bid provisions, and the clerk's audit and approval powers — all constitute a direct exercise of state action; holding further that a hearing before the clerk was required as he exercised these functions). Because of the unusual involvement of the clerk in North Carolina, *Turner* is unlikely to have much bearing on other jurisdictions' power of sale statutes (Colorado aside). Most of the theories of state action have been argued and rejected in the context of a power of sale foreclosure.

The question of state action and that of the requirement for a hearing are distinct. For a representative opinion, see FDIC v. Morrison, 568 F. Supp. 1240 (N.D. Ala. 1983) (finding the lack of personal or *Mullane* notice to be a violation of due process), rev'd, 747 F.2d 610 (11th Cir. 1984) (finding that the mortgagor was not deprived of any property interest because Alabama is a title state).

A query: What if, after a mortgage is executed and recorded on Blackacre, the mortgagor conveys the mineral rights to X. Does the mortgagee, when foreclosing, have to provide actual notice to X that her mineral rights will be extinguished by the decree confirming a power of sale foreclosure? See Davis Oil Co. v. Mills, 873 F.2d 774 (5th Cir. 1989) (holding that actual notice is not required, but that the holder of the minerals has been deprived by state action of an interest entitled to due process when her interest is extinguished by the foreclosure ex parte; however, the holder X may be compelled by statute to file a "request notice" and, failing to do that, can be barred from asserting due process rights to a hearing).

The third method, *strict foreclosure,* once common, is today an ancillary method. We have already discussed this method, in its common law form. It is used regularly today in only two states, Connecticut and Vermont. In Connecticut, deficiency judgments are available. See Dieffenbach v. Attorney General of the State of Vermont, 604 F.2d 187 (2d Cir. 1979) (upholding the constitutionality of Vermont's procedure); Barclay's Bank of New York v. Ivler, 20 Conn. App. 163, 565 A.2d 252, 253-254 (1989). There is a considerable body of case law on its use in Illinois as well. In this latter state it is hedged with statutory restrictions on its use. About ten states have abolished it by statute.

It is reserved for use today in three types of situations: (1) when the mortgagor is insolvent (and thus impervious to a deficiency judgment), (2) when she has little or no built-up equity in the secured property (which equity could be protected or turned into cash by a sale), or where the mortgage being foreclosed was given for the entire purchase price of the property, and (3) when she has abandoned the property or does not appear in the course of the foreclosure action. Thus it is used when the property is worth less than the debt. In addition, it can be used where the mortgagee waives the right to any deficiency. See Citicorp Mortgage, Inc. v. Pessin, 238 N.J. Super. 606, 570 A.2d 481 (App. Div. 1990) (extinguishing assignee of an omitted junior mortgagee's rights with it unless junior paid off senior mortgage debt and reviewing New Jersey case law); Great Lakes Mortgage Corp. v. Collymore, 14 Ill. App. 3d 68, 302 N.E.2d 248 (1973).

Today, strict foreclosure law has sometimes abandoned its reliance on the property as security and extends the right to a deficiency judgment to foreclosing mortgagees. "It has long been the law in Maine that strict foreclosure of a mortgage satisfies the mortgage debt only to the extent of the value of the property at the time of foreclosure. Accordingly, actions were allowed for deficiencies following strict foreclosure." Hammond v. Stiles, 567 A.2d 444, 445 (Me. 1989). On the other hand, if there is a surplus over the debt when the mortgagee sells the property gained through strict foreclosure, then does the mortgagee have to disgorge the surplus? Oceanic Kampgrounds, Inc. v. Camden Natl. Bank, 473 A.2d 884 (Me. 1984) (holding not, because strict foreclosure does not involve a sale of the mortgagor and mortgagee's interest).

As we shall see, strict foreclosure is also used to fix up improperly performed foreclosures of other types, particularly to extinguish the interests of omitted junior lienholders, when justice requires it. Let us turn now to that knotty problem.

## The Problem of the Omitted Junior Lien

The previous discussion of the status of a junior mortgagee defined her as a necessary (but not indispensable) party to the foreclosure of the senior lien.

In the properly conducted senior foreclosure, her interest is wiped out. What if she is omitted from that foreclosure? Because she is not indispensable to it, the proceeding is not a nullity, but now her interest can hardly be said to be wiped out. The proceeding is not res judicata as to her: A person not made a party to an action cannot be bound by its judgment. What can be done for her consistent with the prior proceedings?

# EXAMPLES AND EXPLANATIONS

1. O executes two mortgages. The first, or senior, mortgage is foreclosed by a public, judicially conducted sale. Farwell purchases at that sale. Then the second mortgage was independently foreclosed in the same manner. Murphy purchased at the second sale. Farwell and Murphy do not know of each other's purchase at the time of each sale, but Murphy was the first to find out about the other sale and offers to buy out Farwell's rights. Can she? See Murphy v. Farwell, 9 Wis. 102 (1859).

**Explanation:**   The purchaser at the foreclosure sale of the senior mortgage has an election to make. She (Farwell) has three remedies. First, she can pay off the junior lien and take title free of the omitted lien. This is the most commonly used remedy and is likely to be used if the property is appreciating in value. Second, she can reforeclose, this time including the omitted junior lien or the person holding her rights (Murphy here). In this reforeclosure, the purchaser will become the holder of a revived senior lien — the same lien with which the senior lienholder began the first foreclosure action. Third, she can petition for strict foreclosure against the omitted junior. In this strict foreclosure action, the decree will issue if the court finds that the junior lienor is not prejudiced by being omitted from the foreclosure, as, for example, when the property was already 100 percent mortgaged by the senior lien and so was not valuable enough to provide collateral for the amount of the junior debt. Of this, more in the next paragraph.

In contrast, Murphy holds the rights of the junior mortgagee omitted from the senior sale. She is the "OJ." Her remedies are two in number. First, she can foreclose her lien, or second, she can "redeem" or buy the senior lien. Do you see the conceptual problem with buying the senior lien? (Of this question and these two remedies, more later.)

If the OJ can buy out the purchaser at the senior sale and, at the same time, the purchaser at the senior sale can also buy her out, the situation of an endless round of buyouts is possible. To break this circular pattern of buyouts, the purchaser at the senior sale is given a redemptive priority. (Be clear that this is a redemptive priority and not, strictly speaking, an equity of redemption.) This means that she can buy out the holder of the OJ's rights. Why is the purchaser at the senior sale assigned this priority? Because she not only holds the rights of the senior mortgagee by subrogation at the senior sale but also holds the original mortgagor's rights, including the latter's equity of redemption arising out of the junior mortgage (*not* statutory redemption, which depends on there being a valid decree in foreclosure, from the date of which the statutory redemption period starts to run). Thus when the OJ forecloses, the revived lien of the purchaser is thrown back before the court, but the mortgagor's rights acquired by the purchaser are not thrown back; indeed, they are saved to break the circularity of redemptions that would otherwise result between the OJ and the purchaser. Judgment for Farwell. See generally, G. Nelson & D. Whitman, Real Estate Finance Law §7.15 (2d ed. 1985); G. Osborne, Mortgages §324 (1970).

2. If the procedures required by the foreclosure code require a title search, and the abstractor conducts a search that does not disclose a junior lien on the mortgaged property, can the purchaser at the sale have strict foreclosure against the omitted junior lienor? See Sears, Roebuck & Co. v. Camp, 124 N.J. Eq. 403, 1 A.2d 424, 118 A.L.R. 762 (1938).

**Explanation:**   In the event it is unlikely that another sale would result in bids higher than were submitted in the original (defective) foreclosure or in bids sufficient to satisfy the debt of the omitted junior, the second foreclosure would become a futile act. Strict foreclosure then is an appropriate remedy against an omitted junior, although courts seldom say that it is usual and customary. So where the mortgagor has no built-up equity in the property, or where the property is 100 percent leveraged by the senior mortgage, strict foreclosure is appropriate against the omitted junior. Decreeing strict foreclosure against an omitted junior in these situations is akin to an equity court determining whether the omission prejudiced the rights of the junior. If not, strict foreclosure will be granted. Additionally, if the junior lienor has a cause of action on the note against the mortgagor, she is not left with a remedy. Finally, if she has a cause of action against the negligent abstractor, this rationale has special force since she is left with two remedies. One cause of action lies in assumpsit and another in negligence.

3.  In the preceding problem, what if the OJ is not disclosed in the senior foreclosure because she did not record her interest before the senior mortgagee filed the foreclosure action or any notice of its pendency (up to which time the abstractor searches the title)?

**Explanation:**   The answer to this problem really starts with a question (a somewhat rhetorical one, however): In this instance, should the OJ have to take subject to a lien for the amount that the purchaser at the first sale paid, or redeem the property in the amount of that sale price? How fair is that to the OJ? Not very. She may be forced to put up more than she anticipated to obtain the security for which she bargained. But this unfairness must be balanced against the mortgagor's loss of her built-up equity in the property if no purchaser will bid more than the amount of the senior debt at any sale likely to be subject to the rights of an omitted junior. Strict foreclosure is still likely to be granted.

4. What if an omitted junior has actual knowledge of the senior foreclosure? Should she then get her two remedies of foreclosure and redemption?

**Explanation:** Arguably not. She does not have to be joined as a necessary party to exercise her presale redemption right (hers by contract) and she can also attend the sale and bid. In this situation, she is estopped from foreclosing subject to the revived first mortgage and should be limited to her redemption rights. Put up or shut up should be the judicial response to someone who created this legal mess!

5. ME forecloses on MR's home for good cause. ME purchases at the judicial sale. After the foreclosure decree is confirmed, an OJ appears and petitions to reopen to decree. ME responds that before the decree can be reopened, the OJ should deposit with the court the amount of the senior's (ME's) mortgage debt. Is ME correct?

**Explanation:** No. The omitted junior has an election to make. She has two remedies and can choose one of them. First, she can foreclose her lien; in that foreclosure, she takes the title as she bargained for it (with the senior lien attached to it). However, because the senior lienholder's rights have been transferred by the foreclosure sale to the purchaser at that sale, that lien is revived for the purpose of the junior foreclosure, and the purchaser at the senior's sale becomes the holder of a revived senior lien.

So the presence of the OJ bringing foreclosure forces the purchaser at the sale to disgorge the senior and foreclosing lienholder's rights. But, she will argue, this isn't all that the purchaser has; she has the rights of the mortgagor as well — loosely, these rights are the mortgagor's right of equitable redemption. If those rights too must be disgorged, then the purchaser is forced to disgorge the "title" to the property, not just the senior lien rights, and the OJ will get more than she bargained for. She will get the value of the built-up equity thrown in free. If the property has appreciated in value since the senior lien was executed, this could result in quite a windfall. (Preventing this windfall presents again the question of who can buy out whom — as between the purchaser and the OJ — and which of them has the right to exercise the last right of redemption.)

The revived lien held by the purchaser during the OJ's foreclosure is worth the amount of the outstanding debt. The purchaser becomes a privileged bidder at the OJ's sale — she has the right to bid up to that amount without producing cash. (Remember that she probably has already shelled out this amount of cash at the senior sale.) She is going to get a mortgage that the OJ will then start to pay off, on the same terms applying to the original senior lien.

The amount of this revived lien is the debt outstanding at the time of the senior sale. This results in a windfall to the purchaser if she bid an amount lower than the debt and puts her out of pocket if her bid goes higher than that. The possibility of an omitted junior is thus likely to depress the prices that properties bring in foreclosure.

Second, the OJ can buy out the senior lien rights, now held by the purchaser at the senior sale. This second remedy is not much used. Do you see why? Because it requires more cash than the first remedy (foreclosure of the junior lien).

These are alternative remedies. The forced deposit requested by ME here would turn the foreclosure remedy into a forced redemption. See Bowmar, Mortgage Foreclosure in New York: Omitted Lienors, 22 Real Prop. Prob. & Tr. J. 509, 524-538 (1987). (This is a good discussion, but from a student's point of view, it is replete with discussion of New York statutes and therefore not as crisp on the general issue as it might be. But that's the real world! The view from the local bench is usually more complicated (if you can believe that) than the view from the professor's desk.)

6. If in the preceding paragraph, the foreclosure sale fetched proceeds sufficient to pay the mortgagor a sum, may not the omitted junior impress an equitable or constructive trust on those proceeds not needed to pay off the liens?

**Explanation:** Why not? There is no reason not to do this. It avoids reviving the senior lien and turning the purchaser at the senior sale into a mortgagee by operation of law. Surely the purchaser didn't expect to be turned into a lender by the unexpected appearance of the omitted junior. This remedy conforms to the purchaser's expectation and gives the omitted junior a fund for payment of the junior debt. The trouble is that in practice this is seldom the outcome: The proceeds of the senior sale are seldom sufficient for this purpose. However, the remedy has a conceptual elegance and equitable appeal. See Caito v. United California Bank, 20 Cal. 3d 694, 144 Cal. Rptr. 751, 576 P.2d 466 (1978) (holding that the junior lienor can assert a lien on the surplus).

7. P purchases at ME's foreclosure sale. She goes into possession and improves the property. Time passes. OJ, an omitted junior mortgagee, petitions to open the judgment and elects to foreclose. Can P become a revived mortgagee at OJ's foreclosure sale for the amount of the senior debt, plus the value of her improvements?

**Explanation:** Yes, if the improvements were made in good faith and without knowledge of OJ. In addition, P's revived lien can recover the cost of necessary repairs, taxes, and insurance, as well as the costs of the OJ's foreclosure (but not the costs of the original foreclosure from which OJ was excluded), with a setoff for the rents and profits that P received from the property. If OJ were to redeem, the same values would be added and offset in computing the redemption price.

8. Would your answers to any or all of the previous problems in this section change if for the OJ you were to substitute an omitted mechanic's lienor or lessee of the secured property?

**Explanation:** No. Those who either have improved the property, like the mechanic's lienor, or are entitled to possession, like the lessee, are entitled to at least as much deference as the purchaser at the sale. The problem of the omitted party is a generic one — indeed, a classic one in the law of mortgages.

# Defects in the Foreclosure Sale

A foreclosure sale is an "as is" conveyance of an interest in the secured property. Submission of the high bid at the sale is in effect an offer to purchase, subject to judicial acceptance or an intervening objection that will delay the effect of any preexisting decree. However, the conduct of the sale itself may also create a defect in the title of the purchaser.

A substantial defect in the sale can render the purchaser's interest void. Examples involve the forgery of the mortgage being foreclosed, the foreclosure by a person not the holder of the note, or a sale without the mortgagee's authorization. Other defects render the purchaser's interest voidable, that is, subject to redemption by the mortgagor, but also subject to being extinguished if the interest comes into the hands of a bona fide purchaser. A defect in the authority of a trustee to conduct a private sale, a confusing description of the property subject to foreclosure, the conduct of the sale at the wrong door of the courthouse (as per the notice or the deed of trust), defective (rather than no) notice, are examples of situations giving rise to a voidable interest in the purchaser. Recall the void-voidable title distinction as used in other contexts (for example, in deed defects). These examples are similar to the use of the distinction elsewhere.

When the foreclosure is conducted under the authority of a power of sale in a deed of trust, the trustee is a fiduciary of both the beneficiary and the trustor-mortgagor. As such, she may not "chill the sale," which means that she may not inhibit or suppress the bidding. For example, announcing that the mortgagee will bid the full value of the property while knowing that the bid will actually be much smaller is in effect a conspiracy with the mortgagee to prevent others from bidding. Sullivan v. Federal Farm Mortgage Corp., 62 Ga. App. 402, 8 S.E.2d 126 (1940). And while she may announce the bids of prospective, but absent, purchasers, she steps closer to breaching the fiduciary's scrupulous fidelity to her principals by financing the purchase of the property with a loan to the successful bidder. Not requiring the cash or certified check announced as part of the terms of sale from a bidder, and later financing her bid with a loan, steps over the line. Finally, when she secretly buys at the sale, she is in breach of her duty. She has done what the loan documents do not quite do — acquired an interest in the outcome of the sale and put herself in conflict with the mortgagor. See Boatman's Bank v. Community Interiors, Inc, 721 S.W.2d 72 (Mo. App. 1986), noted in 53 Mo. L. Rev. 151 (1988).

A failure of the foreclosure statute to meet the requirements of the constitution renders the purchaser's interest void. Turner v. Blackburn, 389 F. Supp. 1250 (W.D.N.C. 1975) (this opinion contains a good review of the power of sale foreclosure as found in one state statute).

## The Merger Doctrine and Deeds in Lieu of Foreclosure

When a holder of a less-than-fee interest, such as a mortgagee, acquires the fee, the lesser interest is extinguished by operation of law — that is, extinguished by the common law. Thus it is said, at law (meaning in litigation based on the common law actions), the lesser interest is merged into the greater. In contrast, in equity merger is a matter of intent. See Licursi v. Sweeney, 594 A.2d 396 (Vt. 1991) (holding merger subject to rules of contract, rather than estates).

## EXAMPLES AND EXPLANATIONS

9. Suppose that a mortgagee ME holds both the junior and senior liens. If she forecloses the junior and a third party buys at the sale, is the senior lien extinguished?

**Explanation:**  No. Foreclosure is an equitable action. Merger is thus a matter of intent. A purchaser at the sale presumptively made allowances for the amount of the senior lien when formulating the bid made at the sale. After this calculation is made, the purchaser takes title subject to the senior lien, which is not merged. G. Nelson & D. Whitman, Real Estate Finance Law §§6.15-6.17 (2d ed. 1985); G. Osborne, Mortgages §§273-276 (1970); J. Bruce, Real Estate Finance in a Nutshell 104 (2d ed. 1985).

10. Suppose the same facts as in the preceding paragraph, except that ME buys at the junior sale.

**Explanation:**  Now the senior lien is extinguished, merged into the fee. ME is presumed to have made the same calculation as would a third-party purchaser, but the effect of her purchase is that she is presumed to agree that the land stands for the total debt and the senior lien is extinguished. A second approach to this problem is to ask what ME bought at the sale. Why, the mortgagor's right of equitable redemption, of course. This being so, ME becomes both a borrower and a lender, which, Polonius advised, one should never be. The law takes Polonius's advice and merges the senior lien with the fee simple title. A third approach to this problem involves a principle of judicial economy; ME is in effect forced to foreclose both the junior and the senior liens at the same time. See Licursi v. Sweeney, 594 A.2d 396 (Vt. 1991); Belleville Sav. Bank v. Reis, 136 Ill. 242, 26 N.E. 646 (1891) (finding that the senior lien was extinguished); and see generally Nelson & Whitman, supra, $6.16.

However, if there was an intervening lien at the time of the purchase by the foreclosing junior, her senior lien would not be destroyed. To extinguish the senior lien in this situation would give the intervening lienor a priority that she did not expect and mean that the foreclosing junior would lose a valuable priority, so no merger. Tom Riley Law Firm, P.C. v. Padzensky, 430 N.W.2d 416 (Iowa 1988).

11. Suppose that MR, a mortgagor, acquires both the note and the mortgage of ME, MR's lender. What is the state of MR's title?

**Explanation:**   MR holds the fee simple absolute, in all cases. The doctrine of merger extinguishes the mortgage lien by fusing it (a less than fee interest) into a greater — the fee simple. Neither can MR be both a borrower and a lender at one and the same time. MR's presumptive intent is to extinguish the note and the mortgage. This presumption has a title-cleansing effect; it frees the fee for further alienation. See Wright v. Anderson, 62 S.D. 444, 253 N.W. 484, 95 A.L.R. 81 (1934) (noting that one cannot be both debtor and creditor at one and the same time).

12. Instead of talking about a two-party transaction, think about a three-party one. Suppose that ME and MR execute a brief but enforceable note and mortgage, but that MR conveys her interest to GE, who takes title subject to ME's mortgage but does not assume the personal obligation to pay the note. Later GE buys ME's investment and so acquires the note and the mortgage from ME. Is the note and the mortgage merged into GE's fee simple?

**Explanation:**   Not completely. Although case support is slight, the merger is only partial in this instance. In a falling market, the amount of the debt purchased by GE may be greater than the fair market value of the land that GE earlier purchased. In such a case, GE has rights against MR for the difference between the outstanding debt purchased and the fair market value of the land. In taking title, GE calculated the worth of the land, and so the doctrine of merger might extinguish the mortgage up to the amount of the purchase price, but GE would still have the benefit of her bargain with ME and so have ME's rights against MR up to the amount of the difference money. This protects ME's right to assign her investment in a falling market.

13. Suppose the same facts as in the preceding paragraph, but GE buys the note and mortgage at the same time as she takes title subject to. Merger?

**Explanation:**   Probably. GE makes her deal when closing the transaction and takes without further rights against MR. Is MR a third-party beneficiary of the assignment of the note and mortgage? Is GE presumed to have made the calculations outlined in preceding paragraphs at the closing table and adjusted the price paid MR down accordingly? Will MR have bargained less vigorously, knowing that merger would occur? The answers to these questions are probably yes.

14. Suppose the same facts as in the preceding paragraph, but now GE assumes the obligation to pay the note. Merger?

**Explanation:**   Now the answers to the questions asked in the preceding problem are more clearly yes.

15. Now consider the other side of the chain of title. Suppose that ME acquires the title from a grantee (GE) of the mortgagor (MR). Is ME's mortgage lien merged into her title acquired from GE?

**Explanation:**   It depends. Remember the problems about transfers from the mortgagor. The grantees could either be assuming grantees (ASGs) or nonassuming grantees (NAGs). If ME becomes a NAG, no merger is worked, but if she becomes an ASG, then there is a merger. So mortgagees must be careful (and well advised) in this situation: Their counsel should explain to them that they should only take subject to if they wish to maintain their rights against MR in the future.

16. Suppose ME acquires a deed in lieu of foreclosure from MR. What exactly is conveyed?

**Explanation:**   MR's right of equitable redemption, as well as the fee title. MR could not give up the right of equitable redemption at the outset of the ME-MR mortgage transaction. The common law attorneys used to say, "once a mortgage, always a mortgage"; this doctrine is a way of saying that the redemption rights cannot be waived at the execution of the mortgage. To allow such a waiver would be a clog (another common law term) on the equity of redemption. Later, however, for good consideration, MR can bargain it away. (Courts look closely at this bargain.) MR exchanges it here for the extinguishment of the mortgage lien. But how about the debt? This is not a case of merger, but rather is an instance of a debt discharged by payment (substitute performance) or accord and satisfaction. ME has substituted the land for the debt. See Nelson & Whitman, supra, §§6.18-6.19.

However, in accepting the deed in lieu, a mortgagee must realize that, because the foreclosure on the lien has not gone forward to a decree, any junior liens are not extinguished. Rather, they move up in priority. Thus, the mortgagee accepting a deed in lieu should be careful about forgoing foreclosure, and particularly careful about filing a deed of release for their lien, before ascertaining whether there are junior liens. A title search is necessary to determine this. Janus Properties, Inc. v. First Florida Bank, N.A., 546 So. 2d 785 (Fla. App., 1989) (holding that a junior lien was elevated to senior status when first mortgagee accepted a deed in lieu of foreclosure).

17. MR is in default and she and ME negotiate over the transfer by MR of a deed in lieu of foreclosure. MR wants one of the following three things in the deed: (1) a covenant that MR will receive one-half of the proceeds of any later sale of the property by ME; (2) an estate in fee simple, subject to the condition that ME will not sell the property within a year of the date of execution and will sell it back to MR if the latter finds a purchaser of whom ME approves and to whom ME will lend; or (3) a covenant in the deed that, in any sale, MR will act as ME's broker and receive a commission for this service. As MR's attorney, which of these options would you advise? On what bases would your advise be premised?

**Explanation:** The first option would result in a shared appreciation mortgage, a SAM. See Chapter 19, Alternative Mortgage Instruments, at page 230. The lender would not agree to this unless the appreciation can be realized within a short time. However, the borrower who agrees not to file for bankruptcy or not to contest the acceleration in the loan in bankruptcy may obtain the mortgagee's agreement to share the proceeds on any resale. What if the mortgagor later asserts that this agreement was an equitable mortgage and files suit to impose a lien on the property for the mortgagor's one-half. Mortgagor may have to agree not to sue in this way in order to obtain the mortgagee's consent to this arrangement. While the mortgagee holds the title, what are the mortgagee's rights? Do they hold in a kind of tenancy in common? Does the mortgagor get to review the terms of the sale when it is finally made? If half the proceeds provides the mortgagee with a return in excess of the usury rate, what then? How will one-half the proceeds be calculated, anyway? As half the capital appreciation since the deed was given, half the purchase price, half the cash received at closing, subject to deductions for closing costs, etc.? What about moving this option, if the lender is initially interested, into a fully thought-out SAM?

The second option can be combined with the first in many interesting ways, but, standing alone, the mortgagor's arguments that an equitable mortgage is created become stronger.

The third option is most likely to meet the mortgagee's needs; after all, an institutional mortgagee is in the lending business, not in the business of holding defaulted loan properties.

# Federal Income Tax Consequences

A mortgagee accepting the proceeds of a foreclosure sale, of whatever type, or a deed in lieu of foreclosure, will have to consider whether either ordinary income or a bad debt deduction will result. (What is said here assumes that further recovery of the debt after the sale or acceptance of the deed in lieu is not possible through a deficiency judgment action.) With the acceptance of a deed in lieu, the mortgagee has collected the debt and has not sold or exchanged property (so no capital gain), and if the fair market value of the property is more than the outstanding principal and accrued interest — the mortgagee's "basis" in the debt — ordinary income is realized (if it is less, then the mortgagee is entitled to a bad debt deduction from her ordinary income). Commissioner v. Spreckels, 120 F.2d 517 (9th Cir. 1941).

If the secured property is sold to a third party at the foreclosure sale, and the proceeds of the sale are insufficient to satisfy the outstanding debt — that is, that proceeds are less than the mortgagee's basis — then the mortgagee is entitled to a bad debt deduction in the amount of the difference.

When the mortgagee bids for and acquires the secured property at the foreclosure sale, the mortgagee may realize ordinary income on the difference between its basis in the debt and the fair market value of the property, if that value is greater than the basis. If the value is less, a bad debt deduction results. (*Query:* What if the mortgagee is reacquiring property previously sold to the mortgagor? In this situation, no bad debt deduction will result and no gain or loss results. See I.R.C. §1038(a).)

In the usual case, and perhaps to avoid the realization of income, the mortgagee will bid no more at the sale than its basis in the debt, and so it will bid no higher than the amount of its "credit bid." See I.R.C. §166. As we have seen when discussing omitted juniors, bidding this far, but no further, avoids the legal risks suffered by a sale purchaser who is forced into a reforeclosure by an omitted junior.

# Statutory Redemption

Statutory, as distinguished from equitable, redemption is a postsale right. Several New England states have this right, as well as most states west of the Mississippi River except Louisiana, Nebraska, Oklahoma, and Texas. In all, it is available to mortgagors in 33 states. Many of the major commercial states do not, however, have statutory redemption rights, and some states do not provide this right to a foreclosure conducted under a power of sale, extending a right of equitable redemption or a right to cure the default before the sale, but no statutory redemption afterwards.

Statutory redemption provides a period of time, usually six months, but sometimes as long as two years, in which the person eligible to redeem can pay the sale price and redeem the title. This right is intended to act as a check on low bidding at the foreclosure sale. Its effect may be to depress the bids, however, because would-be purchasers know that they cannot possibly obtain a marketable title until the statutory redemption right expires. The right is alienable by the mortgagor, but the mortgagee cannot levy on it, and often the mortgagor has the right of possession during the redemption period. With some exceptions, as previously noted, it applies to both judicial foreclosure and power of sale foreclosures.

The effect of the mortgagor's exercise of this right is to terminate the title acquired by the purchaser at the foreclosure sale. The mortgagor's title is restored to its status just before the sale, not transferred from the purchaser. As you can imagine, then, the next issue is the extent to which other liens are revived. Some courts hold that all junior liens are revived; some in addition take the position that not only are junior liens revived, but so are senior liens to the extent that they remain unsatisfied by the proceeds of the sale. Still others attach the foreclosing mortgagee's lien, but only to the extent of a deficiency judgment. (As we will see, the third position may be different from the second because many states, in various ways, limit the right to a deficiency.) Fourth, and finally, a few courts have held that the grantee or transferee of a mortgagor has a redemption right that when exercised will not revive junior liens. This fourth position has been roundly criticized as a violation of the rule that no grantee can obtain more than her grantor has to convey. It is, however, an incentive to mortgagees who foreclose to bid the foreclosure sale price up. On the other hand, a provision of the California Civil Code, §729, takes the position that liens extinguished by the sale are not reattached after redemption. Thus junior liens are extinguished and may not later be levied on to satisfy the underlying note.

Often junior mortgagees and lienors are authorized to redeem as well. Often their redemption rights are limited in time (to a period, following a time, during which the mortgagor alone was entitled to redeem). Moreover, they are typically subject to a rule governing the priority of redemptions granting the mortgagor, her grantee or transferee, and juniors the right, in accordance with their original priority of title. Thus senior redeemers can preempt the rights of juniors.

When redeeming, a junior mortgagee or lienor will acquire the rights of the purchaser at the sale. The latter is regarded as the successor to the mortgagor for this purpose. Because the junior may herself be subject to a prior right to redeem, the title she gets upon redemption is more akin to the purchaser's than the revived mortgagor's title because, during the remainder of the redemption period, it is ripening into an absolute title. Absent special statutory language, this ripening accords with the spirit of the statute, provides the full period of redemption to all eligible to redeem, and encourages a foreclosing mortgagee to bid up the sale price. A second reason to regard the redeeming junior as the successor to the purchaser is a matter of judicial economy: The purchaser has all the rights gathered into the foreclosure proceedings, and further judicial action is not needed to confirm the title. If the result were otherwise, the redeeming junior would have to bring an action to foreclose her lien, not just for the amount of the outstanding balance on the junior's note but increased by the redemption amount.[1]

Often only those joined in the foreclosure action can assert a statutory redemption right. See, e.g., Or. Rev. Stat. §23.520 (1987). Thus omitted juniors do not have this right. Portland Mortgage Co. v. Creditors Protective Assn., 199 Or. 432, 262 P.2d 918 (1953). Remember that this right is a creation of statute, and who has it requires close attention to the statute at issue. The following problems are thus offered as a reflection of the types of analysis you might encounter, not because the answers embody a general rule.

# EXAMPLES AND EXPLANATIONS

18a.  MR and ME execute a brief but enforceable mortgage, upon which ME begins foreclosure for good cause. The title of the purchaser at the judicial sale is subject to a one-year right of statutory redemption. Before the sale, MR conveys her interest in Blackacre to GE, who assumes MR's obligation on the mortgage debt. Can GE exercise MR's statutory redemption right?

**Explanation:**  Yes. Unless the statute provides otherwise, you might assume that even a statutory right is freely alienable. In many instances, a

---

1. The result is otherwise in Illinois, but the case authority is old. If the purchaser's title is not transferred to the redeemer, the purchaser may instead become the mortgagor's successor with regard to redemption. At this point, we might have to run the period of redemptions again. Enough, already! A second solution uses the analogy of strict foreclosure. If a junior redeems and the courts of her jurisdiction revive her lien, her debt is extinguished to the extent the value of the land is in excess of the redemption payment. By redeeming, she agrees to this further satisfaction of her debt and agrees to substitute the property for it. This result recognizes that the mortgagor has most likely been denied, in a foreclosure, the full security value of her property. It applies more of that value to satisfy the mortgagor's debt. A third solution is statutory. The Iowa Code requires the redeeming junior to file a statement of the amount of the debt satisfied by the redemption, and if no statement is filed, her whole debt is satisfied. Iowa Code §628.13 (1989).

statutory right of redemption is an opportunity to attempt to refinance the property, and the mortgagor might want to transfer the right to a creditworthy purchaser-assignee. The right should follow the conveyance to GE. It is an implied statutory right, unless it is assumed that the MR-GE transaction was fraudulent in some way.

18b. Assumes the same facts as in the preceding example, except that GE takes a title subject to the mortgage but does not assume the debt. Does your answer to "a" above change?

**Explanation:**   Now GE may not be able to exercise MR's statutory redemption right because GE has not fully stepped into MR's shoes, and only by doing so may she be extended the right to redeem. In other words, one should be concerned with not only what the statute says about alienability of the right, but also with whether the person purporting to exercise the right has contracted for it and stepped into the mortgagor's position. If both conditions are not satisfied, MR retains the right and should seek refinancing assumable by GE.

18c. Now assume that GE takes title after the foreclosure sale. Does this make a difference?

**Explanation:**   GE has no statutory redemption rights. They normally arise at the sale. Why don't we extend statutory redemption rights to GEs who take before the final decree, rather than the sale? See G. Nelson & D. Whitman, Real Estate Finance Law §8.5 (2d ed. 1985). We probably should.

18d. Will a mortgagor have the right to possess Blackacre during the year after the sale?

**Explanation:**   Yes, and so will the grantee or assignee of the right. During the period of statutory redemption, the possession of the property stays with the mortgagor, who has the ability to work the property for rents and profits and so perhaps to eventually refinance the defaulted mortgage. In fact, while possession may be of some benefit to the mortgagor, studies show that very few persons holding statutory redemption rights actually exercise them. But even assuming that they increase the costs of doing business for mortgagees, legislators like statutory redemption nonetheless: The lenders are in a better position to spread the costs over all mortgagors for the benefit of those mortgagors who can and do redeem.

18e. What if GE conveys her interest in Blackacre to VE under an installment land sale contract, and both GE as the vendor under the contract and VE wish to exercise the statutory redemption right. Who has priority?

**Explanation:** GE, as the vendor under the installment land sale contract, has priority of redemption as against her vendee VE. Where two persons both hold the statutory redemption right, the person closest to MR has the prior right.

18f. If ME purchases at the foreclosure sale, can she exercise a statutory redemption right?

**Explanation:** No. Otherwise, the lender would be encouraged to submit a very low bid at the foreclosure sale, sue out a deficiency judgment, and then exercise the statutory redemption right, obtain the title to the property, and resell it. Likely the mortgagee would be made more than whole by this panoply of remedies. The purpose of statutory redemption is to put a check on such low bids, so giving the lender statutory redemption rights would defeat the purpose of the statute.

18g. Is the right of statutory redemption equally applicable to foreclosure sales conducted under a private power of sale?

**Explanation:** Yes in Missouri, no in California. The answer depends upon a reading of the applicable state statute. In general, the private power of sale (usually in a deed of trust) might be expected to give rise to a statutory right to redeem; the private sale requires a check that judicial supervision of other types of foreclosure otherwise would provide.

Some states limit the statutory redemption right in other, diverse ways. Minnesota extends the redemption period when the foreclosure sale price is low. Minn. Stat. §580.23 (1988). Missouri limits the right to foreclosures that result in the mortgagee purchasing at the sale (as well as to power of sale-deed of trust foreclosures). Mo. Rev. Stat. §443.410 (1986). Kentucky permits redemption only when the foreclosure sale price is two-thirds of fair market value. Ky. Rev. Stat. Ann. §426.220 (Michie 1972). In some states the right may be waived, in others it may not. Contrast Kan. Stat. Ann. §60-241(q) (1983) (permitting waiver), with Alaska Stat. §34.20.090 (1985) (requiring that the mortgagor reserve the right).

Critics rail against the right of statutory redemption, claiming that its existence can only depress the bids at any type of foreclosure sale. However, the right has proven a sturdy statutory creature. Only two states have repealed the right since the 1930s — Indiana and New York. Another state, Illinois, recently made calculation of its redemption period more complicated. Ill. Rev. Stat. ch. 110, ¶15-1603(b) (1987), requires seven months from the date on which the residential mortgagor is served with a summons or the court acquires jurisdiction, or three months from the date of the judgment. For an article defending the economic costs of the right to statutory redemption, see Schill, An Economic Analysis of Mortgagor Protection Laws, 77

Va. L. Rev. 489 (1991) (arguing that it serves a function analogous to mortgagor insurance).

Some Midwestern states have recently amended their statutory redemption statutes in response to the farm foreclosure crisis in those states. The redemptive period has been extended for agricultural land to two years and applied retroactively. See Federal Land Bank of Omaha v. Arnold, 426 N.W.2d 153 (Iowa 1988) (in which the retroactivity proved to be a contracts clause violation and singling out certain types of lenders an equal protection clause violation). The extended redemption right permitted redemption at the fair market value, not the sale price as is usual with statutory redemption. Other states have required the lender purchasing at the sale of agricultural land to offer the mortgagor a right of first refusal when reselling the title. Note, A Comparative Study of the Former Owner's Right of First Refusal upon a Lender's Resale of Foreclosed Agricultural Land: A New Form of State Mortgagor Relief Legislation, 1988 J. Corp. L. 895.

# Moratoria on Foreclosures

During the 1930s, several states enacted moratoria on the foreclosure of mortgages and deeds of trust. These statutes were enacted on an emergency basis, for limited amounts of time, and in the hope that after the moratoria period had passed, the value of the property as security for the debt would have been restored by the return of good times. Meanwhile, they permitted mortgagors to remain in possession of the secured property. Such statutes were found constitutional in Home Building & Loan Assn. v. Blaisdell, 290 U.S. 398 (1934) (holding that there is no taking or impairment of contract).

During the 1980s, as regions of the country experienced economic hard times, modified moratoria were again enacted but on a more limited basis, often for residential or farm mortgages. Usually a petition to a court was necessary to obtain "a [six-month] postponement of a threatened foreclosure or other protection from foreclosure, including restructuring of the mortgage debt to eliminate any arrearages" owed a lender — usually, any lender, either an institution or a person. Iowa and Minnesota enacted such statutes. The potential petitioners were the unemployed, the underemployed, or others unable to meet the payments required by the mortgage documents. In regions of the country undergoing economic adjustments, such as the farmbelt or the rustbelt, persons indirectly affected by the economic distress of the region were potential petitioners too, such as the under-, but not unemployed. Putting the matter into judicial hands permitted the court to consider the relative financial strengths of the mortgagor and mortgagee, the mortgagor's other assets, her credit history, her employment prospects, her equity in the secured property, and the prospect that a postponement or restructuring of the debt would achieve some good result. The postponements of foreclosure available in such statutes often merely encouraged institutional mortgage lenders to shorten the period of time, after default but before foreclosure, during which various collection procedures were used.

## Antideficiency Legislation

Most states impose some type of controls on deficiency judgments, even if they are only procedural, with special notice and time limits placed on the action to enforce them. A deficiency judgment is usually a judgment for the unpaid amount of the outstanding debt, recovery of which has been the object of the mortgagee bringing a foreclosure action of some type. A deficiency judgment results from an ancillary action on the note, will be executed on the personal assets of the mortgagor to the extent, again, that the debt in the note has not been satisfied by the proceeds of the foreclosure of the mortgage lien. It is thus a judgment seeking this unsatisfied amount or deficiency from the mortgagor's personal assets (those assets not secured by the mortgage).

Typically, the petition in foreclosure seeks a deficiency judgment in the alternative. If it does not make this request, then the deficiency must be sought within the statute of limitations or within the time after which such an action is barred by laches, unless there is ongoing and related litigation that would interfere with a court's computation of the deficient amount or in which an omitted junior lienholder has sued to reopen the foreclosure decree or to redeem.

Seven states have legislation prohibiting deficiency judgments in one or more (but not all) of the following situations: a purchase money mortgage, a mortgage with a private power of sale, a mortgage foreclosed and subject to short redemption periods, or abandoned property. Most of these statutes were enacted during the Depression. Gelfert v. National City Bank, 313 U.S. 221 (1941) (holding a statute limiting the amount of a deficiency judgment constitutional). Arizona by statute permits a deficiency judgment for waste committed by the mortgagor. Normally a deficiency would be computed only with reference to the debt, and a separate action required of mortgagee for waste.

Sometimes a purchase money mortgage extended by a vendor results in the antideficiency statute being applied, whereas a purchase money mortgage extended by a third-party lender results in that lender being entitled, after foreclosure, to a deficiency judgment. Can you see the sense of that distinction? It must lie in the fear of overpriced property in the former, but not the latter, situation. See Ladd & Tilton Natl. Bank v. Mitchell, 93 Or. 668, 184 P. 282, 284 (1919).

## EXAMPLES AND EXPLANATIONS

19a. Your jurisdiction enacts the following statute: "In all sales of real property by mortgagees and/or trustees under powers of sale contained in any mortgage or deed of trust . . . or where judgment or decree is given to secure the payment of the balance of the purchase price of real property, the mortgagee or trustee or holder of the notes secured by such . . . shall not be entitled to a deficiency judgment." Will this statute apply to commercial transactions as well as residential ones?

**Explanation:** Yes. This statute is a highly edited version of N.C. Gen. Stat. §45-21.38 (1986) (this statute also contains a provision to the effect that the security instrument must show on its face that it is given to secure purchase money; does this imply that the protection of the statute can be bargained away, if not in the normal residential mortgage, in the commercial one?), which was patterned after Or. Rev. Stat. §88.070 (1986). On its face, this statute applies to both types of transactions. Lenders are likely to suggest that development in large commercial transactions will be hindered as a result. Is that so? The argument has a speculative element to it, asking for a measurement of the number of deals that did not take place.

19b. What if after default, a purchase money mortgagee executes and records a deed of release for the mortgage lien and sues on the note, does the statute apply to that suit?

**Explanation:** Yes. Once a mortgage, always a mortgage. The lender cannot escape the reach of the statute by the release, even if it is executed before a default. See Barnaby v. Boardman, 313 N.C. 565, 330 S.E.2d 600 (1985); but see Bantier v. Harrison, 259 Or. 182, 485 P.2d 1073 (1971) (court waived foreclosure of mortgage in jurisdiction with similar statute and permitted a suit on the note). See G. Nelson & D. Whitman, Real Estate Finance Law §8.3 (2d ed. 1985); J. Bruce, Real Estate Finance in a Nutshell 188 (2d ed. 1985).

19c. Does the statute apply to vendor's liens?

**Explanation:** Probably, but they are creatures of equity and if not clearly controlled by the terms of the statute, a crisp answer is impossible.

19d. Does the statute apply to installment land sale contracts?

**Explanation:** Probably, if the case law in the jurisdiction is sufficiently clear that these contracts function as mortgages and so require foreclosure in place of the enforcement of the forfeiture clauses often contained in the contract.

19e. Does the statute apply to junior mortgagees?

**Explanation:** What if the junior is a party to the foreclosure, but the sale produces proceeds insufficient to satisfy the debt of the junior? In such an instance, should not the mortgagee be permitted to release the mortgage lien and sue for a deficiency judgment? If she can't, she lacks an effective remedy, and the statute may unintentionally encourage mortgagor fraud. There is legal uncertainty here. The statute does not on its face distinguish between senior and junior liens. In such an uncertain legal environment, the unsecured lender may be better off than the secured one. A lender may ask for a negative pledge and an agreement not to further encumber in such an environment. See supra pp. 224-225. A similar California statute has been applied only to selling lienholders. Cal. Civ. Code §580(a) (1989).

19f.  Does the statute apply to a junior mortgagee who was originally a purchase money mortgagee, but later is assigned junior status in a subordination agreement?

**Explanation:**  Probably. The subordinating junior executed a purchase money mortgagee, for whom the prohibition on deficiency judgments is express. The statute denying a deficiency judgment to a purchase money mortgagee seems to be defining the term as of the time the mortgage is executed, and the rule should be: Once denied such a judgment, always denied, unless the statutory purpose can be advanced by recharacterizing the transaction after the fact. See Barnaby v. Boardman, 313 N.C. 565, 568, 330 S.E.2d 600, 603 (1985). But there is a split of authority on this issue. See Spangler v. Memel, 7 Cal. 3d 603, 614, 498 P.2d 1055, 1062, 102 Cal. Rptr. 807, 814 (1972), interpreting Cal. Civ. Code §580b (a similar antideficiency statute construed as not prohibiting a deficiency judgment when a purchase money mortgage is subordinated to a later construction loan). The issue between these cases is whether to assign purchase money mortgage status at the time the mortgage is executed or later, when the deficiency judgment is sought. Note, Fair-Value Limitations Applied to the Deficiency Judgments of Sold-Out Junior Lienholders, 23 Loy. L.A. L. Rev. 313 (1989).

19g.  Does the statute apply to mortgagees who take a deed in lieu of foreclosure?

**Explanation:**  Definitely. Unless there is some agreement otherwise, the mortgagee in this instance has made her deal and substituted the property for the debt. Here one might analogize the bargain struck by the mortgagee obtaining a decree for strict foreclosure. No deficiency judgment is available.

20.  If the mortgagee forecloses and then brings a suit for rescission of the mortgage loan agreement because of the mortgagor's misrepresentation of the value of the land, does the antideficiency statute bar such a suit?

**Explanation:**  Not if the misrepresentation amounts to fraud because the statute is meant to bar secondary actions on the loan agreement or contract, not actions based in tort. Kass v. Weber, 261 Cal. App. 2d 417, 67 Cal. Rptr. 876, 879 (1968). A fraud-based cause of action is not one based on the original loan agreement and debt. Bad faith waste of the property would similarly be beyond the reach of the antideficiency statute. Cornelison v. Kornbluth, 15 Cal. 3d 590, 125 Cal. Rptr. 557, 568, 542 P.2d 981 (1975) (the court also holding that good faith waste, brought on by general market decline, is within the reach of the statute).

Another type of antideficiency legislation limits the amount of such a judgment to the "fair value" of the judgment. This is either a limitation of the judgment amount to the difference between the mortgage debt and the fair value of the secured property (setting the value, rather than the foreclosure price, as a floor). This type of statute is a mortgagor's protection against an oversecured mortgagee, particularly one who purchases at her own foreclosure sale. In other situations, the mortgagee is given an incentive to see that the value of the property, found as a matter of fact, is reached by the bidding at the foreclosure sale.

Other statutes have the property appraised and require that the foreclosure sale bring that amount, or some stated fraction, say two-thirds, of the appraised value. See, e.g., W. Va. Code §38-4-23 (1989) (requiring two-thirds or an upset price established by the court). In many instances these statutes were enacted during the Depression. See, e.g., Gelfert v. National City Bank, 313 U.S. 221 (1941) (finding a N.Y. appraisal statute constitutional).

Still another variety of statutes, available in only a few states, provide that the mortgagee must elect either to sue on the note or to foreclose the mortgage lien, but not both. These are so-called one action statutes. A related type of statute, found again in only a few states, requires that a mortgagee sue first to foreclose the mortgage and only afterwards to enforce the note, a so-called foreclose first statute.

# More on Foreclosure Sales: Upsetting the Sale

It is important to remember that, even though statutory redemption is available in more than one-half of the states, all the empirical evidence suggests that it is seldom used by mortgagors. Nonetheless, even though in a rising market the mortgagee can bid low and increase the amount recoverable with a deficiency judgment, it is difficult for a mortgagor to upset the sale. She must show fraud or a gross irregularity in the conduct of the sale; the inadequacy of the sale price, standing alone, is not a basis for avoiding it. Inadequacy coupled with fraud, however, will upset the sale. Ballentyne v. Smith, 205 U.S. 285 (1907); East Jersey Sav. & Loan Assn. v. Shatto, 226 N.J. Super. 473, 544 A.2d 899, 900-903 (Ch. Div. 1987).

A gross inadequacy of price — one shocking to the conscience of the court — is another thing. There are some cases in which inadequacy of the sale price was sufficient in itself to upset a sale. The price in these cases is usually less that 40 percent of the fair market value, and often much less. Ballentyne v. Smith, 205 U.S. 285 (1907) (affirming a refusal to confirm a sale for less than one-seventh of fair market value); Shipp Corp. v. Charpilloz, 414 So. 2d 1122, 1124 (Fla. App. 1982) (sale at $1.1 million not so low when fair market value was in the $2.8-3.2 million range). Does this indicate a judicial reluctance to upset the sale generally? Yes, for even in the instance of a grossly inadequate price, the court must see that the second sale holds the promise of substantially higher bids. Otherwise, the second sale will only add to the amount of the deficiency judgment, which will do the mortgagor no good at all. But see Murphy v. Financial Dev. Corp., 126 N.H. 536, 495 A.2d 1245, 1250 (1985) (finding that foreclosure of property appraised at $46,000, with mortgagee's sale bid successful at $27,000, violated the mortgagee's duty to protect the equity of the mortgagor during the foreclosure process).

Recently one state supreme court, faced with the rule that inadequacy of price so great as to "shock the conscience" of the court would be sufficient grounds for upsetting the sale, even when no irregularity in the sale is shown, abandoned the rule. See Holt v. Citizens Cent. Bank, 688 S.W.2d 414 (Tenn. 1984) (involving property purchased in 1973 for $9000, mortgaged the next year for $8600, purchased in foreclosure for that amount, and sold ten days later in a private sale for $30,000, but holding that the stability of title requires reversal of Tennessee's traditional rule).

# EXAMPLES AND EXPLANATIONS

21a. Consider the typical mortgagor. She purchases a house ten years ago for $100,000 and pays $20,000 down. The rest of the money comes from a third-party, institutional mortgage lender. Thus an $80,000 note and mortgage is executed. The mortgagor lost her job three years ago, goes into default on the note payments, and the mortgagee forecloses a year ago. The debt outstanding on the note is $60,000. The foreclosure results in a high bid of $50,000, made by the mortgagee in a sale conducted in accordance with all applicable statutes.

The fair market value of the house was $150,000 a year ago. Would you advise the mortgagor to use her still-available right of statutory redemption? How likely is it that the mortgagor will obtain the financing to permit her to do so?

**Explanation:**   The statutory redemption right is worth exercising because it only requires that the mortgagor come up with $50,000, the foreclosure sale price, but the prospects of a defaulting mortgagor getting a new loan are dim. Platt, Deficiency Judgments in Oregon Loans Secured by Land: Growing Disparity Among Functional Equivalents, 23 Willamette L. Rev.

37, 49 (1987) (calling the right of statutory redemption "chimerical" and stating: "In realty, most debtors are seldom able to acquire the necessary new financing. New lenders usually are not interested in raising the debtor's Titanic and placing it back in the captaincy of one who has already demonstrated a lamentable inability to avoid hitting financial icebergs."). Still, she may qualify for a consumer loan and getting a $150,000 home for $50,000 may be worth the higher interest rates on such loans.

21b. Assuming that the mortgagor does not exercise a right of statutory redemption and that, further, she knows the mortgagee is offering the house for sale through local brokers for $220,000, what would you advise the mortgagor to do?

**Explanation:** The fact that the price is a small fraction of the property fair market value is insufficient, standing alone, to upset the sale. Here there is no suggestion of fraud and the chances of overturning the sale are (again) low. The mortgagee bargained for the use of the property as security and got what she bargained for in the foreclosure. But see California Joint Stock Land Co. v. Gore, 153 Or. 267, 55 P.2d 1118, 1120 (1936) (overturning a sale). (N.B. In many jurisdictions, the relevant case law will date from the Depression and so may be of questionable applicability to less extreme times.) Where price alone suffices to overturn the sale, the price is often lower than the price here, being about 10 percent of fair market value. A very low price may raise a presumption of fraud in some states, but this is not the general rule.

For example, in Danbury Sav. & Loan Assn., Inc. v. Hovi, 20 Conn. App. 638, 569 A.2d 1143 (1990), the court held that a bid of $98,000 for property valued at $225,000, but subject to a zoning dispute perhaps reducing its value as low as $165,000, was adequate. Those numbers have ratios pretty close to the ratios of the numbers in the Example — but not quite, so the mortgagor has some hope of enjoining the mortgagee's resale.

Further, equitable redemption is unlikely when statutory redemption is available. But not unheard of. State ex rel. LeFevre v. Stubbs, 643 S.W.2d 103 (Mo. 1982) (holding that statutory redemption is remedial in nature and such statutes are to be liberally construed); Blades v. Ossenfort, 481 S.W.2d 531 (Mo. App. 1972). The fact that the house is not yet sold weighs in the mortgagor's favor; no innocent purchaser is yet present, with equities outside the mortgagor-mortgagee relationship. See generally, Washburn, The Judicial and Legislative Response to Price Inadequacy in Mortgage Foreclosure Sales, 53 S. Cal. L. Rev. 843 (1980).

21c. Assume the facts in prior Examples 21a and 21b but in addition assume that the bank is seeking a deficiency judgment against the mortgagor for $10,000 ($60,000 − $50,000). What advice can you now give the mortgagor? If the deficiency is assessed, is she paying twice?

**Explanation:**   Yes. Resisting the deficiency judgment seems possible. Suring State Bank v. Giese, 210 Wis. 489, 246 N.W. 556, 85 A.L.R. 1427 (1933). Deficiency judgments have been refused when the price at the foreclosure sale was "grossly inadequate," but usually the refusal involves an element of fraud in the conduct of the sale. The mortgagor has surrendered her equity in the house, and paying a deficiency would now unjustly enrich the foreclosing mortgagee.

One creative attorney recently argued that the foreclosure bid be used as a basis for a usury computation. Concord Realty Co. v. Continental Funding Corp., 776 P.2d 1114, 1120 (Colo. 1989) (rejecting the argument and holding that in nonconsumer transactions, the interest rate is to be computed from the inception of the transaction, not retrospectively).

# More on Upsetting the Sale: Bankruptcy

Fraudulent conveyance statutes are found in most states and are based on English statutes, the first of which was enacted in the time of Queen Elizabeth I. 13 Eliz., ch. 5, §I (1570). Older statutes generally required that, when a fraudulent intent is proven, a conveyance may be set aside. Later statutes require that if a conveyance occurs within a short time of a creditor's action, it is fraudulent as to that creditor's action.

The federal Bankruptcy Code, 11 U.S.C. §548(a)(2)(A), provides that the trustee in bankruptcy can avoid any transfer made for less than the "reasonably equivalent" value of the property by an insolvent debtor within a year of filing of the bankruptcy petition. The code's definition of transfer is broad and includes foreclosure sales. There is no requirement in the code that a mortgagee's intent to defraud other creditors be shown; the test is an objective one.

For certain types of mortgagors, the one-year period available to upset the sale as a fraudulent conveyance provides another forum in which to test the foreclosure. In Durrett v. Washington Natl. Ins. Co., 621 F.2d 201 (5th Cir. 1980), the court held that a nonjudicial foreclosure sale was a fraudulent conveyance under the now-repealed Bankruptcy Act's statutory equivalent of 11 U.S.C. §548(a). In *Durrett,* the property was worth $200,000 and was sold to the mortgagee on his bid of $115,000, the outstanding amount of the secured debt; thus the bid was for 57 percent of what was the property's uncontested fair market value. The court also stated: "We have been unable to locate a decision of any district or appellate court . . . which has approved a transfer for less than 70% of the market value of the property." This statement is dicta, but has since often been taken as black letter law. In re Jacobson, 48 B.R. 497, 499 n.2 (Bankr. D. Minn. 1985). The Eighth Circuit follows the Fifth. In re Hulm, 738 F.2d 323, 325-326 (8th Cir.), cert. denied,

469 U.S. 990 (1984); In re Lindsay, 98 B.R. 983 (Bankr. S.D. Cal. 1989) (deed of trust foreclosure sale for 64 percent of fair market value set aside). The *Lindsay* opinion provides a good recent review of the *Durrett* case.

Every thesis gathers an antithesis. See In re Madrid, 21 B.R. 424 (Bankr. 9th Cir. 1982), aff'd, 725 F.2d 1177 (9th Cir.), cert. denied, 469 U.S. 833 (1984), often taken to stand for the proposition that the sale price of property in a noncollusive and properly conducted foreclosure is conclusively presumed to be its fair equivalent value for purposes of U.S.C. $548(a)(2)(A). In re Winshall Settlor's Trust, 758 F.2d 1136 (6th Cir. 1985), follows *Madrid*, stating that the "better view is that reasonable equivalence for the purposes of a foreclosure sale under $548(a)(2)(A) should be consonant with the state law of fraudulent conveyances." Id. at 1139. Note, *In re Winshall Settlor's Trust:* The Sixth Circuit's Approach to Reasonably Equivalent Value under 11 U.S.C. $548, 19 Toledo L. Rev. 409 (1988).

More recently, the Seventh Circuit has admitted the possibility of a *Durrett* claim but has refused to accept that case's conclusive presumption of a fraudulent transfer. In re Bundles, 856 F.2d 815 (7th Cir. 1988). "In our view, in defining reasonably equivalent value, the court should neither grant a conclusive presumption in favor of a purchaser at a regularly conducted, non-conclusive foreclosure sale, nor limit its inquiry to a simple comparison of the sale price to the fair market value." Id. at 824. Reasonable equivalence then depends (what else!) on the facts of the each case. Because *Bundles* reversed the judgment of a district court using the rule of *Madrid*, it must be taken as leaning — but not too far — in the direction of *Durrett*.

Recent cases have also shown a tendency to reject the black letter and 70 percent dicta of *Durrett*. In re Adwar, 55 B.R. 111 (Bankr. E.D.N.Y. 1985); In re Fargo Biltmore Motor Hotel Corp., 49 B.R. 782 (Bankr. N.D. 1985) (taking hotel 60 percent occupancy rate, management, and age of structure into account). Of particular interest is the language of In re Clark, 99 B.R. 955 (Bankr. W.D. Mo. 1989), where the debtor's outstanding mortgage debt was $60,000, the market value was $65,000, and the mortgagee bid $45,000 at the sale. Its bid was thus very close to the 70 percent bright line of *Durrett*. The court states:

> In fact this Court suspects that movant deliberately bid 70% of what it believed to be the fast sale value of the property to conform to that perceived safe haven. This Court would suggest two things to mortgage servicing institutions of movant's ilk. First, 70% is not a bright line rule. Instead, *Durrett* . . . said only that any bid below 70% of value has never been approved by the courts. . . . That seems to be somewhat different from saying that a 70% bid is automatically the equivalent of reasonably equivalent value. Second, in the Eighth Circuit, *Durrett* has no effect, and the far more rational doctrine of "reasonably equivalent value" is the law in this seven state heartland. (Citing

*Hulm,* op. cit.) While some pre-set percentage formula is always comforting to those parties who prefer their law measured in feet and inches or dollars and cents, law should only rarely be the cold companion of science, without . . . a modifier of reasonableness. If the practice of law is both an art and a science (as its servants so often state) then the *Hulm* rule is a far better measure than the *Durrett* rule."

Id. at 956-957.

Here, then, in some federal circuits, is a further method to attack a foreclosure sale as a result of which the mortgagor loses a substantial equity in her property.

# EXAMPLES AND EXPLANATIONS

22.  What types of mortgagors will find a bankruptcy filing with a *Durrett* claim useful?

**Explanation:**   Because the threshold showing is that the debtor is in fact insolvent, it is unlikely that many residential mortgagors will be thrown into insolvency merely by the foreclosure. In the commercial sphere, however, where each property is likely to be held by a corporation with the single purpose of managing the property, it is more likely that a foreclosure will result in the insolvency of that corporation. It is in that sphere, then, that a *Durrett* claim will have its greatest impact.

23.  Will a *Durrett* claim apply equally to all types of bankruptcies?

**Explanation:**   The simple answer is that it has been applied in both liquidations and reorganizations of the debtor's estate. It has, however, been most often permitted in Chapter 11 (corporate reorganization) or Chapter 13 (individual reorganization) bankruptcies, rather than in Chapter 7 (liquidation) proceedings.

In one sense, allowing a *Durrett* claim, with its objective test, serves the purposes of uniformity. It puts states without a statutory redemption period on a par with those that have one; for insolvent mortgagors, it provides a one-year period that functions like a statutory redemption period. Yet at the same time, it might be objected that foreclosure sale bidding will be chilled by the knowledge that the sale might be upset during the year after the sale. "Might" because the 70 percent requirement of *Durrett* might spur bidding to at least the 70 percent mark.

24.  What happens to the lien of the mortgagee when the *Durrett* claim is allowed by the bankruptcy trustee, and the sale is set aside?

**Explanation:**   It is reinstated. In re Cole, 81 B.R. 326, 331 (Bankr. E.D. Pa. 1988).

# Notes on Bankruptcy

## The Stay

The effect of filing a petition in bankruptcy is an automatic stay of any nonbankruptcy remedies, including any pending mortgage foreclosure. 11 U.S.C. §362(a). Violation of the stay is contempt of court, and any action taken to violate or avoid it is void. It is effective even without any actual notice of the filing for bankruptcy and continued for an indeterminate time until it is lifted or modified by the court. The mortgagee may have taken the property as security for the debt, presumably to avoid the effect of the mortgagor's insolvency. Nevertheless, her pending foreclosure action can be stopped in its tracks. No future notice of default can be sent, no foreclosure sale conducted, or if already held, confirmed — and even the running of a statutory redemption period is halted and the mortgagee's claim thrown into a pool along with those of other creditors. Her secured status will put her into a line with other secured creditors, ahead of unsecured ones, but the remedy for which she bargained — foreclosure — is denied her.

## Relief from the Stay

To obtain relief from the stay, a mortgagee may request a hearing before the bankruptcy court to show "cause, including the lack of adequate protection, why the stay should be lifted, or to show that the debtor has no further equity in the property or that it is unnecessary to an effective reorganization of the debtor's assets." 11 U.S.C. §362(d)(1)-(2). Section 361 of the Bankruptcy Act provides some illustrations of what adequate protection is; periodic cash payments or additional liens may be provided by the court. Thus the difficulty with alleging inadequate protection is that the court can decree relief that is less than a lifting of the stay but sufficient to provide §361 protection. Creditors wanting the stay lifted generally argue that the debtor has no equity in the property or that the stay is not necessary to formulate a reorganization plan. If relief is granted by lifting the stay, the mortgagee can proceed to foreclose or to finish foreclosure actions stopped by the stay.

Additionally, the stay does not apply to the commencement or continuance of a criminal proceeding against the debtor, the collection of alimony, maintenance or support payments, or a governmental action involving the government's police or regulatory powers or the enforcement of a judgment arising out of any such action. 11 U.S.C. §362(b)(1), (2), (4)-(5).

# Bankruptcy Forms of Action

## Chapter 7

Bankruptcy comes in three varieties. Chapter 7 bankruptcy liquidates the debtor's assets for the benefit of her creditors. The debtor may be either corporate or individual. A court-appointed trustee receives the petition and conducts the liquidation, but the debtor must be actively involved and continuously review her efforts and actions. In a Chapter 7 bankruptcy, the trustee has the benefit of any defense available to a debtor-mortgagor and can become a bona fide purchaser against any mortgage unrecorded at the date of the filing.

## Chapter 11

Chapter 11 is a reorganization of assets for corporate debtors. Under this chapter, the appointment of a trustee is unusual, and the debtor generally remains in possession of the assets of the bankruptcy estate (as all assets subject to the jurisdiction of the court are called). As mentioned previously, in this type of filing an automatic stay can be lifted if the mortgagee has no adequate protection, where, for example, the mortgagor has no equity in a property subject to the pending foreclosure. The act also provides a timetable for presenting a reorganization plan. Currently the debtor must produce the plan within 120 days of the filing of the petition unless the court grants the debtor an extension of time, but after 180 days, any creditor can file a plan too. Thus the debtor usually will have first crack at producing a plan but is under time pressure to do so.

For purposes of the plan, creditors are placed in classes, each with similar types of debts — secured and unsecured, large and small, for instance.[2] Within each class, the debts are restructured in a similar manner, with extensions in maturity dates, changes in payment schedules, or reductions in the interest rate or principal amounts all possible. In addition, the reasonableness of fees and charges involved in debt instruments will be reviewed. See, e.g., In re

---

2. For example, a mortgagee with a deficiency judgment at the time the stay is imposed may not be a one-member class of unsecured creditors unless there is a valid reason for creating such a class. In re Meadow Glen, Ltd. 87 B.R. 421, 424-425 (Bankr. W.D. Tex. 1988). One reason for separate treatment might be that the holder of the deficiency judgment is advancing new funds to the debtor.

Skyler Ridge, 80 B.R. 500 (Bankr. C.D. Cal. 1987) (holding a prepayment charge in a mortgage to be unreasonably high liquidated damages).

Each class of creditors with impaired claims then votes on the reorganization plan, which must be approved not only by one-half the number of creditors in the class, but also by creditors holding two-thirds of the debt in the class. If satisfying all other statutory requirements an approved plan is then confirmed by the court. 11 U.S.C. §1129(a). A plan approved by at least one, but not all classes, is subject to further court review, after which the court may override the objections of the dissenting classes of creditors if it finds that the plan is fair and does not discriminate unfairly against the dissenters. 11 U.S.C. §1129(b)(1). This is often called the "cramdown" provision of the act. Molinaro, The Threat of Cramdown: How Real Is It?, 19 Real Est. Rev. 35 (Fall 1989). The 1978 Bankruptcy Act is detailed in its provisions relating to the fairness of a plan. 11 U.S.C. §1129 (b)(2).

## Chapter 13

Chapter 13 is a reorganization for an individual debtor. She must have regular income, unsecured debts below $100,000, and secured debts under $350,000. These three requirements mean that, for many middle-class debtors, the principal asset of the bankruptcy estate will be a residence. The debtor-mortgagor stays in possession of the property after the stay, and the Chapter 13 reorganization plan must be implemented and completed within three to five years of the filing. After a mortgagee has accelerated the debt under a mortgage covenant, this plan can deaccelerate any mortgage default and reinstate the debt upon the payment of the arrearages in payments, although the authorities and cases split on when the right to deaccelerate is cut off. There is some reluctance to extend it after a foreclosure judgment, but so long as the debtor is still in possession, there is some authority for extending the right. Recently, debtors have attempted to file Chapter 7 proceedings and liquidate their assets to a point where they qualify for Chapter 13 reorganization (bankruptcy wags refer to this gambit as "Chapter 20" — 7 + 13 = 20! Compare In re Saylors, 869 F.2d 1434 (11th Cir. 1989) (confirming a "Chapter 20" plan) with In re Johnson, 904 F.2d 563 (10th Cir. 1990), cert. denied, 111 S. Ct. 994 (1991) (denying confirmation to such a plan).

For a general introduction to the Bankruptcy Code, see Nelson, The Impact of Mortgagor Bankruptcy on the Real Estate Mortgagee: Current Problems and Some Suggested Solutions, 50 Mo. L. Rev. 217 (1985); and for an examination of bankruptcy's effect on the residential mortgagor and possessor or residential property, see Lawrence, At Home with the Bankruptcy Code: Residential Leases, Installment Real Estate Contracts and Home Mortgages, 61 Am. Bankr. L.J. 125 (1987).

# 23

## Real Estate in Trouble

## Workouts

A workout is a term used by real property professionals to mean negotiations aimed at restructuring a mortgage loan for a borrower.

A successful workout, like any negotiation, proceeds in stages. From the mortgagee's perspective, the first stage is to clear away some of the legal underbrush in order to understand the parameters of the discussion. An initial agreement on four items is needed: (1) the validity of the debt (aimed to flush out any defenses to it), (2) the facts constituting the default by the mortgagor, (3) the writings constituting the agreement about the loan (aimed at flushing out whether or not there are oral agreements extrinsic to these documents), and (4) any reservation of rights by either party surviving the present negotiations. Eizenman, Lender Liability: Minimizing Risk in Resolving Troubled Loans, 7 Real Est. Fin. 33, 34 (1990); and more generally, H. D. Chaitman, Law of Lender Liability ch. 3, at 3-1 (1990).

Thus, from the mortgagee's perspective, an initial agreement would conclude that the debt is valid and subject to no defenses; that there is a default based on recited facts; that the documents incorporated by reference are the complete agreement between the parties and that these documents are not subject to parol evidence; and that the lender reserves all other rights under the documents agreed to be that complete agreement. How should a debtor-mortgagor, or his counsel, respond to a lender's request to execute such a four-part agreement before entering into further workout discussions?

As to the default, the mortgagee's recitation of it at the bargaining table must be done deftly because the use of a threat to invoke the remedies to which the default gives rise can trigger a later charge of bad faith. See, e.g., K.M.C. Co. v. Irving Trust Co., 757 F.2d 752 (6th Cir. 1985). The mortgagee must clearly forgo the use of such remedies as long as workout discussions are ongoing.

As to defenses, if the parties cannot agree that there are no defenses, they might at least agree that any litigation resulting from their disagreement be limited in various ways — by agreeing that the resulting litigation (if any) be governed by the law of a particular jurisdiction or (in lieu of the first option) that a particular choice of law rule be used; that a trial by jury be waived; that special or consequential damages are waived, or that arbitration be used.

If there is any disagreement as to what the "complete agreement" between the parties is and what oral agreements exist, the parties still might agree, as a fallback, that there are no oral promises on enumerated subjects (and so on).

# The Terms of the Workout:
# Modifying the Repayment Schedule

Workouts often involve rearranging the payment terms of the loan because the mortgagee realizes that, in many situations in bankruptcy, a court could do the same. The mortgagee, for instance, might agree to forgo missed payments of principal and interest and postpone their due date until the end of the mortgage's term (when they in effect will become a balloon payment) or whenever the property is sold, if that occurs earlier than the end of the term.

In the alternative, the mortgagor may agree to pay whatever he can afford, and the difference between the amount he pays and the amount he owes is added to the principal or else is repayable at an agreed-to date in the future. Or, the interest rate of the existing note can be lowered, but the term extended for a compensating amount: for example, a 12 percent rate, 15-year loan can become a 9 percent, 30-year loan.

If the debtor has other properties free of debt, the missed payments can become a lien against those assets and, with the passage of each due date for a payment, the amount of the lien increased by the payment missed. And so on; the combinations of these suggestions are many, but several may also involve bringing other parties to the table — junior mortgagees, for example, if a modification of a senior mortgage might be a default under their own documents.

# Deed in Lieu of Foreclosure

Often, in its simplest form, the goal of the workout is the conveyance of a deed in lieu of foreclosure. Because this is the least complicated form of workout, this chapter starts with a discussion of such a conveyance. R. Kratovil & R. Werner, Modern Mortgage Law and Practice 581-596 (2d ed. 1981); Lesser & Klug, A Borrower's Guide to Real Estate Loan Workouts, 7 Real Est. Fin. 18 (Summer 1990).

In form, a deed in lieu of foreclosure, given by a borrower-mortgagor to avoid foreclosure, looks like any deed. It has the same components of granting clause, habendum, warranties, testimonium, and attestation provisions. R. Bernhardt, Mortgage and Deed of Trust Practice 281 (1990). Its special purpose, however, is to memorialize an agreement by the mortgagor to avoid a foreclosure action. It is a friendly foreclosure — one achieved by contract. This special purpose, however, raises several problems. Id. at 281-290. Here we address some of them.

The advantages of a deed in lieu are several. The mortgagee avoids the high costs of a foreclosure action. The deed can provide a resolution of disputes flowing out of the foreclosure action as well: actions for a deficiency judgment, attacks on the foreclosure sale, allegations of fraud, duress, and so forth. The potential for time-consuming squabbles between the parties is considerable in a foreclosure action. In contrast, successful negotiation over such a deed can provide an amicable solution to the mortgagor-mortgagee relationship, and when that relationship was longstanding, the deed serves to keep it alive for the future. For a real estate developer and his lender, this may be important. Equally important may be keeping the details of the transaction as confidential as possible so that as little damage as possible is done to the business reputations of the parties. Embarrassment and an impaired credit rating might otherwise result. Finally, the deed may remove the secured property from the bankruptcy estate of the mortgagor. (As we will see, it is necessary to emphasize the "may" in the preceding sentence.) See Boneparth, Taking a Deed in Lieu of Foreclosure: Pitfalls for the Lender, 19 Real Est. L.J. 338 (1991); Note, Foreclosure by Contract: Deeds in Lieu of Foreclosure in Missouri, 56 U. Mo. K.C. L. Rev. 633, 640-643 (1988).

The disadvantages of using such deeds are also numerous. A foreclosure of a senior lien will wipe out the lien of a properly joined junior mortgagee, but the transfer of a deed in lieu has no such effect. Note, Conveyance from Mortgagor to Mortgagee as Foreclosure of Junior Liens, 48 Colum. L. Rev. 955 (1948). Not only that, the mortgagee may also be giving up rights ancillary to the mortgage transaction — rights to a deficiency judgment, to guarantees of the debt, and so forth. Moreover, the mortgagor may later have a change of mind and seek to attack the transfer for any one of a number of reasons or to avoid the transfer by filing for bankruptcy. From the mortgagor's perspective, a bankruptcy liquidation is a second bite of the apple and moreover may be perceived as bringing more money for the property than a foreclosure sale of any type. And the purpose of bankruptcy may not be liquidation of the assets of the bankrupt, but the reorganization of debts as well, depending on which chapters of the Bankruptcy Code are utilized.

An alternative to the voluntary deed in lieu is abandonment of the property by the mortgagor. Abandonment requires an intent to abandon and acts evidencing that intent, such as a failure to perform vital maintenance, to pay property taxes, insurance premiums, or utility charges — or, of course, giving a deed in lieu. However, the tax consequences of abandonment are just as severe under some recent cases; that is, the abandonment is treated just like a sale or other disposition by deed. Arkin v. Commissioner, 76 T.C. 1048 (1981). Why not settle the property amicably on the mortgagee?

The mortgagee who accepts such a deed not only avoids the high transaction costs associated with any type of foreclosure but also, when the fair market value of the property exceeds the debt, acquires the equity of the mortgagor as well. At the time of the mortgage closing, however, recall that the deed in lieu could not be placed in escrow for the benefit of the mortgagee because the establishment of the escrow, with delivery of the deed conditional upon the mortgagor's default in payment of the mortgage debt, would be a clog on the mortgagor's equity of redemption.

Thus there must be a consideration for the granting of the deed in lieu that is separate from that realized in the original mortgage transaction — otherwise the equity is clogged. A mortgagor cannot release or waive the equity as a part of the original transaction, but that is no bar (of course) to its subsequent release. Thus, a deed in lieu cannot be executed at the time of the original mortgage transaction, and even a provision for one in the original loan documents is likely to invalidate the later deed.

Because this equity of redemption is in fact a right of late payment, it does not arise, and so cannot be released, until there is a default that gives rise to the mortgagee's right to foreclose. What is the drafting consequence for a deed in lieu? It is the inclusion, in such a deed, of a recital concerning the prior default.

As to including a recitation in the deed of the consideration, that is also advisable but does present a problem of its own. Remember the rule that "mere inadequacy of consideration is insufficient to avoid a foreclosure sale, unless coupled with evidence of fraud; gross inadequacy of price is needed to avoid a sale, often coupled with evidence of fraud." The rule implies that some consideration must be given. Not stating a consideration leaves a court free, later, to infer that factors involving fraud and duress induced the transfer. So, better to state some consideration, even though a conveyance (of any type) does not require such a statement.

A conveyance made "in full satisfaction and release of the debt evidenced in the note and mortgage" is, from the mortgagor's standpoint, the best that can be obtained. Perhaps the word "satisfaction" is better than "cancellation," unless the mortgagor can produce the cancelled note and mortgage, or those two documents are attached to the deed and referred to there. And, when the mortgagee knows of junior liens on the same property, the word cancellation should be avoided to prevent a merger of the lien and the fee that would promote the junior's status to senior lienholder. On the other hand, for the mortgagee, taking the deed is the equivalent of collecting the debt, but only to the extent of the fair market value of the property at the time of the deed's execution. This may or may not make the mortgagee whole.

What, however, if the mortgagor is not liable on the note? In other words, if the note is nonrecourse, how should the consideration be recited? Here the mortgage lien is granted by one not liable for the debt. Consideration other than the release of the debt will have to be found.

From an income tax perspective, the giving and taking a deed that is silent on the consideration is (for the mortgagor) the equivalent of foreclosure sale, at which the mortgagee bids the fair market value of the secured property, and (for the mortgagee) the collection of the debt up to that value. Commissioner v. Spreckels, 120 F.2d 517 (9th Cir. 1941); and see generally M. Greenberg & N. Wood, Real Estate Tax Guide 296-298 (1988). When the sole consideration is stated as the discharge of some portion of the debt, the conveyance by deed in lieu will be treated as a sale to the mortgagee for the amount of the debt released. Assigning a monetary value to the consideration is thus important for documenting the tax consequences of the sale, for often the consideration will have other elements besides whole or partial release from the debt.

The deed in lieu should also have, as its purpose, the termination of the mortgagor-mortgagee relationship. Ending that relationship is the reason for reciting that the deed satisfies and releases the debt. Further, the rationale for any continuing relationship between the parties should be closely scrutinized. The mortgagor's continued possession of the property, his option to buy the property, or his lease of the premises after giving the deed, all increase the risk that the transaction may be recharacterized as an attempt of the parties to continue their preexisting relationship.

# EXAMPLES AND EXPLANATIONS

1. What are the remedies of a junior mortgagee against the property that has been conveyed to a senior mortgagee by means of a deed in lieu of foreclosure?

**Explanation:** The junior may reasonably argue that he is in the position of a mortgagee omitted from the foreclosure of the senior lien and so has the remedies of an omitted junior. See Chapter 19, Mortgages. These remedies are two in number. First, the junior can foreclose his own mortgage, and second, the junior can redeem the senior mortgage by paying the amount of the outstanding mortgage. Because the second remedy may involve a large cash outlay, it is seldom employed. The first remedy, of foreclosure, is more likely.

2. Assuming that the junior mortgagee seeks foreclosure, what is the priority of the junior lien? Is it moved up in status and is now a senior lien?

**Explanation:**   It could do so only through the doctrine of merger. The doctrine provides that when a mortgagee's lien and the underlying fee come into the same hands, the lien is merged with the fee and is extinguished. Does this doctrine apply to a deed in lieu? It is not likely to in the context of the junior mortgagee's assertion of his rights and remedies.

Thus a mortgagee accepting a deed in lieu, should not assume or take the title subject to its own debt. The debt should be cancelled instead. Safer still, when the senior mortgagee knows of junior lienors, is to release the mortgagor from personal liability on the note but not cancel it.

3. Considering that one advantage of a deed in lieu is often its confidentiality, one might want to avoid a recital of the details of the underlying transaction on the deed itself because the grantee will want to record the deed in the public records. How should this matter be handled?

**Explanation:**   By inclusion of the recitals in an affidavit accompanying the deed, but retained by the title company or legal counsel, rather than on the face of the deed itself.

4. Ben Devon is a developer of commercial properties. One of his properties is the Big Ben Building. It is 60 percent leased two years after its completion. The loan for its construction costs was provided by Builder's Bank. However, it was never taken out by a large insurance company once committed to the building's permanent financing. Instead, Builder's Bank then provided a long-term note and mortgage, for 20 years, at a variable rate of interest three points over its prime rate. The bank's financing is for 75 percent of the fair market value. The mortgage contains a covenant authorizing the use, upon default, of a private power of sale. Builder's note is not in default, although the four most recent payments have been late, and the mortgagor has been assessed late payments on these in the amount of 5 percent of the late payment amounts of principal and interest due.

Ben would like to continue to attempt to lease the property up to normal vacancy rates, which are running at about 8 percent of gross leasable area. However, he is willing to deposit the deed into an escrow pending completion of this last effort. If such an effort fails, he would like to continue to manage the property, perhaps giving a deed with an option to buy the property back, but Builder's resists this idea. No party resists the idea of its attorneys negotiating the terms of a deed in lieu of foreclosure. Ben Devon has other real property interests, not in distress, and the bank is solvent.

The following standard form deed will need modification. How should you use or modify it?

# DEED IN LIEU OF FORECLOSURE

By this deed, the grantor(s), _____, do convey, grant, and release, to the grantee(s), _____, for the consideration of _____, the following interest: _____, in the following described property:

TO HAVE AND TO HOLD, with all appurtenant rights, described as follows:

[legal description inserted here]

The grantor(s) covenant(s) that they have the right to make this conveyance, that they are seised of the property in fee simple absolute, that it is subject to no encumbrances and defects undisclosed at the time of the conveyance, and that they will warrant the grantees the right of quiet enjoyment of the interests conveyed and make such further assurances to them as become necessary to continue such enjoyment.

Given this _____ day of _____, 19_____.

_____
Grantor

_____
Grantor

Attestation: Executed as my/our voluntary acts, on _____, before the undersigned notary.

_____
Notary Public

My Commission expires: _____

**Explanation:** Your first concern might be whether or not there are any outstanding junior mortgages or mechanic's liens filed against the property. Will the junior lien get senior status when the mortgagee of the senior lien takes a deed in lieu? Will a mechanic's lien do the same under similar circumstances? May a quitclaim deed be used as a deed in lieu? If you don't have ready answers to such questions, consult your local title insurer about continuing the lender's coverage (if the latter has a policy) as a mortgagee in possession.

Many a formbook's checklist for real estate transactions contains a list of recitals for a deed in lieu. The following are not recitals, but suggest what subjects and language might be used in some recitals:

1.  The default is or should be specified. (Specifying the late charges due, accrued but unpaid interest, prepayment penalties, and unpaid mortgage escrow amounts should suffice, as well as the assumption by the mortgagee of any unpaid property taxes.)
2.  The consideration should be recited. (A low consideration gives rise to a charge of duress.)
3.  The deed is not an equitable mortgage.
4.  The deed is freely given.
5.  The transfer is made in lieu of foreclosure.
6.  Acknowledgment is made that the transfer is made at the request of the mortgagor (if this is the case).
7.  Attachment is made incorporating by reference a current appraisal.
8.  Disclosure is made of the results of the title search and (if true) a statement that no junior liens exist.
9.  The parties intend by this transfer to terminate the mortgagor-mortgagee relationship.
10.  The parties to the transfer do not intend to merge the lien of the mortgage with the fee simple absolute.
11.  The parties intend to effect mutual releasees of all liability on the debt by means of the transfer.
12.  The parties have been represented in the course of the transfer by independent legal counsel.
13.  The parties do not intend to benefit third parties and expressly reserved their rights against third parties.

Depending on the transaction, all of these recitals may be useful in a deed in lieu, but in particular transactions the use of one might eliminate the need for another. See generally, Bonepath, Taking a Deed in Lieu of Foreclosure: Pitfalls for the Lender, 19 Real Est. L.J. 388 (1991); Madison, Use of Deeds in Lieu of Foreclosure in Defaults and Workouts, 20 Real Est. L.J. 247 (1992); Murray, Deeds in Lieu of Foreclosure: Practical and Legal Considerations, 26 Real Prop. Prob. & Tr. J. 459 (1991).

This is a good case for giving the lender a deed. Perhaps the developer can continue to manage the property after the deed is given, with an option to buy back the property before the end of the maximum amount of time that the bank can hold real property in its own name.

# Surety Bonds

A surety is a person who agrees, often in a document structured to look like a deed, to satisfy the debt or obligation of another (usually known as the "principal"). In the context of a construction loan and agreement, a surety is typically a bonding company specializing in such agreements, and the principal typically is the general contractor.

A surety offers three types of bonds to guarantee the completion of a construction project. (Only in the loosest sense can a bond of this type be labeled as insurance.) First, a *bid bond:* it guarantees protection for an owner whose low bidder fails to perform in accordance with the bid submitted and accepted. There is little use made of such bonds and little litigation, because the project bonded in this way is likely to be bonded in two other, more common ways as well.

Second, a *payment bond:* its function is to guarantee that the payments owed by a general contractor to subcontractors will actually reach the hands of the subs. If the general contractor does not pay subcontractors and suppliers, for example, the surety is obligated to pay them to avoid liens against the project property or claims on the loan proceeds still undisbursed. The surety is not liable on the bond unless the contractor is. Bonds often provide for direct payment by the surety on claims made by a subcontractor or supplier, but restrictions on such direct rights and payments in bond language have been upheld. Hopper Bros. Quarries v. Merchants Mutual Bonding Co., 255 F.2d 147 (8th Cir. 1958). The owner, after all, may wish to be certain that money paid on the bond goes to clear himself of further liability to the sub or supplier. Even when no direct right to file a claim is provided, courts have found one implied on the basis of a common law, third-party beneficiary status of the subcontractor.

The payment bond is usually drafted to protect payments to a certain group of subs and suppliers — say, first-tier subcontractors and suppliers providing materials directly to the construction site. The protected class defined by the bond is a matter for contract interpretation and may or may not be coterminous with the ability of the mechanic's lien laws to reach the project property. See American Institute Architects, AIA Document A311, Labor and Material Payment Bond (1970). (Here, as in other areas of the construction industry documentation, the AIA provides the most widely used forms and annotates them periodically.) The surety is not bound to pay for the services or materials of others not named in the bond; in this respect, a surety is not bound beyond the terms of its bond. Bank loans made to a contractor whose payments are covered by the bond are not covered, and the surety cannot be held liable to the lender.

Third, a *performance bond:* its function is to guarantee that the construction contract will be performed, if not by the original general contractor and subcontractors, then by someone capable of finishing the project according to the original architectural and engineering plans and specifications. Under such a bond, a surety may be called upon to do anything called for in the original construction agreement. American Institute Architects, AIA Document A311, Performance Bond (1970).

A performance bond is often combined with a payment bond in a "performance and payment bond," although when combined, the surety still has two distinct obligations. The surety may meet its bond obligation in several ways: by providing new financing sufficient to complete the project; by finding a new contractor and paying the owner the extra costs associated with the contract between the owner and the new contractor; by entering into a construction contract itself with a new contractor and performing that contract.

Direct rights for subs — the right to file a claim, receive payment, and sue on the bond — are more controversial for performance bonds. Compare Byram Lumber & Supply Co. v. Page, 109 Conn. 256, 146 A. 293 (1929) (finding a direct right), with Fosmire v. National Surety Co., 229 N.Y. 44, 127 N.E. 472 (1920) (denying such a right). The New York court indicates that finding such a right is less difficult with a payment bond. Do you see why? Likewise, some courts find a direct right easier to find when a public facility construction project is involved. Why should this be? See AIA Document A311, Performance Bond, for language negating a direct right.

A fourth product often offered by sureties is a bondability letter, showing that a contractor is bondable. Here, although no bond is actually issued for the project, the surety represents that it conducted its usual and customary investigation of the contractor and finds the latter of sufficient financial and business capacity to be bondable.

# EXAMPLES AND EXPLANATIONS

5. After a project is 75 percent complete, its general contractor abandons work and files for bankruptcy. The general contractor carries a performance bond. A reliable cost estimator states that the total construction costs associated with the project will be 125 percent of the total price of the construction agreement. The construction loan disbursement schedule calls for five additional progress payments. After obtaining a new construction agreement for completion of the project satisfactory to the lender, and after proper notice to the bonding company, how should the surety, the owner, and the construction lender proceed?

**Explanation:**  Assuming that the project is sound as an economic matter, both the surety and the owner have reason to proceed. The surety will surely bring the construction lender into the discussions because a lender may be reluctant to make further disbursements without assurances that the surety is good for the extra 25 percent. "Why should we throw our money into a black hole," the lender might argue, "when we don't see where the extra money is coming from." The surety might provide some assurance without spending any money, for example, by putting the money necessary for completion into escrow, by arranging for a new loan for the extra 25 percent, or by guaranteeing the extra if the original construction lender will advance it. The possibilities are numerous. And, once the extra is guaranteed, the next issue for the negotiations is the payout rate: Should the five remaining progress payments be disbursed from the funds of the original lender, up to the 100 percent, of the original loan agreement, or should each payment be 5 percent from surety funds and 5 percent from the original lender's, or should the surety go first, and the lender complete the payments? Again, the possibilities are numerous, and no one of them is likely to be mandated by the provisions of the bond.

In general, the surety's flexibility in performing on its bond obligation means that it picks up several types of rights along the road to performance by way of subrogation: a right to reimbursement and a right of contribution (from other sureties and, if there are undisclosed and unexcepted liens on the property, from title insurers as well). As it pays materialmen and suppliers on the payment bond, it steps into their shoes under the doctrine of equitable subrogation. As an example of reimbursement, consider that if when the general contractor abandons the site, it was owed money, supplies, or labor, those are now due by the surety stepping into the shoes of the general. Thus, to protect itself, the surety will proceed slowly and cautiously, attempting to tie up as many loose ends as possible; on a construction contract on which work has been paid for, for example, actions that would seem to abandon that contract will not be taken without first attempting to obtain agreements to perform.

Sureties are aggressive in their attempts to recoup their out-of-pocket costs fulfilling their bond obligations. And the courts have limited their remedies in several respects. See International Paper Co. v. Grossman, 541 F. Supp. 1236 (N.D. Ill. 1982) (holding that a guarantor of a corporate loan did not guarantee corporate liability for events occurring after the merger of the corporation guaranteed with another entity).

The subrogation rights of a surety are usually said to arise by operation of law, not by contract; this means, for example, that no Uniform Commercial Code financing statements need be filed by the surety to protect its subrogation rights. First Alabama Bank of Birmingham v. Hartford Accident & Indemnity Co., 430 F. Supp. 907 (N.D. Ala. 1977) (stating that this is true even if the assignee of a covered contractor has filed the assignment of the contractor's construction agreement right to payment). Subrogation is just too hardy a doctrine to be defeated, even by the U.C.C., which does not expressly reject it. Home Indemnity Co. v. United States, 433 F.2d 764 (Ct. Cl. 1970).

# EXAMPLES AND EXPLANATIONS

6. Same facts as in Example 5, except that, in addition, the general contractor assigns his right to progress payments under the contract to a

lender who, on the basis of the assigned contract rights, makes a loan to the contractor. A U.C.C. financing statement is promptly filed. Who has the superior claim on earned, but unpaid, progress payments — the performance bond surety or the assignee of the contractor?

**Explanation:**   The surety. The assignee can take no more than the lender's right to the funds. See National Shawmut Bank of Boston v. New Amsterdam Casualty Co., 411 F.2d 843 (1st Cir. 1969) (holding that the surety has the prior claim on earned, but unpaid, loan disbursements as against the assignee of the contract rights of the general contractor), noted in 64 Nw. U.L. Rev. 582 (1969).

The answer would be the same when, in the course of meeting its obligations on the bond, the surety makes a claim on retainages — those amounts withheld from payment pending a final inspection of the project. Travelers Indemnity Co. v. West Georgia Natl. Bank, 387 F. Supp. 1090, 1093 (N.D. Ga. 1974) (stating that after default the surety's right to unpaid progress payments is superior, but before default the assignee bank prevails). The theory is that the surety is more than a subrogee of the contractor but is also a subrogee of the owner and entitled to any rights that the owner has to the retained funds. While meeting the obligations on the bond, the surety may also have a right to have the retained funds escrowed on its behalf, but the surety acquires its subrogation rights as it fulfills its bond obligations.

Once the assigning contractor satisfactorily performed the work, and a check, intended as payment and made payable to the contractor, is deposited with the assignee, the assignee of the contractor prevails over the surety. Fidelity & Deposit Co. of Maryland v. Scott Bros. Constr. Co., 561 F.2d 640 (5th Cir. 1972).

7. Are consequential damages available from a performance and payment bond surety?

**Explanation:**   Yes, although it seemingly violates the principal that the owner is entitled to recover only the cost of completion stipulated in the construction plans and specifications incorporated into the bond by reference. When nonpayment of consequential damages stands in the way of completion, it is covered by the bond (though not by its literal provisions). See J. J. Brown v. J. L. Simmons, 2 Ill. App. 2d 132, 118 N.E.2d 781 (1954).

# Builder's Risk Insurance

A builder's risk insurance policy is a type of property loss policy for loss or damage to an insured builder's interest in a building or improvement under construction; such a policy covers not only damage to the structure itself, but also damage to construction supplies and materials on the construction site after work has commenced. Does the availability of such insurance limit the liability of a surety issuing a labor or performance bond, or merely control who — the surety or the insurer — performs first? There is also considerable confusion about the subrogation rights of such an insurer when the negligence of an insured party caused the damage on the site. Compare Morsches Lumber, Inc. v. Probst, 180 Ind. App. 202, 388 N.E.2d 284 (1979) (not permitting subrogation), with Baltimore Contractors, Inc. v. Circel Floor Co., 318 F. Supp. 106 (D. Md. 1970) (applying Maryland law and permitting subrogation); Annot., Insurance: subrogation of insurer compensating owner or contractor for loss under "builder's risk" policy against allegedly negligent contractor or subcontractor, 22 A.L.R.4th 701 (1983).

# Federal Tax Liens

The federal government is entitled to a lien "upon all property and rights to property, whether real or personal, belonging to [a delinquent taxpayer]." I.R.C. §6321, 26 U.S.C.A. §6321 (West 1989). Thus the lien can attach to progress payments owed a general or subcontractor who "neglects or refuses to pay any federal tax imposed by the Code." Likewise, a purchaser's right to possession under an installment land sale contract or a lease are also possible subjects of this lien.

To explain briefly the limits of the reach of this lien, consider a taxpayer who dies after the assessment of the lien. May the Internal Revenue Service assert the lien against the value of his life insurance policy? Is the policy "property or rights to property"? The taxpayer is dead when the beneficiary collects the proceeds of the policy, so those proceeds are not available, during the taxpayer's life, to satisfy the tax delinquency. But wait, says the Commissioner: Perhaps the policy had a cash surrender or annuity value during the life of the taxpayer; if so, that portion of the proceeds should be available (and so on). United States v. Bess, 357 U.S. 51 (1958) (holding that the federal lien attaches to the cash surrender value, not the total amount of the proceeds from the policy — a neat middle ground).

This lien comes into existence at the time the IRS district director "assesses" the lien: "the lien imposed by section 6321 shall arise at the time the assessment is made." I.R.C. §6322.

The lien also "shall not be valid as against any purchaser, holder of a security interest, mechanic's lienor, or judgment lien creditor until notice thereof . . . has been filed." I.R.C. §6323.

Read these sections carefully: There is a problem here. What if the lien is assessed, a valid mortgage in a taxpayer's property is recorded, and then the lien is filed? The intervening mortgage lien may be subordinated to the federal tax lien if the "until notice thereof . . . has been filed" clause is given literal effect. This is not the result in most cases. See, e.g., United States v. Bank of Celina, 721 F.2d 163 (7th Cir. 1983) (when several tax lien notices filed, the priority of each lien relates back to date of the first notice); United States v. Bluhm, 414 F.2d 1240 (6th Cir.), cert. denied, 397 U.S. 910 (1969); In re Fargo Biltmore Motor Inn, 49 B.R. 782 (Bankr. N.D. 1985). However, where does the result reached leave the "lien . . . shall arise" language of §6322? See Streule v. Gulf Fin. Corp., 265 A.2d 298 (D.C. App. 1970) (holding that federal tax lien attaches upon assessment, except as to creditors protected by §6323, against whom notice is necessary to achieve priority of federal lien).

Unlike priority of title decisions made under the recording acts of the several states, the actual or constructive knowledge of the IRS's agents of other private liens will not defeat the federal lien. Even if the property changes hands by adverse possession, the adverse possessor has been held to acquire the title subject to the tax lien.

Problems involving the priority of this lien are matters of federal law, except the courts, to the extent permitted by statute, may look to state rules of lien priority when there is no need for a uniform federal rule.

In bankruptcy proceedings, an IRS tax penalty may be avoided by the trustee, but a properly noticed tax lien may not. In re Barry, 31 B.R. 683 (Bankr. S.D. Ohio 1983). Unless the IRS consents to a reorganization or payment plan by the debtor in bankruptcy, the lien need not be discharged by the bankruptcy proceeding. In re Tomlan, 88 B.R. 302 (Bankr. E.D. Wash. 1988) (a Chapter 13 proceeding). When someone other than a debtor, such as a guarantor, partially pays off the lien, that person does not gain the IRS's priority position by subrogation. In re Watkins Oil Serv., 100 B.R. 7 (Bankr. D. Ariz. 1989).

# Fixtures

A fixture is an object of tangible personal property that, when attached to real property, becomes a part of the realty. It refers not so much to a species of objects, but to the legal relationship of an object to the real property. Thus the term "fixture" is seldom generally defined; the latest attempt to do so occurred during the drafting of the Uniform Commercial Code's Article 9, and the drafters there incorporated applicable state law by reference. U.C.C. §9-913(1)(a) (1972).

Whether or not personalty is labeled a fixture has considerable significance in areas of law with which you are already familiar. For example, a fixture normally must be left behind by a tenant at the end of his term. But if the object is found to meet the definition of a fixture, and at the same time is necessary to the tenant's trade or business, it is labeled a "trade fixture" and therefore personalty; as such, it can be disconnected from the leased premises and taken away.

Similarly, when a contract of sale for real property is silent on the matter, classifying the object as a fixture means that the purchaser is entitled to receive the property with that object in place.

Likewise, fixtures are taxable under general real property tax statutes in which the tax is assessed based on the value of the property; trade fixtures and personalty are taxable as such, if such are taxed.

The defined elements of a fixture are three in number: (1) the annexation of the object (its physical connection or incorporation) to the real property, (2) the adaptability of the object to the use of the realty, and (3) the intention of the annexor — or of both the vendor of the object and its annexor-purchaser — that the object become a fixture. See First Wisconsin Natl. Bank v. Federal Land Bank, 849 F.2d 284, 287 (7th Cir. 1988) (stating this test and holding that cranberry vines are fixtures). Teafft v. Hewitt, 1 Ohio 511, 59 Am. Dec. 634 (1853), is the leading case. To some degree, the three elements have been added over time, one on top of another, and in any particular case will vary in importance.

Annexation can be by attachment or, in the instance of a particularly heavy object such as industrial machinery, by gravity. Conversely, a slight attachment might indicate an intent to remove — and so not annex an object — to leased or sold premises. A permanent and intricate attachment of an object may give rise to an annexation by estoppel — a tenant or vendor is then estopped to deny that the annexation was not an indication that he meant to have the object become a fixture.

In early cases, annexation was seen as the controlling element in the definition. However, in later cases involving manufacturing or industrial property, the adaptation of the object to the process representing the dominant and reasonably expected use of the property controls. This is the institutional test, or the assembled plant doctrine (originating in Pennsylvania cases), for determining what is and is not a fixture. Thus an object necessary to a particular use or adapted to that use, for which a larger structure was designed, becomes a fixture under this test.

The third element, intention, is the overarching one, particularly in commercial transactions. Thus a commercial landlord will periodically ask a tenant if there are objects on the leased premises that he intends to remove at the end of the term; or a landlord contemplating the purchase of leased property will ask the tenant if there are items of personalty on the premises subject to the claims of third parties — equipment lessors and the like.

When an object is a fixture under state law, the U.C.C.'s §9-313 applies. While it is not the exclusive source of law for fixtures, it is applicable in the sense that a fixture may also be security included in a real property mortgage or deed of trust. The more specific task of §9-313 is to settle issues of priority between the owner, mortgagee, and the fixturizer — the holder of a lien on the fixture.

Conflicts in the priorities assigned to fixturizers and mortgagees of real property are handled by U.C.C. §9-913. In general, a fixturizer is subordinate to a mortgagee, except that a fixturizer may gain priority over a prior mortgagee when four conditions are met: (1) the security interest in the fixtures is a purchase money security interest, (2) the interest of the mortgagee arises before the objects ("goods" in the U.C.C.) become fixtures, (3) the fixturizer perfects his security interest in those fixtures by filing before the goods become fixtures or within 10 days thereafter, and (4) the debtor (the owner of the fixtures) has an interest in the realty to which the mortgagee lien applies. With these four conditions met, the fixturizer has priority over the mortgagee. U.C.C. §9-913(4)(a) (1972). The overall purpose of this statute is to bring the security interest in fixtures in line with the priority rules in state recording acts.

Otherwise, as between a mortgagee who records and a fixturizer who perfects his security interest with a fixture filing, the first to file has priority. U.C.C. §9-313(4)(b) (1972). This prevents the supplier of the fixturizer from gaining a security interest in the real property on which the fixture is installed.

When the mortgagee is a construction mortgagee, however, the tables may be turned, for a construction mortgagee has priority over a security interest in fixtures if the goods become fixtures before the completion of construction. U.C.C. §9-313(6). This priority is also accorded a takeout or permanent mortgagee stepping into the shoes of the construction lender. Id.; see generally Squillante, The Law of Fixtures: Common Law and the Uniform Commercial Code: Part II: The UCC and Fixtures, 15 Hofstra L. Rev. 535 (1987).

# More on Workouts

We have by now assembled the cast of characters that will be sitting around the workout table: mortgage lenders, guarantors, sureties, fixturizers, general and subcontractors. For the lender, undertaking the negotiations for a workout may be preferable to writing off the loan or suing for a deficiency. Once the discussions are underway, however, there can be no false moves — and certainly no sudden ones. The lender will not want to negotiate with anyone not authorized to deal on the borrower's behalf. Certainly the lender will seldom want to attend any of the borrower's corporate meetings, nor interfere with the borrower's management in any way. Such would be the stuff of lender liability.

Moreover, all of the guarantors and insurers must agree to the workout agreement; otherwise, they will claim that they are prejudiced by it and thereby released from their obligations. This possibility may limit the extent to which a loan can be redocumented at the time of a workout.

Likewise, the workout agreement must be binding for a reasonable length of time, one sufficient to give the borrower time to work out of the financial hole. This will often require independant financial advice, and its providers, whether investment counsel, an accounting firm, or others, will provide another potential defendant if things go badly. But see, e.g., DiLeo v. Ernst & Young, 901 F.2d 624 (7th Cir. 1990) (finding no duty on accountants "to search and sing," disclosing client fraud, in a securities act case); United States v. Benjamin, 328 F.2d 854 (2d Cir. 1964) (containing a good discussion of pro forma statements, id. at 861, and stating: "In our complex society the accountant's certificate and the lawyer's opinion can be instruments for inflicting pecuniary loss more potent than the chisel or the crowbar." Id. at 863.). In addition, where possible under applicable case law, statute of limitations for enforcing the workout agreement may be waived, but here there should be a clear identification of the statute waived.

The attorneys for all involved will be busy documenting agreements as they are made — no agreement should go unmemorialized — and obtaining releases based on prior, possibly inconsistent, conduct: "In exchange for and in consideration of the accommodations and agreements contained herein, the borrower, its sureties, insurers, and guarantors, hereby release the lender for any actions taken to date and all claims arising out of such actions." How effective will such a provision of a workout agreement be? In some circumstances, such a blanket release may be too broad. It may be preferable to waive statutory rights specifically by reference to the statutory citation; if antideficiency statutes are available to the borrower, then those rights should be specifically, voluntarily, and knowingly waived, after the borrower has had the benefit of counsel's advice and with a lender's right forgone in exchange. The law applicable to waivers of statutory protections is likely to be complex — and no legal rules about the enforceability of waivers is likely to be crisp. Bankruptcy proceedings may sometimes be preferable, so let's turn to that subject now.

# Bankruptcy

In the 1970s, a major overhaul of the bankruptcy statutes occurred, resulting in the Bankruptcy Code of 1978, 11 U.S.C. §§1 et seq. Bankruptcy took on new importance with the enactment of the code. As an example, the number of personal bankruptcies jumped way up — from 228,000 in 1979, 455,000 two years later, to over 600,000 in 1989. The pre-1980s stigma attached to bankruptcy was fast dissolving. No sector of the economy learned this lesson faster than the land development industry. For a general introduction, see Symposium, As We Forgive Our Debtors, 65 Ind. L.J. 1 (1989).

In so far as is possible, bankruptcy has two goals, often in conflict but also constantly in front of the courts. See Scott, Sharing the Risks of Bankruptcy: *Timbers, Ahlers,* and Beyond, 1989 Colo. Bus. L. Rev. 183. The first is the rehabilitation of the debtor; bankruptcy today has a redemptive quality, and the glowing terms used to describe it have a religious glow. The goal is a financial fresh start for the debtor. Achieving this requires some risk on the part of creditors. In the case of a Chapter 11 reorganization, this risk is a continuous one because a Chapter 11 reorganization plan requires creditors to exchange their old debts for new ones.

The second goal is equality of treatment for creditors, but equality in this area, just as in the political arena, is illusive and subject to several definitions. Similar claims should be treated similarly, but the pre-Bankruptcy Code status of creditors should be respected as well, and this typically divides creditors into secured and unsecured groups. For example, the statutes avoiding preferences (e.g., 11 U.S.C. §547) discourages creditors from collecting the debtor's assets a short time before bankruptcy; this encourages collective action by creditors in order to maximize the totality of interests held by the creditors as a group. In short, the creditors have to strike a bargain amongst themselves. Another example of recognition of a creditor's pre-Bankruptcy Code status is the lifting of the stay imposed at the filing of a bankruptcy petition when the creditor is not given an equivalent remedy in bankruptcy. See In re Muriel Holding Co., 75 F.2d 941 (2d Cir. 1941) (Learned Hand, J.) (ordering the stay lifted for a mortgage lender who was offered interest-only payment during a renovation and was forced to extend the due date of the last payment); In re Reddington/Sunarrow Ltd. Partnership, 119 B.R. 809 (Bankr. D.N.M. 1990) (a Chapter 11 reorganization). The *Reddington* opinion indicates that bankruptcy proceedings may be preferable to a workout when the creditor receives cash in payment of its debt under a cash collateral order of the court; the cash prevents the total write-off of the loan and immunizes the lender from the liability attendant on the lender's taking possesion of the secured real property. Id. at 813 (discussing *Timbers,* infra).

If the creditors do not reach agreement, the court will strike a bargain for them. In this forced bargain lies the core of the idea of a cramdown: the idea that even a secured creditor's bargain with the debtor can be restructured. See 11 U.S.C. §1122 (for corporate reorganizations) and §1322 (for individual reorganizations). Cramdowns, moreover, can divide a secured mortgage lender's debt into secured and unsecured portions. Note, Modification of an Unsecured Home Mortgage in a Chapter 13 Proceeding, 56 Mo. L. Rev. 841 (1991).

A good example of the tension between these two goals is United Sav. Assn. of Texas v. Timbers of Inwood Forrest Assocs., Ltd., 484 U.S. 365 (1988) (denying an undersecured creditor interest on its collateral as compensation for the opportunity costs of delay caused by the bankruptcy proceeding itself, and holding that a creditor's "interest in property," protected by the statutes (11 U.S.C. §§361-362) and providing relief from the stay, does not include the creditor's right to immediate possession of the secured property); see also In re South Village, 25 B.R. 987, 990 (Bankr. D. Utah 1982) (Maby, J.) Deprived of the state foreclosure remedy, the lender is also forced to bear the costs and risk of bankruptcy. A pre-bankruptcy remedy is destroyed, without compensation. In effect, those costs are thrown into the pool of assets held by all creditors. Another example of this tension is Norwest Bank Worthington v. Ahlers, 485 U.S. 197 (1988), holding that senior creditors could prevent the characterization of a contribution of labor on a family farm as a retention of an equity interest by the debtor. See 11 U.S.C. §1129(b) (authorizing a bankruptcy court to confirm a fair and equitable reorganization plan over the objection of a class of creditors). Thus creditors are not forced to share the debtor's assets with the debtor but can be forced to share the costs of the bankruptcy proceeding itself.

This suggests that, in a Chapter 11 reorganization, the creditors in bankruptcy of a corporate general partner could not be forced to contribute to the future services of the general partner in managing the corporate assets. Rehabilitating the general partner requires that the creditors recognize the contribution, but equal treatment for all creditors does not require recognition. In the real estate field, forcing the general out of the picture is likely to destroy his track record and make him seek another line of work — rehabilitation is forever denied him.

Moreover, any executory contract between the surrounding limited partner and the general partner is likely to be executory and subject to assumption or rejection in bankruptcy. 11 U.S.C. §365(a). See Westbrook, A Functional Analysis of Executory Contracts, 74 Minn. L. Rev. 228 (1989).

Rents are typically treated as cash collateral in a Chapter 11 proceeding and are the subject of a stipulation first acknowledging the lender's interest in postpetition rents, escrowing them, and permitting the debtor to meet necessary operating expenses from the escrow account, holding the balance on account or giving it to the lender to apply to the debt. See Carlisle, Single Asset Real Estate in Chapter 11 — Need for Reform, 25 Real Prop. Prob. & Tr. J. 673, 675-681, 692-704 (1991) (discussing *Timbers* and the assignment of rents, respectively).

# A Concluding Note

The collapse of the lender: Unthinkable in prior decades, but the changing environment for commercial banks and savings banks has made this a possibility today. The status of the workout agreement when the lender is taken over by federal or state regulators is uncertain. The regulators often have the authority to "disaffirm or repudiate any contract or lease" to which the lender is a party and is in the opinion of the federal conservator "burdensome," in order to "promote the orderly administration of the institution's affairs." 12 U.S.C.A. §1821(e) (1990 Supp.) (authorizing FDIC conservators of failed lenders), incorporated by reference into the Resolution Trust Corporation's powers provided in 12 U.S.C.A. §1441 (1990 Supp.). There is not much authority on the meaning of "burdensome" as used in this statute, but one case, Union Bank v. Federal Sav. & Loan Assn., 724 F. Supp. 468, 471 (E.D. Ky. 1989), states that it means unprofitable, undesirable, or failing to conserve the assets of the lender. In the absence of an abuse of discretion on the conservator's part, however, a repudiation of a workout agreement would be hard to overturn in court. But see American Med. Supply, Inc. v. RTC, 1990 Westlaw 58589 (D. Kan, Apr. 26, 1990) (indicating that an invalid repudiation might become grounds for a claim of specific performance). There is no regulatory standard to guide the FDIC-RTC either, but the RTC must have a "strategic plan" for the institution. Arkansas State Banking Commr. v. RTC, 1990 Westlaw 124035 (8th Cir., Aug. 28, 1990) (permitting the RTC to override a state statutory prohibition on branch banking in order to preserve the institution's assets).

Federal regulators take free of many defenses that the borrower might otherwise have against the lender. See, e.g., Mery v. Universal Sav. Assn., 737 F. Supp. 1000, 1004 (S.D. Tex. 1990) (listing fraudulent inducement, fraud, misrepresentation, failure of consideration, duress, defenses based on secret side agreements, duties of good faith and fair dealing, breaches of fiduciary duty, usury, negligence, gross negligence, unfair trade practices violations, and unjust enrichment as defenses of which the regulator is freed). See 12 U.S.C.A. §1823(e) (1990 Supp.), discussed in Garten, Regulatory Growing Pains: A Perspective on Bank Regulation in a Deregulatory Age, 57 Ford. L. Rev. 501 (1989). For a general review of the RTC, see Tucker, Meire & Rubinstein, The RTC: A Practical Guide to the Receivership/ Conservatorship Process and the Resolution of Failed Thrifts, 25 U. Rich. L. Rev. 1 (1990).

# 24

# Installment Land Sale Contracts

An installment land sale contract (ILSC) is an installment purchase device. It is a contract for the sale of real property whose executory period is stretched out over a period of years. The purchaser goes into possession immediately, however, paying little or nothing down, avoiding the payment of closing and settlement costs and the requirements of mortgage lenders. Thus an ILSC is a device that extends credit to some who would not qualify for a conventional mortgage.

In such an arrangement, the vendor need not part with the legal title to the property, enjoys the financial advantage of selling the property at an installment, or higher price, and the tax advantages of selling on the installment method (that is, she will, if complying with the provisions of Internal Revenue Code §453, realize the income from the sale only as she receives it). See Goodman, Tax Ideas: Installment Sales after Tax Reform, 18 Real Est. L.J. 365 (1990).

Traditionally, this device is used by farmers, low-income homeowners, and purchasers of second homes. The vendor of the contract interest retains title to the property, but possession and the obligation to pay taxes and other carrying charges pass to the purchaser. So does the risk of loss, in a majority of states. (The rules applicable to contract of sale generally apply here, so remember that there is a minority view. See Chapter 4.) Probably most ILSCs have provisions placing the risk of loss on the purchaser. See generally Note, Installment Land Contracts: Developing Law in Virginia, 37 Wash. & Lee L. Rev. 1161 (1980). Typical contracts are often found in state codes. See, following Minn. Stat. Ann. §559.21, Form Number 55, Uniform Conveyancing Blanks (1959).

During the extended executory period of ILSCs, both the vendor and the purchaser retain an interest in the property: the vendor the legal title (alienable, mortgagable, subject to levy and sale by her creditors in a majority of jurisdictions, and so forth) and the purchaser an equitable interest (alienable, mortgagable, and, in most jurisdictions, subject to levy and sale by her creditors too). At first glance it may seem strange to you that a majority of jurisdictions treat both parties' interest as subject to lien creditors, but it is possible if the theory is different each time (of this more later). Put this way, it is apparent that the purchaser runs the risk that the vendor's title will be clouded in any one of several ways. To make matters worse for the purchaser, note that, traditionally, the vendor's duty to convey the title at the end of the executory period is independent of the purchaser's duty to make installment payments, although there is some authority limiting this rule. Most states permit the recordation of ILSCs.

ILSCs often contain draconian provisions that have three features: (1) automatic forfeiture of all amounts, paid in toward the price, upon default; (2) retention by the vendor of those amounts as liquidated damages; and (3) termination of the contract upon forfeiture. D & Y v. Winston, 320 Md. 534, 578 A.2d 1177, 1181 (1990). See generally Note, The Changing Status of the Land Contract in Michigan and the Advantages of the Two-Party Mortgage as an Alternative, 28 Wayne L. Rev. 239, 247-248 (1981). In addition, many will contain provisions permitting the vendor to foreclose the purchaser's interest as a mortgagee would a mortgage.

Many state courts still enforce such provisions as written, but, in response to such a hydra-headed provision, some courts have found that the vendor has waived the benefit of the agreement by accepting late payments. Some have reinstated the vendee after a default, or required a vendor to return a portion of the amount otherwise forfeited to the purchaser. This amount is sometimes said to represent the built-up equity of the purchaser in the property, or conversely the amount remaining with the vendor is said to represent the fair rental value of the property for the period of the purchaser's possession. California, Connecticut, and Utah cases have taken this approach. See, e.g., Engstrom v. Bushnell, 20 Utah 2d 250, 436 P.2d 806 (1968); and see generally Note, California Supreme Court: Land Sale Contracts, 60 Cal. L. Rev. 975 (1972); Annot., Vendee's recovery of purchase money, 31 A.L.R.2d 9 (1953). The purchaser still has to sue to recover a portion of the forfeiture; this burden of litigation may mean that the impact of this partial enforcement of the clause is nonetheless draconian.

Other judicial responses have treated the ILSC as the functional equivalent of a mortgage. When the purchaser has paid a considerable portion of the price or the property has increased in value since the execution of the contract, particularly if the purchaser's improvements to the property caused the increase, some courts have used their inherent equitable powers to decree that the property be sold at judicial sale, with the surplus over the debt distributed to the purchaser. A case doing this is Ward v. Union Bond &

Trust Co., 243 F.2d 476 (9th Cir. 1957). See also Skendzel v. Marshall, 261 Ind. 226, 301 N.E.2d 641, cert. denied, 415 U.S. 921 (1973). By no means a majority of states reach this result, but where it is reached, it means that a total, automatic, damage-liquidating, forfeiture provision will be enforceable only through foreclosure. The valuable right gained by the purchaser-mortgagor in foreclosure is the equitable right of redemption, which permits the purchaser first to seek refinancing and then, with the proceeds of the loan, redeem the property under contract.

Most of the courts that have applied this functional equivalency doctrine to turn the contract into a mortgage have done so in factual situations in which the purchaser (1) goes into possession immediately upon executing the contract, and (2) thereafter pays a substantial portion of the contract's purchase price; thus the purchaser has a built-up equity in the property to protect. See McLendon v. Safe Realty Corp., 401 N.E.2d 80 (Ind. App. 1980). In *Marshall,* for example, 71 percent of the purchase price was paid, albeit irregularly, sometimes prepaid. See Goff v. Graham, 159 Ind. App. 324, 306 N.E.2d 758 (1974) (in which an Indiana court permits forfeiture when the purchaser paid about $2500 of a $6200 contract price while renting the property for $6300).

Some of these opinions (including *Marshall*) converting the ILSC into a mortgage do so with a general, and rather spongy, holding to that effect. See also Sebastian v. Floyd, 585 S.W.2d 381 (Ky. 1979), noted in 72 Ky. L.J. 917 (1984); 7 N. Ky. L. Rev. 303 (1980). If a mortgage is established, then is it a lien or title mortgage? Are all the formalities of a foreclosure available to the contracting parties? Is the "mortgagee" entitled to rents pending foreclosure? Or a deficiency judgment requested by the vendor? Is the mortgagor entitled to any applicable statutory redemption right? Even if foreclosure is pruned of the attributes unfavorable to the purchaser, it would be inequitable to return all of the money paid in by the purchaser. The latter would then have received interim possession rent-free, so the purchaser, in return for a forfeiture, should receive back all payments, minus the fair rental value of the property. Durda v. Chembar Dev. Corp., 95 Mich. App. 706, 291 N.W.2d 179 (1980).

Even in jurisdictions with cases like *Marshall* and *Sebastian,* some vendors continue to use forfeiture provisions for their in terrorem value against purchasers who are ignorant of the law involved and the unenforceability of the provisions. Punitive damages should be available against such use, but no case law speaks to this effect directly on point.

In jurisdictions with these cases, when a purchaser mortgages her equitable interest in an ILSC and there is a forfeiture of that interest, the mortgagee is accorded the rights of a junior mortgagee or lienor upon a senior foreclosure. By analogy, such rights should perhaps be extended to such a mortgagee in all jurisdictions.

Where the case law of a jurisdiction would recharacterize an ILSC as a mortgage, the recharacterization need not be automatic and does not mean that forfeiture provisions cannot be drafted fairly and then enforced as written. Provisions for notice of an impending forfeiture, with a time for the vendee to cure the default working the forfeiture or provisions for the vendor's retention of part of the payments as rent and for giving back the excess, would make the forfeiture less harsh.

## Lien Creditors' Right to Reach Contract Interests

When an unsecured creditor of either the vendor or the purchaser obtains a judgment, by statute the judgment typically creates a lien on real, but not personal, property of the debtor. The lien takes a priority attaching when the court clerk in the county where the property is dockets the judgment in the appropriate public record or docket book. In a majority of jurisdictions, the purchaser's interest in an ILSC is real property for purposes of the judgment lien statute. This result is reached as a matter of statutory interpretation or as a recognition of the effects of the doctrine of equitable conversion.

Under these statutes, the vendor's interest is also real property in a majority of jurisdictions. To reach this result, courts have to ignore the equitable conversion doctrine and concentrate instead on the vendor's retention of the legal title until all installment payments are made by the purchaser. The judgment lien attaches, more particularly, to the vendor's lien, itself realty, in the amount of the unpaid installments. Moreover, the vendor's lien is regarded as taking its priority from the time of the execution of the contract. The minority rule is (as you might imagine) that the vendor's interest is personal property. This is just another way of saying that the creditor seeking to attach the vendor's interest will have to bring a second action to execute or foreclose the vendor's lien, thus assigning it to a priority attaching at the time of the execution or foreclosure decree. In a minority jurisdiction, then, any purchaser at the sale of the vendor's interest dare not pay more than the total of existing senior liens and mortgages. The other result under the minority rule is that classifying the vendor's interest as personalty may subject it to the provisions of the Uniform Commercial Code; under such provisions, a financing statement must be filed in order to assert a lien on the property. But this requirement may turn into a procedural blessing when the requirements of foreclosing a code security interest and foreclosing a mortgage lien are compared. The code action is much simpler.

## Bankruptcy

Upon the vendor's bankruptcy, the trustee in bankruptcy may reject the ILSC. See 11 U.S.C.A. §365 (1990). The purchaser must be in possession to "perfect" her interest and must further tender all of the future, unpaid installment payments to avoid rejection of the contract by the trustee. U.S.C.A. §365(i). The purchaser ousted by the vendor's trustee obtains a lien for any payments of the purchase price paid. U.S.C.A. §365(j). This means that it is up to the trustee to determine, when the contract is otherwise silent, what portions of the installments are to be treated as a payment for possession and what treated as a purchase payment. Only with the delivery of a deed does the trustee lose the power to reject the contract. See Epling, Treatment of Land Sales Contracts under the New Bankruptcy Code, 56 Am. Bankr. L.J. 55 (1982).

## Remedies

Upon default of the purchaser, the nondefaulting vendor has (1) any contract action outlined in the ILSC and all contract remedies generally, (2) an action to recover possession of the property, such as ejectment, (3) an action to quiet title, and (4) a foreclosure action.

The nondefaulting purchaser's remedies are those typically associated with a contract: (1) an action for rescission: the recovery of payments made by rescinding the contract and restoring the consideration received under it, (2) a damage action for breach, and (3) an action for specific performance. The third action is limited in the traditional ways, and might in addition require that the contract itself contain an acceleration provision for the nondefaulting purchaser's benefit, or that the vendor's breach be an anticipatory repudiation of the contract.

## EXAMPLES AND EXPLANATIONS

1. VR and VE execute a brief but enforceable installment land sale contract for Blackacre. VR does not have good title at the time of execution. Is VR in default on the ILSC?

**Explanation:** No. VR's duty to present a marketable title is satisfied if VR has a marketable title as of the date of the last installment, at which time VR is bound under the contract to convey the title to VE. Absent some provision for assuring VE as to the quality of the title in the interim, VR is not in default if the title is meanwhile unmarketable. Many courts have stopped their analysis at this point; some, however, have continued and gone on to hold that, even though VR is not in default, neither does VE have to keep making payments without further assurance from VR that the title will ultimately be conveyed. Meanwhile neither party is in breach. Proper drafting should assure that a procedure for providing such assurance is written into the contract.

2. What if VE records the ILSC and the state whose law applies does not have a nonjudicial method for terminating VE's interest in Blackacre? How should VR draft the ILSC to meet this problem?

**Explanation:** VR might attempt to include a contract provision to the effect that, if the contract is recorded, it is void. Such a provision might not survive judicial scrutiny and might be void itself, as being against the public policy of encouraging the recording of contract of law (in jurisdictions where such documents are indeed recordable under applicable recording statutes). A fallback position for VR is not to acknowledge the contract. The lack of acknowledgment will render the contract unrecordable or sometimes, if recorded, render the recording of no effect.

3. Suppose VE under an ILSC purchases a subdivision lot from VR, a developer who has executed a blanket mortgage for construction money for whole subdivision? How can VE protect herself in the event that the construction mortgage goes into foreclosure?

**Explanation:** VE should receive a deed both releasing the lien of the blanket mortgage and reciting the VR-VE agreement, and naming VE, along with the vendor under the contract, as grantees. In the absence of such a deed, VE needs a provision in her contract making it recordable or a provision for giving actual notice to the mortgagee. The contract shown the mortgagee should include provisions requiring VR to notify VE of any mortgage default and assign any right to cure the default to VE.

4a. What if VE improves Blackacre but then goes into default on the ILSC payments? What remedies might a court provide VE?

**Explanation:** First, VE might sue the vendor for unjust enrichment. Anderson v. DeLisle, 352 N.W.2d 794 (Minn. App. 1984) (recognizing this cause of action for the purchaser whose financial difficulties were known to the vendor, and not requiring that the defaulting purchaser allege that the vendor acted fraudulently). In many jurisdictions, however, an allegation of vendor fraud will be necessary. Second, VE also might ask a court to force VR to use foreclosure and distribute the proceeds so that the excess over the debt on the contract goes to VE. VE would have to be sure that the foreclosure sale would fetch this excess. In a third alternative, VE might ask that the court use strict foreclosure, issuing a decree nisi. This would permit VE a time (allotted for exercise of the equitable redemption right) during which VE could compel specific performance of the property subject to the ILSC (and after which forfeiture provisions operate). See Jenkins v. Wise, 58 Haw. 592, 574 P.2d 1337 (Haw. 1978).

If, in the distribution of the proceeds of the sale, VR is entitled under the state's case law to the fair rental value of the property, why shouldn't VE obtain the fair market value of any improvements? Wolf v. Anderson, 334 N.W.2d 212 (N.D. 1983). Remember, however, that after termination of the contract, whether by forfeiture according to its terms, or by the use of a statutory termination procedure, the purchaser loses any cause of action for damages based on the contract; this is the holding of most (early 1900s) cases considering this question. Note, Property Law — Minnesota Applies Unjust Enrichment Doctrine to Contract for Deed Cancellations — Anderson v. DeLisle, 352 N.W.2d 794 (Minn. App. 1984), 12 Wm. Mitchell L. Rev. 393, 396-398 n.32-33 (1986).

4b. Instead of improving Blackacre, VE commits waste and destroys a substantial portion of its fair market value. VR declares a forfeiture of the ILSC and afterwards sues VE for waste. VE defends the latter suit, alleging that once VR declared the contract forfeited, she cannot thereafter sue on it. Is this defense a good one?

**Explanation:** Yes. A vendor has a cause of action in waste against a purchaser in possession so long as the contract relationship continues. Here a vendor would be better advised to have rescinded the contract, rather than exercised her forfeiture right. Horine v. Greencastle Prod. Credit Assn., 505 N.E.2d 802 (Ind. App. 1987). A rescission would return the parties to the status quo ante and require that each party tender back what was originally conveyed at the outset of the contract. For the vendor, the purchaser would have to cure the waste before her tender-back. In this respect, the distinction between forfeiture and rescission is one that the parties might not understand. A cause of action in waste is available only to those with a concurrent and simultaneous interest in the contract. Forfeiture ends the purchaser's interest. Even though the vendor is in ignorance of this legal consequence, the vendor's cause of action in waste is lost at that point, and a later rescission would be of a contract that the vendor has already elected to have forfeited. Meyer v. Hansen, 373 N.W.2d 392 (N.D. 1985); and see Note, A Rescission Approach to Vendor's Damages After Forfeiture of an Installment Real Estate Contract, 74 Iowa L. Rev. 901, 904 (1989). For a state statute permitting vendor a damage action for waste, see Ohio Rev. Code Ann. §5313.10 (Anderson 1989).

5. Suppose that VE sells her interest by means of another ILSC, and the new vendee (VEE) under this second ILSC goes into possession. VEE thereafter makes payments directly to VR. If VEE goes into default on the payments, is VE entitled to notice from VR of the default before VR cancels the ILSC under its default clause? Would your answer change if the original ILSC were assigned and VE and VEE had not executed a separate ILSC? Would your answer to the first question in this paragraph change if VEE paid the amount of VE's equity as down payment on the second ILSC?

**Explanation:** Yes, as to the first question. See Roberts v. Morin, 198 Mont. 233, 645 P.2d 423 (1982). This case held that VE is entitled to notice and has a right to redeem. As to the second and third questions, the answers are also yes; the fact that VE had been paid her equity would make a difference. The failure to execute a second contract is here an implied assignment of all VE's rights under the first contract, and when VE has received compensation for the totality of her interest, so that its remaining worth is at or near zero, strict foreclosure might be an appropriate remedy against VE.

6. What if VE mortgages her interest? What problems arise?

**Explanation:** See Fincher v. Miles Homes, Inc., 549 S.W.2d 848 (Mo. 1977), noted in 43 Mo. L. Rev. 371 (1978). There is no technical reason why a purchaser's interest in an installment contract cannot be mortgaged. There may also be some question about the business prudence of the mortgagee in this situation because the security for the loan is only the purchaser's equitable interest in the contract.

How would the mortgagee modify the usual covenants in the note and the mortgage to protect herself? Probably first and foremost, by charging a higher rate of interest on the proceeds of the mortgage loan. Probably too by insertion of a provision for notice to the vendor of the mortgage and by a further covenant that the mortgagor-vendee will notify the mortgagee of any default in the contract in a timely manner, in order to give the mortgagee time to exercise a right to cure that default; this right would arise under another provision in the mortgage.

Without such provisions, what problems might arise? A forfeiture might occur that would wipe out the ground of the mortgagee's security for its loan; or, in a jurisdiction treating an installment contract like a mortgage, the vendor might foreclose its interest and, as to the vendor's foreclosure, the mortgagee, if not joined in that action, would assume the status of an omitted junior mortgagee, with the two remedies traditional for such parties: reforeclosure or redemption.

In *Miles,* supra, the mortgagee of the vendee's interest recorded, but because the vendor had not recorded, there was some question about the effectiveness of that recording (was it within a valid chain of title?). The mortgagee contended, however, that before the vendee executed a deed of release of her interest, she had to give notice (actual or constructive?) to the mortgagee and, having failed to do that, was entitled to assert her lien against the vendor's title, which, when taken back in the deed of release, was subject to the mortgage lien. In *Miles,* the vendor had actual notice of the mortgage and, because the mortgagee had recorded its interest, mortgagee argued that the vendor knew that the title taken back had its equity attached to it. By analogy, then, the mortgagee is an omitted junior, and the vendor receiving the deed of release is analogous to the purchaser at the foreclosure sale that the deed avoided.

7. What measure of damages is applied to the ILSC?

**Explanation:** If neither VR nor VE wishes specific performance of their rights under the contract, then the underlying contract is still effective, and damages can either be measured by the difference between the contract price and the fair rental value of the property or the benefit of the bargain, both measured at the time of the breach. For a case choosing the former, difference money measure, see Honey v. Henry's Franchise Leasing Corp., 64 Cal. 2d 801, 52 Cal. Rptr. 18, 415 P.2d 833 (1966). VE generally has the burden of proving that forfeiture provides VR with more than difference money or the benefit of the bargain. VR generally has the election of rescinding the contract under the forfeiture provision contained in it. Rescission turns the contract, after the fact, into a lease and gives rise to difference money measure of damages.

8a. If VR seeks forfeiture of the ILSC, can VR also seek damages from VE?

**Explanation:** No. Under the traditional rule, the vendor's bringing a forfeiture action is an agreement to accept the property back as compensation for the purchaser's default. However, the cases are split. Compare Nemec v. Rollo, 114 Ariz. 589, 562 P.2d 1087 (1977), with Goff v. Graham, 159 Ind. App. 324, 306 N.E.2d 758 (1974). And also see the answer to Example 4(a), where it is suggested that an action for waste and forfeiture of the contract are not incompatible.

8b. If VE gave VR her note in lieu of a cash down payment, can VR sue on the note after exercising forfeiture?

**Explanation:** No. See *Nemec,* supra.

9. Is VE's ILSC interest "real property" subject to lis pendens and judgment liens? Or, if VR pledges the right to contract payments, is that "personal property"? What difference does the characterization make?

**Explanation:** The answer to both questions is yes in a majority of jurisdictions, but some doctrinal assumptions must be made.

Yes, as to the first question: VE has an equitable interest in real property that is subject to a judgment lien in jurisdictions that use the doctrine of equitable conversion routinely in contracts for the sale of real property. But see Cascade Security Bank v. Butler, 88 Wash. 2d 777, 567 P.2d 631 (1977) (in which the court said yes, but based its answer on statutory interpretation, rather than the doctrine).

Yes, as to the second question: Recall that a pledge is a bailment (the transfer of possession, without a transfer of title, to the payments), and a reviewing court must be willing to distinguish between the right to transfer the right to the payments from the title to the property. Recall that the distinction is commonly made to justify the use of assignment of rent covenants in mortgages. Once this distinction is made, the right to receive the payments is personal property, and the judgment lien statutes of many (though a minority of) states will not reach it. Another action will have to be brought to attach the vendor's interest.

A second consequence of classifying the vendor's interest as personalty, however, is to bring the right within the scope of the Uniform Commercial Code, §9-102(1). To the same effect: if a U.C.C. security interest is not perfected by filing a financing statement, the assignee of the right to the payments is an unsecured creditor under the code. In re Freeborn, 94 Wash. 2d 336, 617 P.2d 424 (1980). Once the distinction between the right to receive the payment and the title to it is accepted, however, there is still room for holding that if VR suffers a judgment, then VR's interest in the title can be levied and sold to satisfy the judgment because the real property is bound over to satisfy the judgment to the extent that the purchase price under the contract is unpaid. To the extent that VR could assign the right to payment, she can be forced to do so by levy and sale, as to future payments.

## State Legislation

Many states have legislated on some of the problems discussed here. An Oklahoma statute, for example, provides that an ILSC "shall be deemed and held to be mortgages and shall be subject to the same rules of foreclosure and to the same regulations, restraints, and forms as are proscribed in relation to mortgages." Okla. Stat. tit. 16, §11A (1978), discussed in Note, The Decline of the Contract for Deed in Oklahoma, 14 Tulsa L.J. 557 (1979). Florida has a similar statute. Fla. Stat. Ann. §697.01 (1980). With such a statute in its code, a jurisdiction is returned to the questions raised by the general holding of the *Marshall* opinion: If the contract is to be treated as a mortgage, what type of mortgage? Title or lien? Because the statute is probably intended to avoid the drastic effects of its forfeiture provision, the best guess is that the legislature intends an ILSC to be treated as a lien mortgage. Unless the purchaser has little or no equity in the property, the courts are also unlikely to grant her the traditional remedy for a title mortgage default (strict foreclosure).

When after default will the mortgagee be able to take possession of the secured property? Only if the recharacterized contract is treated as a title mortgage, does the "mortgagee" have the right to possession upon default. The intent of the statute is to make the forfeiture provision less, not more, self-executing. Moreover, if the contract is subjected to all the rules relating to mortgages, and not just foreclosure, then the right to possession will be postponed until sometime after foreclosure is complete.

When an ILSC is subject to foreclosure, is it also subject to the ancillary actions such as an action for a deficiency judgment, which usually accompany foreclosure? Probably the legislature meant to say that the contract should be treated as a mortgage only when the impact of the contract's forfeiture terms are harsher on the purchaser than a mortgage foreclosure would be. Thus, just as the mortgagee would not obtain possession any earlier, a deficiency judgment might also be barred when arising from the foreclosure of the recharacterized contract. Offering the mortgagee a deficiency judgment would be the equivalent of saying that she has a cause of action in specific performance of the contract. Considering the markets in which a legislature recognizes that an ILSC is likely to be used, this effect would surely be an unintended result of legislative action.

Other state statutes provide a redemption period — 30 days to a year — and one state (Arizona) provides for a variable redemption period, depending on the amount of payments made. Typically, the period starts to run when the vendor provides a notice of her intent to terminate or cancel the contract. The notice must state the reason for doing so. These redemptive periods, however, are often vague on the procedures to be used in a redemption. They have been used by courts nonetheless to imply a right to refinance and to assign the redemption right. Harder to imply are a purchaser's right to any, even a partial, refund of payments. Wayzata Enters., Inc. v. Herman, 268 Minn. 117, 128 N.W.2d 156, 158 (1964) (denying such a right under a Minnesota statute). During the redemption period, the purchaser has the right to cure the default, and if cured, the contract is reinstated. California limits the vendor seeking forfeiture to actual damages.

An Ohio statute provides that foreclosure, rather than forfeiture, shall be used by a vendor of a property improved by a dwelling when 20 percent of the purchase price has been paid by the purchaser or if payments have been made in accordance with the contract for a period of five years. Ohio Rev. Code Ann. §1313.07 (1987). How should that 20 percent be computed? Twenty percent of all payments due, or 20 percent of payments allocated to principal and interest? If no allocation is made, the former seemed logical; but if an allocation is made, Ohio courts have chosen to count only those portions of a payment devoted to the payment of principal. Durham, Ohio Land Contracts Revisited, 14 U. Dayton L. Rev. 451, 466-467 (1989) (cases cited therein).

# ILSCs and Civil Rights

Often the purchase price of a property sold through an ILSC will be higher than it would be if the property had been sold using a typical executory contract closed within a short time. Afro-American homeowners have recovered, under a federal civil rights statute, damages for racial discrimination that caused their having to pay based on this difference in price. 42 U.S.C. §1982[1]. See Clark v. Universal Builders, Inc., 501 F.2d 324 (7th Cir.), cert. denied, 419 U.S. 1070 (1974) (holding that plaintiffs had made out a prima facie case of racial discrimination, treating black and white plaintiffs differently). *Clark* is discussed in Note, 88 Harv. L. Rev. 1610 (1975). The plaintiffs were a class of over 600 Afro-American homeowners who had purchased homes using ILSCs, when corporate affiliates of the defendants sold homes in comparable white areas using mortgage financing and for prices 20 percent less, with lower profit margins. The plaintiffs did not show that blacks and whites were differently treated with regard to the same housing, only that the defendants operated differently in different markets. They relied instead on the argument that racial discrimination limited the housing supply available to the plaintiffs and thus bid up the price of that housing to a level in excess of what it would be and that the excess profits were illegal under §1982. The rationale for the holding in *Clark* is a combination of a statutory intent to eliminate present racial discrimination by controlling the defendants' sales and, based on the Thirteenth Amendment, the vestiges of Afro-American slavery.

A final thought: If ILSCs are often converted into mortgages for the purpose of extending the protections of foreclosure to the purchaser, it is reasonable to expect that, say, in the context of low-income housing, they will be converted into leases for the purpose of extending the protections given tenants (implied warranties of habitability, good cause evictions, and so forth). See Freyfogle, The Installment Land Contract as Lease: Habitability Protections and the Low-Income Purchaser, 62 N.Y.U. L. Rev. 293 (1987) (arguing that vendors should be liable to purchasers for breaches of an implied warranty of habitability).

# Another Financing Device

In and around Chicago, mortgage lenders often require that their mortgagors execute a deed conveying the secured land to an Illinois Land Trust. The

---

1. This statute provides: "All citizens of the United States shall have the same right, in every State and Territory, as is enjoyed by white citizens thereof to inherit, purchase, lease, sell, hold, and convey real and personal property."

grantee in the deed is the trustee, and this deed is recorded, but the grantors also execute an agreement giving the trustee power to deal with the title in a multitude of ways. The multitude of powers is necessary to deal with a challenge to the trust under the Statute of Uses, but in pertinent part, the powers of the trustee include the authority to sell the secured property upon any default on the note. This agreement is not recorded and is intentionally left off the record.

Meanwhile, the mortgagors-trustor remain in possession of the property. They become beneficiaries of the trust with the right to receive the rents and other income from the property. However, their right is a beneficial or equitable interest in the property that is the subject of this trust; as a consequence, their interest is personal property. As personalty, their interests can be more easily sold. A U.C.C. Article 9 financing statement is filed; upon default, the lender can have possession (U.C.C. §9-503); there is no postforeclosure redemption (U.C.C. §9-506) and no reinstatement right for the borrower (U.C.C. §9-503); and the lender has free access to a deficiency judgment (U.C.C. §§9-504(2), 9-505(2)).

Is this arrangement really a mortgage? See Horney v. Hayes, 11 Ill. 2d 178, 142 N.E.2d 94 (1957) (rejecting equitable mortgage arguments), discussed in Freyfogle, Land Trusts and the Decline of Mortgage Law, 1988 U. Ill. L. Rev. 67, 76.

# PART THREE

---

# *Investing in Real Estate*

# 25

## Real Property Owners and the Internal Revenue Code

## Tax Events

The purchase of a residence is not, from the perspective of the closing table, a tax event with immediate consequences. The closing and transaction costs — for securing the mortgage loan, inspecting the property, securing title search and insurance, paying your attorney — are not deductible expenses. Rather, the closing costs must be added into your "tax basis" in the property. "Basis" is a tax lawyer's term for cost; thus, the tax basis in the property is the purchase price plus the costs of acquisition (closing costs, and so on). The higher the initial basis, the less will be the taxable gain (if any) realized when the purchaser sells to another. From the perspective of the purchaser sitting at the closing table, however, a deduction that tax year would be more valuable than the later advantage. No dice, however: The Internal Revenue Code does not permit it.

Once the purchaser is in possession, the I.R.C. provides various types of tax advantages. The first is an implicit one; that is, the receipt of mortgage loan proceeds, used to finance the purchase, is not the receipt of income and not taxable as such. Second, the code permits the deduction of mortgage interest. I.R.C. §163. (But not the deduction of mortgage loan principal, which makes sense: If the receipt of the loan principal is not income, no deduction should be permitted for its repayment. This is an example of what might be called "tax symmetry," a powerful form for argumentation used by tax lawyers, met often in interpreting the code.) Third, the I.R.C. also permits

353

a further deduction for state and local real property tax payments. I.R.C. §164(a). If the homeowner owns a cooperative apartment through shares in the cooperative and a long-term lease, the deductions for mortgage interest and taxes are available. I.R.C. §216. But these two deductions are not available to renters generally. Likewise, deductions for casualty losses involving a residence are also available on a limited basis. I.R.C. §165.

After a taxpayer takes possession, the recognition of appreciation in the fair market value of the property awaits its sale. The later sale is the taxable event that triggers the code's provisions: The gain goes untaxed until that time. Compare this attitude in the federal I.R.C. with that of the local real property tax assessor and collector. At the local level, unrealized gain in the fair market value of a residence is taxed every year, before the taxpayer has realized any cash from the property with which to pay the local tax. A tax on unrealized appreciated value makes the local tax sound like a very progressive tax indeed, while the federal taxing scheme seems regressive by comparison. (Before you sound the trumpet for the progressive local tax, consider the tax rates and the impact on total income involved at both the state and federal level.)

Unlike business property, a residence — unless we are dealing with a portion of it used exclusively as a home office — cannot be depreciated. See I.R.C. §§262 (prohibiting depreciation for personal or family expenses), 280A (on home offices). Neither are the costs of repairs deductible, §262, although additions and improvements can be added, at cost, to the taxpayer's basis in the property.

Upon the sale of real property, federal taxation can be deferred by use of the installment sale section of the code. I.R.C. §453. If at least one payment of the sales price is received by the taxpayer in a year after the year of sale, gain from that sale is prorated and income realized in the years in which the payment is received. Thus if a vendor takes back a mortgage securing a portion of the purchase price, the income from the mortgage payment is taxed as the payments are received and in the year received. Id. The installment method is a way of deferring tax, not avoiding it; it is a specific example of the code's not taxing income until received.

Not only is federal taxation postponed until sale or other disposition of the property, but also the code offers many vendors of residential real property nonrecognition of gain in the two following, fairly common situations: first, if a transfer of property is made to a spouse, or to a former spouse when the transfer is incident to a divorce. I.R.C. §1041 (this section actually applies to nonresidential property as well). Such a transfer is treated as a gift, and the transferee receives the adjusted basis of the transferor spouse.

The second nonrecognition situation occurs when the sale of a principal residence is followed, within a short time (now two years), either before or after, by the purchase of a new residence. Here the gain, which would otherwise be recognized and taxed in the year of sale, is not recognized to the extent that the purchase price of the new residence exceeds the sales price of the old residence. I.R.C. §1034. This is the "buy up-roll over" rule. It encourages the purchase of ever more expensive housing, although among the general population its impact is unknown.

However, when the taxpayer is able to take advantage of the buy up-roll over rule of §1034, the tax on the nonrecognized gain is deferred, not forgiven. It is deferred to the time when the taxpayer sells a principal residence and does not buy up, but then is taxed only to the extent that the basis of the new residence is less than the sales price of the old. Meanwhile the unrecognized gain on the interim transactions is used to serially reduce the basis of each successive residence purchased. Rier, Tax Ideas: Deferral of Gain on Sale of Former Residence: Exploring All the Options, 19 Real Est. L.J. 61 (1990).

Thus when O buys a residence in Blackacre for $100,000, sells it three years later for $200,000, then buys another residence for $250,000, the gain of $100,000 on the sale of the first property goes unrecognized under §1034. However, the initial basis of the second residence is $150,000 (ignoring closing costs and other adjustments), not $250,000. If the second residence is sold for $350,000 several years later, then the gain of $200,000 ($350,000 − $150,000, the adjusted basis) will go unrecognized if the nonrecognition rules of §1034 are again available to the taxpayer.

And so on — until the taxpayer finally comes to a point in his life when larger or more expensive housing is no longer necessary. And then the code has another provision of benefit to the taxpayer who has reached at least age 55: He may claim a one-time exclusion from income, now to a maximum amount of $125,000, for gain realized on the sale of a principal residence. I.R.C. §121. If either spouse of a married couple filing jointly has attained the age of 55, both qualify for this exclusion. This section can be thought of as the Empty Nesters' Protection Act. Thus, in the example in the previous paragraph, only $75,000 of the $200,000 gain realized on the sale of the $350,000 residence would be taxable. Of that $200,000, $125,000 could be excluded from taxable income under §121. (Let's hope that the empty nesters' exclusion provides them with sufficient funds to buy that condominium in Boca Raton.)

# Business or Investment Property and the Code

An owner of business or investment property, like the owner of a residence, has available deductions for mortgage interest (I.R.C. §163) and state and local real property taxes (§164); however, the business or investment owner also can depreciate the property (§167) and deduct repair and maintenance costs (§212(2)) (expenses for the production of income).

## *Depreciation*

Depreciation is the code-given right to write off or recover the cost of a capital asset. Real property other than land qualifies as a capital asset. Thus the purchase price of the property, adjusted to include closing and settlement costs, is allocated between land and improvements, and the amount allocated to improvements is then divided by the appropriate depreciable life (set out in the code) in order to arrive at the annual depreciation deduction amount. I.R.C. §167.

The §167 depreciation deduction is perhaps the greatest incentive to investment in real property in the code. With its benefits, the investor can reap the benefit without the outlay of cash on a dollar-for-dollar basis. With deductions for repairs, mortgage interest, and local taxes, the taxpayer must actually foot the bill before taking the deduction. Not so here.

Consider: The depreciation deduction is a writing off of the cost of the depreciating asset — generally speaking, this asset is the improvements on the property, but not the land, even land underlying the improvement; land is not depreciable. The deduction permits writing the asset off, at an even rate of 3-5 percent a year over a 27-31 year useful life, down to its salvage value. Considering

1. that the deduction will be computed on the basis of the down payment or cash investment in the property plus the mortgage loan amount used to acquire the property,
2. that, as with residential property, the receipt of the loan proceeds was not a taxable event,
3. that the depreciation deduction is available even if the property is actually appreciating in fair market value, and finally
4. that, for both commercial and residential property, the federal tax-man does not take an interest until there is a taxable event, such as a sale or other disposition of the property,

the depreciation deduction can be large in comparison with the cash outlay needed to become entitled to it.

Consider further that the only thing that will make this deduction less valuable is a cash outlay that is uncompensated for by at least an equal deduction. The one thing that threatens its tax value is the repayment of the mortgage loan principal. Deductions are available for mortgage interest, but not for principal; therefore, when the amortization of principal in the mortgage payment is greater, in any one tax year, than the depreciation deduction, the depreciation deduction is "sheltering income" for the owner or investor.

The shelter ends when the repayment of principal exceeds the depreciation; thus in the early years of loan repayment, when the amortized payments are mostly principal, there is shelter; later there is no shelter because then the principal repayment, which is actually money out of pocket, without an entitlement to a correlative deduction, is greater than the depreciation.

The time at which the shelter ends is often called the crossover point. After this point is reached, the investor owner in a tax-driven transaction is likely to sell; the property with other actual economic value for its owner will hold on. Upon the sale or other disposition of appreciated real property used as the basis for a depreciation deduction, the deductions taken over the course of the taxpayer's tenure will be recaptured. IRC §1245. No good thing lasts forever.

In the last 15 years, Congress has expanded and contracted the tax benefit of the depreciation deduction by extending and reducing the term over which the depreciation may be taken. The high watermark, from the taxpayer's perspective, was reached in 1981; the tax act of that year had the shortest periods on which to base depreciation calculations, so the tax benefit was then the greatest. Terms were then 15 years for some properties; now they are sometimes double that.

## Passive Losses

Recently Congress also added rules limiting the deductions resulting in passive losses to deductions taken from income derived from business or investment properties in which the taxpayer has a similar, passive interest. I.R.C. §469 (enacted in 1986). Deductions, or tax credits, of all types had previously been available to offset income from other activities, even to the extent that tax losses were produced. Now deductions or credits from passive business or investment activities will be disallowed to the extent that they en toto exceed income from all passive activities (exclusive of portfolio income), and so losses from passive activities will not be generally available to offset salary, interest, dividend, and active business income. And, no matter how hard the taxpayer works at collecting rent, for example, it remains classified as passive income, and only passive losses can offset it. To the extent that passive losses cannot be deducted in any one tax year, however, they may be carried forward into future years, when they are again available to offset passive income.

## Tax-Free Exchanges

If the taxpayer's existing property is very valuable, a tax-deferred exchange may be what is needed. I.R.C. §1031. Section 1031 provides that no gain (or loss) will be recognized when the owners of like-kind properties, held for business or investment uses, exchange them. Internal Revenue Service regulations about what constitutes a like-kind property are quite liberal. An investor or developer looking to retire might want to exchange property he now owns for property in the Sunbelt, or for property that requires less time and expense to manage but that has an equivalent value. Further, deferred exchanges, in which the properties to be exchanged are not precisely identified at the time of the agreement to exchange properties is executed, are possible.

See, e.g., Starker v. United States, 602 F.2d 1341 (9th Cir. 1979), sanctioned by I.R.C. provisions enacted in the tax act of 1984 (imposing two requirements: identification of the property within 45 days after the agreement and receipt of the title within 180 days).

## *Capital Gains*

The major difference between traditional tax treatment for residential and that for business or investment real property is the availability of capital gain rates for "real property used in his [the taxpayer's] trade or business." I.R.C. §1221.

The Tax Reform Act of 1986 did not abolish this distinction in the code; however, the act made the distinction inconsequential by making the rates for the taxation of ordinary income and capital gains the same. The capital gains provisions were kept as part of the code; the sections were not repealed. Thus, if the rates again diverge, a major portion of the tax law curriculum in the law schools and a large part of the practice of tax law will reemerge. There are tax lawyers in the I.R.S. and in the law firms waiting with their skills honed, if a little rusty, for that event.

# 26

## *Real Estate Planning: Investment Strategy*

What the real estate attorney calls a complex transaction involving an office building, a shopping center, or an industrial facility is in fact a series of somewhat simpler transactions. You need to have a few ground rules.

Financing for the types of projects previously mentioned requires the capital of entities with different investment objectives — some interested in long-term investments, some short-term. Long-term capital is found in pension funds and insurance companies; short-term capital is found in commercial banks. This capital must be put into the hands of those with the managerial skills to construct the project.

Often no one entity will suffice to do the job: partnerships, joint ventures, and corporations will all be used in some fashion. A combination of entities and/or persons to complete the project is referred to as a syndicate, defined here as a combination of investors and managers, capital and skills necessary to complete the project.

For example, the construction of any project has risks that militate in favor of using the limited liability aspects of corporations. But unincorporated persons and entities can insure against risks too, so use of a corporate form is not inevitable. Moreover, a mortgage lender may take a look at the form of foreclosure available in a jurisdiction and decide that this remedy would be too cumbersome, costly, and time-consuming should trouble develop with the project. Being able to seize corporate shares, in which the lender has a security interest under Article 9 of the Uniform Commercial Code, may be an attractive alternative to foreclosure, and a corporate form for the project's backers may be indicated for this reason.

In this and the next chapter, this book examines the problems of assembling capital and constructing a project. First, however, it presents a preliminary look at the syndicator's concerns with getting the project started. From her perspective, then, a few ground rules need to be set out.

# Rule 1: Buy Only What You Need

There are a few rules of thumb with which you should familiarize yourself. Rule 1 is: Buy only what you need to get started. The less cash you put in, the better your return on cash invested will look. This means that the subdivision developer buys the land but obtains vendor financing, with an additional promise from the vendor to subordinate her priority as a mortgagee. The vendor thus becomes a junior mortgagee, subordinating her lien to the construction lender. See, e.g., Guardian Fed. Sav. & Loan Assn. v. Suskind, 265 A.2d 295 (D.C. 1970).

Another example of the "buy what you need" school of development is the office building developer who purchases the parcel (meaning the soil, the surface, and the air space above the surface — the common law version of real property) on which the building will be located, then immediately sells it, and simultaneously leases it back.

Or, the same developer can lease the land (think of this as the surface component of the parcel defined previously) through a land lease, buy only the rights to the air space (hereafter air rights), and build the building. Or if she wants to buy even less, she leases the air rights too. (In the trade, this is what is known as a ground lease: a right to build on leased ground and in leased air.) See J. Whalen, Commercial Ground Leases 1-2 (1989) (this book contains a useful introduction to ground leases in its first chapter, id. at 1-21). Or, she buys the air rights, then sells them to a third party, who leases them back to her so that she can build.

# A Comment on Ground Lease Negotiations

What sort of motives are involved when parties negotiate the terms of a ground lease? The holder of the fee simple title to the ground, the landlord, may wish to receive income from land that has appreciated, or that she believes will appreciate, greatly in value, but is not yet willing to pay the taxable gain that would be recognized upon a sale of the property. (She may, for example, be near retirement and want a less labor-intensive involvement in the real estate market; she may even be thinking of the lease as an estate planning device, planning to use it as a way of passing the property to her heirs, who can receive it with a stepped-up basis; or she may have no immediate need for liquidity.) The lease preserves her capital asset.

The prospective developer and tenant, on the other hand, wants to own enough property rights to permit her to exercise her managerial and organizational skills. She will also want to limit the recourse of the landlord to the business she organizes within the leased premises and steer clear of putting her personal assets at risk. She wants the lease to be "nonrecourse" except as to the business conducted on the leased premises. Probably, as to the landlord, her request for a nonrecourse lease fits with the landlord's reliance on the cash flow from the project, rather than the personal credit and assets of the tenant, as the basis for making a decision to lease. The tenant will bargain hard for freedom to arrange for financing, including perhaps the right to subordinate the lease to later mortgage liens, and for the right to assign the lease. Will the landlord want to restrict such rights and bargain just as hard the other way? The landlord wouldn't push too hard for such restrictions. Often she doesn't have much incentive to do so, but even if she did, the landlord who involves herself in project decisions runs into the rule in a majority of states that, when a tenant acts as an agent for the landlord who requires or authorizes improvements on the leased premises, a mechanic's lien will attach to the fee simple title; without some affirmative action on the landlord's part, however, a mechanic's lien that is filed because of the actions of the tenant will not attach to the fee. Kobren, Three Perspectives on Ground Lease Negotiations, 19 Real Est. L.J. 40, 50 (1990).

This lease must be drawn up, however, with an eye to make it possible to finance with a construction, and later a permanent mortgage lender. Those lenders may even be in on the negotiations, insisting that they have the right to step in to cure defaults, etc., and to prevent the lease from being forfeited. Like the landlord, the lenders will look primarily to the project's cash flow to repay their loans.

Let's use the office building developer for some further elaboration of the "buy what you need" rule. After you have divided the surface and the air space into different "parcels," think about how the developer might deal with each parcel. Each can be bought outright; bought, then mortgaged; sold and leased back; or leased outright.

Consider the air rights as one parcel. It can be physically subdivided; the condominium regime is an example of such a subdivision. But that can't happen until the building is up; meanwhile, the developer will need to have capital sufficient to carry her to the point of sale of the condominium units.

Meanwhile, it can also be "subdivided" along a time line — split into a present and a future interest. The present interest is the right to possession, given in leases to occupants. The future right is the right to manage the possession of the property as all the present rights or leases expire; it is the landlord's reversion. (This split is the invention not of a lawyer, but of a developer, William Zeckendorf, short on cash for one of his early New York projects.) For example, in any office building lease, the tenant pays for two things of value: (1) the present right to occupy, and (2) the cost to the landlord of postponing the latter's own possession to a future date. These things can be separated; that is, the income stream from the property can be divided into two parts, depending on the aims of patient or impatient investors. Once separated, they can be used as collateral for two separate mortgages, in advance of receipt of the income from the building.

Consider two identical office buildings, each with a single tenant of equal creditworthiness. In Building One, the lease has 3 years to run, but was negotiated 12 years ago and brings in $100,000 in rent annually. Building Two fetches $200,000 in rent from a lease negotiated last year but that has 14 years to run. If the reversion is mortgaged, Building Two will fetch relatively little, while Building One will fetch a lot more; if the present right to occupy is mortgaged, the reverse is true.

Different investors have different aims. One may be interested in the long term; her money will be "patient"; she can accept the benefits of the ground lease. (Pension funds and insurance companies are examples.) She will become the lessor of the ground lease. An investor with less patience will become the holder of the reversion in the air rights. (Savings banks are examples.) And an investor with even less patience (defined here as interested in shorter term investments) will become the recipient of that portion of the income stream representing the present right to occupy, which can fluctuate as individual leases in the building are negotiated.

One further iteration. What if she buys the ground and the air, then sells the air, leases it back, then mortgages the ground before she builds the building? Sells the ground, leases it back, then mortgages the air before she builds the building? The possible combinations are numerous.

How does the building stay legally attached to the land if the mortgagee of the ground lease could foreclose and wipe out inferior (junior) interests, such as the construction mortgagee's lien? One method is a subordination agreement. Another answer lies in exploring the components of the ground lease. It transfers a right to possession to the lessee for a term; that right might include the nonpossessory right to create an interest that attaches the building to the land — an easement of access, or a covenant that attaches to the lease and runs with it, to bind the successors of the ground lessor.

## Rule 1a: Borrow Only What You Need

If there is an existing mortgage on the premises to be purchased and a developer can assume this mortgage, she may be wise to do so. If the property is mortgaged at a low rate of interest, the vendor is willing to remain liable on the existing mortgage, and that mortgage will not be accelerated upon the sale of the property, then the purchaser may be able to use a technique called "wraparound" financing.

This technique requires three documents and works in the following way: First, the vendor gives purchaser a deed, in which purchaser takes title subject to the vendor's existing, low-interest rate mortgage. Second, the purchaser gives the vendor some or all of the value of the vendor's equity in the property and also gives the vendor a purchase money mortgage; this mortgage has a principal face amount based on the current fair market value of the property. Thus the vendor has loaned nothing but has received the benefit of making a mortgage loan for a relatively large amount, and the purchaser pays at the current rate of interest on the wraparound mortgage but has put down relatively little cash and, in effect, has borrowed the credit-worthiness of her vendor. In a third document, the vendor agrees, by contract, to continue to pay off her existing mortgage and pockets the float — the difference between what she receives on the wraparound payments and what she owes on her existing mortgage loan.

The wraparound note and mortgage is in effect a type of junior financing. It can be used when second mortgages or deeds of trust are only available at high rates of interest. It is sometimes called the all-inclusive loan and has been used in this country since the 1930s. (It originated in Canada.) It can be used both as a purchase and sale device, as well as a technique for refinancing.

# Rule 2: Use Someone Else's Money

Why not? Some lenders make it their business to give it to you. In a commercial transaction, the principal of the loan is larger than in a normal residential transaction; concomitantly, the number of lenders available to make these larger loans is smaller. See Charing Cross Corp. v. Comfed Mortgage Co., Inc., 25 Mass. App. 924, 516 N.E.2d 1178 (1987). Not only are the loans larger, the loan to value ratios are also larger, and once familiar with the world of commercial lending, a lender may tend to seek larger loans within this universe of transactions because the administrative costs are constant over the bulk of commercial loans. Moreover, there is a panache to making the largest loans; being the mortgagee of the Sears Tower, the TransAmerica Building, or the World Trade Center has a value to the lender involved. There is also a certain panache in making certain types of loans: shopping malls, Texas office buildings, and Los Angeles shopping centers have all had their time basking in the sun of lender approvals.

A higher percentage of debt to fair market value is available in real property investments than is available elsewhere, in other forms of invest-ments. This percentage is sometimes called leverage (although this term is used in a slightly different way when talking about "leveraged depreciation"; see infra, page 368). Leverage is valuable because it permits a developer to control large properties with small amounts of cash investments. This in turn reduces her risk if nonrecourse mortgages are used. Such mortgages are common in commercial lending, both for business and tax reasons. High leverage also increases the developer's pretax return on the cash she does invest, as well as providing her with noncash expenses, such as depreciation, resulting in a post-tax "shelter" for her cash flow.

# EXAMPLES AND EXPLANATIONS

1a. You have found a parcel of land on which small storekeepers rent space but toward which the financial district of a city is moving. O purchased the land with its improvements two years ago for $2 million, but the land, if improved with a ten-story office building "constructed to the limit of the zoning envelope" for the land, would be worth $10 million. Construction costs for the building are about $8 million dollars. C is willing to provide the $8 million for these costs.

O purchased the land with $100,000 down and financed the balance with a mortgage for $1.9 million, at 9 percent for 20 years, with M. After two years, the mortgage has an outstanding balance of $1.875 million; it is, in the jargon, "paid down" only a little.

You find you can purchase the property for $2.5 million dollars. In the two years that O has owned the property, interest rates have risen to 12 percent. What should you do?

**Explanation:** You have two options. You can first attempt to convince M to subordinate her mortgage lien to C's; or, second, convince C to provide you with a wraparound mortgage, in which you agree (by covenant or in a sidebar contract) to continue to pay off M's loan. (The wraparound loan is discussed in more detail in Chapter 30 on construction loans.) Either way you will be using both M and C's money, not your own. However, each lender has risks, for which you probably will have to compensate them as well as provide legal protection. What sorts of protection do you foresee the lenders requesting? How will you respond to their requests?

1b. Still, as things stand, you will have to come up with cash to buy out O's equity in the property — to the tune of $625,000. How can you avoid this?

**Explanation:** By renting the property with a ground lease for your project. O will continue to own the property, but you can demolish the stores and construct your building with the proceeds of C's loan. This lease might contain an option to buy the lessor's property at some future date and following some specified procedure, but meanwhile you buy only what you can afford and rent the rest. Again, however, C will need to know that you will continue to pay the rent to O and that, if you don't, C can step into your shoes and cure any default in the lease.

By applying the two principles formulated thus far, the project that looks just beyond your financial reach can be made feasible.

# Rule 3: Be Skeptical

## *Examining the Setup for Rental Property*

The third rule of thumb in making real estate investments is be skeptical. Every setup (sometimes also called a pro forma) is a statement of income and expenses. Today the use of personal computers and their attendant software enable any user to produce elaborate and professional looking setups. This is all the more reason to look closely at this document. A setup may be just that! See Martin, Nine Abuses Common in Pro Forma Cash Flow Projections, 18 Real Est. Rev. 20 (Fall 1988).

A setup may be seen as a series of graphs with two axes. It has a vertical x-axis, that provides details of income and expenses in any one year. It also has a horizontal y-axis, that provides a series of annual statements and predictions for each item of income and expenses, year by year, until the property is scheduled for sale. Thus analysis of any one year moves down one of the x-axes with the setup, while moving along one of the y-axes provides a comparison of the same income or expense item over several years.

1. In studying a set-up look first for automatic increases in (say) rental income. If it increases at 5 percent a year, that is a good indication that a lease-by-lease analysis has not been done. If the leases are too long, they will limit income growth; if too short, they make income flow uncertain. A lease-by-lease analysis may not show rent concessions as, for example, when a lessee has rent abated for the first four months after moving in or has rent abated every January. Further inquiry of the tenants will show these concessions, and an estoppel letter from them will be necessary to make sure that the inquiries produce the truth.

However, no lease-by-lease analysis will show the credit rating of the tenant. A high rent may be charged a tenant whose credit rating is low, thus making the setup look good, when in fact the income flow is unstable. On the other hand, a lower rent may be appropriate when the tenant's credit rating is higher.

2. In the situations contrasted in the previous paragraph, it would be inappropriate for a lender to use a debt service ratio (comparing income to debt) in a fashion blind to the credit ratings of the tenants. A higher loan principal might be justified by the blind use of the ratio, but the possibility of default might be greater too.

Another example. If the building is a small one, the usual rules of thumb on vacancy rates for rental real property investors may not apply. A large apartment building may properly be assigned a vacancy rate of 5 percent — that is, 5 out of every 100 units will likely be vacant at any one time. However, if the building has only 4 units in it, the rate will be 75 percent, 50 percent, or 25 percent, depending on the number of vacant units.

At any rate, applying a 5 percent rate to such a building is a meaningless gesture. And, in a single tenanted building, a vacancy rate is meaningless.

3. Expenses exceed income in the long-term. That is, expenses rise in older buildings as they age. Spending 40 cents of expenses for each dollar over the first 10 years, an owner can count on double that if the building is over 30-40 years old.

For example, if you know that the ratio of expenses to net operating income (before mortgage payments are made) is .396 for the first 10 years, and then .571 for the second 10 years, then if expenses are estimated to grow at 5 percent a year, what should the expected income growth look like?

$$[.396 \times 1.05^{10}] = .677$$

If .677 has to be .571 of income in 10 years, then

$$\frac{.677}{.571} = \$1.19$$

Or, a dollar of expenses in 10 years will produce $1.19 of income. So income of $1.00 today must grow at a 2 to 3 percent annual rate to keep pace with rising expenses.

4. Collection losses, leasing commissions, and the value of tenant improvements should be computed into the setup. Any noncash, imputed income should be deducted as well. (Remember, however, that imputed income can be added in later, when the tax benefits are computed.)

5. The longer the y-axis for any item, the less reliable it is likely to be because it is more prediction than fact. However, the longer the y-axis in general, the greater the resale value (sometimes called the recapitalization rate) will be because the property will have time to appreciate. If the investment requires the recapitalization to be profitable, then particular attention must be paid to the method used to compute the resale value. How tied to known market facts is it?

Examine now the setup analysis for the office building discussed previously:

### Setup or Pro Forma Analysis

| | | |
|---|---|---|
| Income | | |
| Floors 2-10 (office) ($16,000 monthly/floor) | $144,000 | |
| First floor (commercial) (monthly) | +17,500 | |
| | $161,500 | |
| | ×12 | |
| Total annual income | | $1,938,000 |
| Vacancy rate (at 5%) allowance | | −100,000 |
| | | $1,838,000 |

Operating costs and expenses

| | |
|---|---|
| real estate taxes | $500,000 |
| utilities | 75,000 |
| janitorial | 60,000 |
| insurance | 80,000 |
| repairs (at 5%) | 100,000 |
| management (at 5%) | + 100,000 |
| | $915,000 |
| Net before financing | $923,000 |

Having this much information, you should now (1) determine the reasonableness of the assumptions behind these numbers, and (2) do the further calculations to determine whether the project is a worthwhile one. What do you say?

## The Difference between Income and Cash Flow

After you have skeptically examined all of the components of the income flow that a property will generate, you may well find that in the early years of a project, there will be negative (income) or losses. The Internal Revenue Code recognizes this fact and provides a way of generating a "cash flow" when the income stream is negative. So after tearing down the income stream depicted in the setup, your next task is to find out if the benefits conferred by the code provide enough benefits to turn the negative income into a positive cash flow. See, e.g., Mead v. Borough of Fort Lee, 170 N.J. Super. 167, 406 A.2d 177, cert. denied, 82 N.J. 263, 412 A.2d 770 (App. Div. 1979).

These benefits typically will be three in number: (1) the deduction for mortgage interest payments (see I.R.C. §163), (2) the deduction for state and local taxes on the property (I.R.C. §164), and (3) the deduction for depreciation (I.R.C. §§167-168). Together, these provide an amount of deduction that "shelter" a taxpayer's income to the extent the deductions reduce the tax liability of the developer. If the deductions add up to "D," then the tax savings will be D × b%, where b is the tax bracket in which the taxpayer finds herself. Thus if federal income tax is computed at the 28 percent rate, D × .28 is the amount of the tax benefit that may change the negative income or loss into a positive cash flow.

Of these three types of deductions, the depreciation deduction is particularly important. It is true shelter for income because, unlike the other deductions mentioned, it involves no cash outlay by the taxpayer. The others do: A taxpayer has to pay the mortgage interest to the lender before she can take the deduction; she has to pay the tax man before she can deduct the amount of the taxes. She does not have to pay out to anybody before she can take the depreciation deduction. Moreover, the amount of the deduction is computed as a percentage of her investment in the property plus the amount of her mortgage on it. This is leveraged depreciation. Kronke, How to Calculate Real Estate Return on Investment, 2 Real Est. Rev. (No. 4) 105 (1973).

Thus it is often said that while the depreciation deduction is more than the mortgage and tax deduction, the sheltering of income continues, and the taxpayer should retain the property. Once it is less, the shelter is over, and the taxpayer should sell the property — all this assumes, of course, that the deal is a tax-driven one and that the property is not valuable for some other reason.

Some types of development are deemed particularly worthy of a tax subsidy. For example, if the property is a certified historic structure being rehabilitated, or low- or moderate-income housing, tax benefits in the form of tax credits are available in the code as well. These credits are given in addition to the ones already described. See I.R.C. §469.

A credit is better than a deduction. The latter is an amount subtracted from income to determine the amount of taxable income; the credit is a percentage of taxable income subtracted from the tax liability once computed.

Why is the resulting number labeled the "cash flow" and not income? Because it is money saved, not money given to the taxpayer. It is not cash in hand; rather, it is a subsidy within the code, but not a direct payment to the taxpayer. Thus the income generated by a project is the measure of the amount of money in the investor's pocket before federal income taxes are paid; cash flow is the measure of the amount of money in an investor's pocket after taxes.

This distinction between income and cash flow is a vital one because the real property development that breaks even or goes into the black only after taxes is said to be tax-driven. The best deals are the ones that make economic sense: their profit levels are positive to begin with and are only enhanced by the tax benefits. Guess which transactions are *not* widely available for investment and which transactions are syndicated through some investment entity or in some sense "go public"?

# Nonrecourse Mortgages

Much commercial mortgage lending today is conducted through the use of documents in which the mortgagor has no personal liability on the loan; the property alone is security for the loan. Thus it is said that the mortgage loan is nonrecourse and the mortgage in rem. This is usually accomplished with a covenant in the note. See, e.g., Bankers Credit Serv. of Vermont, Inc. v. Dorsch, 231 Va. 273, 343 S.E.2d 339 (1986). This covenant is to the effect that the noteholder covenants not to sue the maker, waives any rights to a deficiency judgment after foreclosure, and generally waives her rights against the mortgagor personally.

The covenant is also accompanied by statements to the effect that the mortgagor expressly only secures the loan with the property and does not incur personal liability. The objective of the covenant is to limit the mortgagee to foreclosure as the exclusive remedy for defaults in payment, as well as to limit her ability to receive insurance proceeds, condemnation awards, or an assignment of the leases and/or rents from the property. The covenant also usually states that the intention of the parties is not to release or discharge the debt.

Why is the last statement necessary? Because in some jurisdictions, there may be a question as to the validity of such a "mortgage." Remember that a mortgage is usually regarded as an agreement ancillary to the debt, so that if there is no personal liability, hence in some sense no debt, there is nothing to which the mortgage can attach. How sensible is such an argument? Not very. If the lack of any personal liability were to mean the lack of in rem liability, why use a mortgage? The parties should not be presumed to have used a superfluous document. If both types of liabilities are removed, the mortgagee can hardly see her way clear to do the deal. Indeed, the mortgagor has then been unjustly enriched and the mortgagee unreasonably impoverished. Would a court turn away a mortgagee's suit (against a mortgagor denying liability of the property in foreclosure) for unjust enrichment on a theory of quasi-contract? At this late date, too much commercial convention supports the use of nonrecourse mortgages.

Regardless of the presence of a nonrecourse covenant, mortgage lenders are continually searching for ways to feel secure and be assured of repayment of the loan. First, such a covenant may be used in a transaction also using guarantees by the borrower — that is, in transactions in which the borrower personally guarantees the repayment of the mortgage interest or guarantees to make up operating deficits (excluding debt principal) for the business to be conducted on the secured property. Often such guarantees "burn off" or expire when the project reaches a certain level of cash flow or when the top portion of the loan is repaid. St. Claire, Nonrecourse Debt Transactions: Limitations on Limitations of Liability, 19 Real Est. L.J. 3, 28-29 (1990). Probably in the first instance, and certainly in the second, the Internal Revenue Service would not challenge the nature of the debt as a nonrecourse one. Cf. Overland Park Sav. & Loan Assn. v. Miller, 243 Kan. 730, 763 P.2d 1092 (1988) (holding guarantor liable on nonrecourse debt). Second, a mortgage lender might require the placement of private mortgage insurance to insure repayment of the loan, so that the status of the debt is still secure. Third, a general partner will often offer a personal guarantee, offering to be treated as personally liable, for the nonrecourse debt of the partnership. Nonrecourse covenants may also be drafted so that they do not apply when the mortgagor commits fraud, is found to have made a mispresentation on the loan application, or diverts loan proceeds to other projects or receives rents after a default activating an assignment of rents clause. Cf. In re Mills, 841 F.2d 902 (9th Cir. 1988) (interpreting bad faith waste as not barred by California antideficiency statute), and Cornelison v. Kornbluth, 15 Cal. 3d 590, 542 P.2d 981, 125 Cal. Rptr. 557 (1975) (holding that this statute bars mortgagee's suit for waste involving financial difficulties of mortgagor, but not a suit for caused by the bad faith actions of the mortgagor).

# EXAMPLES AND EXPLANATIONS

2. What if a title insurer misses a mechanic's lien in the course of its title search, pays off the lien to satisfy a claim under its policy, and then sues the nonrecourse mortgagor for the lien amount?

**Explanation:**  Judgment for the mortgagor. The prohibition on the deficiency judgment in the insured mortgage precludes suit by the title company, as the subrogee of the rights of the insured mortgagee, from suing to recoup the amount of the claim based on the mechanic's lien. Berks Title Ins. Co. v. Haendiges, 772 F.2d 278 (6th Cir. 1985).

3. Nonrecourse mortgages have several types of business uses. Can you identify situations in which they are likely to be used?

**Explanation:**   Nonrecourse mortgages are likely to be used in speculative markets, particularly markets in danger of a downturn. In the 1930s, for example, when the banks and the government acquired many properties in foreclosure, nonrecourse covenants in a mortgage note were used to encourage potential purchasers to assume ownership, which many would do only if the risk of a further downturn in the economy was assumed by the vendor. Another speculative market in which such covenants are used is oil and gas drilling; financing documents contain such covenants to encourage the wildcatter to develop such properties.

Nonrecourse covenants are often used in three other situations: (1) when the parties to a mortgage transaction have had no prior dealings with each other, (2) when the value of the real property taken as security for a loan is in dispute (its use here permits the transaction to stay open-ended as to the fair market value, and (3) when a nonrecourse covenant is traded in exchange for an equity participation by the lender.

In the context of a loan to a limited partnership, the nonrecourse nature of the mortgage is necessary if the limited partners are to be able to attain a tax basis in the secured property that includes a pro rated amount of the mortgage. The explanation goes something like this: Limited partners are not typically liable for partnership losses, so when personally liable for mortgage loans, the increased basis is unavailable. However, if no partner, general or limited, is liable personally, all are eligible for the increase in basis. The lack of a risk of loss adds to the certainty of their interest, against which depreciation and deductions may be taken by each partner pro rata. See I.R.C. §752(a)(2) and regulations issued under authority of this section.

# 27

## Tax Events: Tufts *and* Lyon

## Basis Problems: Receipt and Cancellation of Mortgage Debt

The receipt of mortgage loan proceeds is not usually a taxable event; the recipient borrower is not taxed upon the disbursement of the loan because there is an obligation to repay it. His balance sheet is not enriched because the receipt of the proceeds is balanced by the obligation to repay them. There is symmetry to this view. Moreover, if at some later time, there is a sale of the property, the taxpayer recovers his initial investment in the property free of any tax. However, over and above that recovery, there is a taxable event, and the gain or loss realized or recognized is the difference between the "amount realized" on the sale and the adjusted basis of the taxpayer-owner of the property. I.R.C. §1001(a).

To calculate a taxpayer's adjusted basis, one must first compute his basis in real property. It is typically the cost of the property — the purchase price plus the costs of acquisition, or closing and settlement costs. This is sometimes called the cost, initial, or unadjusted basis of a taxpayer. In contrast, a taxpayer's adjusted basis is the initial basis, reduced by the amounts to take account of depreciation and other tax benefits, and/or increased to reflect improvements or other infusions of capital into the property (for example, to reflect the financing costs of modernizing or adding onto it from time to time).

Moreover, if a mortgagor is forgiven the obligation to repay all or part of the loan, then the Internal Revenue Service also considers that this is a taxable event. The issue is the "amount realized" when the debt is cancelled for the original mortgagor and assumed by the purchaser or other transferee of the property. Consider the following case on this issue. It is one of the cornerstones of the real estate industry.

# Commissioner of Internal Revenue v. Tufts[1]

The Facts: A taxpayer became a general partner with others in a project for the construction of a garden apartment complex in the suburbs of Dallas, Texas. Originally, a builder (Clark Pelt) and his wholly owned corporation formed a general partnership for the purpose of constructing the apartments. Later, the taxpayer and three other "relatives and friends" of Pelt were made general partners too. The partners contributed very modestly in cash to the project, which was highly leveraged — the loan to value ratio was close to 100 percent and a $1.8 million nonrecourse note and mortgage financed the project. The local economy went into decline, and the income from the project was never sufficient to cover the payments on the mortgage. Little if any of the outstanding principal of the mortgage was paid off.

The partners held on for three years, and in each year they took mortgage interest, local tax, and depreciation deductions on the project. After three years, their adjusted basis was $1.45 million. They then sold the property. The purchaser paid nothing down, but "assumed" the outstanding mortgage debt. At the time of the sale, the property was worth $1.4 million. The taxpayer then declared a $50,000 loss — the difference between $1.45 and $1.40 million. The IRS claimed that they had a gain of more than $350,000. This gain was the difference between the outstanding mortgage balance assumed by the purchaser and the adjusted basis of the partnership in the project.

The Authorities: In Crane v. Commissioner, 331 U.S. 1 (1947), the Supreme Court held that Beulah Crane, a taxpayer who had inherited an apartment house from her husband, attempted to run it for eight years, but then sold it for $3000 plus the purchaser's promise to assume the outstanding mortgage on the property, "must include the unpaid balance of the mortgage in the computation of the amount the taxpayer realized on the sale." *Tufts,* supra, at 302. Beulah declared that she had a gain of just $3000 and that she had just sold her "boot" — the tax term for her equity in the property in excess of the outstanding mortgage debt.

The Court found Beulah Crane's position "absurd." It used two theories to destroy Beulah Crane's position. First, she had been entitled to reduce her basis in the apartment house from the amount of cash she invested plus the amount of the mortgage. When she sold, tax symmetry required that the amount realized be computed in the same manner, that is, by including the outstanding amount of the mortgage. This is the so-called tax benefit theory of *Crane.* Its underlying rationale is that taking the tax benefits of ownership requires that, upon disposition of the property, the taxpayer not suddenly switch to an accounting method based on a later-computed fair market value. The use of this theory was good, nay great, news for real

---

1. 461 U.S. 300 (1983), noted in 45 U. Pitt. L. Rev. 803 (1984), 18 Ga. L. Rev. 1 (1983).

property investors: They found out that implicitly the Court validated their depreciation computations based not on their actual investments, but on their actual investments plus the amount of the mortgages carried by their project.

Second, Beulah Crane received an economic benefit when she was released from the obligation to repay the mortgage loan. See Anderson, Federal Income Tax Treatment of Non-Recourse Debt, 82 Colum. L. Rev. 1498 (1982). This economic benefit is rooted in the notion that, with the value of the property equal (as in *Crane*) or greater than the amount of the outstanding mortgage, the taxpayer will act to avoid the mortgagee's taking the property by foreclosure; that is, it is to the economic benefit of the mortgagor to avoid the mortgagee's using its foreclosure remedy. Thus, even with the property subject to a nonrecourse mortgage, a taxpayer will treat the debt as if it is a personal obligation and so, when disposing of the property, taxable gain results.

Beulah's property was worth about a quarter of a million dollars, more than the balance on the outstanding mortgage. The Court added: "Obviously, if the value of the property is less than the amount of the mortgage, a mortgagor who is not personally liable cannot realize a benefit equal to the mortgage. Consequently, a different problem might be encountered where a mortgagor abandoned the property or transferred it subject to the mortgage without receiving boot." This is the famous footnote 37 of the *Crane* opinion. It recites the facts of *Tufts* and, moreover, it seems based on the economic benefit theory of *Crane:* If a nonrecourse mortgage debt is $150,000, and the property securing it is worth $100,000, the mortgagor will get no economic benefit from retaining the property if he can walk away from it and cancel a $150,000 debt by letting the mortgagee have a $100,000 property on which to foreclose.

In the *Tufts* opinion, the Court said its goodbyes to footnote 37, while reaffirming what it found to be the inner logic and broader rationale of *Crane*, which "teaches that the Commissioner may ignore the non-recourse nature of the obligation in determining the 'amount realized' upon disposition of the encumbered property." 461 U.S. 300, 309 (1983). The "amount realized," a term found in I.R.C. §1001, is the statutory peg on which the Court hangs its hat. The Court emphasizes the relationship between the amount realized and the adjusted tax basis accounting that permitted the *Tufts* taxpayer to realize tax benefits in taking depreciation and other property-related deductions. These adjustments in the tax basis of the property took an initial basis of $1.8 million, down to about $1.45 million, "on the understanding" that upon later disposition of the property, the I.R.S. could recover any gain.

Tax symmetry was again part of the rationale for validating the I.R.S.'s computation of the amount realized. This time, however, the Court downplayed the economic benefit found in the *Crane* opinion and substituted the view that the nonrecourse financing of the project was a "true loan"; that is, the Court focused on the initial soundness of the loan and the partnership's obligation to repay it. Thus, a "true loan" is one that reflects the actual fair market value of the property at the time of the taxpayer's acquisition of it. When later the taxpayer's debt was forgiven, and he had been operating, in the meanwhile, on the same "basis" (absolutely no pun intended) as he has since acquiring the property, the same accounting must be used to compute the amount realized. If the adjusted basis of the taxpayer was then $1.45 million and the $1.8 debt had not been paid down when the loan was forgiven by a purchaser's assumption of it, then the difference is the "amount realized."

Thus the taxpayer like Tufts, who adjusts the basis of a property using the mortgage amount, cannot turn around upon disposition of the property and calculate a loss based on its fair market value when the mortgage debt is cancelled. If fair market value is no part of the original calculation, it cannot be part of the second.

This is also realistic. After all, if the partnership did not repay, would it continue to do business? No, for then, what lender would deal with it? *Tufts* then emphasizes the tax benefit theory of *Crane,* along with the idea of a true loan — one reflecting market realities when made.

If the implicit holding of *Crane* was good news for investors, its economic benefit theory had them troubled. The reason for worry was that the benefit could be computed after the transaction was completed — after the taking of title, when all the documents embodying the bargain were already negotiated. In contrast, the "true loan" theory relied on the obligation to repay. That was fixed at the outset of the transaction, at the closing. Thus *Tufts* is a holding that gives tax certainty to the documents in which the investor's bargain is struck. Knowing that the tax consequences of a bargain are clear at the outset is great news for an investor; he can then calculate his bargain by including them. For the investor, *Tufts* is better news than was *Crane,* good as it was.

And *Tufts* sounded another, basic note of reassurance: to the effect that nonrecourse debt may constitute part of a taxpayer's basis in real property under I.R.C. §167, so long as the fair market value of the secured property reasonably approximates the amount of the debt. This is the way *Tufts* has been used as authority. See, e.g., Estate of Barron v. Commissioner, 798 F.2d 65, 68 (2d Cir. 1986). Thus losses and depreciation may be calculated on the amount actually invested in the property in cash, plus the amount of the mortgage loan for the property. In this way real property is able to generate "shelter" — the generation of tax benefits large in comparison with the cash investment made. Recall that the I.R.S. didn't question the *Tufts* taxpayers taking the tax benefit of the depreciation and using it to offset their other income, even when they did not make any capital contributions to the partnership. They were "sheltering" this other income by participating in the partnership. See generally Allan v. Commissioner, 856 F.2d 1169, 1172-1174 (8th Cir. 1988).

The other reassuring, and implicit, holding of *Tufts* was its validation of Clark Pelt's transfer to his "relatives and friends" of the tax benefits of his apartment project. The I.R.S. did not question the legitimacy of such a deal.

Allowing a developer to "sell" his tax benefits by forming a partnership can be, for the cash-strapped developer, quite a deal.

Justice O'Connor concurred in the result in *Tufts*, but thought that she had a better method for accounting for the taxpayer's gain. She would have treated the disposition transaction in *Tufts* as two transactions: first, a real property transaction, traditionally the generator of capital gains (or losses, as the case may be); and second, as the forgiveness and cancellation of debt, which results in ordinary income. Under the facts of *Tufts,* there was no capital gain and there may have been a capital loss in the property transaction, but in the second, debt transaction, the cancellation of the taxpayer's debt certainly results in ordinary income of over $350,000. O'Connor prefers this bifurcation of the taxpayer's exit transaction, but comes to her result as an expression of *Crane* as well as Treasury regulations following it.

What is the initial tax basis for the purchaser of the property securing the debt in *Tufts*? All that has been said so far assumes that an investor will never be called on by the IRS to show that his interest is not a sham or that his mortgage included in basis is not based on market realities. See, e.g., Deegan v. Commissioner, 787 F.2d 825, 827 (2d Cir. 1986) (holding that a taxpayer may not include in his basis any liability that for any economic reason is not genuine debt). Some semblance of a close mortgage market relationship should be maintained, or else the Commissioner will seek to show, for example, that the mortgage is really the functional equivalent of some other type of transaction and therefore not a "true loan."

In this regard, see Estate of Franklin v. Commissioner, 544 F.2d 1045 (9th Cir. 1976) (holding that a sale-leaseback transaction, with a fixed re-purchase price and in which only $75,000 changed hands when the property was worth reputedly $1.2 million, was functionally an option to purchase). The *Franklin* opinion emboldened the incoming Carter Administration to propose I.R.C. regulations that would have required partnerships to show the Commissioner that the mortgaged value of their assets is not speculative. Those regulations died in a firestorm of protest by real property investors. Nonetheless, the opinion remains as a reminder that the investor abusing the code can be called to account; it does, however, use a postclosing method of analysis, which is implicitly disapproved by the Court's use of the true loan rationale in the *Tufts* opinion.

Cases like *Tufts* teach that a taxpayer disposing of property has to treat the amount realized on the sale or other exit transaction in a way similar to its treatment at the start and during his ownership. Tax symmetry requires this. Cases like *Franklin* tell us that upon acquisition, however, a taxpayer may be called on to show to the I.R.S. that the value of the property reflected in its tax treatment after purchase reflects its actual fair market value at the date of acquisition. Tax realism requires this. Were it otherwise, in a declining market for real property, a taxpayer in trouble with his mortgage lender could dispose of the secured property for an inflated value if he could find some high-bracket or high-income taxpayer who can use the high basis to shelter other income. Rather, each new owner must show that the debt he "assumes" is realistically secured by the property. Thus, the purchaser of the garden apartments in *Tufts* must show the I.R.S. that the debt assumed and the property securing the debt are in synch; otherwise, his initial basis (on which his depreciation will be computed for his federal income tax returns) will be its fair market value at the time of his acquisition.

# EXAMPLES AND EXPLANATIONS

1. A developer purchases Blackacre, with a fair market value of $1.4 million. It takes out a 90 percent note and nonrecourse mortgage for $1.26 million. It pays the loan down to $1.15 million and adjusts its basis in the property to $.9 million. The fair market value of the property declines to $1 million. Now comes default and foreclosure: At the foreclosure sale, the property is sold for $1 million. What is the developer's tax liability? How is this case different from *Tufts*? Does the difference (if any) matter?

**Explanation:** It is $.25 million. Does the fact that the basis is below the fair market value matter? No, although the distinction between what might be capital gain ($1.0 − .9 = $.1 million) and what might be ordinary income ($1.15 − $1.0 = $.15 million) is now clearer. Justice O'Connor, in her concurring opinion in *Tufts,* suggested that this distinction makes sense, but the majority opinion did not adopt it. The taxation of what O'Connor would call the ordinary income liability of the taxpayer, on the $.15 million, is settled after *Tufts*.

2. Same facts as in the previous example, but instead of a foreclosure sale, the developer gives the lender a deed in lieu of foreclosure. The fair market value of Blackacre when the deed is executed and delivered is $1 million. What is the developer's tax liability?

**Explanation:** The very same. *Crane* comes very close to the situation of a deed in lieu, and there is little ground to distinguish this problem from that case. See Rev. Rul. 90-16, 1990-8 I.R.B. 5.

# The Sale-Leaseback

V gives a deed to Blackacre to P, who at the moment he accepts the deed, becomes a lessor and gives V back a lease. Thus V becomes a lessee. Possession of the property does not change hands. V continues as the "owner," now in possession of the premises as a tenant, often with an option to repurchase the title in the future. What are the legal consequences of these two transactions? First, the P-lessor becomes the titleholder. He gets to depreciate the property. That, in itself, is quite a tax benefit.

As a general proposition, the I.R.S. does not like to see a market for tax benefits develop. If one taxpayer decided to collect all of the tax benefits of his neighbors and claim them on his own return, the I.R.S. would have some extremely negative things to say about the preparation of his tax forms during any audit. (Imagine the taxpayer saying to his neighbor: "Hi! I see you lost some valuable bushes on your lawn. Were you planning to take that loss as a tax deduction this year? If not, can I buy your deduction from you?") If, however, taxpayers do a sale-leaseback transaction, the trade is just as real but perfectly legal. (Or, if as we will see later, parties all come together within a legal entity called a partnership, this type of trading is on just as sound a footing.)

What's wrong with trading this tax benefit, you ask? Someone has to take the deduction, so what does it matter who? The answer is, it doesn't matter if (and this is a very BIG if) both V and P are taxed at the same marginal rates or take the depreciation according to the same schedule. But if this assumption doesn't apply, it does matter from the IRS's perspective, because the sale-leaseback is at the same time a raid on the public treasury.

So, here is the basic, benefit-trading, sale-leaseback. The two transactions take place in close sequence, at the same closing. The advantages to the initial owner involved in the transaction are considerable. Consider:

1. That as a lessee, he has the equivalent of 100 percent loan to value financing; as a mortgagor, he would have to pay a down payment, loan closing costs, and so forth. See generally Fox & Halperin, Tax Considerations in Refinancing Real Estate: The Wrap-Around Mortgage and the Sale and Leaseback, 1 J. Real Est. Tax. 17 (1973).
2. That as a lessee, all payments are deductible as rental business expenses; as a mortgagor, only interest payments are deductible.
3. That as a lessee, he avoids the onerous acceleration clauses found in mortgages. In fact, this may be just one of several protections extended to tenants after the revolution in landlord tenant law that has occurred during the past several decades. As a mortgagor, on the other hand, statutory protections are available in the state foreclosure code, but there is no protection for the owner's built-up equity in the property.

Other differences between using a lease and a mortgage are the following:

| Lease | Mortgage |
| --- | --- |
| Lessor depreciates property. | Mortgagor depreciates property. |
| Usury limits inapplicable. | Usury applicable. |
| Summary process available. | Foreclosure available. |
| Lessor has sublease-assignment controls. | Due on sale clause applies. |

See generally Black, Sale-Leaseback Transactions: Advantages and Disadvantages, 3 Prob. & Prop. 23 (May/June 1989); then, for a more detailed discussion, see Homburger & Andre, Real Estate Sale and Leaseback Transactions and the Risk of Recharacterization in Bankruptcy Proceedings, 24 Real Prop. Prob. & Tr. J. 95, 98-103 (1989).

Look at the following four diagrams of the typical sale and leaseback transaction and think about which lease looks most like a mortgage.

In the first diagram below, recognize that the vendor and the lessee are really the same person, or legal entity, and that the same is true for the purchaser and the lessor. By transferring the title to P, however, they have assigned the tax benefits involved with depreciation of the property also to P.

$$\frac{V^{or}}{L^{ee}} \xrightarrow{\quad deed \quad} \frac{P}{L^{or}}$$
$$\xleftarrow{\quad lease \quad}$$

This first diagram is the basic transaction.

$$\frac{V^{or}}{L^{ee}} \xrightarrow{\quad land\ sale\ K \quad} \frac{P}{L^{or}}$$
$$\xleftarrow{\quad lease \quad}$$

Would the I.R.S. think this second transaction was a sham? Arguably not. Do you see why? What business reasons might a purchaser-lessor have for using this form of the transaction? Taking into account the basic definition of an installment land sale contract, with its long executory period, this form of the transaction might be particularly useful when the purchaser requires the long executory period to set up other aspects of the transaction, such as compliance with the complex regulatory structure of the securities market. Suppose that registration with the Securities and Exchange Commission was necessary if the purchaser was to obtain the purchase price by selling shares in the entity that was to take title to the property.

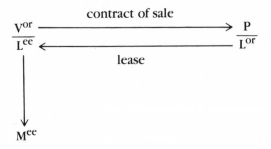

The third diagram presents the facts of Estate of Franklin v. Commissioner, 544 F.2d 1045 (9th Cir. 1976), in which the I.R.S. argued successfully that the transaction was a sham and that the $V^{or}$-P sale and $V^{or}$-$L^{or}$ leaseback to the $L^{ee}$ (also the original $V^{or}$) was, in its two-step totality, really a mortgage transaction.

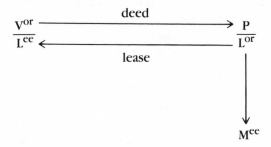

The fourth diagram presents a transaction closely resembling that of the following leading case.

# Frank Lyon Co. v. United States[2]

The Facts: A state-chartered, federally insured commercial bank in Little Rock, Arkansas, wanted to build itself a headquarters office building. It initially proposed to finance the project with bonds, but Arkansas usury limits prevented the bank from bringing the bond to market at current rates. Federal banking regulators also objected to the bank's holding title to all of that real property, but preapproved a sale and leaseback in which (1) the titleholder would be an independent third party, and (2) the bank would have a re-purchase option after the fifteenth year of the leaseback.

Thereafter, after a series of bids to finance the project by several investment bankers and negotiations with several of them, the bank choose Frank Lyon Co., whose principal business was not banking, but rather the retailing of major appliances. Lyon agreed to a rent reduction, accepted a bank counterproposal, and invested $500,000 of its own money in order to get the nod.

After construction was begun, Lyon engaged in a sale and leaseback with the bank and, after that, assumed in its own name a construction note and mortgage, and later a permanent mortgage, for the office building. (Both lenders had preapproved the Frank Lyon Co. as a participant in the transaction.)

That transaction proceeded in at least five steps:

1. Title to the office building was transferred from the bank to Lyon. The bank retained title to the underlying land.

---

2. 435 U.S. 561 (1978).

2.  Lyon assumed the note and mortgage obligations and became personally responsible for payment of the debt that they represented. The debt was further secured by an assignment of Lyon's interest in the lease and the bank subordinated its interest in the ground to the permanent mortgage.
3.  The bank leased a fee simple absolute in the land to Lyon, reserving a ground rent at a nominal level for a 25-year term, but after 25 years, the rent level, starting at $100,000, jumped up in $50,000 increments every fifth year.
4.  Under the leaseback of the building, the rent was just sufficient to pay off the permanent mortgage note as the debt it represented came due over the first 25 years of the lease term; after that, over each five years of the lease, the annual rent was reduced to $300,000 — a 50 percent reduction.
5.  The bank had, in its lease for the building, an option to repurchase the building after the 11th, 15th, 20th, and 25th year of the term, at a fixed price equal to the unpaid, outstanding balance due on the permanent mortgage note, plus Lyon's initial, $500,000 investment, plus 6 percent interest on that investment.

In sum, Lyon held the fee simple to the building and the air rights, the bank held the fee to the land, while Lyon held a lease to the land.

The I.R.S. said that the transaction was a disguised mortgage and denied Lyon a depreciation deduction.[3] The United States District Court found for the taxpayer, the Eighth Circuit reversed (finding for the I.R.S.), and the Supreme Court granted certiorari.

The Court's opinion, authored by Justice Blackmun, assumed that the opinion in the Eighth Circuit, on appeal here, conflicted with an opinion from the Fourth Circuit. See American Realty Trust v. United States, 498 F.2d 1194 (4th Cir. 1974). *American Realty Trust* is a case involving a hotel in Palm Beach, Florida. The hotel was owned by Harry Helmsley. Florida hotels are seasonal with heavy business in the winter, but Harry experienced some poor seasons and his business was cash-poor as a result. He arranged a sale-leaseback of the hotel with a real estate investment trust (for more on these, see page 417, infra). The court upheld the transaction and turned away the I.R.S.'s argument that this was really a mortgage transaction because Helmsley produced evidence of a valid business purpose for the transaction, a purpose found not in the documents, but in the business environment

---

3. The I.R.S. has a choice among two methods for recharacterizing a sale-leaseback. First, it can proceed as it did in *Lyon,* attacking the transaction as a disguised mortgage. Second, it can challenge its validity as an exchange of property under I.R.C. §1031(a). As to the second method, see Leslie Co. v. Commissioner, 539 F.2d 943 (3d Cir. 1976). The second has been the least successful method for the Service.

for Florida hotels. The Fourth Circuit, in other words, looked beyond the documents of the sale and leaseback to validate the transaction.

In contrast, the Eighth Circuit in *Lyon* had looked at the documents alone: the lease consideration was limited; the option prices in the leaseback did not take account of the possibility of appreciation in the fair market value of the bank building, or inflation; the condemnation award provision in the lease reminded the court of provisions found in mortgages; rental payments looked like mortgage payments in level and amount; and the bank controlled disposition of the real property. The Eighth Circuit looked at the documents, while the Fourth looked at the business context in which the documents were drafted. This is the nub of the conflict between the circuits that the Supreme Court opinion in *Lyon* sets out to resolve.

The primary factor validating the transaction was that Lyon was primarily liable on the note and mortgage, first to the construction lender (a commercial bank) and then to the long-term, or permanent, take-out note and mortgage. Thus the sale-leaseback, considered as a whole, was an extension to the bank of Lyon's creditworthiness. What the Court does not say, however, is that when the purchaser-lessor is personally liable for mortgage financing, the sale-leaseback is not a sham. Rather, the opinion goes on to consider additional factors.

Second, Lyon undertook a risk that the rental value of the building would recoup its investment, noting that the decreasing rent under the ground lease would not. That is, the return to Lyon on his initial investment was contingent on the bank's not exercising its option to repurchase in the building lease.

Third, the opinion notes that the I.R.S. is likely to lose little revenue because of a sale-leaseback. Someone will take the depreciation deduction at issue in this case, so what does it matter to the I.R.S. whether it is Worthen Bank or Lyon? That is, the arguments of the I.R.S. seeking to recharacterize a sale-leaseback must overcome an initial preference that the parties be allowed to cast a transaction as they wish, particularly when the Treasury will not likely lose revenue if the Court decides for the taxpayer. If the transaction is a wash, as far as the public treasury is concerned, why should the I.R.S. care to pierce the veil thrown over the deal by the documents used to close the transaction? This suggests that the bank traded its depreciation and mortgage interest deduction to Lyon, in exchange for its rent deduction taken as a business expense; this trade is made in the assumption that if the bank continued to hold the title, it would lease some of the building. If the taxpayers involved in the sale-leaseback are taxed at different marginal rates, however, this trade is not a wash so far as the public treasury is concerned. And if the sale-leaseback is a wash, why do it? Answering this question is what sends the Court's opinion in search of a business purpose for the transaction. If there is a preference that in the tax-wash transaction, the documents control (that is, that the parties to it are to be permitted to structure it the way they see fit); the burden on the government to upset the transaction as documented will be great.

Fourth, the transaction here is not the simplest, two-party type of sale-leaseback, and the opinion makes much of the three-party nature of the transaction. Should that make much difference? See particularly the case of Helvering v. Lazarus Co., 308 U.S. 252 (1939). *Lazarus* was a two-party sale-leaseback. Such a transaction lacks the reality check that the presence of a third-party, institutional mortgage lender provides; otherwise, the sale portion of the transaction may be for an inflated price, and the lease payment insufficient to cover Lyon's mortgage payment liability. This fourth factor is used in this opinion to distinguish the *Lazarus* case. Surely the Court doesn't mean to say that two-party transactions are more likely to be recharacterized than are three-party ones? It must be the reality check rationale that makes the distinction important.

What the court does not emphasize is important too — and it may well be controlling in some jurisdictions when a state court is asked to recharacterize a sale-leaseback as a mortgage. If the lease contained high initial rental payments, which taper off at the end of the term, and the lease permits the lessee to exercise an option to purchase the title for a nominal sum at the end of the term, such a lease can readily be considered a contract of sale for the property. The lessee would be considered less than rational if he did not exercise the option. The lessee would be under an economic compulsion to do so — thus argued the I.R.S., unsuccessfully, in this case.

The Supreme Court's test for the transaction differs considerably from the Eighth Circuit's. The *Lyon* opinion holds:

> [W]here, as here, there is a genuine multiple-party transaction with economic substance which is compelled or encouraged by business or regulatory realities, is imbued with tax-independent considerations, and is not shaped solely by tax avoidance features . . . , the government should honor the allocation of rights and duties effectuated by the parties.

The Court is generous in its holding. Few transactions are not "encouraged" by business motives. Similarly, few transactions will be "solely" driven by the tax code. The facts of *Lyon* make much out of the regulatory necessity for doing the transaction as a sale-leaseback, but the Court suggests that business realities can be just as important. In the course of the opinion, Blackmun seems very impressed by the personal liability of Lyon on the construction and permanent loans, and by the presence of third-party lenders, presumably as a type of reality check on the economics of the deal. This will doubtless encourage third-party loans to finance sale-leaseback purchases. The I.R.S. appears to have been given a high burden of proof for future litigation.

If you think that any one factor is dispositive, read the paragraph of the opinion reprinted below.[4] This reading should free you from the mistake of relying on any one factor.

Still, the holding is capable of two interpretations: (1) the documents control, unless there is no business purpose; or (2) when a business purpose is present, the documents control.

Consider further: If the deal goes sour and litigation results, should damages for loss of the tax benefits be given? What if the vendor-lessee decides that recharacterization as a mortgage is a real possibility under state law? Recall in this connection the low option price in *Lyon*. When the purchaser-lessee is really found to be a mortgagee, he should be forced to foreclose. The vendor-lessee might have this question settled in a cause of action for a declaratory judgment. What would the purchaser-lessor's response be? A breach of contract suit, seeking consequential damages. The purchaser expected that he would obtain a tax benefit, which recharacterization will deprive him of. Many states refuse to include tax benefits either as a component of or as an offset for contract damages. The tax benefit is a matter between the taxpayer and the government, not a matter between the contract parties. But this rule flies in the face of the economic reality that the transfer of tax benefits

---

4. This paragraph recites the factors the court found important: "We . . . find . . . [the Court of Appeals opinion] incompatible with the substance and economic realities of the transaction: the competitive situation as it existed between Worthen [Bank & Trust Co.] and Union National Bank in 1965 and the years immediately following; Worthen's undercapitalization; Worthen's consequent inability, as a matter of legal restraint, to carry its building plans into effect by a conventional mortgage and other borrowing; the additional barriers imposed by the state and federal regulators; the suggestion, forthcoming from the state regulator, that Worthen possess an option to purchase; the requirement, from the federal regulator, that the building be owned by an independent third party; the presence of several finance organizations seriously interested in participating in the transaction and in the resolution of Worthen's problem; the submission of formal proposals by several of those organizations; the bargaining process and period that ensued; the competitiveness of the bidding; the bona fide character of the negotiations; the three-party aspect of the transaction; Lyon's substantiality and its independence from Worthen; the fact that diversification was Lyon's principal motivation; Lyon's being liable alone on the successive notes to City Bank and New York Life; the reasonableness . . . of the rentals and of the option prices; the substantiality of the purchase prices; Lyon's not being engaged generally in the business of financing; the presence of all building depreciation risks on Lyon; the risk, borne by Lyon, that Worthen might default or fail, as other banks have failed; the facts that Worthen could "walk away" from the relationship at the end of the 25-year primary term, and probably would do so if the option price were more than the then-current worth of the building to Worthen; the inescapable fact that if the building lease were not extended, Lyon would be the full owner of the building, free to do with it as it chose; Lyon's liability for the substantial ground rent if Worthen decides not to exercise any of its options to extend; the absence of any understanding between Lyon and Worthen that Worthen would exercise any of the purchase options; the nonfamily and nonprivate nature of the entire transaction; and the absence of any differential in tax rates and of special tax circumstances for one of the parties — all convince us that Lyon has far the better of the case." 431 U.S. at 582-583.

is one feature of the whole transaction. See Harris v. Metropolitan Mall, 112 Wis. 2d 487, 334 N.W.2d 519 (1983), noted in 1985 Wis. L. Rev. 375.

# Some Background for Accountants (Others May Read Too!)

The Financial Standards Accounting Board (FSAB) is an arm of the American Institute of Certified Public Accountants and the trade association regulatory body for certified accounting firms. It is the source of standard accounting procedures for its industry. Over the last several decades, it has permitted accountants to report separately the liabilities of wholly owned subsidiaries of publicly traded corporations. Accounting Principles Board, Op. No. 18, The Equity Method of Accounting for Investments in Common Stock (which permitted non-real estate corporations to report the book value minus outstanding debt as the net assets of the subsidiary on the parent's balance sheet). This encouraged those corporations to hold the title to mortgaged real property in the name of subsidiaries. Thus the debits on a subsidiary's balance sheet were not incorporated into that of the parent corporation. This means of avoiding consolidation of the balance sheets was changed in 1980 by the FSAB's Statement of Financial Accounting Standards No. 94.

One might expect that the corporate reaction to this change in generally accepted accounting procedures would be the increased use of the sale-leaseback as a means of keeping real property mortgage liabilities off a corporation's balance sheet. But the FSAB anticipated this. It issued, in late 1988, stricter accounting standards for sale-leaseback transactions. See FSAB, Statement of Financial Accounting Standards No. 98. Under Statement 98, to avoid being tagged as a corporate liability, a leaseback to a corporation must be an operating rather than a capital lease. An operating lease is a noncapital lease. It is a residual category of leases. A capital lease is one meeting one or more of the following criteria: (1) title to the leased property is transferred to the lessee at the expiration of the term; (2) the lessee has an option to purchase the property at a bargain price; (3) the term of the lease is 75 percent or more of the property's useful economic life; the discounted present value of the minimum lease payments is 90 percent or more of the present fair market value of the property. Farragher & Reinstein, Accounting for Real Estate Sale-Leaseback Transactions, 20 Real Est. Rev. 90, 91 (1990).

Any lease that is not a capital lease is deemed to be an operating lease and can be reported by a corporation's accountants as the rental of property.

The vendor-lessee engaging in a sale-leaseback is a vendor in need of cash. The prudent vendor will use Rule 1, presented at the beginning of this chapter, but he will use it in reverse. He will sell only what he needs to sell: his land, the improvements on it, or both. (Perhaps just selling and leasing back his personal property will do — the weight of sale leaseback reported opinions involve personal property.) So it is legitimate to consider how the transaction will fare in two unexpected forums: first, if it is subjected to an income tax audit by the I.R.S. which might attempt to argue that the two transactions, considered as a whole, are really a disguised mortgage, or, second, if the whole transaction becomes subject to the jurisdiction of a bankruptcy court or trustee.

## More on Sale-Leasebacks: The Bankrupt Lessee

Commercial leases typically provide that upon the insolvency or bankruptcy of the lessee, a default occurs and the lease is automatically terminated. In Queens Boulevard Wine & Liquor Corp. v. Blum, 503 F.2d 202 (2d Cir. 1974), the court held that the termination provision was unenforceable. This holding was incorporated into 11 U.S.C. §541(c) of the new Bankruptcy Code four years later. The code also restricts the effect of anti-assignment provisions often contained in commercial leases.

The filing of a bankruptcy petition automatically stays the hand of any court order by which the lessor attempts to recover possession of the property or damages for the lessee's remaining in possession. 11 U.S.C. §362. Instead, the lessor's remedy is to force the trustee[5] to elect either to assume or reject the lease within 60 days of the filing. 11 U.S.C. §365(d)(3).

The trustee makes this decision to assume or reject the lease on the basis of "business judgment." If the lease has a rent well below going rates, the lease normally will be assumed; if the rent is higher than going rates, it likely will be rejected. "Business judgment" is not a defined term in the code. The black letter statement comes from Group of Institutional Investors v. Chicago, Milwaukee, St. Paul & Pac. R.R., 318 U.S. 523 (1943).

Section 365(d)(4) deems the lease rejected unless the trustee makes this assumption or obtains an extension of the 60-day period. Rejection results in the trustee's and lessee's surrender of the property. Upon rejection, all rents and charges accruing since the filing must be accorded a status in bankruptcy superior to unsecured claims. On the other hand, an assumption requires an express order of the court and is made without modification of the lease's provisions. It also requires the curing of all existing defaults and compensation for all losses occurring because of the defaults, or else provision of "adequate assurance" (not defined in the code) that both the cure and the compensation will occur. In the past, adequate assurance has meant a

---

5. "Trustee" here refers to a trustee in bankruptcy, a court-appointed official functioning much the way a magistrate might in a civil matter. The trustee is charged with gathering the debtor's assets into an "estate," the fund from which creditors will be paid.

consideration of the debtor's financial statement, his personal guarantors, and his past income stream.

A second alternative of the trustee is to try to recharacterize the sale-leaseback as, in its totality, a mortgage. The effect of the automatic §362 stay is the same: The renamed mortgagee is barred from pursuing any type of foreclosure. Secured creditors are preferred over unsecured ones in any bankruptcy proceeding. That's as it should be: the former bargained for a better place in the line to be paid. However, under Chapters 11 and 13 of the code, §§1123 and 1322, the trustee can modify the provisions of the security instrument. Modifications can include deacceleration of any remedy available to the purchaser-lessor. In addition, if the debt is greater than the value of the security, the secured creditor can find himself partially unsecured to the extent of the excess. Thus the secured creditor's claim on the bankrupt's estate can be limited to the value of the property. 11 U.S.C. §506(a).

Moreover, mortgage liens can be invalidated in bankruptcy. Invalidation converts a secured creditor into an unsecured one with a lower priority on the pay list. For example, a transfer of a lien after the filing can be invalidated or, if prior to the filing, can be found to be a fraudulent conveyance under state law. 11 U.S.C. §548(a)(1).

A third avenue for the trustee is to recharacterize the sale-leaseback as a joint venture. Thus the venture will be ongoing, and the trustee can avoid the now joint venture agreement as an executory contract that will, like the lease, be subject to the assumption or rejection provisions of the code. An executory contract is not defined in the code. Executory duties under a contract can either be substantial in relation to the whole performance or else involve nonmonetary duties, more generally involving a relationship based on continuing personal trust. However, here the trustee cannot assume nondelegable contractual duties, unless the debtor is not in possession of the property. If the debtor remains in possession, a nondelegable duty can be assumed.

What now of the termination provisions in the lease? If that provision remains a part of the now joint venture agreement, the venture may be over before it gets started. Compare 11 U.S.C. §365(c)(1)(A) with §365(e)(2)(A)(i).

The arguments against recharacterization of the sale-leaseback are several. First, the legislative history of §365 does not single out leases involved in a sale-leaseback for any special treatment. Its "assume or reject" powers apply to "any rental agreement to use real property." Second, later prospective mortgagees of the vendor-lessee may perform and rely on a title search. This notice-type argument is countered by the notion that recognition of the sale-leaseback may create a superpreference not envisioned by the Bankruptcy Code. No wonder, then, that the legislative history of §365 is silent. Third, the bankruptcy trustees and courts should respect state contract law; the parties have the freedom to do the deal as they wish, and reformation of a contract requires evidence of mutual mistake or fraud. Fourth, the rules governing equitable mortgages are intended for mortgages executed defectively by the parties; applying these rules in the context of bankruptcy raises problems not anticipated by these rules and that the rules were not designed to address. Fifth, if equitable mortgage rules apply, then other equitable principles may estop the vendor-lessee from asserting that the transaction was a mortgage after engaging in it. Wouldn't, for example, the doctrine of estoppel by deed (with warranties) put the fee title back into the purchaser-lessor's hands?

# EXAMPLES AND EXPLANATIONS

3. If the typical bankruptcy provision in a commercial lease is unenforceable, then what drafting suggestions do you have for the commercial landlord?

**Explanation:** No guarantees, but how about the following ideas as the basis for further drafting?

a. The lessor might be provided with a right to review the financial statement of a lessee on a periodic basis, and if the net worth shown is negative, landlord may cancel the lease.
b. If the lessee's net worth is 10 percent less than it was upon the last periodic review, landlord may cancel or require an additional security deposit for the rent.

The troubling aspect of these suggestions is that a trustee or court might take the cancellation to be the equivalent of a bankruptcy termination clause. In addition, while provisions drafted on the basis of these suggestions do give the lessor early warning of the lessee's financial woes, an automatic cancellation of the lease might be regarded as a fraudulent conveyance. While that indeed would present an additional problem, the conveyance here occurs when the lease is executed — in a long-term lease, that is likely to have happened prior to the time just before the filing for bankruptcy and during which the conveyance is deemed fraudulent. 11 U.S.C. §548.

4. If the vendor-lessee in a sale-leaseback mortgaged his leasehold before he goes bankrupt, what is the status of the leasehold mortgagee?

**Explanation:** If the vendor-lessee is found to be the holder of the fee simple absolute, then the purchaser-lessor becomes a first or senior secured creditor or mortgagee under an equitable mortgage. In turn the leasehold mortgagee becomes the holder of a second or junior mortgage lien.

5. If a trustee in bankruptcy "rejects" the lease, what is the effect on the lessee? Can he stay in possession?

**Explanation:** Once the property leaves the estate of the debtor, 60 days or less after the filing, one court has held that it goes into the hands of the party in possession — that is, the debtor. In re Knight, 8 B.R. 925, 929 (Bankr. D. Md. 1981) (involving a residential lease). Rejection by the trustee is not the equivalent of a breach of the lease. Were it otherwise, the rejection would give rise to eviction and that would hardly further the redemptive objectives of bankruptcy. But see In re Hepburn, 27 B.R. 135 (Bankr. E.D.N.Y. 1983) (sending the landlord under a rejected lease into state court to evict).

6. In the second of the prototypical sale-leasebacks presented previously, the deed from the vendor-lessee to the purchaser/lessor is replaced with an installment land sale contract (often called a contract for deed, remember). If the vendor is later in bankruptcy, how is this contract to be treated?

**Explanation:** Either as an executory contract or as a mortgage. An executory contract is not defined in the code, so the issue is a relatively open one. See In re Booth, 19 B.R. 53 (Bankr. D. Utah 1982) (coming down on the lien side of the issue). Previously in these materials, we have seen state courts treat the installment land sale contract as a mortgage. Most of these cases involve the enforcement of forfeiture provisions, but bankruptcy courts might see their holdings in a broader perspective.

Another way to look at this issue is to examine the common law doctrine of equitable conversion in the law of the applicable state. Would that state's equity courts treat this contract for a deed as performed, or not? See In re Cox, 28 B.R. 588, 591 (Bankr. D. Idaho 1983).

A further issue is whether it makes a difference what type of bankruptcy proceedings — liquidation or reorganization — is involved. *Booth* may be more useful to the reorganizing debtor under Chapter 11 (corporate) or Chapter 13 (individual) than the liquidating one (Chapter 7). The code contains some incentives to use reorganization rather than liquidation.

# Avoiding Recharacterization

How can the purchaser-lessor avoid recharacterization? The following methods are useful, but no one of them standing alone will be determinative.

1. By the lessor's not exercising a great deal of control over the business of the lessee.
2. By reciting that the transaction is not a mortgage, nor a loan, nor a joint venture, but indeed a sale and leaseback. Reciting the business purpose for the transaction can't hurt either.

3. By not using the terms of mortgage law, for example, interest rate, prepayment premium, escrows, and so forth.

4. By avoiding any duty to repurchase on the vendor-lessee, untying the repurchase price from the initial amount of the consideration for the deed, by pricing the property at the then fair market value by some recognized method of appraisal, and by giving third parties an opportunity to bid for the repurchase, with the vendor-lessee having an option or right of first refusal after that bidding. *Sed quere* whether the holding in *Lyon* doesn't sanction the use of small repurchase prices when the business reasons for the sale-leaseback are substantial.

5. By requiring extra types of collateral or security, personal guaranties, or letters of credit by the lessee. Such techniques are sometimes referred to as credit enhancement. Justice Blackmun appeared impressed by them in *Frank Lyon*.

# 28

# General and Limited Partnerships

The premier device enabling the trading of tax benefits between persons who don't need them (the developer, syndicator, or organizer of the association) and those who do (the high-income investor) is the partnership, particular the limited partnership. It makes the sale and leaseback look like a horse and buggy standing beside a sleek racing car.

The general partnership is a collection of mutual agents — each partner is the agent of every other — for a specified business purpose. Absent an agreement to the contrary, no partner is entitled to compensation for the conduct of ongoing partnership affairs.

A partnership is not an entity for federal income tax purposes. Thus no taxable event can occur at the partnership level; rather, taxes are paid by the partners individually. And, just as it is not a taxable entity, the partners can pass the tax benefits of the partnership's activities through to the individual partners. Thus it is often said that the partnership is a conduit or pass-through device for tax benefits.

This is not to say that no tax decisions are made at the partnership level. In fact, many tax planning decisions are taken at that level. Decisions on choosing the tax year, electing the method of depreciation, and choosing the accounting methods for the partners are indeed made by the partnership as a whole. In addition, the characterization of the tax benefits associated with the partnership, as a gain, loss, deduction, credit, or otherwise, is made at the partnership level. However, although a business expense deduction is characterized as such at the partnership level, its benefit is taken by the partners individually. Thus the partnership is an aggregation of its partners in so far as tax benefits are concerned, and the benefit of the Internal Revenue Code's provisions accrues to the partners individually. Yet the code treats the partnership as a legal entity in many other important respects.

Contrast the partnership with the corporation. The latter is a legal entity in its own right for purposes of paying federal income taxes. As a result, the income it receives is taxable at the corporate level, as well as when it is distributed to shareholders as dividends. The partnership avoids such double taxation. Neither can the shareholders deduct corporate losses attributable to their shares; likewise, there is no pass-through of corporate tax benefits.

# Uniform Partnership Acts

The partnership had its origins in the tenancy in partnerhip — a form of concurrent estate devised when legislatures did not hand out corporate charters as a matter of course. See Weidner, A Perspective to Reconsider Partnership Law, 16 Fla. St. L. Rev. 1, 3-10 (1988). (Professor Weidner is the reigning king of law review authors on partnership matters.) It was, then, against this common law background that the drafters of the Uniform Partnership Act (UPA) and the Uniform Limited Partnership Acts (ULPA, and in 1976, RULPA, the revised ULPA) worked. The former applies to general partnerships, the latter to limited ones. See Elfin, Revision of the Uniform Partnership Act, An Analysis and Recommendations, 23 Ind. L. Rev. 655 nn.1-2 (1990) (reporting that the UPA is typically adopted without much change, but is modified more than usual in Alabama, Georgia, and Nebraska).

No basic definition of a partnership (that is, no definition that is not a non-sequitur) is provided in either act because none was thought needed. "A partnership is an association of two or more persons to carry out as co-owners a business for profit," states UPA §6.

These acts quickly gained national acceptance and were adopted in all states except Louisiana. See Shapiro, The Need for Limited Partnership Reform: A Revised Uniform Act, 37 Md. L. Rev. 544, 545 (1978). Today UPA has been modified substantially in a few states, like Georgia, and RULPA has been adopted in somewhat over 30 states (elsewhere ULPA is available). Moreover, a major revision of UPA is in the works, proposing mostly clarifying additions to the act. See Weidner, The Revised Uniform Partnership Act Midstream: Major Policy Decisions, 21 Toledo L. Rev. 825 (1990), reporting a further embrace of the legal entity theory of partnerships discussed infra, new rules on dissolution and winding up a partnership, and an elaboration on the fiduciary duties of partners.

These acts are "tiered": absent a controlling provision in a limited partnership agreement, then ULPA or RULPA controls, and if that act does not resolve the problem, UPA controls. Also, absent a provision contra in a general partnership agreement, UPA controls. This tiering reflects a preference for interpreting the acts as a series of default rules. That is, unless the partners agree otherwise, by default or the silence of their agreement, the rule of the act controls. There are provisions of the acts, however, to which it is inappropriate to apply such an interpretation. For instance, UPA §21 imposes fiduciary duties owed by each to every other partner. The partnership agreement that abrogated the right of a partner to sue for a breach of a fiduciary duty, such as the duty of good faith and of loyalty, would violate basic principles of the law of agency (elsewhere embodied in the acts) that courts have traditionally enforced. While a partnership agreement might further define and elaborate on a partner's fiduciary duties, they cannot be eliminated by agreement. Their existence, though perhaps not their scope, is mandatory.

Also probably mandatory are the rules in UPA §§33-43 on winding up a partnership and the restrictions on a partner's withdrawal from the entity.

A general partnership may be based on an oral agreement; no written one is necessary. This is true in many, but not all, states. See Bellware v. Wolffis, 154 Mich. App. 715, 397 N.W.2d 861 (1986) (holding that the failure of a general partnership to file a required certificate is no bar to suit between two partners). A limited partnership, however, must everywhere file a certificate of limited partnership with the state before the partnership is established. RULPA §201.

# The Theory of the Partnership

In the nineteenth century, the organizational problems raised by a partnership were governed by two distinct theories. Weidner, A Perspective to Reconsider Partnership Law, 16 Fla. St. L. Rev. 1, 4 (1988). The first and most traditional theory was that the partnership was the aggregate of its partners' actions — no more and no less. The aggregate theory of partnership leaves no room for defining behavior or actions that can be attributed to the partnership itself, regarded as an entity separate and distinct from the actions of the partners. Defining the partnership itself as a legal entity, with a life of its own, is the task of the second theory, known (as one might expect) as the legal entity theory. The intent of the drafters of these acts was to establish the legal entity theory of the partnership for situations in which it was thought necessary that the partners be able to deal collectively with the outside world. To this end, a person as used in the act was defined as including "individuals, partnerships, corporations, and other associations." UPA §2. Moreover, the nature of the partner's interest is a "share of the profits or surplus" and, as such, is personal property. UPA §26. That is, the partner's interest is distinct from the partnership's assets.

Within the partnership and among the partners, however, the aggregate theory sometimes controls. The partnership itself is defined as an "association," not a legal entity. UPA §6. The two theories coexist uneasily in the UPA, the first of the acts offered for state adoption. The first principal drafter,

Dean William Ames of Harvard, was a proponent of the legal entity theory, while his successor, Dean William D. Lewis of Pennsylvania, completed the drafting and supported the aggregate theory.

As a further example of the act's use of the legal entity theory, consider a conveyance to a partnership. At the turn of the century, there was uncertainty as to whether the partnership could take title to real property in its own name, or whether it had to hold in the name of all partners. The UPA provides that "any estate in real property can be acquired in partnership name" and, if so acquired, "can be conveyed only in the partnership name." UPA §8(3). No "words of inheritance" — for example, "and her heirs" — are required when the partnership takes title, and the entire estate of the partnership's grantor passes to the partnership as grantee, unless a contrary intent appears. UPA §8(4). See Pinellas County v. Lake Padgett Pines, 333 So. 2d 472 (Fla. App. 1976).

This conveyancing result is reenforced by UPA §§9 and 10. Section 9 provides that "every partner is an agent of the partnership" — the legal entity theory embraced on, it turns out, a rationale of apparent authority, unless the partner acting has no authority to do so and the person with whom she deals has knowledge of this lack of authority. UPA §9(1). See Hodge v. Garrett, 101 Idaho 397, 614 P.2d 420 (1980) (lack of authority of partner to bind the partnership causing a void contract). Section 10 states that "any partner may convey real property" held in partnership name, "unless the partner's act binds the partnership under paragraph (1) of §9" or unless the grantee is a bona fide purchaser. A problem lurks here. Section 9(1) may not "bind the partnership" to the conveyance when the "unless" clause controls. Thus §10 gives less confidence to a purchaser of partnership property than probably was intended.

Old conveyancing habits die hard. Partnership conveyances often continued to be executed in the names of the partners. Besides inertia, requiring each partner to convey away partnership property may serve the function of an estoppel letter. See generally H. Reuschlein & W. Gregory, Agency and Partnership 317-336 (1979).

# Limited Partnership Documents

Today there are two documents generally used to establish a limited partnership. The first is the certificate of partnership. Its provisions, detailed in the various acts, should be consulted, depending on the type of partnership being formed. It is the charter of the association. The second is the partnership agreement. It is akin to the bylaws of the association.

The limited partnership is not a collection of mutual agents. It is, rather, a partnership in which some partners (the limited partners) delegate the management of partnership affairs to others (the general partners). Brooke

v. Mt. Hood Meadows Oregon, Ltd., 81 Or. App. 387, 725 P.2d 925 (1986) (holding that limited partners cannot compel general partner to distribute profits). The general partner is often a corporation set up for this specific purpose and is often run as a close corporation. See ABA Committee on Corporate Laws, Close Corporation Supplement, Model Business Corporation Act, reprinted at 37 Bus. Law. 269 (1981) (note, however, that the Model Business Corporation Act underwent modifications in 1983). Unlike a general partnership, a limited partnership requires that a certificate of limited partnership be filed with the state. Deporter-Butterworth Tours, Inc. v. Tyrell, 151 Ill. App. 3d 949, 503 N.E.2d 378 (1987) (holding that until a certificate is filed, all limited partners are treated as general partners).

# New Uses for Old Forms

After the Second World War, the Internal Revenue Code found new uses for the limited partnership.

Three principles worked this transformation: First, the partnership is a device for deferring taxes. Depreciation and the early losses of the project shelter the partner's other income and defer taxes on it until recapture upon a profitable resale. This principle was validated in *Tufts*. See Rhodes, Real Estate Limited Partnerships: Selected Tax Considerations, 72 Nw. U.L. Rev. 346 (1977); Weidner, Realty Shelter Partnerships in a Nutshell, 8 Ind. L. Rev. 899-902, 907-912 (1975). Limits on this shelter were added by the 1986 Tax Reform Act. Follain et al., The Impact of the 1986 Tax Reform Act on Real Estate, 17 Real Est. Rev. 76 (Spring 1987).

Second, it is a device for exercising leverage. In business jargon, leverage usually means the developer's power to control many assets without paying cash for them. Yet leverage has a second definition often used in the trade: It is the addition of the amount of partnership mortgages, along with cash investments, to the partners' tax basis for partnership assets. This use of leverage was validated in *Tufts*. See supra, page 374.

As an example of this second type of leverage, assume that a 20-member limited partnership purchases a property worth $1 million and that LP owns a 5 percent interest in this partnership. If the partnership paid $200,000 down and financed the rest of the price in an $800,000 note and mortgage transaction, LP paid $10,000 for her 5 percent interest, but to this cash investment she can add $40,000, for a $50,000 basis in the partnership's property. Against this basis, LP can depreciate her pro rata share of the depreciation taken, as well as her share of any losses, until her basis is zero. See Treas. Reg. §1.752(e) (partner's share of partnership liabilities).

Third, the partnership is a device for converting ordinary income into capital gains. This third principle works only when there is a disparity between (lower) capital gain and (higher) ordinary income tax rates. There has been no such disparate treatment in the 1986-1992 period, but that may change any time.

These three principles have had different impacts over time. As to the first, for example, Congress has changed the rates of depreciation permitted by the Internal Revenue Code every two years or so during the years 1969-1986. In general, the rates were accelerated in the tax reform acts enacted up to 1981, which was the high point in the use of accelerated depreciation as a method of favoring investment in real property. That year, some properties were permitted depreciation schedules over a 15-year life, taking double depreciation each year. The rates were then "deaccelerated" until 1986, when straight line depreciation was required for commercial property over a 31.5-year life, and for residential property over a 27.5-year life. Thus the quality of the shelter has varied with the passage of the various revenue measures enacted by Congress over the past 20 years. This is discussed in more detail later in this chapter (see pages 412-417).

The second principle, leverage, has been limited since 1986 by the code's requirement that a taxpaying limited partner's leveraged depreciation or losses be defined as "passive losses" and, as such, be only used to shelter "passive gains." See I.R.C. §469. See infra, pages 414-415.

The third principle is still embodied in the code, but is now mooted by the uniformity of capital gain and ordinary income rates. None of the code sections that implement the distinction between these two types of income were repealed in 1986, and a change in the rates will make the distinction an important one once again.

Partnerships remain an important entity even after 1986. There are two reasons for this. First, no one has figured out a more flexible way to hold title to real property. Second, at the same time that Congress imposed the passive loss and other code restraints on real property development, it reduced its individual federal income tax rates to a level (31 percent) lower than its corporate rates (34 percent).

# The Limited Partnership

Morrissey v. Commissioner, 296 U.S. 344 (1935), held that an organization recognized under state law as a trust or partnership may still be treated as a corporation for tax purposes if it possesses several typical corporate characteristics. In 1960, the I.R.S. promulgated the so-called Kintner Regulations. United States v. Kintner, 216 F.2d 418 (9th Cir. 1954). These regulations pointed to the six corporate characteristics at issue:

1. the presence of two or more associates;
2. an objective to carry on a business for profit;
3. continuity of life;

4. centralized management;
5. limited liability; and finally
6. free transferability of interests.

The first two characteristics are held in common by both corporations and partnerships and so will not be further discussed. The last four characteristics are considered in the current leading case on the income tax considerations in the formation of limited partnerships. This case is discussed in the section that follows.

# Larson v. Commissioner[1]

The facts of *Larson* present a fairly typical limited partnership agreement involving a corporate general partner and several limited partners interested in a passive investment.

*Larson* involved two partnerships holding title to California properties. One property was a student apartment house located near a state university, and the other was an orchard. Each partnership had a corporate general partner. The general partner was very thinly capitalized, with assets ranging from around $20,000 in one tax year to nearly $50,000 in another.

The apartment house partnership was comprised of eight limited partners (including Larson) and the corporate general partner. It purchased the apartment house for $450,000, payable in a nonrecourse note for that amount to the vendor.

As the opinion states the test of the Kintner regulations, an "organization will be taxed as a corporation if, taking all relevant characteristics into account, it more nearly resembles a corporation than some other entity. This will be true only if it possesses more corporate than noncorporate characteristics."

Then the opinion reviews the four characteristics. As noted previously, there are six in the regulations, but the first two are common to both corporations and partnerships and so were not considered here. The four corporate characteristics considered in *Larson* are: (1) continuity of life, (2) centralized management, (3) limited liability, and (4) free transferability of interests.

The first, continuity of life, is easily won by the taxpayer. The partnership agreement could limit the life of the entity to a set term. In addition, the court found that the bankruptcy of the general partner would have, as a matter of operation of law embodied in California's UPA, dissolved the partnership. Dissolution is a term referring to the point at which a change in the relations among the partners occurs "by any partner ceasing to be

---

1. 66 T.C. 159 (1976), noted in 8 U. Tol. L. Rev. 500 (1977), 11 U. Rich L. Rev. 743 (1977), J. Tax. (Aug. 1976), at 66.

associated in the carrying on" of the business. UPA §29. Any partner's ceasing to be associated changes nothing immediately; it only signals the beginning of the winding up of the partnership. UPA §30. What distinguishes a partnership, in other words, is the right of partners to choose their associates, while such a right is denied corporate shareholders. Each partner's right to choose her associates is enforced by the right of "any partner" to "cease being associated" and dissolve the partnership. Do the associates have this easy exit? If so, there is no continuity of life.

The regulations provide that

> if the death, insanity, bankruptcy, retirement, resignation, or expulsion of any member will cause a dissolution of the organization, continuity of life does not exist. If the retirement, death, or insanity of a general partner of a limited partnership causes a dissolution . . . , unless the remaining general partners agree to continue or unless all remaining members agree to continue the partnership, continuity of life does not exist.

26 C.F.R. §301.7701-2.

There are some interesting assumptions buried in the Tax Court's analysis of the regulation. One is that California's UPA controls its silent limited partnership act and a partnership agreement silent on the same subject. Two, "member" is taken to mean either a general or limited partner, when the structure of the two-sentence regulation implies that the first quoted sentence applies to general, and the second to limited, partnerships. Three, the verb "agrees" to continue the partnership, found in the unless clause, gives the I.R.S. an opportunity to argue that if the partners would have no reason not to agree to continue after an event dissolving the partnership, there is continuity of life. Often a partnership agreement will provide that the partners are authorized to agree to a continuance of the entity after a dissolving event, but make it plain that they do not agree to do so at the formation of the partnership. The opinion turns away the Commissioner's argument, saying that the term "dissolution" in the regulation seems keyed to the legal relationship between the partners, rather than some more pragmatic term such as "termination."

As to the second characteristic, centralized management, the court states that this characteristic "will not be met if the general partner has a meaningful proprietary interest" in the entity. A general partner with such an interest is more akin to an owner-manager, rather than to a member of a corporate board of directors. The taxpayer loses here: The general partner had an interest, but it was subordinated to that of the other partners, who had the right to remove her in the partnership agreement. The subordination and right to remove provisions of the agreement bolstered a finding that the entity had centralized management. Round two goes to the Commissioner, and it's now a 1-1 tie going into the third round.

The third characteristic, limited liability, is negated when the general partner has personal liability for the debts of the partnership. The use of nonrecourse provisions in mortgage notes secured by the partnership property will usually make no one in the partnership personally liable. The regulations are typically negative in their phrasing: The general partner has no personal liability "when he has no substantial assets (other than his interest in the partnership) and when he is merely a dummy," the mere agent of the limited partners. 26 C.F.R. §301.7701-2. The opinion first turns this portion of the regulation around, rephrasing it positively: "In other words, personal liability exists if the general partner either has substantial assets or is not a dummy." *Larson,* 66 T.C. 159, 180 (1976). (The writer feels a whipsaw headache develop when reading this part of the opinion.) As one might expect, the general partner is not found to be a dummy. Why, you ask? The opinion goes technical on its readers to answer that question. It is because the limited partners have reserved a right to remove the general but, by implication, have not reserved the right to direct her day-to-day administration of the partnership business. The more drastic right does not include the operational or executive right. End of discussion.

End of case. When the taxpayer wins the third round, she has won two rounds and her entity is a partnership for tax purposes, having negated two of the four relevant corporate characteristics.

But the *Larson* court continues. Its discussion of the fourth characteristic of transferable interests is brief but clearly focuses on the partnership agreement. Here the limited partner is permitted to transfer her interest with the consent of the general, whose consent may not be unreasonably withheld. Not good enough. Suppose that the transfer of an interest could only be made to another partner, or that the partnership had a right of first refusal on any transfer, or that the general partner with a substantial proprietary interest could not transfer her interest at all — these techniques might avoid corporate status. The final round is won by the I.R.S., but it has already lost the case. Winning the last round does not win the Commissioner the fight. To continue the simile, remember that this is not a war in which the winner of the last battle is victorious. The Marquis of Queensbury, not the Duke of Wellington or Napoleon, provides the better analogy for the verbal sparring between Commissioner and taxpayer here.

# EXAMPLES AND EXPLANATIONS

1. Does the *Larson* opinion define a partnership?

**Explanation:**  No. Because the regulations under consideration in this case require only that the "association" negate two of four corporate features to be classified as a partnership. A partnership is thus only defined as "not a corporation." By the way, the UPA, ULPA, and RULPA are no more helpful in this regard.

2. Are each of the corporate characteristics reviewed by the opinion given equal weight?

**Explanation:**   Yes, the approach is what the *Larson* opinion describes as a mechanical one. Each characteristic is assigned equal weight. MCA, Inc. v. United States, 685 F.2d 1099, 1101 (9th Cir. 1982).

3. Must a majority of the corporate characteristics be negated in fact as well as in practice, or is it sufficient that the document creating the entity negate two of the four characteristics?

**Explanation:**   The latter. The association is classified as a partnership for tax purposes in its own documents, not by its operating procedures. The Kintner regulations themselves present opportunities for doing the former, but the *Larson* court by and large turns these aside. In contrast, Zuckman v. United States, 524 F.2d 729 (Ct. Cl. 1975), did not: *Zuckman* examined the partnership methods of operation, not just its documents.

4. What types of projects will want to negate which characteristics?

**Explanation:**   The answer to this question can only be given by example. A partnership with a small number of limited partners may wish to control the transferability of its interests, but may not care so much about negating centralized management (that being a fact anyway). On the other hand, the presence of a large number of limited partners will make centralized management much more important — the entity will not attempt to negate this characteristic, and so will rely on negating continuity of life and free transferability of shares.

5. The syndication industry puts great stock in this opinion. Is that reliance justified? Is the *Zuckman* analysis of industry standard operating procedures hidden among the opinion's discussion of the four corporate characteristics?

**Explanation:**   One answer is yes, amid the discussion of *Larson's* third characteristic (limited liability). But if that method is used for one, who's to say that it cannot be used for all equally weighted characteristics. Consider for a minute the *Larson* partnership agreement's provision on the right to remove the general partner. This right is used once to support the Commissioner's arguments but again, a second time, to uphold the taxpayer's arguments. When the same provision cuts both ways, the case surely must be regarded as a close one. In truth, isn't the entity reviewed in *Larson* barely a partnership?

Finally, notice how capitalizing the corporate general partner helps the taxpayer with two of the four characteristics — with both negating centralized management (by providing the general with a substantial proprietary interest in the partnership) and limited liability (by providing substantial assets). The point is lost in the *Larson* opinion because, in its discussion of limited liability, it used an alternative analysis for discussing limited liability — to the effect that the corporate general partner is "not a dummy" or straw entity. However, this shows how easy it is to qualify as a *Larson* partnership.

The syndicators of limited partnerships nevertheless place great reliance on this case.

## The Aftermath of *Larson*

The I.R.S., disappointed with the holdings in this opinion, attempted to modify its regulations. It published new regulations at 42 Fed. Reg. 1038 (1977). These proposed regulations eliminated what the Service considered the bias in the Kintner regulations against the corporate form. In particular, they eliminated the two-to-two result that resulted in a partnership. Later, after a political firestorm, the I.R.S. withdrew its proposals. See 42 Fed. Reg. 1489 (1977).

In 1978, President Carter proposed amendments to the Internal Revenue Code to accomplish much the same, this time proposing that the code be amended to treat a limited partnership with more than 15 limited partners as a corporation, unless substantially all of its assets were low-income housing. After another politically charged debate, these amendments failed to pass. Later still, the Service proposed regulations that would have treated as a corporation any limited partnership in which no member was personally responsible for the entity's debts. Those proposals were withdrawn in their turn in 1982.

## The Implications of *Larson* for the Partnership Agreement

The limited partnership agreement that, by its terms, provides that the partnership is dissolved upon the bankruptcy of the general partner, such that the partners would then be able to demand the return of their contributions, negates the corporate characteristic of continuity of life. Moreover, the continuity of life provision can be negated by stipulating that the partnership will continue for a definite number of years — usually a number somewhat greater than the terms of mortgages securing or contemplated for partnership property. Further, when the agreement makes clear that the general partners are the moving forces behind the partnership's business, are unrelated and independent of the limited partners, and have substantial assets to satisfy the obligations of the partnership, the corporate characteristic of limited liability is negated as well. The agreement negates the limited liability characteristic by (in many cases) affirming the idea of centralized management — but so what? To qualify as a partnership, only two corporate characteristics need be negated.

The limited partnership is a vehicle for the general partner to attract investment in her project. Investments are known as "contributions" in RULPA. Capital contributions to the partnership are often made by limited partnerships in several cash payments, made according to a schedule set out in the provisions of a note given to the partnership at the outset of its existence. This procedure is sanctioned by RULPA §§501 and 502. Remedies available to the partnership upon a limited's default in the terms of payments are usually severe, often including forfeiture and sale of the defaulting partner's interest, either to other limited partners or third parties.

Contributions by limited partners may also be in the form of services. Usually the types of services contributed are those that may be rendered without the person doing so being deemed in "control" of the business of the partnership. RULPA §303. Acting as a contractor, agent, or employee of the partnership, consulting or advising the general partner, acting as a surety for the partnership, acting to amend the partnership agreement are permitted ("safe-harbored") under this section. RULPA §303(b). So is voting on the major business decisions of the partnership, such as leasing, mortgaging, or selling its property. Such safe-harbors were provided by RULPA after cases, such as Delaney v. Fidelity Lease Ltd., 526 S.W.2d 543 (Tex. 1975), found limited partners liable as general partners because as officers of a corporate general partner they took control of the business. RULPA §303 was drafted in response to those cases.

Capital contributions by the limited partners are entered on separate capital accounts kept for each partner. A capital account starts with whatever contribution a partner makes at the outset, is increased by any taxable income received, and decreased to the extent of any tax benefit received and any distribution of cash made by the partnership. It is maintained for each limited partner at the partnership level. I.R.C. §704(b). Its purpose is to determine whether the allocation of profits and benefits has, under the Treasury's Regulations, a "substantial economic effect," a very complicated subject that must be left to a course in partnership taxation. But it is the justification for keeping these accounts. Suffice it here to say that the purpose of the regulations is to insure that the tax benefits of the project are taken by those who bear its business risks (by contributing appropriately). When a partner's account is negative upon a dissolution and winding up of the partnership, that partner will have to pay those with positive accounts or take a reduced share in the final distribution of profits or bear an increased share of final losses, finally balancing the risks and the benefits of holding a partnership share. The safest course for the partnership is to allocate the tax benefits pro rata, to the extent of each partner's contribution; assigning all the tax benefits to the limited partners, with the general being paid entirely on a fee basis (hopefully a fee deductible by the other partners) is risky. Similarly, the allocation of tax benefits should be made in the partnership agreement; it should not be made in midstream as one limited partner or another needs the benefit, or made orally. If the I.R.S. determines that the allocation is without substantial economic effect, the partnership agreement allocation will be overridden, and the Service will reallocate it in accordance with each partner's capital contribution.

# Master Limited Partnerships

A master limited partnership, or MLP, is a limited partnership, qualified as such under the limited partnership act in effect (either ULPA or RULPA) whose interests or units are traded publicly on a major stock exchange or over the counter. It concedes the ability of an interest holder to trade her interest freely, and so acknowledges the last corporate characteristic discussed in *Larson*. Nevertheless, it is managed as a limited partnership and retains the ability to avoid the double taxation imposed on a corporation. Its units are registered with the federal Securities and Exchange Commission.

Remember that a limited partnership is a conduit for tax benefits — depreciation, deductions, and losses — that are generally greatest in the start-up years of a real estate project. Without the start-up deductions and losses, the tax benefit of this type of entity diminishes considerably. When this point in the project's administration is reached, the line reflecting the tax benefits dips below the ascending line of rents and profits generated by the project. When this crossover point is reached, the interests in the limited partnership are held, if at all, for their income-generating capacity. At this point, high-income, high-bracket taxpayers may wish to sell their interests. Converting the traditional limited partnership into a MLP enables them to do so.

In the early 1980s, the reduction in the highest income tax bracket, from 70 percent of income taxed to 50 percent, also decreased the incentive of high-income, high-bracket taxpayers to seek this tax shelter as much as they had formerly. Now often several limited partnerships, whose projects were generating taxable income, were rolled into one master limited partnership, and the shares of the former partnership were exchanged, in a tax-free exchange under I.R.C. §1031, for a unit of the publicly traded MLP. Thus, a combination of the reduced tax rates in the 1982 Tax Reform Act and the aging of older limited partnerships established in the 1970s, created the environment in which MLPs could thrive. The 1986 Tax Reform Act gave these entities a further reason for being, and so we will return to this subject again later in the chapter (see infra, pages 415-417).

# Reviewing the Limited Partnership Prospectus

Some warning signs of a bad deal — defined here as one that is tax-driven, rather than one that makes economic sense — are outlined below. See generally R. Stanger & K. Allaire, How to Evaluate Real Estate Partnerships

(1987); Kelner, Real Estate Tax Shelters: How to Tell a Good Deal from a Bad Deal, 25 Clev. St. L. Rev. 44, 57-69 (1976).

1. The type of project. Is it one that is often syndicated? If so, an examination of several prospectuses is warranted.

a. Garden apartments. These are the type of project most often syndicated. They have a short life. Real depreciation, not just tax-related depreciation, occurs. They are built for a short life, and so maintenance expenses can often rise faster than rents. They are occupied by short-term tenants, and the high turnover requires an on-site manager. If rising mortgage interest rates make homeownership impractical for tenants, however, they may be a good subject for syndication. Quaere, though, whether they are a good investment. In a review of the performance of six large public limited partnerships, 67 percent of the cash invested went into the purchase of apartment house properties, but the investment units were found to be worth 10 to 89 percent of unit cost and no partnership studied had increased the value of its units. Of course, in the meanwhile, tax benefits had been distributed as well, but the signs of a risky investment are still present because in this age of two-year cycles for tax reform, no tax benefit can be counted on forever. Thompson & Williams, What is My Partnership Investment Worth?, 20 Real Est. Rev. 26, 29 (1990) (using an 8 percent capitalization rate appraisal to value the partnership's assets).

b. Office buildings. These are built for a longer life (30-50 years) but often need new fixtures within 10 years or so of construction. Their leases tend to be for longer terms than those for garden apartments and are often "net leases" — meaning that any increases in the costs of taxes, insurance, and utilities are passed along to the tenants. (A lease that passes increases in all three items named above is called a "triple net lease.") The tenants themselves are businesses whose major expenses are for personnel; rent is a relatively minor line item on their ledgers. Moreover, the best property managers tend to be attracted to office buildings — the work is easier. However, the leasing period may be lengthy in overbuilt markets. In some markets recently, the vacancy rate for new construction has topped 20 percent, but that may indicate that bargains can be had just as well as indicating a danger sign. In such markets, front-end "rent holidays" may be offered as an inducement to lease; in some markets, rent concessions for the first year are customary. Check the local situation on this. Moreover, a 5 to 7 percent vacancy rate in a building rented to one, or even a few, major tenants represents less lost value than it would be in a building not dominated by a few tenants. A landlord may even be tempted to renew a lease at a lower rent than have a major tenant move out.

c. Shopping centers. Here land (a nondepreciable asset) is a major component of the project's fair market value. Thus few centers are syndicated. Net leases make the deductions smaller too. But once again, the tenants are stable and long-term. The property is often preleased too — that is, major anchor tenants, such as larger department stores, are committed to the center in advance of construction. They will want to install the fixtures in their space themselves, and many both improve and maintain it. Appreciation in value is computed with income multipliers or capitalization rates and so will be slow. This is an investment for patient money, if you can find a project to invest in.

Moreover, for any type of property, there may be a real estate investment trust, or REIT, which specializes in holding one type of property. (REITs are discussed in detail at the end of this chapter.) This is particularly true of shopping centers. Any such comparable investment vehicles should be checked.

2. A project resyndicating through the prospectus. This is a warning sign, not an absolute bar to making the investment. Before investing, further research into the resale value of the project is warranted. If the resale or terminal value is computed with an income multiplier or a capitalization rate, it may not reflect the fair market value of the project and need to be checked by comparison with a market data appraisal using comparable properties.

3. Heavy loading of front-end fees. Syndicators live by fees, but a project can die by them. One recent study of public limited partnerships that performed poorly shows that such fees represented 21 to 27 percent of the price of an investment unit. Thompson & Williams, What is My Partnership Investment Worth?, 20 Real Est. Rev. 26, 31 (1990). One way to short-circuit an examination of each and every fee is to divide the paid-in capital (the sum of all cash investments) for the project by its net operating income (gross income reduced by all expenses, but not by mortgage carrying costs). The result is a type of price-earnings ratio for the partnership.

4. A constant income-expense ratio over time. If income can be expected to rise over time, so can expenses. The conservative prospectus will estimate both as rising over time, particularly if the real depreciation rate of the project is steep.

5. A long pay-in or investment period for limited partners. If the partner-investors are given too long a time to invest, their investment objectives might change, and the partnership investment might not fit their needs. This would mean they might not invest as promised, and the partnership's collection costs in enforcing the notes the investors give will rise. The shorter the pay-in period, the better.

6. The resale or reversionary value. If a capitalization rate is used to value the project, the longer the period before the project is resold, the less likely it is the project will prove to be a good investment. See generally, McMahon, Applied Tax Finance Analysis of Real Estate Tax Shelter Investments, 27 B.C. L. Rev. 721 (1986).

7. The track record of the syndicator or general partner or partners. Has she experience with similar types of property? A track record with lenders? Successful first deals tend to lead to the successful second ones. Information

on the background of the syndicator is usually found in an attachment or addendum to the syndication prospectus, but remember that only projects deemed similar by the syndicator are included. A computerized search of periodicals, using the name of the syndicator, may be helpful in discovering what the background portions of the prospectus do not disclose. In particular, an examination of the length of time the syndications are held is worthwhile. If the holding periods are long, this may be an indication that it takes a long time to justify the terminal or resale value of the project. On the other hand, it may be that the property is a particularly good one and valuable in generating "passive" income — with which to offset passive losses — after the effective dates of the Tax Reform Act of 1986.

# EXAMPLES AND EXPLANATIONS

6. The owner of about 50,000 acres of rural timberland asks your advice about whether or not it is a good idea to establish a limited partnership to hold and manage this land and the logging operations on it. The predominant type of timber on the land is thingagummy pine, which can be used for both building supplies and wood pulp. When the building trades slack off, the price of pulp tends to rise, so the venture would be a stable business. If clear cut, the land would be timbered over in about 15 years. Would such land make good partnership property? What criteria would you use to make this decision?

**Explanation:**    This is not the type of property that is likely to be syndicated very often. The value of the property is largely land, which is not subject to depreciation; thus that tax benefit is not available for transfer between partners. Second, the logging operation that brings in the profits is likely to require personal rather than real property. Even sawmills are portable today. Thus the large start-up losses present in real estate development are not likely to be available here. Third, the increase in land values is not likely to be great, so the asset of the partnership is not likely to appreciate to the point that makes investment attractive to those interested in more than the logging. Fourth, logging is labor intensive, and the liabilities that therefore might flow from the operation indicate that a corporate structure that offers limited liability might better suit it. Overall, this is not a good prospect for a partnership, but if the logging is the precurser of a change in land use so that some of the traditional tax benefits accorded real property apply, a closer look might be warranted.

# The Internal Rate of Return

Many of the foregoing criteria will depend on your evaluation of the reasonableness of using an internal rate of return, or IRR, as a method of computing the return on the cash invested. But no matter what you think of its use, IRR remains an industry standard, so you need to understand the following premises about it. (A helpful understanding of the subject can be attained by regular reading of the articles occasionally published by the quarterly Real Estate Review.)

1. It is a type of capitalization rate.
2. It permits the syndicator to present the project without making any assumptions about its future marketability.
3. It acknowledges the tax benefits and permits those benefits to be reflected in the value given the project.
4. It is like a mortgage interest rate in that it assumes that the investor will be receiving income that must be reinvested at the same rate as was the return on the initial investment.

Thus the IRR is represented by x in the following equation:

$$I(x) - (TB + ROI)x = 0.$$

$I$ = the initial investment (the purchase price of a unit),
$TB$ = the tax benefits of the investment, discounted to present value,
$ROI = CD + TV,$ both discounted to present value, where
$CD$ = cash distributions of the partnership, and
$TV$ = terminal value of the project; thus

$$I(x) = (TB + ROI)x.$$

Putting the equation this way shows that the IRR is used twice. Its first use is as a rate of return on an imaginary savings account into which are put the tax benefits and the cash distributions of the partnership. This is an imaginary account because the deposits into it are of the tax benefits, and these are not the result of a cash transaction; rather, the deposits are of money saved on taxes, not money earned. The rate of return on this account is then used again, as a discount rate that reduces the final value of the savings account to the amount of the initial investment (I in the equation above).

This is not an algebraic equation. Rather, it is arrived at through trial and error: in short, through using a given percent to build up the account using the IRR, and then by using the same percentage rate to discount the value of that account back down to the initial investment.

The IRR is in fact two rates of return: (1) a rate of return on an initial investment, and (2) the annual rate of return on a continuous reinvestment process.

The IRR assumes that an investor will be making a series of discrete reinvestments of tax benefits and cash distributions during the life of the project. How reasonable is this assumption? To the extent that the reinvestment involves tax benefits, the answer is, reasonable enough. It is reasonable because the so-called reinvestment is of tax savings, not earnings or legal tender. Further, it will not become cash until the project is sold, and meanwhile, the tax benefits are dependent on the partnership's holding onto the project; in that sense, they are held captive by the project. The tax benefits are soft money that cannot be spent except as permitted by the code, cannot be banked, and are confiscated by the I.R.S. if not used on the tax return for a given year. Thus they might as well be "reinvested" in the project; the I.R.S. provides no alternative.

All of this says, implicitly, that the reinvestment assumption is not appropriate so far as cash distributions are concerned. That is legal tender, it can be banked, and the I.R.S. will not confiscate it at the end of the tax year. Thus the IRR is most appropriate in the tax-driven deal, but to the extent that an investor wants good economics to drive the deal, she should remain skeptical of its use.

One response to the IRR is to break it down into components — that portion of it attributable to

- cash distributions,
- tax benefits, and
- the terminal value.

The IRR computation will treat each as equally important, but they are seldom equal in fact. If a project uses long-term net leases with creditworthy tenants, then perhaps using an IRR is appropriate; shopping centers and office buildings are good examples of such types of projects.

Of course, once you have computed the IRR for one project, the result is meaningless if you cannot use it again to compare similar projects. But you have to find the similar projects, which may prove just as difficult as understanding the IRR to begin with.

## Holding the Syndicator to Account

One of the major differences between partnership agreements drafted from the limited partner's perspective and those drafted from the syndicator's or general partner's is that the former will contain many warranties about the property and the transaction that the latter will not contain. If and when the deal goes sour, the general partner will want to argue that, if the warranties do not cover precisely what went wrong, the express warranty will replace any implied warranties or common law fiduciary duty to which the general partner might be held. The Uniform Partnership Act requires that an accounting be made periodically, and it is unlikely that this right can be waived in the agreement and exculpate the nonaccounting general partner. UPA §19-22.

The duty to account for the profits is the overriding principle, but, nonetheless, the general partner is entitled to reasonable compensation for her services. However reasonable that compensation might be, she cannot retain it if it is not disclosed to the other partners.

Usually, a general partner is a fiduciary for the limited partners. Ebest v. Bruce, 734 S.W.2d 915, 921-922 (Mo. App. 1987) (finding that the general partner's receipt of tax advice was not a defense). Nondisclosure of partnership business by the general partner can also be a breach of fiduciary duty. For example, even if a resale price for partnership property is reasonable in market terms, if a breach of fiduciary duty is involved — as where the general partner has sold to an entity in which she is interested — often no damages need be shown in a suit by the limited partners. The breach is actionable regardless of the damages sustained. This example contains a breach of two such duties: first, the duty of loyalty, breached by the self-dealing, and second, the breach of the duty to disclose. See Dixon v. Trinity Joint Venture, Ltd., 49 Md. App. 379, 431 A.2d 1364 (1981); but see Quinn-L Corp. v. Elkins, 519 So. 2d 1164 (La. App. 1987) (taking over construction loan of partnership to prevent foreclosure was not a breach of fiduciary duty).

The same breaches might occur if the general partner purchases a property in a corporate name and then flips the property to the partnership for a profit, undisclosed to the partners. Bassan v. Investment Exch. Corp., 83 Wash. 2d 922, 524 P.2d 233 (1974), noted in 50 Wash. L. Rev. 977 (1975). The situation here is often styled as the general partner's duty not to compete with the partnership.

This duty not to compete may even survive the withdrawal of the breaching partner or the dissolution of the partnership. See Leff v. Gunter, 33 Cal. 3d 508, 658 P.2d 740, 189 Cal. Rptr. 337 (1983).

Quite often, the general partner will be held to these fiduciary duties because she alone is able to evaluate the partnership's projects. She will be able most easily to reconstruct the financial analysis done for the project. The duty to account and disclose arise (the Securities Acts' liability aside for the moment) only after the limited partner makes the investment. Realistic assessment of the project can be made only when the project has a track record, however short. Thus, until some two years into the project's operation, the general partner is functioning like a broker. Meanwhile the tax benefits of the project may blind the limited partner to its economics. The general is in a unique position to take advantage, and fiduciary duties are the anodyne for that advantage.

# Securities Acts' Liability

For larger partnerships, the registration of the partnership with the Securities and Exchange Commission is typical and gives rise to a duty of due diligence, imposed on a general partner participating in the preparation of the registration statement. See 15 U.S.C. §77k(a) (Securities and Exchange Act of 1933, §11). Thus, if the terminal value assigned partnership property is misleading, the general partner would have breached a duty to make a reasonable investigation of the appraisal method used to arrive at this value. Negligence is the ground for an investor's cause of action under this section.

Section 11 can also snare any expert — attorney or accountant — participating in the preparation of the registration statement because it does not require that there be privity of contract between the expert and the investor or limited partner.

Another section of the Securities Acts creates liability not only for a registered partnership interest but for offering to sell a security, registered or not. See 15 U.S.C. §77k(b)(3). Privity of contract is required with the investor, but some courts have extended this section to experts, as "participants" in the sale, when the data they prepare is relied on by the limited partner making an investment decision.

Section 10b and Rule 10b-5 of 1934 Act impose liability for reckless conduct in the preparation of data or reports, for any registered or exempt offering, that results in any material misrepresentation of fact about the project. These are antifraud protections for investors. For liability based on fraud, a professional's errors and omissions policy may not provide coverage.

The Racketeer Influenced and Corrupt Organization Act (RICO), 18 U.S.C. §1961, is also a way of sweeping all "aiders and abetters" of a misleading prospectus into one action. RICO may prove appealing to plaintiffs because punitive, treble damages are available and attorneys' fees and costs are recoverable for the successful plaintiff. See Engl v. Berg, 511 F. Supp. 1146 (E.D. Pa. 1981) (a suit by a limited partner against the general).

Common law professional malpractice liability is also possible, in negligence, for misstatement of the investment potential of a partnership interest. White v. Guarante, 43 N.Y.2d 356, 401 N.Y.S.2d 474, 372 N.E.2d 315 (1977) (where an accountant was held liable to a partnership for audit and tax services).

For attorneys, this is an area of law in which legal and business advice seem intertwined. It is permissible to give business advice, but it should be properly structured and offered in the context of a particular transaction. And, as in any field of law, although the giving of advice may be proper, exculpation of liability for otherwise actionable advice is not.

## Real Estate and Tax Reform

In the 1970s and 1980s, in intervals of two years or so after 1974, the Congress has enacted major amendments to the Internal Revenue Code. Known variously as tax reform acts (TRAs), they included major provisions affecting the federal income taxation of real property development. Up to 1981, the provisions liberalized the treatment accorded developers. That year turned out to be the watershed.

For example, real property improvements were depreciated according to an accelerated schedule authorized in the 1981 TRA. The accelerated cost recovery system there permitted real property of all types (excluding land, of course) to be depreciated over 15 years. The system made the gleeful and arbitrary assumption that property had a useful life of 15 years and that each year its value lost 1/15 of its cost. Further, the depreciation allowed was recovered under the rapid "175 percent declining balance" method, which meant an additional tax benefit: It permitted about 12 percent of the property's depreciable cost to be deducted each year. After 1981, however, Congress lengthened the recovery period. It was 19 years in 1985.

Then, in 1986, the recovery period was increased to 27.5 years and 31 years for residential and nonresidential properties, respectively. For this purpose, "residential" means a structure deriving 80 percent or more of its rental income from dwelling units. This lengthening of the recovery period more than cut in half this tax benefit.

Post-1981 TRAs restricted other tax benefits accorded developers, until finally the impetus for several reforms came together in the Tax Reform Act of 1986. Amendments to the Internal Revenue Code, heretofore considered in the alternative, were enacted cumulatively.

By 1985, the I.R.S. examined 377,000 income tax returns for signs of abusive tax shelters — up 52 percent since 1981 — and, as a result of these audits, assessed $2.2 billion in fines and assessments on overdue taxes. The total investment in publicly syndicated limited partnerships involving real property was $4.5 billion in 1983, $5.7 billion in 1984, and $7.1 billion in 1985. The size of the average syndication also increased. It was $20 million in 1983 and $50 million in 1985, with the largest offering involving more than $300 million in 1985. In the last year, the threat of tax reform put a damper on the volume of private commercial real property transactions.

Some argued that marketing interests in large partnerships to a larger number of investors, in lower tax brackets, in smaller units or interests, was a step toward making these entities the major vehicle for providing capital for real property development. Such arguments were hotly disputed, however, by those who questioned the suitability of limited partnerships for this purpose and the unregulated nature of the market for partnership interests.

# The 1986 Internal Revenue Code Amendments

Four of 1986's major changes in the Internal Revenue Code will be discussed here. First, the rates of taxation were changed in two ways. The 1986 Act equalized the tax rates applicable to both ordinary income and capital gains.

It also reduced the tax rates for individuals so that, for the first time in a long time, the rate for individuals was lower than the corporate rate.

Second, a taxpayer's deduction for losses from a property was limited to the amount the taxpayer had at risk in the property. This "at risk" limitation had long applied to nonreal property activities, but real property development had heretofore been exempted; the 1986 TRA removed the exemption, repealing I.R.C. §465(c)(3)(D).

Thus a taxpayer's deductions are generally limited to her cash contributions to (say) a partnership, the adjusted basis of the property contributed, and mortgage amounts (pro rated for her interest in the partnership) for which she is personally liable. I.R.C. §465.

The personal liability requirement is a tough one because the real estate developers have, for reasons found in the partnership taxation chapters of the I.R.C., used nonrecourse mortgages to finance improvements to property syndicated and held by limited partnerships. Nonrecourse mortgages are a way of establishing limited liability of the limited partners without writing this feature of their investment into the certificate or the partnership agreement. To write it into either of those two places would throw into jeopardy the limited liability aspect of its associational form under *Larson* — the so-called partnership would run the risk of being taxed at the associational level as a corporation. Better to rely on the partnership acts and the mortgage documents.

Fortunately, Congress did not leave the limited partnership industry to fall between the horns of the I.R.C.'s provisions. It provides an out. See I.R.C. §465(b)(6). "Qualified nonrecourse financing" may be included in a taxpayer's at-risk basis. It is financing given by a third-party mortgagee with three attributes: a mortgagee (1) regularly making real property loans, (2) unrelated to the taxpayer unless the loan is commercially reasonable and is made on terms that an unrelated individual would extend, and (3) not the recipient of a fee with regard to the loan transaction. See generally Note, The Tax Reform Act of 1986 and its Effect on Real Estate Tax Shelters, 40 Ark. L. Rev. 567, 576-580 (1987).

Third, the 1986 Act limited the deductions for passive losses. I.R.C. §469. Prior law had permitted a taxpayer to use losses attributed to her limited partnership interest as a deduction from otherwise taxable income derived from activities in which the taxpayer actively participated. The 1986 Act limited this passive loss deduction to be taken only against other passive income. Passive income does not include portfolio income, the latter being income not derived from the ordinary course of a trade or business. Moreover, under this act all rental income was presumed passive, no matter how hard the taxpayer worked to collect it, but subject to an exemption that allows the deduction of passive losses against active income up to $25,000 for an individual taxpayer. Passive losses not used in one tax year may be carried forward indefinitely, however, into future years. Even if they are not deductible one year because the taxpayer materially participates in a partnership's activity, they may be carried forward into a tax year in which the taxpayer partner is passive.

The intent of Congress in enacting this third reform is to deny a tax shelter for salary and portfolio income. During the holding period for real property improvements, passive losses can only shelter passive income. This limitation will not apply, however, to losses incurred upon the sale or other disposition of the improvement; losses at that point are real enough and can offset any type of income. Note, supra, 40 Ark. L. Rev. at 580; and see Goldberg, The Passive Activity Loss Rules: Planning Considerations, Techniques, and a Foray into Never-Never Land, 15 J. Real Est. Tax. 3, 4-11 (1987).

This reform reduces the tax benefit trading potential of limited partnerships.

Fourth, the 1986 Act restricted the deduction for mortgage interest. I.R.C. §163(d)(3). Interest expenses incurred in a trade or business in which a taxpayer actively participates remains generally fully deductible. However, a deduction for investment interest expense is restricted. Where the taxpayer has only a limited business interest, such as that of a limited partner, a Subchapter S shareholder, or any other business activity in which the taxpayer does not materially participate, no deduction is permitted if the deduction would exceed the income from the limited business interest. Only to the extent that investment income exceeds investment expenses is related interest deductible. Deductions lost in this manner can be carried forward.

The act also put in place new tax credits for the construction of low-income housing and for the rehabilitation of historic and older structures.

The net effect of the act, however, would likely have been to depress the fair market values of properties with an element of syndication value (value reflecting the tax benefits conferred by prior law). Estimates were that the fair market value of office buildings would decline 16 percent and that of apartment buildings 8 percent. Fortunately, the enactment of the 1986 Act coincided with falling interest rates in mortgage capital markets, so that the economic effect was hardly noticed. Follain, Hendershott, & Lang, The Impact of the 1986 Tax Reform Act on Real Estate, 17 Real Est. Rev. (No. 1) 76, 83 (Spring 1987). Hardly noticed, that is, except by syndicators or promoters of large limited partnerships. They noticed, and the rate of syndications was cut in half for the first several years after the enactment of the act.

# The Consequences of the 1986 TRA

There are, of course, many people (tax attorneys and accountants) who are paid well to spend their time devising perfectly legal methods of avoiding or deferring taxation. One of the ways in which they immediately went to work at the end of 1986 was to devise ways of putting passive income and passive losses together into one entity — these became known as master limited partnerships (MLPs), whose assets included older, well-established projects as well as just-established younger ones. See supra, page 405. At one time often separate, one-project limited partnerships were combined into one entity. The former threw off income, the latter losses. Interests in these partnerships are traded on major stock exchanges. The value of assets held by such entities doubled in 1987. (There was also some use of MLPs in the corporate world by corporations with realty assets, such as Burger King, Pillsbury, and the Boston Celtics.)

Congressional response to MLP growth was quick. Amendments to the I.R.C. in 1987 included §7704. This section denied the largest MLPs — the ones traded on stock exchanges or other secondary markets — the ability to shelter passive income with passive losses from other sources. It provided that income from such MLPs was portfolio, not passive, income. This, of course, denied these large MLPs the very function for which they were created. Section 7704 more generally denied the applicability of the Kintner regulations when classifying MLPs as either a corporation or a partnership. For the first time, public trading of an entity's interests was used as the dispositive criteria. Critics of §7704 were equally quick off the mark. Adler, Master Limited Partnerships, 40 U. Fla. L. Rev. 755 (1988). Most corporations, it was argued, are not traded on the public exchanges and are subjected to taxation at the corporate level. Moreover, this section taxes widely traded interests, available to the small investor, but does not tax syndications that are not so widely traded and so are available only to wealthy investors. Perhaps a better approach would have been to impose requirements on MLPs similar to those met by REITs. Such requirements would have the entity pass on a high percentage of its income to the holders of its interests.

A second response was to establish partnerships for holding equity rather than mortgage debt. That generates passive income too. Smith, Syndication Topics: Actively Pursue Passive Income: Planning for 1987, 17 Real Est. Rev. (No. 1) 12(Spring 1987). This will reduce the IRR and perhaps make it less valuable as a method of evaluating an investment. Any investor would have a greater role and risk as an equity participant and, concomitantly, would have a reduced role as a lender.

Yet a third response, at the partnership level, might be to characterize an activity as a lease, which is inherently passive, rather than as the provision of services to a partnership. I.R.C. §469(e)(3). Similarly, the use of ground leases may increase. Partnerships may also purchase partnership assets in sale-leaseback transactions so that, as purchaser-lessor, its rental income will be classified as passive. If a partnership owns its own office building among its other assets, it can convert the building into a commercial condominium, use one floor as its office (owning that unit in fee simple absolute and taking depreciation on it), lease the other units for passive income, or take dealer status and sell them for active income. Partnerships are flexible enough to adjust!

The net effect of the TRA's passive loss rules will likely be to increase, rather than decrease, the use of limited partnerships to generate income because it is passive income. What would otherwise be portfolio income will become passive income over time.

## Investment Trusts: An Alternative Investment Vehicle

Real estate investment trusts, or REITs, are business trusts formed for holding either mortgages or the fee simple to real property. They are tax-free intermediaries (as governed by I.R.C. §856-860) if they: (1) distribute a very high (95 percent) of their net annual income to shareholders; (2) derive at least 75 percent of their gross income from real property, without engaging in short-term holdings of real property interests (no speculative, quick-turnover investments, in other words); and (3) have 100 or more shareholders. Most of the large REITs have shares that are traded on the major stock exchanges.

Thus REITs are a specialized type of mutual funds for real property investments. Often they are established by a bank or insurance company, but many are stand-alone entities.

REITs have had their ups and downs. In the early 1970s, they were aggressive lenders, but in the climate of the 1974-1975 recession, many failed. (In times of high interest rates, however, they can be a very profitable investment vehicle.) As a result, the number of REITs in existence at present is smaller than in the mid-1970s. Nonetheless, while mortgage REITs have had their hard times, some ownership REITs have done well long-term, in part because they have specialized in holding title to one type of property. The final word, then, on REITs? Specialized, but worthwhile, investment vehicles.

# 29

# *Real Property Transfer Taxes*

Until 1968, transfers of real property were subject to a federal excise tax. When Congress repealed the tax that year, many state and local governments took up the cudgels. See, e.g., 30 Del. Code §5401 (1989); Md. Code Ann. art. 81, §287A (1987) (authorizing both state and county transfer taxes). In the large commercial transaction, structuring the transaction to save on these transfer taxes is worth the planning time involved. Thus when a one-project corporation holds title to land to be developed, the sale of corporate stock, rather than the sale of the land itself, may avoid the tax altogether.

As you read these materials, keeps two caveats in mind. First, the tax payment will only be one among many considerations influencing the structure of a transaction. As an example, take the decision to transfer corporate stock, rather than real property corporate assets, as presented in the previous paragraph. This decision may be reversed and a transfer of the property itself arranged if the corporation is in a business generating toxic wastes. Their cleanup might be pursued by environmental regulators armed with statutory liens. Any assumption of the stock might thereafter render the stockholder liable for the cleanup, even if the corporation had divested itself of the polluted property before the purchaser acquired the stock.

A second caveat: The following problems are only meant to suggest the range of transfer tax problems. Nothing succeeds in this area like consulting the state statute or local ordinance in question. Problems unique to the wording of the statute or ordinance are bound to arise.

## Defining the Property Taxed

Sometimes the unit of property to be taxed is in dispute. For example, in a transfer affecting a condominium regime or a subdivision, when the transfer tax rate is progressively steeper as the consideration for a transfer increases, an attorney will argue that the rate of taxation should be computed on the sale of each individual unit or parcel, rather than on the sale in the aggregate of all units or parcels in the project.

## Exemptions

Often there are statutory exemptions from the tax for intrafamily transfers and for transfers to a partnership. See, e.g., Ocean Harbor Assocs. v. Director of Revenue, 565 A.2d 893 (Del. Super. 1989) (litigating the applicability of a more limited exemption for a transfer to a partnership in which the transferor has a pro rated interest in the property in the same proportion as he previously owned the property); Gottfried, Inc. v. Wisconsin Dept. of Revenue, 145 Wis. 2d 715, 429 N.W.2d 508 (Ct. App. 1988) (litigating the question of whether a trustee-to-beneficiary exemption extends to a corporation-to-shareholder transfer).

## Buy-and-Hire versus a Package Sale

State transfer taxes are often levied on the value of the property transferred. In the setting of the residential subdivision, a developer may thus choose to transfer the land parcel to the purchaser in its undeveloped state. The alternative is to sell the completed house, together with the underlying land. The sale of the undeveloped parcel alone can be transferred for a lower tax and the developer can have a contractual agreement with the purchaser that he will construct the house on the parcel after the transfer.

Recently, Pennsylvania amended its transfer tax statute. The amendment included within the definition of the value of the transfer, "the actual consideration for or actual monetary worth of any executory agreement for the construction of . . . improvements." 72 Pa. Stat. Ann. §8101(C) (1989). This tax on executory construction agreements has been attacked but upheld, on constitutional grounds. Pennsylvania Builders Assn. v. Commonwealth of Pennsylvania, Dept. of Revenue, 122 Pa. Commw. 493, 552 A.2d 730 (1989), aff'd, 524 Pa. 134, 569 A.2d 928 (1990). What further transfer tax planning would you suggest?

First, the purchaser might be given an option to execute a construction agreement after the transfer. Because this option is not executed at the time of the transfer, there is no outstanding agreement and no tax due computed on the basis of its worth. However, this arrangement may not be sufficiently secure from the developer-vendor's perspective. After all, the purchaser may not take up the option and instead have some other builder construct the home. If, however, the developer's profit is built into the contract of sale for the unimproved parcel, the purchaser could be given an option to build the house at cost. A third arrangement would be to require that the purchaser enter into a construction agreement with one of a selected group of builder-developers.

The advantage of a transfer tax used to be its easy administration. The price on the deed when recorded was the amount on which the tax is computed. That goal remains, but how will the Pennsylvania revenuers involved in the problems previously recited know whether a construction agreement is attached to a transfer of a land parcel? What happens if there is an agreement, but construction is started, yet never completed?

## Transfers of Mortgaged Property

In the instance of mortgaged property, transferred without releasing the mortgage debt, which is assumed by the transferee, the consideration will not appear on the face of the deed. In New York City, a tax is imposed on the transfer of "any economic interest" in real property, and the vendor is liable for transfer taxes and may deduct any preexisting mortgage debt assigned or assumed from the "net consideration" on which the tax is computed. Park Ten Assocs. v. City of New York Dept. of Finance, 136 A.D.2d 307, 526 N.Y.S.2d 962 (1988), modified, 74 N.Y.2d 628, 541 N.Y.S.2d 979, 539 N.E.2d 1100 (1989). However, the developer-vendor who mortgages property just before transferring it to a corporation that is to hold the title during its development, is likely to find that the *federal* income tax consequences more than offset the local transfer tax savings. See I.R.C. §357.

In any event, the transfer of real property to a one-project corporation may still be a taxable transfer. In Maryland, a transfer involving "actual consideration paid or to be paid" occurs when the holder of title to real property transfers that title to a corporation of which he is the sole shareholder. Dean v. Pinder, 312 Md. 154, 538 A.2d 1184 (1988). "Actual" consideration is not, the opinion said, a limiting term. Rather, the corporate authorization to mortgage the property and the subsequent availability of mortgage credit to the corporation may be actual consideration. So may be the benefit of limited liability for the corporation.

## Corporate Asset Transfers

One statute imposes a 2.2 percent transfer tax on the "transfer of an economic interest in real property." If a contract of sale is silent on the payment of such a tax, it is customary for the vendor and the purchaser to split the payment fifty-fifty. D.C. Code §45-923 (1989). Such a transfer "occurs upon the conveyance, vesting, granting, bargaining, sale, or assignment, directly or indirectly, of a controlling interest by 1 or more persons and by 1 or more transactions within any 12-month period, in any corporation, partnership, association, trust or other unincorporated entity." Id.

A "controlling interest" is more than 50 percent of the (1) votes given all classes of stockholders in a corporation, (2) capital or profits of a partnership, association, or other incorporated entity, or (3) the beneficial interest in a trust, whether or not the entity is multitiered, as when a corporation owns an interest in a partnership.

# EXAMPLES AND EXPLANATIONS

1. How can payment of this real estate transfer tax be avoided?

**Explanation:** First, how about a transfer of a 50 percent interest, with the remaining 50 percent transferred 367 days later?

Second, how about amending the partnership agreement or corporate charter to require that no major transfer of its real property assets occur without the consent of all partners or shareholders? Any purchaser would then arguably become the owner of a minority interest, but still have a significant control over the partnership's or corporation's activities.

Third, how about the use of long-term leases? If a lease of 99 years is the equivalent of an assignment, then how about a 98-year lease?

Finally, wouldn't such a tax statute encourage the use of various types of mortgages? A shared appreciation mortgage, for example? A convertible mortgage, in which the debt is repaid by an interest in the property?

Transfer taxes on mortgages present some special problems. See Examples 2 through 5 that follow.

2. When a transfer tax is levied on the amount of any mortgage loan given in exchange for a mortgage lien on real property, should an assignment of rents and profits be part of the amount of the mortgage when computing the tax due?

**Explanation:** Not if the assignment is additional security for the payment of a mortgage loan. An assignment of the underlying leases on which the rents are due might be treated differently. See Taxpayer Servs. Div., Technical Servs. Bureau, N.Y. State Dept. of Taxation and Finance, TSB-M-89-(6.1)-R, Tax on Mortgage (Aug. 3, 1989), at 1-2.

3. If a transfer tax includes the amount of a mortgage, is a tax due when a future advance clause is used, after the original closing on the mortgage lien, to advance additional loan proceeds?

**Explanation:** Maybe. See id., where the state tax department states that the tax is due only if the mortgage is "new." How would the state or recorder police this (if the tax is due)? It would be difficult.

4. Is a new tax due if the security for the mortgage is changed?

**Explanation:** Probably not, unless the replacement security is worth substantially more than the original, or unless the whole transaction is a scam to avoid the tax — as where the property provides security with the intention that the lien will later be foreclosed.

5. A New York statute imposes a transfer tax on the recording of a mortgage, in the amount of about 2 percent of the amount secured by the mortgage. N.Y. Tax Law §250 (1988). This is a tax on the privilege of recording, not on the mortgage lien itself, although the imposition of the lien is a precondition to finding that a tax is due. Citibank, N.A. v. State Tax Commn., 98 A.D.2d 929, 470 N.Y.S.2d 920 (1983). In some instances, this tax must be paid by the mortgagee and not passed through to the mortgagor. How feasible is it to police the pass-through? In what situations will this tax be difficult to administer?

**Explanation:** Mortgage documents that increase the amount secured without imposing a new lien, that extend an existing lien to additional property, or that replace an existing mortgage raise the issue of whether the document *imposes* a lien. Clearly a document that discharges or releases a lien does not create a taxable recording. Probably neither does a replacement nor an extension of a lien, but an increase in the amount secured will probably be taxable to the extent of the increase. Casting the transaction to achieve the right tax result is easy: There should be no extinguishment of an old, or separate creation of a new, mortgage lien, but rather the recordation of a document referencing the old lien. Note, Deferred Mortgage Recording: Weighing the Risks and Benefits, 2 Hofstra Prop. L.J. 389 (1989).

However, computation problems remain. What if the mortgage documents are not immediately recorded and are partially paid off when the recording does take place later? If this is a tax on the privilege of recording, the benefits of recording are not available for the full amount, and so the outstanding amount at the time of recording should be the basis for the tax computation. Downtown Athletic Club v. State Tax Commn., 280 A.D.363, 113 N.Y.S.2d 485 (1952).

How about a wraparound mortgage? Will it be taxed at its face amount or the amount of the true loan? The latter. First Fiscal Fund Corp. v. State Tax Commn., 40 N.Y.2d 940, 390 N.Y.S.2d 412, 358 N.E.2d 1037 (1976) (holding that the tax is to be computed without reference to the underlying mortgage).

What if the document has no face amount or secures future advances after the closing, at which only a portion of the value of the property is advanced? The statute states that the full fair market value of property is the basis for computing the tax due at the recording. N.Y. Tax Law §256 (unless the taxpayer submits an affidavit as to the amount secured). When a tax is due on a later transfer by a deed in lieu of foreclosure to the mortgagee, it is paid this second time on the value of the transfer and measured by the value of the property to the mortgagee.

A final, cautionary note: Don't lose sight of the important protections afforded by recording when looking to avoid a mortgage recording tax. A loss of priority could result from delaying a recording. In addition, the mortgage will lack the prima facie evidentiary value it would otherwise have. Further, if the mortgagor goes bankrupt in the interim, the putative mortgagee will appear before the bankruptcy trustee as an unsecured creditor. 11 U.S.C. §362. In addition, the mortgage recorded within 90 days of the bankruptcy might be subject to challenge as a preferential transfer and invalidated on that ground. 11 U.S.C. §547.

# Recording Fees

Recording fees should not be confused with transfer taxes. These fees are often levied on a per page basis. Thus, a construction loan mortgage for a condominium or residential subdivision will affect many units or parcels and will be released as they are each sold. In this situation, perhaps the most common form of avoidance of recording taxes is the recordation of a Master Document, to which reference can be made in later deeds and mortgages. The same economy is realized by recording a Master Set of Covenants, Conditions, and Restrictions for a subdivision or condominium and incorporating it by reference in the deeds to individual parcels or units.

When the recording fee for a mortgage is computed on the amount secured, a mortgage with a note with an open-ended principal amount raises the issue of whether to compute the fee on the amount currently advanced or on the amount that might in the future be advanced. In the Matter of the Application of Home Sav. Assn. for Exemption from Ad Valorem Taxation in Wyandotte County, 806 P.2d 1023 (Kan. App. 1991) (holding that the amount actually secured at the time of recording is the proper basis for computing the fee).

# 30

## *Construction Agreements and Finance*

## The Construction Process

Construction involves three essential parties: an owner of the property to be developed, an architect, and a general contractor. The owner traditionally performs three distinct and separate steps prior to construction. She first conceives the project, then hires an architect who designs it, and finally (with or without the architect) supervises the hiring of a general contractor.

The contractor may be selected by competitive bidding, by negotiation, or by selection (or some combination of these three processes). The owner's construction agreement with the contractor requires that the project be delivered to the owner-developer for a lump sum, at cost plus a (fixed) fee, or for a guaranteed maximum cost (with provisions for the owner and the contractor to share the savings if the project is built for less). This agreement can be either bid competitively by several contractors or negotiated with one contractor.

Once selected, the general contractor receives the completed construction drawings from the architect, who in turn often reviews the implementation of the construction agreement through administration of the agreement and/ or a series of inspections. These inspections occur at designated points in the process, for example, when the foundation is complete, when the first floor is laid, when the framing is done, and so on. These are all times at which the owner will have to accept the work of the contractor. See generally, Krotovil, Mortgage Lender Liability-Construction Loans, 38 DePaul L. Rev. 43, 44-46 (1989).

In some sense, then, the architect as an inspector becomes a project overseer, but not its supervisor. The word "supervise" was eliminated from American Institute of Architects' documents in the mid-1970s. See, e.g., AIA Document B-141, §1.5.4 (1977) (AIA documents for architectural services and construction agreements are the contracts on these subjects most widely used in the United States). If anyone supervises, it's the general contractor. See generally, Halper, Negotiating Architectural Contracts, 17 Real Est. Rev. 65 (Summer 1987); Jones, Contracts for Construction and Design Services: An Overview for Lenders and Owners, 4 Real Est. Fin. 20 (Fall 1987).

This traditional procedure undertakes all of these steps one at a time, completing the preceding one before undertaking the next. From the owner's perspective, it has the advantage of permitting a precise determination of what the project will look like and what it will cost, made in advance of any construction on the project.

This chapter has two aims. First, it seeks to build on the title and recording problems that you encountered in earlier chapters dealing with noncommercial transactions, and second, it seeks to introduce you to a new set of persons involved in the construction process — architects and construction personnel — through a discussion of their contractual rights. Thus it takes both a property- and a contract-oriented approach to its subject.

## An Architect's Duty to Prepare Plans and Specifications

Because of liability exposure and rising costs, architects have been narrowing their roles to that of designers. J. & J. Elec., Inc. v. Gilbert H. Moen Co., 9 Wash. App. 954, 516 P.2d 217 (1973). State codes sometimes provide special statutes of limitations for suits on architectural design defects. See, e.g., Minn. Stat. Ann. §541.250 (ten-year statute of limitations). The majority of courts considering the issue have decided not to impose implied warranties for fitness of or strict liability for design services rendered owners. Board of Trustees of Union College v. Kennerly, Slomanson & Smith, 167 N.J. Super. 311, 400 A.2d 850, 853 (Law Div. 1979). Query whether this would be the result if the defective architectural plans were produced from a stock supply or reproduced in great quantities and sold, perhaps through the mails. Id. at 853 (dicta). Unlike other professionals such as attorneys and doctors, the architect may be hired to produce an exact result, that is, a building that fits within the zoning envelope, is a certain size, with a certain access and elevation, and so forth. The exactitude of the employment militates in favor of a finding of an implied warranty. Likewise, when the architectural designer also builds the house, an implied warranty of habitability for the benefit of the owner may be appropriate. For a minority rule case finding an implied warranty, see Tamarac Dev. Co. v. Delamater, Freund & Assocs., P.A., 675 P.2d 361 (Kan. 1984).

Thus any liability of the architect must be based on an express contract duty or, on the contract as a whole, in tort. In a few states, like Michigan, the architect has been characterized as owing a fiduciary duty to her employer. When a duty is imposed in a contract, the injured party can either bring a cause of action for breach of the contract, in contract, or for breach of the duty, in tort. Compare Bernard Johnson, Inc. v. Continental Constructors, Inc., 630 S.W.2d 365 (Tex. App. 1982) (recognizing a cause of action for negligent performance of a contract duty), with Lesmeister v. Dilly, 330 N.W.2d 95 (Minn. 1983) (refusing to recognize this cause of action).

The design defect that is also a violation of a building or a housing code is sometimes identified as architectural negligence per se. Roy v. Poquette, 515 A.2d 1072 (Vt. 1986) (involving an engineer).

# The Architect's Duty to Supervise

This is an unsettled area of law. Architects have also been narrowing their role as project overseers. Today, absent a contractual duty, an architect is not required to supervise construction. If the supervisory duty is present in an agreement with an owner, the standard of care is that of "a professional skilled architect under the same or similar circumstances in carrying out his technical duties in relation to his services undertaken by his agreement." Aetna Ins. Co. v. Hellmuth, Obata & Kassabaum, Inc. 392 F.2d 472 (8th Cir. 1968).

The narrowest supervisory duty of an architect during construction is to assure that the project is built in substantial conformity with the plans and specifications. This duty has the virtue of tying the architect to plans that she has already presented to the owner. Schreiner v. Miller, 67 Iowa 91, 24 N.W. 738 (1885) (a leading case, with a discussion of the architect in his traditional role of project supervisor); Day v. National U.S. Radiator Corp., 241 La. 288, 128 So. 2d 660 (1961) (holding that supervision of boiler installation was outside the architect's duty when the boiler blew up and injured a worker on the project site).

Broader duties of supervision, broader than to assure conformity with the design, have been found in a duty to inspect and approve the work of the general contractor. Pancoast v. Russell, 148 Cal. App. 2d 909, 307 P.2d 719, 722-723 (1957). An architect has also been found liable in negligence for a failure to install a guardrail on the project site, Geer v. Bennett, 237 So. 2d 311 (Fla. Dist. App. 1970), and for the collapse of sheeting and shoring work in an excavation for a project, Erhart v. Hummonds, 232 Ark. 133, 334 S.W.2d 869 (1960). Contra, Day v. National U.S. Radiator Corp., supra. Thus followed, in a redrafting in standard owner-architect's agreements, the previously mentioned elimination of the word "supervise," so that the courts would not be called on to construe it.

# EXAMPLES AND EXPLANATIONS

1. When an owner-architect agreement provides that the architect "will not be required to make exhaustive or continuous on-site inspections to check the quality or quantity of work" (the phrasing of AIA Document B-141, §1.5.4), does the architect have a duty to supervise a roofing subcontractor constructing a roof?

**Explanation:**   This contractual language does not preclude a court finding that the architect has a limited duty to supervise, so a contract cause of action by the owner is still possible. See J. & J. Elec., Inc. v. Gilbert H. Moen Co., supra, from which the contract language is taken. A first issue is how the cause of action, if it comes to that, should be pled? In contract, in tort for negligence, or in tort for the negligent performance of a contractual duty? See Note, Architectural Malpractice: A Contract Based Approach, 92 Harv. L. Rev. 1975 (1979).

Finding out which cause of action is permitted is no easy research task. The case law of a state might focus on one theory but not preclude any other. Yet on the determination sometimes depends the successful assertion of a defense or the measure of damages available.

No matter how the architect's duty is pled, she has a duty to render the supervisory service with the care reasonable under the circumstances. If the design is in some sense novel or untried, closer supervision may be required. Bayuk v. Edson, 236 Cal. App. 2d 309, 46 Cal. Rptr. 49, 54 (1965).

So no matter what the theory, an architect has a duty to inspect for design defects (e.g., to find out whether the windows specified in the drawing have a two-inch gap at the top and will cause leaks and consequent damage if left that way), but no duty to inspect the construction. R. J. Reagan Co. v. Kent, 654 S.W.2d 532 (Tex. App. 1983). Anyway, as a matter of judicial economy, it may be better for the owner to sue the subcontractor directly.

2. What if in the first problem the architect had no notice of the roofing contractor's deviation from the plan and specifications for the roof?

**Explanation:**   In and of itself, the lack of notice may not matter in a cause of action for negligent supervision. Compare Lotholz v. Fiedler, 59 Ill. App. 379 (1895) (holding the architect liable for hidden deviations from a plan), with Paxton v. Alameda County, 119 Cal. App. 2d 393, 259 P.2d 934 (1953) (architect with notice liable).

3. The ultimate control over job progress is the right to stop the work. What if the architect has that right?

**Explanation:**   The right to stop work has provided the basis for imposing a duty to supervise. Compare Miller v. DeWitt, 37 Ill. 2d 273, 226

N.E.2d 630, 633 (1967) (architect's failure to advise shoring up a renovation project roof, collapsing on contractor's employees and injuring them, was negligence when the right to stop work was express in the owner-architect agreement), distinguished in McGovern v. Standish, 65 Ill. 2d 54, 357 N.E.2d 1134 (1976) (architect's right to reject or correct materials is not a right to stop work and does not result in negligent failure to supervise in action on injury of contractor's employee), with Reber v. Chandler High School Dist. No. 202, 13 Ariz. App. 133, 474 P.2d 852, 853-854 (1970) (rejecting the holding of *Miller*). Notice that, under the holding in *Miller*, an express duty in the owner-architect agreement is extended to the separate agreement between the owner and the general contractor as well. The parties probably did not intend this, or else why use separate agreements?

4. If the architect cannot be held liable under a duty to supervise, then what other later acts, performed by an architect in the course of the construction process, might render her liable?

**Explanation:** Two examples are a negligent issuance of an inspection certificate and a negligent disbursal of a retained amount under a construction agreement.

5. If an architect has a limited duty to inspect a project for design defects, should she also serve as a construction lender's inspector at the same time?

**Explanation:** No, not without some expansion of her contractual duties, unless gross negligence or bad faith is involved. A prudent lender will require a direct contractual link with an inspecting architect.

# Documenting the Process

This is a process dominated by standard forms, modified to suit the project underway. The most prevalent forms are those maintained by the American Institute of Architects (AIA). These forms were last modified and republished in 1987. The American College of Real Estate Lawyers (ACREL) has published commentary on the AIA forms and, because the AIA forms are architect-oriented, its commentary is useful when representing an owner or developer. The Associated General Contractors of America and the Engineers Joint Contract Documents Committee each publish a set of forms, representing yet other points of view. See Shapiro, The 1987 AIA A201 General Conditions: An Owner's View, 24 Real Prop. Prob. & Tr. J. 523 (1990).

# EXAMPLES AND EXPLANATIONS

6a. Sometimes a comparison of forms leads nowhere. A good example is the AIA provision that the architectural drawings remain the property of the architect. General Conditions A-201, attached to basis AIA owner-architect agreement A-101 or A-111 (1987). The ACREL recommends that all drawings are the property of the owner. How should an attorney facing a negotiation over this question respond?

**Explanation:**   By sorting out the interests involved. The owner has an interest in seeing that the same building, or a building with the same architectural detail, isn't erected next door. Moreover, the owner is paying for the services of the architect. "Ah, ha!" says the architect. Services are what the owner gets, not the drawings (which are only the product of the service). Further, the architect knows that there is no such thing as a completely original building and that she will use some of the features included in the owner's building again. Moreover, she is proud of her design and does not want the owner copying it in locations and sites for which it is not appropriate. Finally, the architect is responsible for the design and liable for any defects in it; its reuse, under circumstances over which she has no control, extends that liability.

6b. Taking each of the interests described above into account, what middle course between the *meum* and *tuum* of the AIA and ACREL provisions can you suggest?

**Explanation:**   The extreme view of an owner's rights is that the owner can assign the right to use, or reuse, the architectural plans to some third party for her own use. To this the architect might object that the proposed reuse of the plans in another location might be unsuitable for any of several reasons having to do with the site, the type of use proposed for the building, and so forth. The architect, however, might be given a right to refuse reuse of the plans, through procedures established to obtain the architect's consent to reuse. The right to refuse reuse cannot be executed unreasonably, however. A less extreme view of the owner's rights is that the owner has an interest in using the plans on a continuing basis in connection with her own use and with the occupancy of the premises; she does not wish to go back to the architect each time maintenance or renovation of the premises is undertaken. The owner may also wish to use the plans for any planned addition to the project. The more the project is likely to be altered in design by later changes or the more likely the plans are to be put into unskilled hands, the more likely the architect is to insist on retaining some rights in the plans.

When assigned initial ownership rights in the plans, the architect might be willing to negotiate over her rights in the plans when (1) an indemnity for the use of the plans in other projects or on other projects or sites is involved; (2) a mortgage lender insists on the right to use the plans to complete the project or to undertake activities necessary to protect its rights under the covenants of the mortgage; all the while, the architect may insist on retention of the right to use the plans on other projects; or (3) the architect is in default on the design contract. Circo (ed.), The Role of Lender's Counsel in the Design and Construction Process: Contract Review, Conditional Assignments, and Related Due Diligence, 24 Real Prop. Prob. & Tr. J. 556, 563 (1990).

# Construction Lending

At some point, probably by the time the owner receives architectural drawings and during the selection of a general contractor, the owner-developer is discussing financing the project with two major, and very different, types of lenders.

Since World War II, construction lending reflects a blend of the investment objectives of these two types of lenders. The first type are the construction lenders, the lenders who make short-term loans for the money used in the construction process. The difference between these loans and the residental mortgage loan is that the loan is not disbursed all at once. Rather, it is disbursed in stages, with fees and interest collected from the lender's own funds and added to the amount due the lender when at the closing it "sells the loan" to the takeout, or permanent, lender.

The latter is the second type of lender. This permanent lender has a longer-term investment objective: It provides the long-term financing for the project, in the form of a note and mortgage on the by-then improved property. This financing may be for a term of 20-25 years.

Both types of lenders will be necessary to "do the deal" that involves the improvement and construction of commercial real estate, whether it is an office building or a shopping center. In those commercial real estate markets considered very "hot" or popular with permanent lenders, it may be possible to close a construction loan transaction, knowing with certainty a takeout lender will materialize. But most lenders, being of a conservative or risk-averse bent of mind, would rather not proceed that way. Most, if not all, short-term construction lenders will want to know that a committed permanent lender is lined up to "take them out" at the completion of the construction process.

And, considered closely, tying the construction note and loan to the presence of a permanent lender makes good sense for the following reason: The construction mortgage might technically create a mortgage lien, which secures the debt and can be foreclosed upon default. But the security is a half-built building. What's that worth? Commercial real property is valued for its income stream — the rents and profits from tenants — and without that stream on line, the building is valueless. Unless partial occupancy permits can be secured from the appropriate local government, a 40 percent completed construction process is just as worthless as one 90 percent completed.

Thus the commitment for the takeout loan, in the hands of the construction lender and the developer, is the best security for the construction loan — not security in the technical sense, to be sure, but the best assurance of repayment. The purchaser at a foreclosure sale obtains the privilege of completing the construction process.

The takeout lender's commitment is accompanied by another document, negotiated between the developer and the two lenders. This is the buy-sell agreement: Its subject is the transfer of the lien of the construction lender to the permanent one, in exchange for the permanent lender's funding the loan — in effect, repaying the construction lender the proceeds of the latter's loan. It provides a description of that closing and details any preconditions that the permanent lender thinks must be met before the transfer of the lien.

One final use for the takeout commitment lies in the statutes and regulations governing national banks. The Federal Reserve Act prevents federally chartered commercial banks from specializing in real property lending by restricting such loans to a percentage of all its loans or of the bank's assets. However, if a loan is made with a binding refunding agreement — such as a takeout commitment — and has a term of 60 months or less, it is not regarded, for regulatory purposes, as a real estate loan.

## Doing the Deal Backwards: The Loan Application Process

This is the pattern: The developer collects a commitment to lend from the permanent lender and then shows it to a construction lender as an inducement to extend the construction loan. This commitment is attached to the application to the construction lender. Also attached are the many documents necessary to close the takeout loan: the note and mortgage that will be used, the type of title insurance policy required by the takeout lender, and so forth.

During the application process for the construction loan, the lender will also want to see the many documents necessary to build the building. These include the construction agreement with the general contractor, the contractor's agreements with subcontractors, the agreement for disbursement of the loan and inspection of the work in progress, the forms required for certifying progress payments and disbursements, and the leasing agreements with major tenants.

Thus all the documentation for the construction lending process, from beginning to end, is agreed on beforehand. The parties don't just agree to act reasonably and adjust their differences as they go along. That would be an invitation to litigation. No documentary surprises here — avoiding them is the major purpose of the application process.

The process has two steps. A review of the completed building's rentable space will yield a square footage from which can be projected a rental income. That income is then capitalized to determine the fair market value of the building. That fair market value is then compared with the values around it — a rough reality check for the appraisal process. Then the construction budget is reviewed to determine if the cost of the building is within its market value — well within. Construction lenders generally expect to make $1.25 for every dollar that they lend.

The construction costs under review are broadly defined. They include not only the costs of the actual construction (so-called hard costs) but also the costs of obtaining all regulatory approvals for the construction and all payments to architects, engineers, and (of course) attorneys involved in the planning of the building (so-called soft costs). Hard plus soft costs equal the total cost of construction. The total must be within the fair market value of the building.

Thus a construction lending transaction is completed by assembling all the documents necessary to it, starting with the documents needed in the future and working back to those needed in the present to close the construction loan.

## The Subordination Agreement

Quite often the time between a developer's acquisition of the land and the closing on the construction note, mortgage, and loan agreement is long enough so that the developer will not want to have a substantial amount of money tied up in the purchase of the land. The developer may either be thinly capitalized or else be carrying a large inventory of land parcels, using each parcel only as needed. The solution to this problem is to finance the land acquisition with a mortgage. However, interest rates on raw land tend to be higher than for improved property, loan-to-value ratios lower, and the term of the loan shorter. The developer's response to this situation is typically an attempt to obtain her financing from the vendor, in the form of a purchase money or take-back mortgage. Another response is the use of an installment land sale contract; the contract contains an option to convert it into a deed when the construction loan is funded, when the proceeds of that loan are available to pay off the contract obligation of the purchaser.

Whichever method is used, the installment contract or the takeback mortgage, there is either an express provision in the contract or a reference to a sidebar agreement in the mortgage, to the effect that the vendor will subordinate her interest in the property — either the lien of the mortgage or her vendor's lien under the contract — to the later lien of the construction lender. A subordination agreement is a contract to shift the priority of a senior lien to a less preferred status, junior to the lien of a later identified development or construction lender. It can be either a provision of a contract of sale, the escrow instructions, a mortgage, or a separate agreement. The construction lender will require a first lien on the land, and the subordination agreement is a method of achieving that and, at the same time, permitting the developer to put as little cash as possible up for the land acquisition.

If the subordination clause or agreement is sufficiently precise as to the type of lien that is to attain priority over the vendor's, the later subordination — meaning now a reversal of the priorities that would otherwise be established under the recording acts — can be automatic. A subordination agreement should include a statement of the maximum amount of the construction loan, the purpose of the loan, its interest rate, its term, its monthly payment, as well as a warranty that the disbursal of the loan will be applied to the particular project. Incorporating a particular mortgage form by reference is also a good idea.

Here is a skeletal subordination agreement of this type:

## SUBORDINATION AGREEMENT

This agreement, made this day *[date]* between *[developer]* and *[purchase money vendor, mortgagee, or lienholder]*, recognizes that the developer is about to execute a *[construction agreement, note and mortgage, referenced herein]*, and that a condition precedent to obtain the proceeds of this construction loan is the lender's obtaining a lien on the real property superior to that of the vendor, NOW THEREFORE the vendor agrees that he consents to and approves all provisions of the construction note and mortgage securing this note, and all agreements governing the disbursal of the proceeds of this loan. Vendor further unconditionally waives, relinquishes, and subordinates his lien in favor of the lien of the construction mortgagee.

A nonautomatic subordination agreement would require that the vendor take a second look at the construction loan note, mortgage and agreement, with an eye toward reviewing it for compliance with the earlier (and vaguer) agreement. Such a subordination is known as an executory subordination.

If the vendor does not have this opportunity to take a second look, a court asked to review the automatic agreement is asked an all-or-nothing question: Is the agreement enforceable? Or, is it too vague, or does it lack a material term and fail for indefiniteness? Would you expect a court to look more closely at an automatic or an executory subordination? Obviously a court is less likely to second-guess a vendor who has had the opportunity herself to review and approve the construction loan documents, and so the executory subordination will receive a more cursory judicial review.

If a subordination agreement requires that the proceeds of the construction loan be applied to the vendor's parcel, then the diversion of the funds to pay off the vendor is a payment for land, not for construction. To the extent that funds are so used, the vendor can benefit and still assert a breach of the subordination agreement. Is this fair? The diversion prohibited is one to the developer's other projects, unrelated to the vendor's land. The result of such a breach is a rereversal of the priorities, reestablishing the original priorities. Not a complete reordering of the priorities, but only to the extent of the breach. What about the diversion of construction loan proceeds to pay for fees and commissions owed by the developer-borrower for the project on the vendor's parcel? Often a lender will become a third-party beneficiary of provisions inserted in the subordination agreement for this purpose. For example, the vendor and the developer may agree that "the construction lender in making disbursements pursuant to the note, mortgage, and construction agreement does not represent that it will, and is under no obligation to, see that the disbursements are used for the purposes agreed to." Sometimes, too, language is inserted, in larger, boldface type, warning the vendor that some of the loan proceeds may be expended "for purposes other than improvement of the secured property."

The agreement must be executed and implemented before any default on the subordinated lien occurs. When the lienor preferred in the agreement takes advantage of the subordination, she must search the public records for documents that would prevent her from assuming the agreed-to priority.

Any agreement to subordinate to a junior lien is also, by implication, an agreement to subordinate to any lien superior to the preferred one. For example, an agreement to subordinate to a third mortgage is also an agreement to subordinate to a second mortgage. See generally Lambe, Enforceability of Subordination Agreements, 19 Real Prop. Prob. & Tr. J. 631 (1984); Abbott, Some Basic Priority Problems in a Land Development Project in Mississippi with Emphasis upon Power of Sale Foreclosure Procedures, 50 Miss. L.J. 665 (1979), providing commentary on Grenada Ready-Mix Concrete, Inc. v. Watkins, 453 F. Supp. 1298 (N.D. Miss. 1978) (an opinion with a good review of the cases to that date).

# EXAMPLES AND EXPLANATIONS

7a. A vendor taking back a mortgage agrees that she will record this mortgage just after the construction note and mortgage are recorded. The developer and the land vendor make no other agreement. What type of subordination agreement is this? Automatic or executory?

**Explanation:** It looks automatic. These are the facts involved in Middlebrook-Anderson Co. v. Southwest Sav. & Loan Assn., 18 Cal. App. 3d 1023, 96 Cal. Rptr. 338 (1971). Commentary on this case is found in Lambe, supra, at 638-641. See also Carolina Builders Corp. v. Howard-Veasey Homes, Inc., 72 N.C. App. 224, 324 S.E.2d 626, review denied, 313 N.C. 597, 330 S.E.2d 606 (1985).

Moreover, the case law is well developed on the minimum terms required for a subordination agreement that is capable of specific performance: For example, required is a maximum principal amount, interest rate, and term for the construction mortgage; a use to which the construction loan funds will be put; and maximum loan-to-value ratios (to provide the subordinating vendor with an equity cushion). See, e.g., MCB Ltd. v. McGowan, 86 N.C. App. 607, 359 S.E.2d 50 (1987) (holding a subordination that does not specify the interest rate or principal amount of later loan void for indefiniteness as a matter of law). If any material details of the agreement are left for future agreement, an automatic subordination may be void.

7b.  If the agreement on the order of recording is taken to be a type of subordination agreement, then what terms should a court incorporate by implication into this agreement?

**Explanation:**  The implied terms might come from the actual knowledge of the construction lender. However, in *Middlebrook-Anderson,* supra, there is also the suggestion that, as a matter of policy, the lender is best able to bear the risk of diverted funds and, as an expert in construction lending, bears the duty to achieve a clear agreement on the extent of lien priority for the subordinating vendor. See also Handy v. Gordon, 65 Cal. 2d 578, 422 P.2d 329 (1967). There is some suggestion in this case that automatic subordinations are not a prudent business practice for a lender.

8.  If the agreement to record in a certain order is found to be an automatic subordination agreement, is one of the terms of this implied automatic subordination a warranty by the lender not to permit the diversion of the loan proceeds from the development on the vendor's parcel?

**Explanation:**  The typical parties to the subordination agreement are the vendor and the developer (soon-to-be-borrower). Is the lender the third-party beneficiary of their agreement? In the case of the agreement to record in a given order, the construction lender has to be an active participant in the execution of the agreement, but isn't that activity required to implement any type of subordination agreement, express or implied? The answers to all of these questions are uncertain, but their very existence militates against a court's making an implied agreement out of the recording order in the first place. Having found an implied agreement, however, the court is going to have to further clarify its terms.

Other theories of the lender's responsibility for diversion of loan proceeds might vary the results. Is the lender an agent of the vendor, policing the use of the proceeds? As the vendor's agent, the lender will owe fiduciary duties to its principal, which in some jursisdictions might short-circuit the need to show damages upon a breach of the agency agreement. Is the lender in breach of an implied contract to police the use of the funds? Consequential damages will be permitted if the breach is found. Does this breach lie in tort — the breach of a duty of due care in lending? If so, then foreseeability will be a crucial issue, and the burden of proof is cast on the subordinating vendor.

9. If a jurisdiction will void a subordination agreement for failure to include a material term, will it also deny specific performance of such an agreement?

**Explanation:** Yes. Roskamp Manley Assocs. v. Davin Dev. Inv. Corp., 184 Cal. App. 3d 513, 229 Cal. Rptr. 186, 190 (1986). There is, however, authority to the contrary. Note, Real Estate Finance-Subordination Clauses: North Carolina Subordinates Substance to Form — *MCB Ltd. v. McGowen,* 23 Wake Forest L. Rev. 575, 592-595 (1988) (collecting the cases).

# Subordination and Lien Circuity

Subordination agreements sometimes create situations that result in a circuity of liens. Every lien is superior to one another as well as inferior to one another.

For example, O conveys a mortgage lien to A, who agrees to subordinate the lien to a later construction loan lien. A records only her lien, not the agreement. O conveys a lien to B. B records. O then conveys a third lien to C, who is a qualifying construction lender under the subordination agreement and records.

Every grantee has promptly recorded. Thus under any type of recording act, there is a circuity of liens. In this instance, a circuity is created by the subordination agreement. See supra pages 176-178.

Some courts have assigned priority to B, then to C, and lastly to A. An agreement to subordinate to a third lien is also an agreement to subordinate to the second. B, after all, knew nothing (at least through the records) of the A-C agreement and so should not suffer on account of it. C is assigned the next slot on the list of priorities because she bargained to step ahead of A, who is left to bring up the rear.

Is this a good solution? Perhaps, but B is preferred in a situation in which she did not expect to go first and so is given a windfall priority. C, on the other hand, expected to go before A, at least to the extent of A's lien. C's expectation can be put as a matter of subrogation: C expected to step into A's shoes.

Thus the better solution is Grant Gilmore's, which is the solution preferred by the weight of modern authority: first, to set aside the amount of A's lien, which C expected to precede; second, to pay out of the amount set aside in step one the amount of A's lien, to (1) C, up to the amount of her claim, and then (2) to A, to the extent there is any remaining balance within the amount set aside; third, to pay out to B any amount remaining after A's claim is set aside and paid out as before; and fourth, to pay out any balance remaining after the first three steps are taken, to C, up to the amount of her claim, and then to A.

The first step prevents B from realizing any windfall. It also first enforces the subordination agreement to the extent possible out of a claim of which B had constructive knowledge through the records. It enforces the agreement, to the extent possible, without violating B's expectations. Then B is paid. Then the agreement is enforced again, as to the remaining balance.

This method also carries the sub rosa message that, for the agreement to be enforced fully, it should be promptly recorded.

# EXAMPLES AND EXPLANATIONS

10a.  B in the foregoing text is often a provider of construction services claiming the protection of the mechanic's lien statutes. A is the purchase money lienor and the landowner from whom O buys the land. And C is a construction lender-lienor.

A's lien is in the amount of $4 million, B's $1 million, and C's $4 million. At the foreclosure sale, O's property is sold for $5 million. Who gets paid what?

**Explanation:**   C is paid $4 million, and B $1 million. But the steps are different in the two methods advanced here. Make sure you review those steps, infra pages 437-438.

10b.  If O diverted $1 million from the construction site on A's former parcel, would your answers change?

**Explanation:**   There is authority that says yes, and that, to the extent of the diversion, C does not step into A's shoes and is not preferred over A. Thus A would still have priority over C and B, to the extent of the $1 million.

However, the weight of this authority is diminished when there is no express warranty that C will police O for A's benefit in the subordination agreement. Thus a few cases imply such a warranty. It is something for which A could have, but did not, bargain; and C, not being a party to the original O-A agreement, is not bound to it. Thus, in the view of the majority of courts considering the issue, C has no duty to police O for A's benefit.

The majority view is bolstered by cases on other, related issues: for example, whether a lender has a duty to inspect a construction site to make sure of the quality of the construction for the benefit of its later purchaser — quality in this context is often measured by the housing code or the implied warranty of habitability. Most cases answer that the lender has no such duty. Only when the lender clearly violates prudent lending practices is such a duty likely to be imposed.

In view of the problems with which subordination agreements confront lenders, some may not even review such agreements; rather, they may prefer that the agreements be reviewed by the title insurance company closing the loan. The likely effect of such a refusal if nothing more is said to the title company is for the insurer to treat every agreement as executory.

# The Wraparound Mortgage

When a project needs renovation or modernization, or the developer needs new financing for any other reason, the financing is often provided by a wraparound loan. It is a mortgage that has a subordinate and subsequent lien on real property as to which a superior lien remains unsatisfied. It is not, however, a standard form junior mortgage. It is different in three respects. First, in addition to the mortgage covenants and the note, a third document is executed between the borrower and the lender. This third document is often in the form of a rider to the mortgage, providing that the borrower will continue to pay all installments and charges due the superior mortgagee as they become due and payable, in order to keep the superior mortgage from going into default.

The other two distinctive features of the wraparound loan are found in the note. The first of these is the note's principal amount. It is the sum of the outstanding amounts due on the superior loan and the new funds advanced upon this refinancing. The principal of the wrapping, subordinate loan thus appears much greater than it is in fact, because only the funds actually disbursed are at risk; they are secured, meanwhile, by the equity in the property built up since the execution of the superior mortgage.

The third feature differentiating a wraparound mortgage is the note's interest rate. It will usually be higher than the first or other superior mortgage, but lower than the current market rate. Thus, the wraparound is used to preserve the prior extension of credit at lower rates than those currently available. (Of course, a due-on-sale or further encumbrance clause in the superior mortgage may throw a crimp into the use of the wraparound loan.) This third feature explains the economic incentive to use such a loan.

Here is an example of a wraparound agreement:

## WRAPAROUND MORTGAGE AGREEMENT
## OR RIDER

This agreement is made with reference to a mortgage [the wraparound note and mortage] dated _____ between _____, the mortgagor, and _____, the mortgagee. The secured property is subject to a lien described as follows: [the senior mortgage(s)]. Mortgagor agrees to comply with all covenants, terms, and conditions of the senior mortgage, except the requirement to make all payments of principal and interest, which payments mortgagee agrees to pay when due, so long as the mortgagor shall not default on any other term.

Mortgagor agrees further that, to the extent mortgagee makes payment on the senior mortgage, mortgagee shall be entitled to a pro rata lien on the secured property and be subrogated to the rights of the senior mortgagee. Upon default by mortgagor under the senior mortgage, the mortgagee hereunder may pay, compromise, or settle the claims of the senior mortgage.

To the extent not previously assigned, all rents and profits from the secured property are hereby assigned to the mortgagee as further security for the debt to him. Any default in the senior mortgage is also a default hereunder.

Mortgagor shall notify the senior mortgagee of the right of mortgagee hereunder to make all payments directly to said senior mortgagee, and also request that said senior mortgagee notify the mortgagee herein of any default in the senior mortgage. Any amount found in violation of the applicable usury laws shall be applied in reduction of principal of the notes secured by this mortgage.

This type of financing has been in use since the 1930s. In the 1970s, however, its use became widespread as real estate investment trusts used it, in part as an accounting tool to increase the amount of income carried on their books. The wraparound mortgage also has other names: It is sometimes known as the hold-harmless, the all-inclusive, or the overriding mortgage.

Another use for the wraparound loan occurs upon a sale of the real property, as purchase money financing. Here the vendor gives the purchaser a deed to the property, and the purchaser executes a wraparound note and mortgage, along with a third document, a mortgage rider or agreement in which the vendor is obligated to continue to pay off the first mortgage, still outstanding and unsatisfied after the title is transferred. The purchaser takes title subject to the outstanding, third-party mortgage lien and gives the vendor, as a downpayment, the value of her equity in the property, over and above the amount of the fair market value necessary to secure the outstanding lien. The principal amount of the wraparound loan is the market value of the property, and the purchaser pays interest on the face amount of the wraparound loan, often at current rates of interest (often higher than the rate on the wrapped, superior mortgage note). Here the vendor, promising to continue to pay off the superior mortgage, receives the payment on the wraparound loan, passes along monies necessary to keep the superior loan from going into default, and pockets the difference.

In this second, purchase money use of the wraparound loan, the vendor is really functioning as a lender; she is essentially lending her creditworthiness to the purchaser — which is why a purchaser might use this device. It is a means to avoid borrowing in one's own name or using one's own line of credit if that line is stretched thin.

Wraparound loans can be tiered, so that there are many subordinate, and wrapping, loans, each one used in connection with a refinancing of the property or with a transfer of its title.

# EXAMPLES AND EXPLANATIONS

11a. If the wraparound mortgage lien is foreclosed, what is the amount of the credit bid permitted the junior, wraparound lender? Is it the face amount of the wraparound loan or the amount actually disbursed by the junior mortgagee?

**Explanation:** The amount of the credit bid (the amount permitted a foreclosing mortgagee in a bid not requiring cash or a certified check at the sale) is but the tip of the iceberg of a larger problem, which probably can't be addressed until we know whether the wraparound lender, or a third-party purchaser, is the successful bidder at the sale.

11b. So then, what if the wraparound lender is purchaser at the sale?

**Explanation:** It probably does not matter. Because the senior lien is not affected by this foreclosure, a credit bid of either the face amount of the loan or the amount of the "true loan" (the amount actually disbursed) will permit the wraparound lender to take the title subject to the senior lien; it in effect will free the title of any equitable interest created by the rider or agreement on the part of the developer or vendor to continue to pay the wrapped, outstanding superior loan. No matter what the bid, the wraparound lender gets her bargain: the ability to take possession and the title subject to the senior lien, and hence the right to assume the mortgage payments on the senior lien herself.

However, because either the face amount or the true loan amount will have this effect, the lesser should probably be used. Its use is less mischievous. Consider that a credit bid of the face amount may wipe out the obligation of the wraparound borrower (to the wraparound lender) to repay the superior lien — so a wraparound lender is ill-advised to bid the face amount. Worse, doing so may result in a claim by the wraparound borrower on the "proceeds" of the foreclosure sale. If the lender is eventually required to back up her credit bid with cash, the borrower may claim the proceeds in excess of the amount actually disbursed or outstanding on the wraparound loan as her own. Indeed, this claim is stronger when a third-party purchaser pays cash in excess of the true loan amount of the wraparound loan.

11c.  Consider then, what if a third party does purchase at the foreclosure sale, paying cash at the sale?

**Explanation:**   In this latter situation, the proceeds in excess of the true loan should go to repay the superior lien before being given to the borrower: That is, the person conducting the foreclosure should recognize that in the foreclosure of a wraparound loan, the mortgage rider or agreement to repay outstanding debts creates an implied obligation to distribute the proceeds of the sale to the superior mortgagee (or mortgagees) before giving any proceeds to the wraparound borrower. This implied term of the rider may be thought of as an implied agreement to repay the superior loan upon foreclosure of the wraparound lien. The weakness of this analysis is that it results in a windfall repayment of the superior lienholder's debt. However, the alternative is to tempt the borrower to force a default and foreclosure on the wraparound mortgage in order to get at the proceeds, bid in cash by an unsuspecting purchaser. Subjecting the distribution of the proceeds to the implied term permits that purchaser to take the property as debt-free as possible, and uses each and every dollar bid to free the title of the superior lien. Depending on how much is bid, however, remember that the purchaser will still take the title subject to superior lien (or liens).

# Usury

Usury involves (1) a loan, or a forbearance on money lent, (2) repayable absolutely, made for (3) interest in excess of the maximum statutory rate, and (4) made with the intent of exceeding that maximum. A 1980 federal statute, a provision of the Depository Institutions Deregulation and Monetary Control Act of that year, preempted state usury statutes for most first-lien residential mortgages securing real property unless the state legislature, within a three-year period, overrode the federal preemption. Fourteen states did so. See Wechsler, Survey: Real Estate Transactions, 35 Syracuse L. Rev. 589, 589-591 n.10 (1984) (reporting that Colorado, Georgia, Hawaii, Idaho, Iowa, Kansas, Maine, Massachusetts, Minnesota, Nevada, North Carolina, South Carolina, South Dakota, Wisconsin, and Puerto Rico overrode the federal preemption in order to continue their state usury statutes in effect). The federal statute was enacted to permit the introduction of adjustable rate mortgages, as well as to smooth the flow of mortgage capital across state lines. The availability of consumer protection statutes, as well as concepts of implied covenants of good faith and fair dealing and rules about unconscionability, made usury protection less crucial to many borrowers. See Goldstein, Unconscionability: Some Reconsiderations with Particular Reference to New-Type Mortgage Transactions, 17 Real Prop. Prob. & Tr. J. 412, 416-417 (1982).

Thus, in about one-fifth of the states, usury statutes continue to apply as before. However, each statute contains exceptions, and even if the usury ceiling applies, a search for exceptions is necessary; the one for corporate loans is perhaps the most used exception in real property transactions. This exception has been expanded in many statutes to cover loans to limited partnerships. In some states, exceptions exist for particular types of lenders; in others, exceptions are made for particular types of mortgage loans, for example, federally subsidized or underwritten loans.

However, even in states accepting the federal preemption, noninstitutional loans for the purchase of a residence, intrafamily real property loans, nonowner occupied residential loans, junior mortgages on residential property, and loans secured by residential real property made for purposes other than the purchase of the property must still be scrutinized for usury violations.

Taking the four elements of usury in reverse order, consider first the necessary *intent*. The word here means an intent to require more than the maximum rate, not an intent to violate the law per se. Actual subjective intent need not be shown, so that a loan agreement with a statement of an interest rate greater than that permissible, is sufficient proof of usurious intent. Usury can thus be presumed from a loan agreement usurious on its face, except when an honest mistake was made; then the presumption of usury can be rebutted. However, a mistake in interpreting the usury law is no defense (even if the mistake is honestly made).

Usurious intent is sometimes measured by looking back over the term of the loan at the effective annual rate of interest. Thus, to factor in discounts and points, the courts may apportion such charges over the loan term, or else compute the interest rate on the declining balance of the loan after this apportionment. However, for other purposes, it is often also measured by the intent evidenced in the loan documents.

Interest is compensation for the use of borrowed funds, so that a lender is not *exacting interest in excess of the maximum rate* when charging reasonable fees for closing and settlement services and passing those fees along to the appraiser, credit reporting agency, surveyor, property insurer, attorney, title insurer, or recorder of deeds. See County Sav. & Loan Assn. v. Freeman, 534 S.W.2d 903 (Tex. 1976), noted in 13 Hous. L. Rev. 773 (1977) (a discussion of closing fees).

As to *a loan or forbearance on money lent,* the courts often talk of being realistic, preferring to examine the substance of the transaction over its form; however, they routinely allow a price differential for installment sales. Allowing a higher price for property bought on time effectively removes many installment land sale contracts from scrutiny under the usury laws.

A *borrower's absolute obligation to repay* exempts a lender from the usury laws when the loan is repayable only upon the happening or nonhappening of a bona fide contingency. An advance of money as an investment, subject to the risk that it will be lost if the enterprise fails, is not a loan subject to the usury laws. If there is a genuine risk that the lender can wind up with less than she invested, there likewise is no loan.

What techniques can you think of to avoid the impact of an applicable usury statute? A borrower, of course, can always shop for a loan in a state with a lenient usury statute. Both borrower and lender might consider (1) the sale and assignment of the mortgage note at a discount; (2) the use of a sale and leaseback transaction; (3) the use of an installment land sale contract; (4) a sale and repurchase transaction with the lender; (5) a wrap-around mortgage; or (6) some contingent compensation and/or equity partici-pation by the lender in the project. To survive recharacterization as a loan in a later equitable proceeding, however, there should be business as well as legal reasons for the use of any alternative transaction.

If the wraparound mortgage described in the previous section is used to acquire land by a developer-purchaser, is there a usury problem present in the calculation of interest on an amount that the vendor-lender-purchase money mortgagee did not actually advance?

Assuming that no mortgage note is usurious on its face, probably no usury is present in the wraparound mortgage because the vendor has not exacted a prior advantage under the existing first lien loan and has, in fact, advanced credit, but not cash, worth the face amount of the wraparound loan. If the purchaser took out a mortgage in her own right and later refinanced with a wraparound junior mortgage, she is in effect mortgaging her own existing creditworthiness and so typically is not paying more than the usury statute permits. In neither case is there a "loan" present. The wraparound loan is instead a sale of credit, but one in which the vendor assists the purchaser to obtain the land — the purchaser is not paying interest on money not advanced, and cases finding usury when a lender calculates the interest on nondisbursed principal are not applicable. Cf. Stuchin v. Kasirer, 237 N.J. Super. 604, 568 A.2d 907 (App. Div. 1990) (holding that no usury existed in wraparound, 9 percent loan that also provided for interest rate of 24 percent after default).

# The Role of the Subcontractor

In the contractual and financing schemes just described, the construction lender is presented with a project that is, by the end of the loan application procedure, fully documented; that is, the owner-developer will have executed a construction agreement with the general contractor. The latter, in turn, will have entered into agreements with the various subcontractors and build-ing trades needed to construct the project.

These agreements with the subs are, in fact, the backbone of the general contractor's estimates for completing the project. The latter's having them in hand gives her, and in turn the lender, confidence that the project can indeed be built for the amount stated in the general contractor's agreement with the owner.

In general, the sub knows that her bid, if accepted, will become the basis of the construction agreement. What if the sub's cost estimates are wrong, and her services cannot be delivered for the price stated? There is likely to be economic loss up the line — from the sub who will have to absorb the mistake or pass it along, to the general contractor who will have insufficient loan funds to call on, to the lender, whose loan may become insecure as a result.

Mistakes in cost estimates by subs are likely also to cause delay on the job site. As a result, the general contractor may become liable to the owner under liquidated or actual damage provisions in the construction agreement. She may also suffer damages in her own right, as a result of having to pay for labor and equipment for a longer period than anticipated. Often in such instances, with no physical injury or accident associated with the loss, the damages are purely pecuniary or economic. Are these economic damages recoverable? Prosser states that economic losses are not recoverable in negligence. W. Prosser, Torts 665 (4th ed. 1971). For some cases from one state on design professionals, see Prichard Bros., Inc. v. Grady Co., 407 N.W.2d 423 (Minn. App. 1987) (architect not liable in negligence when duty imposed by contract); Waldor Pump v. Orr-Schelen-Mayerson & Assocs., 386 N.W.2d 375 (Minn. App. 1986) (engineer liable in negligence to subcontractor to draft reasonably competent plans); D & A Dev. v. Butler, 357 N.W.2d 156 (Minn. App. 1984) (architect not liable for delay in completing plans).

If the subcontractor cannot recover her damages through her agreement, but has added uncompensated value to the project, she may file a mechanic's lien. The presence of such a lien in the public records may cause the lender not to issue the next disbursement of the loan, and further delays and damages can result from that. Usually any disbursed payment to the mechanic made by check has a waiver of lien rights on the check, above the space on the back for an endorsement.

# Mechanic's Liens

## Statutory Origins

These liens are statutory creatures. Their purpose is to provide payment for work performed or materials supplied in construction, repair, or improvement of real property and so to encourage that improvement. More fully, perhaps, their purpose may be said to protect those "mechanics" (the general contractor's subcontractors, and perhaps even sub-subs) who add value to property but who do not deal directly with the titleholder (including the holder of most present and future interests) for whom the improvement is made. For those who deal directly, their usual remedy is to negotiate directly over fees and to sue for breach of their employment contract.

These liens were unknown to the common law, although it is easy to regard them as an equitable remedy for unjust enrichment, and the property titleholder who benefits from an improvement will be unable to convey free of the lien after accepting the services or materials of the protected mechanic.

The first such lien statute was enacted by the Maryland General Assembly, at the suggestion of Thomas Jefferson and James Madison, to induce mechanics to work on the construction of the new capital city of the Republic. Md. Laws, 1791, ch. 45, §10. In 1803, Pennsylvania was the second state to enact such a law. It applied to certain areas in Philadelphia. In contrast, the first Georgia law on the subject was enacted as an ordinance of the City of Savannah in 1820. All states now have such statutes. An up-to-date compilation is found in Secured Transactions Guide (CCH), §§8301 et seq. (1989).

Generalizations about these statutes are hazardous, but *in general* they are established by a recording of the lien by the mechanic. The description of the property to which the lien is to apply must be specific. Upon filing, the lien applies to both land and the improvements on it. Sometimes the lien is effective upon recording, but sometimes its effectiveness relates back to the "commencement of the work" — a term often defined as the commencement of any work on a project, not just of a particular mechanic's work on the improvement.

Where the relation-back principle is used, a lender making the first disbursement for a construction loan will check the construction site to ascertain one of two things: first, that no materials have been delivered to it, and second, that no signs of work are visible on it. Either event might give rise to a mechanic's lien. The lender may even take pictures of the site on the closing or disbursal date. Sometimes, as in Florida, the relation-back principle is used only when a notice of a lien is filed in advance, and then only against intervening parties with constructive notice of this filing. The lender won't want the soil disturbed if its excavator can claim the benefit of a prior lien.

Although construction mortgage lenders customarily attempt to protect themselves against a loss of priority to mechanics, the mechanic's lien laws of many states go further and provide expressly that when the mortgage is recorded prior to the commencement of construction, it is assigned a priority over any mechanic's lien arising during construction. This is often referred to as the majority, or "priority," rule. See Kratovil, Mortgage Lender Liability-Construction Loans, 38 DePaul L. Rev. 43, 45 n.6 (1989). With such a statutory provision in effect, one might better refer to the mechanic's lien law as the construction lenders law and dispense with mechanic's lien waivers (the latter will seldom happen). The rationale for such a provision is that no mechanic would be working on the construction site unless the lender were willing to provide the loan, so why not encourage such loans with just this type of provision? Eleven states follow a different rule. See infra this page. In Missouri, for example, a construction mortgagee by definition is deemed to have subordinated its mortgage to mechanic's liens on the same project. Sometimes the mortgagee's control over the disbursement of the loan, or direct disbursement to the mechanic, is given as the reason for such a (minority) rule. See, e.g., H. B. Deal Constr. Co. v. Labor Discount Center, Inc., 418 S.W.2d 940 (Mo. 1967).

There have been numerous attacks on the constitutionality of these statutes, most of which have been rebuffed. See Note, Constitutionality of Mechanic's Lien Statutes, 34 Wash. & Lee L. Rev. 1067 (1977). In the last several decades, however, several states have redrafted their statutes in response to Sniadach v. Family Fin. Corp., 395 U.S. 337 (1969), and its progeny.

## Scope and Inclusiveness of Mechanic's Lien Statutes

The definition of mechanics protected by these lien statutes has tended to become more inclusive over the years. For example, the original Savannah law protected only master masons and carpenters. Today, in some jurisdictions, an architect, surveyor, landscape architect, engineer, or urban planner may be covered as well. As a result, many statutes cover both those with direct contracts with the owner and those without such contracts. Thus one method of delineating the scope of a lien statute is to include specific occupations and trades. But see Branecky v. Seaman, 688 S.W.2d 117 (Tex. App. 1984), writ refused (distinguishing between an architect who draws the plans, who is not protected by the statute, and an architect who draws plans and supervises construction, who is).

Another method of assessing a lien statute's scope is to examine the number of contractual links between the person claiming the lien and the owner. About half the states use the degree of removal from contractual privity with the owner as the measure of coverage. In these states, the general contractor and her subcontractor are covered, or the subs of the subs are covered, or (even) the sub-subs of the subs are covered. In the other half of the states, the lien covers any mechanic who adds value to an improvement.

If the applicable statute reaches the third tier of subcontractors mentioned above, so generally will a construction lender's system of direct disbursement by check, with an endorsement line on the back under a waiver of lien.

Today many state statutes give the construction lender priority over the workers paid with its proceeds. Eleven states do not clearly accord this preference under their statutes. They are Alaska, Colorado, Illinois, Indiana, Iowa, Maine, Missouri, Montana, Oregon, Virginia, and Wyoming. California provides a limited priority for construction lenders.

## *Stop Notices*

In some states giving the construction lender this preference, mechanics have the option of filing a stop notice with the lender, indicating that they are unpaid for work done or materials supplied. After this filing, the lender pays the person supposedly meant to pay the filing mechanic at its peril. This stop notice procedure is a recognition of the fact that, if the mechanic is to be paid once the construction deal goes sour, it is to the loan proceeds that the mechanic must look. The action to foreclose the lien asserted in this way must be brought within a certain time of the filing, or else the lien is lost. California and Washington have stop notice procedures in their statutes.

## *Enforcement*

Mechanic's liens generally are enforced or perfected by judicial foreclosure. If several mechanics each obtain a judgment and the funds for satisfying all of them are insufficient, there is no effective method of allocating priority among the protected mechanics themselves. In some states, each takes equally; in others, a reverse order of contractual privity with the owner is used. This need for express prioritizing is a result of the legal fact that, in many states, if one mechanic gains priority over the construction lender, all mechanics on the same project do too.

# EXAMPLES AND EXPLANATIONS

12. Is title insurance adequate to protect against mechanic's liens?

**Explanation:**  Not in its standard form policies. Special endorsements are needed. Title insurers will often insist on site pictures and complicated escrow procedures handled by the title insurer itself. Because many title insurers found in the mid-1970s that their escrow procedures were insufficient protection, they will also insist on bring-down title searches before each disbursement. Such searches update a prior search, presumably made just before the last disbursement.

13. An excavator deposits top soil at a construction site. The soil has been taken from elsewhere and transported to the site. Upon noticing the pile of top soil, what should a lender considering a construction loan application do?

**Explanation:**  Obtain a lien waiver from whoever delivered the soil. Rupp v. Earl H. Cline & Sons, Inc., 230 Md. 573, 188 A.2d 146 (1963).

14. Is a lien available for demolition work necessary to make way for an improvement expressly covered by the applicable mechanic's lien statute?

**Explanation:** Probably not. When the statute reaches only so far, the courts are unlikely to extend it without statutory authority. They are used to mechanics grasping at any theory to receive payment and are only too likely to send them to the legislature instead.

15. How about a swimming pool contractor who files a lien obtainable by any person "improving a building"?

**Explanation:** No lien. While a mechanic's lien statute is remedial and so should be liberally construed, its reach should not be extended beyond its plain meaning. The meaning of "building" is a structure intended for occupancy and shelter. Moreover, the legislative history of many mechanic's lien statutes includes a series of broadening amendment to add new lienable structures and services; perhaps the matter is best left to future legislative action. If swimming pools are to be lienable, the legislature should say so. Freeform Pools, Inc. v. Strawbridge Home for Boys, Inc., 228 Md. 297, 179 A.2d 683 (1962).

16. If the mechanic's work violates applicable setback or other land use control laws, can the cost of rendering the improvement legal be set off against the amount of the lien?

**Explanation:** Yes. If the mechanic resorts to the law, she is bound to have done her work in conformance to applicable law, unless misled by the owner into installing a noncomplying improvement.

17. If a material supplier files a security interest on a fixture, may she also have a mechanic's lien?

**Explanation:** Not in California. When a lien is uncertain, an Article 9 UCC filing is the backup protection, as it might be for demolition work or the construction of temporary work necessary for use on the job site.

For the mechanic, it is safe to say that obtaining satisfaction of this type of lien is a legal minefield that requires legal counsel to get through it safely. The simple mechanic's lien law is a non sequitur.

# Loan Participations

The permanent lender is likely to seek other lenders to help it fund its loan. This involves a sharing of the risk of default, raising capital to meet its loan closing and funding commitments, and a sharing of the benefits of the long-term investment. It is in effect a partial assignment of its status as a mortgagee.

The nature of the assignment is the subject of an agreement called the participation agreement.[1] It is drawn up between the original lender, often called the lead lender, and the participating lenders. The lead lender is often classified as either an assignor of an interest in the mortgage lien itself — the most common characterization — or as the agent of the rest of the participants, a debtor of the participants (who are its creditors), a joint venturer for the purpose of making the loan, or a trustee. The plethora of descriptions gives some idea of the complexity of the relationship established. See, e.g., Manchester Bank v. Connecticut Bank & Trust Co., 497 F. Supp. 1304 (D.N.H. 1980) (finding that a participation is not a security for purposes of the federal securities laws).

Absent an agreement otherwise, buying a loan participation is the purchase and sale of an undivided interest in the note itself — but not an interest in the lien, with the consequent right to enforce the lien should that become necessary. Hence, for this purpose, the loan participant is described as an assignee. The alternative is describing the participant as one with the right to receive mortgage payments passed along by the lead lender; this description creates contract remedies in the participant but leaves the right to deal with the mortgagor exclusively with the lead lender. (Recently this method of describing the relationship has surfaced in the bankruptcy context.) The legal title to the lien is retained by the lead lender, and the latter has the only recorded interest in the secured real property. Participation agreements are not customarily recorded.

Absent an agreement otherwise, the participants and the lead lender are presumed to share in the proceeds of the loan on a pro rata basis. When the proceeds of the loan are insufficient to repay each participant its agreed share, each participant and the lead again share the available proceeds on a pro rata basis. This is the majority rule. (A minority rule, used in a few states, provides that the order of assignment controls: first to participate, first in right.)

Two exceptions to the pro rata rule arise. The first occurs when the lead lender provides a guaranty of repayment to the participant; then only the participants share pro rata, before the lead is repaid. Thus participants go first, pro rata, followed by the lead lender. Two computational variations on this first exception exist: The pro rata computation preceding distribution does, or does not, include the lead's share. The second exception occurs when

---

1. Today the participation agreement generally represents both the terms governing the relationship between the participant and the lead lender. In the past, however, it was common to issue the participant a certificate of participation, as well as to execute a participation agreement.

the participations mature at different times. Then, the order of maturity determines the priority of each participant's pro rata distribution.

The participation agreement will normally require the lead lender to share all information provided by the mortgagor with the participants, but precludes the latter from dealing directly with the mortgagor. Sometimes the mortgagor is required to send information to the participants, who nonetheless can only communicate back through the lead. The lead lender also generally warrants ownership of the loan, regulatory compliance of the loan, and the insured status of the loan and the property. Most loans are assigned on a nonrecourse basis, except as to any specific warranties given by the lead lender in the participation agreement. Further assignment of the loan participation is restricted, as is further modification in the loan documents, without the approval of (respectively) the lead and the participants. See Penthouse Intl., Inc. v. Dominion Federal Sav. & Loan Assn., 665 F. Supp. 301 (S.D.N.Y. 1987), rev'd, 855 F.2d 963 (2d Cir. 1988), cert. denied, 490 U.S. 1005 (1989) (where the assignment of a participation provoked litigation when the deal collapsed).

Recent federal opinions, issued in the context of litigation conducted by federal regulators taking over the lead lender, indicate a reluctance to find a fiduciary duty owed by the lead lender to the participants. See, e.g., Northern Trust Co. v. Federal Deposit Ins. Corp., 619 F. Supp. 1340, 1344 (W.D. Okla. 1985). The participation agreement is sometimes said to control this matter, and a fiduciary duty will not be inferred from an otherwise silent agreement. See, e.g., Colorado State Bank v. Federal Deposit Ins. Corp., 671 F. Supp. 706 (D. Colo. 1987).

The primary function of the lead lender is to continue to service the loan. For this it receives a fee. In the normal event, this is little problem for the participant, but the participant's right upon the mortgagor's default is critical and often is the subject of negotiations between the lead and the participants. If the lead lender is severely restricted in its rights in dealing with the mortgagor, the latter will not be able to efficiently work out of the default. For example, the right of the lead to draft and accept a deed in lieu of foreclosure is usually not very clear in these agreements. See generally Threedy, Loan Participations — Sales or Loans? Or Is That the Question?, 68 Or. L. Rev. 649 (1989). In Caronlet Sav. & Loan Assn. v. Citizens Sav. & Loan Assn., 604 F.2d 464 (7th Cir. 1979), the court found in the lead's right to service the loan a right to modify its terms.

# An Updated Construction Model

The last half of the 1960s saw an increase in inflation. The costs of energy soared after 1973. In the early 1980s, interest rates for both construction and permanent loans reached all-time high levels. These pressures on construction costs — plus a building boom in oil-patch and Sunbelt cities, the availability of foreign capital for real estate investments, and the rebuilding of inner cities — has caused the construction industry to search for new arrangements in order to build more quickly. In some overbuilt regions, these arrangements also saw developers go bust more quickly.

One result of these pressures was reflected in the so-called fast track. Instead of an architect preparing a complete set of construction drawings and supervising the bidding process all at once, the process is condensed (but only in markets heated up by the pressures listed previously) — financing, design, and construction activities are combined. For a general description of the fast track, see K. Sabbagh, Skyscraper 13-15 (1990).

The construction process itself is hard to shorten, but the time involved in planning for it can be. Because this planning time leads up to a lender's commitment, it is crucial for locking in loans at predictable, manageable rates.

Thus, two steps are often taken to shorten the planning time. First, the general contractor is brought into the planning earlier, to review the architectual drawings for construction problems. This early review is an attempt to locate problems before they get to the job site. As such, it uses the contractor's experience on other projects with the capability of the building trades and with what products are available commercially (as opposed to ones requiring special manufacturing). It can also provide an early estimate of costs, particularly in areas where costs might run unexpectedly high. While the general contractor is not selected by competitive bidding this way, the benefits of this early consultation may more than compensate for whatever savings would have otherwise resulted.

The contractor's involvement in this planning may be based contractually on a cost plus a fee basis (the fee being a percentage of the construction costs or fixed), on a cost plus fee credited against a lump sum or guaranteed cost budget, or on a lump sum, guaranteed cost, or other construction agreement. If there is no construction agreement in force and the general contractor is working for the owner-developer on some other basis, then one further step that the developer can take to assure a fast track for the project is to execute the first contracts needed for construction herself. Examples might be contracts for site preparation, excavation, or demolition on the site, with a provision in these agreements providing for later assignment to the general contractor, once selected.

Second, the construction drawings can be done in sections, and let out for bids as they are completed. This saves a good deal of time. Bids are received in sequential batches and reviewed by both the contractor and the architect. While traditionally the general contractor assembles and selects the subcontractor, under this aspect of fast tracking the owner still benefits from seeing the competitive bids submitted by the subs while also participating directly in the process and receiving whatever early warning signs of cost over-runs develop.

Only the more sophisticated owner-developer can fast track a project because it requires continuous owner involvement. It also overlaps the design and construction process, resulting in time savings as well as a certain amount of healthy competition between the design and construction professionals.

# EXAMPLES AND EXPLANATIONS

18.  As a construction lender, what types of lending procedures will have to be modified for projects on a fast track? What if an architect and contractor are joint venturers or partners in providing fast track services to owners? What advice should owners faced with such arrangements be given?

**Explanation:**   A fast track construction process is reviewed briefly in Fisher, Fast Track Construction: A Legal Quandary, Prob. & Prop. (Mar.-Apr. 1990), at 28. When on the fast track, the architect likely will become more than usually concerned about liability for her construction cost estimates. More generally, the allocation of the risk of cost overruns is also likely to become a hot topic for negotiations between the parties.

Charting and scheduling the various subcontractors is another concern. Much more attention will be paid to such charts, as well as to devising shorter timetables for handling change orders and disputes. Generally, the role of the architect and the construction manager will be increased, giving them a greater role in approving change orders and resolving disputes. Schenk, Construction Wars: Part II: Risk and the Construction Manager: A Continuing Development, 24 Real Prop. Prob. & Tr. J. 593, 606-608 (1990). Thus far, however, no set of fast track forms is generally available.

# 31

## Shopping Center Covenants

## Real and Equitable Covenants

Before discussing covenants that define the types of goods that may be sold or businesses that may be conducted on leased premises in a shopping center, a brief review of the law of real and equitable covenants is in order. In your first-year courses, you probably studied schemes of real or running "residential only" covenants in the context of the suburban residential subdivision. See, e.g., Neponsit Property Owners' Assn., Inc. v. Emigrant Indus. Sav. Bank, 278 N.Y. 248, 15 N.E.2d 793 (1938). For a real covenant to run with the land, the legal requirements were three in number: the original parties to it must intend that it run, it must "touch and concern" the land, and the covenantor and covenantee and their successors must be in privity of estate.

In the context of shopping centers, you perhaps studied cases involving the second element of a running covenant, litigating the issue of whether anticompetitive covenants touch and concern the land. Coomes v. Aero Theatre & Shopping Center, Inc., 207 Md. 432, 114 A.2d 631 (1955); Whitinsville Plaza, Inc. v. Koteas, 378 Mass. 85, 390 N.E.2d 243 (1979) (involving a drug store). In equity, the third requirement is replaced with an inquiry into whether the party against whom the covenant is to be enforced has notice of it. This is no big deal for a recorded lease because the recording acts themselves have the effect of imparting constructive notice. Further, you may be relieved to learn that there is no litigation on, or authority for, enforcing the common law requirements for a running or real covenant in the context of a shopping center. This is probably so because the center's landlord typically restricts his tenants' rights to sublease or assign their leased premises, thereby directly conducting all releasing of the center's premises himself.

A real or running covenant, however, can attach to interests other than the fee simple absolute of a residential lot in a subdivision. For example, restrictive covenants can attach to leases. See, e.g., Thurston v. Minke, 32 Md. 487 (1870).

Consider the following scheme of covenants set within the legal framework for a small, ten-store, strip shopping center, with a small department store for a magnet or anchor tenant (MAT).

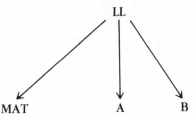

LL leases first to MAT, then to A, and then to B. In his lease, A is given an exclusive right to sell shoes in the center and, at the same time (and in the same lease), promises not to sell toys. In his lease, B is given an exclusive right to sell toys and similarly promises not to sell shoes.

1. Should MAT be included in the general scheme of covenants? Definitely not. MAT is likely to be an anchor or magnet tenant, with a broad line of goods. To give MAT an exclusive for its current line would unduly restrict the developer's power to obtain a good tenant mix.

2. Suppose that A opens a toy department in his shoe store. B sues A to enforce the restrictive covenant A made with LL. This covenant is contained in a prior lease, and B the subsequent lessee may enforce it on the theory that the covenant was retained by LL for B's benefit and that when B obtained the benefit of it in his lease, he also obtained the power necessary to enforce it. Thus, if LL could obtain judgment against A, so can B. Judgment for B.

3. Now suppose that B opens a children's shoe department in his toy store. A sues B to enforce the covenant B made with LL. A has a more difficult time formulating a theory for his suit. The difficulty arises from the fact that a prior lessee is seeking to enforce a covenant not in existence when he executed his lease. How can this difficulty be overcome? There are three approaches or theories. If, for example, LL expressly promises A that his exclusive will be enforced by the extraction of restrictive covenants on retained, unleased premises and subsequent lessees, then the burden of that covenant attaches to the retained premises and burdens future lessees. (Landlords will not often want to make such a promise in their first leases, so this theory often does not work.) Can such a promise, however, be implied when A is given an exclusive that is implemented by a restrictive covenant binding B?

If not, a second theory that A might use is that the exclusive use covenant in A's deed implies that LL promised to burden retained premises with a covenant not to compete with A. This implied reciprocal negative servitude runs with the unleased premises to burden future lessees who are charged with notice of it. Such notice can be obtained through a search of the records, but this works only where all leases are recorded and B can be put either on actual notice through a title search or on constructive notice if the deed is recorded and B does not search. A second way in which B can be put on notice is through an inspection of the premises in the center, B noting that A is operating the only shoe store. The inspection then charges B with an inquiry, either in the records or directly of A, to ascertain what his rights are. It is unlikely, however, that a walk through the center by a prospective tenant would show more than a confusing plethora of retail efforts.

One last theory for A is that A is the third-party beneficiary of the restrictive covenant made by B. Here LL is taken to have inserted the covenant in B's lease for A's benefit. This theory applies when (as in prudent drafting) LL takes care to state that A can enforce the covenant, or when the prior exclusive use covenant gives rise to an inference that LL intended B's restriction to benefit A. The possibility of liability under this theory will make a landlord all the more careful about extending any right to sublease or assign a lease.

## The General Plan of Covenants

A shopping center landlord would like to be able to follow the market as the tenants seek to rent, and so fashion a mix of tenants out of those who present themselves. However, this approach presents a problem. Cf. Werner v. Graham, 181 Cal. 174, 183 P. 945 (1919). This case's holding seems to require that the developer of the center have the general scheme of covenants in place before the first lease is signed. In this way, the benefit and the burden of the scheme attach to all premises at the same time. As a practical matter, this means that a master set of covenants should be recorded. For covenants dealing with a tenant's hours of operation or sign display, say, this is no problem. Should the rule apply also to exclusive use and restrictive line-of-business covenants? Arguably not. The holdings like *Werner* are concerned with residential subdivision covenants, in which all users promise to use their premises in the same way and rely on all other users or owners to abide by the covenant too. Not so in a shopping center, where the developer should be permitted to formulate the tenant mix as the leasing proceeds.

In other jurisdictions, the general plan or scheme of covenants need not be preconceived by the developer or landlord. (At least there is no authority for imposing such a requirement.) Here the leases to the center, taken together and as a whole, can themselves become the general scheme. Cf. Snow v. Van Dam, 291 Mass. 477, 197 N.E.2d 224 (1935). Thus, although each lease must be written (the Statute of Frauds applies to it and to all of its components), the center's landlord acquires the flexibility to devise the scheme as he leases the shops, mixing the right combination of tenants as they present themselves. Here too, each tenant has the obligation to determine from those leases that came before whether or not he fits into that mix without infringing on the rights of prior lessees.

In still a third set of jurisdictions, the approach is different. Here the focus is on the status of the last-entering tenant. He is put on notice of facts that are evident from a reasonably diligent physical inspection of the center. Cf. Sanborn v. McLean, 233 Mich. 227, 206 N.W. 496 (1925).

There is some definitional problem here because the last entry into the center may be on a prior chain of leases, or may be the last entry in chronological order of leasing. If the last entry is responsible for inspecting the center to determine whether any conflicts exist between the prior lessees' uses and his own proposed use, it is possible that the last entry means last lease, rather than the last chain of leases. If all the leases are recorded, then how one defines last entry is a way of defining who is put on notice and to whom this possessory notice is to be imputed, thus defining the extent of the title search that the last lessee will have to perform. If, for example, the last chronological entry is on a prior chain of leases, but satisfies himself that his proposed use is within the ambit of permitted uses on his chain of leases, then the question arises whether he has made a sufficiently diligent investigation, or whether he is also put to determining from a search of the records whether any other chain of leases conflicts with his use. In the context of the large shopping center this latter type of search can be expensive, burdensome, and inconclusive (in that, no matter how proficiently conducted, they may not show unrecorded leases and unrecordable subleases). It makes little sense to put such a search burden on the last lessee on a prior chain of leases.

No matter what the extent of the search is, however, the likelihood of a *Sanborn* problem arising in a shopping center context is remote. The problem in *Sanborn* was whether parcel owners who had a deed containing no restrictive covenant were nonetheless bound to observe one because their neighbors were mostly restricted at a time when the common grantor of all the parcels in the subdivision was long gone from the scene. The common landlord of a center's stores, or his agent, is always on the scene. If two identical exclusive use covenants, say, are contained in leases to different lessees, the landlord would be around to rectify or redress the situation, and the lessees are not left to argue amongst themselves about their common retail territory. Still, if an injunction and not just damages is wanted, the tenant will have to be a party to any action by the objecting tenant.

# EXAMPLES AND EXPLANATIONS

Consider a more complicated scheme of covenants, as follows:

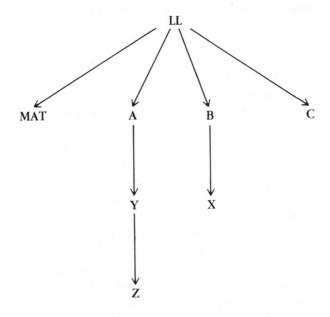

A is given an exclusive on shoes (and promises not to sell toys); B has an exclusive on toys (and promises not to sell clothes); C sells sneakers; X sells hobbies (and, at LL's insistence when consenting to the sublease, promises not to sell shoes); Y sells hiking boots; Z sells puzzles. The chronological order of leasing is A, B, C, X, Y, and finally Z. X, Y, and Z are all sublessees of a portion of their sublessor's leased premises. Their sublessors continue to operate on the remainder of the premises.

1. A sues C to enforce his "shoe exclusive." What result, and why?

**Explanation:**  A has to formulate his suit according to one of the theories presented in the previous discussion of the prior lessee's suit. The issue is a matter of lease interpretation. Once given his exclusive, A relies on LL not to lease in the future to a use that infringes A's rights. This is the reciprocal negative servitude, burdening C's lease. A is also the beneficiary of LL's implied promise and can sue to enforce it against any lessee deriving his rights from LL, who cannot transfer in future leases more rights than he (LL) has. Judgment for A.

2. Y sues C to enforce A's "shoe exclusive." What result, and why?

**Explanation:**  This is a more difficult case, even though a prior lessee is suing a lessee on a subsequent chain of leases. Y's line of goods fits within the definition of A's line, so that A cannot object. However, LL might have standing to object. Why would A rent to Y in the first place, unless he thought that Y's line of shoes would not compete with his own. The A-Y lease further defines A's exclusive, and if Y's line is no threat, then why are C's sneakers?

The general issue between C and Y is whether A's lease is to be read as it was written or, in the alternative, as it is implemented by the lessee who benefits from it. If it becomes clear as A operates his business that his is an adult, leather-soled, business shoe store, he has defined the benefit that the "shoe exclusive" provides him. Thus, in sneakers versus boots, the question is whether the exclusive is to be interpreted as written or as implemented. One suggested approach is to define LL's foreseeable objective — to create a tenant mix that maximizes the flow of potential customers in the center — that complementary stores achieve as easily as competitive ones. Thus exclusive use provisions that prove broader than necessary should be defined and narrowed by the actual conduct of a business. The process of cutting back the exclusive use covenant is akin to the location of an easement by the dominant user, or any agreement between neighbors to settle a boundary dispute by acquiescence. Once defined by its implementation, both the land-lord and the store lessee might be given the opportunity to utilize the unused increment in the exclusive use covenant to carve out submarkets in order to refine further the optimum mix of tenants. Judgment for C.

If the line between sneakers and boots proves too difficult to draw, as a matter of lease interpretation, then the court may look for other ways to handle the matter. One way is to suggest that Y, as the last store owner entering into a lease, was bound (knew or should have known) that his lease might conflict with C's. This is a notice provided him not by merely inspecting the leases from which his derives, but from a physical inspection of the leased premises then in use. Y's investigating his lease is insufficient to protect him, C argues, because he (Y) is also bound by possessory facts. Facts based on possession trump written lease provisions. The focus of this argument is on the status of the latecomer, rather than the rights derived by Y and C. Again, judgment for C.

On a practical level, this problem should be anticipated in the Master Covenants as a matter for LL alone, or for the center management (often a real estate broker) or the Merchant Owners Association (MOA) if the developer is not on the scene. LL, the manager, or the MOA should be designated the exclusive decision-maker for such issues, or the matter should be one to which binding arbitration is the exclusive remedy. On another level, this problem indicates why covenants over subleases and assignments often become a stick-ing point for negotiations. Shopping center lessors prefer to restrict the assignability of their lessees, primarily so that they can capture the built-up equity in the rental value of the premises, but also so that when they deal directly with the next lessee, no question of whether the restrictive use cove-nant runs with the assignment arises.

3. When A gives his customers toys as favors when they buy shoes, B sues A. What result, and why?

**Explanation:** Judgment for B, on the theory that LL retained a benefit (the right to lease in ways not competing with A) that he passed on to B in the LL-B lease. Whether A is selling toys raises the issue of whether there is such a thing as a "free" toy in this context, but in a sense, this issue is irrelevant to B's suit because B is alleging not that A is a competitor, but that he is interfering with B's business. That allegation is one that sounds in tort; this suit is a tort action or, more precisely, a tort action in which the duty and its breach are defined in and shown by a contract (or lease). As an evidentiary matter, this may be a hard case for B to prove. A lessee who causes a flood that causes another lessee to shut down would be the easy case. Perhaps a scene of parents dragging their children past the toy store saying, "You got your toy for the day from the shoe salesperson, so let's go home," would be the best evidence. The tort basis of the suit, however, opens up the possibility of consequential damages.

4. Seeing the wisdom of A's marketing, B opens a children's shoe department in his toy store. Now A sues B. What result, and why?

**Explanation:** If LL were the plaintiff, the lease interpretation issue would be whether B has violated the terms of his lease: Does "clothing" include shoes? With A the plaintiff, a prior lessee is suing a subsequent one. One of the three theories discussed previously for such suits must be adopted so that this suit can proceed.

If we combine the facts of this and the previous Example, then what B does here raises an estoppel issue: whether B's actions estop him from bringing the first suit. Beyond that issue, the court must also decide whether LL's implied promise to A not to rent in the future to a shoe store operator is (1) binding on B when B makes some express promise not to sell certain lines of goods, like clothes, and (2) narrowed by any possessory facts that B can discover about A's business (for example, that he is selling only adult wingtips and pumps). A might argue that the benefit of a broad exclusive is of value to him whether or not he actually uses it to sell all lines of shoes, because he can carve out submarkets (for example, in the hiking boots lease to Y, who might rent part of A's space to sell a specialized type of shoe).

5. X, the hobby store owner, sues Z, who sells puzzles. What result, and why?

**Explanation:** The issue here is this: if Z is clearly not within the exclusive use covenant given to A (some things are obvious, and this one is) then is a sublessee, like Z, who derives his rights through A's lease, implicitly limited to selling goods falling within the exclusive? Does an exclusive use covenant contain an implied covenant not to sell other goods? Some people make a hobby of doing puzzles. Again, the reliance of all tenants on the landlord or the manager to attain the best tenant mix indicates that there is, or should be, an implicit promise contained in every exclusive use covenant that restricts the lessee to the uses falling within the covenant. Not only is the landlord bound to honor the exclusive in his future leasing but so is any sublessee — which would preclude Y from renting to Z, whether or not Z's use infringes X's rights. Judgment for X.

On the practical level, all of these problems point out the business need for a shopping center's landlord to retain a tight control on subleases and assignments. This not only gives the landlord the control over future build-up in the rental value of the premises, but it also allows the center's manager or landlord to achieve the optimum mix of tenants. Finally, when the landlord or manager does not maintain decision-making authority over covenant interpretation and enforcement, questions of privity and standing will arise in many of the foregoing Examples.

# 32

## Commercial Leases

This chapter returns to many of the ideas you encountered in your first year of law study. There, however, your focus was likely on the residential landlord-tenant relationship, with the many tenant protections fashioned by courts and legislatures over the last several decades.

Most likely, an important part of this study was the implied warranty of habitability (IWH). Many of its protections, however, do not apply in the context of commercial leasing. Knapp v. Simmons, 345 N.W.2d 118 (Iowa 1984); Restatement (Second) of Property §5.1, at 176 (Reporter's Note).

Nevertheless, the same inequality of bargaining power and expertise that prompted courts to impose an IWH in a residential setting may still remain in commercial leasing. On the other hand, some courts are employing the IWH in the commercial context. Davidow v. Inwood North Professional Group — Phase I, 747 S.W.2d 373 (Tex. 1988) (finding an implied warranty of fitness for a particular use by a commercial landlord). See generally Note, The Unwarranted Implication of a Warranty of Fitness in Commercial Leases — An Alternative Approach, 41 Vand. L. Rev. 1057 (1988); Note, Landlord-Tenant — Should a Warranty of Fitness be Implied in Commercial Leases?, 13 Rutgers L.J. 91 (1981).

## Shopping Centers

### Some Background

The American shopping center is a unique form of land development. The Guinness Book of World Records has the date of the first one as 1908, in the community of Roland Park, Baltimore, Maryland. Some of the early ones, in the 1930s and 1940s, were built to serve as downtowns for established suburbs — Upper

Darby Center and Suburban Square around Philadelphia, Highland Park in Dallas, and River Oaks in Houston. The first centers built to serve communities yet unbuilt — but of course built by the developer of the community — were established by J. C. Nichols around Kansas City, Missouri. (James Rouse carried on and expanded this tradition with the new town of Columbia, Maryland.) Architect Victor Gruen established the suburban development pattern with Northland Center around Detroit, and later, in 1956, with the first enclosed mall, Southdale Center in Edina, Minnesota, outside of Minneapolis. The central cities responded (politics was not far removed from these developments) with renovated downtowns, complete with streets closed to traffic and strewn with benches and potted trees. James Rouse has spearheaded such developments, relying on both public and private financing. See Gillette, The Evolution of the Planned Shopping Center in Suburb and City, 51 Am. Planning Assn. J. 449 (Aug. 1985). An excellent shorter history of the shopping center is found in K. Jackson, Crabgrass Frontier 257-261 (1985).

The largest North American centers today are the Del Amo Fashion Center, in Torrance, California, with over 3 million square feet; the West Edmonton Mall, in Edmonton, Alberta, Canada, with over 4 million square feet; and, under construction as this is written, Megamall, in Bloomington, Minnesota, all of 9.5 million square feet (that's the equivalent of 78 football fields).

The shopping center also offers a wonderful case study for two subjects that you probably discussed during your first-year property course:[1] the law of real covenants and landlord-tenant law. See, e.g., Whitinsville Plaza Inc. v. Kotseas, 378 Mass. 85, 390 N.E.2d 243 (1979) (discussing anticompetitive covenants); Doo v. Packwood, 265 Cal.App.2d 752, 71 Cal.Rptr. 477 (1968). The shopping center lease is the documentary vehicle for this discussion. It is a unique blend of the two subjects.

---

1. You may also have encountered the shopping center in your course on constitutional law. There the focus was on the "public" functions of the center as a community center, to which people espousing various causes of general concern wish access—to exercise advocacy rights, to recruit, or to solicit money. Although these cases are an outgrowth of Marsh v. Alabama, 326 U.S. 501 (1946) (a case involving a company town), Amalgamated Food Employees Local 590 v. Logan Valley Plaza, 391 U.S. 308 (1968), is the first United States Supreme Court opinion to address the issue of free speech in a shopping center. There the center attempted to enjoin peaceful labor picketing in a suburban setting. Because, the opinion states, the center serves as the functional equivalent of "the business block," with free access to the public, the state may not enforce its trespass laws in such a way wholly to exclude members of the public wishing to exercise First Amendment rights. The Court, however, did not deny that the owners had the right to make "reasonable regulations governing the exercise of First Amendment rights on their property." Id. at 320. Four years later, in Lloyd Corp. v. Tanner, 407 U.S. 551 (1972), the fact that the dispute in *Logan Valley* related directly to the use of the center, with no suitable alternate means of communication available, was elevated to a constitutional requirement; only with such facts present will the right of the center developer or owner to exclude yield to the First Amendment right. A controversial pair of decisions, these. *Lloyd* is discussed in Note, The Public Forum from *Marsh* to *Lloyd*, 24 Am. U. L. Rev. 159 (1974).

## *Leasing Shopping Center Space*

The negotiations for leasing space in a shopping center or mall can be extremely complicated. See, e.g., Halper, Restoration Clauses in Shopping Center Leases, 15 Real Est. Rev. 66 (Winter 1986). They often start with a simple letter of intent, such as the following:

June 1, 19____

Louie Lessor
1234 Mall Parkway
River City, Maryland

Dear Sir:

In response to your request that we express our interest in leasing space in the White Heat Mall, a shopping center to be constructed by you at the intersection of Urban and 150th Ave., River City, please be informed that we have a definite interest in such a lease on satisfactory provisions, including (but not limited to) the following:

1. The space shall be approximately ____ in area.
2. The minimum monthly rent shall be one-twelfth of $____ per square foot, multiplied by the number of square feet in the premises.
3. This minimum rent shall apply against the percentage rent of ____% of gross sales.
4. The term shall be ____ years.

The provisions of the lease shall be subject to the review and approval of our legal counsel. This letter is not intended to be contractual in nature but is only an expression of some of the major terms that we would discuss with you before entering into a lease.

Very truly yours,

Theresa Tenant<br>President, Super Drugs, Inc.

---

Then things got interesting. Hudgens v. NLRB, 424 U.S. 507 (1976), overruled *Logan Valley.* Enter federalism: The Supreme Court of California decided that its state constitutional free speech rights protected the rights of high school students to protest a United Nations resolution against Zionism. The United States Supreme Court let this holding stand, deciding that federal due process and takings clauses, asserted to protect the center's property rights, were not offended. PruneYard Shopping Center v. Robins, 447 U.S. 74 (1980).

In the 1980s, six state supreme courts have declined to provide free speech rights on center property. Two more have in dicta indicated that they would rule the same way, while two (California and Washington) have contrary holdings. Note, Speech Activists in Shopping Centers: Must Property Rights Give Way to Free Expression?, 64 Wash. L. Rev. 133, 138-140 n. 43-45, 56 (1989), calling the holding of *PruneYard* into question because of later-decided Unites States Supreme Court takings cases.

What other provisions would you suggest for this letter? For suggestions, see Cal. Continuing Educ. for the Bar, Commercial Real Property Lease Practice 7, 73-77 (1976 & Supp. 1982). Consider, for example, that the center is not yet constructed. What preclosing conditions would this indicate?

# Title Problems

If the discussion of a lease goes forward, two legal aspects loom large. The first concerns the status of the title of the developer. As in every discussion, the construction and permanent mortgage lenders for the project will insist on a first lien as security for their loan(s). Preexisting mortgage liens will have to be subordinated to their lien(s). The powers of either preexisting or senior mortgagees over the leasing scheme, the set of covenants controlling the use of the leased premises, and the powers of the developer, the leasing manager, or merchants' association present specialized applications of the priority of title rules considered in past chapters of this book.

The takeout mortgage lender for the center, in particular, will have likely reviewed the mixture of retail stores to be used in the center. That lender probably will have also reviewed the form of the leases to be used. The reason for the review is that the lender wants to assure itself that the stores will generate the sales volume sufficient to make the center a success or, if the takeout mortgagee must take over the center, that the center can be made successful. Such a mortgagee, once in possession, or such a mortgagee's grantee will have limited rights because, if a lease is prior in time to the mortgage documents, the mortgagee has no right to disturb the lessee. Why? Because at the time of the execution of the mortgage and note, the mortgagee took as security for the note only the landlord's reversion. So long as a senior lease is not in default, the lessee is secure in her possession of the premises, and the mortgagee is bound by lease's terms.

However, if the mortgage documents are prior in time, a mortgagee in possession will have the right to evict a lessee upon default and for the same reason: The mortgagee's security includes the right to lease the premises. And so the junior lessee must attorn (or recognize the rights of the mortgagee in possession as the landlord) or be subject to eviction. See Annot., Rent — mortgagor and mortgagee, 105 A.L.R. 744 (1936). How well do these rules work for the mortgagee? Not very well. Most likely the mortgagee forced to take possession of the center does not want the tenant walking out during the takeover. Attornment suggests a principle of mutuality — if the landlord or her successor has the option of ousting junior leases, so has the lessee the option to abandon. Particularly when the affected junior tenant is a major one in terms of retail sales volume or square footage in the center, this is not a desirable legal outcome. It will have to be modified by contract in the lease.

The lender will also want to review the set of use covenants common to all lessees. The subjects for such covenants are many and varied, but might concern business hours, types of advertising and sign display, and the timing of sales. A tenant should review the status of these covenants to make sure that none conflict with its proposed use of and operation on its premises. In addition, a prospective tenant wants to know that there is a manager, easily available or on-site, who is charged with making a continuous effort at leasing and whose leasing activities bind the owner and the mortgagee of the property.

Some use covenants will not be common to all lessees. These will likely have to do with the uses to which other lessees may (or in some cases must) put their premises, as well as the uses that others are prohibited from engaging in. One tenant may have been promised that it will be the only jewelry store, the only men's clothier, and so on. Another may have promised not to engage in competition with a lessee operating a food store, by selling groceries. A prospective tenant will have to know of any conflicts between its proposed use and prior lessees' uses. In this connection, remember that the leases used are likely to contain a long enough term that, under the applicable recording act, they will be recordable. A quick method for a prospective tenant to get a handle on the problem is to ask the landord to warrant that no violation of existing use covenants exists. If the landlord balks at this, then a further, and reasonable, investigation will be required, i.e., a title search, or a walk through the center to look for potential problems.

## Contract Problems

There will be many contractual problems to consider as well, and many complicated lease clauses to draft. See generally Pollack, Clauses in a Shopping Center Lease, 20 Prac. Law. 63 (Dec. 1974). Consider the following contract problems.

# EXAMPLES AND EXPLANATIONS

3. How long should the term be? How should it be stated?

**Explanation:** Landlords are likely to resist terms longer than five years, so a short primary term, followed by several options to renew the lease, is becoming the norm.

4. Shopping centers typically open in either the spring or the fall. What problems arise because of this fact?

**Explanation:** The rent cannot be annualized on the basis of the first months of operation. (The landlord will likely want the percentage rent paid more frequently than annually.) This is particularly true if the opening is in the fall because the Christmas shopping season starts during those first months. Perhaps a special base rent should be negotiated for the start-up period.

5a. Shopping center leases are typically "triple net" leases. This means that taxes, insurance, and utility costs and/or increases are passed along to the tenant. See, e.g., Valencia Center, Inc. v. Publix Super Markets, Inc., 464 So. 2d 1267 (Fla. App.), rev. denied, 475 So. 2d 696 (1985) (absent express lease provision, the landlord is under a duty to pay taxes on leased premises); see generally Lower, Passing Through Costs to Tenants Raises Complex Problems, 20 Real Est. Rev. 45 (Spring 1990).

As to taxes: The landlord will be able to provide a list of taxes paid over the last several years and will know to whom they were paid. With that information, the prospective tenant is in a position to make a preliminary list of the taxing authorities to which the premises are subject. Investigation of the structure of local government will check and round out this list. Taxes can be annually or periodically assessed and levied. The resulting lease provision might list the anticipated taxes and make plain whether special assessments, and other substitutes for real property taxes, are included as well. If the building is under construction, the date on which the landlord can start to pass through the taxes will become important. The billing period for the pass-through is important as well: Will the taxes be passed along as levied, or in anticipation of the levy, or after it? And how will the tenant's pro rata share be computed — on a ratio of the tenant's square footage to the total square footage of the project, or according to the value of the lease as a portion of the landlord's rent roll?

5b. As to utilities: Should the landlord negotiate for the right to provide electricity to each tenant? The landlord might add a surcharge as utility charges are passed along to the tenants. If the landlord provides such services, the further issue is whether the landlord undertakes (expressly or implicitly) a duty to provide a certain level of service. The landlord may want to exculpate herself from any such duty. Should the tenant seek to obligate the landlord to provide a certain number of kilowatts? The modern office or commercial space requires a good deal of computers and electronic equipment that, at some minimal level, should never be completely without power and that require a controlled range of temperatures in order to function.

5c. As to other charges: The landlord will want to pass along maintenance charges as well. She will want to define maintenance as broadly as possible: "All costs and expenses of every type and nature, including appropriate reserves." If the center is an enclosed mall, the landlord will want to include a charge for the depreciation of the HVAC system. If the previously quoted language were used, it would remain unclear whether a depreciation charge, or a charge to pass through the administrative expenses for billing. and collection of common area charges, or a bad debt reserve would be permitted.

5d. Whether the pass-through is for taxes, insurance, utilities, or maintenance, a tenant's charge is computed as a fraction of the total charged the center. This fraction has the gross leasable area of the tenant's premises as its numerator. The denominator will be either the gross leased area or the gross leasable area of the center. Which denominator will the tenant typically prefer? Which the landlord? And what is at stake in the discussion?

**Explanation:** The landlord will prefer the gross leased area, and the tenant the gross leasable area. (These labels can get confusing, so remember that the tenant is negotiating to pay the smaller fraction of the total cost, while the landlord is negotiating to have the tenant pay the larger fraction.) At issue is the question of who bears the burden of vacant space in the center, a matter vital to the survival of the project as a whole.

5e. A net lease has become more common as the shopping center industry has grown. How can a tenant induce efficiency in a landlord offering such a lease?

**Explanation:** The tenant should negotiate a cap or dollar amount ceiling on the amounts that the landlord can pass through in any computational period. Thus will the landlord be given an incentive to stay within the limits imposed.

# Restrictive Use Covenants

Much like general schemes of restrictions used in the context of suburban residential subdivisions, a larger shopping center is today subject to a scheme that restricts the individual merchant tenants to particular lines of business. Consider the following provisions:

During the term of this lease and any extensions or renewals thereof, the lessee shall use the premises as a drugstore and for no other purpose.

The lessee will use the premises as a drugstore.

The premises are leased for use as a drugstore.

What differences do you detect in the wordings? What consequences follow from each? What if the verb "use" were fleshed out a bit, and the verbs were "use, occupy, and operate?" What difference would that make in the first two provisions? See Carrollton Central Plaza Assocs. v. Morse Shoe, Inc., 1989 U.S. Dist. LEXIS 5842 (E.D. La. 1989).

Another problem: If the tenant is making a promise here and not just giving a warranty, what of the developer-landlord? What promise is she making? If she restricts a tenant to certain uses, does she implicitly promise that she will not in the future compete with that use or in the future rent to any tenant who will compete with it? Your first-year study of implied and reciprocal negative servitudes should warn you that the landlord retains what she has not previously transferred and in the future can lease for other uses, but she cannot rent for the same use unless the first tenant clearly has a nonexclusive right to put the leased premise to a certain use. The developer thus retains the right to lease in the future, but only as to noncompeting uses. She makes this promise not to compete in exchange for the tenant's promise to abide by the restriction.

However, the scheme of shopping center covenants does not work entirely like a series of restrictive covenants in a residential subdivision. This is so because the merchants in the center are not using their leased premises in just one way, but in many. So the developer's promise not to compete needs qualification: She may be promising (in those weasel words of the attorney) not to compete unreasonably. Those qualifying words are sometimes necessary because in some lines of goods, more than one outlet may be better. Dress shops, shoe stores, and jewelers — judging by their frequency in many larger shopping centers — are examples of this phenomenon.

This flexibility is also necessary because sometimes, as a developer is constructing a center, she does not know precisely which lines of goods will provide the best mix of tenants. In the words of art that have attached to the law of real covenants, the developer does not have a predetermined "general scheme" in mind. The best scheme sometimes is partly determined with the selection of the "anchor" or other major tenants,[2] but it also sometimes awaits the lease-up period, just before the takeout or permanent loan is closed. Putting the right mix of tenants together is a matter of timing, luck, and hard negotiations. The first tenant to lease in the center will have to trust the developer to obtain the best mix of leases.[3]

The developer's overall aim in imposing these restrictions is to create a mix of tenants that will maximize the number of people attracted to the center. It is hoped that this flow of people will patronize more than one store

---

2. An anchor tenant is typically the lessee of the largest amount of the space in the project. In an office building, it executes a lease for a space large enough to provide security for the landlord; that is, the tenant's rental payments offer a reasonable certainty that the carrying costs of the project can be met. In a shopping center, an anchor tenant may serve this function, but its presence there may also draw a crowd to the center. It serves as the economic magnet for the center, dealing in a larger number of lines of goods and services so that the center's targeted consumers will be given a reason to shop there.

3. The idea of working the leasing process backwards applies here as well as when negotiating permanent and construction loans for a project: The higher rents are paid by the smaller tenants, so that the landlord's profit margin is typically higher when renting to a card shop rather than to a department store. The latter "leases in bulk" at an annual square footage rate that may even be a loss leader for the developer. Those losses will have to be made up so that the project achieves overall profitability at the expense of the other, smaller lessees. Thus some initial square footage is typically set aside for small, specialized shops.

in the center. This scheme creates a mutual exchange of customers, which in turn creates the legal consideration that imposes on each merchant the duty to abide by the developer's restrictions. A variant on this theory of consideration has it that a major or anchor tenant (often a department store) pays a lower rent, and little or no maintenance fee, because it acts as a magnet to attract people to the center for a first purchase, thus creating a customer flow past the smaller stores.

Thus there are two rationales for the scheme of restrictions in the center. One is the developer's implied promise not to compete unreasonably; the other is the reciprocity of benefit based on customer flow. The best mix of leases is one that gives the developer total discretion, but in order to attract big name shops, the developer will likely have to give some of this discretion away in the form of anticompetitive covenants. If the first tenant is a large department store, a general covenant giving it the exclusive right to deal in "general department store wares" will give it a virtual veto power over further leasing. More particularity in the drafting will be required, if indeed the developer and its lenders will permit the first tenant any covenant on this subject.

# EXAMPLES AND EXPLANATIONS

A developer lessor executes a lease with a major anchor tenant for 90,000 square feet. The anchor tenant pays its own taxes, insurance premiums, and utility charges. It also pays a flat maintenance charge for the mall attached to the tenant's department store.

Subsequently the developer executes a lease with Googles, Inc., of 5000 square feet "for use only as a retail, but not a discount, business and only for the business of an optician, selling eyeglasses and frames."

6. Is the developer thereafter prohibited from leasing a shop in the center to an optometrist?

**Explanation:** A close case, but the reference to the type of goods tips it in the tenant's favor. Better to get such things clear during the negotiations for the lease and avoid such disputes.

7. Googles' lease was amended to provide in addition that "the lessor agrees that, during the term of this lease, it will not lease to any other tenant in the center for the purpose of carrying on the business of an optician and/ or optometrist and the tenant will use the premises for no other purpose whatsoever."

The developer, before the beginning of Googles' term, leases other premises — consisting of 25,000 square feet in the center — to Super Drugs, Inc., a chain of drug stores. The Super Drug store in the center will include a discount optical department. Now what is your answer?

**Explanation:** Googles had not yet obtained the benefit from the exclusive use provision when Super Drug's prior lease was executed, so it has been held that the landlord has not violated the promise because that promise was binding only during the term of the lease. Klein v. Equitable Life Assurance Socy. of the United States, 477 N.E.2d 1190 (Ohio App. 1984). How fair is this result? In the context of a shopping center, which requires a lot of advance planning to achieve the right mix of commercial uses, it seems dry.

The landlord's objective of achieving the right mix of tenants means, most likely, a constantly changing mix of tenants as one lease replaces another. Thus the landlord should attempt to include in any lease an exception for the rights of any preexisting lessee, as in "the landlord will not *hereafter* execute any lease permitting the tenant to operate [here including a description of the instant tenant's use]. . . ." In addition, any exclusive use should terminate when the tenant ceases to sell the protected line of goods or to engage in the protected business, or if the tenant leaves the center altogether.

8. What if Super Drug's lease provided that, "with the exception of the rights conferred under the landlord's lease with Newsstands, Inc., the tenant has the exclusive right to sell magazines"? What is the problem with this language from the landlord's perspective?

**Explanation:** What if Newsstands, Inc., moves out of the center? Can the landlord lease the premises to another newsstand? Unless the lease exception covers both the use on the premises and the preexisting lease, the answer will probably be no.

9. If the Super Drug lease were executed after the start of the term in the Googles' lease, who should police the exclusive right to operate an optical business in the center? Would your allocation of the duty to police change if the developer warranted to the tenant that there were no competing uses in the center on the date the lease is executed?

**Explanation:** The tenant with the "exclusive" use provision is usually assigned the duty to police it, and that answer does not change in the face of a warranty such as the facts suggest. Note, however, the developer has violated her express promise as to the type of business, but not as to the market served: Super Drug will operate a *discount* business. In the original lease provision, the restrictions on use were twofold: a tenant's promise to use the premises as a optical shop and also a promise to conduct a retail, as opposed to a discount, business. When the restriction on the type of business was changed into an "exclusive," the reference to a distinction between retail and discount business was not abandoned, so that, all other aspects of the negotiations being held constant, the developer (implicitly) retained the right to rent to a discounter; her retention of this right was for the exclusive.

Does this make sense? The contrary argument is that dropping the lease amendment broadened the tenant's permissive uses, and so the developer retained less, not more. See generally Belvidere South Towne Center, Inc. v. One Stop Pacemakers, Inc., 54 Ill. App. 3d 958, 370 N.E.2d 249 (1977) (citing various definitions of a drug store).

What is the general lesson here? For the landlord, it is that a description of the types of goods included in an "exclusive" use restriction should be avoided; a description of the type of business to be carried on provides the landlord with greater flexibility in negotiating future leases. See Silverman, Pitfalls in Shopping Center Lease Use and Exclusive Clauses, 20 Real Est. Rev. 60, 61-62 (1990) (arguing that, for example, an exclusive for food consumed off-premises will present problems in leasing later to a supermarket). The distinction between describing the goods and the business can get fuzzy: An exclusive for the operation of a gift shop may later preclude a department store.

10. If the shopping center developer polices the use restrictions on the leases, and each lease calls for forfeiture of the lease "upon any violation of a covenant contained herein," may the developer also be allowed a remedy of injunction, barring the tenant's continued sale of the violative line of goods, or one of damages, if the tenant continued to do so?

**Explanation:** A good question, but if the lease is silent on other remedies, its terms (draconian though they might be) govern. Presumably the parties knew how to negotiate a different agreement. The landlord might argue that the more drastic and inclusive remedy includes any lesser ones by implication. Unless the tenant wants to move out, she is unlikely to resist the effects of such an argument.

The more general question remains. Why don't landlords negotiate leases in which some defaults work a forfeiture, but others don't, instead giving rise to a claim for damages? (Landlords don't; they seem to want the lease arranged so that, with any default, the tenant is out on her ear.) A violation of a use restriction is a good place within a lease to provide something less than forfeiture. See generally Saltz, Do Tough Landlord Lease Forms Really Pay Off?, 20 Real Est. Rev. 55 (Summer 1990).

11. Googles installs two video games on its leased premises. The games account for about 5 percent of the gross sales on the premises. The developer then proposes to lease premises to Super Drug, but first sues to terminate the Googles lease. In this suit, what result, and why?

**Explanation:** Judgment for Googles. The video games are not a change of use but are instead incidental to the main business of the shop, as shown by the comparative revenues from the games and the optical business. See

Ray-Ron Corp. v. DMY Realty Co., 500 N.E.2d 1163 (Ind. 1986), noted in Krieger, Property Survey 1987, 21 Ind. L. Rev. 343, 344-346 (1988).

Once a shopping center is built and leased, the landlord's continuing ability to control the mix of tenants will depend on her ability to control subleases and assignments; thus a tenant's subleasing and assigning the lease will usually depend on the landlord's consent, "such consent not unreasonably to be withheld," as the common clause used in leases has it. See Warmack v. Merchants Natl. Bank of Fort Smith, 612 S.W.2d 733 (Ark. 1981) (finding that a shopping center landlord's desire for a good tenant mix is a proper reason for withholding consent). Thus, in the context of the shopping center, there is a close connection between use restrictions and subletting-assignment clauses.

# Implied Covenant of Continuous Operation

The traditional rule is that without an express provision in a lease for continuous operation of the tenant's business, such a covenant will not be implied, even when the lease does contain a rent covenant consisting of an obligation to pay both a base rental and a percentage of the gross sales. Annot., Lease of store as requiring active operation of store, 40 A.L.R.3d 971 (1971). This rule is applied even when the tenant had an exclusive use restriction in its lease, and thus the landlord was restricted from leasing to another tenant in the same line of business. If the landlord had severely restricted a tenant's ability to sublease or assign her lease, however, a continuous operation covenant might be implied; and similarly, if the tenant has the right to sublet or assign, no implied covenant would likely be found. See generally, Comment, Percentage Lease: Is There a Need to Imply a Covenant of Continuous Operation?, 72 Marq. L. Rev. 559, 569 (1989) (arguing that no need exists if good drafting anticipates problems).

However, if the tenant were an anchor or magnet tenant, the rule might not be applied: With a magnet tenant, continuous operation is necessary to make the center an economic success. Moreover, when any tenant — but particularly a magnet one — is paying a low base rent and a high percentage rent, the implication might be made. Fifth Ave. Shopping Center, Inc. v. Grand Union Co., 491 F. Supp. 77 (N.D. Ga. 1980). When coupled with an exclusive use restriction, or a provision requiring that the tenant be open for business at specified hours, such an implication is more likely still.

What if the center has no anchor or magnet tenant? Recently, in Slater v. Pearle Vision Center, Inc., 376 Pa. Super. 580, 546 A.2d 676 (1988), the court used the "doctrine of necessary implication" to imply a covenant of continuous operation in a strip shopping center. The tenant's lease required that she agree to open 90 days after the landlord's approval of the tenant's work letter (an addendum to the lease describing the tenant's improvement of interior space), to use the entire premises for its business, and to exclude from the definition of a tenant's "abandonment" of the premises periods up to 60 days for repairs and remodeling. Beyond these specific lease provisions, the opinion emphasizes the economic interdependence of the tenants on one another and the need to function as one entity.

# EXAMPLES AND EXPLANATIONS

Building on the facts already supplied in Examples 6-11, suppose that the rent covenant in the Super Drug lease called for a term of 15 years, with 5 options to renew the lease for 5-year renewal terms and a minimum rent of $200,000, with a percentage rent based on gross sales, triggered annually by sales of $400,000 during the first 15 years and $300,000 after that. The only other relevant provision of the lease provides that the premises are "to be used and operated as a drug store and for no other purposes whatsoever."

12. Business is bad, and Super Drug seeks to cease operations, but is willing to pay the minimum rent and look for a sublessee. Can the developer insist that Super Drug continue operations?

**Explanation:**   No. Super Drug is not the anchor tenant, and thus not a magnet to attract customer flow into the center. No implication of a duty to operate can be taken from the percentage rental, in part because the base rent does not seem insubstantial or nominal. See Walgreen Arizona Drug Co. v. Plaza Center Corp., 132 Ariz. 512, 647 P.2d 643 (Ct. App. 1982); Keystone Square Shopping Center Co. v. Marsh Supermarkets, Inc., 459 N.E.2d 420 (Ind. App. 1984); Fay's Drug Co., Inc. v. Geneva Plaza Assocs., 98 A.D.2d 978, 470 N.Y.S.2d 240, 241-242 (1983), order aff'd without op., 62 N.Y.2d 886, 478 N.Y.S.2d 867, 467 N.E.2d 531 (1984); Annot., Lease of store as requiring active operation of store, 40 A.L.R.3d 971 (1971). If the base rent were nominal and the tenant an anchor, the answer might be different. First American Bank & Trust Co. v. Safeway Stores, Inc., 151 Ariz. 584, 729 P.2d 938, 940 (Ct. App. 1986) (insubstantial base rent implied a duty to operate); Ingannamorte v. Kings Super Markets, Inc., 55 N.J. 223, 260 A.2d 841 (1970) (duty to operate implied for lease of anchor tenant paying percentage rental). Thus, when the base fixed rent is substantial, no implied covenant to operate continuously is likely to be found, whereas if the fixed rent is insubstantial in comparison to the percentage rent, an implied covenant is more likely.

Before you memorize the foregoing rule as black letter law, consider whether the parties could indicate an intent to agree otherwise by the landlord's first making improvements to the premises and then agreeing to a substantial fixed base rent, with a comparatively small percentage rent? You will have to admit that the possibility of implying a continuous operation covenant rises with the landlord's helping out with the improvements. If the landlord financed the improvements for the tenant, on the other hand, your answer would probably stay the same. R. Schoshinski, American Law of Landlord and Tenant 234 (1980).

13. Six months short of 20 years later, Super Drug's annual sales hover around the $250,000 figure and have been at this level in each of the last 5 years. The developer sues Super Drug, alleging breach of an implied covenant to operate diligently so as to trigger the percentage rental provision and asking to terminate the lease. What result?

**Explanation:** Judgment for Super Drug. See Mercury Inv. Co. v. F. W. Woolworth Co., 706 P.2d 523 (Okla. 1985). See also Dayton Hudson Corp. v. Macerich Real Estate Co., 812 F.2d 1319 (10th Cir. 1987). When the only result of a lease default is forfeiture, the courts are unlikely to imply the default because of its harsh consequences. Again, should the landlord negotiate a less-than-forfeiture remedy and insert it in the lease? Landlords, presented with this type of problem, often do not do that. The forfeiture remedy is too appealing a hold on the tenant.

14. The Super Drug lease prohibits its assignment without the express written consent of the landlord. The parent company for Super Drug decides to reposition itself in its market and to close all of its Super Drug stores. The lease provisions give Super Drug the right to discontinue operations at any time by sending a notice to that effect 90 days in advance; within 90 days after the mailing of this notice, the developer could then elect to terminate the Super Drug lease. (The landlord's right to terminate is often called a "recapture" provision.)

Super Drug provides the developer with the 90-day notice of its intent to discontinue operations, but the developer does not elect to terminate the lease within 90 days after its receipt of the notice. Super Drug then agrees to sublease to Disco Drug, another drug store chain wishing to establish a presence in the center's market area. Super Drug informs the developer that it will exercise its second and third options to renew in a timely manner. The developer refuses to renew Super Drug's lease or recognize its sublessee and sues to terminate Super Drug's lease, often known in this situation as "the head lease." In this suit, what result?

**Explanation:** Judgment for Super Drug. If the sublease to Disco is distinguishable from an assignment, the right to sublease remains in Super Drug's arsenal of leasehold rights. If the developer did not elect to terminate, the cessation of operations does not destroy that right to sublease, not otherwise restricted in the lease. See Joseph Bros. Co. v. F. W. Woolworth Co., 844 F.2d 369 (6th Cir. 1988) (percentage rent provision inapplicable after sublease); F. W. Woolworth Co. v. Plaza North, Inc., 493 N.E.2d 1304, 1307 (Ind. App. 1986); see generally R. Schoshinski, American Law of Landlord and Tenant 579-589 (1980).

15. If Disco Drug subleases from Super Drug in order to curtail competition in the market and does not intend to operate a store in the center, would your answers to the previous Examples change?

**Explanation:** Yes. Even when a base, fixed, or minimum rent is substantial, a tenant is liable for discontinuing operations when to do so would only inflict economic injury and not serve a business purpose for the tenant. Berkeley Dev. Co. v. Great Atl. & Pac. Tea Co., 214 N.J. Super. 227, 518 A.2d 790 (Law Div. 1986); R. Schoshinski, supra, at 235. If it subleased to prevent the developer's leasing to a third-party competitor in the center, would any answers change? Yes again: The anticompetitive intent gives rise to a landlord's suit in tort. Id.

16. If the Super Drug lease contains a provision that permits (but does not require) the landlord to relet the premises after the tenant abandons them, does the presence of that provision affect the landlord's rights? How?

**Explanation:** Yes. The permissive reletting provision is inserted by landlords who wish to make it plain that they are reletting on behalf of the tenant, and not on their own behalf. The clause is thus a method of preserving the landlord's right to sue on the lease for damages. At the same time, however, the clause is also a basis for a court's declaration that the landlord has an implied duty to mitigate the tenant's damages. See Sandor Dev. Co. v. Reitmeyer, 498 N.E.2d 1020 (Ind. App. 1986); Hirsch v. Merchants Natl. Bank & Trust Co., 166 Ind. App. 497, 336 N.E.2d 833, 836 (1975).

17. If Super Drug takes over 90 days to remove its fixtures to prepare the premises for Disco, is that a breach of an implied duty to operate the premises found in the restrictive use provision?

**Explanation:** No. Assuming that the court would imply a duty to operate out of the restrictive use provision, the right to redecorate or ready the premises for a sublessee is incidental to the right to sublet and should be protected on that account. Monmouth Real Estate Inv. Trust v. Manville Foodland, Inc., 196 N.J. Super. 262, 482 A.2d 186 (App. Div. 1984), cert. denied, 99 N.J. 234, 491 A.2d 722 (1985).

18. The developer and Super Drug settle their several disputes by inserting an express covenant for continuous operation into the lease. Prior to the effective date of the lease amendment, however, the parent company of

Super Drug changes its corporate policy of geographic expansion and decides that henceforth it will not operate in the area of the shopping center. Super Drug files suit for an injunction, asking the court to decide whether it may assign its lease.

**Explanation:**   Super Drug may not now assign its lease. Steel Ltd. Partnership v. Caldor, Inc., 850 F.2d 690 (4th Cir. 1988). A mandatory injunction is the typical remedy in such a case, but may the developer also have damages? Yes, in Hornwood v. Smith's Food King No. 1, 772 P.2d 1284 (Nev. 1989). The loss of value for the shopping center developer during the time the tenant's portion of the center is "dark" is a consequential damage that the tenant could reasonably have foreseen and for which it is liable. The damages awarded in *Hornwood*, however, involved an anchor tenant, which is unusual; injunctions are the usual remedy in these cases. Future opinions will likely address the issue of whether damages may be given to a developer against a nonanchor tenant, particularly if the courts continue to make much of the "economic interdependence of all tenants" in a center, as the opinion did in Slater v. Pearle Vision Center, Inc., 376 Pa. Super. 580, 546 A.2d 676 (1988). In the alternative, the courts might continue to examine the position of a tenant in a center before imposing damages for a violation of a continuous operation covenant. In a strip center, as in *Slater*, each tenant's storefront is equally visible, but each one's going "dark" has an impact that depends on the square footage of the leased premises.

# The Percentage Rental

During the 1930s, large chain stores used to offer landlords a percentage of the revenues of the operation conducted on the premises as a method of protecting themselves from the effects of the Depression. M. Friedman, 1 Friedman on Leases 158 (2d ed. 1983). After the Second World War, however, such clauses were beneficial to landlords in the rising economy and rental markets — and they have been used to protect landlords from economic changes ever since. Halper, Structuring Shopping Center Leases, Prob. & Prop. (Jan.-Feb. 1989), at 29, 30-31.

A preliminary to negotiations over this clause is the appraisal of the leased premises' fair rental value, on which a fair rent can be based. With that accomplished, the developer-landlord will attempt to get the tenant to pay an amount as close to that rental figure as possible. (And, to the extent that the percentage rent is inadequate protection against inflation, the landlord will want to readjust the base rent periodically.) This reduces the overall risk to the landlord by guaranteeing her a floor, base, or minimum rent, and makes any percentage rental, computed as a percent of sales, gravy to the landlord. The tenant resists, wanting as low a base rent as possible, as well as the smallest percent of sales as possible.

The relationship between the two types of rent plays off the landlord's need for a secure cash flow (say, to pay her permanent mortgagee) against her desire to participate in the success of the center and the tenant's desire to have a fixed rental obligation versus her willingness to share the profits with the landlord.

# EXAMPLES AND EXPLANATIONS

19. That said, the next question is: Should the percentage rent be calculated as a percent of gross or net sales?

**Explanation:** The industry standard is gross sales. Were it not so, the landlord would become involved in the accounting procedures used to establish the difference between net and gross. This the landlord does not wish to do. Neither does the tenant want the landlord involved in such calculations, for that would reveal to the landlord the tenant's profit margins, likely to be regarded as the latter's closely held secret.

20. What should gross sales include?

— cash sales?
— credit card[4] or charge account sales?
— discount[5] sales?
— layaway sales?
— installment sales?
— sales made to a store employee at a discount?
— sales made from vending machines?
— sales made through a franchise operating in the store?
— returns?
— sales made on charge accounts that are overdue?

What is each party interested in here?

**Explanation:** The landlord is pushing for the broadest definition of gross sales, in part because it will be the easiest to administer. (She is thinking

---

4. See Cocke v. Pacific Gulf Dev. Corp., 594 S.W.2d 545 (Tex. Civ. App. 1980) (holding that a credit card discount was not included in a "gross revenue" percentage lease).

5. Park Central Dev. Co. v. Roberts Dry Goods, Inc., 11 Ariz. App. 58, 461 P.2d 702 (1969) (holding that trading stamps were not discounts and so were not deductible from gross revenues).

of making the "unedited" cash register tapes the basis of the computation.) The tenant is pushing for as many exemptions as she can get.

21. What would be the landlord's likely response to the tenant's push for exemptions?

**Explanation:** Her response would be to place a ceiling or cap on the dollar amount of each and every exemption.

22. Once gross sales is defined, the next step is to determine the computational period. What should that be?

**Explanation:** Over the long haul, this is not the pressing matter that a definition of gross sales is, but ending the computational year in the middle of the Christmas shopping season makes no sense (because doing so would not take account of January merchandise returns). It would be better to pick a low point in the sales cycle — say the middle of the summer in the Sunbelt or the dead of winter in the Frostbelt.

23. With the computational period fixed, the frequency of payments based on the percentage will have to be determined. What will each side want here?

**Explanation:** The landlord will want frequent payments, say on a monthly basis, and the tenant will want to make quarterly or less frequent ones. The more frequent the payments, the more the tenant will push for a periodic readjustment to reflect the possibility that the payments may not reflect the rent due over a longer period — say the fact that monthly payments may not reflect the annualized rent due.

24. How would your answers in the preceding Examples change if the lease were for a freestanding building to be used by a bank, a fast-food restaurant, a theater, or a photo-developing kiosk? (The use of a portion of the parking lot for similar uses is one method of increasing the rent flow in older centers.)

**Explanation:** A freestanding lessee is likely to construct its store in the center of the parking lot. Because of the financing problems inherent in this type of construction loan, a sale-leaseback is often used as a financing device for this type of development.

The landlord will need to oversee the placement of this improvement so that it does not interfere with utility access to the center or, if it does, to reserve easements to service the affected lines. Use restrictions in the lease are likely to be narrower than for other tenants in the center, but such restrictions should not apply to lenders or leaseback investors who have to take the premises over to recoup loans or investments.

Exterior appearance will have to be regulated so that the tenant is not permitted to introduce a disharmonious exterior, although the interior of the premises, particularly if shielded by smoked glass on the windows to reduce parking lot glare, is unlikely to be of much concern to the landlord.

Customarily, such leases will still be triple-net, but as to water and sewer utility charges, a pass-through should be computed either on the basis of square footage if the use has a low consumption rate, as with a bank, or on the basis of a separate meter if the use has a high consumption rate, as with fast-food franchises. Such freestanding lessees should probably carry their own insurance, and because the landlord's manager will have less control over the premises, the tenant should indemnify the landlord for all premises liability.

# A Note on Antitrust Law

Shopping center landlords sometimes require that their tenants agree not to operate a similar store within a certain radius of the center, either under its name or any other name. DiSciullo, Geographic and Product Markets for Radius Clauses under the Rule of Reason, 19 Real Est. L.J. 121 (1990). If the radius is reasonably limited and the same tenant is not prevented from operating in other lines of business, then the radius clause will be upheld and is not a violation of the federal antitrust statutes. However, if the covenant regulates the price or quality of goods that a tenant may carry, whether the clause is of benefit to either the landlord or the tenant, it will likely be subject to attack. Compare National Super Markets, Inc. v. Magna Trust Co., 212 Ill. App. 3d 358, 570 N.E.2d 1191 (1991) (covenant precluding grocery store being operated within one mile of shopping center is not per se illegal under §1 of the Sherman Act), with Drury Inn-Colorado Springs v. Olive Co., 878 F.2d 340, 343 (10th Cir. 1989) (restrictive covenant on developer's remaining land called for no other hotel with room rates within 20 percent of beneficiary's hotel rates violates §1 of the Sherman Act: "When we plant the restrictive covenant in this garden, it withers under Sherman's glare."). The attack is likely to come from the Federal Trade Commission, which has been very active in this field over the years. Sears, Roebuck & Co., 89 F.T.C. 240 (1977).

In response to a radius clause of three to five miles, the tenant will ask that existing stores, and renewals of any existing leases, be excepted. The landlord's likely response to that is to ask that those existing facilities, if excepted, not be enlarged substantially. How about advertising? If the radius clause is otherwise valid and sale advertising is permitted under the lease, a tenant advertising a sale at another location without also holding it in the center may run afoul of the covenant.

Crucial to the validity of radius clauses is the determination of the affected market. If it extends geographically beyond the radius described in the clause — the area in which a consumer might naturally look for the goods or services described in the clause — the market impact will be lessened pro tanto, and the clause will become easier to defend. See, e.g., Drabbant Enters. v. Great Atl. & Pac. Tea Co., 688 F. Supp. 1567, 1579 (D. Del. 1988).

# Bankruptcy and the Shopping Center Lease

Upon the shopping center tenant's bankruptcy, the unexpired lease is subject to the automatic stay (11 U.S.C. §362) imposed upon any proceeding against the tenant and, assuming that the stay is not lifted, is treated as an asset of the bankrupt's estate, and the trustee in bankruptcy is then entitled to either assume or reject the lease. 11 U.S.C. §365(a). Neither an anti-assignment covenant nor a covenant stating that the lease is forfeited upon the tenant's bankruptcy will prevent the trustee from exercising this §365 right. The trustee has the right to reject a lease when, in the exercise of business judgment, it is prudent to do so. An assumption must be made by express court order, within the statutory time frame, or rejection is presumed. 11 U.S.C. §365(d)(4). A trustee may also assign the lease. 11 U.S.C. §365(f).

The foregoing powers are not unique to leases subject to bankruptcy court jurisdiction. However, when a trustee seeks to assume, or assume and assign, a shopping center lease that has been in default, she must beforehand provide the landlord with adequate assurance of future performance. This expressly includes (1) a showing of the source of future rent, and, in the case of an assignment, a showing that the financial condition of the assignee is similar to that of the lessee at the time of the execution of the lease; (2) assurance that the percentage rent will not substantially decline in the future; (3) assurance that the assumption or assignment will not cause a default in "any other lease, financing agreement, or master agreement relating to the shopping center"; and (4) an assurance that the assumption or assignment "will not disrupt any tenant mix or balance" in the center. 11 U.S.C. §365(b)(3)(A)-(D).

For purposes of invoking this special protection given shopping center landlords, a landlord must establish that indeed a shopping center is involved. The term is not defined in the Bankruptcy Code. A master lease and covenants, fixed hours of operation, common areas, and joint advertising are elements of such a showing. Contractual interdependence is required among tenants. The landlord's common ownership, joint parking facilities, even the existence of an anchor tenant are insufficient. In re Goldblatt Bros., Inc., 766 F.2d

1136, 1140-1141 (7th Cir. 1985); In re Joshua Slocum, Ltd., 99 B.R. 250, 256-257 (E.D. Pa. 1989).

# EXAMPLES AND EXPLANATIONS

25. You check into a hotel. You buy traveler's checks at the front desk. There you receive a discount coupon for dinner in the hotel's restaurant and another coupon for a free drink in the hotel bar. You go up to your room with two keys: One unlocks the door to the room and the other a locked cabinet in which are snacks, sodas, and other foods, available for an extra charge. You select a cable movie on the TV, knowing that this will add six dollars to your bill. The hotel is operated under a percentage lease on "gross sales and receipts." Which of the foregoing purchases, coupons, and extra charges should be included in the calculation of gross rents and receipts for purposes of calculating the percentage rent due?

**Explanation:** Partial answers are provided by the case law. See Papa Gino's of America, Inc. v. Broadmanor Assocs., Ltd., 5 Conn. App. 532, 500 A.2d 1341 (1985) (permitting a tenant to deduct used restaurant coupons from gross sales); McComb v. McComb, 9 Mich. App. 70, 155 N.W.2d 860 (1967) (holding that the sale of traveler's checks was included). Considering the last holding, you can see why hotels have recently moved toward the locked cabinet approach to a refreshment bar in the room. But see Cocke v. Pacific Gulf Dev. Corp., 594 S.W.2d 545 (Tex. Civ. App. 1980) (holding that the TV rental was included), which explains why extra channels are provided for movie viewing in a hotel room.

# Office Building Leases: A Negotiating Problem

You have recently passed the bar examination and are establishing your first office. After examining the market for commercial office space in Metropolis, you send the following letter to Bill Friend, a local real estate broker, in response to a call informing you of available space in the Downtown Building:

Dear Bill:

On behalf of myself and a partner to-be, I write to make a draft proposal to lease office space in the Downtown Building, as set forth below:

| | |
|---|---|
| Premises: | Approximately 6000 sq. ft. on the 7th floor. |
| Base Rent: | $26.00 per rentable sq. ft. per annum inclusive of all services. If ownership of the building should change, all tenant |

deposits will be transferred to new owner(s) and returned to tenant under lease terms, and tenant will review management contract to assure no change in management services.

Term:                    10 years.

Lease Start:             September 1, 1993.

Annual Escalations:      Tenant will pay pro rata share of real estate taxes and building services attributable to premises, excluding special assessments or special taxes above actual costs for year after start of lease. Operating costs shall exclude: (1) capital improvements and costs incurred as result of said improvements; (2) any special services and expenses for retail space; (3) costs of government-mandated improvements; (4) costs arising from disputes with other parties; (5) costs of operating parking services; (6) costs incurred by Lessor as property owner; (7) costs for which Lessor is compensated by management fee; (8) costs to benefit specific tenant or not passed through to all tenants; (9) costs used to generate rental or other income. Tenant will have right to audit Lessor's expense records, with an opportunity to copy relevant documents and use reasonable space for audit. Tenant will pay for such audit unless audit shows discrepancy. On first anniversary of lease and each anniversary following, base rent shall be increased by 20 percent of annual CPI increase for the preceding year.

Rent Abated:             Lessor agrees to abate the first seven months rent.

Tenant Allowances:       Lessor agrees to finish the space per plan attached as Exhibit A including those items identified by space planner as provided by Tenant at Lessor's sole cost to be presented in work letter.

Options to Expand:       In the third and fifth year of lease, Tenant shall have option to expand premises leased to all available space on 7th floor. Tenant reserves right to exercise this option on all or any part of available space.

Options to Extend:       Tenant shall have option, on three months' advance notice, to extend the primary term of this lease at 8 percent off fair rental value, with Lessor providing services including but not limited to painting, carpet cleaning, replacing deteriorated fixtures, etc.

| Services: | Lessor shall provide the following: (1) cleaning and janitor services; (2) electronic access to premises at Lessor's expense on a 24-hour, 7-day-a-week basis, with lobby attendant on duty daily to 12 midnight; (3) professional, first-class building management; (4) at least eight parking spaces. |
| HVAC: | HVAC shall be provided Monday-Friday, 8 AM-8 PM, and Saturday 8 AM-2 PM, except for any holidays, at average temperatures causing no damage to Tenant's computers, word processing, and copying equipment. At all other times, Lessor shall supply HVAC at cost. |

This proposal is nonbinding and is made subject to modification or withdrawal at any time prior to its acceptance and the execution by the parties of a lease agreement.

Very truly yours,

John B. Tenant
Attorney at Law

In reply a month later, Bill Friend has just sent you the following letter:

Dear John:

Thanks for your patience in waiting for Larry Lessor's response to your approach to the rental of space in the Downtown Building on Market Street. Larry is pleased to submit the following terms whereby your firm would lease space in his building:

| Area: | Approximately 6125 rentable sq. ft. on the 7th floor, as set forth in Exhibit A. |
| Term: | 7 years. |
| Commencement: | September 1, 1993. |
| Base Rental Rate: | $28.50 per sq. ft., full service. In addition, at start of fourth lease year, the then-escalated rent shall be increased by $3.00 per sq. ft. |
| Rent Abatement: | Lessor shall waive full monthly base rent for first five months for proposed lease. |
| Improvements: | Tenant shall accept premises "as is" and receive a credit of $4.00 per rentable sq. ft. of office space to be applied to costs incurred in construction of Tenant's office. |
| Escalation: | Annually Tenant shall pay pro rata share of actual operating expenses and real estate tax costs over a base of CY 1992. Base rental shall be adjusted at the beginning of January 1994 and each year thereafter based on 30 percent of corresponding CPI percent increase for all urban consumers, with 1988-1990 as 100, published by U.S. Dept. of |

|  | Labor, Bur. of Labor Statistics, for Metropolis SMSA. |
|---|---|
| HVAC: | Lessor shall provide HVAC in season between 8 AM-6 PM, Monday-Friday, and between 9 AM-1 PM Saturday, except for holidays observed by the state or federal government, and at other times at a to-be-determined rate. |
| Access: | 24 hours daily by at least one elevator. |
| Parking: | Lessor shall provide Tenant with right to lease monthly parking contracts in ratio of one contract for each 1000 sq. ft. leased. |

This proposal is submitted subject to modification, code requirements, or withdrawal at any time, with or without notice, prior to time at which landlord and tenant execute a more definitive and comprehensive written agreement applicable to the leased space in the Downtown Building. Meanwhile we look forward to our continuing discussions in this regard. Please do not hesitate to contact us with any questions or comments you may have with regard to the above terms and conditions.

Sincerely yours,


William B. Friend
Downtown Real Estate Brokerage, Inc.
AGREED AND ACCEPTED BY: _____
Date: _____        Title: _____

After this exchange of letters, what points remain to be negotiated between landlord and tenant? How would you propose to resolve them? See Tunis, Protecting Tenant Interest in Lease Negotiations, 20 Real Est. Rev. 44 (Spring 1990).

# *Index*

Accounting standards, 386-387
Agreement to reconvey, 223
All-inclusive loan. *See* Wraparound financing
Attorney review clauses, 9, 72-73, 181, 465

Bankruptcy
  automatic stay, 313, 334
  cash collateral, 334-335
  cramdown, 315, 334-335
  deed in lieu of foreclosure, 319
  Durrett v. Washington Natl. Ins. Co., 310-313
  executory contract, 335
  federal tax liens, 330
  foreclosure, 282-283, 297, 310-316
  forms of action, 314-315
    corporate reorganization, Chapter 11, 314, 335
    individual reorganization, Chapter 13, 315
    liquidation, Chapter 7, 314
  fraudulent conveyances, 310-313, 389
  generally, 310-316, 333-336
  installment land contract, 340-341, 390
  lender liability, 334
  limited partnership, 403
  loan participation, 450
  preference avoidance, 334
  sale-leaseback transactions, 387-389
  shopping center leases, 482-483
  statutory redemption period, 283, 303, 330
  surety bonds, 326
  termination clauses, 389
  title insurance, 191
  vendee's liens, 110
  vendor's liens, 113
Builder's risk insurance, 328-329
  subrogation rights, 329

Certificate of title, 181
Chain of title
  abstractors and, 171-172
  foreclosure, 296
  generally, 171-176

idem sonens, doctrine of, 182
Model Marketable Title Act
  adverse possession, 198
  boundary agreements, 199
  chain of marketable record title, 200
  constitutionality of, 198-199
  example of, 196-197
  foreclosure deed, 201
  generally, 195-204
  installment land sale contract, 200
  party wall agreements, 199
  reciprocal negative easements, 199
  root of title, 197-198, 200, 201
  quitclaim deed, 201
  tax deeds, 200
  wild deeds, 200
  recording acts, 171-176
  title abstracts and, 171, 181
  title search and, 171-172, 181
  Torrens system, 205
  warranties of title, 122
Circuity of interests,
  generally, 176-178
  subordination agreements, 437-439
Commercial leases. *See also* shopping center leases
  generally, 463-486
  implied warrant of habitability, 463
  office building leases, 483-486
Construction
  architects
    design defect, 427
    duty to inspect, 425, 427-428
    duty to supervise, 427-429
    implied warranties for fitness, 426
    implied warranty of habitability, 426
    liability, 453
    negligence, 429
    right to refuse reuse of plans, 430
    statute of limitations, 426
  fast track, 452-453
  financing
    all-inclusive loan. *See* Wraparound financing
    binding refunding agreement, 432
    buy-sell agreement, 432

487

Construction (*continued*)
fast track, 452-453
fixtures, construction mortgagee, 332
generally, 431-453
hard costs, 433
hold harmless loan. *See* Wraparound financing
installment land sale contract, 433
land acquisition, 433
loan application process, 432-433
loan participation
    agency, 450
    bankruptcy, 450
    fiduciary duties, 451
    generally, 449-451
    pro rata rule, 450
mechanic's lien,
    enforcement, 448
    fixtures, 449
    judicial foreclosure, 448
    land use control laws, 449
    priority, 446
    relation-back, rule of, 446
    statutes, 438, 445-449
    stop notices, 448
    subcontractors, 445
    subordination, 447
    title insurance, 448
    Uniform Commercial Code, 449
    waivers, 446, 448
overriding loan. *See* Wraparound financing
purchase money mortgage, 433
short-term financing, 431
soft costs, 433
subcontractors, 444-445
    liquidated damages provisions, 445
subordination agreements,
    automatic subordination agreement, 436
    constructive notice, 438
    diversion of loan proceeds, 436, 438
    example of, 434
    executory subordination, 434
    generally, 433-439
    lender, duty to inspect, 438
    lien circuity, 437-439
    nonautomatic subordination agreement. *See*
        executory subordination
    priority, effect on, 433-434
    recording acts, 437
    specific performance, 436
    third-party beneficiary, 436
takeback mortgage. *See* purchase money
    mortgage
takeout financing, 431-432
usury
    adjustable rate mortgages, 442
    consumer protection statutes, 442
    federal preemption, 442-444
    generally, 442-444
    installment land sale contract, 444
    sale-leaseback transaction, 444
wraparound financing
    credit bids, 441
    due-on sale clause, 439

    example of, 439
    foreclosure, 441-442
    generally, 439-442
    purchase money mortgage, 440
    real estate investment trusts, 440
    usury, 444
Contract of sale,
agency relationship, 67-68
    covenant of good faith, 67-69
contingency clauses,
    generally, 45, 64-73
    subject to attorney review clause, 72-73
    subject to existing mortgages clause, 70
        price term, definiteness of, 70
    subject to financing clause, 65-69
        agency relationship, 67-68
        available financing, 69
        duty of good faith, 67-69
        material terms, 65, 67
        option to purchase, relationship to, 69
        satisfactory financing, 69
    subject to rezoning clause, 71-72
    subject to sale of prior residence clause, 70
destruction of property, 45, 107
equitable mortgages, 222
escrows, 128
generally, 4, 43-53
installment land sale contract and, 337
interference with a prospective advantage, 110
junior liens and, 247
listing agreements, 22
price term, definiteness of, 70
remedies for breach
    affirmation, 108
    election of remedies, 107-108
    foreclosure of liens, 108
    jury trial, 108-109
    measure of damages, 109
    rescission, 107-110
        assignable nature of right, 108
        consideration, failure of, 107
        destruction of property, 107
        duty to restore, 109
        improvements, 108
        mutual mistake, 107
        unjust enrichment, 108
    restitution, 108
risk of loss,
    English rule, 43
    equitable conversion, doctrine of, 44-46
        criticism of, 46-47
        legal Title, 44
        Massachusetts rule, 46-47
        option to purchase, 44
        specific performance, 44-45, 46
        waste, 44
    generally, 43-53, 125
    installment land sale contract, 337
    insurance policy
        constructive trust, 51-53
        endorsement, 51
        escrow, 52
        generally, 43, 51-53

proceeds trust, 53
  subrogation rights, 51
  title trust, 52-53
  trust theory, 43
marketable title, doctrine of, 43
Massachusetts rule, 46-47
  abatement of purchase price, 46-47
merger, doctrine of, 125
Uniform Vendor Purchaser Risk Act
  abatement of purchase price, 49-50
  applied to option to purchase, 48
  destruction, defined, 50
  generally, 47-51
  rationale of, 47
  right of possession, 49
  specific performance, 48
  terms of, defined, 48-51
Statute of Frauds, 58
"subject to" clauses, 64-73
transfer taxes, 421
vendee's liens, 110-112, 113
  assignable nature of, 110
  bankruptcy, 110
  bona fide purchaser, 110-111
  foreclosure of, 111
  priority, 112
  proportionate equitable conversion, 111
  Statute of Frauds, 111
vendor's liens, 112-113
  assignable nature of, 113
  bankruptcy, 113
  bona fide purchaser, 113
  priority, 113
Curative statutes, 176, 202-203

Deed in lieu of foreclosure
  abandonment as alternative, 320
  antideficiency legislation, 306
  bankruptcy, 319
  consideration, 320
  equity of redemption, 320
    clog on equity of redemption, 320
  escrow, 320
  example of, 323
  federal income tax consequences, 321, 378
  foreclosure, 294-298
  generally, 296, 318-324
  merger, doctrine of, 321-322
  mortgages, 220, 267
  omitted junior liens, 288-293
  recitals in, 324
  remedies, 321-322
    merger, doctrine of, 322
    reforeclosure, 321
  transfer taxes, 424
Deed of bargain and sale, 7
Deed of trust. See also Mortgages
  generally, 215, 219, 226
  power of sale foreclosure, 286
Deeds
  acknowledgment, 118
  attestation clause, 118

components of, 116-119
covenants of. See Warranties of title
delivery of
  acceptance, 123
  agency, 123
  condition on delivery, effect of, 124
    vendor's lien, 124
  escrow
    agency relationship, 127
    bona fide purchaser, 132-133
    contract of sale, 128
    generally, 127-133
    instructions, 127-130
    irrevocability, 128
    marketable title, 130
    misdelivery of, 132-133
    mortgages, 127-128
    relation back, doctrine of, 128
    risk of loss, 131-132
    Statute of Frauds, 128
    time is of the essence, 130-131
  generally, 123-126
  manumission, 123
  proof of, 123
  recording, 123
  seisin, 123
  slander of title, 124
descriptions in
  base lines, 135-138
  boundary descriptions, 139
  courses control distances, Rule of, 140
  generally, 135-144
  Jeffersonian survey. See rectangular survey
  metes and bounds description, 135, 139-141
  monuments, 140, 143
  principal meridian, 135-137
  ranges, 135-138
  reasonable certainty, rule of, 140
  rectangular survey, 135-139, 140, 142
  standard parallels, 135-138
  townships, 135-138
habendum clauses, 116, 118, 139
implied warranty of habitability
  "as is" clauses, 154
  broker misrepresentation, 149-150
  builder's liability for defect, 145, 147
  commercial real property, 158, 463
  disclaimer. See waiver of
  duty to disclose defects, 148
  generally, 145
  habitability, defined, 146
  lender liability, 155-157
  measure of damages, 150-152
  mitigation of damages, doctrine of, 147, 151
  nonbuilder vendor, 148
  statute of limitations, 145, 153
  statutory basis for, 145
  subsequent purchasers, 152-154
  vendor fraud, 149
  waiver of, 146, 154-155
indenture, 119
merger, doctrine of, 125
negligent preparation of, 125-126

Deeds (*continued*)
  quitclaim, 117
  seisin, 120
  Short form deeds, 116, 118
    example of, 118
  slander of title, 125, 159-161
  Statute of Uses, 117
  Uniform Recognition of Acknowledgements
    Act, 118
  warranties of title,
    assignability, 121
      American rule, 121
    bona fide purchasers, 120
    burden of proof, 121
    chain of title, 122
    defenses, 122
    English warranty, 120
    future warranties, 120
    generally, 116, 118, 119-123
    general warranties, 119
    measure of damages, 121
    present warranties, 120
    special warranties, 119
    statutes of limitations, 120, 122

Enfeoffment, 3, 5
Equitable conversion, doctrine of, 5, 22, 44-46,
    340, 345, 390
Equity of redemption, 218-222
Escrow
  agency relationship, 127
  bona fide purchaser, 132-133
  contract of sale, 128
  generally, 127-133
  instructions, 127-130
    example of, 129-130
  irrevocability, 128
  marketable title, 130
  misdelivery of deed, 132-133
  mortgages, 127-128
  relation back, doctrine of, 128
  risk of loss, 131-132
  Statute of Frauds, 128
  time is of the essence, 130-131
Executory interests, 5
Executory period, defined, 63

Financing. *See also* Construction, financing
  cash flow, 367
  debt to fair market value, 363
  federal tax consequences, 367
    depreciation deduction, 367-368
    sheltering of income, 367
    tax credits, 368
  ground lease, 360-362, 364
    cash flow analysis, 361
    components of, 362
    condominiums, 361
    default, right to cure, 361
    mechanic's liens, 361
    nonrecourse, 360-362
    recourse, 360

  subdivisions, 361
  subordination clause, 361-362
  internal rate of return, 408-410
  land leases, 360
  leverage, 363
  loan to value ratios, 363
  mortgage in rem. *See* nonrecourse mortgage
  nonrecourse mortgages, 363, 368-371
    deficiency judgment, 369, 370
    equity participation, 370
    foreclosure, 369
    personal guarantees, 369
    subrogation clauses, 370
  pro forma. *See* setup
  real estate investment trust, 382
  sale-leaseback transaction, 360
  setup, 365-366
    example of, 366
  subordination clauses, 360, 364
  syndication, 359, 402
  wraparound financing, 362-364
    purchase money mortgage, 363
    take subject to clause, 362
Fixtures
  annexation, 331-332
  assembled plant doctrine, 331
  construction mortgagee, 332
  generally, 330-332
  priority of lien, 332
  security interest, 331-332
  Uniform Commercial Code, 331
Foreclosure
  acceleration of debt, 279-283
  accord and satisfaction, 297
  anticipatory repudiation, 279-280
  antideficiency legislation, 304-307
    appraisal statutes, 307
    deed in lieu of foreclosure, 306
    deed of release, 305
    deficiency judgments, 304, 306
    foreclosure first statute, 307
    installment land sale contract, 305
    junior mortgagees, 305
    misrepresentation, 306
    one action statutes, 307
    purchase money mortgage, 304-306
    private power of sale, 304
    rescission, 306
    subordination agreement, 306
    vendor's liens, 305
  bankruptcy, 282-283, 297, 310-316
    automatic stay, 313
    cramdown, 315
    Durrett v. Washington Natl. Ins. Co.,
      310-313
    forms of action, 314-315
      corporate reorganization, Chapter 11, 314
      individual reorganization, Chapter 13, 315
      liquidation, Chapter 7, 314
    fraudulent conveyances, 310-313
    statutory redemption period, 283, 303
  collection procedures, 279-280
  deacceleration, 282-283
  decree nisi, 284, 285

deed in lieu of foreclosure, 294-298
  clog in equity of redemption, 296
  deed of release, 297
  right of equitable redemption, 296
  shared appreciation mortgage, 297
defects in foreclosure sale, 293-294
  "as is" nature of, 293
  bona fide purchasers, 293
equitable mortgage, 297
equitable redemption, doctrine of, 295, 296, 309
federal income tax consequences, 298
  credit bid, 298
  omitted junior liens, 298
fraudulent conveyance statutes, 310
generally, 279-315
Graf v. Hope Building Corp., 280-282
liquidated damages provision, 281
merger, doctrine of, 294-298
  accord and satisfaction, 298
methods of, 283-288
  judicial foreclosure, 283-285
    credit bid, 284
    order of priority, 284
    statutory redemption, 299
  power of sale foreclosure, 285-286
    antideficiency legislation, 304
    burden of proof, 286
    constitutionality of, 286
    deed of trust, 286
    statute of limitations, 286
    statutory redemption, 287, 299, 302
  strict foreclosure, 288
moratoria on, 303-304
  constitutionality of, 303
notice requirement, 280
omitted junior liens, 288-293
  circularity of redemption, 290
  constructive trust, 292
  deed in lieu of foreclosure, 321
  equity of redemption, 289, 291-292
  lessee's, 293
  mechanic's liens, 293
  strict foreclosure, 290-291
  subrogation, 289
right to prepay, 280
Soldiers and Sailors Relief Act, 282
statutory redemption, 298-303, 307-310
  bankruptcy, automatic stay, 313
  deficiency judgment, 309-310
  equitable redemption, 309
  farm foreclosure, 303
  inadequacy of price, 307-308
  priority of redemptions, 299
  private power of sale, 302
third-party beneficiary theory, 296
writ of quia timet, 279
Fraud, 166

Grantor-grantee index, 174
Ground lease, 360-362
  cash flow analysis, 361
  components of, 362
  condominiums, 361

default, right to cure, 361
mechanic's liens, 361
nonrecourse, 360-362
recourse, 360
subdivisions, 361
subordination clause, 361-362

Idem sonens, doctrine of, 182
Illinois Land Trust, 348-349
  financing statement, 349
  Statute of Uses, 349
  Uniform Commercial Code, 349
Installment land sale contracts, 337-349
  automatic forfeiture, 338, 339
  bankruptcy, 340-341
  blanket mortgage, 342
  burden of litigation, 338
  burden of proof, 345
  civil rights, 348
  deed of release, 344-345
  default, right to cure, 344, 347
  deficiency judgment, 339, 347
  election of remedies, 345
  equitable conversion, doctrine of, 340, 345
  equitable right of redemption, 339, 342, 344
  equitable title, 338
  executory period, 337
  financing statement, 340, 346
  foreclosure, 338, 347
  forfeiture, 338-339, 343
  functional equivalency, doctrine of, 339
  implied assignment of rights, 344
  judicial sale, 338
  legal title, 338
  lien creditors, 340
  liquidated damages, 338, 339
  lis pendens, 345
  marketable title, 341
  measure of damages, 345
  mortgage, relation to, 338
  omitted junior lien, 344
  recording statutes, application of, 338, 342
  reforeclosure, 344
  relationship to contract of sale, 337
  remedies, 341-346
    acceleration clauses, 341
    anticipatory repudiation, 341
    purchaser's remedies, 341
      breach, 341
      decree nisi, 342
      rescission, 341
      specific performance, 341, 342, 347
      unjust enrichment, 342
    vendor's remedies, 341
      contract remedies, 341, 343
      ejectment, 341
      foreclosure, 341
      quiet title, 341
      strict foreclosure, 344
      waste, 343
  risk of loss, 337
  state legislation, 346-347
    redemption periods, 347

Installment land sale contracts (*continued*)
  statutory redemption, 339
  strict foreclosure, 344
  termination of contract, 338
  Uniform Commercial Code, 340, 346
  vendor's duty, 338
  vendor's lien, 340
Internal Revenue Code
  amount realized, 373, 375
  at risk limitations, 414
  basis, 353, 373
  buy up-roll over rule, 355
  cancellation of mortgage debt, 373
    nonrecourse loan, 374-376
  capital gains, 358, 397-398, 413
  Commissioner v. Tufts, 374-378, 397
  Crane v. Commissioner, 374-377
  deductions
    mortgage interest, 354, 355, 367,
      415
    real property taxes, 354, 355, 367
    repair costs, 355
  depreciation
    accelerated cost recovery system, 413
    business property, 355-357, 367-368,
      398
    generally, 355-357
    investment property, 355-357
    leveraged depreciation, 368
    residential property, 354
  economic benefit theory, 375-376
  federal tax liens, 329-330
    bankruptcy, 330
    notice of, 330
    priority of title, 330
    subordination, doctrine of, 329
  generally, 353-358, 412-417
  installment sales, 354
  internal rate of return, impact on, 416
  Kintner Regulations, 416
  leverage, 397-398
  like-kind property exchange, 357
  master limited partnerships, 416
  nonrecognition of gain, 354
  nonrecourse mortgages, 414
  passive losses, 357, 398, 414, 416-417
  personal liability requirement, 414
  portfolio income, 416
  real estate investment trusts, 416
  sale-leaseback transactions, 379-386, 416
    acceleration clauses, 379
    deductions, 379
    Frank Lyon Co. v. United States, 381-386
    loan-to-value financing, 379
    mortgage, compared to, 379
    real estate investment trust, 382
    sham transactions, 380
  tax benefit theory, 374
  tax credits, 368, 415
  tax-free exchanges, 357
  tax reform, 412-417
  tax shelter, 376, 415
  true loan theory, 376

Leases
  ground leases, 360
  land leases, 360
  net leases, 406
  sale-leaseback, 360
Liens, junior
  alternatives to, 247
    contract of sale, 247
    installment land sale contract, 247
    sale-leaseback, 247
    wraparound financing, 247
  deficiency judgments, 246
    waiver of, 246
  equity of redemption, 245
    clog on, 247
  foreclosure proceedings, 243-244, 246
  generally, 243-247
  marshalling, doctrine of, 243-244
  priority of title, 244
  relativity of title, 245
  right to redeem, 243
  subrogation, 246
Lien circuity. *See* Circuity of interests
Livery of seisin, 3, 4

Marketable record title acts, 7
Marketable title, doctrine of, 3, 7, 43
  specific performance, 43
Marshalling, doctrine of, 243-244, 250
Misrepresentation, 166
Model Marketable Title Act, 195-204
  adverse possession, 198
  boundary agreements, 199
  chain of marketable record title, 200
  constitutionality of, 198-199
  example of, 196-197
  foreclosure deed, 201
  installment land sale contract, 200
  party wall agreements, 199
  reciprocal negative easements, 199
  root of title, 197-198, 200, 201
  quitclaim deed, 201
  tax deeds, 200
  wild deeds, 200
Mortgages
  adjustable rate mortgage (ARM), 230, 256,
    259
  alternative mortgage instruments, 230-231
  amortization, 227
  application for, 237
    consideration, 237
    lender liability, 237
    specific performance, 238
  assignment of rents, 271-272
    attornment clause, 271
    executory agreement, 272
    subordination agreement, 271
  assumption of debt, 249
    deed covenant, 251
    personal liability, 249
    Statute of Frauds, 251
    surety, 249

balloon payment, 227, 228, 229, 231, 318
covenants, 218
deed in lieu of foreclosure, 220, 267
deed of trust, 215, 219
defaults, power to cure, 220
dragnet clauses, 236-237
   parol evidence, 236
   strict construction, 236
   waiver of, 236
due-on-sale clause, 229
equitable mortgages, 222
   burden of proof, 222
   contract of sale, 222
   deed in fee simple absolute, 222
   foreclosure, 222
   lien theory, 222
   parol evidence, 222
   sale-leaseback, 225, 389
   "support" mortgage, 225
   title theory, 222
   vendor's liens, 113
   warranty deed, 223
equity of redemption, 216, 218-222, 245
   clogs in the, 220, 221, 247
   junior lienholders, 245
   waiver of, 220, 221
escrow accounts, 238-241
   agency relationship, 241
   contract duty, 241
   trust relationship, 240-241
   uniform covenants, 239-240
estoppel, doctrine of, 224
Federal Home Loan Mortgage Association
     (Freddie Mac), 213, 239, 254, 280
Federal National Mortgage Association (Fannie
     Mae), 213, 239, 254, 280
foreclosure, 216-217
future advance mortgages, 231-234
   actual notice, 234
   constructive notice, 232, 235
   disbursement, 235
   example of, 231
   mandatory. *See* obligatory advances
   mechanic's lien, 235
   obligatory advances, 231-235
   optional advances, 232-235
   recording acts, 232, 235
   "stop notice" law, 233
   subordination, 232
good faith dealing, doctrine of, 221, 239-240
Government National Mortgage Association
     (Ginnie Mae), 213
graduated payment mortgage (GPM), 231
history, 211-213, 216, 218
implied assumption agreement, 255
interest computation, 226-227
internal rate of return, 230, 416
inverse order of alienation, rule of, 250
lien
   covenants of, 226
   terms of, 226-230
lien theory of, 216-217, 222
marshalling, doctrine of, 250

mortgagee in possession, 270-271, 272-274
   appointment of receiver, 270
   attornment clauses, 271
   duty to account, 272
   environmental liability, 270
   foreclosure, 270-271
   leases, 270
   standard of care, 270
   waste, 270
negative pledges, 225
part performance, doctrine of, 224
privity of contract, 218
privity of estate, 218
promissory note, 215, 225-226
   right to prepay, 226
   terms of, 225-226
purchase money mortgage, doctrine of, 224
receiverships, 272-278
   agency relationship, 272
   assignments of rent clause, 272
   elements of proof, 273
   federal bank receivers, 276-278, 335-336
     avoidance powers, 335-336
     *D'Oench, Duhme* doctrine, 276-278
   Interrelationship with Mortgagee in
     Possession, 272-273
   Subrogation, 274
regulation of, 211-212, 227, 230
remedies, 218-220
   judicial confirmation, 219
   judicial foreclosure, 219
   power to cure default, 220
   private power of sale, 219
   right to receiver, 220
   specific performance, 220-221
   statutory right of redemption, 219, 221
   strict foreclosure, 219
reverse annuity mortgage (RAM), 230
roll-over mortgage, 231
secondary mortgage market, 212-213, 270
securities implications, 212
shared appreciation mortgage, 229, 231, 297
"subject to" clauses, 249, 250
   sale by foreclosure, 249
surety relationship, 249
terms of, 226-230
title theory of, 215-217, 222
transfers by mortgagee, 263-270
   assignment of mortgage, 263
   bona fide purchaser. *See* holder in due course,
     doctrine of
   confession of judgment, 265
   defenses, 263, 268-270
     personal defenses, 268
     real defenses, 268
   duty of inquiry, 267
   first in time rule, 266
   holder in due course, doctrine of, 263, 265,
     268-270
   implied warranty of repayment, 266
   merger, doctrine of, 267
   negotiable nature of note, 263-266, 269
     acceleration of debt, 265

Mortgages (*continued*)
   nonrecourse, 265
   priority of title, 267
   tender of payment, 269
   voidable deed, 267
   void deed, 267
   transfers by mortgagor, 250-263
      assumption of existing mortgage, 249-255
         deed covenant, 251
         defenses, 255
         derived right or contract theory, 251-254
         discharge rule, 253
         financing, 262
         foreclosure, 252
         implied, 255
         personal liability, 249
         statute of frauds, 251
         subrogation, 251
         third-party beneficiary theory, 251-254
      chain of derived rights, 252
      derived right of contract theory, 251-253
      discharge rule, 253
      due-on-sale clauses, 255-263
         acceleration of debt, 256-262
         adjustable rate mortgage, 259, 262
         assumption agreements, 259
         automatic enforcement, 256
         burden of proof, 258
         commercial mortgage loans, 262
         creation of junior lien, 257
         defined, 258
         Escrow, 262
         exceptions to, 257
         federal regulation of, 256-261
         Garn-St. Germain Act, 257, 259-260, 262
         general partnerships, 262
         history of, 256
         Illinois land trusts, 262
         installment land sale contract, 260
         preemptive effect of federal regulation, 256, 258
         prepayment penalty, 258, 261
         sale-leaseback transaction, 263
         showing of insecurity, 256
         waiver, 261
      FNMA-FHLMC uniform mortgage covenant, 254
      implied assumption agreement, 255
      inverse order of alienation, rule of, 250
      marshalling, doctrine of, 250
      nonassuming grantee, 252, 254
      remote, assuming grantee, 252-254
      "subject to" existing mortgage, 249
         parol evidence rule, application of, 251
      surety, 249, 253-254
   uniform covenants of, 226, 254
   use restrictions, 218
   variable rate mortgage, 228, 230, 256

Negligence
   abstractor, 7

Partnerships
   agency, 393, 395, 396
   continuity of life, 399-400, 403
   contributions, 404
   dissolution, 399-400
   estoppel letter, 396
   general partnership, 393
   leverage, 397-398
   limited partnership, 393, 396-397
      bankruptcy, 403
      characteristics of, 399-401
      tax consequences of, 398-405
         Kintner Regulations, 398-399, 402
         Larson v. Commissioner, 399-405
   master limited partnerships, 405, 416
   professional responsibility
      attorney advertising, 15
      attorney review clauses, 9, 72-73, 183-184
      conflict of interest, 11
         scrivener's exception, 13
      dual representation, 10, 12, 13
         scrivener's exception, 13
      ethical considerations, 10
         DR 5-105(A)-(D), 10-12, 14
         Model Rules of Professional Conduct Rule 1.7, 10-11
      exemption from brokerage regulations, 16
      generally, 9-17, 126
      grievance procedures, 16
      independent professional judgment rule, 12
      malpractice, 204, 412
      negligent preparation of deed, 125-126
      reverse competition, 15
   purchase option
      equitable conversion, doctrine of, 44
      Statute of Frauds, 58
      Uniform Vendor Purchaser Risk Act, 48
   securities law liability, 411-412
   tax consequences, 393, 397-398
      Kintner Regulations, 398-399, 402
      Larson v. Commissioner, 399-405, 414
   theory of, 395-396
      aggregate theory of partnership, 395
      legal entity theory, 395-396
   Uniform Partnership Acts, 394-395

Quitclaim deed, 7, 201

Real estate brokerage
   agency relationship, 19-20, 38-39
      chain of agency, 20
   brokers
      employment agreement, 19
      fiduciary duties, 31-35
         consumer protection statutes, 33, 37
         disclose material facts, duty to, 31-32, 34, 36-37, 38
         good faith, duty of, 31-33
         interference with prospective advantage, 34
         investigate, duty to, 37

loyalty and self-dealing, duty of, 31-33
misrepresentation, duty to purchaser, 35-40,
    149
regulation of, 33, 37, 40
remedies for violation of, 33
licensing requirements, 40-41
listing agreement, 19
regulation of, 33, 37, 40-41
commission, 19, 21, 22-23
    antitrust implications, 22
    "no closing, no commission" rule, 29-31
        Ellsworth Dobbs, Inc. v. Johnson, 30-31
    "ready, willing and able," 27-29
    "usual and customary fee," 22
    vendor's liability for, 27-31
listing agreements
    agency relationship, 24
    antitrust implications, 22
    as broker's employment agreement, 19, 59
    contract of sale, 22
    contractual nature of, 21
    defined, 20-22
    equitable conversion, doctrine of, 22
    exclusive agency listing agreement, 22-25
    exclusive right to sell agreement, 22-25
    extension clause, 26-27
    Multiple Listing Service, 25-27, 38
    net listing agreement, 23
    open listing agreement, 22-25
    procuring cause doctrine, 26
    regulation of, 20
    relationship to commission, 21
    Statute of Frauds, 20, 59
    terms of, 21-22
    "withdrawal from sale" clause, 27
Real estate investment trust, 382, 407, 416
    tax consequences of, 417
Real estate syndication
    garden apartments, 406
    generally, 359, 402, 406-407
    net leases, 406
    office buildings, 406
    real estate investment trust, 382, 407
    Securities Acts' liability, 411-412
    shopping center, 406
    syndicator liability, 410-411
Recording acts, 3, 163-179
    acknowledgment, 175, 202-203
    assignment of mortgage, 263
    bona fide purchaser, 165, 172-173
        shelter rule, 173
    chain of title, 171-176
    circuity of interests, 176-178
    conditional delivery, impact of, 182
    consideration, 165, 167-169
    constructive notice, doctrine of, 163, 164, 175,
        178
        assumption of mortgages, 254
        future advance mortgages, 232
        holder in due course, 269
    curative statutes, 176, 202-203
    donees, 166

earnest money, 168
effective recording, 174
fees, 424
first in time, first in right, 164-165, 176
"for value" requirement, 167-169
    preexisting debt, 171
grantor-grantee index, 174-175
index, status of, 178
judgment holders, 170-171
lien creditors, 169, 170-171
New Jersey rule, 177
notice function, 164
notice statutes, 165
    bona fide purchasers, 165
    consideration required, 165
    donees, 166
out-of chain document, 175
parties in possession, 178-179
priority of title, 164-166, 176-177, 178, 270
race-notice statutes, 165, 166
race statutes, 3
searching of records, 163
self-proving nature of recording document, 163
shelter rule, 173
subsequent purchasers, 163, 169-170
    bona fide purchasers, 173
    leases, 169
    mortgagees, 169
subordination agreements, 177
tax liens, 177
tract index, 175
wild card deed, 15


Sale-leaseback transactions
    accounting standards and, 386-387
    bankruptcy, 387-390
    equitable conversion, doctrine of, 390
    equitable mortgage, 389
    estoppel by deed, doctrine of, 389
    generally, 360
    installment land sale contract, 390
    recharacterization, 388, 390-391
    tax consequences of, 379-386
        acceleration clauses, 379
        deductions, 379
        Frank Lyon Co. v. United States, 381-386
        loan-to-value financing, 379
        mortgage, compared to, 379
        sham transactions, 380
Shopping center leases
    anchor tenant. See magnet tenant
    antitrust implications, 481-483
    attorney review clause, 465
    attornment clauses, 466-467
    bankruptcy, 482-483
    contract issues,
        generally, 457-469
        triple net leases, 468-469
    covenants
        anticompetitive covenants, 455, 464, 471
        antitrust laws, 481-482

Shopping center leases (*continued*)
    duty to inspect, 458
    exclusive right to sell, 456
    generally, 455-462
    implied covenant of continuous
        operation, 474-478
    implied reciprocal negative servitudes, 457,
        459, 470
    master set of covenants, 457, 460
    real covenants, 455-456, 464
    recording of, 457
    restrictive use, 457, 467, 469-474
    Sanborn v. McLean, 458
    Statute of Frauds, 458
    third-party beneficiary theory, 457
  duty to operate, 475-477
  equitable covenants, 455
  estoppel, 461
  exclusive right to sell clauses, 456-457, 460
  exclusive use covenants, 457, 462
  history of, 463-464
  lease interpretation, 461
  lease negotiation, 463, 465-466
  magnet tenant, 456, 470, 474
  necessary implication, doctrine of, 474
  percentage rental, 475, 478-481
  priority of title, 466-467
  reciprocity of benefit, 471
  right to sublease or assign, 455, 460, 462,
      474-478
  tenant mix, 457, 462, 470-471
  title problems, 466-467
Specific performance, 43
Statute of Frauds, 5, 20, 55-61, 251
  contract of sale, 58
  deeds, application to, 56
  exceptions to, 59-61
    equitable estoppel, doctrine of, 59-60
    part performance, doctrine of, 59-60
  listing agreements, 59
  material terms, 57
    price term, 57
  option to purchase, 58
  recording, relationship with, 56
  Statute of Uses, 56
  writing requirement, 56
Statute of Uses, 4-5, 56, 349
Subordination, doctrine of, 360
Surety bonds, 324-328
  bankruptcy, 326
  bid bond, 325
  bondability letter, 326
  direct for subcontractors, 326
  payment bond, 325
  performance bond, 326
  performance and payment bond, 326
  subrogation, doctrine of, 327-328


Title abstractor, 183-184
  attorney liability, 183-184
  liability of, 183-184
  measure of damages in action against, 183

  negligent misrepresentation, 183
    bond requirement, 184
    regulation of, 184
  rule of reasonable foreseeability, 183
  statute of limitations, 183
    discovery rule, 183
Title abstracts, 3, 7, 15, 181-184
  attorney review, 181
  certificate of title, 181
  chain of title, 171, 181
    idem sonens, doctrine of, 182
  conditional delivery, impact of, 182
  grantor-grantee index, 174
  privity of contract, 183
  rule of reasonable foreseeability, 183
  title plant, 181
  Torrens system, 205
  tract index, 175
  transfer of mortgagee's interest, 267
Title insurance, 7, 184-194
  bankruptcy, 191
  conditions and stipulations of, 185, 189-190
  duty to defend, 185, 189-190
  exceptions to coverage, 185
  exclusions, 189
  indemnification, function as, 185
  litigation insurance, 15
  marketability of title, 184, 190
  measure of damages, 185, 192-194
  policy,
    example of, 186-188
    highlights of, 188-190
  risk of loss, 192
  Schedule A, 184
  Schedule B, 184-185
  subrogation right, 190
  terms of, 184, 188-190
Title plant, 181
Title registration acts. *See* Torrens acts
Title search, 7, 181
  acknowledgment, 202-203
  attestation, 202
  chain of title, 171, 181
    idem sonens, doctrine of, 182
  curative statutes, 202-203
  foreclosure proceedings, 243
  grantor-grantee index, 174-175
  Model Marketable Title Act, 195-204
    adverse possession, 198
    boundary agreements, 199
    chain of marketable record title, 200
    constitutionality of, 198-199
    example of, 196-197
    foreclosure deed, 201
    installment land sale contract, 200
    party wall agreements, 199
    quitclaim deed, 201
    reciprocal negative easements, 199
    root of title, 197-198, 200, 201
    tax deeds, 200
    wild deeds, 200
  standards of, 203-204
  tract index, 175

Torrens acts, 7, 205-208
  abstract of title, 205
  chain of title, 205
  contracts of sales and, 206
  curtain principle, 206
  deeds and, 206
  fund principle, 206
  land court, 207
  mirror principle, 206
  quiet title action, 207
  title insurance industry, 207
Tract index, 175, 205
Transfer taxes
  assignment of rents and profits, 422
  avoidance of, 422
  condominium, 419-420
  corporate asset transfers, 421
  deed in lieu of foreclosure, 424
  executory construction agreements, 420-421
  exemptions, 420
  future advance clauses, 422
  generally, 419-425
  mortgaged property, 421, 424
  property taxed, 419-420

  recording of mortgage, 423-424
  shared appreciation mortgages, 422
  wraparound mortgages, 423

Uniform Commercial Code, 359
Uniform Vendor Purchaser Risk Act, 47-51
  rationale of, 47

Warranties of title, 116-123
Workouts, 317-318, 332-333
  antideficiency statutes, 333
  federal regulation of lenders, 335-336
  fixtures, 332
  lender liability, 317, 332
  payment terms, 318
  releases, 333
  repudiation, 336
  statute of limitations, 222
  waiver, 333
Wraparound financing, 362-363
  purchase money mortgage, 363
  take "subject to" clause, 362